Political parties and the European Union

This panoramic survey of the European political landscape analyses and assesses the ways in which Europe's political parties have responded to the European Union.

Its combination of different approaches in one volume mirrors the complexity of the issues involved:

- *Case studies* in Part I examine the history of the main parties in the major member states as well as their positions on European integration.
- In Part II *comparative approaches* offer new perspectives on a number of parties across the EU by analysing, for example, the position of various Green parties on political integration.
- The chapters in Part III focus on *supranational* aspects by examining party politics at the European level.

The contributions make clear that, despite a clear trend towards political convergence, the specific political circumstances of individual member states remain immensely important. *Political Parties and the European Union* offers an up-to-date guide to the diversity of national traditions and cultures that have shaped the political parties across Europe.

It provides an excellent overview of party politics in the EU and will be an ideal companion for courses on the European Union, in comparative political studies and European politics in general.

John Gaffney is Professor of French and European Politics at Keele University.

Political parties and the European Union

Edited by John Gaffney

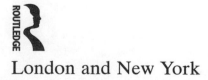

London and New York

First published 1996
by Routledge
11 New Fetter Lane, London EC4P 4EE

Simultaneously published in the USA and Canada
by Routledge
29 West 35th Street, New York, NY 10001

© 1996 John Gaffney for selection and editorial matter
© 1996 the contributors for the individual chapters

Typeset in Times by
Keystroke, Jacaranda Lodge, Wolverhampton.
Printed and bound in Great Britain by
Clays Ltd, St Ives plc

British Library Cataloguing in Publication Data
A catalogue record for this book is available from the British Library.

Library of Congress Cataloguing in Publication Data
A catalogue record for this book has been requested.

ISBN 0–415–09059–8 (hbk)
ISBN 0–415–09060–1 (pbk)

Contents

Tables

Contributors

David Bell is Senior Lecturer in the Department of Political Studies and Head of Department at the University of Leeds, and the author with Byron Criddle of *The French Socialist Party* (Oxford, Oxford University Press, 1988) and of *The French Communist Party* (Oxford, Oxford University Press, 1994).

Martin Bull is Senior Lecturer in Politics and Contemporary History and Associate Director of the European Studies Research Institute at the University of Salford. He has published widely in the area of Italian and comparative politics, and has edited (with Paul Heywood) *West European Communist Parties After the Revolutions of 1989* (London, Macmillan, 1994).

Alistair Cole is Lecturer in the Department of European Studies at Bradford University. He has published widely in journals covering French and European politics, including the *European Journal of Political Research*, *Political Studies*, *West European Politics*, *Modern and Contemporary France* and *German Politics*. His most recent book is *François Mitterrand: A Study in Political Leadership* (London, Routledge, 1994).

Catherine Fieschi is Lecturer in French and European Studies at Aston University and a doctoral candidate in Political Science at McGill University, Canada. She is the recipient of the Social Sciences and Humanities Research Council of Canada doctoral scholarship. Her research focuses on movements of the extreme right in Europe as well as on comparative political theory.

John Gaffney is Professor of French and European Politics at Keele University. He is the author of, *inter alia, The French Left and the Fifth Republic* (London, Macmillan, 1989) and *The Language of Political Leadership in Contemporary Britain* (London, Macmillan, 1990); and co-editor of *Political Culture in France and Germany* (with Eva Kolinsky, London, Routledge, 1991), *The Language of Political Leadership in Contemporary France* (with Helen Drake, Aldershot, Dartmouth, 1995) and *French Presidentialism and the Elections of 1995* (with Lorna Milne, Aldershot, Dartmouth, 1995).

Stephen George is Jean Monnet Professor in the Department of Politics at the University of Sheffield. He is the author of *Politics and Policy in the European Community* (Oxford, Oxford University Press, 1985, 2nd edition 1991), *An Awkward Partner: Britain in the European Community* (Oxford, Oxford University Press, 1990, 2nd edition 1994) and *Britain and European Integration since 1945*

(Oxford, Basil Blackwell, 1991); he is the editor of *Britain and the European Community: The Politics of Semi-Detachment* (Oxford, Oxford University Press, 1992) and joint editor (with Simon Bulmer and Andrew Scott) of *The United Kingdom and EC Membership Evaluated* (London, Frances Pinter, 1992).

Richard Gillespie is Professor of Iberian and Latin American Studies at the University of Portsmouth. He is the author of *The Spanish Socialist Party* (Oxford, Oxford University Press, 1989), editor of *Mediterranean Politics* (London, Pinter, annual) and co-editor of *Democratic Spain: Reshaping External Relations in a Changing World* (London, Routledge, 1995).

Deborah Haythorne is Departmental Administrator in the Department of Politics, University of Sheffield, from which she graduated with a BA degree. She previously worked as Personal Assistant to Richard Caborn when he was MEP for Sheffield, and subsequently when he became MP for Sheffield Central.

Simon Hix is a doctoral student at the European University Institute, Florence. He has published several journal articles and book chapters on political party theory, the transnational party federations and comparative approaches to the study of the EU. He formerly worked as a political consultant on EU affairs.

Michael Holmes lectures at University College, Cork and in the Centre for Peace Studies in Dublin, and was previously Lecturer in Politics at University College, Dublin and at the University of Limerick. His doctoral research is on the Irish Labour and Democratic Left parties and their attitudes towards European integration. He has published on a number of issues concerning Ireland's relations with the European Union, and also on Irish foreign policy and the politics of the Irish football team.

Robert Ladrech is Lecturer in Politics at Keele University. His research interests currently focus on transnational party development in the European Union and the institutional development of the European Parliament, in particular its relations with national parliaments. His work on these issues has been published in the *European Journal of Political Research*, the *Journal of European Integration* and the *Journal of Common Market Studies*.

Ulf Lindström obtained his doctorate in political science in 1983 at the University of Umea, Sweden. Since 1987, he has been with the Department of Comparative Politics, University of Bergen, Norway, while also serving as Associate Professor of Politics in Helsinki and Abo, Finland. Among his previous publications are *The Scandinavian Party System* (with Sten Berglund, Lund, Studentlitteratur, 1978) and *Fascism in Scandinavia 1920–1940* (Stockholm, Almqvist and Wicksell, 1985).

Richard Moeller is a Ph.D. student and part-time Lecturer at the University of Edinburgh. His main research area is comparative political systems in Western Europe and specifically the political parties of Germany. He is completing his dissertation on the relationship between the West German Social Democrats and the East German Socialists during the 1980s. He has worked in the US Senate in Washington.

Peter Morris is Senior Lecturer in Politics at the University of Nottingham where his principal interests are in the politics and contemporary history of France and

Britain. His publications include *Consensus Politics from Attlee to Thatcher* (with Dennis Kavanagh, Oxford, Blackwell, 2nd edn, 1994), *Histoire du Royaume Uni* (Paris, Hatier, 1991) and *French Politics Today* (Manchester, Manchester University Press, 1994). He has co-edited a *Biographical Dictionary of French Political Leaders since 1870* (Brighton, Harvester Wheatsheaf, 1990) and translated *The Republic of de Gaulle* (Cambridge, Cambridge University Press, 1993). In 1988–9 he held the Elie Halevy Chair at the Institut d'Etudes Politiques in Paris.

William Paterson is Founding Director of the Institute for German Studies, University of Birmingham. He was formerly Professor of Politics at the University of Warwick before moving to Edinburgh in 1990 as Director of the Europa Institute. He also chaired the University Association for Contemporary European Studies from 1989 to 1994. Professor Paterson has written and edited many books and articles on German and European themes. He is active in Anglo-German relations and is a regular participant in the Königswinter Conference.

Wolfgang Rüdig is Reader in Government at the University of Strathclyde, Glasgow, Scotland. He is the author of *Anti-Nuclear Movements: A World Survey of Protest against Nuclear Energy* (Harlow, Longman, 1990) and editor of *Green Politics One* (1990), *Green Politics Two* (1992) and *Green Politics Three* (1994) (all Edinburgh, Edinburgh University Press). He is currently completing books on the British Green Party and the comparative politics of global warming.

James Shields is Lecturer in French Studies at the University of Warwick. He has published a large number of articles and book chapters on contemporary French politics, with particular reference to the extreme right, and on aspects of eighteenth- and nineteenth-century French literature and thought.

Julie Smith is a Hanseatic Scholar at the University of Hamburg. She is currently researching for an ESRC-funded Ph.D. thesis on the European Parliament. Her publications include *Citizens' Europe? The European Elections and the Role of the European Parliament* (London, Royal Institute of International Affairs, 1994) and *Voice of the People: The European Parliament in the 1990s* (London, RIIA, 1995).

Lars Svåsand graduated from the University of Bergen in 1972 and is currently Professor in Comparative Politics. He has published articles, chapters and books on political parties, particularly party organizations. His most recent work is *Challenges to Political Parties: The Case of Norway* (co-edited with Kaare Strom, Ann Arbor, MI, University of Michigan Press, 1995).

Susannah Verney has a Ph.D. from King's College, London. She is currently Visiting Fellow in Mediterranean Politics at the University of Bristol, UK, Visiting Research Fellow at the University of Bradford, UK and Lecturer in Political Science at the Beaver College Study in Greece Programme, Athens, Greece. She has published many articles and book chapters on Greek relations with the EU and other aspects of contemporary Greek politics.

Roger Woods is Reader in German, Nottingham University. He studied German at Reading, Tübingen, London, and Oxford Universities. He is the author of, *inter alia*, *Ernst Jünger and the Nature of Political Commitment* (Stuttgart, Akademischer Verlag, 1982); *Opposition in the GDR under Honecker, 1971–85: An Introduction and Documentation* (London/New York, Macmillan/St Martin's Press, 1986). He is also co-editor with M. Gerber of *The End of the GDR and the Problems of Integration* (Lanham, NY and London, University Press of America, 1993), *Understanding the Past, Managing the Future: The Integration of the Five New Länder into the Federal Republic of Germany* (Lanham, NY and London, University Press of America, 1994). He has just completed a study entitled *The Conservative Revolution in the Weimar Republic* (Macmillan, 1996).

Preface

One of the most intriguing and enjoyable aspects of editing *Political Parties and the European Union* has been the way in which our research area changed as the project progressed. The project was begun because it was considered that some of the political, and especially party political, aspects of European integration had been somewhat neglected. As will be seen from several of the chapters in this volume, in many countries of the European Union political activity itself has intensified during the 1990s, bringing political parties to the fore, and countering many of the purely economic or institutional developments within Europe with partisan activity in the local, regional, national, intergovernmental and supranational areas. In terms of both deepening and widening the Union, and in some cases even of membership itself, the debates within and between national political parties, as well as in the party groups in the European Parliament, have reflected the growing politicization of the European integration process. From the Danish referendum 'no' in 1992, to the perceived 'democratic deficit' within the Union's institutions; from the demands for a 'social' Europe to the ways in which the Union is responding to the economic recessions of its member states, the political parties of Europe have been drawn deeper into the European debate, at the same time as 'Europe' itself has entered decisively into national political debates.

In order to understand these developments, we have adopted three interrelated perspectives: case studies addressing the ways in which major political parties have responded to the European Union and European integration; comparative studies which appraise the political parties in one country (or in the case of Scandinavia a group of countries), or else parties from the same political family across the Union; and finally, studies focusing upon the specifically European activity of parties either in European elections, transnational federations or in the European Parliament. In this way, we hope to offer a comprehensive view of party political activity within the European framework.

There are, of course, omissions in a project of this type. There are over eighty parties represented in the European Parliament, and well over one hundred in the national parliaments of the Union; it is therefore impossible to include all of them in one volume. Even some countries of the Union have been neglected owing to constraints of space; and as the Union widens, such omissions will themselves multiply. Nevertheless, this volume provides a comprehensive framework for understanding the ways in which party politics has responded to the European Union. As regards other works which offer complementary perspectives on these issues one should cite in particular the works of Kevin Featherstone, David Hanley, Stanley Henig and

Emil Kirchner (see bibliography of Chapter 1, pp. 27–30). Earlier versions of the chapters in this volume were presented at a workshop and a conference at Aston University in 1993 and 1994, and at a series of panels at conferences of the Political Studies Association (UK) and the European Community Studies Association (USA) in 1993, 1994 and 1995 as well as a series of individual presentations at conferences and research seminars.

I should like to thank Professor William Paterson of the Institute for German Studies, Birmingham and Dr Vincent Wright of Nuffield College, Oxford for their encouragement and help in identifying and contacting some of the specialists who then joined the project. I must also thank the European Parliament, the University Association for Contemporary European Studies and the Languages and European Studies Department at Aston University for supporting financially many of the panels and conferences involved in the project, and the Center for European Studies at Harvard University, its library and administrative staff for their assistance while I was researching for the background to the book in 1992 and 1993. I also wish to thank all of the contributors to the volume for their advice, enthusiasm and patience. I would also like to thank Routledge Publishers for their interest in the project and in particular Caroline Wintersgill, the politics editor, for her interest, advice and collaboration. Finally, I should like to thank Julie Ramsden for her invaluable administrative and secretarial expertise in organizing workshops and conferences, and in helping to prepare the manuscript for the publishers.

John Gaffney
Birmingham, December 1995

Abbreviations

AL	Alternative Liste (Alternative List, Germany)
APO	Ausserparlamentarische Opposition (extra-parliamentary opposition)
C	Centerpartiet (Swedish Centre Party)
CAP	Common Agricultural Policy
CDS	Centro Democrático y Social (Social and Democratic Centre, Spain)
CDU	Christlich-Demokratische Union (German Christian Democrats)
CERES	Centre d'études de recherche, et d'éducation socialistes (Centre for Socialist Study, Research and Education)
CFSP	Common Foreign and Security Policy
CGIL	Confederazione generale italiano del lavoro (Italian Confederation of Labour)
CGT	Confédération générale du travail (General Confederation of Labour)
CiU	Convergència i Unió (Convergence and Unity, Catalonia)
CPSU	Communist Party of the Soviet Union
CSP	Confederation of Socialist Parties
CSPEC	Confederation of Socialist Parties of the European Community
CSU	Christlich-Soziale Union (Bavarian Christian Democrats)
DC	Democrazia cristiana (Italian Christian Democratic Party)
DGB	Deutscher Gewerkschaftsbund (Federation of German Trade Unions)
DKP	Deutsche Kommunistische Partei (German Communist Party)
DL	Democratic Left (Ireland)
DNA	Det Norske Arbeiderparti (Norwegian Social Democratic Party)
DVU	Deutsche Volksunion (German People's Union)
EC	European Community
EcoFin	EC Council of Economic and Finance Ministers
ECSC	European Coal and Steel Community
EDC	European Defence Community
EDG	European Democratic Group
EDU	European Democratic Union
EEC	European Economic Community
EFA	European Free Alliance
EFG	European Federation of Green Parties
EFTA	European Free Trade Association
ELD	Federation of European Liberals and Democrats
ELDR	European Liberals, Democrats and Reformers

EMS	European Monetary System
EMU	Economic and Monetary Union
EP	European Parliament
EPC	European Political Co-operation
EPEN	Ethniki Politiki Enosis (National Political Union, Greece)
EPP	European People's Party: Federation of Christian Democratic Parties of the European Community
ERM	Exchange Rate Mechanism (of the European Monetary System)
EU	European Union
EUCD	European Union of Christian Democrats
EUT	European Union Treaty
FDP	Freie Demokratische Partei (Free Democratic Party)
FF	Fianna Fáil
FG	Fine Gael
FN	Front National (French Extreme Right Party)
FP	Folkpartiet (Swedish Liberals)
FRG	The Federal Republic of Germany. Also West Germany prior to 1990.
FYROM	Former Yugoslav Republic of Macedonia
GATT	General Agreement on Tariffs and Trade
GDE	Groupe des droites européennes (Group of the European Right)
GDP	Gross Domestic Product
GDR	The German Democratic Republic. Also East Germany prior to 1990.
H	Høyre (Norwegian Conservative Party)
IGC	InterGovernmental Conference
IU	Izquierda Unida (United Left, Spain)
K	Kekustapuolue (Finnish Centre Party)
KF	Konservative Folkeparti (Danish Conservatives)
KK	Kansallinen Kokoomus (Finnish Conservative Party)
KKE	Kommounistiko Komma Ellados (Greek Communist Party)
KPD	Kommunistische Partei Deutschlands (Communist Party of Germany)
KRF	Kristelig Folkeparti (Norwegian Christian People's Party)
LI	Liberal International
LP	Labour Party (Ireland)
MEP	Member of the European Parliament
MRG	Mouvement des radicaux de gauche (Left-wing Radicals, France)
MRP	Mouvement républicain populaire (French Christian Democrat Party, Fourth Republic)
MSI	Movimento Sociale Italiano (Italian neo-fascists)
NATO	North Atlantic Treaty Organisation
ND	Nea Dimokratia (New Democracy, Greece)
NPD	Nationaldemokratische Partei Deutschlands (National Democratic Party of Germany, neo-Nazis)
NSDAP	Nationalsozialistische Deutsche Arbeiterpartei (National Socialist German Workers' Party, Nazi Party)
Oth	Others
PASOK	Panellinio Sosialistiko Kinima (Panhellenic Socialist Movement, Greece)
PCE	Partido Comunista de España (Communist Party of Spain)

PCF	Parti communiste français (French Communist Party)
PCI	Partito comunista italiano (Italian Communist Party)
PD	Progressive Democrats (Ireland)
PDS	Partito Democratico della Sinistra (Democratic Party of the Left, formerly Italian Communist Party)
PES	Party of European Socialists
PFN	Parti des forces nouvelles (French extreme right)
POL.A	Politiki Anoixi (Political Spring, Greece)
PP	Partido Popular (People's Party, Spain)
PPI	Italian Popular Party
PS	Parti socialiste (French Socialist Party)
PSDI	Parti socialista democratico italiano (Italian Democratic Socialist Party)
PSI	Partito socialista italiano (Italian Socialist Party)
PSOE	Partido Socialista Obrero Español (Spanish Socialist Workers' Party)
QMV	Qualified majority voting
RPR	Rassemblement pour la république (French Gaullist Party, 1976–)
RV	Radikale Venstre (Danish Social Liberals)
S	Socialdemokratiet (Danish Social Democratic Party)
SAP	Socialdemokratiska Arbetarparti (Swedish Social Democratic Party)
SEA	Single European Act
SED	Sozialistische Einheitspartei Deutschlands (Socialist Unity Party of Germany)
SF	Sosialistisk Folkeparti (Danish Socialist Party)
SFIO	Section française de l'internationale ouvrière (French Socialist Party, 1905–69)
SI	Socialist International
SP	Senterpartiet (Norwegian Centre Party)
SPD	Sozialdemokratische Partei Deutschlands (German Social Democratic Party)
SPV	Sonstige Politische Vereinigung (Alternative Political Association, Germany)
SRP	Sozialitische Reichspartei (Socialist State Party)
SS	Suomen Sosialdemokraattinen (Finnish Social Democratic Party)
SV	Sosialistisk Venstreparti (Norwegian Socialist Party)
TD	Teachta Dàla (member of the Dàil, the lower house, Ireland)
UDF	Union pour la démocratie française (French Centre-Right Party Confederation)
UDR	Union des démocrates pour la république (French Gaullist Party, 1968–76)
UGT	Unión General de Trabajadores (General Workers' Union, Spain)
UN	United Nations
UNR	Union pour la nouvelle république (French Gaullist Party, 1958–67)
V	Venstre (Danish Liberals)
WEU	Western European Union

1 Introduction

Political parties and the European Union

John Gaffney

THE POLITICAL PARTY IN CONTEXT

The subject of this book is the relationship between national political parties and the European Union (EU).[1] One of the prerequisites for a nation's membership of the European Union is democracy; one of the characteristic features of West European democracy is party government. The countries that joined the EU in the 1980s, Greece (1981), Portugal and Spain (1986), had each been subject to recent dictatorships. Their return to democracy was not only a prerequisite to EU membership, the opposite was also true: membership of the EU was itself seen as the guarantee of democracy in these Mediterranean states. The entry of these three countries in the 1980s demonstrated that it was not the economies but the polities of the member states which constituted the decisive factor in the European Union's identity. This remains true in the 1990s: it was the political convergence between the European Union and the applicant states of Norway, Finland, Sweden and Austria, just as much as their economic compatibility, which distinguished them from the politically unstable countries of the former Warsaw Pact. The political parties of all EU members and would-be members are therefore crucially implicated in the politics of Western Europe and the European Union.[2]

There is a paradox here. The institutions, actors and processes in the European Union, from its inception in 1958 until today, all have extensive literatures.[3] It is also worth pointing out that the literature on the EU, although less than forty years old, is vast by any standards, dwarfing many other subjects studied in the social sciences. The literature on political parties *per se* is vast also. The literature on political parties in the Union, however, is minimal. We can say, therefore, that very little of the literature on integration is on political parties, and very little of the literature on political parties is on integration. This book will rectify this to some degree; more importantly, it will contribute to an explanation of the paradox, for there are reasons for the lacunae in European Union research on political parties, reasons that are partly related to misperceptions about their role and influence. In this chapter we are concerned with the role of the political parties on the European stage. We shall take into account the nature of the modern political party, the significance of Europe for the national parties, the parties' contribution to the processes of European integration, and the factors which encourage or restrict that contribution.

Political parties have always played a decisive role in democratic politics. On the one hand, they provide 'linkage' between institutions and constituencies within the polity; they are 'agencies for forging links between citizens and policy makers'. On the other hand, they constitute the essential site for the creation of a culture, ideology or doctrine which reflects and creates ideas intended to become governmental policy and ultimately the law of the land, and thus part of the normative values of society.[4] In the context of European integration, some national political parties regard Europe as of little significance; some of those which do regard it as significant find it difficult to maintain or transmit such a view to a wider national or European constituency; some are hostile to Europe precisely because they consider it undermining of the national political culture which gave rise to them and their values; some consider Europe to be so significant and formative of future political society that they have contributed to the development of parallel European parties which may take over from their national parties lock, stock and ballot box if ever the political structures of a united Europe, reflecting the evolution of national cultures, supplant or transcend those of the national polities.

The political party is essentially a national and local phenomenon. It is made up of many elements. It contains an elite from which it normally draws its leadership (sometimes individuals who turn out to be of exceptional historical significance); it contains activists of varying degrees of effectiveness and supporters of varying commitment. A party may have a discourse or discourses which contribute to or hinder its effectiveness and identity. It has a public image and a history; it generates sets of policies which then inform and direct it; it has a set of myths which underpin it; it has resources and money, connections with governments, relations to movements or organizations that gave rise to it (geographical, class-based, professional and so on); it has a series of relationships with the wider national culture and beyond. All of these elements interact with one another. Some of them have played a major role in the area we are examining. Nearly all of them, however, play a different role or have a different degree of influence depending upon the national environments the parties find themselves in: according to the national political circumstances of each party, individuals may have more influence, local activists less; relations to institutions will be different; relations to pressure groups and interest groups will vary. Moreover, many of the ideas which underpin the political activity of political parties are locally as well as nationally based; even ideological outlook often has a very local formative context. Attention to the national and local environments of the political parties is, therefore, crucial to an understanding of how the parties perceive, and behave towards, Europe.

In the context of the EU, the question of the role of the political parties needs to be addressed at two further levels. First, a proper assessment of their historical significance, and actual influence and involvement is necessary. Such an assessment is appropriate in part simply because, as we have pointed out, the place and role of political parties in the European context is underresearched. The second and related level on which the issue must be addressed is that of the received scholarly view that the role of the political party has in general been usurped by other political actors, and particularly so in the case of the EU; and that to emphasize the role of the political parties in the European political process is, in fact, misleading. According to this view, interest groups, elites and other groups with access to restricted knowledge, skills and networks, and to the national and transnational bureaucracies, are in the main the actors who are responding to and attempting to shape micro- and macro-economic forces, and the political responses to them. In this forceful process, the political parties are of very secondary importance. Before addressing the first level of inquiry – the impact on European integration, real or potential, of the political parties – before, in fact, it is worth addressing – we must address the second, the relevance of parties.[5]

Is it not true that the parties used to be major actors in the political process generally and are now no longer? Is it not true that as national economies become more integrated and the economic process itself more complex, the political parties simply do not have the expertise to claim or undertake a concerted involvement in transnational politics? Is it not true, therefore, that analysis of the functioning of the EU and of the decision-making process can be made largely without reference to the input of the political parties at either the national or supranational level? Is it not also true that given public disaffection and partisan dealignment, the political parties themselves can no longer even claim the status of the voice of their social and political constituencies? The dealignments, reduction in party identification, electoral abstentionism, especially for elections to the European Parliament, suggest that perhaps omitting parties, relatively speaking, from the study of the political process is justified, and compounded by their decreasing relevance both as expressions of aggregate interests and as the organizers and articulators of discrete and shared ideologies. There are historical, sociological and institutional reasons for the shift in significance of the political parties in the politics of advanced capitalism and representative democracies. The broad view, however, that their importance has diminished, is misplaced; it is the more diffuse and changing nature of their influence which needs to be assessed, in order that their proper place and potential in the political process of European integration be identified, and therefore that the process itself be better understood.

Before asking what political parties do in the European context, we need to identify what they do generally, what they are. Political parties are the organized expression of some of the cleavages within society, and they compete or co-operate with one another in order to, at least, influence the political process, at best, attain governmental power. In more or less historical order, the main politically expressed cleavages in European society have been those of religion, nationalism and social class.[6] The religious question implied significantly differing visions of the world (indeed, of the universe), essentially between Catholics and Protestants, Anglicans and non-conformists, or the clergy on the one hand, and those in favour of a secular state on the other. These conflicts, from the Reformation onwards, took different forms in different countries. In the European context, the continent divided very roughly into a Protestant Northern Europe (the Scandinavian countries, Great Britain) and a Catholic Southern Europe (Portugal, Spain, France and Italy). Several countries experienced significant internal religious cleavages, dividing the country into religiously distinct regions; this was essentially the case of Holland, Belgium and Germany. Common to all of the countries involved was the importance of the actual or desired relationship of the church to the state, and therefore of the degree and type of participation of each within the polity. The social impacting of the religious cleavage predates the rise of the modern political party by several centuries; it remained, nevertheless, one of the formative contexts of political activity throughout Europe.

Coming later than the religious cleavage in most countries but with more decisive influence upon the structuring of the modern political party, the rise of nationalism in the nineteenth century accompanied the consolidation of the state. One of the effects of such consolidation was the assertion of the sway of developing national parties over localized aggregated interests. This was, essentially, the sway of the centre against the periphery, the state against the regions. In many cases, in particular in countries such as Britain, France and Spain with a strong centralized state, this meant the concerted suppression of strong regional parties. Concomitant with the assertion of the national over the local, capitalism gradually became the politico-economic status quo throughout most of Europe, and those with capital were able to command dramatically more political influence than those with only their labour.

The most decisive cleavage to have structured political organization in the twentieth century has been that of class. The bourgeois parties of the nineteenth and twentieth centuries, often small cadre parties despite their national focus, responded with differing degrees of success to the rise of the mass working-class parties as industrialization and urbanization spread. The decisive factor here was the way in which the parties responded to the uneven though relentless extension of the suffrage. As the suffrage spread, many of the older parties themselves evolved into mass parties. The class cleavage has been fundamental to the creation of party 'families' along the left–right spectrum, and has created identifiably similar parties in most European countries: communist parties, social democratic parties, liberals, conservatives and the ultra-right, being the main ones. The exceptions and qualifications to such classifications, however, are so many that they threaten to disprove the rule. Where on a class spectrum would one place the main Irish political parties, Fine Gael and Fianna Fáil? How does Christian democracy fit into a class cleavage analysis? Liberal parties often fit neatly into one class category as regards economic policy and another as regards social policy. Perhaps identifying the 'true' underlying organizing principle of political parties is impossible: trying to decide where or sometimes whether the Italian Christian Democrats should be placed on the right of the political spectrum; where to put the Giscardian Union for French Democracy, the former Italian Communists, the Scottish Nationalists, the Ecologists; whether the liberals should be in the centre or on the right, and so on; these questions are perhaps more interesting than the ultimate resolutions of such difficulties. This is so for two important reasons.

First, although the class cleavage is strong, the national specificities of each European country mean that the 'families' perspective will always involve more exceptions than rules. For example, the German SPD and Spanish Socialists claim membership of the same family – that of social democracy and the Socialist International – and yet they differ significantly. There are historical reasons for the divisions on the right of the political spectrum between, say, secular conservatives and liberals, or Gaullists and Christian democrats. It is true that the generally comparable political and economic evolution of Western European countries has created political parties which can be compared, and which clearly organize themselves into families, for example in the European Parliament. All of them, however, even the highly controlled communist parties between 1920 and the death of Stalin in 1953, evolved in the overwhelmingly influential environment of their own national, linguistic and political cultures.[7] Watching the Irish Fianna Fáil or the British Conservatives seeking out their 'place' in the European Parliament context is illustrative of both the richness and the diversity of the wider European political context and of the profoundly national character of the political parties themselves.

To sum up, all the political parties in the European context come from political traditions that are shared by all of the European countries: the many-sided influence of Christianity; kingship and monarchical rule; the rise of nationalism; the shift from feudalism to an emerging capitalism; the rise of democracy; a strong secularism; the assertion of human rights; the assertion of both individual and collective values; strong currents of militarism, authoritarianism and violent political conflict both within and between the nation states; the gradual extension of the principle of political, social and economic rights to all members of society. Each of the political parties is also born of political traditions which distinguish it dramatically from every other party for reasons of the time of its emergence and development; its leadership, membership, constituency and language; the electoral system; the intensity of rival ideologies and organizations; economic developments; international relations; local experiences. All political parties are in a relationship to other political parties in the European context, and operate in a context in which the inheritance of a shared culture is matched by the equal inheritance of a multitude of differentiating cultures. We might also add that what is perceived as shared is often radically divergent, such as the differences between social democracy in Northern and Southern Europe;[8] and what is perceived as different often conceals similarity, such as the contributions of both Protestantism and the Catholic tradition to human and individual rights.[9] Both the collusion and the tension between these various differences and similarities only seem to increase as Europe integrates economically and politically: identifying the complexity of such similar and divergent political experiences of Europe is a necessary prerequisite to a better understanding of it. The notion of various cleavages helps us understand European political parties, on the condition that we see them as the context in which each of them has developed, rather than as the characteristics which define them. This brings us to the second reason for questioning the notion of cleavage as an organizing principle for our study.

The validity of analysis by cleavage can only be sustained if we bear in mind the semantics involved in the definition of social science terms; that is to say that social structures, cleavages and so on are not realities but metaphors which help us understand the complexities of political and social reality. In many instances the three cleavages we have mentioned, religious, national and class, have developed and acted upon political parties simultaneously, creating political parties of unique character. This means that each political party is not simply a reflection of social problems and cleavages but is a *sui generis* political reality which organizes and acts within given social, economic, geographical and other conditions, and which has developed and responded with a particular degree of success to a range of influences, some of which offer constraints, others challenges.[10] It is essential to bear this in mind when analysing political parties in the context of European integration. If we remember our earlier point regarding Fianna Fáil's attempts to locate its appropriate place in the European Parliament, we can say that it is not just a question of the combination of cleavages which interlock slightly differently from other parties; having been forged in the heart of Irish nationalism, it is irrevocably itself and nothing else. In a sense, comparative analysis is of interest as much because things are not the same as because they exhibit similarities, and this complexity is integral, not peripheral, to the way in which Europe has integrated.

NATIONAL POLITICAL PARTIES IN EUROPE

As we have seen from our discussion in the previous section there is, over and above the sociological and historical perspective, what we might call the political specificity of each political party. Its experience, responses, leadership and internal and external relationships will be different from those of all other parties.[11] Politics is itself a formative factor of political action, just as are social and historical experience.[12] In the context of our analysis, this means that how the members and leaders of each political party behave, whether and how they seize opportunities, cope with or exploit their past, their national cultures and so on, will affect their party's fortunes. We should, therefore, see political parties as voluntarist. As such, they must respond to public opinion or sections of public opinion and voice appropriately the demands of political constituencies; they must offer the prospect of power in some form, even if it is only in the minimalist form of consequential political action; they must exhibit effective political leadership both of their political constituencies and within their political organizations.

In the national context, political parties respond to public opinion in two ways: reflecting it (or parts of it), and then making appeals to it (or parts of it) in order to gain votes and representation. In the context of Europe, however, it is arguable whether such a constituency, such 'opinion', exists at all. We shall discuss this question in more detail below; here we can simply note that electorates still respond essentially to national and local politics, and there is only ever the faintest echo of what we might call a European public opinion. The parties cannot offer power at this level, and although their leaders may be effective and seen to be so at the European level, they invariably act via national governmental and inter-governmental channels. In most areas of political activity these are the only channels there are. It is arguable, for example, that the only clearly audible voices over the question of European political union in the 1980s were those of individual national leaders such as Helmut Kohl and François Mitterrand and, in enthusiastic reply to their initiatives, those of the party groups in the European Parliament.

This of course is not to deny the processes taking place at the European level to which political parties should and do respond. Indeed, this is the political dilemma. The economic integration of late twentieth-century Europe is accelerating, and is having wide-ranging, profound and long-term political and social effects. There are, however, few established political relationships and institutions in which or through which the political parties can respond to these developments. Consequently, many national political parties do not have rigorously informed positions on such issues as European monetary union, social cohesion, European industrial policy, the enlargement of the European Union; even such basic issues as a European trans-port policy are often beyond the vision of any single political party. What each does is to respond in a variety of affirmative or negative ways to policy input by other informed actors such as the European Commission, expert economic opinion or even the national party's own groups in the European Parliament, so often seen as an outside entity.[13] Such lack of involvement has repercussions. Only in the 1990s, for example, did the European Parliament become an important target for lobby-ists; for a long time it was regarded as politically marginal compared, for example, to the Commission. In many respects, the lack of expertise in such areas as those listed above (EMU, industrial policy, etc.) draws the political party into accepting advice not from inside itself, but from outside bodies who can lay claim to specialist knowledge but not political legitimacy: think tanks, interest groups, European cartel organizations, and so on. Trade unions sometimes represent interests better than do political parties at the European level. It is also true, however, that trade unions are only a fraction of the interests which do operate at the European level, the majority representing business.[14]

One of the consequences of varying expertise in the European area within or among the political parties, particularly those whose Euro-enthusiasm is cool, is that those individuals in the parties who do have specialist knowledge – e.g. of monetary union, or of the implications of the Maastricht Treaty – will gain influence in the party in this area because of their rare knowledge and will invariably be Euro-enthusiasts, thereby emphasizing a view which will not necessarily reflect the national leadership's position. Pro-Europeans, therefore, may profit from significant strategic political advantage when issues become potentially significant, because of their specialist knowledge. A good illustration of this is the constant tension between the British Labour group in the European Parliament and the party's national headquarters. Discrepancy of influence also happens between the parties, so that a party more knowledgeable about the EU, such as the German SPD, may have significant influence over a less knowledgeable sister party such as the Spanish Socialists or the British Labour Party (this was the case for both parties during the 1980s). Such varying influence and expertise raises the question of the historical background to such influence and involvement in European integration, to which we now turn.

HISTORICAL OVERVIEW

One of the essential conditions for European integration was the political convergence achieved in Western Europe after 1945.[15] When we compare the Europe of post-1919 with that of post-1933 and post-1945, the differences are striking. Before 1914, the United Kingdom and the Scandinavian countries were evolving liberal democratic states. France had adopted a form of republicanism which had been relatively stable since 1870, although strong anti-republican movements remained. Germany's polity, like Russia's, was imperial, with Parliament's role real, although severely restricted. Most European countries had elite groups supportive of democratic institutions. In post-1933 Europe the situation was, from a democratic point of view, far worse. In the United Kingdom, Belgium, Holland and Scandinavia liberal democracy was still intact, but in Germany, Italy, Greece, Portugal and Spain, various forms of fascism and authoritarianism dominated; in France republicanism was vigorously contested, both from the left and right, and not so vigorously defended by its own supporters. Most of the countries of Eastern Europe too were generally subject to various forms of dictatorship, and in the Soviet Union the revolution of 1917 had gradually given way to Stalin's dictatorship, in fact, another form of Russian imperialism.

After 1945, in contrast, Italy and France adopted similar republican constitutions, and both West Germany and Austria accepted liberal and effective forms of parliamentarianism. In the immediate post-war years, the three main political parties in the majority of European countries, the communists, socialists and Christian democrats, were themselves largely convergent in both domestic and foreign policy; and in France, until the onset of the Cold War in 1947, they even formed governing coalitions together. In most West European countries, political parties thrived and contributed to the stability and prosperity of the countries involved. Pressure gradually built upon the authoritarian regimes in Portugal, Spain and later Greece to adopt unequivocal forms of political liberalism. For the first time in modern European history, in fact, political convergence was such that it was possible to imagine a European political entity without using Roman or Napoleonic models of empire.

It is also the case that within the framework of post-war reconstruction and American financial aid (the Marshall Aid Plan), the West European countries were forced to accept broadly compatible monetary and fiscal policies. Under American influence and the pressure of the Bretton Woods agreement (1944) which led to the General Agreement on Tariffs and Trade (GATT, 1948),[16] they were also obliged to adopt broadly compatible methods of economic planning. In the 1950s and 1960s the West European economies all expanded significantly. We can say, therefore, that whereas the 1919 settlement began to disintegrate even before it was applied, the post-1945 settlement was remarkably successful, even though its basis in international law was in fact much weaker. The OEEC (Organization for European Economic Co-operation) was set up in 1948 to administer economic recovery. The Council of Europe established in 1949 was a political organization intended essentially to co-ordinate US aid and discreetly encourage integration, but had few powers. From 1951, with the creation of the European Coal and Steel Community (the ECSC) the economic integration of what was to become the European Community truly began.[17] The European Economic Community was created within this overall process of convergence. The fact that the integration process produced effective institutions designed to respond to economic integration and co-operation rather than political union is highly significant and would colour the way in which European integration took place from then on.

As regards political activity, democracy and the party system during the war years had not withstood the onslaught of fascism, except in the UK and in neutral Ireland, Sweden and Switzerland. The political parties had been destroyed and many party members imprisoned and murdered, particularly those who had become involved in resistance activity. In fact, the only party whose structure had enabled it to withstand the state terrorism of Nazism had been the Communist Party. Having been swept aside by the fascist experience, some pre-war parties disappeared completely; some were rekindled after 1945 and became more thoroughgoing mass parties; other new parties were created. The majority of parties in countries such as France, Germany, Holland, Belgium and Italy were simply restarted in 1945. In the UK and the neutral countries, the parties had not had to face Nazism. In the case of the UK, this situation saw the development at the party political level – on both the left and right – of a somewhat facile self-regard which was itself a reflection of a national sense of robust political superiority over Europe's capricious democratic culture. Such political arrogance would prove misplaced, and contributed to the lateness of Britain's contribution to political exchange at the European party political and doctrinal level. Irrespective, however, of who survived and how, what re-emerged in 1945 was the party system itself. The old political party system was the only model of political organization available, and, of course, in the post-fascist period took on for a brief moment an almost sacred status.[18] The social democratic parties reformed. The communist parties, because of their anti-fascist war record, did very well at elections (especially in France and Italy) and therefore rejoined the parliamentary system as major players. Traditional conservatives realigned and modernized, the centrist liberal and radical parties re-emerged, then declined somewhat when faced with social democratic competition. The new parties were formed with differing degrees of success in the different national contexts; Christian democracy, for example, was highly successful in Germany and Italy, but unsuccessful in France, non-existent in the UK. Some individuals, such as the French resistance leader de Gaulle, disdained what they perceived as the inadequacy of the political parties, their self-interest and unheroic nature. But generally the parties were popular, and came back in force based upon old networks and procedures, developing and consolidating the democratic politics of the pre-fascist period. It is clear that de Gaulle envisaged a different kind of political organization, more populist and less sectarian; but the debate as to precisely what political organizations might replace the political party was never engaged with any seriousness.

Right across the political spectrum the response to party government was positive and supportive. The communists in most West European countries encouraged their constituencies to help get their countries back on their feet. Even after the onset of the Cold War from 1947, communist parties worked within the parliamentary system, especially at local level. Christian democratic parties were the proof that the Catholic hierarchy in Italy, Germany, France and Belgium had decided to work with and within liberal democracy. The case of the German SPD is a good illustration of how social democracy, too, was prepared to work within the system. The post-1945 SPD attitude to the FRG stands in startling contrast to the SPD's attitude to Weimar in the 1920s; only after 1933, when it was too late, did social democracy realize that liberal democracy was worth defending. Linked to these developments was the systematic elaboration of attitudes to concomitant developments in Eastern Europe in the post-war period. By the summer of 1946, it was becoming shockingly clear to liberals, social and Christian democrats alike how quickly non-communist parties were being restricted and then suppressed under orders from Moscow.

Christian democrat parties were all pro-European; seven of the twelve governments signatory to the North Atlantic Treaty in 1949, however, were social democrat governments or coalitions which included social democrats.[19] A general pro-Europeanism fitted (more or less) the fundamental internationalism of social democracy, and allowed the discourse of first the Dutch, then the Belgian, the Italian, French and German social democrats, and later the Italian communists, to evolve in a pro-European direction. Conversely, the task of maintaining and enhancing national identities also often fell to social democrats, especially in Germany, given the division of the country and the generalized discrediting of the nationalist pretensions of the ultra-right. The evolution of Western Europe, therefore, placed most political parties in similar situations, allowing them to contribute at various levels and in a range of institutions in such a way that although regional, national, intergovernmental and supranational developments added complexities to the life of political parties which they had previously not known, they were not, generally speaking, incompatible with one another.

We need to counter what appears to have been a kind of domino effect of allegiance to Europe with three observations, each of which underscores our earlier points concerning the vigour of national influences. The first is that within the overall evolution of a sympathetic Europeanism there were 'pockets of resistance': the French and Portuguese communist parties and the French Gaullists are the best examples. At the risk of oversimplification, it was generally the case after 1945 that the right was more pro-European, the left less so. Moreover, some political parties went through successive phases of pro- and anti-Europeanism: the British Labour and Conservative parties have swapped trenches more than once on the question of Europe; the Greek and Danish parties, the Irish Fine Gael and the majority of Spanish parties all have histories which modify the idea of a seamless pro-European development. Second, the pro-Europeanism of most political parties in Europe has been relatively weak compared to their national allegiances and preoccupations. Immediately after the war, for example, national reconstruction was a priority, as was the establishing of national welfare and education systems, and so the focus of political activity remained fundamentally that of the nation state. Third, and this point is related to the preceding two, the strength of pro-Europeanism was fragile given the vigour of national allegiance, and the still fragile legitimacy of Europe's political and economic institutions.

There was also a wider international relations perspective to these developments. It is arguable whether, strictly speaking, the distinction in political science between 'high politics' (foreign policy, defence, diplomacy) and 'low politics' (domestic policy, economic policy) is a valid one when applied to politics in general.[20] Political processes and policy issues interact with one another all the time. Moreover, for certain governments, and especially for certain interest groups and citizens, various policy issues will become paramount at various times. In the UK, for example, in the 1980s, nuclear disarmament and the poll tax were two issues which mobilized protest and dissent. The high/low politics distinction is not particularly helpful in characterizing them. Nevertheless, if we bear this general caution in mind, in terms of the European Union the distinction is quite helpful, in that for the nation states of Western Europe, what had traditionally been 'high politics' virtually disappeared after 1945. This had major effects upon party activity regarding European integration. To put it simply, Western Europe's foreign policy aligned itself with that of the USA.[21] There was no risk of war between West European countries (even though the aftermath of such thinking still existed, as was demonstrated by the Anglo-French Dunkirk Treaty in 1947 against the non-existent threat of another German attack). With the emergence of the USA from the Second World War as the world's major economic and military power, and the USSR as the second world power now in control of half of Europe, and both in possession of nuclear weapons, Western Europe was unequivocally embedded in a superpower relationship. For the most part, the West European states occupied themselves with purely domestic issues and with economic co-operation at the foreign policy level, so simple were the fundamental foreign policy choices.[22] To assert this is not to minimize what was at stake. The choices were, of course, as simple as they were stark; and all political actors knew that the most likely battleground of a Third World War would be the European landmass. The question of superpower allegiance, therefore, did not distract greatly from national concerns; the sympathies of the Western communist parties were known but these too were also forcefully concerned with domestic issues. Even for pro-Soviet communists, it was recognized that allegiances were distributed, as it were, according to geo-political realities, and apart from momentary and isolated cases (for example in post-war Greece, or post-colonial Portugal) there was never the possibility of a Western communist party preparing the proletariat to rise, let alone rise and meet its Soviet liberators.

Between the political parties generally, the question of how truly European was their Europeanism did not arise until after the EEC was established. Even then their pro- or anti-Europeanism was often just a function of their need to demarcate themselves from adversaries (for example, the French Gaullists versus the Giscardians throughout the second half of the 1970s). In a word, in the post-1945 period political parties were not very interested in asserting either their nationalism *or* their internationalism. Their concerns were domestic; essentially of the who-gets-what welfarism kind. Even when we consider the general national allegiances of the political parties, and even the extremist nationalism of parties of the ultra-right, or at various moments in its history the French Gaullist Party, such nationalism was essentially for domestic consumption. In the case of the Gaullist Party, for example, there was always more of a true contrast between its industrial policy and that of, say, the French Socialists than there was between their respective views on national sovereignty and France's place in the world.

To summarize, the political parties were key actors in national reconstruction after the war. At the international level, however, except for the question of German rearmament in the early 1950s,[23] superpower politics did most of their thinking for them. To the small extent that 'Europe' did influence domestic political issues, it was generally supported; to the extent that it informed foreign policy, with the possible exception of attitudes towards post-war Germany, it generated little interest either in the political parties or among citizens. What transnational co-operation there was, was largely the work of political individuals and elites.[24] In fact, it is arguable that the effectiveness of pro-integration individuals and elites was greater given the uncontentious nature of a generally agreed West European foreign policy, protected by the United States.

PARTIES AND INDIVIDUALS

The revival of the political parties in the aftermath of the Second World War as well as, paradoxically, their fragility, contributed to a significant phenomenon often seen as evidence of the weakening of the political parties in the European area, namely, the role of individuals. On the contrary, the activism of these individuals cannot be understood outside the context of the political parties.

Changes within the power relationships and organizing structures of political parties are the product of the activities of individuals, particularly of those in a strategic relationship to the party elite and leadership or those who themselves constitute the leadership. Where parties are convalescent and are overwhelmingly preoccupied with the national economy and with re-establishing the autonomy of the state, as well as with their own political legitimacy, individuals can play an influential role in shaping them. After the war, parties, like all other political, social and economic organizations, were in a state of reconstruction. Significantly, it was individuals in countries where this process was at its most fragile (Germany, Italy, France) who had the greatest influence on European integration.

Against the background of such incomplete political structures at all levels, the activity and political effects of individuals could take on inordinate significance. The classic example is, of course, Jean Monnet, who, in the late 1940s and early

1950s, had a dramatic effect upon European integration. It is true that he was a 'faceless bureaucrat', unelected and without a personal partisan allegiance, and whose strategy was what Paterson has called 'elite capture' rather than democratic incrementalism.[25] Nevertheless, Monnet is also the exception that proves the rule. The network of relationships in which Monnet's ideas and initiatives so flourished was indeed that of individuals, but individuals all of whom were themselves party politicians; and it is this relationship, the synergy between an unimpeded bureaucracy of committed technocrats, and a range of individuals from party elites in or close to democratic political power in their own national context, which enabled such inroads to be made into the integration process. This was to be the case up until the confrontation in 1965 between French president de Gaulle and the other EEC countries;[26] that is to say between a highly legitimated individual and a pro-integration elite. De Gaulle, by asserting the primacy of intergovernmentalism over supranationalism, was also challenging the inordinate influence of a number of individuals who had gained influence throughout Europe in the aftermath of the Second World War. Until this confrontation, most of the individuals involved in the early stages of the 'European idea' had been party men with similar and relatively unchallenged outlooks on such issues as political institutions, the role of elites, the elaboration of policy, the role of the state, the importance of political doctrine and so on. These individuals undertook concerted action in an opportunistic environment due to the flux at all levels of political activity: governmental, policy making, doctrinal and institutional.

One of the major contributions to the European debate was, therefore, by individuals, but individuals from within political parties. Some were members of parties which traditionally were very controlling of individuals (usually, the more left-wing, the more controlling); some of parties which allowed a considerable degree of autonomy to individuals. Occasionally, the parties which were controlling allowed individuals great leeway on the issue of Europe, or else allowed a degree of autonomy to individuals because the party was itself pro-European Community (the PCI once it had become pro-European, and the French MRP, are very different examples of such cases). On the other hand, where the European Community issue was perceived as being of secondary consequence, autonomy was also tolerated, for example, in the case of British Labour Party individuals at various times during the 1960s. In some cases, of course, individuals were of such consequence that their pro- or anti-European Community activism was not under the party's control. Even when the official decisions of a party organization were neutral, indifferent, or even hostile *vis-à-vis* Europe, the individual activity of well-placed persons has played a role. The activity and interventions of Robert Schuman in the MRP in the 1940s in France, of Paul-Henri Spaak and the Belgian Socialists in the 1950s, or Edward Heath and the British Conservatives in the 1960s are three of the best examples. Conversely, highly active pro-European individuals could be marginalized by a party organization hostile to the European Community (or indeed those hostile themselves marginalized by a party organization turned sympathetic to further integration; Tony Benn and the British Labour Party, various Gaullist barons and the RPR in the 1980s are illustrative examples). Identifying the pro-European or anti-European stance taken by the official organs of the political party is therefore inadequate to an explanation of the political party's European views, since it does not necessarily reflect the activity and influence of individuals within the organization, one of the major factors affecting the evolution of attitudes over time. In the more Euro-sceptical 1990s, in contrast to the Euro-enthusiastic 1980s, the role of nationalistic individuals in national political parties, whether or not they were party leaders, played a significant role in the parties' attitudes towards the EU (for example, individuals in the influential 1922 Committee of the British Conservatives). In the case of an anti-European like Philippe Séguin in the French RPR, the European debate itself acted as a vector of his own rise within his party in the early 1990s after a decade of pro-European consensus in the party. And throughout the EU member states, the 1990s have witnessed the rise to prominence of various parties of the ultra-right whose defining rhetorical characteristic, at least, has been anti-Europeanism. Whatever the influence of individuals, and however the debate shifted – from the 1960s onwards involving a dynamic tension between intergovernmentalism and supranationalism – the shared background of nearly all of them was their party activity.

PARTIES AND GOVERNMENTS

Because of the assertion of intergovernmentalism in European political relations, political activism, lobbying between parties on the European issue and the involvement of party individuals in the establishing of networks of influence in European Union institutions are, in fact, all secondary to the influence gained via party control of national government. It is, therefore, essentially via governments that political parties influence European affairs.

Perhaps the best recent positive example of the interrelationship between individual, party and government is the case of the French Socialist president, François Mitterrand (president, 1981–95). In the course of Mitterrand's leadership of the French Socialist Party (1971–81), before he became president and the party gained a parliamentary majority and formed a government, the party often held a hostile view of the EC. This view changed during the 1980s through President Mitterrand's gradual alignment with an earlier pro-EC party position, one held by former Socialist Party leaders such as Guy Mollet. Mitterrand's Europeanism was politically effective because it was based upon a tradition within the party, and not simply because he had always been personally pro-European. He was able to highlight and encourage pro-Europeanism to such a degree that during the left's tenure of power in the 1980s it dwarfed most other policy orientations.

By the same token, however, it could be argued that the Mitterrand example – the fact that he changed the dominant view in the party from his powerful position as president – demonstrates the lack of party influence on governmental affairs, and its subordination to individual influence. And, of course, party members themselves often argue that this is so. Resolutions or manifesto promises are always very unevenly translated into governmental policy and legislative output. On the European issue this point is borne out by the experience of many political parties where majority party opinion has been overridden. Both of these views are in fact true. Mitterrand did have enormous influence, not simply because he was president but because he had been the party's presidential candidate and treated as a source of great wisdom; he could not have ridden so hard in a pro-Europe direction had not such a view expressed a strong tradition within the party.

It is not simply strong national executives who reorientate party positions on

Europe. The EU itself seems to draw political parties in and convert them (and individuals too) to the European cause. This is very noticeable with left-wing political parties, especially, although not exclusively, once they are in government. The British Labour Party's position on membership of the European Community when it took office in 1974 is illustrative. The party had been stridently anti-EC before being elected. In office, Prime Minister Wilson used a national referendum on membership in 1975 to distance the party from the consequences of its anti-EC policy. The 'yes' vote in the referendum kept the UK within the EEC while allowing the Labour Party itself to continue for the next decade with its highly ambivalent attitude towards integration. The Spanish Socialists' attitudes to NATO before and after coming to power, and the Greek Socialists' attitudes to the European Union before and after coming to power are equally rich examples of this ambivalence where a government is faced with European issues. In all these cases, once in government, previous official party positions ceased to have the same significance. Nevertheless, minority opinion in the party, especially if the government has only a small majority, can be of considerable influence, partly because the minority opinion is often so vehement. A good example of this is the significant role the anti-Europeans in the British Conservative Party played in undermining the confidence and position of the Conservative government under John Major in 1992 and 1993 during the tortuous ratification of the Maastricht Treaty, and subsequently in the run up to the 1996 intergovernmental conference.

The influencing or attainment of national government, the exercise of national power, and the implementation of policy at national level have been the central organizing principles of party activity since their creation. We shall discuss below the problem of whether parties still exercise power in the same way as they once did. We can say here, however, that such organizing principles make them ill equipped to transcend their role and organize at the European level, other than through intergovernmental channels, and these often only through the influence of individual leaders and party elites well placed to exercise such influence.

ELITES AND OPINION

Regarding the role of individuals and of governments, three further points can be made here. The first is that it is invariably individuals from the party elites who wield the influence we referred to above. That is to say that, almost by definition, the influential individual must be in an influential position (this may not always involve office; former influence is often determining). This normally means, but again not invariably, that the individual concerned will be a member not only of the party's elite but of the country's social elite also. Many studies demonstrate that it is not only in parties with a patrician tradition or element (the British Conservative Party, for example) but also within leftist parties that the higher the position in the party, the higher the social status of the individual concerned. This is a commonplace in political sociology. What it means for our study, however, is that Europe will normally be perceived as an elite issue. This in turn means that the political rhetoric of opposition to these individuals or policy positions will often draw upon a kind of populist claim against the essentially elitist concerns of a minority whose personal education and background have often been such that they know Europe and have personal contacts in countries other than their own. The combination of the anti-Europe stance and anti-elitist style of the Gaullist, Charles Pasqua, during the 1992 French referendum on Maastricht, is a good example of how Europe and a perceived elitism can be conflated and attacked as if they were mutually dependent. Negative perceptions are compounded by a traditional perception of the European Union as an economic rather than a political entity, in a word, a rich man's club.[27]

The second observation is related to the first and concerns the question of elites and their vulnerability to opinion. We mentioned above that one of the organizing principles of political parties was to represent and reflect the views of various constituencies and liaise between the electorate and government.[28] As regards Europe, the observer is faced with a dilemma. In relation to which government or aspect of government might the European political party perform? In relation to which citizens might the political party perform? The answer to both questions arguably is none: the political party has no European government, no European citizens to mediate between or to intercede on behalf of. In terms of opinion's reaction to Europe, it cannot really be said that such opinion is European opinion, but rather national opinion about Europe. How European, then, should a political party's European opinion be? Because Europe can be perceived as a faraway place (even though all Europeans are in it), and as the concern of the elites, the political parties and the whole political class can be momentarily perceived, and rejected, as constituting that elite. This can have dramatic consequences, as was demonstrated by the Danish 'no' to the Maastricht Treaty in 1992, in which growing disaffection with the political class generally was accentuated still further through the contentiousness of a referendum issue concerning Europe. This happened in France, too, during the referendum campaign for treaty ratification in September 1992; most French political parties and majority opinion, even in the Gaullist Party, were in favour of ratification. The 'yes' vote, however, won the barest of majorities, demonstrating once again the political effects of a perceived lack of popular consultation on the European issue, and the capacity for Europe to generate a groundswell of hostile opinion in particular circumstances. In fact, the Danish referendum triggered, in other member states, a whole series of oppositions to European integration and/or the way it was being driven.[29]

The third observation relates to the two major strands of political activity in the European Union's institutions, namely, intergovernmentalism and supranationalism: in *both* cases political party influence goes via national government. In the case of intergovernmentalism, this is because the actors in the European Council and Council/s of Ministers are drawn from the governments of the member states;[30] in the case of supranationalism because the main agency of nomination to the Commission is the national governments. The influence of the parties upon the European Parliament is great, and it is true that here political party influence is not refracted through government. The political significance of the EP, however, is small compared to that of the Council and the Commission. The struggle for political control, power and accountability in the European Union since the 1950s was shaped by the relationship between the Commission, the Council of Ministers (and, since 1974, the Council of Ministers and the European Council) and the national governments. In this way, the potentially direct involvement of political parties was partly screened out. Nevertheless, there have been significant developments in the scope of the parties' influence via the European Parliament, and it is to these that we now turn.

POLITICAL PARTIES AND THE EUROPEAN PARLIAMENT

A European Parliament with delegated representatives from each of the national parliaments existed from 1958 onwards. A major change occurred in 1979 with the institution of direct elections to the European Parliament every five years. As we said above, the Parliament's powers remain largely consultative and very restricted, and real power in the EU resides in the hands of the Council and the Commission.[31] More importantly, and in the context of a European Parliament not considered as a major site of power by either the citizens or the governments of the European member states, its legitimacy remains fragile and its relevance, even its desirability, contested.

One of the fundamental differences between the European Parliament and the intergovernmental institutions of the EU is the Parliament's concerted attempt to organize itself, and therefore the future of Europe, along partisan rather than territorial lines, responding to, one might say encouraging, ideological cleavages at the European level. This in part arises from the deep belief, especially in the two main groups, the socialists and the European People's Party (Christian democrats), that such has been the effective and democratic way to organize national polities, distinguishing them from authoritarianism, one-party states and dictatorships; thus, therefore, should the future Europe be organized. It is interesting in terms of political organization and of ideology, but especially in terms of political culture, that what is being envisaged is a transposition of a political *modus vivendi* from the national to the supranational level.

It is true of course that 'ideologizing' the European dimension is not the only organizational principle in the EU, nor even its main one. In fact, in many ways it is a somewhat idealistic endeavour, and over the past thirty years has been seen even as quixotic in the face of the irresistible pull of national concerns: whenever a social, economic or territorial crisis has occurred, the political parties invariably reflect their perceived national interests. There is an overwhelmingly strong national focus in the EU. To date, this has been only slightly mitigated by the attempts to cleave the EP ideologically or by partisan input into the Committee of the Regions.[32] But although the integration of national economies has in many ways driven the history of the EU, ideas about political organization, desirable institutional structures, social policy, political co-operation, wealth distribution and so on have all involved ideological considerations. Even the creation of an economically strong Europe is seen by most political parties in terms of the 'kind of world we want to live in'. The point here is that it is not a question of whether Europe has developed or will develop along national rather than partisan lines, or of establishing which of these is the true political fault-line dividing politically organized interests from one another, but that both exist and have a strong claim to representation at the European level.

We said above that there was something idealistic about trying to organize the European Parliament along ideological lines. This is because of the EP's institutional weakness, rather than because this does not reflect a European reality. Potentially, the ideological organization of the EP is of great significance, and is not only about how the present should be reflected politically at the European level, but how the future might be enacted institutionally and politically. It is conceivable to imagine Europe in this way, particularly as regards policy elaboration and the organizational conduct of political elites. The question of who such formations represent ideologically, however, remains. What are the European constituencies represented by such Euro-parties? What does it mean in partisan terms to be European? Where is the linkage? The problem for those trying to push political activity on to the European level, and given that this is the level at which economic activity principally operates, is that politically the nation state still possesses decisive vitality, both as a site of activity and as a player in international relations. Not only has it survived, quite illogically; it remains a mobilizing political force of enormous cultural strength, and it is creative in that political change (such as the development of Franco-German relations over the last fifty years) occurs along channels in which the nation state is critically implicated.[33] The expression of popular sovereignty, moreover, remains most obvious at this level. The *raison d'état* as a mobilizing factor in political action also remains decisive at a whole variety of levels; and although this usually depends upon the strength and influence of the nation state involved, smaller states, too, manifest similar traits. Political parties from a shared 'space', then, share more than territory: they share dispositions, cultural attitudes, language; we might say they share secrets which bind them to one another, so that even in ideological conflict they can feel the same pull of say, in the Irish case, allegiance to a united Ireland; in the UK case, the sense of being unlike continental Europeans; in the Danish case, the shared weight of the country's fearful proximity to Germany; in the case of the French, a fundamental conviction of France's own polity offering the blueprints for European political organization, and so on and so on; and in the case of all the member states, the exigency of defending jobs, industries and the infrastructure of national economies.[34]

We can speculate, therefore, that one of the reasons why the political parties are perceived as being less than centrally relevant in the European context is that here they do not perform one of the essential functions of the political party, that of linkage; that is to say, on European issues they do not act as channels between citizens' interests and governmental or supragovernmental institutions. Generally speaking, the European Parliament has organized itself as if it were the legislature of a supranational state. The irony is that, in spite of certain gestures by national parties (e.g. drawing up a common manifesto with sister parties), the elections to the EP themselves are fought almost wholly along national lines, and according to national issues; and it is only when they are conducted in this way that they actually generate any interest. This is more the case in some countries than in others, but is the general rule in all of them.

Moreover, the EP's legitimacy is low (voting turnout is relatively low, around 60 per cent across Europe in the last four elections), its powers are restricted and the relationship of the parties in Parliament to the national parties is also problematic. The British Labour Party is a good case in point and reflects one of the fundamental dilemmas of European integration. In the European Parliament, the British Labour group was the largest both in the Parliament and in the socialist group (forty-five MEPs in the 1989–94 legislature, sixty-two in the 1994–99 legislature). It was enthusiastically pro-integration, and often radical in its approach (for example, its opposition to Allied involvement in the Gulf War of 1991). In both these respects it was, however, out of step with the national party to which it was subordinate. There exists perpetual tension between the two levels of activity, and the national party constantly has to stress the subordination, sometimes insubordination, of its satellite in Strasbourg. In France too, many of the highly respected French Socialist MEPs were quite unceremoniously replaced in the 1994 elections by new candidates who reflected the changed configuration within the party at national level.

In a sense, the European Union expresses the contradictions of European politics: the Parliament is organized into adversarial transnational political families (socialists, Christian democrats, etc.) which themselves are highly sensitive to their national origins; the Council expresses national interests, yet from governments themselves formed along lines of ideological and policy choice. The Commission, with a European mission on the one hand, and nationally designated commissioners on the other, liaises with each, and therefore enjoys decisive influence, yet also has the most fragile legitimacy of any of the EU's main institutions.[35] Moreover, in the ideologically defined European Parliament, there is collusion and consensus in many instances between parliamentary groups (especially between the socialists and Christian democrats) in order to find solutions, execute parliamentary business and enhance the status and effectiveness of the Parliament, or of the integration process itself. This means that both ideological and territorial distinctions have superimposed upon them another set of divisions, between the view which wants the Parliament and the Union to work, to prosper and to increase its powers, and one which does not; between lies a range of intermediate opinion concerning the scope of the European Parliament, and the desired latitude of the Union.

There are, then, three fundamental problems regarding party political activity at the European level. The first is that there is both a perceived and a real lack of relationship between the European citizen and the party as an expression of aggregated citizen interests. Voting in European elections is usually just a form of expressing a view of national governments.[36] By organizing itself into partisan rather than territorial groups, the European Parliament demonstrates its desire to be a policy-orientated institution. This, however, brings us to the second problem, already mentioned, which is that whatever it may or may not be (an expression of national interests, an agency of ideologies), and however legitimate it may or may not be, the EP has little power, and therefore its lack of perceived importance is compounded. The EP was given second reading powers by the Single European Act and limited co-decision by the Maastricht Treaty, and has since seen more lobbying by interest groups; before, the focus was much more exclusively on the Commission. The political parties, however, remain largely outside the whole culture of lobbying and specific interest group representation, and are therefore uninformed or less informed by it and about it.[37]

In terms of parties developing an identity in the European Parliament and elsewhere, a third fundamental problem is that traditional political identities are themselves shifting, if not diminishing. They remain recognizably unchanged only within extremist or supersensitive nationalist parties. Nevertheless, at a time when groups are not only trying to work together, but to *identify* themselves in order that they can work together, identity is as important as it is problematic. Strong coalitions are still formed in the European Parliament, even though differences between them are invariably resolved by consensus negotiation. Most of these coalitions involve, however, only loosely related ideological issues: health and safety, the environment, workers' rights, industrial policy, social dumping. We might argue that the only fundamental difference between the two main groups in the European

Parliament involves degrees of *laissez-faire* versus degrees of state intervention in the economy. Even here, however, the socialists are far more free market than traditionally they were, and the Christian democrats were never free marketeers of the Friedmanite type. If the EP does develop and strengthen along partisan lines, therefore, it will be along new ideological lines based less upon old divisions and more upon doctrinal reference points as yet unclarified. The extent to which political parties both effectively reflect and aspire to exert influence upon such reference points will depend significantly upon their ability properly to identify the cleavages that will count in future partisan conflict.

This convergence between the ideological families is sometimes such that, at the European level, policy differences are minimal, and the search for consensus, the driving force of the European Union itself, is the norm in terms of European Parliament activity. With the collapse of the Soviet Union in the early 1990s, the ideological cleavages which often forced parties to organize themselves in relation to a political spectrum running from – to simplify – capitalism to communism, have given way to other cleavages (income, age, profession, lifestyle, religion, etc.). These have existed for a long time, but are arguably insufficient in themselves to reorganize the party political system. They do, nevertheless, have salience, and potentially more effect in the post-Cold War era. The parties therefore face a crisis of orientation, and perhaps even of identity, of a kind they have not before encountered. For it is one of the ironies of European integration and of the role of the political parties, that at the very moment they begin wrestling with the question of their supranational or transnational legitimacy and role, their legitimacy and role *per se* are undergoing major revision.

POLITICAL PARTIES IN THE 1990s

One of the striking features of national party responses to the European Union is the manner in which most parties of EU member states are or else have become pro-European Union. This is not always the case, but is a strong tendency within EU politics. By the 1990s, only a handful of communist and extreme right-wing parties remained uncompromisingly anti-EU. It is not, however, a question of straightforward acceptance or rejection. The British Conservatives were thrown into confusion in the early 1990s by the strength of minority anti-European Union feeling in a party generally accepting of the European Union. The classic examples of hostility are, as we mentioned earlier, the French and Portuguese Communist Parties. Nevertheless, it is indeterminable whether a party like the PCF, with its blend of chauvinist nationalism and pro-Soviet internationalism, should be *necessarily* opposed to the European Union. The EU can in principle engender allegiance or hostility from any ideological perspective. Even such fundamental hostility as the PCF's became muted when the party was in a strong position to oppose it, as it was when power sharing in national government with the Socialists between 1981 and 1984. Once in government, parties' views, as we have seen, seem to converge on the EU. The question we need to consider here, however, is the extent to which such convergence reflects the political parties' relationship to their constituency.

Since the 1960s (a period of relative political party stability), issues have arisen in acutely political form: disarmament, women's rights, the siting of power stations or of motorways, the provision of nursery facilities, abortion rights, racism; these have often taken political form and 'crested' by means of 'single-issue' groups. The political party was often seen as incapable of or unwilling to take on these issues, which could rise dramatically on the scale of public attention (and as often dramatically fall). This development has been witnessed, and with similar degrees of intensity, in all of Western Europe. Perhaps the most striking example of such a movement (if one can describe the environment as a single issue) was the German Greens, a movement so successful it became a political party – only to face all the internal dilemmas and organizational and strategic failures faced by political parties. It is perhaps worth adding here a word on the widely accepted thesis by Otto Kirchheimer on the 'catch-all' party, and the way in which political parties in the post-war period widened their appeal in an attempt to become all things to all voters.[38] Given the rise of single-issue politics, we need to add the observation that catch-all political parties clearly do not catch all.[39] If we consider, however, that single-issue groups and political parties are both responses to their environment and to one another, it is arguable that this is not, in fact, evidence of the decline of political parties but of changes in modes of political activity. Perhaps, stretching the semantics, we can say that the political party cannot represent the whole, that it is by definition anti-totalitarian and partisan.[40]

Party identification, along with party membership, has fallen dramatically in the last thirty years across Europe. Allegiances are less intense, more liable to change, and generally seen as less relevant than they used to be. The socio-economic changes of the 1960s, moreover, found reflection within the political system in the 1970s and 1980s. Schematically, we can say that relative affluence and the development of consumerism and the tertiary sector (60 per cent of employed Europeans were in service industries by the 1990s) led to major shifts in individual and group *perceptions*, not least in terms of class and party loyalties. Attitudes to political parties in terms of identification, loyalty and activism underwent major changes in this period, a loosening of ties being the dominant characteristic of change. Affluence and social mobility accentuate dealignment. In fact, throughout Europe by the 1990s only a fraction of the adult population were members of a political party and usually only a tenth of the membership of any political party is involved in any activism.[41] With shifts in the social cleavages in West European societies, changes that were accompanied by falls in church attendance and therefore changes in religious cleavages, the whole coupled with a partisan dealignment and the widely held belief that political parties do not address issues relevant to even their target constituencies, it is not surprising that a whole series of factors suggest system volatility: short-lived 'surge' or 'flash' parties, the rise of single-issue politics, abstentionism, the struggle between modernizers and traditionalists within most political parties, are just a few examples.[42] Nor is it surprising that in such a political environment, developing a coherent and forceful attitude to Europe, whether pro or anti, gives way in many political parties to a strategic caution borne of real uncertainty. Anti-European Union feeling exists as a potential threat to consensus in many parties and to the support they do have. Nevertheless, in the European political class or classes, pro-European feeling has been a generalized and gradual response to a generalized and gradual pro-European Union culture within Europe. Such a culture is, however, notoriously difficult to measure. Such instruments as the publication *Eurobarometer* can only approximate to a monitoring, not offer an understanding of feeling concerning Europe and European integration.[43] The triggering of a range of unexpected responses to Europe throughout Europe by and after the Danish referendum of 1992 is evidence of how unpredictable European opinion on Europe can be.

The hostilities engendered in various national public opinions by the ratification of the Maastricht Treaty by the member states in 1992 and 1993 began unravelling the growing sense of political integration that had been building up over the previous five years or so. Denmark, France, Britain and Germany all experienced major anti-European Union reactions to Maastricht once the Danes had demonstrated that popular opinion could have a major impact. It is probable that much of this feeling against Europe and the European Union was a form of sanction, not of the principle of further integration but of the process; a process which was not integrated into the democratic procedures of sanction or endorsement by national polities, or by the European population as a whole. We face here a dilemma, therefore, because the *agencies* of political communication in this area, which should act as forums of debate, aggregators of interest and opinion, 'transmission belts', 'linkage mechanisms' or 'shock absorbers' in the integration process are the political parties, and for all the reasons we have given, the parties are struggling with their role. The irony here, and an added complication in terms of analysis, is that opinion polls and surveys show that Europe is not a major concern for Europeans as far as political identification and even policy preferences are concerned. There is, therefore, a lack of political representation as regards Europe; this is matched by a lack of interest on the part of the public except in the form of anti-Europeanism; and the political organization caught in this Catch-22 is the political party. What then should the political parties be doing in this context to resolve the paradox?

CONCLUSIONS

Theories of neo-corporatism have questioned the relevance of the political party in advanced industrial democracies. It is doubtless the case that corporatist structures within a democracy are evidence of the extreme complexity of modern representative democracies.[44] The crucial point, however, is that that is where they are: in democracy, not outside it. The political parties used to perform many of the functions now performed by neo-corporatist relations. We return to our original observation. Governments use avenues other than the political party to mediate and organize interests in society. At the European level, where the parties are even less in evidence than at the national level, the question becomes even more pertinent. Lobbies, interest groups, consortia, cartels and professional associations are all in a systematic relation to the European Union's institutions, offering expertise and communication channels to the European Union's structures; even the European Parliament's committees increasingly use these rather than party expertise in their elaboration of legislative proposals. In a sense, the kinds of policy decisions which governmental and other agencies need to take are either too complex for the political parties, or too specialized, or both. One of the major problems, therefore, is the political parties' suitability as sites of expertise in areas such as economic and monetary union. One of the ways the political parties have responded to this is through the use of think tanks which, moreover, particularly in parties of the left, constantly face accusations concerning their undemocratic nature and place within the party political process.[45]

Yet political parties have endured. If exclusive neo-corporatism and single-issue theories of political activity were correct, the political party should have disappeared at least two decades ago. In fact, throughout the twentieth century, political parties have remained one of the enduring institutions, and come to characterize representative democracy. Many of them have tried to adapt to new forms of leadership, to the media age, to a looser trade union connection, to the multiplicity of sources of all kinds of information and so on. They remain, on a continent still dominated by the nation state, the only avenue to formal political power. In terms of other kinds of more responsible, more democratic structures, moreover, alternatives remain of rudimentary relevance.[46] In terms of their relations to institutions and to one another, however, political parties face, if not an identity crisis, then at least serious questions of adaptation to modern politics.

It is true that political parties are often the target for the expression of disapproval by citizens, especially if they are associated with the national government. Nevertheless, the opposite is also true. No form of organized political relation and expression has yet developed which can pick up half-formed waves of opinion as well as the political party, and this even though the political party is perpetually in tension between its rally quality and its need to organize itself in order to survive over time.[47] The political party remains the best organization to express and channel politically the conflicts between classes, religious groups or regions. Even today, political parties generally remain part of the broader movements which gave rise to them, whether professional, ideological or territorial. Often it is shifts within these, for example the movement of trade union-based parties towards more citizen-based parties, which cause the apparent crises within parties. But they endure in the absence of alternatives, and in stark contrast to the political chaos of countries in which a party system has not been established or has been destroyed.

The parties adapt and persist. It is true that party identification is now low in all countries in the European Union, and a further period of adaptation is to be expected: how is a party to incorporate the expertise necessary to govern highly complex economies and societies? How is it to represent interests properly? How is it to adapt to social and demographic changes? How can it express the views of its potential members, supporters and voters? How is it to do all these things in an integrating Europe? In a word, how is it to change in order to survive the transformations in party identification? Invariably, however, it is the political parties themselves which remain major contributors to the debating of these questions, and invariably remain players in any imagined solutions.

One of the reasons why the political party faced such problems of identity and direction at the national level during the second half of the twentieth century was because of the internationalization of national economies. The European Union itself was a response to this economic internationalization. The dilemma has been that the nation state remains the organizing agency of this internationalized activity, and while the parties have become less important in decision making at the national level, they cannot, for all the reasons given, replace the inadequate national focus with a significant input at the international level. The economic integration of Western Europe, in spite of the slowdown in the early 1970s and again in the early 1990s, has continued at a dramatic pace.[48] Similarly, social integration (travel, educational exchanges) has intensified (with concomitant politico-administrative measures concerning immigration, drugs and police activity). The irony, and the danger for democratic politics, is that the political equivalents of these integrative processes – transnational parties – are only gradually forthcoming, and shakily at that, and their future effectiveness is not assured. A further point to make here is that as the European Union expands, which it has been doing continuously at roughly ten-yearly intervals, economic and social integration will continue. Political integration, on the other hand, will be – because of the difficulties of organizing a larger Union – *de facto* less easy. The political parties therefore will face more challenges the more integration – economic, social or political – proceeds.[49] Nevertheless, political parties have, as we have said, endured; indeed their staying power is one of their chief features.

It is no doubt the case that the political parties are undergoing change. Nevertheless, it is possible that this change is being misunderstood because the nature of political parties has itself been misunderstood. Maurice Duverger's analysis of political parties is perhaps the most influential characterization of political parties, dividing political parties essentially and chronologically between small, elitist cadre parties on the one hand, and mass parties on the other, the latter being bureaucratized, organized and 'structured' by activists.[50] It is arguable, however, with the rise of the media and the spread of a more diffuse political culture, that the mass party essentially needs not activists in order to survive, but professionals. Pizzorno makes the interesting point that strong political parties are perhaps evidence of an unstable political regime,[51] that is to say that the more difficult it is for a community to express itself politically, the more disciplined and strongly articulated the political parties need to be. It follows that in a more stable and sophisticated polity, the political parties will inevitably be weaker. A related point is that the party system pre-dates the mass parties of the late nineteenth and twentieth centuries. In many ways the system itself was already there in the age of cadre parties. If the kind of mass party politics Europe has known for a century transforms itself in order to absorb and respond to the lessons of mass society – the media, different forms of education, more social and geographical mobility, and so on – that is to say, if the mass party as we have known it declines, even disappears, this does not necessarily mean that the system itself is in decline, or that the safeguards it brings to the democratic life are being undermined. Duverger was not in a position to see that the political convergence across Europe inherent in the post-war period would favour those political parties which used the techniques of the old cadre parties: a strong relationship to the media; a diffuse ideology; control of the party by elites; issue politics; and a dialogue with constituents. Kirchheimer's implicit critique of Duverger should be seen in this context, that perhaps the cadre party and the catch-all parties, in many ways the antithesis of one another, have a great deal more in common with one another than would appear.[52] This is in part what is happening at the level of the trans-European federations and party groups in the European Parliament. The bureaucratic mass party has given way to a party in which an elite of professionals organizes for particular purposes such as winning elections and developing policy. The organization, however, through its membership and recruitment policy is, unlike the old cadre parties, open and, unlike the mass parties, in constant contact with large swathes of opinion, rather than with activists.

In the future, then, political parties face challenges at both the national and the European level: first, whether at the symbolic level they can offer themselves as encapsulating 'an idea', a political morality, a vision and so on, strong enough to sustain their popularity; second, whether they will continue to canalize opinion and, as formerly, offer the prospect of political power and policy implementation. We can expect the parties' contradictory development to continue; they will continue to face questions concerning their value as well as accusations of their growing irrelevance until they adapt successfully to new circumstances. The question of Europe, and how the political parties respond to it, will be a part of this fascinating process.

NOTES

1 I should like to thank David Bell, Helen Drake and Bruce Graham for their comments and suggestions on an earlier draft of this chapter.

2 We use the term European Union to refer to the institutional framework set up by the Rome Treaty of 1957 establishing the European Economic Community, later called the European Community. The Union of which the Community is itself one of the pillars formally came into being after November 1993, when the Treaty on European Union (the Maastricht Treaty) came into force. Strictly speaking, the Community still exists within the Union, but just as EC replaced EEC as the accepted term, so the EU replaced the EC. The European Commission put it like this:

> Transformation of the Community into a European Union does have political signifi-cance. It reflects the wider dimensions of the new Treaty. The Union is founded on the European Communities, but also reflects the desire of the member states to establish a political union, creating Union citizenship and extending the Community's activities into new fields such as foreign and security policy, defence, judicial and home affairs. It echoes the phrase from the preamble of the Treaty of Rome 'an ever closer union among the peoples of Europe'. It is important to note that the European Union is not a legal body, whereas the European Community is. The new Treaty stresses the Union's single institutional framework, but it embraces a wider range of policymaking procedures than those laid down in the European Community treaties. The European Council of Heads of State and Government provides the impetus for the development of the Union and defines general political guidelines. (Background Report: *The Maastricht Agreements: Some Questions and Answers*, Commission of the European Communities, ISEC/B10/92, 2 April 1992, p. 2.)

In this volume we use the term 'integration' to refer to degrees of co-operation within the Union. For a historical overview of the treaties see N. Nugent, *The Government and Politics of the European Community* (London, Macmillan, 1991, 2nd edn), pp. 34–49.

3 See bibliography for the background literature on this topic, bearing in mind that essentially there are two literatures, one on political parties and one on the European Union.

4 K. Lawson, *Political Parties and Linkage* (New Haven and London, Yale University Press, 1980), pp. 3ff. On identification of goals, elite recruitment and mobilization see K. Von Beyme, *Political Parties in Western Democracies* (Aldershot, Gower, 1985), pp. 13ff.

5 The view that political parties were no longer as central to political studies as they once were was in part the result of the influence of economic approaches upon the study of politics. In the case of EC/EU studies, until the 1990s, political parties as either case studies or comparative studies were almost entirely unresearched.

6 There is an extensive literature on parties and cleavages. For a succinct discussion see J.-E. Lane and S. Ersson, *Politics and Society in Western Europe* (London, Sage, 1991, 2nd edn), pp. 25–31; D. Seiler, *Les partis politiques en Europe* (Paris, PUF, 1982), pp. 13–19; and S.M. Lipset and S. Rokkan, 'Cleavage structures, party systems and voter align-ments', in P. Mair (ed.), *The West European Party System* (Oxford, Oxford University Press, 1991), pp. 91–138.

7 For a comprehensive analysis of such developments seen from the perspective of a

shared language, see F. Saint-Ouen, *Les partis politiques et l'Europe* (Paris, PUF, 1990). See also H. Drake, 'Political parties and European integration', *Modern and Contemporary France*, No. 47, October 1991, pp. 74–9.

8 Against this, of course, we could equally demonstrate the striking similarities between the policy goals, internal organization and leadership styles of the northern social democratic parties. For a description and analysis of this see S. Padgett and W. Paterson, *Social Democracy in Post-War Europe* (London, Longman, 1991), pp. 126–76.

9 See G. Hermet, 'The citizen individual in Western Christianity', in P. Birnbaum and J. Leca (eds), *Individualism* (Oxford, Clarendon Press, 1990), pp. 116–40.

10 The best concise assertion of this important point is G. Sartori, 'The sociology of parties: a critical review', in P. Mair (ed.), *The West European Party System* (Oxford, Oxford University Press, 1991), pp. 150–82. See also, H. Daalder, 'The "reach" of the party system', in ibid., pp. 78–90, and Lane and Ersson, *Politics and Society*, pp. 25–31.

11 Because of the strong influence of Moscow on the parties of the Third International between 1920 and the mid-1980s, communist parties are more of an exception to this exceptional rule.

12 See Sartori, 'The sociology of parties'.

13 On the work of these groups see the chapters by Ladrech and Hix in this volume. See also G. Tsebelis, 'The power of the European Parliament as a conditional agenda setter', *American Political Science Review*, vol. 88, no. 1, March 1994, pp. 128–42.

14 It is also difficult for trade unions to organize effectively at the European level because of the 'structural asymmetries' of their national conditions of activity. See P. Guerrierri and P. Padoan, *The Political Economy of European Integration* (London, Harvester, 1989), p. 49.

15 See, *inter alia*, D. Urwin, *The Community of Europe* (London, Longman, 1991), and D. Arter, *The Politics of European Integration in the Twentieth Century* (Aldershot, Dartmouth, 1993).

16 For a thorough discussion and critique of the prevailing view of the influence of Marshall Aid, see A.S. Milward, *The Reconstruction of Western Europe, 1945–51* (London, Methuen, 1984), especially pp. 90–125.

17 In terms of integration, the main point to stress is that the UK refused to join the ECSC in 1950, and in 1955 withdrew from the EEC negotiations, leaving France, Germany, Italy, the Netherlands, Belgium and Luxembourg to create the ECSC and EEC on their own. It is worth pointing out that the UK's attitude was based largely upon its assumption of the continuing economic weakness and political instability of its continental neighbours.

18 See L. Blum, *A l'échelle humaine* (Lausanne, Mermod, n.d.), pp. 63ff. For Blum, the parties were essential to the proper re-establishing of democracy; their fundamental rationalism helped guard against the illegitimacy of authoritarian leadership.

19 Padgett and Paterson, *Social Democracy*, pp. 224 and 250; and A. Dalthrop, *Politics and the European Community* (London, Longman, 1982), pp. 89–93.

20 S. Hoffmann, 'Obstinate or obsolete: the fate of the nation state and the case of Western Europe', *Daedalus*, No. 95, Summer 1966, pp. 862–915.

21 There was some high politics in the form of the Western European Union. This, however, followed NATO's European policy almost completely, and, in fact, was of little relevance given the Atlantic Alliance and NATO. For an excellent discussion of this issue see M. Kahler, 'The survival of the state in European international relations', in C. Maier (ed.), *Changing Boundaries of the Political* (Cambridge, Cambridge University Press, 1987).

22 The significant foreign policy issue in the 1940s and 1950s for Belgium, France, the UK (the latter joining the EEC in 1972) and in the 1970s, Portugal (which joined in 1986), was the question of decolonization. The question of Europe did not generally divide the parties, whatever their views, other than where it impinged on this issue.

23 See A. Clesse, *Le Projet de la CED du plan Pleven au crime du 30 août. L'histoire d'un malentendu européen* (Baden-Baden, Nomos, 1989); F.N.E. Fursden, *The European Defence Community: A History* (London, Macmillan, 1980).

24 Pro-integration movements such as the European Movement (1948), which attempted to

transcend the national political parties, were set up to counter these tendencies. In their first few years they were arguably successful. The European Movement was a pressure group and a talking shop whose principal aim was to raise consciousness of European integration and stimulate national parties and governments regarding European issues. In this sense it was a complement to mainstream democratic procedures and structures. It never triggered a mass movement, and integration remained an elite activity. In a sense the Community that emerged from the Rome Treaty of 1957 shortcircuited the European Movement and any potential it had to become a mass movement. Monnet's Europe was essentially a bureaucrat's Europe in which the unelected Commission would dominate. It is arguable, however, that given the political realities of post-war nation state politics which we have discussed above, this was the only supranational Europe on offer. See M. Kolinsky and W. Paterson, *Political Movements in Europe* (London, Croom Helm, 1976).

25 See K. Featherstone 'Jean Monnet and the "democratic deficit" in the European Union', *Journal of Common Market Studies*, vol. 32, no. 2, June 1994, pp. 149–70; see also D. Brinkley and C. Hackett, *Jean Monnet: The Path to European Unity* (London, Macmillan, 1991), and J. Monnet, *Mémoires* (Paris, Fayard, 1976).

26 For an interesting contemporary discussion of the context of the veto see John Lambert, 'The constitutional crisis 1965–1966', *Journal of Common Market Studies*, vol. 4, no. 2, 1965, pp. 195–228.

27 This perception has diminished, particularly since the entry of poorer countries – Portugal, Spain and Greece. Nevertheless, the view is still a significantly strong one.

28 See G. Sartori, *Parties and Party Systems* (Cambridge, Cambridge University Press, 1977), pp. 56–64.

29 For a general discussion of the relation of parties to opinion in the EU context, see M. Slater, 'Political elites, popular indifferences and community building', in Loukas Tsoukalis (ed.), *The European Community* (Oxford, Blackwell, 1983), pp. 69–93. See also Michael Greven, 'Political parties between national identity and Eurofication', in Brian Nelson, David Roberts, Walter Veit (eds), *The Idea of Europe* (Oxford, Berg, 1992), pp. 75–95.

30 There are one or two exceptions to this rule in countries where non-party individuals can be given ministerial office, such as France; however, such individuals invariably join a political party subsequently.

31 This situation is compounded by the fact that few major national politicians are significantly involved in the work of the European Parliament, whether or not they stand as MEPs. See *inter alia*, C. Tugendhat, *Making Sense of Europe* (London, Viking, 1986), p. 14. It is worth pointing out, however, that the EP has seen a gradual increase in its powers since its creation. In the 1994 legislature, its most demonstrable power, ratifying the composition of the Commission, drew public awareness to its potential influence.

32 On the Committee of the Regions see Treaty on European Union, Title II, Arts 198a–c (Luxemburg, Official Publications of the European Community, 1992). See also Andrew Scott, John Peterson and David Millar, 'Subsidiarity: a "Europe of the regions" v. the British constitution', *Journal of Common Market Studies*, vol. 32, no. 1, March 1994, pp. 47–66.

33 See S. Hoffmann, 'Reflections on the nation-state in Western Europe today', in Tsoukalis *The European Community*, pp. 21–37.

34 See eleven papers presented to European Consortium of Political Research, Workshop on National Political Systems and the European Community, University of Essex, March 1991.

35 A further complicating factor from the mid-1990s onwards has been the increasingly partisan profile of the commissioners. For a general overview of the Commission's legitimacy, see H. Drake and C. Pradeilles, 'Political legitimacy and the European Union: choosing the Commission President', paper delivered to the Economic and Social Research Council Conference, Evolution of Rules for a Single European Market, 8–11 September 1994, Exeter, UK.

36 See *inter alia*, J. Lodge (ed.), *Direct Elections to the European Parliament, 1984* (London, Macmillan, 1986), *The 1989 Election of the European Parliament* (London, Macmillan,

1990) especially the introduction, and *The 1994 Election of the European Parliament* (London, Frances Pinter, 1995).

37 See, *inter alia*, H. Wallace, 'Negotiation, conflict, and compromise: the elusive pursuit of common policies', in H. Wallace, W. Wallace and C. Webb (eds), *Policy Making in the European Community* (Chichester, Wiley and Sons, 1983), pp. 43–80; S. Mazey and J. Richardson, 'Interest groups and European integration', Political Studies Association Conference Paper, Belfast, 1992; S. Andersen and E. Eliassen, 'European Community Lobbying', *European Journal of Political Research*, vol. 20, 1991, pp. 177–87; W. Grant, 'Pressure groups and the European Community: an overview', in S. Mazey and J. Richardson, (eds), *Lobbying in the European Community* (Oxford, Oxford University Press, 1993), pp. 27–46; P. McAlcavey and J. Mitchell, 'Industrial regions and lobbying in the structural funds reform process', *Journal of Common Market Studies*, vol. 32, no. 2, June 1994, pp. 236–48.

38 O. Kirchheimer, 'The transformation of the Western European party systems', in J. LaPalombara and M. Weiner (eds), *Political Parties and Political Development* (Princeton, Princeton University Press, 1966), pp. 177–200.

39 See S. Wolinetz, 'The transformation of Western European party systems', in Mair, *The West European Party System*, pp. 218–31.

40 For an interesting discussion of this see Blum, *A l'échelle humaine*, pp. 68ff.

41 See Lane and Ersson, *Politics and Society*, pp. 144–8.

42 See K. Lawson and P. Merkl (eds), *When Parties Fail* (Princeton, Princeton University Press, 1988).

43 *Eurobarometer* (Brussels, European Commission). *Eurobarometer* is a survey-based biannual publication. Since January 1994, a new monthly survey, *L'Europinion*, has also been published.

44 See Lane and Ersson, *Politics and Society*, pp. 36–9. For a theoretical appraisal of the whole subject see A. Cawson, *Corporatism and Political Theory* (Oxford, Blackwell, 1986).

45 J. Gaffney, 'Political think tanks in the UK and ministerial *Cabinets* in France', *West European Politics*, vol. 14, no. 1, January 1991, pp. 1–17. It is perhaps worth pointing out that in the USA there is no tradition, on the left or the right, of party hostility to think tanks.

46 One thinks of a computer-literate citizenry voting on issues, perhaps even legislating from home via personal computers, or, at the other extreme, of J.-P. Sartre's revolutionary but highly unstable groups-in-fusion. Neither of these two examples can be considered as feasible alternatives to party politics and government in the prevailing political cultures in Europe.

47 See B.D. Graham, *Representation and Party Politics* (Oxford, Blackwell, 1993).

48 See L. Tsoukalis, *The New European Economy: The Politics and Economics of Integration* (Oxford, Oxford University Press, 1993).

49 At a governmental level there has been diffusion of economic activity by the privatizations and deregulations which took place across the member states throughout the 1980s, especially in the UK; nevertheless, the overall economic integration of the Union has continued. Although European political co-operation has been given a treaty basis by the Single European Act (Title III, Act 30), it is not remotely as developed or co-ordinated as the economic activity within the Union.

50 M. Duverger, *Political Parties* (London, Methuen, 1976) original published in 1951; R. Michels, *Political Parties* (New York, Dover, 1959).

51 See Von Beyme, *Political Parties*.

52 For a discussion of this issue see Graham, *Representation*, pp. 63–6. See also A. Panebianco, *Political Parties: Organization and Power* (Cambridge, Cambridge University Press, 1988).

SELECT BIBLIOGRAPHY

Amin, A. and Dietrich, M. (eds), *Towards a New Europe? Structural Change in the European Economy*, Aldershot, Edward Elgar, 1991.

Andersen, S. and Eliassen, E., 'European Community lobbying', *European Journal of Political Research*, vol. 20, 1991, pp. 177–87.

Arter, D., *The Politics of European Integration in the Twentieth Century*, Aldershot, Dartmouth, 1993.

Attinà, F., 'Parties, Party systems and democracy in the European Union', *International Spectator*, vol. 27, 1992, pp. 67–86.

Avril, P., *Essais sur les partis politiques*, Paris, Payot, 1990.

Bartolini, S., *Party Politics in Contemporary Western Europe*, London, Cass, 1984.

Blum, L., *A l'échelle humaine*, Lausanne, Mermod, n.d.

Borella, F., *Les Partis politiques en Europe*, Paris, Seuil, 1984.

Brinkley, D. and Hackett, C., *Jean Monnet: The Path to European Unity*, London, Macmillan, 1991.

Budge, I. and Keman, H., *Parties and Democracy: Coalition Formation and Government Functioning in Twenty States*, Oxford, Oxford University Press, 1990.

Bulmer, S., 'Domestic politics and European Community policy-making', *Journal of Common Market Studies*, vol. 21, no. 4, June, 1983, pp. 349–63.

Charlot, J. and Lancelot, A. (eds), *Les partis politiques*, Paris, Colin, 1972.

Clesse, A., *Le Projet de la CED du plan Pleven au crime du 30 août: l'histoire d'un malentendu européen*, Baden-Baden, Nomos, 1989.

Cole, A., *French Political Parties in Transition*, Aldershot, Dartmouth, 1990.

Coombes, D., *Politics and Bureaucracy in the European Community*, London, Allen & Unwin, 1970.

Dahl, R.A., *Political Opposition in Western Democracies*, New Haven and London, Yale University Press, 1966.

Dalthrop, A., *Politics and the European Community*, London, Longman, 1982.

Dalton, R.J., *Citizen Politics in Western Democracies: Public Opinion and Political Parties in the United States, Great Britain, West Germany, and France*, London, Chatham House Publishers, 1988.

Dalton, R.J. et al., *Electoral Change in Advanced Industrial Democracies: Realignment or Dealignment?*, Princeton, Princeton University Press, 1984.

Donegani J.-M. and Sadoun, M., *La démocratie imparfaite. Essai sur le parti politique*, Paris, Gallimard, 1994.

Duverger, M., *Political Parties*, London, Methuen, 1976, original published in 1951.

Epstein, L.D., *Political Parties in Western Democracies*, New Brunswick, NJ, Transaction Books, 1980.

Eurobarometer, Brussels, European Commission.

Featherstone, K., 'Looking towards the 1984 European elections: problems of political integration', *Journal of Common Market Studies*, vol. 22, no. 3, March 1984, pp. 269–82.

Featherstone, K., *Socialist Parties and European Integration: A Comparative History*, Manchester University Press, 1988.

Featherstone, K., 'Jean Monnet and the "Democratic deficit" in the European Union', *Journal of Common Market Studies*, vol. 32, no. 2, June 1994, pp. 149–70.

Fox Piven, F. (ed.), *Labour Parties in Post-industrial Societies*, Cambridge, Polity, 1991.

Fursden, F.N.E., *The European Defence Community: A History*, London, Macmillan, 1980.

Gaffney, J., *The French Left and the Fifth Republic*, London, Macmillan, 1989.

Gaffney, J., *The Language of Political Leadership in Contemporary Britain*, London, Macmillan, 1991.

Gallagher, M. et al., *Representative Government in Western Europe*, New York, McGraw Hill, 1992.

George, S., *Politics and Policy in the European Community*, Oxford, Oxford University Press, 1991, 2nd edn.

Graham, B.D., *Representation and Party Politics*, Oxford, Blackwell, 1993.

Grant, W., 'Pressure groups and the European Community: an overview', in S. Mazey and J. Richardson (eds), *Lobbying in the European Community*, Oxford, Oxford University Press, 1993, pp. 27–46.

Greven, M., 'Political parties between national identity and Eurofication', in B. Nelson, D. Roberts and W. Veit (eds), *The Idea of Europe*, Oxford, Berg, 1992, pp. 75–95.

Guerrierri, P. and Padoan, P., *The Political Economy of European Integration*, London, Harvester, 1989.

Hanley, D. (ed.), *Christian Democracy in Europe: A Comparative Perspective*, London, Frances Pinter, 1994.

Henig, S. (ed.), *Political Parties in the European Community*, London, George Allen and Unwin, 1979.

Hermet, G., 'The citizen-individual in Western Christianity', in P. Birnbaum and J. Leca (eds), *Individualism*, Oxford, Clarendon Press, 1990, pp. 116–40.

Hoffmann, S., 'Obstinate or obsolete: the fate of the nation state and the case of Western Europe', *Daedalus*, No. 95, Summer 1966, pp. 862–915.

Holler, M.J., *The Logic of Multiparty Systems*, Dordrecht/Boston/Lancaster, Kluwer Academic Publishers, 1987.

Hurwitz, L., *Contemporary Perspectives on European Integration: Attitudes, Non-governmental Behaviour, and Collective Decision Making*, New York, Greenwood Press, 1980.

Hurwitz L. and Lequesne C. (eds), *The State of the European Community: Policies, Institutions and Debates in the Transition Years*, London, Longman, 1991.

Jacobs, F. et al., *European Political Parties: A Comprehensive Guide*, Longman, Harlow, 1989.

Kahler, M., 'The survival of the state in European international relations', in C. Maier (ed.), *Changing Boundaries of the Political*, Cambridge, Cambridge University Press, 1987.

Katz, R.S., *A Theory of Parties and Electoral Systems*, Baltimore, Johns Hopkins University Press, 1980.

Keating, M., *The Politics of Modern Europe*, Aldershot, Edward Elgar, 1994.

Kesselman M. et al., *European Politics in Transition*, Lexington, MA, D.C. Heath, 1987.

Kirchheimer, O., 'The transformation of the Western European party systems', in J. LaPalombara and M. Weiner (eds), *Political Parties and Political Development*, Princeton, Princeton University Press, 1966, pp. 177–200.

Kirchner, E.J. (ed.), *Liberal Parties in Western Europe*, Cambridge, Cambridge University Press, 1988.

Kolinsky, M. and Paterson, W., *Political Movements in Europe*, London, Croom Helm, 1976.

Lane, J.-E. and Ersson, S., *Politics and Society in Western Europe*, London, Sage, 1991.

Laver, M. and Hunt, W. Ben, *Policy and Party Competition*, New York, Routledge, 1992.

Lawson, K., *Political Parties and Linkage*, New Haven and London, Yale University Press, 1980.

Lawson, K. and Merkl, P. (eds), *When Parties Fail*, Princeton, Princeton University Press, 1988.

Layton-Henry, Z. (ed.), *Conservative Politics in Western Europe*, New York, St Martin's Press, 1982.

Lee, J.J. and Korter, W., *Europe in Transition*, Austin, University of Texas Press, 1991.

Lemaire-Prosche, G., *Le PS et l'Europe*, Paris, Editions universitaires, 1990.

Listhaug, O., McDonald, S.E. and Rabinowitz, G., 'A comparative spatial analysis of European party systems', *Scandinavian Political Studies*, vol. 13, no. 3, 1990, pp. 227–54.

Lodge, J. (ed.), *Direct Elections to the European Parliament, 1984*, London, Macmillan, 1986.

Lodge J. (ed.), *The 1989 Election of the European Parliament*, London, Macmillan, 1990.

Lodge J. (ed.), *The 1994 Election of the European Parliament*, London, Frances Pinter, 1995.

Mair, P., McAleavey, P. and Mitchell, J., 'Industrial regions and lobbying in the structural funds reform process', *Journal of Common Market Studies*, vol. 32, no. 2, June 1994, pp. 236–48.

Mair P. (ed.), *The West European Party System*, Oxford, Oxford University Press, 1991.

Merkl, P. (ed.), *West European Party Systems*, New York, The Free Press, 1980.

Michels, R., *Political Parties*, New York, Dover, 1959.

Monnet, J., *Mémoires*, Paris, Fayard, 1976.

Muller-Rommel F. (ed.), *New Politics in Western Europe: The Rise and Success of Green Parties and Alternative Lists*, Boulder, CO, Westview Press, 1989.

Muller-Rommel, F. and Pridham G. (eds), *Small Parties in Western Europe: Comparative and National Perspectives*, London, Sage, 1991.

Nelson, B. et al., *The European Community in the 1990s*, Oxford, Berg, 1992.

Nugent, N., *The Government of Politics of the European Union*, London, Macmillan, 1994, 3rd edn.

Padgett, S. and Paterson, W., *A History of Social Democracy in Post-War Europe*, London, Longman, 1991.

Panebianco, A., *Political Parties: Organization and Power*, translated by Marc Silver, Cambridge, Cambridge University Press, 1988.

Parlement européen, Direction générale des études, *Les partis politiques dans la CEE et l'unification européenne*, Parlement européen, Luxembourg, 1988.

Peters, B.G., *European Politics Reconsidered*, London/New York, Holmes and Meier, 1991.

Pridham, G. and Pridham, P., *Transnational Party Cooperation and European Integration*, London, George Allen and Unwin, 1981.

Roussellier, N., *L'Europe des libéraux*, Paris, Complexe, 1991.

Saint-Ouen, F., *Les partis politiques et l'Europe. Une approche comparative*, Paris, PUF, 1990.

Sartori, G., *Parties and Party Systems*, Cambridge, Cambridge University Press, 1977.

Scholten, I. (ed.), *Political Stability and Neo-corporatism: Corporatist Integration and Societal Cleavages in Western Europe*, London, Sage, 1987.

Seiler, D.-L., *Les partis politiques en Europe*, Paris, PUF, 1982.

Seiler, D.-L., *Les partis politiques*, Paris, Armand Colin, 1993.

Shackleton, M., 'European Community between three ways of life', *Journal of Common Market Studies*, vol. 29, no. 6, December 1991, pp. 575–601.

Shackleton, M., 'The internal legitimacy crisis of the European Union', Edinburgh, European Institute, Occasional Paper, 1994.

Sjöblom, G., *The Roles of Political Parties in Denmark and in Sweden, 1970–1984*, Copenhagen, Institute of Political Studies, University of Copenhagen, 1985.

Smith, G., *Politics in Western Europe*, London, Heinemann, 1989.

Spinelli, A., *The Eurocrats: Conflict and Crisis in the European Community*, Baltimore, Johns Hopkins University Press, 1966.

Stammen, T., *Political Parties in Europe*, Connecticut, Meckler Publishing, 1981.

Treverton, G.F. (ed.), *The Shape of the New Europe*, The Council on Foreign Relations Press, 1991.

Tsebelis, G., 'The power of the European Parliament as a conditional agenda setter', *American Political Science Review*, vol. 88, no. 1, March 1994, pp. 128–42.

Tsoukalis L. (ed.), *The European Community*, Oxford, Blackwell, 1983.

Tsoukalis, L., *The New European Economy: The Politics and Economics of Integration* Oxford, Oxford University Press, 1993.

Tugendhat, C., *Making Sense of Europe*, London, Viking, 1986.

Urwin, D., *The Community of Europe*, London, Longman, 1991.

Von Beyme, K., *Political Parties in Western Democracies*, Aldershot, Gower, 1985.

Wallace, H., Wallace, W. and Webb, C. (eds), *Policy Making in the European Community*, Chichester, Wiley and Sons, 1983.

Ware, A., *Citizens, Parties and the State: A Reappraisal*, Cambridge, Polity, 1987.

Wilson, F.L., *European Politics Today: The Democratic Experience*, Englewood Cliffs, Prentice Hall, 1990.

Wolinetz, S.B. (ed.), *Parties and Party Systems in Liberal Democracies*, London, Routledge, 1988.

Zetterholm S. (ed.), *National Cultures and European Integration*, Oxford, Berg, 1994.

Part I
Case studies

2 The German Social Democrats

Richard Moeller

The German Social Democrats (SPD) have held a broad spectrum of attitudes and policies in regard to Europe. Under the direction of distinctive leaders, the party has maintained approving as well as disapproving viewpoints of European integration for numerous reasons. The breadth of these convictions makes for an interesting examination of the internal dynamics of the German Social Democrats and their philosophy towards Europe. This chapter characterizes the relationship of the Social Democratic Party of the Federal Republic, and later a reunited Germany, to the European Union. Each section covers a specific period in the development in the Social Democratic Party's policy and attitude regarding European integration. The first part of this chapter examines the creation of the SPD and the pro-German policies exemplified by its first post-war leader, Kurt Schumacher. The shift in policy from a negative to a positive view of an integrated Europe is then explored. The SPD's inter-German relationship and Willy Brandt's *Ostpolitik* illustrate the distinctive support for integration and recognition of a divided Germany. Finally, examination of the party's handling of reunification will explain SPD arguments for and against Maastricht and the specifics leading up to the European Union.[1]

HISTORICAL BACKGROUND

The SPD originated from the creation of the Socialist Workers' Party of Germany at Gotha in 1875, combining an organization that had been founded by Ferdinand Lassalle and led by August Bebel and William Liebknecht. Most of the early support for European unity by the SPD came in the form of workers' unions, and in 1866 the Leipzig Programme of the General Association of German Workers stated that a united and centralist German nation state would be the beginning 'of a solid European state'.[2] In 1891 the party's new programme adopted Marxist objectives; yet the tension between revolutionary and revisionist ideas reflected ideological conflicts which would be echoed years later by Rosa Luxemburg and Eduard Bernstein. In 1912 Otto Hue, leader of a miners' union, suggested a 'concerted policy for the exploitation of European iron resources by means of a trade policy linking to the East . . . and the formation of a Franco-German iron and steel community'.[3] Before 1914, most of the support for broader European relations was confined to a group of right-wing SPD revisionist intellectuals who were connected with the journal *Sozialistische Monatshefte*.[4] In 1914 the SPD voted for war credits. Rosa Luxemburg, as an opponent of war, broke away from the SPD and helped to form what was later to become the Communist Party (KPD).

After the First World War the idea of European unity strengthened dramatically. In the SPD's Heidelberg basic programme of 1925, Rudolf Breitscheid added a referendum stating that the SPD 'stands for the creation of a European economic unit, which has on economic grounds become urgent, for the formation of the "United States of Europe", in order thereby to attain the solidarity of interests of all continents'.[5] Yet by the late 1920s the SPD had lost much of its integration momentum; and despite much external discussion during this time regarding the League of Nations and the Briand Memorandum on European unity, the SPD mentioned the subject only in passing in its 1929 *Jahrbuch*.[6]

During the 1930s, the SPD was concerned about Hitler's growing strength, fought in opposition to the Nazis, and was eventually suppressed with many members being jailed.[7] During the war many SPD members went into exile, taking with them, as it were, the fear of nationalism. There was also general agreement that the nation state had become redundant, and that European politicians, especially socialists, should 'work for a European future'.[8] The chairman of the exiles in London, Hans Vogel, argued that a 'Europe that continues to remain fragmented into a few dozen separate states, politically and economically, will in the future continue to be the real source of danger in the world'.[9]

THE POST-WAR SCHUMACHER ERA, 1945–52

Many factors contributed to the actions of post-war German politicians in opposing West German participation in a range of European institutions, despite the fact that they continued to express the pro-European views discussed above.[10] The most important factors were the four-power occupation of Germany and the progressive fusion of the three Western zones amid the growing rift between the East and the West. The SPD now had to take on board a much more urgent situation. On 22 April 1946 the Social Democrats in the Soviet zone of occupation were forced to join with the Communists, and by May 1949, the Allies had agreed to the *Grundgesetz* (Basic Law) which established a new West German state. Immediately following this, the creation of the East German state was announced.

Post-war SPD policy was defined by the emergence of Kurt Schumacher at the Kloster Wennigsen conference of October 1945 as the first post-war leader of the party. In his biography of Schumacher, Lewis Edinger states that there was 'no doubt in the minds of Schumacher's closest associates that he made every major decision affecting the national policy of his party between 1946 and 1952'.[11] Schumacher had a particularly acute national consciousness. He was able to exercise a respectable amount of moral authority due to the courage with which he had opposed the Nazis and his imprisonment in the Dachau concentration camp. His political audience recognized that his own sense of patriotism had not been tainted by Nazism and that he bore no responsibility for its actions. Rather, Schumacher saw re-establishing German unity and parliamentary values as his most important post-war task. He gave a higher priority to German reunification than to any moves towards Western European integration.

Schumacher's statements during this period reflected a traditional internationalist faith; however, what he most desired was German reunification with equal status in relation to other nations. In 1946, he stated: 'Social Democrats cannot conceive of a new Germany as an isolated and nationalistic Germany. They can only envisage

Germany as a component of Europe, but they wish this Germany to be not a pariah but an equal.'[12] For Schumacher, European integration was inextricably bound up with the German question. He stated: 'There is no German question which is not at the same time also a European question.' The official policy of the SPD contained a challenging objective, and one that would prove to be too idealistic. The April 1948 conference in Düsseldorf declared that the goal of the SPD remained 'a united, democratic Germany in freedom and peace', and one which 'in common with the social democrats of all countries strives for the league of free peoples in the United States of Europe'.[13] Schumacher's goal of a united Germany in a united Europe was in stark contrast to the unfolding events of East–West relations.

The SPD opposed the creation of the Council of Europe in 1948. Despite the fact that Konrad Adenauer, as CDU/CSU chancellor, was prepared to accept Council membership, Schumacher was not. Schumacher also opposed Adenauer's acceptance of a separate West Germany and Saar entry into the Council. Schumacher saw this as the legitimation of the separation of the Saar from West Germany, a separation he believed to be disastrous for the cause of German unity.

However, the post-war reactions of the SPD to proposals for European co-operation were not always negative. Schumacher had welcomed the Marshall Plan, and was satisfied with West Germany's status within it. Furthermore, other members in the SPD took a less rigid view of West Germany's place in European arrangements. SPD executive Carlo Schmid distanced himself from Schumacher. While Schmid supported German reunification as the main goal, and opposed European unity merely for defensive purposes, he did not seem to be so insistent on the socialist character of a new European entity.[14] Schmid also talked about a European federal state having its own supranational organs, including a directly elected European Parliament with supranational party groupings.[15]

On 9 May 1950 the Schuman proposal for a European Coal and Steel Community (ECSC) was greeted by Schumacher with marked ambivalence. Schumacher's hesitation was to be replaced with critical opposition as the details of the proposal were negotiated. On 20 April 1951 the SPD executive published a seven-point memorandum regarding the details of the Plan. The SPD insisted that the Schuman Plan should cover 'all democratic Europe, including Britain and Scandinavia', apparently in order to strengthen the cause of social democracy.[16] Paterson explains this shift by reference to four factors: concern at the non-participation of Britain (which would make prospects for socialist policies in West Germany less hopeful); suspicions and prejudices against France across much of the party; the advice of experts such as Fritz Henssler, Professor Fritz Baade, Professor Nolting and Dr Viktor Agartz, suggesting that West Germany had been denied full economic equality; and the connection which had been established between Adenauer, French agreement to the Schuman Plan and rearmament under the European Defence Community (EDC).[17]

The biggest obstacle to Schumacher's opposition stance was not internal party criticism, but the position of the trades union leaders.[18] All the major trades unions in West Germany were confederated into the Deutscher Gewerkschaft Bund (DGB). In the post-war period this organization had not associated itself with the SPD and even at times distanced itself from it. In response to the Schuman proposal, the DGB put forward a communiqué expressing its approval of the ECSC. Schumacher felt that union opinion was disloyal to the SPD. The SPD also criticized the lack of powers for the ECSC Assembly, as it had earlier criticized the Council of Europe for not being sufficiently supranational. The fundamental strategy of the SPD was 'opposition with a nationalist tone', and it sought to characterize Chancellor Adenauer as simply a tool of the Allies.[19]

OLLENHAUER'S LEADERSHIP, 1952–63

With the Soviet Union's interest in proposing talks on German unity and the establishment of a neutral state, in March 1952, the SPD felt that participation in the EDC would threaten any potential for German unity. Yet in March 1953 the EDC treaties were passed by a simple majority in the Bundestag. The SPD, along with a few members of smaller opposition parties, petitioned the Constitutional Court for a decision on the constitutionality of the treaties.[20] The SPD argued that any German military contribution implied an alteration of the Basic Law. However, after the election in September 1953, Adenauer was able to secure the qualified majority he needed, with the SPD no longer controlling the one-third of the assembly required to petition the Court. The SPD's legal course of action was thus rendered futile.

However, in August 1954, the French Parliament refused to ratify the Treaty. The SPD was therefore able to consider the initiative of Sir Anthony Eden which eventually led to the creation of the Western European Union (WEU). The SPD found the WEU more acceptable than the EDC because it involved Britain, although it objected to the fact that West Germany was being absorbed in a military alliance system as if there were no other Germany.

Now that the defence issue had been more or less arranged, the SPD leadership was able to consider and support European integration. Schumacher's death in August 1952 contributed to wider changes in the party's opposition style. His successor, Erich Ollenhauer, was more concerned to keep the SPD in step with public opinion and the party united. Ollenhauer, faced with economic prosperity, considered socialism less important than Schumacher had.

FROM EUROPEAN OPPOSITION TO SUPPORT, 1955–65

A number of other factors contributed to the shift in SPD policy from opposition to support. The trades unions were in favour of the ECSC, and in the post-Schumacher period the SPD enjoyed much closer co-operation with the DGB. Furthermore, past SPD policies had been unsuccessful and electorally enigmatic. The party was forced to recognize the popularity of the European ideal among the public, and specifically the younger generation. Moreover, succumbing to public pressure, the SPD's parliamentary group gained political power *vis-à-vis* the party's executive, which prompted a more favourable attitude to European integration. In addition, the Saar was reunified with Germany in January 1957, which generally reduced tensions.

SPD members in both the ECSC Assembly and the Council of Europe contributed to creating a more popular attitude towards European integration within the party. Some of the prominent SPD members who did so were Herbert Wehner, Fritz Erler, Karl Mommer and Willi Birkelbach.[21] The result was a general 'deideologicization' within the party. The SPD came into regular contact with Jean

Monnet, and in October 1955 entered into Monnet's Action Committee, thus demonstrating an end to an opposition strategy. By this time, according to Paterson, 'a state of bipartisanship was achieved' in European policy, except in some areas of defence.[22]

The Social Democrats supported the Euratom proposal and the creation of the European Economic Community (EEC). The SPD pressed for a common monetary, financial and investment policy, yet it was worried about the non-participation of Britain and the EEC's inadequate democratic procedures. The SPD began to show support for supranationality, while emphasizing the need for more democracy.

THE EUROPEAN ECONOMIC COMMUNITY

The SPD had voted for the EEC in order to create a large free trade area and not in order to divide Western Europe into two competing economic groups. It was concerned about the restrictive geographical focus of the EEC and declared that it desired 'no Continental Europe of Six which brings about full political integration at the cost of friendship and contacts with other European states'.[23] Moreover, the SPD was prepared to be more accommodating to the positions of Austria, Scandinavia and Britain, by sacrificing some of the rigidities of the EEC.[24]

At the end of the 1950s, the SPD attempted a bipartisan approach in order to emphasize its own credentials for power. The Bad Godesberg Programme of 1959 stressed a modernized domestic agenda adapting to the new economic situation in West Germany. Most importantly, the party dropped the Marxist rhetoric of its earlier years (thereby making the most dramatic split with its past). The Bad Godesberg Programme stated that 'economic development calls for collaboration between the European states', and 'regionally-defined inter-state communities need not lead to isolation from the rest of the world'.[25] The Bad Godesberg Programme showed dedication to the ideals of the EEC and Euratom; however, the party was still cautious on defence and specified that a reunited Germany should be part of a European security system.

In June 1960 Herbert Wehner gave a speech which demonstrated SPD acceptance of the importance of West German credibility in the eyes of its allies. This indicated a shift of support in favour of the Western defence system in order to increase domestic confidence in the SPD's handling of foreign affairs. SPD ideology in the field of foreign policy thus entered a new phase, breaking away from its past reservations.

In response to the nationalistic foreign policy of President de Gaulle and his veto of Britain's EEC entry application in 1963, the SPD became quite critical. Ollenhauer criticized the fact that the French had signed a treaty of friendship with West Germany during the same year, leaving the impression that it supported de Gaulle's nationalistic action.[26] The SPD also criticized de Gaulle's 'empty-chair' policy during the 1965–66 EEC crisis over the maintenance of the national veto in the Council of Ministers. The SPD defended the provisions of the Treaty of Rome and rejected the revisions demanded by France. On 29 November 1965 Fritz Erler stated that German interests were better served within the Community than they would be if Germany were to go it alone and risk complete isolation.[27] The Social Democrats felt that their critical stance on French actions had strengthened their position in the West German Government.

During the early 1960s, the SPD argued for a 'Europe of the Peoples', which it contrasted with the existing 'Europe of the Nations'. The SPD also initiated a bill for the direct election of the thirty-six West German Members of the European Parliament at the same time as the Bundestag elections were being held; this move, however, failed.[28] Furthermore, the SPD sought to give more prominence to the resolutions of the European Parliament in the negotiations of the Council of Ministers. The SPD was concerned at the increased competence of the Council and the Commission while the Parliament remained weak.

THE BRANDT PERIOD, 1966–74

After the elections of 1965, Willy Brandt achieved greater influence within the SPD. In the 'Grand Coalition' government of 1966, Brandt served as foreign minister. However, both he and Wehner, as minister for all-German affairs, were given the responsibility of concentrating on *Ostpolitik* rather than West European integration. With the experience of being mayor of West Berlin through the period of the construction of the Berlin Wall, Brandt's principal concerns were directed towards the East. Brandt's attitude towards a federal EEC remained very ambiguous. For example, when he spoke of 'European Union' his conception was far looser than normally understood.[29] In a speech to the Council of Ministers in September 1968, Brandt stressed a need for an 'economic union' based mainly on co-ordination and consultation. He emphasized the need for more powers to be given to the European Parliament, a view to be shared and often repeated by SPD representatives in the years to come.

Brandt's political career began during the Weimar Republic, not as a member of the SPD but in a smaller left-wing party, the SRP (Sozialistische Reichspartei). While the Nazis controlled Germany, Brandt had been forced into exile in Scandinavia. This time of exile seems to have left Brandt with a broad-based view of Europe and integration. However, to many his plan for a wider cultural identification was vague and without any legal recommendations.

Again, in November 1967, the SPD's support for the further development of the EC and for its enlargement to include Britain was interrupted by de Gaulle's second veto on UK entry. In response, the SPD initiated a proposal demanding that the Council of Ministers vote on the principle of negotiations being opened with four prospective new member states. In line with the other political parties of West Germany, the SPD believed that proper European unity depended on the participation of both France and Britain. In the 1968 SPD Conference in Nuremberg, the SPD passed a resolution stating that the 'aim remains to extend [the] Community by means of accepting other European countries, especially Great Britain, Ireland and the Scandinavian countries, and to build up the Community politically in the long term'.[30] With the resignation of de Gaulle in 1969 and his replacement by Georges Pompidou, the prospects for new EC decisions appeared encouraging. On 28 September of the same year, Willy Brandt was elected, becoming the first post-war SPD chancellor. After his election, Brandt attended a summit at The Hague for EEC heads of government in which he pressed for progress on the SPD's European objectives. Brandt felt that without Britain and the other states that were seeking entry, Europe could not be what it should be. Brandt also pushed for economic and even currency union, development of political co-operation in foreign policy with a view to the subsequent creation of a 'political community', and the enhancement of the EC's own institutions. Brandt was able to obtain agreement on each of his topics. He was also given credit for persuading Pompidou to support further integration.

On 13 May 1970 at the SPD Conference in Saarbrücken, Brandt maintained that the EC could and should become the 'decisive impulse' in more areas of life, 'for shaping our society'.[31] The SPD pushed for further collaboration in foreign policy and security matters. The first foreign policy discussion on 19 November 1970, entitled 'European Political Co-operation' (EPC), brought the Six together in Munich. These discussions were later to become regular features of EC policies. Moreover, European Parliament budgetary powers were increased in response to prolonged demands for increased democratic accountability within the EC. EC enlargement was successfully ratified in the West German Bundestag on 21 June 1972, which demonstrated the FRG's commitment to British, Irish and Danish accession. The EC Summit in Paris on 19–20 October 1972 reflected the significant progress that had been made since 1969.

THE SCHMIDT PERIOD, 1974–82

The EC was suffering from extreme economic difficulties when Helmut Schmidt succeeded Brandt as chancellor on 16 May 1974, following the Guillaume spy scandal.[32] The oil crisis had undermined progress towards any degree of economic and monetary union. The British were pressing, under the newly elected Labour government, for a renegotiation of the terms of entry agreed in 1972. Schmidt agreed to support some of the British demands, and the December 1974 summit in Paris allowed changes in the EC's system of budgetary contributions. There was also progress on the EC's regional policy and the principle of direct elections to the European Parliament. The SPD expressed support for the entry of Greece, Portugal and Spain after the fall of their dictatorial regimes.

In a *Foreign Affairs* article in 1970, Schmidt argued that the lesson to be drawn from the previous 'sobering' decade of repeated failures of European initiatives was one concerning the world's economic problems. He argued that a pragmatic approach to solving these economic problems should be the primary concern of the EC states. Schmidt's most notable European achievement was his pressing for the establishment of the European Monetary System (EMS). The EMS was agreed at the December 1978 summit, and the communiqué stated that it was intended to have a stabilizing effect on international economic and monetary relations.

The SPD supported, albeit critically, the Tindemans Report on European Union in 1976. The SPD asserted that some of its provisions had in fact been drawn directly from ideas previously espoused by SPD leaders. Specifically, Tindemans had accepted Brandt's suggestion that the economically stronger EC states might integrate more quickly than others. The SPD accepted the overall objective of the report, but proposed changes to emphasize social democratic concerns. Moreover, at its November 1977 Hamburg conference, the SPD reaffirmed its commitment to a 'federal European Union' with a democratic constitution. The Social Democrats believed that democracy in the EC should be increased on the basis of a three-tier plan, giving the directly-elected Parliament more powers *vis-à-vis* the Council and the Commission.[33]

The Social Democrats adopted a European election manifesto at a 'European Congress' of the party on 9–10 December 1978, which assembled the 'political and moral' guidelines for the party in European matters from the principles of the Bad Godesberg Programme. The Programme argued for an 'EC charter of civil rights' to protect citizens across member states, 'humane and balanced growth', full employment via the establishment of a thirty-five hour week, industrial democracy, economic convergence to overcome regional and social inequalities and 'economic and monetary union' on the basis of a European Monetary Fund. The manifesto also argued for increased European Parliamentary power to allow for amendments to any part of the EC budget, to enable it to pass bills, to require its approval for any treaty changes, to enable it to appoint the members of the Commission after their nomination by the Council, and that the Council itself should return to majority voting as provided for in the Treaty of Rome.

Schmidt's pragmatic economic views were not shared by all the members of his coalition government. FDP foreign minister Hans Dietrich Genscher, with his Italian counterpart Emilio Colombo, put forward an initiative for a new European Act leading to 'European Union'. This initiative was, for the most part, concerned with institutional constructs; however, the SPD was more concerned with the recession and the budgetary problems of the EC. The FDP proposed that the decision-making structures of the EC and those under 'European Political Cooperation' should be combined to create a common security and foreign policy, that there should be a move towards majority voting, and that the powers of the Council should be strengthened. However, Klaus Hänsch, an SPD MEP, questioned in July 1982 how 'dusty old phrases from the early 1950s' could enthuse anyone.

THE OPPOSITION PERIOD, 1982–89

The Social Democrats were forced into opposition at the end of 1982 when the Free Democrats crossed the floor of the Bundestag to install Helmut Kohl and the CDU/CSU in power. The 1980 elections had given the FDP a boost, enabling it to take more assertive policy positions. The market-orientated policies of the FDP economic minister Otto Lamsdorf provoked criticism from the trades unions and from within the SPD party itself. Intra-coalition conflicts concentrated on unemployment and the failure of the government to solve this problem. Schmidt was also under criticism for using personal influence in relation to US missiles in West Germany. On 17 September, the FDP ministers resigned and less than one month later switched their allegiance to the CDU/CSU, exercising successfully, for the first time, the 'constructive vote of no confidence' provided for in the Basic Law. The SPD was thus in opposition, with only 38.2 per cent of the vote, followed by the Greens with 5.6 per cent.

Opposition affected SPD domestic policy as well as their policy on the EC. Emotionally charged debates ensued over environmental and nuclear matters. Pre-1980 thinking on defence, the environment and international relations was challenged. The 1984 European manifesto of the SPD reflected these new attitudes, especially on the left of the political spectrum. Specifically, in regard to EC policy, the SPD believed that institutional reform was needed and that the decision-making procedures of the Community should be reformed in order to:

I. Give the European Parliament stronger control on the budget, the right to initiate legislation, the right to co-determine EC policies, and the right to consultation before a new Commission is named.

II. Compel the Council of Ministers to reach decisions by set deadlines, to limit the authority of the Council to make changes or even veto legislation.

III. Increase popular participation in the policy-making process, and to establish a uniform voting system in European elections.[34]

The European Community should seek co-operation with non-member states in line with the SPD's new agenda of 'the development of Europe into a peace community, in which social peace within, peace with nature, and external peace are realized'. The SPD joined the growing peace movement by discussing the dismantling of nuclear missiles on both sides of Europe, and the objective of a chemical- and nuclear-free zone in central Europe.

As leader of the Social Democrats since 1983, Hans-Jochen Vogel became more assertive on European policy during the Milan summit in July 1985. Vogel argued that the Kohl government was not pushing its EC partners enough and not achieving results. Vogel had stated that the Milan summit would be one of Kohl's last chances to do justice to his claims on taking office. The SPD had criticized Kohl for exercising a veto when the agricultural ministers had discussed grain prices, the first veto to be applied by a West German government. Kohl was also criticized for leaving the British proposals isolated. Vogel described his party's frustrations by stating that the 'European ideal . . . is in danger of being destroyed by national egoism. Bureaucracy is running riot.'[35] Vogel believed that Europe had one last chance to maintain its influence in the face of the superpowers and the economic might of Japan.

The Social Democratic Party shifted its policy of promoting the integration of a left-wing 'social' Europe after its electoral defeat and in response to the Greens and the peace movement. This policy would remain the same under its many chancellor-candidates. As Kevin Featherstone states, it seemed as though the SPD activists were 'more excited by the nuclear issue, than they were by European integration'.[36]

The SPD spent much of the late 1980s concerned with the impending 'Europe 1992'. Specifically, the SPD spent considerable effort pushing its policy of creating a 'European social area'. Hans-Jochen Vogel stated in 1988 that the leaders of the Social Democratic Party of Germany 'have always linked their assent to the demand that the social effects of the internal market must also be taken into consideration and the market must develop into a European social area'.[37] The SPD desired a European effort to promote employment, as the Commission had promised in 1985 in its 'Co-operative Strategy for Growth and Employment'. Moreover, the SPD argued that this co-operative strategy was under attack by conservatism and that the 'European Social Democrats and Socialists [should] continue to press for it'.[38] The SPD shared with other socialist parties a desire that 'Europe 1992' should bring with it a 'Europe of social progress'. Their fear was of a Europe of capital, based on the lowest economic common denominator, and representatives of industry and conservative politicians who saw 1992 'as the greatest deregulation measure in economic history'. Vogel stated: 'what is frightening for us . . . is that capitalist circles quite evidently regard Europe 1992 as a chance to undermine or deregulate social achievements'.[39] Vogel believed that removing 'alleged' disadvantages in competition would reduce the high standards of protection, safety rules and the social rights of workers to mere cost factors and parameters.

Ernst Breit, president of the European Trade Union Confederation and chairman of the German Trade Federation, warned that introducing a deregulation campaign against social rights under the pretext of completing the European internal market must not become the Trojan horse used by conservatives who wanted to change the system and turn back the wheel of history. Vogel affirmed:

> But it is high time we ... used all our combined strength to create a European social area together with the European internal market, in which technical and economic progress goes hand in hand with social progress ... It is up to the Social Democratic parties ... to bring about step-by-step improvements in the European social system, which is only sketched out in the present EC Treaty and the Single European Act. Europe must not be a Europe of businessmen – it must become a Europe of social progress![40]

The Social Democrats indeed had defined objectives. Behind their industrial policy was the primary goal of the 'ecological renewal' of the economy. According to the SPD, the new catalyst for finally completing the common market called for in the Treaties of Rome was worldwide recession and the fear that Europe could no longer compete with Japan, the United States and the newly industrialized Asian nations. Yet Europe was heading in the direction of a more free-market system. Despite the fact that the SPD feared social decline and ecological repercussions, it could not slow the free marketism at work. It responded rhetorically:

> We may agree or disagree with these views. But there can be no doubt that the completion of the internal market will open new opportunities for the Community's industrial and services sector and that the more productive use of economic resources resulting from stronger competition within Europe will also strengthen the Community's position in international competition.
>
> So the European process of integration will remain an arduous one. But it can no longer be stopped. We German Social Democrats want Europe. Throughout the 125 years of our party's history we and all the European forces of Social Democracy have always stood for international understanding and co-operation. Even in our 1925 Heidelberg party programme we declared our aim to be the 'United States of Europe'.[41]

UNITY

In 1989 the Social Democratic Party found itself at a watershed. As a result of Kohl's (CDU) and Genscher's (FDP) quick actions to embrace the growing movements towards reunification and the 'systematic SPD campaigns to spread a sense of insecurity and envy in regard to ... the cost of unity',[42] the ruling parties were able to take advantage of the openings offered by the movement in East Germany. The SPD had been more deeply affected by the division of Germany than the other parties. Before the erection of the Wall in 1961, the SPD was a party in favour of reunification. But that changed. SPD policy, identified with Willy Brandt and Egon Bahr, became a policy of 'change through rapprochement'.[43] In the late 1980s, SPD chancellor candidate Oskar Lafontaine was critical of the so-called pan-German aspirations of the ruling parties. He favoured a separate citizenship for the GDR and the FRG. At the very beginning of the break up of the GDR, the SPD leadership was composed of intellectuals who favoured reform, but separate GDR statehood. For all intents and purposes, this policy was accepted by the SPD. Then came the massive protests and in the rush to unity the SPD was left out. Willy Brandt tried to press the party to follow this movement, but Lafontaine could only stress the practical difficulties of unity.

This ambivalence towards the treaty for reunification once again divided the SPD. Lafontaine opposed the treaty, but Vogel and the economic spokesman Wolfgang Roth saw this as a mistake. The episode inevitably undermined Lafontaine in the run up to the December election of 1990, and gave the impression that the party was divided and uncertain. The SPD had hoped that its support for détente (*Entspannung*) would become increasingly popular as Gorbachev set out to end the Cold War. But they had not reckoned with the time bomb of the reunification issue. The policy known as 'change through rapprochement' (*Wandel durch Annäherung*) was characterized by the Kohl government as 'change through chumming up' (*Wandel durch Anbiederung*). And with Kohl forcing the banks to fall in with the currency reform, the SPD was left appearing to criticize reunification. To many voters, however, reunification was a family matter.[44] For the SPD, the all-German election of December 1990 was to be a disaster. The SPD won only 239 seats in the Bundestag compared to the CDU/CSU with 319, which, combined with the FDP's 79, gave the coalition the clear majority.[45]

A NEGATIVE RELATIONSHIP

Throughout the post-war years, the SPD has changed its stance significantly on perhaps the two most significant events to occur in post-war Germany: the reunification of Germany and European integration. The SPD's attitude to each of the two issues has had an indirect and negative impact on the other. As the SPD increasingly favoured European integration, this negatively affected its emphasis on German reunification. The positive emphasis which the SPD gave reunification during the Schumacher years negatively influenced its stance on integration. Schumacher saw the re-establishing of German unity and parliamentary values as his most important post-war task.[46] In 1952 Ollenhauer, who had taken over the role left vacant by Schumacher's absence, moderated the SPD's position, keeping the party in step with growing public opinion.[47] Paterson states that 'with the entry of the SPD into the Monnet Action in October 1955 . . . [t]here was no doubt . . . that priorities had been reversed. German reunification was relegated from the major to a relatively minor theme in the SPD's European policy.'[48] However, within the party, some speakers like Carlo Schmid continued to maintain that efforts towards reunification must precede efforts towards Western European integration.[49]

In the early 1960s, the SPD was quite critical of the Gaullist notion of Europe which rejected Britain and was hostile towards the United States. The SPD stated that this idea of Europe lacked supranationality and democratic control.[50] The SPD called for a 'Europe of the Peoples', pushed for the fusion of the EEC, Euratom and the ECSC,[51] and for increased rights for the European Parliament. Notwithstanding this, a prominent member of the SPD, Kurt Mattick, argued that treaties relating to Europe should contain a mention of German reunification (a notion which was to become less important in a few short years).[52]

By the 1970s, the party strongly supported a 'European Union'. Its foreign policy stance had been influenced greatly by the *Ostpolitik* of Brandt. Under the leadership of Egon Bahr, its most dramatic change of heart in relation to Europe and reunification occurred in the mid-1960s and was accepted as policy by the SPD in the 1970s and beyond. Bahr called for an end to the policy confrontation of 'all or nothing' with respect to the German question. Rather than working to overthrow the GDR, Bahr suggested that attempts be made to change it. Change, he believed, would only be possible through a policy of rapprochement. The policy implied a de-emphasis of the single-minded pursuit of Western unification and an emphasis on solutions that would include the whole of Europe. Brandt felt that in order to achieve this policy, a 'European Peace Order' would be necessary.[53] European peace implied, to the SPD leadership, playing down the reunification option and emphasizing the permanence of the Federal Republic.[54] In the context of Europe, this policy did not mean that the SPD concentrated more of its efforts on Western Europe. The reverse was the case: the SPD began to concentrate much more on inter-German affairs and to push for European unity. This push for unity in the 1970s and much of the 1980s came in the form of increased European Parliamentary powers and expansion of the Community to include Greece and Portugal. Brandt's suggestion that the economically stronger nations of the EC might integrate more quickly than the others exemplified the dramatic turnaround in SPD policy. This attitude intensified during the SPD's 'second phase of *Ostpolitik*' in the 1980s, with expanded communications and negotiations with the East German ruling party.[55] The SPD called for the CDU/CSU to modify its stance demanding the collapse of East Germany and to work with the East Germans, pragmatically accepting a divided Germany. This agenda lost the SPD support in the wake of the 'bombshell' of German reunification and the elections of 1990.

The SPD's complete transformation in relation to reunification and European integration is indeed interesting to examine. The events of 1989 and 1990 characterized the severe difficulty of the party in defining its objectives for future policies in Europe and a reunited Germany.

MAASTRICHT

SPD criticism of Maastricht was focused on specific details and not general attitudes to the treaty. For example, in an article in *Die Welt*, Björn Engholm (SPD leader 1992–3) and Oskar Lafontaine (SPD chancellor candidate of 1990) criticized the planned economic and currency union, arguing that 'economic unity without political union in Europe is similar to the disastrous drive of the over-rushed German-German currency union'. Engholm demanded 'regulation of political union and democratization of the European formation'. The CDU countered the SPD's argument and spoke of the SPD misunderstanding of the realities in Europe and of its obvious electioneering tactics.[56] Moreover, in March 1992 Lafontaine argued that the SPD should not support the Maastricht Treaty. He put forward seven points that related to the lack of European parliamentary powers.[57] He argued that unless certain conditions were met, the SPD should not back Maastricht. Despite limited objection from within the party, the SPD was in a precarious position. Criticism of Maastricht could imply that the SPD did not support the Treaty, just as it was perceived as not having supported reunification.

After reunification, however, most statements from the SPD on European integration were quite positive. In an *SPD-Bundestagsfraktion* article entitled 'The Social Democratic Party's proposition towards perspectives of European integration', the party stated that 'a democratic and federal Europe remains the right answer for the economic, social and ecological challenges of our time . . . [and after] German unification, we want to hold on to the continuation of European integration'. Despite the party's concern about an enlarged bureaucracy, 'single regulations that [had] not been reached' and a treaty that was a 'compromise', the SPD maintained that Maastricht was 'a significant step in the process of European unification'.[58]

In an interview with the then SPD leader Björn Engholm, dated 16 March 1992, in the *Stuttgarter Zeitung*, questions were asked regarding the position of the SPD *vis-à-vis* Maastricht. Engholm stated the sentiment of the party:

> The Social Democratic Party has . . . questions on single agreements, but never the whole question. It is always our understanding that a united Germany needs a strict and clear integration in the European Community. We want a European Union. We want to eliminate the ambiguous situation through the realization of political union especially through a strengthening of the political rights of the European Parliament. The EC is the only stable structure that we find in Europe today.

Engholm added:

> Without the aid of a robust EC, I see no evolution of the young nations to become new democracies and new market economies. That is the only formative line that we have for the Eastern states today. Deepening and enlargement of the Community are not contradictory. The EC first of all must open to the EFTA nations. This should occur by 1995. The next step would then be an opening to the Central European nations. We should, however, in no way excite the aspirations of distant Eastern Europe about joining the EC. That would strain these countries. The European Union cannot extend from Gibraltar to the Chinese border.[59]

Björn Engholm was forced to resign as SPD leader on 3 May 1993. He had admitted that he had failed to tell the whole truth in 1987 to a committee investigating a dirty tricks campaign mounted against him by the Christian Democrats.[60] His replacement after the interim leadership of Johannes Rau, Rudolph Scharping, expressed similar views to Engholm in statements on Europe. Even though Scharping was close to Brandt, and used the same slogan of promising to 'dare more democracy', he had to concentrate on restoring the SPD's image, which had been damaged by the Engholm incident and the party's poor performance in the German elections of 1990.

Helmut Schmidt stated that the new SPD leader was 'here with a clear perspective'.[61] However, as Scharping told the *Süddeutsche Zeitung* before he was elected party leader, 'forming a government in Bonn will only be possible when the party is clearly stronger than it is now'. He added that this would require 'popularity, imaginativeness and credible policies'.[62]

CONCLUSION

The Social Democrats dealt with Maastricht with a noticeable degree of conver-gence with the Christian Democrats. Especially in the area of Europe, the SPD had resisted the temptation to impair the government by utilizing its majority in the Bundesrat. The major factor contributing to this convergence was the SPD's potential and 'preference for leadership in a Grand Coalition' in 1994.[63] The centre-right swing of the party since reunification can be attributed to this desire. With all of the domestic troubles in Germany, the SPD had seen Europe as the area upon which to agree and democracy and integration were seen as the factors which would guarantee a peaceful Europe.[64]

One of the most important explanations for Europe gaining such prominence in Social Democratic policy thinking was the SPD's qualified rejection of the nation state. Regions and their competence in democratic participation were seen to be of prime importance to the future of European integration, and the transfer of state functions to Brussels was to prepare EC members for the future in a world society.[65] Much like the government in Bonn, Social Democrats saw regional integration as part of a universal trend, of which the European Union was one element.[66]

The EU was to play a key role in post-(Eastern)bloc politics and it would take on its share of responsibility in the development of self-determination in former Soviet-controlled states.[67] The EU was the role model as well as an institutional foundation for dispute management through established co-operation, interdependence and integration.[68] The EU's social, monetary and democratic dimensions were seen to be especially helpful in solving Eastern European problems.[69] Since these were also the main problems in the EU's internal processes, the SPD combined the two areas of public debate in order to push its own point of view. While the overarching leitmotif of Social Democratic European policies remained that of a basic consensus plus specific demands, the SPD emphasized the pan-European aspects of integration much more strongly than any of the governing parties: 'We want the Community's further development to be oriented towards an all-European perspective.'[70] The SPD favoured both the strengthening of European integration and extending the Union towards EFTA and Eastern European countries.[71] Despite the fact that the SPD put special emphasis on integrating Eastern Europe into the Union, they were only going a little further than the government.[72]

The general direction and the results of Maastricht had been welcomed; yet the Social Democrats criticized the fact that individual member states were still far too dominant in the Union's decision-making process. They demanded internal reforms to fit in with their vision of a federation;[73] responsibility for EU security matters should rest not with the Council alone but also with the Parliament. This had been the main area of contention between CDU/CSU and FDP on the one hand and SPD on the other, both before and after 1989. Yet the European Union was not to become a cornerstone of defence in the 1990s. The Union was to retain its civilian character in order to achieve the primary aim of economic and political integration, and so that Eastern Europe's association would not be jeopardized.[74] Similarly to the government parties, the SPD did not reject the idea of European defence altogether; it merely saw it more in terms of a long-term project.[75] The evolution of some form of broad security identity, including military matters, was seen to be inevitable. But it was a long way off and disarmament would have to come before integration.

The SPD repeatedly stressed that the European Community had become the driving force for a broader union.[76] While the United States of Europe was the long-term goal, the EU was to transform itself into a political union accompanied by a monetary and economic community.[77] There were few differences between the government parties and the SPD, merely a divergence in emphasis and priorities.

For the Social Democrats, the European elections of June 1994 were a welcome event and the party anticipated a successful result. Rudolph Scharping had been riding high in the polls and the party looked to be heading for victory. But the CDU and its Bavarian sister party the CSU together took 38.8 per cent of the vote, more than they had won in the 1989 European elections.[78] The Social Democrats took only 32.2 per cent, a full 5 percentage points less than in 1989.[79] At a meeting of the party's presidium, there was no hiding the SPD's depression following the election results; Rudolph Scharping broke a tea cup, something seen in Germany as a sign of luck, but failed to cheer up his colleagues. But as Scharping made clear, the Social Democrats were in no mood to accept defeat. Scharping stated that he had gone through hard times in his political life, that those times had not discouraged him, and nor would the European election results.

Of concern to the Bonn Government was the support of the liberal FDP, the linchpin of the coalition, which fell decisively below the 5 percentage points needed under German electoral law to make it into parliament. The FDP's loss of a crucial 1.5 per cent thus meant a loss of all its seats in the European Parliament. More than 6 per cent of the German electorate opted for smaller 'other' parties, nearly twice as many as in 1989. Some marginal comfort could be found here for both the Social Democrats and the Liberals. The turnout for the European elections was low. However, the rise of the Federation 90-Green Party support by nearly 2 percentage points (to 10.1 per cent) meant that the SPD would have to deal with an increase on both its right and left flank.

The CDU/CSU/FDP coalition was restored to power for a fourth term in the national elections of October 1994. Yet the victory was by the slenderest margin (10 seats more than the combined opposition parties). The CDU/CSU lost 25 seats (from 319 in 1990 to 294). Despite the loss, the SPD fared dramatically better than it had in the 1990 elections, with a gain of 13 seats (from 239 in 1990 to 252).[80] The SPD result was an unmistakable improvement on its dismal performance four years earlier which had been blamed on its lack of enthusiasm for reunification.[81]

Scharping said that Kohl's shaky majority would not last a full term. 'If we don't govern now we will with great certainty do so in 1998 or even earlier', he told his party following their narrow defeat. He also called the reaffirmed coalition a 'coalition of losers'.[82] Scharping pointed to an increased vote for the SPD, which when combined with the party's strength in the Bundesrat and *Länder*, amounted to a stronger than usual role for a party coming second in an election.

As far as European policy was concerned, the election had little impact on Kohl's established Euro-federalist policy, which was generally backed by the Social Democrats.[83] Both parties pushed for faster integration and worked towards preparation for more incorporation of the East and North, to be discussed at the 1996 review of the Maastricht Treaty.

The German Social Democrats continued to propose a more powerful European Parliament *vis-à-vis* the European Commission and Council with the knowledge that, after the June 1994 results, the Social Democrats throughout Europe would still have the largest representation in Strasbourg.[84] Moreover, in July 1994, Klaus Hänsch, the German Social Democratic MEP, was elected with a clear majority (365 out of 534 votes cast) as president of the European Parliament. Hänsch was one of the twelve deputies who stood up to the governments of the member states in the course of the preparatory work on Maastricht in 1991 and insisted on greater powers for the European Parliament. He made it clear that he would make full use of the additional powers accorded to Parliament by Maastricht.[85] Members of the SPD continued to criticize Chancellor Kohl's government for what they saw as tactical errors in his negotiations.[86] However the SPD was not prepared to let the ensuing legislative procedure fail and the party began to look for a way to force the government into combining aspects of a political union with the democratization of political structures. In Engholm's view, Maastricht was a success, if not quite as successful as it would have been if Social Democratic demands had been listened to.[87]

NOTES

1 This chapter is based on the comprehensive account by Professor William E. Paterson of the SPD and European integration up to the late 1960s. The author would like to thank him in particular. This work also draws upon Kevin Featherstone's findings up to the 1980s. The author would like to thank the *Deutsche Gesellschaft für Auswärtige Politik*, particularly, Frau Gisela Gottwald; the Information Office of the European Parliament in Bonn; European Advisor Klaus Suchanek of the SPD; Frau Lindau Bauer at the Archive Centre of the SPD; and Frau Ute Kuhlmann at the *Europa Archiv*.
2 Kevin Featherstone, *Socialist Parties and the European Integration* (Manchester, Manchester University Press, 1988), p. 142.
3 William E. Paterson, *The SPD and European Integration* (Farnborough, Saxon House, 1974), p. 1.
4 Ibid.
5 Internal SPD paper on past party policy on Europe, 18 May 1979. Cited in Featherstone, *Socialist Parties*, p. 142.
6 Paterson, *The SPD*, p. 2.
7 For a good view of the Social Democratic mentality before and after the Nazi regime, see L. Edinger, *Kurt Schumacher: A Study in Personality and Political Behaviour* (Stanford, Stanford University Press, 1965).
8 Socialist Vanguard Group, *Calling All Europe* (London, 1942).
9 SPD paper, May 1979; cited in Featherstone, *Socialist Parties*, p. 143.
10 Paterson details these 'conditioning factors' in his section 'The post-war era 1945–49': Paterson, *The SPD*, pp. 4–14.
11 Edinger, *Kurt Schumacher*, pp. 112–17.
12 SPD paper, May 1979; taken from *Nach dem Zusammenbruch-Gedanken über Demokratie und Sozialismus* (Hamburg, Karl Strutz, 1946), p. 46. Cited in Featherstone, *Socialist Parties*.
13 Ibid., p. 144.
14 Carlo Schmid, *Erinnerungen* (Munich, Scherz, 1980).
15 Featherstone, *Socialist Parties*, pp. 145–6. See also Hans Peter Schwarz, *Vom Reich zur Bundesrepublik. Deutschland in Widerstreit der aussenpolitischen Konzeptionen in der Jahren der Besatzungsherrschaft 1945 bis 1949* (Berlin, Luchterhand, 1966).
16 Paterson, *The SPD*, p. 66.
17 Ibid., p. 65.
18 Ibid., p. 57. Also in J. Lodge *The European Policy of the SPD* (London, Sage, 1976), p. 14.
19 Ibid., p. 66.
20 Ibid., pp. 79–82.
21 Ibid., p. 118.

22 Ibid., pp. 118–19. Paterson asserts that one of the main influences was SPD realization that the ECSC had become identified in the public mind with the preservation of German prosperity.

23 *Jahrbuch der Sozialdemokratischen Partei Deutschlands, 1958–59* (Bonn-Bad Godesberg: Neuer Vorwarts-Verlag Nau, 1959), p. 25. Subsequent *Jahrbücher* cited in Featherstone, *Socialist Parties*.

24 Ibid., p. 27.

25 *Grundsatzprogramm der Sozialdemokratischen Partei Deutschlands*, Bad Godesberg Congress 13–15 November 1959; section entitled 'International Gemeinschaft', cited in Featherstone, *Socialist Parties*, p. 151.

26 *Jahrbuch der SPD 1962–63*, pp. 21–2.

27 *Jahrbuch der SPD 1964–65*, p. 51.

28 *Jahrbuch der SPD 1962–63*, pp. 23–4.

29 Both Paterson and Lodge expound on this point. See Paterson, *The SPD*, p. 146.

30 *Parteitag Nürnberg 1968 v. 'Perspektiven'* 2 (d). Cited in Featherstone, *Socialist Parties*, p. 154.

31 *Jahrbuch der SPD 1970–72*, pp. 39–40.

32 One of Brandt's closest personal advisers, Günter Guillaume, had long been a spy for East German intelligence; he was secretly privy to negotiations over the inter-German transit accord and the Basic Treaty.

33 'Beschluss des Hamburger Parteitages zur Europapolitik', 15–19 November 1977, SPD, Bonn. Cited in Featherstone, *Socialist Parties*.

34 Ibid., p. 161.

35 *Politik*, 4 May 1985.

36 Featherstone, *Socialist Parties*, p. 163.

37 Hans-Jochen Vogel, 'The challenge of 1992', in Dankert and Kooyman (eds), *Europe Without Frontiers: Socialists on the Future of the European Economic Community*, (London, Mansell, 1989), p. 85.

38 Ibid., p. 86.

39 Ibid.

40 Ibid., p. 88.

41 Ibid., pp. 91 and 109.

42 Peter H. Merkl, *German Unification in the European Context* (Philadelphia, PA, Penn State University Press, 1993), p. 139. For a detailed explanation see the chapter 'Hesitating in sight of the goal', p. 136.

43 William Paterson, 'Foreign and security policy', in G. Smith, William Paterson and Peter H. Merkl, *Developments in West German Politics* (London, Macmillan, 1989) p. 202.

44 Stephen Padgett and William Paterson, 'The rise and fall of the West German Left', *New Left Review*, March 1991, p. 73.

45 Timothy Garton Ash, *In Europe's Name* (London, Cape, 1993), p. 640.

46 Lewis Edinger, *Kurt Schumacher* (Stanford, Stanford University Press, 1965), p. 168.

47 Deutscher Bundestag, *Verhandlungen*, 7 February 1952, p. 1, section 1C.

48 Paterson, *The SPD*, p. 125.

49 Carlo Schmid in SPD Parliamentary Party, *Mitteilungen für die Presse*, 17 November 1955.

50 'SPD gegen Übertragung des Gaullismus auf Europe', *Stuttgarter Zeitung*, 16 August 1960.

51 '7-Punkte Programm Willy Brandts', *Neue Zürcher Zeitung*, 11 July 1964.

52 *Neue Zürcher Zeitung*, 7 March 1963. *Deutsche Zeitung*, 11 and 18 March 1963.

53 Willy Brandt, 'Für ein geregeltes Nebeneinander', 2 July 1967, in W. Brandt, *Aussenpolitik Deutschlandpolitik Europapolitik* (Berlin, Berlin Verlag, 1968), p. 85.

54 Notably, the European Peace Order involved exchanging renunciation of force agreements with the Soviet Union, Poland, Czechoslovakia and including the GDR fully in the process. Yet Brandt stipulated that his administration would not view East Germany as a foreign country (*nicht Ausland*). Nevertheless, the fact that he failed to mention 'reunification' in his speech and quite openly acknowledged the existence of two German

states demonstrated the belief that he was ready to put the immediate benefits of co operation with the GDR ahead of any aspiration of a reunited Germany. See Boris Meissner, *Deutsche Ostpolitik 1961–1970* (Cologne, Verlag Wissenschaft und Politik, 1970), pp. 380–3.

55 For example, the SPD negotiated a *Sicherheitspartnershaft* (security partnership) with the SED in connection with chemical- and nuclear-free zones in Central Europe.

56 'SPD auf Distanz zu Maastricht', *Die Welt*, 6 March 1992.

57 'Lafontaine empfiehlt der SPD die Ablehnung der Verträge von Maastricht', *Frankfurter Allgemeine Zeitung*, 6 March 1992.

58 'SPD-Antrag zu Perspektiven der europäischen Integration', *Die SPD im Deutschen Bundestag. SPD Bundestagsfraktion Artikel*, No. 1568, 16 June 1992.

59 'Wir wollen die Schieflage der Gemeinschaft beseitigen. Interview mit Björn Engholm zur Europapolitik', *Stuttgarter Zeitung*, 16 March 1992.

60 Called the 'desk-drawer' affair, a friend of Engholm's who resigned in March 1993 as Schleswig-Holstein's minister of social affairs, had paid a CDU aid as a thank you for tipping off the Social Democrats about the dirty campaign against them in 1987. Engholm said that he had misled the committee about when he had learned that the CDU was running the campaign.

61 *Bonn General-Anzeiger*, 26 June 1993, p. 3.

62 *The New York Times*, 'German opposition party chooses a new leader', 24 June 1993, p. A11.

63 Author's interview with William E. Paterson, 23 November 1993.

64 SPD, 'Außen-, Friedens-, und Sicherheitspolitik', Beschlüsse des Parteitages in Bremen, 28–31 May 1991, p. 8.

65 Oskar Lafontaine, *Deutsche Wahrheiten. Die nationale und die soziale Frage* (Hamburg, Hamburg Verlag, 1990), p. 96.

66 SPD, *Grundsatzprogramm der Sozialdemokratischen Partei Deutschland*, Bonn, 1989.

67 Gerd Walter, 'Vorschlag für eine politische Einigung der Staaten in Europa', in Matthias Barthe and Margaret Johannsen, *Zur Zukunft Deutschlands. Reden vom 2. internationalen Ost-West-Workshop über Gemeinsame Sicherheit*, Hamburger Beiträge zur Friedensforschung und Sicherheitspolitik, No. 44, January 1990, p. 42.

68 Egon Bahr, 'Aussöhnung statt Recht', interview in *Freitag*, 6 December 1991.

69 Walter, 'Vorschlag für eine politische Einigung', p. 42.

70 SPD, 'Außen-, Friedens-, und Sicherheitspolitik', p. 12.

71 SPD, 'Der neue Weg, Regierungsprogramm 1990–94', Beschlossen vom Parteitag am 28 September 1990 in Berlin.

72 Karsten Voigt, 'Europa jenseits der Entspannungspolitik. Protokollband des 7. Internationalen Humbolt Kolloquims zur Friedensforschung', *Berliner Beiträge zur Friedens- und Konfliktforschung*, April 1991, p. 64.

73 SPD, 'Außen-, Friedens-, und Sicherheitspolitik', p. 9.

74 Voigt, 'Europa jenseits der Entspannungspolitik', p. 64.

75 Lafontaine, *Deutsche Wahrheiten*, p. 82.

76 SPD, 'Außen-, Friedens-, und Sicherheitspolitik', p. 9.

77 SPD, 'Von der Konfrontation der Blöcke zu einem Europäische Sicherheitssystem. Positionspapier zu den sicherheitspolitischen Aspekten der Einigung Deutschlands im Rahmen der Europäischen Integration', Presservice der SPD, Bonn, 25 April 1990, p. 2.

78 *The Economist*, 18 June 1994, p. 43. The CDU took 32 per cent and the CSU took another 6.8 per cent.

79 Ibid.

80 The CDU/CSU received 41.5 per cent of the vote with the SPD with 36.4 per cent and the FDP with 6.9 per cent. See 1994 results in *The Guardian*, 18 October 1994, p. 13. For results and comments on 1990 vote see Merkl, *German Unification*, p. 159.

81 Steve Crawshaw, 'Kohl claims victory by a whisker', *The Independent*, 17 October 1994, p. 1.

82 David Gow, 'Kohl home by slim margin', *The Guardian*, 17 October 1994, p. 1.

83 Exception to this convergence is the SPD stance on a common defence policy. For arguments on the idea of a 'grand coalition' in the area of Europe see David Gow, 'Kohl's flame still burning', *The Guardian*, 18 October 1994, p. 24.

84 Interview with Karsten Voigt, Bonn, 15 February 1995.
85 Peter Hort, 'The new president of the European Parliament: Klaus Hänsch', *Deutschland Magazine*, October 1994, p. 35.
86 Erich Hauser, 'Das "Monster" von Maastricht', *Frankfurter Rundschau*, 18 February 1992.
87 Engholm, in the *Stuttgarter Zeitung*, 16 March 1992.

SELECT BIBLIOGRAPHY

Ash, Timothy Garton, *In Europe's Name*, London, Cape, 1993.
Bahr, Egon, 'Aussöhnung statt Recht', Interview in *Freitag*, 6 December 1991.
Brandt, Willy, 'Für ein geregeltes Nebeneinander', 2 July 1967 in W. Brandt, *Aussenpolitik Deutschlandpolitik Europapolitik*, Berlin, Berlin Verlag, 1968.
Brandt, Willy, 'Welche Antworten gibt Europa?' *Zukunft*, No. 8, August, 1992.
Carl, Willi, 'Gerhard Schmid MdEP. Das dänische Ja stabilisert Europas Einigungsprozeß', press release, *Thema Europa. Medienservice der SPD. Abgeordneten im Europäischen Parlament*, 19 May 1993.
Dahrendorf, Ralf, *A Widening Atlantic?* New York, Council of Foreign Relation Books, IV Series, 1986.
Deutscher Bundestag, *Verhandlungen*, 7 February 1952, p. 1, section 1C.
Edinger, Lewis, *Kurt Schumacher: A Study in Personality and Political Behaviour*, Stanford, Stanford University Press, 1965.
Featherstone, Kevin, *Socialist Parties and European Integration,* Manchester, Manchester University Press, 1988.
Friedrich Ebert Stiftung, 'Peres für aktivere Rolle Europas', *Info Magazin*, January–March, 1993a.
Friedrich Ebert Stiftung, 'Zukunft der europäischen Sozialdemokratie', *Info Magazin*, January–March, 1993b.
Hänsch, Klaus, 'Vertiefung der Gemeinschaft und gesamteuropäische Zusammenarbeit', *Europa Archiv*, pp. 13–14, 1993.
Hänsch, Klaus, 'Vertiefung oder Auflösung', *Europäischer Medienservice*, vol. 13, no. 1, 25 January 1993, p. 2.
Hort, Peter, 'The new president of the European Parliament: Klaus Hänsch', *Deutschland Magazine*, October 1994.
Jacobi, Otto, *Sozial Demokratie als gewerkschaftliche Perspektive in Europa. Ein Plädoyer*, Friedrich Ebert Stiftung Publication, Reihe Eurokolleg 21, 1992.
Krieger, Wolfgang, 'Die Deutsche Integrationspolitik im postsowjetischen Europa', *Europa Archiv*, p. 18, 1992.
Lafontaine, Oskar, *Deutsche Wahrheiten. Die nationale und die soziale Frage*, Hamburg, Hamburg Verlag, 1990.
Lippert, Barbara, *German Unification and EC Integration: German and British Perspectives*, London, Frances Pinter, 1993.
Lodge, Juliet, *The European Policy of the SPD*, Sage Research Papers in Social Sciences 90–035, vol. 5, London, Sage, 1976.
Meissner, Boris, *Deutsche Ostpolitik 1961–1970*, Cologne, Verlag Wissenschaft und Politik, 1970.
Merkl, Peter H., *German Unification in the European Context*, University Park, PA, Penn State University Press, 1993.
Padgett, Stephen and Paterson, William, 'The rise and fall of the West German Left', *New Left Review*, March 1991.
Paterson, William, 'Foreign and security policy', in G. Smith, William Paterson and Peter H. Merkl, *Developments in West German Politics*, London, Macmillan, 1989.
Paterson, William E., *The SPD and European Integration*, Farnborough, Saxon House, 1974.
Pond, Elizabeth, 'Germany in the New Europe', *Foreign Affairs*, vol. 71, no. 2, 1992.
Rosolowsky, Diane, *West Germany's Foreign Policy: The Impact of the Social Democrats and the Greens*, New York, Greenwood Press, 1987.
Scharping, Rudolph, interview on European affairs, *Südwestdeutschen Rundfunk*, channel 1, 27 July 1992, 8.05 am.

Schmid, Carlo, in SPD Parliamentary Party *Mitteilungen für die Presse*, 17 November 1955.

Scweitzer, Carl-Christoph and Karsten, Detley, *The Federal Republic of Germany and EC Membership Evaluated*, London, Frances Pinter, 1990.

SPD, 'Außen-, Friedens-, und Sicherheitspolitik', Beschlüsse des Parteitages in Bremen, 28–31 May 1991.

SPD-Bundestagsfraktion, '*Karsten D. Voigt: Realismus und Verantwortung. Deutsche Außenpolitik am Beginn einer konzeptionellen Erneuerung,*' 1378, 27 May 1992.

SPD-Bundestagsfraktion, *SPD-Antrag zu Perspektiven der europäischen Integration*, 1568, 16 June 1992.

SPD-Bundestagsfraktion, *Wieczorek-Zeul. Die EG braucht die Erfahrung der skandinavischen Staaten*, 256, 2 February 1993.

SPD, *Der neue Weg, Regierungsprogramm 1990–94*, Beschlossen vom Parteitag am 28 September 1990 in Berlin.

SPD, 'Von der Konfrontation der Blöcke zu einem Europäische Sicherheitssystem. Positionspapier zu den sicherheitspolitischen Aspekten der Einigung Deutschlands im Rahmen der Europäischen Integration', Presservice der SPD, Bonn, 25 April 1990.

SPD Vorstand, *Europa. Eine historische Chance für Deutschland: 10 vernünftige Gründe, die für Maastrict sprechen*, undated publication.

SPD Vorstand, *Politik. Mehr Öffentlichkeit für die Europäische Politische Union*, Berlin, 1 October 1991.

Stares, Paul B., *The New Germany and the New Europe*, Washington, DC., Brookings Institute, 1992.

Stevens-Ströhmann, Rosalind, 'German Unification and Europe's Integration', *The World Today*, October 1991.

Vogel, Hans-Jochen, 'The challenge of 1992', in Dankert and Rooyman (eds), *Europe Without Frontiers: Socialists on the Future of the European Economic Community*, London, Mansell, 1989.

Voigt, Karsten, 'Europa jenseits der Entspannungspolitik. Protokollband des 7. Internationalen Humbolt Kolloquims zur Friedensforschung', *Berliner Beiträge zur Friedens- und Konfliktforschung*, April 1991.

Walter, Gerd, 'Vorschlag für eine politische Einigung der Staaten in Europa', in Matthias Barthe and Margaret Johannsen, *Zur Zukunft Deutschlands. Reden vom 2. internationalen Ost-West-Workshop über Gemeinsame Sicherheit*, Hamburger Beiträge zur Friedensforschung und Sicherheitspolitik, no. 44, January 1990.

3 The German Christian Democrats

William Paterson

THE CHRISTIAN DEMOCRATIC UNION

The first two decades in the history of the Federal Republic were dominated by the Christian Democratic Union (CDU) and its Bavarian ally, the Christian Social Union (CSU). The Christian Democrats were similar to parallel groupings which appeared in other European countries but as a successful conservative biconfessional party they represented a new departure in Germany. Although the party was consciously biconfessional, its core membership was preponderantly Catholic.

The pro-European policy of Konrad Adenauer, the first chancellor and leader of the CDU, appealed across the confessional divide. Its greatest appeal was to Catholics but it also appealed to Protestants who were looking for an antidote to the extreme nationalist positions taken up by many German Protestants during the Hitler era. Those middle-class German Protestants who still clung to nationalist positions felt much more at home in the Free Democratic Party (FDP) which had a German national wing identified with Thomas Dehler.

Adenauer's Europeanism revolved around a deep but narrow complex of sympathies and antipathies. His Europe was a Western Catholic Europe radiating out from his beloved Cologne. Symbolically, from Adenauer's house in Rhöndorf it is possible to look only westwards over the Rhine. This Western Europe was seen to rest on the basis of a Franco-German entente.[1] Adenauer's enduring anti-communism implied a close identification with the policy of the United States and an unwavering hostility towards the Soviet Union. In the field of external relations it was possible for Adenauer to shape a coherent policy out of this bundle of conflicting prejudices; there was at that time no tension between his reliance on the French in the field of European integration, and on the Americans for security. The French were content to follow the American lead in security matters in the face of the Soviet threat, and the Americans were the most committed supporters of Western European integration.

Adenauer's foreign policy was a clear cut option for the West; he believed that Germany's interests were essentially identical to those of the Western powers as a whole and that they would be willing to grant Germany a genuine partnership by gradually dismantling the discriminatory status of the occupation regime. This had to be preceded by an unmistakable German option for the West, for only then would the Western powers trust Germany enough to lift the discriminatory legislation. Adenauer's genius was to see that the emergence of Germany as a political force had to be identified with the pattern of co-operation that was being established in the

Western world. This meant, above all, a willingness by Germany to make concrete concessions to the French, the main opponents of Germany's rapid return to major importance, in return for France's intangible trust and goodwill; without these no progress could be made.

Adenauer's greatest disappointment was the failure of the plans for a European Defence Community. These plans would have taken Western Europe far along the road towards a federal state, but were rejected by the French National Assembly in August 1954. In taking Germany into the Common Market and Euratom, Adenauer was faced with opposition, not from the Social Democrats, but from his erstwhile coalition partners, the Free Democrats, and with distinct reservations from his economics minister Erhard. Ludwig Erhard's reservations were basically economic. He was committed to the creation of a free trade area and was much less prepared to trade economic concessions against political benefits. Erhard was supported by his state secretary Müller-Armack and some sections of business opinion, but no one could challenge Adenauer in terms of support in the CDU and he was quickly brushed aside.

More important perhaps than his victory over domestic opposition was Adenauer's insistence on major concessions to the French in the negotiations; he saw that without these concessions the weak French government of Guy Mollet could not lead France into the EEC. Walter Hallstein, who became president of the Commission of the EEC, was the chief German negotiator and Adenauer's closest foreign policy confidant. This period represents the high point of Adenauer's success.

This ended in the 1960s. Adenauer's foreign policy had been weakened by the attitude of President John F. Kennedy's administration, which made it clear that it intended to press for a detente with the USSR, despite the continued division of Germany. Unity with the West was thus not necessarily seen to be identical with a concern for German reunification. In this situation de Gaulle acted as a catalyst of the forces of change. If he had limited himself to asserting French interests within the existing framework, he would not have threatened the cohesion of Germany's foreign policy. But he presented a rival programme, a competing vision of a future Europe. His advocacy of *l'Europe des états*, rather than a supranational Europe, and of the eventual solution of the German problem within the framework of an East–West detente, appealed to different groupings in the Federal Republic, though there was no consensus in support of the total package.

On the other hand, his challenge to the United States, his attack on NATO and his animus against the supranational elements of the European Community embarrassed the German government. It threatened to disrupt the links between the bases of Adenauer's foreign policy: between security alignment with the United States and the entente with France, and between the Franco-German rapprochement and the commitment to European integration. Faced with these antinomies, Adenauer was much less happy than he had been among the certainties of the 1950s. After an attempt to deny the tension between these competing views, he indicated that while West Germany must continue to depend on the United States for security, Germany's interests in West European integration lay with France and thus with de Gaulle. This implied a lesser commitment to supranationalism and an endorsement, however unwilling, of the French exclusion of Britain – a major blow to the Community idea. This endorsement was symbolized by Adenauer's insistence on signing the Franco-German Treaty, against considerable internal opposition, just after the French veto on British entry in January 1963.

THE GAULLISTS VERSUS ATLANTICISTS

In the period between 1963 and 1966 the CDU/CSU was polarized in European policy terms between the Gaullists and the Atlanticists. It was essentially a struggle between the 'ins' and 'outs'. The 'ins' held the major ministries, the 'outs' – Konrad Adenauer and Franz Josef Strauss – were respectively in retirement and disgrace. The 'outs', however, were party chairmen: Konrad Adenauer of the CDU and Franz Josef Strauss of the CSU. They carried on a continual guerrilla campaign against the government, accusing it of placing too much emphasis on the Atlantic relationship, of neglecting France and of turning its back on the commitment to supranationalism. The Atlanticists were headed by three prominent Protestant politicians, the federal chancellor, Ludwig Erhard, who had succeeded Adenauer in 1963, the foreign minister, Gerhard Schröder, and the defence minister, Kai-Uwe von Hassel. Erhard had been lukewarm about the foundation of the EEC and would have preferred a larger free trade area. As Protestants, it is probably fair to say that they had a less strong emotional commitment to the values and countries of the original Community than Catholic members of the CDU. However, their policies were motivated less by any lack of enthusiasm for France than by the need, which every West German government has felt, of not letting their policies drift into conflict with those of the United States. In any case the force of the Gaullist attack was blunted by its own incoherence, which originated in the contradiction between support for very close links with France and for supranationalism, given Gaullist attitudes to supranationalism. It was also the case that no West German politician at that time would have risked serious conflict with the United States, given West German security dependence on that country.

KOHL AND THE EUROPEAN VOCATION OF THE CDU

After assuming office as chancellor in October 1982, Helmut Kohl put European integration back at the centre of the CDU's discourse. By then the steam had long run out of *Ostpolitik* and there was correspondingly less mileage to be gained in opposing it. Kohl's European posture was largely modelled on Adenauer's. They are both Catholics from that part of Germany that is unmistakably part of Western Europe and which borders on France. The geographical distance from Cologne to Ludwigshafen is not great; but more importantly, these are both areas where the key project was seen as Franco–German reconciliation.[2] In an essay written on the centenary of Adenauer's birth, Kohl wrote 'The only way to do justice to Adenauer's legacy is to treat it as a command to do likewise.'[3] Kohl signalled the change of policy priorities by visiting Paris and Brussels within a week of his advent to power.

In his early years as chancellor, Kohl's European policy was largely declaratory. Even at that time, however, a return to the Adenauer priorities was clear. There was a continued emphasis on the Franco–German relationship as the central motor of European integration, and Kohl cultivated a close and enduring relationship with François Mitterrand. This seemed less striking at the time since his predecessor, Helmut Schmidt, had had very close relations with Giscard d'Estaing. Their priorities were somewhat different, however. Both Giscard and Schmidt were intergovern-mentalists rather than integrationists, and the Franco–German relationship was seen as a necessary spine at a time when American leadership could no longer be relied upon. Kohl and Mitterrand, by contrast, were both committed integrationists and they saw Franco–German relations as the motor of integration.

Progress in this direction was initially very slow, given the intergovernmental character of the European Community in the early 1980s; the first real initiative, the Genscher–Colombo Plan and the resulting Solemn Declaration, was identified with the Free Democratic Party. The British budgetary issue remained a major obstacle in the way of further progress, and much effort was devoted to its removal, which was largely accomplished by President Mitterrand at the Fontainebleau summit of 1984. Kohl and Mitterrand were both well aware of the British prime minister's opposition to further integration and, given that unanimity was the decision rule of the European Community, they bided their time and put relatively little effort into launching schemes for deeper integration in those early years.

At the Milan summit conference of June 1985, a Franco–German proposal was put forward for a Draft Treaty on European Union. Despite its ambitious title, which echoed the European Parliament's plan of the previous year, it was a fairly modest document concentrating, like the Solemn Declaration, on the extension of European political co-operation. Its force had in any case been weakened by the use by Ignaz Kiechle, the CSU German agriculture minister, of a veto in the Agricultural Council only a month earlier. Given that the draft paper envisaged the extension of majority voting in the Council, the use by the German government of a veto for the first time did much to undermine the German position at the summit.

In the latter part of the 1980s the environment for realizing plans for further integration improved dramatically. The first catalyst was the Single European Act of 1986. Its major impact lay in the introduction of majority voting in the Council of Ministers. Formally, this was introduced only in a limited number of articles largely to do with the implementation of the Single European Market, but in practice positions were widely traded and majority voting was contagious. Although unanimity remained the rule for institutional change, it was now embedded in a Community where majority voting was frequent and the price of isolation potentially high. The capacity of a single state to block progress was thus dramatically reduced.

THE IMPACT OF GERMAN UNITY

If the Single European Act provided the potential for further change, it was the prospect and eventual achievement of German unity that paved the way for far-reaching change. Kohl's reaction was to embrace and accelerate unity, but to insist that a unified Germany must be anchored in a much deeper Europe.

German unity was accomplished at breath-taking speed between the fall of the Berlin Wall on 9 November 1989 and 3 October 1990. Progress towards anchoring Germany in a deeper Europe began even during the talks on unity. President Mitterrand, after a short period where he appeared to return to balance of power thinking, had by December 1989 come to the conclusion that German unity was inevitable, and at the Strasbourg summit of December 1989 the initial moves which led to the setting up of the Intergovernmental Conferences on Political and

Economic and Monetary Union were being discussed, and the drive towards the new treaty on European Union, which was finally negotiated at Maastricht in December 1991, was dominated by Franco–German co-operation.

There were, however, significant differences of emphasis. For President Mitterrand and a number of Germany's neighbours economic and monetary union was the main goal since their major concern was that the disparity between Germany's economic strength and their own was likely to widen even further. Even as things stood, they felt that Germany, especially in monetary policy through the Bundesbank, had an enormous influence on its neighbours. Economic and monetary union would be a way of making that influence reciprocal and giving other countries a handle on German economic power. Chancellor Kohl and the Christian Democratic Union were prepared to support economic and monetary union in order to assuage French fears, but were always aware of the lack of enthusiasm of the Bundesbank and insisted on a number of conditions:

> There are certain things that we hold to be indispensable, such as convergence of economic policies and prosperity levels, budgetary discipline by all Community governments and an independent European central bank committed above all to monetary stability.[4]

For Kohl and for the CDU in general it was equally important that progress should be made towards political union: 'The Treaty on Political Union in its scope and objectives must not take second place to the Treaty on Economic and Monetary Union.'[5] Their view was that this must entail movement in the direction of a more federal Europe: 'Europe will be a federal Europe – it will not be a unitary Europe.'[6]

CORRECTING THE DEMOCRATIC DEFICIT

Kohl and the CDU were particularly concerned to see the powers of the European Parliament strengthened. This was a position which, although shared by other German parties to a greater or lesser extent, formed a much more central part of CDU discourse. In the negotiations that led up to the Maastricht Treaty, it was argued for strongly, not only by Kohl, but by Egon Klepsch, the CDU MEP who was at that time president of the European Parliament. The CDU was also committed to the development of a common foreign and security policy, though it gave a much greater priority to the maintenance of a defence connection with the United States than did either the French government or the SPD:

> To strengthen the European pillar of the Alliance, and to develop the security dimension within the Community, it would be logical to make use of the Western European Union. It will be vital to keep in close touch and to maintain a close dialogue with our friends and partners in the United States in order to make sure that no misunderstandings can arise.[7]

EUROPOL

Chancellor Kohl was the first leader to suggest the creation of a EUROPOL, a supranational European police agency: 'that would be able to operate without let or hindrance in all the Community countries in important matters such as the fight against drug barons or organised international crime.'[8] In practice, this proposal ran up against the entrenched interests of the *Länder* in Germany and the reservations of other member states, and progress towards greater judicial and police co-operation at Maastricht was less than Kohl would have wanted.

Alongside its advanced position on deepening, the CDU has been markedly committed to widening. Like all other German parties, it has wished to see a Northern enlargement, but the strength of its commitment to an Eastern enlargement and to bringing the countries on Germany's eastern rim into the Union is distinctive:

> As a young man after the war, in my own part of Germany on the border between France and Germany, I was able to see how an age-old enmity between two nations was overcome. Friendly links were established between governments; more importantly, the people themselves, and the young people especially, became friends. We would now dearly like to see the same thing happening with our Polish neighbours. We now have a border of hundreds of kilometres between our two countries and we do not want to see prosperity barriers arising in Europe between the rich and the poor, the haves and the have nots. It is not only a question of matching prosperity levels. It is important to ensure that people can get together again. This is why we have opened our borders to our neighbours – Czechoslovakia and Poland – and we should be delighted to see all other EC countries following suit as soon as possible.[9]

THE GERMAN–BRITISH RELATIONSHIP

Chancellor Kohl and the CDU more generally have traditionally privileged the Franco–German relationship. The relationship with the British government and the Conservative Party was always much less warm and, with the exception of the period when the Conservatives were led by Edward Heath, there were quite sharply diverging views on the desirability of deeper European integration. Under Mrs Thatcher, those divergences widened. In the mid-1980s, there was still enough common ground to agree to the Single European Market and the single European Act. The working out of the Single European Act and the way in which it encouraged deeper integration led Mrs Thatcher to become even more intransigently opposed to further integration. This predisposition was heightened by the speech of Jacques Delors to the British TUC in the summer of 1988. Mrs Thatcher was now launched on a path that led from her Bruges speech in September 1988 to her 'No, no, no' speech in the House of Commons after the Rome summit in October 1990. She responded to the onset of German unification by opposing it at every point and trying unsuccessfully to enlist the aid of President Mitterrand in what was quite clearly a doomed enterprise.[10]

Against this background, it is hardly surprising that Chancellor Kohl welcomed John Major, whom he referred to in his Edinburgh speech as a 'eine Glucksache für Europa' (a fortunate occurrence for Europe). Europe had played a key role in Mrs Thatcher's fall, provoking Geoffrey Howe to mount his fatal attack on her in his speech in the House of Commons on 13 November 1990. This was followed almost immediately by the decision of Michael Heseltine to provoke a leadership election. In the subsequent elections, a key role was played by Tristan Garel-Jones, foreign office minister with special responsibility for the European Community. Garel-Jones articulated and organized ministerial discontent with Mrs Thatcher's policies. At the heart of this anxiety was the perception that Mrs Thatcher's policies were deeply damaging to the United Kingdom interest, that, in pursuing autonomy with increasing fervour, she was in danger of excluding Britain from any real influence in the Community and putting real and tangible interests at risk. Her anti-European rhetoric had also undermined the Conservative aim of appearing the most European of the major parties in Britain and ceded that role to the Labour Party. Garel-Jones, Chris Patten, Michael Heseltine, William Waldegrave and Douglas Hurd were the strongest proponents of a pro-European strategy but the view that Mrs Thatcher had marginalized Britain was widely shared. In the event, the leadership election was won by John Major who was identified with neither a pro- nor an anti-European faction; his campaign organizer, Norman Lamont, was thought to be a mild Eurosceptic.

In office, John Major was much influenced by Chris Patten, the most Christian democratic of Conservatives, and he quickly developed a strategy designed to reverse the perceived marginalization. In essence, this involved forging a strong relationship with Chancellor Kohl on the basis of both cultivating strong personal ties and abandoning intransigent opposition. This new policy was announced in Bonn in March 1991 where John Major talked to the Konrad Adenauer Foundation of his aspiration of placing Britain 'at the heart of Europe'. Kohl reciprocated Major's sentiments in his speech in Edinburgh in May 1991, and throughout that year close relations between the United Kingdom and Germany were regarded as important priorities for both sides. Chancellor Kohl played a very helpful role for John Major in the negotiations, especially in relation to the opt out on the Social Chapter where he backed Major's position. Kohl was subsequently to become increasingly disillusioned with his investment in British–German relations as the Eurosceptics increased their influence in the Conservative Party after the Danish referendum in June 1992 and Major's position moved to accommodate them. He had originally believed that as John Major's tenure in office lengthened he would increasingly be able to play a positive role in relation to European integration. This view was later revised by all the significant figures in the CDU and Kohl continued to look for external support to France and to meetings of Christian Democratic leaders which preceded summit meetings.

THE CDU AND MAASTRICHT

The Maastricht negotiations were something of a disappointment to Kohl and the CDU. On political union progress was very slight. Parliament gained some additional powers, notably in relation to the approval of Commission appointments, but progress in other areas, especially towards common foreign and security policy, was minimal. The one exception was that of economic and monetary union where the Treaty on European Union was exceptionally ambitious. Unfortunately for Kohl this also proved to be the area that was sensitive domestically. Just before the Maastricht negotiations, *Bild Zeitung*, Germany's most popular tabloid, ran a campaign in defence of the deutschmark which struck a chord in German public opinion, which has since the 1970s been reluctant to see the deutschmark given up.

The ratification of Maastricht, although it took place against the backdrop of a public opinion that was becoming less enthusiastic about European integration, did not produce the same factional struggle in the CDU, as it did in the British Conservative Party. It did, however, lead to division with the Bavarian sister party, the CSU.

The resolutions on European policy of the CDU at Düsseldorf on 25–28 October 1992 give a fair picture of opinion inside the CDU. The CDU remained committed to the ideal and apprehensive about nationalism and its excesses to a degree which found no echo in the British Conservative Party:

> The Treaty of Maastricht marks the beginning of the critical phase in the process of European unification. If we should fail now to implement the unification of Europe we are threatened by a relapse into old-style nationalism and rivalry. The radicals of the right and the left are equally eager to whip up fear of Europe and nourish the illusion that the great problems of the future may be solved by the unaided efforts of one nation alone. We must not idly stand by in a situation in which the structures and developments of Europe increasingly serve to excite apprehension among the people, obliterating their awareness of the chances which unified Europe has to offer. The Christian Democratic Union of Germany has decided to accept this challenge: It is our stated aim that Germany should be European. Germany needs the European Union.[11]

It was also committed to adoption of a European Constitution:

> The European Union must be given a constitution which embodies its fundamental ideas. Being the manifesto of a liberal society, it must contain a code of fundamental rights, a regulation demarcating the decision-making authority of the various institutions of the Union, and a system by which the competences of the Community on the one hand and its member nations with their federal states, regions, and communes on the other, are circumscribed unequivocally in conformance with the principle of subsidiarity. The constitution of the Union should restrict the activities of its governing bodies to the necessary minimum, listing them in concrete terms in a catalogue.[12]

While it thus reaffirmed its traditional goals a new post-Maastricht line more closely in tune with a guarded public opinion was also apparent:

> United Europe must protect and promote the national identity, the culture, and the lifestyle of each nation or country. If the principle of subsidiarity is observed scrupulously we shall be protected from the excesses of reglementation, bureaucratic perfectionism, and centralism. It must become the guiding principle of all EC organs.
>
> In this context, it will have to be investigated what rights could be conferred back to the member countries, their federal states, and/or their regions.[13]

THE DISCUSSION SURROUNDING THE NEW CDU BASIC PROGRAMME

The CDU adopted a new Basic Programme at its conference in Hamburg on 23 February 1994. In the months before there had been intense speculation about possible changes in its European policy focusing especially on the question as to whether the goal of a federal Europe would be preserved. In an apparently inspired leak the *Frankfurter Allgemeine Zeitung*, the Conservative daily whose own position is more nationalist and Eurosceptical than that of the CDU, suggested that the new programme would drop the aspiration of creating a federal state in favour of emphasizing the permanence of the nation states.[14] In the event, the programme represented more continuity than change: 'We wish a strong Europe that secures the future of the nations . . . we wish to strengthen federalism in the European Union.'[15]

THE EUROPEAN ELECTION

The CDU's election programme for the 1994 European election represented a further presentational adjustment to prevailing public opinion. Voters were asked to strengthen Germany and Europe. The CDU was referred to as 'the German European Party'. There was scarcely a mention of institutional development. Point nine, the last point in the programme, referred to the necessity of organizing Europe on a free, democratic, federal, subnational basis. This was, however, flanked by a strong rejection of overregulation, bureaucratic perfectionism and centralism. Subsidiarity was strongly emphasized.[16] In general, as elsewhere, the election was fought on domestic themes and the CDU presented it as a plebiscite for the chancellor. The CDU increased its percentage share from 37.7 per cent to 38.8 per cent, but its seats went up from twenty-four to thirty-seven as the number of German seats went up from seventy-eight to ninety-nine. The CDU/CSU together won forty-seven seats.

THE CHRISTIAN SOCIAL UNION

The Christian Social Union was probably the most 'European' party in the early decades of the Federal Republic. In a sense this was unsurprising given the generally higher level of support among German Catholics for the ideas of European integration. Despite the post-war inflow of refugees into Bavaria, the confessional balance of Bavaria after 1945 remained unchanged and the CSU remained a largely Catholic party in membership and electoral support.[17] In the early years of the Federal Republic, the CSU was relatively inactive in pushing its ideas on European integration since these were sufficiently close to those of Konrad Adenauer for it to have confidence in him representing its views. The model that lay behind such pronouncements as it did make was of a federal Europe. The ideas were distinctive in the degree to which they stressed the Christian character of Western Europe and its function as a bulwark against the spread of communism.

Strauss's resignation as defence minister in 1962, and the retirement of Adenauer in 1963 propelled the CSU into adopting a much more active policy on European integration. Foreign and European policy making at governmental level was now in the hands of the Protestant triumvirate of Erhard as chancellor, Schröder as foreign minister and von Hassel as defence minister, who were perceived by Strauss and Adenauer as being too close to the United States, too keen on detente and not sufficiently committed to the realization of the European idea.

In the years after 1964 Strauss developed his European strategy further.[18] This had a number of components. Of central importance was the assertion of a much more independent and much more equal role for Europe between the superpowers:

> A united Western Europe should be the first step [*Vorstufe*] on the way to the United States of Europe, a United States of Europe which should include the peoples of Central and Eastern Europe. United Europe should adopt the

position of an independent power between the United States and the Soviet Union and thus secure the preponderance of free society in the global political powerplay.[19]

This central role for Europe would be based on a European political federation with its own means of defending itself: 'A United States of Europe with its own nuclear deterrent under supranational control would form the second essential pillar of a Western defence community in alliance with the USA.'[20]

The development of a federal Europe to include the peoples of Eastern Europe would make possible the solution of the German question – Strauss referred to this as the Europeanization of the German question:

> Above all it [i.e. a United States of Europe] would provide the one framework which would make possible the reunification of Germany and avoid all its latent dangers. Germany needs Europe more than any other country. . . . In contributing to the formation of a European federation, Germany herself would find a new identity.[21]

These various strands were bound together by profound anti-communism and reflected a fear that the United States would sacrifice German interests in an attempt at accommodation with the USSR. This hostility to the USSR led to Strauss pinning a great deal of hope on the China card, i.e. the belief that continued disagreement with China would constrain the Soviet Union in Eastern Europe and help keep the 'German option' open. This view was encouraged by the Chinese, who hoped that the formation of a united Western Europe would act as a bulwark against the Soviet Union.

A major weakness of the CSU approach, however, was the fact that it was ultimately unacceptable to France. Although de Gaulle welcomed the emphasis on European independence, the CSU's espousal of supranational institutions and common nuclear defences was anathema to successive French governments. In the Grand Coalition, the CDU/CSU ministers were fairly evenly balanced along Gaullist/Atlanticist lines. This, combined with day-to-day political exigencies and the fact that Strauss was tied up with his responsibilities as finance minister, meant that the CSU kept a fairly low profile on European issues between 1966 and 1969.

THE CSU OUT OF POWER IN BONN

The early years of the social–liberal coalition were dominated by *Ostpolitik*. The CSU therefore concentrated less on advocating a stronger Western Europe and more on opposing *Ostpolitik*. Their policy of strong anti-communism and pro-German unification rhetoric brought tangible domestic political benefits. It helped to establish the CSU as a potential fourth 'conservative' party throughout the Federal Republic, although Strauss's attempt to capitalize on this after the 1976 election, when he broke up the joint parliamentary party for a short time, foundered on resolute CDU opposition. In Bavaria itself these ideas and opposition to *Ostpolitik* helped the CSU to make significant inroads for the first time into the nationally minded electorate of the Protestant corridor of Franconia. In terms of European policy the CSU was relatively muted. On agricultural policy it vigorously opposed the Mansholt Plan and generally took a strongly pro-agriculture line close to the German Farmers' Union.[22] It was very critical of the EMS on the grounds that it would encourage the weaker EC states to become too dependent on Community funds. Strauss and the CSU were very close to a number of large industrial and technological interests, particularly in the modern sector, and the CSU was active in opposing any plans for co-determination at a European level, as put forward by the SPD-led government. This closeness to agricultural interests and to modern industry is a hallmark of the CSU. In this strategy the disadvantages for modern industry of costly support for agriculture were minimized by the existence of the CAP.

After the collapse of the SPD/FDP government the CSU was able at least potentially to increase its influence on European policy through Ignaz Kiechle, agriculture minister after 1983. Kiechle's position created difficulties for the CSU in 1984 because of the agreement of the West German government to cuts in dairy production. The difficulties that this created for the CSU ensured that Kiechle took the lead in supporting a West German veto on cuts in cereal prices in 1985.[23]

THE TRANSFORMATION OF CSU POLICY

The marked Europeanism of the CSU in the three founding decades of the Federal Republic began to cool slightly in the 1980s. Franz Josef Strauss became increasingly critical of a European Commission which he perceived as inefficient. He was also interested in developing closer relations with the British Conservatives, with whom he shared a common agenda of anti-socialism and ensuring that the European Community did not become a vehicle for socialism by the back door through re-distribution, harmonization and the expansion of the public sphere. In pursuit of his strategy of locating the CSU on the right of the political spectrum, Strauss was happy to allow the CSU to be described as conservative, and the Basic Programme of the party stresses this conservative character.[24] This was never a position that could have been adopted by the CDU, which stresses its loyalty to Christian democratic principles. The CSU and the United Kingdom Conservatives also shared a common scepticism about the second enlargement of the European Communities and its potential effect on Community finances. They were also worried about the capacity of those countries to play a role as full members of the Community. Franz Josef Strauss, in stark contrast to Helmut Kohl, shared Mrs Thatcher's aversion to the European Parliament which he slightingly referred to as a *Plauderbude* (talking shop).

Strauss's objections to the European Community in the first half of the 1980s were largely tactical, and policy priorities changed with the advent of the Single European Act in 1986. His critique had been framed in a period during which the European Community was perceived to be in the doldrums, and the priority now became to reformulate European policy in a period of rapid Community development. Strauss talked to Mrs Thatcher of a 'train that cannot now be stopped'. CSU priorities shifted to ensuring an active Bavarian presence at the federal and European level. This change of emphasis was also related to the reform of the CAP in 1986–87, which put tremendous pressure on the Bavarian government, and its response to its agricultural supporters, that agriculture was a matter to be decided at the European level, was simply not accepted. The fury of its agricultural clientele was an important impetus in encouraging the Bavarian government to maximize opportunities for influencing European policy at the federal and European level A Brussels office was opened in December 1987 and a new European ministry was legally established in June 1988. The Single European Act necessitated the agreement of the *Länder*, and Bavaria took the lead in using the European issue as a way of recalibrating state–federal relations. The *Länder* suggested in a Bundesrat resolution of 21 February 1986 on the ratification of the SEA that their agreement to ratification of the SEA would be dependent on improvements to the policy-making machinery in the FRG and to *Länder* representation in international institutions such as the EC. In the Bundesrat's first debate on ratification on 16 May 1986 the *Länder* sought to introduce an article providing for their constitutionally guaranteed *Mitwirkung*, including the inclusion of *Länder* representatives in West German negotiating teams at the Council of Ministers. Although this campaign was led by Bavaria the resolution was passed unanimously. In the event, the federal government agreed to legal provision for restricted *Länder* participation in policy making, and the Bundesrat ratified the SEA in December 1986.

THE CSU AND YUGOSLAVIA

The CSU's opportunity to affect *la grande politique* of the European Community has been severely constrained in recent years. The death of Franz Josef Strauss in 1988 robbed it of its only major figure who was interested in wider issues and who possessed the contacts (Mrs Thatcher, for example) to play an independent role on the international stage. After unification, its horizon narrowed and it continues to be confronted with a situation in which the Foreign Ministry seems set to remain the permanent preserve of the party (the FDP) with which it possibly has even less in common than with the SPD. During the late 1980s the CSU took a markedly more pro-American line than other German parties; this has continued into the 1990s, with the CSU in stark contrast to the thrust of Franz Josef Strauss's Gaullist phase being less enthusiastic about the substitution of a European defence identity for NATO.

The other external issue on which the CSU has taken a stand is on former Yugoslavia. Bavaria has very close links with Croatia which reflect the presence of Croatian migrants, history and the shared Catholic religion, and the CSU was particularly active in pressing for the recognition of Croatia and Slovenia – one of the few issues on which it was able to influence Foreign Minister Genscher. The CSU has continually taken a strongly anti-Serbian line in the European Parliament. This position has been especially identified with Otto Von Habsburg, a CSU MEP. At his urging the CSU members of the European Parliament have continually called for military action against Serbia. They took particular satisfaction from the European Parliament Resolution of February 1994 which called for the implementation of the NATO ultimatum against Serbian military power in Bosnia.

Bavaria and the CSU also have close relations with Albania, Bulgaria, Slovakia and the Ukraine, although in the case of the Ukraine, as with Croatia, they are beginning to have second thoughts, concerned that the Ukraine regime is too undemocratic and that its anti-Russian stance might lead to conflict.

THE BAVARIAN CHALLENGE TO GOVERNMENT EUROPEAN POLICY

Traditionally the Christian Social Union, the CDU's Bavarian partner, has been even more European than the CDU. Its position began to change after unification and Edmund Stoiber, the Bavarian minister president, has begun to articulate a policy on European Union closer in some respects to that of the British Conservatives than the CDU. CSU pronouncements on European Union hardened considerably over the summer of 1993 when Max Streibl, Franz Josef Strauss's successor as minister president, stepped down. Streibl had fairly undefined views on Europe beyond a strong attachment to a Europe of the regions which formed a centrepoint in the CSU's policy from 1988 to 1992. His successor, Edmund Stoiber, placed himself consistently on the right of the CSU.

Stoiber first made his dissent on Europe public in an open letter to Helmut Kohl on 3 September 1993. He pointed to the lack of transparency and clarity in the EU system which contributed to a lack of popular acceptance. Stoiber argued in favour of subsidiarity as a corrective, but at this point he also argued in favour of strengthening a multi-chamber European Parliament and giving the EU Commission more clearly the appearance of a government, although he also stressed the necessity of preserving the identity and capacity for action of the Member States. In his governmental declaration of 22 October 1993, Stoiber focused almost exclusively on Europe and in a very controversial interview with *Süddeutsche Zeitung* on 2 November, Stoiber delivered a blistering attack on the European Union. The speech and the interview replayed a number of familiar themes reminiscent of the British Conservatives on the tendency of the EU Commission to over-intervene and to over-regulate. There were, however, a number of distinctive themes. In the interview he specifically stressed Bavaria's statehood and the necessity of this remaining uncompromised. Historical parallels were drawn and Stoiber suggested that Bavaria had been an unwilling participant in the Imperial Reich after 1871.

Stoiber did not restrict himself to underlying Bavarian populist resentments, however, but presented a wider German national alternative to Helmut Kohl which might appeal more widely across the Federal Republic. He stressed the necessity for pursuing a policy based on clear majority support in public opinion, and related this directly to the decision of the Federal Constitutional Court of 12 October 1993, which had argued that legitimation of European integration should take place at the national level and that every step should be accompanied by clear parliamentary support. Stoiber also suggested that support for an integrated Europe had been tied up with German division and the experience of the Second World War. He argued further that this stance, which he identified with the generation of Helmut Kohl, was now outdated and that Germany should identify a much more specific role for itself based on national interest, a discourse readily familiar to those who have followed the European policy of the British Conservative Party.

The theme of national interest, while accepted as self-evident in Britain, has not normally been explicitly articulated in post-war Germany. The shaming experience of the Nazi regime and its hypernationalism had made the language of national interest unusable. Germany's policy was to work from within multilateral institutions and to seek to develop a common interest that would clearly not be against Germany's interests; but the brutal language of national interest was avoided.

Stoiber's speech thus provoked furious criticism and he was accused of high treason by Heiner Geissler, a former Secretary General on the left of the CDU. Stoiber subsequently made a number of speeches critical of the European Union, including one in Brussels itself.

In placing Europe at the centre of his discourse Stoiber was pursuing a number of goals. Within Bavaria, he was attempting to consolidate the position of the CSU by mobilizing nationalist populist currents of opinion. This was especially important in the light of the European elections in June 1994, where the CSU would have to secure 5 per cent overall in Germany, a target more difficult to achieve in a unified and larger Germany. The pressure was therefore on to get out the votes in Bavaria. More widely, Stoiber was attempting to occupy the space to the right of the CDU on European policy throughout the Federal Republic. Franz Josef Strauss had also often pursued a policy of mobilizing right-wing opinion throughout the Federal Republic. The major difference was that Strauss was a figure taken seriously, even if not equally popular throughout the Federal Republic, while Stoiber remained an ambitious provincial politician. The content of Strauss's distinctive appeal was also markedly different from that of Stoiber. Externally Strauss concentrated on opposition to *Ostpolitik*, while internally he pursued a range of right-wing policies. Stoiber attracted little support from any CDU politicians, but he intended his sceptical views on Europe to attract support from ordinary voters inside and beyond Bavaria; by articulating them he put pressure on the embattled Chancellor Kohl's central policy flank of support for European Union by being the first member of a mainstream party to act as a focus for popular discontents with the European project. It was precisely the fear that Stoiber might weaken popular support that accounted for the shrill tone of denunciation of his pronouncements by the political elite.

Stoiber's views received enthusiastic backing from Peter Gauweiler, the environment minister in the Bavarian government. Gauweiler had been the member of the CSU who had first taken a populist Eurosceptic line during the Maastricht debates, when he referred to the proposed single currency as 'esperanto money'. Gauweiler also produced a long list of measures that, according to his views of subsidiarity, should be repatriated to Bavaria. In Spring 1994 Gauweiler was compelled to resign as environment minister over alleged corruption, though he remained in the *Landtag* and continued to head the CSU in Munich. Out of office, Gauweiler became increasingly Eurosceptical, making common cause with Manfred Brunner, the leader of the Alliance of Free Citizens, a party explicitly formed to combat the Maastricht Treaty. During the campaign for the European election, Gauweiler went even further and appeared on a joint platform with Brunner and Jörg Haider, the controversial Austrian extreme right-wing politician.

The CSU has always pursued a dual strategy of governing Bavaria and being in permanent alliance with the Christian Democratic Union at the federal level. Within the federal government, finance minister Theo Waigel became the most prominent CSU representative and acted as principal German negotiator on the economic aspects of the Maastricht Treaty. He and the other CSU members of the governing coalition thus remained bound by the constraints of governmental policy. It is important to remember, however, that the federal government is much smaller than its British counterpart and that, apart from a very few junior ministers outside the Cabinet, there is no equivalent to the huge number of members of the government that are such a characteristic feature of the Westminster scene. The relationship between the government and the legislature is thus less close than in Britain, a difference symbolized by the role of the prime minister as the leader of his or her party in the House of Commons, a role carried out by a parliamentary party leader in Germany, where the government members symbolically sit above and facing the Bundestag, while in Britain they sit alongside other members on the government benches. As members of a joint parliamentary party with the CDU, the CSU Bonn members of the Bundestag are, nevertheless, under different pressures from their Bavarian colleagues; but the constraints are less binding than those which apply to their governmental colleagues.

In a report on the work of the CSU *Landesgruppe* in Bonn to the CSU party committee in Deggendorf on 18 March 1994, its chairman, Michael Glos MdB, struck a tone in relation to Europe which hovered between the loyalty of his governmental colleagues and the Euroscepticism of his minister president. On the broad aims of external policy, the report offers a ringing endorsement to NATO and stresses that WEU should be developed as a European pillar of NATO, a position quite compatible with that of the British Conservatives. It gives much more prominence to the stabilization of Russia than would now be accorded by the other coalition partners: 'The stabilisation of Russia is the determining German and European interest in the east of the Continent. It is, therefore, necessary to see a stable security order in Europe with Russia.'[25] Traditionally in Germany Conservatives, including Bismarck, have seen Russia as an order-creating power (*Ordnungsmacht*) and have sought alliance with Russia, even when it was of a different ideological persuasion as in Weimar, while liberals have tended to see Germany's role as encouraging democratic processes in Central Europe, against Russia if necessary.

The report endorsed the goal of European integration as a *Staatenverbund*, a league of states, rather than the federal goal still endorsed by the CDU. The report also warned against overharmonization by the Brussels bureaucracy.[26] Those positions were, however, qualified by other sections in the report which endorse all proposed German legislation in relation to the Single Market.[27] Despite the commitment to a *Staatenverbund*, the proposals for the 1996 IGC stress effectiveness, greater parliamentary control and increased use of qualified majority rules, positions normally identified with Euro-enthusiasts. The commitment to Russia as an order-creating power is qualified by the need to encourage the reform democracies of Central Europe and to deny Russia a veto on their development.

THE CSU IN THE EUROPEAN ELECTION

The CSU manifesto for the European election of 1994 extended the policy of facing both ways. It was certainly less Eurosceptical than Stoiber's earlier pronouncements. This was only to be expected, given the fact that both Christian Democratic parties were fighting on a common all-German list. By this time, too, the Republicans and other right-wing groups, to whose potential voters Euroscepticism had been designed to appeal, were obviously losing in electoral appeal.

The manifesto contains a very enthusiastic endorsement of European monetary union, and Theo Waigel and the CSU are given the credit for the siting of the European Monetary Institute and a future European Central Bank in Frankfurt. The passage on monetary union attempted to deal with the emotional attachment to the deutschmark by including a picture of a shining coin and the assertion that EMU prevents speculation against the deutschmark until it can be replaced by something equally strong. There was very little on European institutions apart from an endorsement of federalism, subsidiarity and the rather contradictory notion that the EU was a league of states (*Staatenverbund*). Subsidiarity is understood primarily in the sense of returning powers to Bavaria and Germany from Brussels. A conservative note is struck in the passages which emphasize the need for Europe to be competitive and to strengthen internal security. There are also appeals to reduce the unfair burden Germany is shouldering as the main net payer into the European Union budget and as the destination for most refugees and asylum seekers.

The result of the election was extremely satisfactory for the CSU, which increased its share of the vote from 45.4 to 48.9 per cent and its MEPs from seven to eight. The SPD dropped marginally from 24.2 to 23.7 per cent. Most satisfyingly for the CSU, the Republicans dropped from 14.6 per cent in 1989 to 6.6 per cent, while the FDP dipped from 4 to 3.3 per cent. The CSU is thus likely to continue to diverge from the CDU policy and to derive some of its inspiration from the British Conservatives.

CONCLUSION

In an essay written in 1994 Anthony Nicholls argued that since German Unity the prevailing 'Rhineland' position on Europe in Germany now had to contend with an alternative 'Frankfurt' position. The Rhineland position 'means working closely with the core members of the European Union, the original signatories of the Treaty of Rome to intensify European integration. . . . At the heart of this policy is the Franco-German axis.'[28] The Frankfurt position argues that:

> Germany cannot ignore the fact that it is now a nation-state again, and that it has interests and responsibilities which cannot be palmed off on supranational bodies like NATO or the European Union. . . . In addition they have a jaundiced view of the Franco-German alliances. . . . Nor do they believe that the European Union itself has much further scope for development in terms of integration, though many of them would like to see it substantially enlarged. Maastricht is regarded as a confused and misguided treaty, and in particular the concept of monetary union is regarded as Utopian.[29]

The Rhineland position still adequately characterizes the CDU and more especially the federal chancellor, Helmut Kohl. The Frankfurt position which Nicholls identifies with the *Frankfurter Allgemeine Zeitung* and the Bundesbank, which is located in Frankfurt, do, however, have a significant influence on the Rhineland position. The *Frankfurter Allgemeine* is Germany's most influential conservative organ of opinion and its views do find a considerable resonance in the CDU. That the views of the Bundesbank need to be taken into account by the CDU is self-evident. It will also have to take account of the views of another highly respected institution, the Federal Constitutional Court. On 12 October 1993 the Federal Constitutional Court delivered a ruling on the constitutionality of the Maastricht Treaty which, while it endorsed the constitutionality of the treaty, stressed that the states were 'Masters of the treaties' and the European Union was a *Staatenverbund* (league of states).

The CDU as a governing party makes policy within the iron triangle of government, party members and the electorate. There are some signs of a lessening of enthusiasm in public opinion, but unlike the United Kingdom the party membership still seems ready to support the status quo (Rhineland position). We have, however, moved some distance from the situation of a decade ago where the election manager of the CDU could describe 25 per cent of his members as 'Euro freaks'. Public opinion is thus only likely to have an effect on governmental policy when it is reflected as in relation to economic and monetary union by an ally (Bundesbank) within the governing loop; but already the change in public mood has brought about some presentational changes.

Although constrained by the exigencies of permanent coalition with the CDU, the CSU position appears much closer to Frankfurt than the Rhineland. Both the CDU and the CSU have felt their positions vindicated by the result of the European election and are therefore likely to persist with their present positions. In the short to medium term the position of the CDU is least likely to change since it is informed by the core convictions of a dominant chancellor. The CSU's position is avowedly tactical but, in the longer term, it is likely that their more Frankfurt view will lead to some modification of the Rhineland view of the CDU when the generation of Volker Rühe assume the topmost leadership positions.

NOTES

The research on which this chapter rests was undertaken in the context of an ESRC grant, reference R000234004, on Germany's role in the new Europe which the author is undertaking with Professor Simon Bulmer.

1 W. Weidenfeld, 'Die Europapolitik', *Konrad Adenauers Politische Studien*, vol. 1, 1979, pp. 33–40.
2 See A. J. Nicholls, 'Germany and the European Union: has unification altered Germany's European Policy?', *International House of Japan Bulletin*, vol. 14, no. 3, 1994, pp. 1–7.
3 H. Kohl, 'Konrad Adenauer. Erbe und Auftrag', in H. Kohl (ed.), *Konrad Adenauer 1876–1976* (Germany, Belser Verlag, 1976) p. 75.
4 H. Kohl, *Our Future in Europe* (Edinburgh, Europa Institute/Konrad Adenauer Foundation, 1991), p. 14.
5 Ibid., p. 12.
6 Ibid., p. 7.
7 Ibid., p. 15.
8 Ibid., p. 16.
9 Ibid., pp. 12–13.
10 M. Thatcher, *The Downing Street Years* (London, HarperCollins, 1993), pp. 790–1, 813–15.
11 Resolutions of the Congress of the CDU, Dusseldorf, 25–28 October 1992, Resolution A1.4.
12 Ibid., A1.6.
13 Ibid., A1.7.
14 *Frankfurter Allgemeine Zeitung*, 28 August 1993.
15 *Grundsatzprogramm* adopted at the 5th Party Conference of the CDU on 23 February 1994, pp. 68–9.
16 *Europa-Gut für Deutschland*, European Election Manifesto, CDU, Bonn, 1994, p. 7.
17 A. Mintzel, *Die CSU. Anatomie einer konservatiuen Partei* (Cologne, Westdeutscher Verlag, 1972).
18 F. J. Strauss, *The Grand Design* (London, Weidenfeld and Nicolson, 1965).
19 Cited in A. Mintzel, *Geschichte der CSU. Ein Überblick* (Cologne, Westdeutscher Verlag, 1977).
20 Strauss, *The Grand Design*, p. 9.

21 Ibid., p. 9,
22 See S. Bulmer and W. Paterson, *The Federal Republic of Germany and the European Community* (London, Allen and Unwin, 1987), pp. 241–4.
23 Ibid., p. 24.
24 *Grundsatzprogramm der Christlich-Sozialen Union in Bayern*, CSU Landesleitung, Munich, 1993, p. 143.
25 Report to CSU Party Committee, Deggendorf, 18–19 March 1994, p. 16.
26 Ibid., p. 17.
27 Ibid., pp. 15–16.
28 Nicholls, 'Germany and the European Union', p. 1.
29 Ibid., pp. 1 and 2.

SELECT BIBLIOGRAPHY

The literature here is extremely sparse. Volume 1 of the Adenauer memoirs has appeared in English.

Adenauer, K., *Memoirs, 1945–53*, London, Weidenfeld and Nicolson, 1966.
Bulmer, S. and Paterson, W., *The Federal Republic of Germany and the European Community*, London, Allen and Unwin, 1987.
Bulmer, S. and Paterson, W., *Germany and the European Union*, Basingstoke, Macmillan, 1996.
Luecker, H. A. and Hahn, K. J., *Christliche Demokraten bauen Europa*, Bonn, Europa Union, 1987.
Strauss, F. J., *The Grand Design*, London, Weidenfeld and Nicolson, 1965.

4 The French Socialists

Alistair Cole

The French Socialist concept of Europe has been marked by a measure of ambivalence. Historically, Europe was valued insofar as it prolonged the internationalist traditions of French socialism, but it was feared because of the diminution of national sovereignty it implied. The dynamic tension between these two imperatives has resurfaced throughout the history of the Socialists' relationship to Europe. In this chapter, we shall consider first the historical relationship between French socialism and the European Community; second, the evolution of Socialist policy towards the EC during the 1980s; before, third, concentrating upon the specific sphere of EU institutional reform; and finally, considering how the internal dynamics of the French Socialist Party have had an impact upon the party's relationship with the EU.

FRENCH SOCIALISM AND EUROPE IN HISTORICAL PERSPECTIVE

By tradition, the French Socialists were internationalists (rather than mere Europeanists), proudly claiming the heritage of Jean Jaurès and the Second International. During the interwar period, the SFIO[1] had supported the League of nations; this support was transformed into support for the United Nations (UN) in the immediate aftermath of the Second World War. When the UN proved itself incapable of providing a genuine mechanism of collective security with the onset of the Cold War, the socialists declared themselves resolutely pro-European. The unification of Europe was portrayed by SFIO leader, Guy Mollet, as a means of strengthening the West against the Soviet threat: Europeanism and Atlanticism were mutually reinforcing.[2] In fact, the party was split between federalist Europeans, fervent Atlanticists, and those occupying a median stance, such as Mollet. During the Fourth Republic (1946–58), the SFIO declared itself an enthusiastic supporter of Europe, aligning itself with the main initiatives culminating in the Treaty of Rome of 1957. The exception to the party's pro-European stance was the proposed European Defence Community (the European Army), first proposed in 1951, which was intended to accompany German rearmament. This was finally defeated by the French National Assembly in 1954, splitting the SFIO into two factions. The opposition of a minority of SFIO deputies secured the fate of the treaty. A legacy of anti-Germanism continued to manifest itself within the party's ranks; the EC itself was envisaged as a corset to prevent Germany from dominating the continent.[3]

Beneath the party's supranational discourse, ambiguities and inconsistencies remained. The Socialist-led government of Guy Mollet (1956–57) performed a leading role in negotiating and ratifying the Treaty of Rome, and yet Mollet was instrumental in writing safeguards into the treaty to limit transfers of national sovereignty. And while the SFIO stressed the economic advantages to be gained from a free market, there remained a feeling of unease at being affiliated with a liberal, capitalist association of nations.[4]

Prior to François Mitterrand's election as president in 1981, Socialist attitudes towards European integration were influenced by factors pulling the party in different directions. These included the party's traditionally pro-European stance; the heritage of past Socialist policy making in the sphere of European policy; the relationships maintained with other parties, notably the French Communist Party (PCF), and internal dynamics within the Socialist Party itself. Once Mitterrand became leader of the PS (Parti socialiste) in 1971, the firmly pro-EC, pro-Atlantic stance of Mollet's SFIO gradually gave way in the early 1970s to a tougher anti-Americanism, and to an apparently more reserved attitude towards the European Community. This reflected a partial socialist acceptance of the Gaullist foreign policy legacy, and a tactical accommodation by the new PS leader Mitterrand to reach an agreement with the PCF.

The party's new radicalism towards Europe was developed in a series of policy documents: the 1972 party programme *Changer la vie*, the PS–PCF common programme of June 1972, the final motion carried by the Bagnolet congress of December 1973. A reluctant acceptance of the European Community in these documents was combined with a primordial emphasis on the national character of the future French socialist experience, and, most revealing, with a *gaullien*-style belief in the superiority of the French experience over those of its European counterparts.[5] The party's discourse relating to Europe was designed to reinforce the idea (not least for the consumption of the PCF) that a Socialist government in France would be fully in control of its own destiny and that the victorious left would not face insurmountable barriers from European capitalism, or a hostile European Community. But in spite of the critical tone adopted by Mitterrand's PS towards the European Community during much of the 1970s, we should stress that neither Mitterrand's own European credentials, nor those of most of his party were in doubt: a commitment to the European ideal comprised one feature of continuity throughout Mitterrand's long political career.[6] The party as a whole was firmly supportive of the European Community. This was in spite of the flowering of a particular type of political rhetoric in certain sections of the party that confused socialism and national independence in a manner inimical to the EC. The Europe advocated by French Socialists was consistent with French *dirigiste* traditions. This was revealed in the PS manifesto for the first direct elections of the European Parliament in 1979, which outlined a series of demands that recurred throughout the 1980s: the need for common EC policies in key industrial sectors (such as iron and steel, shipbuilding, textiles and aerospace), the necessity for a coherent European social policy, and reform of the CAP.[7] Beneath the party's socialist rhetoric of the 1970s, it was easy to discern an underlying thread of pro-European realism; this was expressed, for instance, in the party's majority support for the direct election of the European Parliament. Socialist European policy was a delicate tightrope exercise throughout the 1970s. Mitterrand managed to ensure a minimal pro-European position which isolated manifest opponents of the EC, in the CERES faction and elsewhere, but which distanced itself from traditional notions of supranationalism.

THE EVOLUTION OF SOCIALIST POLICY TOWARDS THE EC, 1981–94

Prior to Mitterrand's election as president, the European Community had rarely been debated upon its own merits, but was subordinated to the imperatives of internal politics. The main themes which had underpinned Mitterrand's discourse throughout the 1970s remained present in his 1981 campaign: these included the enactment of the social provisions of the Treaty of Rome, the development of common industrial policies, the reform of the CAP, the promotion of European economic independence (including protection for sectors menaced by imports from the USA and Japan), and the establishment of rules for regulating the activities of multinational companies.[8]

Any assessment of the French Socialist Party and the EC during the Mitterrand presidency must distinguish between the activities of the various Socialist governments, and the policy positions and attitudes adopted by the party itself. During the early period of the Mitterrand presidency, it was difficult to distinguish between the two: both the party *stricto sensu*, and the government were largely absorbed by domestic policy. At this early stage, Europe was conceived of primarily in terms of policies, rather than institutional reform: this order of priorities was outlined in the French government's Memorandum on the Revitalization of the Community of October 1981. The memorandum called for united European action in a wide variety of spheres, including economic policy, industrial policy and a co-ordinated EC-wide economic relaunch to combat rising unemployment.[9] The central proposal – EC-wide reflation – was dismissed with a mixture of bemusement and ironic disbelief by France's EC partners, all pursuing tough anti-inflation policies. Only after it had become clear that France's partners had no interest in following his 'socialist' lead was Mitterrand forced to deal with Europe as it existed in reality.

President Mitterrand's neo-Keynesian attempt to reflate the French economy after May 1981 was clearly at odds with the economic policies pursued by France's main trading partners. The failure of Mitterrand's initial activism revealed unambiguously that French economic policy, facing grave problems domestically, was not for export. And yet the European dimension was central to domestic economic policy. For most observers, unilateral Keynesian reflationary policies were no longer possible for a medium-sized nation such as France in an interdependent world economy. The critical turning point in Mitterrand's first presidential term arose in March 1983, when the president was forced to arbitrate between two opposing economic policies in a move which set the course for the rest of his presidency. The choice lay between whether to remain within the European Monetary System (EMS), devalue the franc for the third time and accept a tough anti-inflationary economic package; or else to withdraw from the EMS, adopt protectionist measures for French industry and continue on the reflationary path traced since May 1981. After much hesitation, Mitterrand chose the former course of action, confirming thereby that France could neither isolate itself through adopting protectionism, nor indefinitely pursue different economic policies from those of its main trading partners. Mitterrand's acceptance of the European constraint, however reluctantly, dictated a policy choice based on that of economic convergence with France's EC partners, most especially West Germany. For this reason, the idea of a socialist Europe was definitively buried with the third devaluation in March 1983.

At a lower level, this debate occurred within the party: the PS was split between those who advocated reluctant acceptance of the new austerity policy in support of the president, and those, such as J.-P. Chevènement, who contested the foundation of such a policy in the name of national independence and the pursuit of Socialist objectives. Chevènement's alternative economic strategy would have involved a leap into the unknown; his critics contended that it would have marginalized France within Europe, and resulted in even tougher austerity measures to defend the franc. Moreover, any protectionist measures would have invited retaliation from France's principal trading partners. And yet the party leadership was clearly disoriented by the magnitude of the economic U-turn of 1982–83 and initially sought solace in the belief that the change in economic policy would only prove to be a temporary affair. Once it became apparent that the new economic direction was to be a permanent feature of government policy, the party leadership reluctantly adjusted its political message and supported the government. Its status as the main presidential party limited its margins of manoeuvre. The new economic policy formally prevailed at the party's 1983 congress.[10]

While officially supportive of the new economic direction, however, party policy simultaneously advocated neo-Keynesian measures of European-wide economic relaunch at variance with government policy. Such concerns peppered the PS manifesto for the 1984 European elections, which also urged co-ordinated EC industrial policies to fight off the challenges of Japan and the USA.[11] The PS continued to portray Europe in terms of a conflict between the forces of progress and the Right, a conception which had been transcended by Mitterrand's espousing the European cause in key speeches such as that to the German Bundestag in January 1983, or that to the Strasbourg Assembly in May 1984. In time, however, the Socialists followed the lead provided for them by their president. Once the PS had officially accepted the turning point implied by March 1983, it was virtually condemned to follow the President of the Republic on related issues; this was expressed notably, for example, by PS support for the Single European Act in 1986, notwithstanding severe misgivings from sections of the party.

The Single European Act was accepted without any real public debate within the PS, through solidarity with President Mitterrand before the 1988 presidential election.[12] In various later policy documents, however, the PS denounced the 'liberal' interpretation of the Act which sought to transform the EC into an arena for 'naked deregulation'. In its 1989 European manifesto, for instance, the party specifically criticized certain measures introduced by the Act, such as the ending of exchange controls, and certain effects of fiscal harmonization.[13] The 1989 manifesto argued that the effects of the Single Market 'could be negative in the short term', and urged that the Single Market be accompanied by measures to combat unemployment. The party was adamant upon the need for the Social Charter to accompany moves towards the Single Market. In essence, the PS was unwilling to allow the EC to be reduced to an 'extended free trade zone' of the type advocated by Mrs Thatcher, an interpretation vigorously rejected by Mitterrand as well. The party's official support for the Maastricht Treaty stemmed in part from the belief that the 'Social Chapter' rectified the free market excesses of the Single European Act.

Similar preoccupations reappeared in the party's 1994 manifesto, *Changeons l'Europe*. The party's stance on the EU indicated a realization that it was necessary to go beyond the liberal ethos of the Single European Act and the Maastricht Treaty. Michel Rocard, the new Socialist leader, affirmed in September 1993 that 'there is a Europe of the left and a Europe of the right'. The party was conscious that many traditionally left-wing voters had voted against the Maastricht Treaty in France's September 1992 referendum: in March 1994, the party's European affairs spokesman (Gérard Fuchs) appealed for the support of 'many of those who had voted No as well as those who had voted yes in the Maastricht referendum'.[14] At the party's National Convention in April, the old theme of a Europe of the left was voiced strongly from certain sections of the party. For instance, former premier Laurent Fabius urged the party to concentrate upon national and European strategies for growth, employment and social protection, and not to bore the electorate with technical and specialist discourse of European integration and intergovernmental conferences.[15]

Faced with evidence of diminishing European idealism within the French electorate during the post-Maastricht period, the party pleaded for a Europe that responded to ordinary people's anxieties. To this end, the PS advocated the creation of a Europe-wide minimum wage; a concerted anti-unemployment strategy (notably by a reduction in the working week); and a European-wide Keynesian policy of economic relaunch. These proposals were broadly in line with those espoused by the congress of the European Socialist party in November 1993.[16] It might be contended that issues such as employment, economic growth, social protection, community preference and interventionism are the classic staple of social democratic European fare. These themes have forced their way back onto the party's European agenda. This has been facilitated by the party's return to opposition. But party leader Rocard traced the limits of this process in his speech to the PS National Convention of April 1994. Any deviation from the path of closer European integration would be 'electorally damaging, economically dangerous, strategically irresponsible, and politically immoral'.

THE FRENCH SOCIALISTS AND EC INSTITUTIONAL REFORM

During the early phase of the French Socialist government (1981–83), French policy was underpinned by attention to the prerogatives of national sovereignty. The government consistently favoured concern with policies over institutions, preferring to maintain the institutional status quo, rather than envisage endangering the national safeguards obtained by Guy Mollet and General de Gaulle.[17] The issue of majority voting was particularly sensitive, since it appeared likely that majority votes during this period would go against France. The party supported the 1966 Luxembourg compromise, which allowed any member state to oppose a veto on issues of 'vital national interest'. The French government – like the British – was cautious over initiatives aimed at EC institutional reform, such as the Genscher–Colombo reform proposals of 1981, the Spinelli initiative of 1982 or the European Parliament's draft European Union Treaty (EUT) of 1984.[18] Throughout his presidency, Mitterrand remained favourable, *grosso modo*, to an intergovernmental model of EC decision making, as had Presidents Giscard d'Estaing, Pompidou and de Gaulle before him. In the interests of enhanced European integration and the pursuance of French policy objectives (notably in relation to social and monetary policy), however, Mitterrand proved more willing than any of his predecessors to consent to, and indeed initiate, reforms of the EC's institutional structures.[19]

The standard adopted by the party closely followed the government's priority concern with policies rather than institutions. In its 1984 manifesto, the PS was reluctant to deal with the issue of Community reform; it denounced the European Parliament's draft European Union Treaty as a 'federalist constitution'. There was, however, a notable discrepancy between the attitude of the PS leadership in Paris, and the more integrationist approach adopted by Socialist MEPs in Strasbourg. There was considerable reluctance on the part of the PS Euro-deputies to follow orders to vote against the Spinelli initiative in 1984.[20] Given its affirmed anti-federalist stance, the (national) party was understandably shaken by Mitterrand's pledge to support the Parliament's draft European Union treaty in his speech to the Strasbourg Assembly in May 1984.

The major institutional reforms contained in the Single European Act and in the Maastricht Treaty lie outside of the boundaries of the present chapter. To recall briefly, the Single European Act gave the European Parliament the power of co-decision with the (intergovernmental) Council in relation to the measures needed to bring about the Single European market by 1 January 1993, an important step in the direction of supranationality.[21] But the Act left largely intact the intergovernmental basis of decision making within the Community: the Council of Ministers remained the key institution, and the rule of unanimity was retained for all matters except those relating to the Single Market. In practice, however, the momentum created by the Act led to the virtual abandoning of the unanimity rule, and the advent of majority voting as the norm within the European Council. Paradoxically, the only attempt to ressurrect the veto since 1986 has been the French threat to veto the EC–USA compromise agreement over GATT. The Maastricht Treaty, analysed below, went further in the direction of supranationality, without fundamentally challenging the intergovernmental basis of the Community.

In the following section, we shall consider the evolution of official Socialist attitudes towards the Commission, the European Parliament, and the concept of political and economic union.

The supranational institutions: the Commission

The Socialists' initial reluctance to envisage any major reform of EC institutions masked a suspicion of the supranationalism inherent in the European Parliament, the European Court of Justice and the Commission. The interventionist economic policy initially pursued within France brought the Socialist government into frequent conflict with the Commission. Complaints against the French assumed two charac-teristics: that it was adopting protectionist measures contrary to the Treaty of Rome, and that it was channelling state aid to lame duck industries.[22] The Commission's veto in 1991 of the take over of the Canadian aerospace company de Havilland by the state firm Aerospatiale was met with ill-disguised fury by the French government.[23] Throughout the period leading up to the Maastricht summit agreement of December 1991, the Socialists' flowery rhetoric favouring European integration was somewhat difficult to reconcile with attacks against the supranational pretensions of the Commission, even though headed by Frenchman Jacques Delors after January 1985. The French negotiators in the intergovernmental conferences preceding Maastricht were determined to ensure that the Commission's power should remain limited, and that it should be excluded from the proposed common foreign and security policy, much to the dismay of Delors. Indeed, the Maastricht Treaty fell well below the expectations of Delors, since it rested too firmly on the existing intergovernmental bases of EC decision making. The Commission emerged as a favoured object of criticism for both sides in the Maastricht referendum campaign of September 1992.

The Parliament

The French Socialists consistently took a minimalist view towards the powers of the European Parliament: this reflected a long preoccupation with national sovereignty, as well as the centralizing traditions and the notion of the indivisibility of the French Republic. There was also the belief that it was preferable to strengthen the inter-governmental Council of Ministers, rather than the near-impotent Parliament. In the pre-Maastricht negotiations, Mitterrand originally proposed more joint meetings of parliamentarians from the European Parliament and from national parliaments. These meetings would perform a purely consultative role, with the Parliament thereby deprived of its existing powers.[24] In both the Single European Act and the Maastricht Treaty, Mitterrand was obliged to accept rather more authority for the European Parliament than he had initially intended.

Mitterrand's reluctance was shared by his party. The relative isolation of the French stance was illustrated at a joint session of European parliamentarians in November 1990 in Rome: this conference was attended by representatives of the European Parliament (one-third) and the national parliaments (two-thirds). The conference overwhelmingly adopted a text calling for co-decision for the Parliament with the Council. The confusion reigning within the PS was illustrated by the fact that all other European socialist parties accepted the Rome text, while the PS opposed it.[25] Simultaneously, a Fabius–Dumas amendment to the party's 1990 European manifesto urged that a new European Senate be created, to be composed of representatives of the national parliaments, as well as MEPs, in order to rectify 'the worrying loss of power' of national parliaments to Community institutions.[26]

Political union: beyond intergovernmentalism?

President Mitterrand's European model contained strong elements of intergovern-mentalism, although 'federalist' developments were welcomed when they promoted French interests. Among Mitterrand's advisers there was a determination to limit the supranational aspirations of the Commission president, Delors, as well as to resist attempts to make the European Parliament more democratic and to extend the scope of its competence unduly. At the Maastricht summit of December 1991, Mitterrand accepted *some* strengthening of the Commission and the European Parliament.[27] But this was counterbalanced by the summit's expressed aim of moving towards a single European currency by 1999 and provisions for the new common foreign and security policy, both of which excluded the Commission and (initially at least) strengthened the role of the European Council.[28] In contrast, by accepting, even promoting a European central bank, Mitterrand approved a major step towards supranationalism in the sphere of monetary policy.

Definite moves towards monetary union, the creation of a European central bank and a single currency were the primary French economic objectives at Maastricht. Mitterrand calculated that a single currency and a European central bank would allow the French a greater influence over monetary policy, currently monopolized by the German Bundesbank. The final treaty locked the EC more firmly into economic integration (the objective of a single currency by 1999) than it made real concessions to the principle of political union. To this extent, it responded more accurately to French priorities than to German ones, notwithstanding the pivotal role performed by Helmut Kohl in the run up to the summit.

As on other occasions, party policy evolved in line with presidential preoccupations, albeit imperfectly. The PS European manifesto of November 1990 represented the party's fullest statement of European policy for almost twenty years.[29] The PS manifesto stressed the need for common social, economic and monetary policies within the EC, as well as an 'external affirmation' of the Community on the international scene. The party refused any early enlarging of the EC to encompass the new democracies of Eastern Europe, but declared its support for Mitterrand's proposed European Confederation as the most effective means of responding to the collapse of communism.[30] While the PS manifesto called for a European central bank, and a single currency, this bank would have to operate 'within the context of orientations given by the relevant political authority': any moves towards monetary union and a single currency must be accompanied by real democratic controls. The party remained suspicious of technocratic influences which the process of economic and monetary union seemed destined to strengthen.

SOCIALIST PARTY DYNAMICS AND THE EU

Socialist Party dynamics have had a bearing upon PS attitudes towards the EC in several ways: we shall consider the relationship between President Mitterrand and the PS as the presidential party; the relations between the national PS leadership, and the socialist group in Strasbourg; and the extent of intra-party dissent over Europe within the PS.

President–party tensions

In the Fifth Republic, the presidential party has tended to exist in a subordinate relationship to the president.[31] In fact, there were more or less subtle differences of emphasis over Europe between Mitterrand and his party; these were aggravated as his presidency wore on. On occasion, the party found it difficult to predict Mitterrand's shifts in attitude over Europe. It was observed above how in 1984 the party's anti-federalist discourse rested uneasily alongside Mitterrand's commitment to the Parliament's draft European Union Treaty. These nuances became apparent during the 1984 European election campaign, incumbent upon the different functions performed by party and president. As head of the PS list in 1984, party leader Jospin centred the PS campaign on the theme of opposition to a Europe dominated by the right, and advocacy of a 'socialist' Europe. This was far from the logic of Mitterrand's declared European crusade announced in May 1984, which transcended notions of left and right in pursuit of European integration. A similar conclusion was valid for the 1989 European campaign. To some extent, the roles performed by Mitterrand and the PS leadership were functionally differentiated: as head of the PS list, Jospin (and later Fabius) sought to rally the left-wing electorate; as president above the fray and as a senior European head of state, Mitterrand attempted to project himself as an unrivalled European statesman. By 1994, when the relationship between party and president had virtually collapsed, Socialist leaders suspected Mitterrand of actively supporting the rival centre-left list led by Bernard Tapie.

As Mitterrand's presidency progressed, the issue of Europe caused growing dissension between president and party; this did not stem primarily from differing substantive perceptions of European integration, but from the belief that Mitterrand's repeated manoeuvres were damaging the Socialist Party's interest. The PS leadership barely concealed its exasperation, for instance, that President Mitterrand decided to put the Maastricht Treaty to an unnecessary referendum in September 1992. The conditions surrounding the 1994 European campaign aggravated matters further. The poor PS performance in the European elections of 1984 (20.8 per cent) and 1989 (23.4 per cent) revealed that Europe was hardly propitious territory for the Socialists. But these votes flattered the party's 1994 total: with 14.48 per cent, the Socialist Party recorded its weakest national score in any election since Mitterrand had taken control of the party in 1971. The verdict appeared as a damaging indictment of Michel Rocard's leadership of the Socialist Party since April 1993, dealing a fatal blow to his chances of standing in the 1995 presidential election. This was grist to Mitterrand's mill; the president scarcely bothered concealing his belief that Jacques Delors would make a better PS presidential candidate than Rocard, his hereditary enemy within the Socialist Party. In 1994, the PS list only narrowly outpolled the rival centre-left list led by the radical Bernard Tapie.[32] The PS total was eroded by the proliferation of minor lists encouraged by the non-decisive nature of European elections, and the existence of an electoral system based on proportional representation. Aside from Tapie's list, the Socialists faced competition from the list headed by J.-P. Chevènement, former leader of the CERES faction, ex-Socialist minister, and ardent opponent of the Maastricht Treaty; Chevènement's weak performance (2.54 per cent) revealed the limits of overt anti-Europeanism within the traditional Socialist electorate.

Relations between Paris and Strasbourg

French Socialist Euro-deputies have always performed a prominent role within the European Parliament, where the PS forms an influential member of the European Socialist group, the largest since the 1989 European elections. From 1989–94, the French Socialist Jean-Pierre Cot achieved a high profile as president of the socialist group within the European Parliament. According to Cot:

> The relationship between the Socialist Party's national leadership and the European deputies is a very relaxed one. The Paris leadership imposes few directives on its European deputies and leaves them with considerable freedom of manoeuvre. This was not always the case, however, especially between 1979 and 1984, when the party's European deputies were more subject to central party control. Since 1984, there has not been one occasion when the central party has had to impose its views upon the European party.

The PS national leadership has in the past affirmed a right of oversight and control. In a policy statement adopted by the party's directing committee in 1978, for instance, the PS declared that 'French Socialist MEPs are naturally subjected to the exercise of party discipline'.[33] In practice, the Socialist group in Strasbourg has enjoyed considerable autonomy, and has revealed itself to be consistently more federally inclined than metropolitan deputies. The evolution of official party policy towards firmer support for European integration comforted the position of most Socialist MEPs.

The major influence exercised by the national party over its European delegation occurs at the level of candidate selection, rather than through any crude attempt to control the voting record of the Socialist MEPs. French MEPs are elected by a fixed national list system of proportional representation. The top fifteen or so places on the PS list normally secure election. The distribution of places on the PS list is determined by complex negotiations between the party's main factions, with each awarded places in proportion to its strength within the party. In 1994, the new PS leader Rocard was largely unable to escape from this method of procedure, despite his call for the rebuilding of the Socialist Party (shattered by its 1993 defeat) upon new, non-factional bases.

Neither the European socialist group, nor the French delegation are monolithic. Divisions among French Socialist MEPs occasionally stem from their metropolitan factional allegiance, but these are rare. As a general rule, PS MEPs have been less afflicted by factional rivalries than their metropolitan counterparts. A more common source of division relates to conflict between the European socialist group and the position adopted by the French delegation. When there is an open conflict between the French delegation and the group, a proportion of MEPs will invariably side with the group, rather than the delegation. Within the European group itself, the French Socialists have occupied a clearly identifiable minority position in relation to several key policies, such as agriculture, the location of the European Parliament, and the importance of civil nuclear energy. Apart from these specific issues, where the national interest prevails, Cot believes that the French delegation is 'at the very heart of the group's activities'.

Intra-party tensions

From the creation of Mitterrand's PS in 1971, the real line of division over Europe was not fully reflected within the party's official factions: while the left-wing CERES was consistently minimalist towards the EC, the other main groupings contained within their ranks fervent Europeans, as well as determined opponents of European 'technocracy'. The diversity was greatest among Mitterrandists (for instance between J. Delors and P. Joxe), while the Mauroy and Rocard groups were more consistently pro-European. Party divisions over Europe were thus cross cutting. They were observable in relation to a broad spectrum of policies and conceptions of Europe. In the ensuing section we shall consider several key themes: supranationality versus national sovereignty, the role of Germany, and economic and monetary union. These are by no means exhaustive.

Supranationality versus national sovereignty

The Socialist Party contained the full range of positions along the supranational–national continuum: from avowed federalists in the tradition of Jean Monnet, such as Jacques Delors; to those such as Mitterrand, for whom enhanced political integration ultimately remained a form of intergovernmentalism; to those such as

Chevènement, who refused any (further) delegations of national sovereignty to EC institutions. In the course of the 1992 Maastricht referendum campaign, the median position articulated by President Mitterrand represented the mainstream within the party. Socialist divisions over Maastricht had to be placed in context: in terms of Socialist deputies, voters and party members, pro-Maastricht sentiment within the PS outstripped that of any other French party.[34] In fact, after a prolonged period of rather artificial consensus over Europe from the mid-late 1980s, the collapse of communist regimes in Eastern Europe, followed by German unification and the Maastricht Treaty, provoked renewed divisions within all French parties.[35] The poor showing in the 1994 European election of the list sponsored by Chevènement's Mouvement des citoyens suggested the limits of an overtly anti-integrationist appeal within the Socialist electorate.

The role of Germany

German unification provoked an underlying source of (rarely avowed) tension over Europe within the PS. Among the left-wing ex-CERES faction, there had long existed an almost pathological distrust of Germany and German intentions.[36] Chevènement's opposition to the Maastricht Treaty stemmed above all from the belief that Republican France must not succumb to German domination, in the monetary, political or economic spheres. Other Socialist politicians were less overtly anti-German; French governments since 1981 had reasserted the centrality of the Franco-German partnership within the EU, and President Mitterrand not only established a 'special relationship' with Helmut Kohl, but was associated with each of the initiatives culminating in moves to greater European political and economic integration at Maastricht. And yet, fears of the economic and political weight of the unified German state permeated French governments, as well as sections of the Socialist Party, and were expressed by both sides in the Maastricht referendum campaign.[37] The changing balance of power occasioned by German unification continued to work through its effects on traditional notions of Europe.

Economic and monetary union

At an official level, Socialist Party policy was one of resolute support for the Maastricht Treaty, including moving towards monetary union by 1999. The commitment to economic union illustrated the extent to which Mitterrand had fully integrated the European constraint into his conception of France and Europe: it testified to the irreversible nature of the U-turn undertaken in 1983 and to the new confidence felt in future French economic performance. PS divisions over monetary union were scarcely surprising, given that the party remained divided over the EMS and the turning towards austerity in 1983. Party opponents of Maastricht argued that the EMS already tied all other countries to the German mark, and, thereby, to German economic policy. Full economic and monetary union would render this process irreversible, thereby depriving French governments of their residual economic sovereignty.[38] This was another version of the political voluntarism versus economic constraints debate engaged within the party in 1983. Although majority party opinion firmly backed the Maastricht Treaty, party declarations tended to imply that economic and monetary union was vital because it was a means of recovering control over economic policy from the grasp of the Bundesbank, and that the future European central bank would be subjected to political dictates.

CONCLUSION

In the absence of a socialist Europe, definitively buried in March 1983, the French Socialists insisted upon the importance of social, economic and industrial counter-weights to a predominantly liberal and capitalist European Union. The French Socialist attitude towards Europe has been, by and large, one of committed Europeanism. The PS was less divided over ratification of the Maastricht Treaty, for instance, than any other French party. The most overtly anti-European elements left the PS to join Chevènement and the Mouvement des citoyens. But there have also been persistent expressions of dissatisfaction with the EU. French Socialists continue to contest the notion of a free market, monetarist European Union that many see as consolidated by the Maastricht Treaty. They have consistently supported the notion of a more interventionist Europe, willing to protect European social conditions and jobs from outside competition. And along with their European counterparts, French Socialists have advocated with greater insistence an EU-wide programme of Keynesian relaunch to lift Europe out of the present recession. Freed from the constraints of being a governing party since March 1993, the PS has shown a new awareness of problems of unemployment and social deprivation, which were ignored or underplayed by the Single European Act and Maastricht Treaty. With the PS in opposition, a left-wing register has resurfaced, bemoaning the inadequacies of social and economic policy, and criticizing the interference of the Commission in industrial and trade policy. These signs testify to a well-ingrained tradition: expressions of firm support for European integration sit rather uneasily alongside a critical stance towards much of the reality of the European Union as it exists. To some extent, French Socialist attitudes are in tune with a distinctive national approach to the EU. The tough stance adopted towards the GATT negotiations in 1993, for instance, tended to unite left and right, while politicians of all colours are more likely to call for protection or Community preference than are their Anglo-Saxon counterparts. A residual statist and interventionist tradition continues to permeate French European policy, although governments of left and right have had to accept that the Single European Act and the Maastricht Treaty establish a liberal, capitalist Europe with limited sovereignty for national economic policy making.

Looking back at the Mitterrand presidency, we can see that the old dream (entertained by some Socialists at least) of the French Socialist Party acting as an inspirational guide for others to imitate had to be shelved after the economic U-turn of 1983. French socialism was called to order by external constraints. The party's recognition of the European constraint represented more than a mere choice in favour of the EU. Acceptance of the need for economic convergence also testified to the economic transformation that had occurred during the Mitterrand presidency. Fundamentally pro-European throughout its history, it remains the case today that the French Socialist Party is less tempted by the sirens of anti-Europeanism than other European Socialist Parties.

NOTES

1 Section française de l'internationale ouvrière, the party's official title from 1920–69.
2 See G. Prosche, 'L'identité européenne du parti socialiste français', *Revue du marché commun*, 1990, pp. 49–56.
3 J. Kergoat, 'Le long combat des socialistes français', *Le Monde*, 8–9 November 1991.
4 See P. Gerbet, 'Les partis politiques et les communautés', in J. Rideau, et al., (eds), *La France et les communautés européennes* (Paris, LGDJ, 1975), pp. 81–5.
5 This was especially the case for the final motion of the extraordinary Bagnolet European congress. Reprinted in *Le poing et la rose*, supplement to no. 73, August 1978.
6 A. Cole, *François Mitterrand: A Study in Political Leadership* (London, Routledge, 1994), pp. 116–32.
7 Reprinted in *Le poing et la rose. Special responsables*, no. 81, 3 May 1979.
8 See L. Chauvin, *L'idée d'Europe chez François Mitterrand*, DEA thesis, Paris, Institute of Political Studies, 1989, pp. 49–51.
9 'The hopes and holes in Mitterrand's plan', *The Economist*, 17 October 1991.
10 Motion I, *Le poing et la rose*, no. 102, October 1983; *Le Monde*, 31 October 1983 for details of congress debates.
11 'La volonté de la France, une chance pour l'Europe', *Le poing et la rose*, no. 108, June 1984.
12 On this aspect, see V. Le Guay, 'Les partis français saisis par l'Europe', *Quotidien de Paris*, 2 July 1987.
13 'Manifeste socialiste pour l'élection européenne', *Vendredi*, no. 18, 12 May.
14 A. Logeart, 'Le PS propose que l'Europe soit dotée d'un président élu pour un ou deux ans', *Le Monde*, 16 March 1994.
15 P. Robert-Diard, 'En route', *Le Monde*, 19 April 1994.
16 P. Lemaître, 'Les socialistes européens feront campagne pour une communauté forte', *Le Monde*, 9 November 1993.
17 See E. Hayward, 'The French Socialists and European institutional reform', *The Journal of European Integration*, vol. 12, nos. 2 3, 1989.
18 For details of these initiatives, see E. Wistrich, *After 1992: The United States of Europe*, (London, Routledge, 1991), pp. 37–40.
19 See H. Drake, 'François Mitterrand, France and European integration', in G. Raymond (ed.), *France During the Socialist Years* (Aldershot, Dartmouth, 1995), pp. 32–63.
20 This point was stressed in an interview with Jean-Pierre Cot, 30 March 1993.
21 The SEA also decreed that the European Council would be able to oppose the Parliament only by unanimous opposition to its decisions. Both provisions exceeded French proposals. For a simplified summary of the Act's provisions, see N. Nugent, *The Government and Politics of the European Community* (London, Macmillan, 1991), pp. 48–9.
22 M. Scotto, 'La France est-elle dans le collimateur de Bruxelles?', *Le Monde*, 23 February 1983. The Germans were particularly irritated by French subsidies to the nationalized steel industry.
23 *Le Point*, 17 October 1991.
24 M. Duverger, 'L'heritage européen', *Le Monde*, 26 April 1991.
25 Ibid.
26 'PS: les malgré nous de l'Europe', *Le Figaro*, 16 December 1990.
27 The European Parliament was to be invested with the power of co-decision in four policy spheres: research, the environment, consumer affairs and the Single Market. The Parliament would retain its right of veto over the accession of new members and the signing of association agreements, as well as a new right of veto over international agreements and changes in its electoral procedure. The Parliament was to be given the right to invest the Commission, in addition to its ultimate right of no confidence in the Commission. To the dismay of Delors, the Commission did not emerge greatly strengthened, although its legitimacy was reinforced, insofar as it was henceforth to be invested by the European Parliament.
28 The decision to move towards a single currency would in principle be taken either by a

qualified majority vote within the Council in 1996, or, failing sufficient economic convergence, by a minority of countries determined to go ahead with a single currency by 1 January 1999. The common foreign and security policy provisions kept foreign policy firmly in the hands of national governments; decisions relating to EC competence to intervene in foreign policy affairs would require first a unanimous vote within the Council; qualified majority voting would apply to details of implementation thereafter.

29   *Le Monde*, 21–22 October, 23 November 1990.
30   Mitterrand's idea of a European Confederation, associating existing EC member states, the EFTANS and the new Eastern European democracies (including the USSR) was first raised in December 1989, as his response to the events of Eastern Europe. The format of the confederation would allow the new democracies to associate themselves with the EC, without threatening the cohesion of the existing EC structure. Mitterrand's confederation evoked a lukewarm response elsewhere.
31   See A. Cole, 'The presidential party and the Fifth Republic', *West European Politics*, vol. 16, no. 3, 1993, pp. 49–66, for detailed analysis.
32   The Tapie list polled 12.05 per cent.
33   Cited in C. Verger, *Les deputés socialistes français du parlement européen*, thesis, Paris, Institute of Political Studies, 1982, p. 10.
34   Of the many articles to this effect, see D. Buchan, 'Wrong end of the Maastricht stick', *Financial Times*, 3 September 1992. Around one-fifth of declared PS electors voted against Maastricht on 20 September 1992, a lower proportion than in any other party. And only five deputies campaigned for a 'no' vote.
35   See, *inter alia*, M.-P. Subtil, 'L'Europe en procès. Les partis entre le pragmatisme et la peur de l'inconnu', *Le Monde*, 14 March 1991.
36   This sentiment was expressed by Alain Minc who argued that 'there is no European problem, only a German one' in a colloque organized by Chevènement's club République moderne. Cited in *Le Monde*, 4 April 1989.
37   On this aspect, see the editorial by Serge July in *Libération*, 31 August 1992.
38   See, for instance, Chevènement's interview with *Le Quotidien de Paris*, 3 September 1992.

SELECT BIBLIOGRAPHY

Chauvin, L., *L'idee d'Europe chez François Mitterrand*, DEA thesis, Paris, IEP, 1989.
Cohen, S., 'François le gaullien et Mitterrand l'européen', *Histoire*, no. 143, April 1991, pp. 30–6.
Cole, A., *François Mitterrand: A Study in Political Leadership*, London, Routledge, 1994.
Cot, J. P., 'Etre français et européen, *Autrement*, no. 122, May 1991.
de Bussy, M.-E., 'Les socialistes . . . sous la Ve République', in J. Rideau, et al., *La France et les communautés européennes*, Paris, LGDJ, 1975.
Drake, H., 'François Mitterrand, France and European Integration', in G. Raymond (ed.), *France During the Socialist Years*, Aldershot, Dartmouth, 1995.
Featherstone, K., *Socialist Parties and European Integration*, Manchester, MUP, 1988.
Gerbet, P., 'Les partis politiques et les communautés', in J. Rideau, et al., *La France et les communautés européennes*, Paris, LGDJ, 1975.
Hayward, E., 'The French Socialists and European institutional reform', *The Journal of European Integration*, vol. 12, nos. 2–3, 1989.
Jenson, J., 'Strategic divisions within the French left: the case of the first elections to the European parliament', *The Journal of European Integration*, vol. 4, no. 1, 1980.
Kergoat, J., 'Le long combat des socialistes français', *Le Monde*, 8–9 November 1991.
Kourliandsky, J-J., 'Europe: le grand chantier du président', *Cosmopolitiques*, no. 5, December 1987, pp. 33–46.
Lemaire-Prosche, G., *Le PS et l'Europe*, Paris, Editions Universitaires, 1990.
Lemaire-Prosche, G., 'L'identité européenne du parti socialiste français', *Revue du marché commun*, no. 343, January 1991, pp. 49–56.
McCarthy, P., *France-Germany, 1983–1993: The Struggle to Cooperate*, London, Macmillan, 1993.

Mitterrand. F., *Réflexions sur la politique extérieure de la France*, Paris, Fayard, 1986.

Moreau Defarges, P., 'J'ai fait un rêve ... le président François Mitterrand, artisan de l'union européenne', *Politique Etrangère*, no. 2, 1985, pp. 359–74.

Nugent, N., *The Government and Politics of the European Community*, London, Macmillan, 1991.

Parti socialiste, 'Pour une Europe en marche vers le Socialisme', Motion adopted at the Congrès national extraordinaire du parti socialiste, Bagnolet, 1973, *Le poing et la rose*, Supplement to no. 73, August 1978.

Parti socialiste, 'La volonté de la France. Une chance pour l'Europe', *Le poing et la rose*, no. 108, June 1984.

Parti socialiste, 'Manifeste socialiste pour l'élection européenne', *Vendredi*, no. 15, 21 April 1989.

Pinto Lyra, R., *La gauche en France et la construction européenne*, Paris, LGDJ, 1978.

Wells, S. J., 'Les politiques étrangères de Mitterrand', *Commentaire*, no. 11, Autumn 1988, pp. 655–66.

5 The French Gaullists

James Shields

DE GAULLE AND EUROPE: A CERTAIN IDEA OF THE NATION STATE

On 5 September 1960, General de Gaulle held a press conference at the Elysée Palace, the president's official residence. Questioned on his vision of Europe some three years after the signing of the Treaty of Rome, he gave an unequivocal reply:

> The construction of Europe, that is its union, is clearly a necessity . . . In such a domain, however, we must proceed not on the basis of dreams, but on the basis of realities. So what are the realities of Europe? What are the pillars on which it can be built? They are quite simply its States – States which are certainly very different from one another, each with its own soul, its own history and its own language, its own misfortunes, its own glorious achievements and its own ambitions, but States which are the only entities with the right to command and the power to be obeyed. To imagine that we can build something above and beyond these States which will work effectively and enjoy popular support is an idle fancy.[1]

These remarks encapsulate the essence of de Gaulle's thinking on Europe throughout the period of his presidency (1959–69), and are consonant with his pronouncements on the future of Europe from as early as the 1940s.[2] They express clearly his unshakeable belief in the nation state as the only legitimate source of political authority and his hostility to European integration on the supranational model envisaged by Jean Monnet and Robert Schuman, which found widespread support in European post-war thinking. Those 'more or less extra- or supranational bodies' which serviced the European Community (EC) might have their 'technical value', de Gaulle conceded, but since they lacked an authentic political mandate, they could not provide effective fora for decision making on important issues.[3] Authority to formulate and implement policy resided solely in the democratically elected governments of member states. In May 1962, during another press conference, de Gaulle famously provoked the resignation of the five Mouvement républicain populaire (MRP) ministers in his government, when he attacked the project of European integration as so much 'myth, fiction and posturing', and derided its advocates as 'Volapükists' and dreamers.[4]

It was this attitude of unyielding hostility to any form of supranational authority which defined from the outset de Gaulle's stance towards the Community and its institutions. On his accession to the presidency in January 1959, he had honoured France's commitment to the Common Market for the economic benefits which it could bring, particularly in the farming sector through the elaboration of the Common Agricultural Policy (CAP) and, more broadly, through the exposure of French industry and commerce to external competition as a spur to modernization. With its ties of economic co-operation and the communal interests underlying its foundation, the EC also offered a theatre in which France could foster a special (and controlling) relationship with Germany and aspire to play a leading role in the new European order. It has been argued that, following the failed attempt to upgrade France's status within the integrated military command structure of NATO in 1958, de Gaulle had recourse to the EC as a means of extending French influence and furthering his foreign policy objective of *grandeur*.[5] What such participation in Europe did not imply, however, was any sacrifice of French national sovereignty or self-determination: these were absolute values for de Gaulle, and not subject to negotiation.

This resistance to the federal model of European integration has become a defining feature of Gaullism in the 1960s, occasioning the charge that de Gaulle laboured under an archaically nationalistic conception of France and that, failing to resolve the conflict between national independence and a European vocation, he betrayed a fundamentally anti-European cast of mind. As one acerbic critic of de Gaulle's foreign policy, ex-premier Paul Reynaud, put it: 'He wanted France to be at the head of Europe whilst not wanting there to be a Europe!'[6] To argue as much, however, is to misrepresent the nature and extent of de Gaulle's Europeanism. Insist though he might upon French self-determination, de Gaulle recognized that, in the new order emerging from the Second World War, such 'self-determination' in the fullest sense was no longer possible; 'independence', he acknowledged, could have nothing to do with 'isolation'.[7] Nor, he contended, should Europe exist solely as an economic market serving a few advanced Western states. De Gaulle's was a much grander vision of a Europe stretching 'from the Atlantic to the Urals', able to assert its independence from the United States and emerge as a 'third force' in a world polarized by NATO and the Warsaw Pact.

This conception of *la grande Europe* depended for its coherence and effectiveness upon political co-operation with a view to common policy making in certain areas. It was in defining the modalities of this co-operation that de Gaulle marked himself off so insistently from the federalists and from France's more integrationist Community partners. De Gaulle was not closed to the possibility that Europe might one day fulfil the requirements for a 'national' identity; but, within 'the conditions of our time', he argued, supranationalism was an experiment conducted 'in the domain of speculation', a 'Utopian construct' lacking the legitimacy born of common historical experience, collective consciousness and a shared body of social and cultural values.[8] European political union, he protested, must be on a *confederal* basis: it must be 'an association of nations within a confederation of States', achieved through intergovernmental co-operation rather than the development of supranational institutions.[9] Though de Gaulle denied ever having called, as commonly alleged, for a *Europe des patries*, the formula was not one he repudiated.[10] While the terms 'coopération', 'association', 'confédération', 'union' recurred with tireless frequency in his prescriptions for the construction of Europe, those of 'intégration' and 'fusion', with their connotations of 'idéologie' and 'technocratie', drew his most savage criticism. Fearing that the Brussels Commission would become the instrument of an American-dominated Europe, he denounced 'all those systems which, under cover of "supranationality", or "integration", or "Atlanticism", would in fact keep us under a well-known hegemony'.[11]

The institutional framework within which de Gaulle's 'European Europe' should exist was quite different from that provided for in the Treaty of Rome, and would require that the latter be revised. The Fouchet Plans of 1961–62 set out a blueprint for the sort of intergovernmental co-operation which de Gaulle wished to see among the Six. This had to be flexible, allowing each member state to retain sovereignty over its own affairs and, crucially, a right of veto over Community decisions in the Council of Ministers. As early as 1953, de Gaulle had sketched out the institutional arrangements required for the 'political' Europe which he envisaged: 'an organic council of Heads of Government meeting periodically and sharing common services to help them formulate their decisions in the political, economic, cultural and military spheres', in conjunction with a 'deliberative assembly'.[12] The Fouchet Plans built upon and amplified these basic prescriptions, recommending a Council of Community heads of state or government meeting several times a year, where unanimity would be the rule in decision making; a political Commission, based in Paris and composed of top foreign office civil servants, helping the Council to draw up and implement its resolutions; and a parliamentary assembly of indirectly elected national delegates with a strictly 'deliberative' status.[13]

In order for Europe to exercise due control over its own foreign policy and play a mediating role between the power blocs of West and East, it was necessary that common policy be worked out in the areas of foreign affairs and defence (although de Gaulle had strongly opposed the project of a European Defence Community (EDC) in 1954 on the grounds that it surrendered too much control over French national security).[14] When the Fouchet proposals were rejected by France's EC partners as a thinly disguised attempt to replace the integrationist goals of the Treaty of Rome with a purely intergovernmental arrangement, de Gaulle sought closer bilateral co-operation with Germany, concluding a Franco-German Friendship Treaty in 1963 which provided for regular meetings of heads of government and ministers to discuss, *inter alia*, foreign affairs and defence matters. In compensating for the failure of the Fouchet Plans, this attempt to underscore a solidarity of interests between France and Germany did not, however, signal any new readiness on de Gaulle's part to relinquish the merest portion of French independence in decision making on major issues. The introduction of qualified majority voting as the norm in the Council of Ministers, anticipated in the Treaty of Rome and due to come into force on 1 January 1966, provoked a French boycott of the Council for six months in 1965 (the so-called 'empty chair policy'), until the Luxembourg Compromise of January 1966 allowed France to retain a veto on questions where French vital interests were judged to be at stake – a veto which de Gaulle exercised in 1967 to oppose (for the second time) Britain's admission to the Community, in the face of strong support among the other five members for the British application.[15]

THE GAULLIST PARTY AND EUROPE: FROM THE UNR TO THE RPR

This brief overview of de Gaulle's stance on Europe provides the essential background for any consideration of the Gaullist Party's relationship to the EC and subsequent European Union (EU). Throughout de Gaulle's presidency, the 'certain idea of France' which he defended in his dealings with EC partners informed the policies

of the Gaullist Party in its successive guises as the UNR, the UDV[e] and the UDR.[16]
While the question of Europe generated considerable debate within the other parties
(with the notable exception of the consistently anti-European French Communist
Party), the Gaullists provided a unified base of support for the president's policies
and initiatives.

There are several reasons, beyond political persuasion, which explain this unity
of the Gaullist Party around de Gaulle's European vision. The first is the highly
personalized relationship of disciplined support which existed between the General
and his *compagnons*: whatever de Gaulle's ambivalent attitude towards 'his' party,
its primary function was to form the nucleus of parliamentary support for his
government.[17] The second is the fact that Europe fell within the *domaine réservé* of
foreign affairs and defence, where policy making was a presidential prerogative,
according to de Gaulle's interpretation of the Constitution. The third is the fact
that de Gaulle's policies on Europe, however irksome for his EC and Atlantic
partners, commanded general support in French public opinion as consciousness
of the European issue heightened through the 1960s.[18] Basking in a reflected public
approval which judged de Gaulle, for all his intransigence, to be a 'determined
supporter of European unification',[19] the party steered the same course between
independence from and commitment to Europe. As the manifesto for the 1967
legislative elections insisted, the Gaullist objective was 'neither isolation nor narrow
nationalism':

> A country can be part of an alliance such as the Atlantic Alliance and still be
> independent. A country can be part of an economic community, such as the
> Common Market, or of a political community, such as the united Europe which
> we wish to see, and still be independent.[20]

While de Gaulle might claim public endorsement for such heavily qualified
'Europeanism', it left him open to attack from his more *communautaire* adversaries.
In the 1965 presidential election, the MRP, still smarting from the 'volapük' outburst
three years earlier, put up the centrist candidate, Jean Lecanuet. Campaigning on
a strongly pro-European platform, Lecanuet won 15.6 per cent of the vote, robbing
de Gaulle (with 44.7 per cent) of outright victory on the first ballot.

As successor to de Gaulle in 1969, Georges Pompidou proved a more accommodating statesman, presiding over some improvement in relations with the United
States and clearing the way, finally, for the admission of Britain to the Community.
As part of his 'change within continuity' platform, the new president also lent support
to the project of economic and monetary union as a means of strengthening the
Community within a confederal framework. On the principle of self-determination,
however, Pompidou kept faith with his predecessor and enjoyed the same unity
of purpose within the Gaullist Party. It was not until the presidency was lost by
the Gaullists in 1974 to the decidedly pro-European and more Atlanticist Valéry
Giscard d'Estaing that this unity of purpose was called into question, with important
consequences for the Gaullist Party's relationship to Europe.

The first major threat to the cohesion of the Gaullist position on Europe came
over the passage of a Bill in France, in June 1977, ratifying direct elections to the
European Assembly. Though this was anticipated in the Treaty of Rome, member
states had been reluctant to implement it, preferring until then to proceed with an
Assembly made up of delegates from the national parliaments. Despite Gaullist

misgivings about the type of Assembly being proposed and the method of election, outright opposition to the ratification was initially confined to a few old-guard Gaullists led by Michel Debré, chief architect of France's Constitution and first prime minister of the Fifth Republic. They claimed that a directly elected European Assembly, contriving to divide a French national sovereignty which was by definition indivisible, breached the Constitution of the Fifth Republic. Such an Assembly, in extending the bounds of its competence, would transform itself into a constituent body inimical to the interests of France, which it would seek to tie into a federal Europe and subject once more to American hegemony. An arguably better-founded charge relating to the method of election was that, since France would have fewer members of the Assembly per head than smaller states, the French would have proportionally less control over their destiny in European decision making. Enlisting the key terms of 'classical' Gaullism in support of his cause, Debré set up a Committee for the Independence and Unity of France to co-ordinate opposition to the proposed elections.

While Debré's campaign had limited impact on the Gaullist Party and public opinion at large, it coincided with a more decisive sequence of political events: Jacques Chirac's resignation as prime minister to President Giscard d'Estaing in August 1976, his relaunch of the UDR as the new Rassemblement pour la République (RPR) in December of the same year, and his election in March 1977 as mayor of Paris, a power base from which to prepare his 1981 presidential bid. Determined to apply maximum pressure on Giscard, while remaining technically within the presidential majority, Chirac came out forcefully in December 1976 against any extension of the European Assembly's powers. Though he conceded support in principle for direct elections, and though he had, as prime minister, been party to the government's initial approval of the project in July 1976, he now set out his opposition to the elections and refused RPR support for the Bill, on the grounds that it provided insufficient guarantees to ensure the preservation of French national independence.

The ensuing debate revealed splits within the Gaullist party between ultras of Debré's persuasion and pro-Europeanists, such as Jacques Chaban-Delmas and Olivier Guichard, who favoured full participation in the Community while opposing any drift to supranationalism. Chirac, for his part, sided increasingly with the ultras, warning that the proposed European Parliament would usher in a federal super-state. Calling for postponement, the RPR withheld its support from the Bill, which was pushed through the National Assembly without a vote (by means of Article 49 of the Constitution) and signed by President Giscard d'Estaing, with a clause attached restricting the European Assembly's powers to those provided for in the Treaty of Rome.[21]

The debate over direct elections to the European Assembly had two important consequences for the new Gaullist Party under Chirac. First, it gave a glimpse of the growing divergence of positions within the party on the European question, though the use of Article 49 spared the Gaullists from registering their divisions in a parliamentary vote. Second, it presented Chirac with an early opportunity to distinguish the RPR from its centre-right and distinctly pro-European coalition partners, and to reoccupy the Gaullist high ground on the issue of French national sovereignty. In so doing, it set the RPR leadership, at odds with more moderate voices within the party, on a course of opposition to Europe. Though the unity of the

RPR was formally maintained, fissures had been opened which would become more apparent, and more damaging, in the campaign for the first direct elections to the European Assembly in 1979.

THE EUROPEAN ELECTIONS OF 1979

The European elections of June 1979 marked a critical point in the RPR's attempt to define its position on Europe ten years on from the departure of de Gaulle. The period leading up to the elections was one of sustained confrontation between Chirac and President Giscard d'Estaing on the question of Europe, as on other matters. The conflict centred by turns on the Spanish and Portuguese applications for membership of the Community (opposed by Chirac on the grounds that Iberian competition would destroy the fruit farming and wine growing south-west of France); the European Commission (accused of incompetence and of damaging the French economy by failing to protect France against cheap imports from outside the EEC); the United States (ever poised to exert its hegemony over a federal Europe); the West German Chancellor Schmidt (for suggesting that the new European Assembly might see some increase in its powers); and President Giscard d'Estaing himself (taxed with colluding in the creation of a supranational Europe and deceiving the French as to his real intentions). Arguing that the Community was being turned into a large free-trade zone with no protection for French jobs or goods, Chirac waged a campaign high on Gallic chauvinism. Over it hung the ever-present spectre of supranationalism and the perceived threat of extended powers for the new European Assembly, seen as presaging the transfer of decision making from the Council of Ministers to a quasi-federal body.[22]

The conflict came to a head in November and December 1978, when a special congress of the RPR called on President Giscard d'Estaing to secure a declaration from the other heads of state, due to meet in Council on 4–5 December, that the powers of the European Assembly would be strictly limited to those laid down in the Treaty of Rome. When Giscard declined, Chirac, recovering from a car accident in the Paris Cochin hospital, issued the so-called *appel de Cochin* in which he berated the president and his newly formed Union pour la démocratie française (UDF) as 'le parti de l'étranger', ready to sell out French national interests in the marketplace of an enlarged, pro-American Europe. In an obvious attempt to echo de Gaulle's famous appeal of 18 June 1940 against the armistice with Nazi Germany, Chirac called upon Frenchmen everywhere to respond to the threat of national extinction by resisting 'the partisans of surrender and auxiliaries of decadence':

> That is why we say NO.
> No to the politics of supranationality.
> No to economic subservience.
> No to the eclipse of France on the international stage.
> We give our full support, yes, to the organization of Europe. We wish, as much as anyone, to see Europe take shape. But it must be a European Europe, where France can pursue her destiny as a great nation. We say no to a France reduced to the status of vassal in an empire of merchants, no to a France abdicating today in order to disappear tomorrow.[23]

This melodramatic appeal (with its evocation, as Giscard retorted, of 'a dis-gruntled, introspective, shivering France', at risk of becoming the 'old maid of

Europe')[24] was intended to rally the Gaullists. Instead, it had the effect of exacer-bating the disagreements between Chirac and some of the barons in the party, who objected to his immoderately negative stance. The Gaullist minister of justice and effective head of the RPR ministerial team, Alain Peyrefitte, took issue with Chirac's 'extreme remarks' in an open letter to the parliamentary party, and was suspended from the RPR for six months as a result.[25] Another long-serving Gaullist and former secretary-general of the UDR, Alexandre Sanguinetti, blamed Chirac's advisers[26] for his increasingly authoritarian leadership style. When Chirac responded by renewing his attacks on the president, the 'foreign party' and the Community (denouncing the 'Eurocracy' of the 'Brussels system', with its 'thousands and thousands of stateless civil servants'),[27] Peyrefitte again intervened, this time to defend President Giscard d'Estaing and the government's European policy as a faithful extension of de Gaulle's foreign policy objectives.[28] The disagreements reached their most potentially damaging point when, in late April 1979, a number of moderate RPR deputies led by Michel Cointat, criticizing the 'anti-European spirit' of the Gaullist list and its deviation from de Gaulle's intentions, threatened to field a dissident list of *gaullistes européens* for the June elections.[29]

None of these expressions of dissent sufficed to make Chirac alter course. Resolved to turn the European elections into an indictment of Giscard's domestic and foreign policies alike, and confident that he could carry the party with him in his aggressively nationalist stance, Chirac refused invitations to form a joint list with the UDF. Instead, he headed a List for the Defence of France's Interests in Europe (DIFE), reserving the number two position for Michel Debré as a way of countering the latter's threat to field his own – still another – dissident list.[30] Such was the Gaullist leadership's hostility to the whole process in which they were engaged that they made provision for a system of rotation in the European Assembly (the so-called tourniquet system) for all eighty-one members of the list, thereby contriving to ensure that none would spend long enough in Strasbourg to 'go native' among the Euro-federalists.

The DIFE was opposed on the centre-right by the Giscardian Union for France within Europe (UFE) list, headed by the popular pro-Europeanist Simone Veil, which claimed to represent the truly Gaullist position by defending participation in the Community as the best means of furthering the national interests of an essentially independent France. The results of the election vindicated this approach, opening a wide gap between the Giscardians and the Gaullists. With just over 16 per cent of the poll, Chirac's list won fifteen of the eighty-one French seats in the new European Assembly, against twenty-six for the Giscardian list (27.6 per cent), twenty-one for the Socialists and Left Radicals (23.6 per cent) and nineteen for the Communists (20.6 per cent).[31]

This was a humiliating defeat for the RPR and a serious personal setback for its leader. Within a Gaullist electorate wedded to the idea of a positive role for France in Europe,[32] a substantial minority refused to give even grudging support to Chirac's Poujadist-style campaign, which threatened to undermine the governing alliance to the advantage of the left-wing opposition.[33] An estimated 39 per cent of the Gaullist vote in the 1978 legislative elections swung away from the RPR, bolstering the presidential majority and confirming the UDF as potentially the most powerful electoral force in France.[34] Though the swift dismissal of his team of advisers allowed Chirac to resist pressure for his own resignation as party leader, the RPR had been exposed once again as a party divided on its conception of Europe. A year later, the divisions revealed by the European debate were to find more telling expression still when Michel Debré and Marie-France Garaud both announced their intention to stand, against official Gaullist backing for Chirac, in the presidential election of 1981.

THE EUROPEAN ELECTIONS OF 1984 AND 1989

The defeat sustained in the 1979 European elections left the Gaullist Party with the need to reassess its stance on Europe and, more pressingly, to rethink its relationship with the UDF and its whole strategy for regaining ascendancy on the right. The process of revision which followed culminated in June 1983, when the central committee of the RPR approved what amounted to a complete volte-face on Europe. Calling for 'a vital new momentum in the construction of Europe', Chirac argued that there was now a greater risk of Europe disintegrating than evolving towards a superstate, and that such disintegration would endanger all of de Gaulle's early achievements within the Community and deprive France of so many political and economic benefits. Stressing the need for closer co-operation in defence and security matters, and for greater economic and monetary solidarity among member states, he proposed that France maintain its commitment to the European Monetary System (EMS), that common policy be worked out in areas such as arms production, energy and high-technology industry, and that options for a common European defence system be considered.[35]

Underlying this clear change of course by the RPR leadership were a number of pragmatic considerations. Chief among these were the lessons drawn from the defeats of 1979 and 1981. The failure of the Cochin appeal to mobilize support against Giscard's European policy, followed by the abject performance by Michel Debré (1.7 per cent) in the first round of the 1981 presidential election, showed the symbolic references of historic Gaullism to be ill-adapted to the political imperatives of the 1980s. With 16 per cent in the 1979 European poll, the RPR had fallen far short of the baseline from which Chirac had to set off in the first round of the 1981 presidential election if he was to have any prospect of success in the second. Eliminated on the first ballot of that election with only 18 per cent (against 28.3 per cent for Giscard and 25.9 per cent for Mitterrand), Chirac was forced to take account of the need to extend his appeal to the crucial middle ground occupied by Giscard.

The election of a Socialist president and parliamentary majority in 1981 altered the French political landscape, defining a common enemy against which the whole of the right and centre-right could unite. Given the clear majority of RPR and UDF voters in favour of a joint list for the European elections of 1984,[36] and the approach of the 1986 legislative elections as the occasion for the right's anticipated return to government, the political importance for the RPR of bridging its differences with the UDF was manifest. Having convinced an initially reluctant UDF leadership of the merits of an alliance, Chirac used an extraordinary party congress on 3 March 1984 to call for faithful allegiance from the RPR to a joint list (the Union of the Opposition for Europe and the Defence of Liberties) which would serve as a springboard for the right's return to power. To ensure this allegiance, the RPR list gave prominence to a younger generation of Gaullists, such as Alain

Juppé and Alain Carignon, whose 'Chiraquian' credentials were well-attested and who articulated a more progressive vision of Europe than some of their die-hard Gaullist *compagnons*.[37]

Given Giscard's pronounced Europeanism and the role which he had played as president in bringing about the institutional changes so opposed by the Gaullists in the late 1970s, the formation now of a joint list with the UDF seemed little short of a capitulation by Chirac's party. It was not, however, underwritten by a joint electoral programme. After a brief statement of common aims, the parties remained free to develop their separate manifestos. In a wide-ranging document (significantly entitled *L'Europe, une volonté*), the RPR trod a cautious line between its erstwhile opposition to the construction of Europe and its commitment to co-operation with the UDF. Since the directly elected European Assembly had not opened the way, as feared, for the creation of a European superstate, the Gaullists were able to effect their 'conversion' without disavowing their earlier concerns. Though the emphasis was now on conciliation, Chirac's party still made clear its opposition to European integration and its anxieties over the extension of the Community to Spain and Portugal, upholding the Luxembourg Compromise and the right of veto in the Council of Ministers. In the run-up to the elections, Chirac acknowledged the 'divergence' between himself and Simone Veil in terms which stressed the abiding importance of the concessions extracted by de Gaulle in 1966: 'So, what separates us? The fact that Mme Veil wishes to see more decisions taken on the basis of majority voting. My own view is that the Luxembourg Compromise is a good compromise and that we should stick to it.'[38]

Despite such concerns, the 1984 European elections in France largely sacrificed the question of Europe to domestic considerations.[39] Delivering a mid-term verdict on the first Mitterrand presidency, the elections saw the joint UDF–RPR list under Simone Veil win 42.9 per cent of the vote and forty-one seats (twenty-one to the UDF, twenty to the RPR), against 20.8 per cent (twenty seats) for the Socialists, 11.3 per cent (ten seats) for the Communists, and 11 per cent (ten seats) for the Front National (FN).[40] This was a relative success only for the alliance of the right. With 43 per cent of the vote, it fell far short of the outright majority for which it had hoped. More significantly, the absence of a separate RPR list created an opening for the FN which, with its National Opposition Front for a *Europe des patries*, sought to strike an ultra-Gaullist pose and to harvest what anti-European, anti-Veil or 'anti-system' feeling there was on the right. This was a tactic to which the RPR electorate proved particularly susceptible. A SOFRES survey carried out in May 1984 showed 37 per cent of RPR voters to be 'in sympathy' with Le Pen, while another SOFRES poll indicated 33 per cent of RPR sympathizers among those expressing an intention to vote for the FN.[41]

In the short term, the European elections of 1984 allowed the RPR to negotiate a truce on Europe with its centrist allies and to redefine its European strategy at a moment when French public opinion, though exercised mostly by the domestic implications of economic recession, seemed overwhelmingly pro-European.[42] Within a longer-term perspective, however, the results of the 1984 European and 1986 legislative elections,[43] with the limited success of the UDF–RPR alliance and the emergence of a potent new force on the far right, did little to resolve the problems of identity and direction within the Gaullist party. These remained to be confronted afresh. The moment chosen for this new process of self-assessment was, unsurprisingly, the period following Chirac's defeat by Mitterrand in the 1988 presidential election and preceding the municipal and European elections of 1989. The presidential failure of 1988 dealt a severe blow to the right, whose divisions had been translated in the first round into a three-way contest between Chirac (19.9 per cent), Barre (16.5 per cent) and Le Pen (14.4 per cent). In particular, it called into question the leadership of Chirac, soundly beaten in the second ballot by Mitterrand (54 per cent to 46 per cent).[44] The prospect of another seven years in opposition led to demands for reform, or *rénovation*, on the right. The case was put most forcefully by some younger Gaullist modernizers such as Michel Noir and Alain Carignon, who pressed with certain UDF colleagues for the creation of a new single party to mobilize the whole of the right and centre-right. Their initiative was met by stern resistance from more orthodox Gaullists such as Michel Debré and Charles Pasqua, who denounced any trend towards fusion with the UDF as a betrayal of their political identity.[45]

Though the *rénovation* debate was not primarily focused on Europe, it contributed to the atmosphere of division in which the campaign for the 1989 European elections was fought by the RPR and UDF.[46] Disagreement over tactics and leadership resulted in two lists being presented: a joint UDF–RPR list under Giscard d'Estaing and a centrist list under Simone Veil. The fielding of a third list by the *rénovateurs* was only averted when the secretary-general of the RPR and number two on the joint list, Alain Juppé, threatened Gaullist dissidents with expulsion from the party.[47] While Chirac once again defended the joint list as imperative, others in the RPR feared that the party had been outmanoeuvred, leaving the UDF as the dominant partner in control of two separate lists and enhancing Giscard's claim to be the natural leader of a federated right. It was of considerable symbolic significance in this respect that Giscard's list featured two notable names: those of Charles de Gaulle and Alain Pompidou, grandson and son respectively of France's two former Gaullist presidents (while a single RPR dissident, Jean-Louis Bourlanges, figured on Veil's centrist list). Since both lists were characterized by their integrationist emphases (supporting a new treaty, economic and monetary union, stronger Community institutions and a European defence policy), they left the FN once again to pose as the champion of French identity and proponent of a Gaullist-style *Europe des patries*.[48]

As in the presidential election of the previous year, the results illustrated graphically the problems of division besetting the right: with 28.9 per cent, the UDF–RPR list won twenty-six seats, against seven seats (8.4 per cent) for Veil's list and ten seats (11.7 per cent) for Le Pen, who again made inroads into the Gaullist constituency.[49] To promote the cause of unity, Giscard urged MEPs from the two mainstream lists to sit together in the European Parliament, but a similar pattern of dispersal occurred as in 1979 and 1984, the Gaullist MEPs combining with the Irish Fianna Fáil in the European Democratic Alliance, and the UDF splitting into the European People's Party and the European Liberal, Democratic and Reformist Group.

TACTICAL CHANGE AND POLICY REVIEW

The 1984 and 1989 elections marked two distinct stages in the RPR's tactical shift on Europe. Though in both cases a joint UDF–RPR list was fielded, the nature of the alliance in 1989 differed in important ways from that of 1984. For the first time in 1989, Chirac and his party formed part of a list headed by the once demonized Giscard d'Estaing (with Chirac even agreeing to be president of the list's national support committee); for the first time, too, they now agreed to sink their differences with the UDF in a joint electoral programme. In the resulting UDF–RPR platform, *Pour une Europe unie*, the Gaullists' old anxieties over European integration were nowhere in evidence; instead, the manifesto called for a 'truly united Europe', 'politically strengthened' and with 'greater powers of legislation and control' for the European Parliament. To that end, it argued, a new treaty was required to redefine the powers of the European Council, Commission and Parliament. In addition, the time had come for a common (parallel) European currency, a common foreign and security policy, and for harmonization of policy in a range of other areas, such as immigration and asylum, the fight against terrorism, education and training, and research and technology.

Both symbolically and politically, these were major concessions for the Gaullist party. In particular, they appeared to signal a common will among the leaders of the right and centre-right to embrace the process of European union which, following the Single European Act of 1986, would take concrete form in the Treaty on European Union signed at Maastricht in 1992. While some discerned in this a 'spectacular conversion', the shedding by the RPR of an 'archaic nationalist image', others saw an 'unnatural alliance' between two quite different conceptions of Europe, a cynical trade-off for mutual political advantage between 'European federalists' and 'diehard nationalists'.[50] With the RPR relinquishing its own 'space', the two figures on the right who benefited most from the 1989 European election were Giscard (architect of the UDF–RPR united front) and Le Pen (whose party, with an increased share of the vote, retained all ten of its seats in the European Parliament). The RPR's virtual eclipse between the opposing visions of Europe articulated by Giscard and Le Pen was further accentuated by the high-profile Europeanism of Simone Veil's centrist list. The failure by the Gaullists to convey a message of their own, through the signing of a joint manifesto in which the UDF was clearly the driving force, gave new urgency to those within the RPR protesting that the party had lost its way on Europe.

Alive to the danger in this, the RPR used the period following the 1989 European election to define its position on Europe in isolation from its UDF partners. The process culminated in December 1990, when the party's National Council approved a new manifesto, *Pour l'union des États de l'Europe*. Despite the obligatory references to the preservation of 'national realities', the dangers of federalism and the desirability of widening as well as deepening the Community, the manifesto called for: a 'negotiated transfer' of 'elements of sovereignty' where the wider interest of the Community was clearly at stake; an 'urgently needed extension of the role and power of those institutions which have an undisputed legitimacy: the European Parliament, European Council and Council of Ministers'; a 'harmonizing' of European foreign policy and a 'renewed alliance' between Europe and the United States.[51]

The meetings of the RPR's political bureau which accompanied the drafting of the new manifesto set out a diversity of positions which the official version could only partially reflect. These were not echoed, moreover, by any wider debate within the party at large. Nor did they resolve what some more vocal opponents within the RPR saw as the most pressing challenge to de Gaulle's legacy. For how was progress to be made from an economic market towards a more politically unified Europe without accepting the very limitations on national self-determination which the Gaullist party had always steadfastly refused to countenance? As the debate over the ratification of the Maastricht Treaty was to demonstrate, the problem of Europe could no longer be buried by the RPR leadership in carefully worded formulae and a marriage of convenience with the Giscardian centre-right.

THE MAASTRICHT REFERENDUM

France's ratification of the Maastricht Treaty in 1992 provided the occasion for an unprecedented display of disunity within the RPR. The background can be briefly outlined. In 1986, Chirac's 'cohabitation' government[52] endorsed the Single European Act which paved the way for a new Treaty, agreed by the twelve member states at Maastricht in December 1991 and signed in February 1992. In May and June 1992, a series of parliamentary votes in France ratified the Treaty and made provision for the changes to the Constitution which it would entail (notably over economic and monetary union, external border controls, and the question of a European 'citizenship' extending the right to vote and to stand in municipal and European elections to EU citizens residing in another member state). These votes were carried by a combination of Socialist and UDF support in both chambers, with the Communists opposing and the Gaullists largely abstaining.[53] The decision to submit the Treaty to referendum as the final stage in the ratification process was announced on 3 June 1992, following its narrow rejection in the Danish referendum, and the date was duly set for 20 September. A debate which had been confined to the National Assembly and Senate would now be conducted in the public domain (a significant factor in Mitterrand's decision, since the outcome seemed a foregone conclusion and the campaign would surely expose the divisions and rivalries within and among the parties of the right).[54]

If the prospect of a resounding 'yes' vote proved short-lived (the anticipated 65 per cent support for the Treaty in June had given way, by late August, to the threat of a potential 'no' majority),[55] that of a divided right proved all that Mitterrand could have hoped. The referendum campaign shattered the veneer of unity behind which the 1984 and 1989 European elections had been fought, laying bare serious divisions within the UDF (where opposition to the Treaty was led by the maverick deputy from the Vendée, Viscount Philippe de Villiers) and, more predictably, within the RPR (where Philippe Séguin and Charles Pasqua formed an unlikely alliance to campaign vigorously for a 'no' vote in the face of support for the Treaty from the party leadership). One outcome of the *rénovation* debate of 1988–89 had been the concession by the RPR leadership of the right to form *tendances* or factions – a well-established practice among French Socialists and part of the very definition of the UDF confederation, but a novel departure within the highly centralized 'command structure' of the RPR.[56] Séguin and Pasqua had already tested this new 'right' at the party's national conference in 1990, tabling a motion which accused the leadership of allowing the RPR to lose its direction in the wake of the 1988 presidential defeat and which called on Chirac to resign as party leader in order to concentrate on his (third) bid for the presidency in 1995. Winning over 30 per cent of the delegates' votes on that occasion (just short of the support which would have forced Chirac's resignation), they had tapped into a substantial reservoir of disquiet about the party's identity, its relationship, on the one hand, with a durable FN (stable at around 10–12 per cent of the national vote) and, on the other, with its once junior UDF partners (who for the first time enjoyed stronger representation than the RPR in the National Assembly).

Now, through their 'Rally for No in the Referendum', Séguin and Pasqua extended their defiance beyond questions of party leadership and strategy to embrace the whole issue of France's place within Europe and the extent to which closer European integration was compatible with the preservation of national sovereignty. The parliamentary debates over the constitutional amendment saw Séguin emerge as a forceful orator, championing the principle of national sovereignty in grand Gaullist tones. Throughout the passage of the reform text and in the ensuing referendum campaign, he elaborated a carefully nuanced position, taking pains to distinguish between his support for the 'construction of Europe' and his opposition to 'l'Europe de Maëstricht', denounced as 'federalism on the cheap, fundamentally anti-democratic, falsely liberal, and technocratic through and through'.[57] The Maastricht Treaty, Séguin argued, was incompatible with the Constitution, with French national self-determination and with democracy itself (defined, in a much-invoked Gaullist phrase, as 'inseparable from national sovereignty'). It was a fiction to claim, moreover, that monetary union would promote economic prosperity, as it was a fiction to pretend that the suppression of the nation state would guarantee 'perpetual peace' within Europe.[58] The sustained vigour with which Séguin mounted his opposition to the treaty culminated in a televised debate with President Mitterrand at the Sorbonne on 3 September, marking the RPR deputy for the Vosges out as the leading light in the 'no' camp and a potential rival to Chirac for the leadership of the party and, ultimately perhaps, for the presidency itself.

While Séguin sought to occupy the heights of classical Gaullism in his opposition to Maastricht, Pasqua set his objections in a less lofty perspective. His rejection of the treaty was couched in a more populist and xenophobic register, castigating the proponents of a Europe without internal borders and of voting rights for foreigners in French municipal elections, and equating the repudiation of Maastricht with that of the Mitterrand presidency as a whole.[59] Denouncing the 'craven consensus' and 'ostrich politics' of the French Socialist government and the European Commission, the leader of the RPR group in the Senate used his alliance with Séguin to rally extensive support among RPR members and voters, and to appeal beyond them for the rejection of the treaty by the French electorate at large.

In the face of such a resolute 'no' campaign, Chirac prevaricated before coming out in lukewarm support of the treaty. In reality, his choice was so restricted as to leave no obviously viable course open to him. Having initially called for a refer-endum, he could not now take refuge in a call for abstention; nor could he afford to alienate the pro-European centre-right (so crucial to his presidential prospects) by opposing the treaty outright; nor, finally, could he risk accentuating the divisions within his own party by coming out in unqualified support. While Séguin and Pasqua urged their leader to reject the treaty, the influential centrists François Léotard and Charles Millon warned that they would withhold support from any future presidential candidate who had not given 'a clear commitment to Europe'.[60] Concerned to limit the potential damage to himself and his party, Chirac kept a low profile throughout most of the campaign, allowing Séguin and Pasqua freedom to wage their anti-Maastricht campaign and conceding to RPR members and electors the right to vote as they saw fit. While the more federalist elements in the treaty (a timetable for full economic and monetary union with the creation of a single currency, and reciprocal voting rights for EU citizens in municipal and European elections) exceeded the natural bounds of Gaullist support, Chirac was anxious to avoid the accusation of obstructionism and to preserve a common front with the UDF in the run-up to the March 1993 legislative elections. His own position was summed up in the ambivalent assertion, before an audience of some 2,000 party cadres on 4 July, that he would cast a 'clear-headed but unenthusiastic' vote in support of the treaty.[61]

Though keen to avoid active campaigning, Chirac was in the end obliged to defend not only his own declared position on Maastricht but, by implication, the very legitimacy of his place within the Gaullist leadership succession. Invoking the higher interests of France as his reason for rallying to a cause which President Mitterrand had made his own, he contrived to present the treaty as the culmination of de Gaulle's European vision, while Séguin and Pasqua tirelessly denounced it as the very antithesis of that vision. The image of a Gaullist leader engaging in open debate with subordinates over the General's legacy confirmed the centrifugal forces at work within a movement once defined by its centralized leadership. It demonstrated, too, the extent to which the Gaullist vision of Europe had become blurred and open to conflicting interpretations.

The narrow endorsement of the Maastricht Treaty in the referendum of 20 September (51 per cent to 49 per cent) spared Chirac an embarrassing personal defeat at the hands of Séguin and Pasqua. Even so, exit polls showed that a clear majority of RPR voters had rejected their leader's example.[62] Of those who had voted for Chirac in the first round of the 1988 presidential election, an estimated 64 per cent followed Séguin and Pasqua in opposing the treaty.[63] Though subject to some caution, more interpretative analyses of the vote suggested that the RPR, under the sway of the anti-Maastricht campaign, had approached the referendum as a party still imbued with the Gaullist cult of the nation state and of French exceptionalism. Questioned in a BVA exit poll on the reasons for their vote, 60 per cent of RPR 'no' voters cited the loss of national sovereignty, while 56 per cent feared handing France over to Brussels technocrats.[64] In separate SOFRES polls conducted in advance of the referendum, a majority of RPR supporters averred that France had derived little or no benefit from membership of the Community (53 per cent) and that the construction of Europe would ultimately destroy French identity and values (54 per cent).[65]

Faced with such a groundswell of opposition to his own position, Chirac sought a vote of confidence from the party executive in the days immediately following the referendum.[66] Though his leadership was endorsed by 95 per cent in a hastily convened meeting of the party's National Council (from which Séguin and Pasqua pointedly absented themselves), the referendum campaign had dramatized the gulf between the party leadership and a substantial majority of the Gaullist rank and file. Above all, it had shown the double dilemma confronting Chirac as party leader: how to keep faith with the difficult legacy of de Gaulle within the context of a France and a Europe much changed since the 1960s; how to hold his movement together and exert his appeal as *rassembleur* across a mainstream right more openly fragmented now than at any time since the foundation of the Fifth Republic. As the only major party leader to abdicate responsibility for laying down an official party line, Chirac sought the path of least resistance. Within six months of parliamentary elections and two and a half years at most before the presidential contest, his grudging support for the Maastricht Treaty smacked more of calculation than of conviction, raising wider questions about the extent to which the European issue had been subordinated in France to domestic political pressures and to the presidential ambitions of individual political actors.

AFTER MAASTRICHT: THE EUROPEAN ELECTIONS OF 1994

After the drama of the Maastricht referendum, the European elections of June 1994 presented the RPR with the task of assuaging its divisions over Europe and projecting a coherent image in the last national ballot before the 1995 presidential election. Though these were to be the most significant European elections yet, given the increased powers of the European Parliament provided by the Maastricht Treaty, the agenda was once again largely set for the RPR by domestic political considerations. The campaign was conducted in a political environment radically altered by the landslide victory of the right in the parliamentary elections of March 1993 and the nomination of Edouard Balladur as prime minister at the head of a second RPR–UDF 'cohabitation' government.[67] The initial popularity of Balladur and his emergence as a prospective presidential candidate posed a delicate problem for Chirac. The absence within the UDF of a convincing presidential front-runner and the potential range of Balladur's appeal over the centre-right, with his conciliatory approach on European and other issues, gave Chirac more incentive than ever to seek an accommodation with his old adversary, Giscard d'Estaing, thereby keeping open his route to the centre-ground.

Seen in this light, Chirac's decision to press for a joint UDF–RPR list and his agreement to the nomination of the reputed federalist Dominique Baudis (UDF) at its head were widely interpreted as part of a larger trade off: by making concessions to the Europeanist core within the UDF and affirming the RPR's commitment to the construction of Europe, Chirac would remove a potential obstacle to centrist support for his candidacy in the second round of the forthcoming presidential election.[68] The RPR's nomination to second place on the list of Hélène Carrère d'Encausse, erstwhile president of the National Committee for the Ratification of the Maastricht Treaty, was a significant gesture too, shoring up Chirac's claim to a genuinely progressive vision of Europe. The joint list was sealed by a common programme committing Gaullist MEPs to sit alongside their UDF partners in the same centrist group (the European People's Party) in the Strasbourg Parliament. As in 1989, the programme bore the marks of the UDF's overriding influence and the RPR's compliance, calling for progress on economic and monetary union, the free circulation of goods, capital and persons, the development of a common European foreign and security policy in co-operation with NATO, and institutional reform to strengthen and democratize the European Union, including a further extension of the European Parliament's powers and greater control by national parliaments over European decision making.[69]

Though there was fulsome approval from UDF leaders for the RPR's 'swift and sympathetic' endorsement of Baudis,[70] Chirac's stance was far from commanding universal support within his own ranks. When the political bureau of the RPR was called upon to ratify the nomination at its meeting of 7 April 1994 (with the notable absence, again, of Séguin and Pasqua), it was the occasion for a vigorous debate. To those who argued that the RPR should head the joint list, or even field a separate Gaullist list altogether, Chirac replied that a united front remained a necessity and that the RPR already enjoyed control of the premiership and the presidency of the National Assembly. The case which he put for ceding leadership of the list to the UDF's nominee, as reported in *Libération*, carried more than a suggestion of calculated opportunism:

> The French could not care less about political in-fighting and have other problems to worry them. They have no time for squabbling and would not understand it if the majority were split over Europe. The European Parliament does not have much power; so there is no good reason to fall out with our partners over Europe. The Prime Minister was anxious that we should field a joint list. In any case, the platform which we have signed with the UDF is not our vision of Europe. All we are doing is giving a mandate for five years to our MEPs.[71]

Despite such (revealing) protestations in favour of 'union', the results of the election on 12 June showed a right and centre-right still deeply divided over Europe. With a modest 25.6 per cent of the vote, the UDF–RPR list secured twenty-eight seats from an expanded French quota of eighty-seven, while the anti-Maastricht lists of de Villiers and Le Pen gained 12.3 per cent (thirteen seats) and 10.5 per cent (eleven seats) respectively.[72] Acknowledging the strength of the anti-European vote on the evening of the elections, Chirac issued a written statement in which he noted 'the growing incomprehension and suspicion of French public opinion towards the construction of Europe'. This, he declared, was a problem 'of which account must be taken'.[73]

These remarks signalled something of the difficulty facing Chirac as a prospective presidential candidate in the wake of the divisions opened up by the Maastricht referendum. While anti-Europeanism could be no platform on which to construct a presidential campaign, there was more electoral gain to be had from opposition to Europe in the early 1990s than in the late 1970s; yet Chirac found himself constrained to strike a positive, statesmanlike stance, with no hint of the aggressive nationalism which once characterized him. Making a virtue of necessity in his strategy to woo the centre, he left de Villiers and Le Pen free to exploit anti-European sentiment on the right, not least within his own party. Of all the major electoral constituencies, that of the RPR proved the most volatile on the European issue. Analysis of the 1994 European election suggested that a considerably higher proportion of RPR than UDF sympathizers had transferred their support to de Villiers; the transfer of votes to Le Pen's list, though negligible by comparison, showed a still wider divergence between the two components of the mainstream right.[74] Of those RPR sympathizers who had voted 'no' in the Maastricht referendum, an estimated 45 per cent chose again to reject their leader's example by endorsing de Villiers' list, with only 42 per cent coming into line in support of the UDF–RPR list. More tellingly perhaps, of RPR sympathizers who had voted 'yes' in the Maastricht referendum, 14 per cent none the less opted for de Villiers' list in preference to that of Baudis.[75]

These statistics testify to an intractable problem for Chirac and, more broadly, to the difficulty confronting the mainstream right as a whole on the European question. Viewed over the span of some fifteen years, Chirac's record on Europe had been largely one of damage limitation. While straining to renounce his formerly aggressive chauvinism, he failed to replace this with a convincing Europeanism. By abandoning his early attempts at differentiation and pursuing a policy of convergence with the UDF, Chirac sought to avoid confrontation and to use the European issue for domestic political leverage among his centrist allies. The 'union' which became a key component in his strategy not only failed to mobilize the whole of the right and centre-right in successive European elections: it fell from 43 per cent of the vote in 1984 through 28.8 per cent in 1989 to a low point of 25.6 per cent in 1994.

As the right and centre-right in France increasingly became the battleground in the debate over Europe, the emergence first of Le Pen then of de Villiers drew off swathes of support from the UDF–RPR alliance, and in particular from Chirac's party. With the Giscardian centrists articulating their long-held Europeanism and de Villiers carving up the anti-European vote with Le Pen, Chirac was left occupying something of a void in terms of European policy and image. Failing to communicate a coherent vision, he restricted himself to seeking political advantage through personal appeal and electoral opportunism. For all their solemn pledge to sit in the same parliamentary group ('It is by this means that the interests of France within Europe will be most effectively defended'),[76] it was significant that the Gaullists and Giscardians went their separate ways in Strasbourg once again in 1994, the fourteen Gaullist MEPs opting, as before, for the European Democratic Alliance and the UDF, with one exception, for the European People's Party.[77]

GAULLISM WITHOUT DE GAULLE: A PROTEAN LEGACY

Once a rallying theme, Europe proved the most openly divisive issue for the Gaullist Party in the early 1990s. While the RPR, like its UNR and UDR predecessors, had always encompassed different political leanings and *courants* (economic *dirigistes* and liberals, social conservatives and progressives, etc.),[78] the party showed itself to be more divided over Europe than on any other issue; more divided on this issue, too, than any other French political party. On the face of it, de Gaulle's European policy amounted to a simple set of exigencies: national independence and *grandeur*, the assertion of French interests and optimization of French influence, to be achieved in large part through a tightly controlled relationship with the EC and NATO. What appeared simple in principle, however, proved much more complicated in practice, requiring all the conviction and idiosyncrasy of its author to balance anti-supranationalism with a genuine belief that Europe should be more than an economic market, that it should have a coherent 'political' identity. The essence of Gaullism, as Peter Gourevitch has noted, is not its clarity but rather its 'judicious use of confusion and ambiguity'.[79] Questioned by journalists on his attitude to Gaullism during a trip to the United States in 1983, Jacques Chirac replied: 'Gaullism is a pragmatic way of thinking, not a doctrine. It has changed with a changing world. No one knows what General de Gaulle would say if he were here today, but I think he would say the same as I do.'[80]

These remarks go to the heart of the problem for today's Gaullist leadership. Gaullism may not be a doctrine, but it does represent a particular political programme, or at the very least a set of core priorities and policies, informed by the time and circumstances in which they were conceived. There is little in the Gaullist canon to guide the RPR in its response to events which have fundamentally altered the European scene in recent years, focused most dramatically in the fall of the Berlin

Wall and German reunification. While the collapse of communism disrupted the geo-political profile of Europe, participation in the Gulf War in 1991 and the integration of the Franco-German Eurocorps into NATO in 1993 set France on a new footing within the Atlantic Alliance, with far-reaching implications for French security policy.[81] In line with Chirac's calls since the mid-1980s for a 'vital strategic coupling' of the American and European defence systems (a now recurrent theme in RPR policy documents on defence and security), these developments mark new stages in what Jean Baudouin has called the *dégaullisation* of French foreign policy.[82]

While the protean nature of Gaullism may be a virtue for Chirac, it is, as the debate over Maastricht showed, a potentially damaging one. On the European question more than any other, de Gaulle still exercises a remarkable hold over French thinking. More striking still is the breadth of interpretation with which the Gaullist message has come to mean all things to all sides: not only the RPR, but the UDF, the Socialists, and even the FN claim legitimacy for their stances on Europe (official and dissident alike) by reference to a variously interpreted, and reinterpreted, Gaullist model.[83] As the formal heirs to Gaullism, the RPR has come to suffer more than it benefits from this weighty legacy: in its attempt to keep faith with its Gaullist heritage and adapt to an evolving France within an evolving Europe, it has ended up facing in several directions at once. A telling demonstration of the problem was provided by the departure from the party in 1989 of the influential Yvan Blot, who joined the FN on the grounds that Le Pen's 'ideas today are closest to those of de Gaulle', and the defection some months later of Jean Charbonnel, who rallied to the presidential majority on the grounds that 'the Gaullist legacy is better assured today by President Mitterrand and his government than by the opposition'.[84] Though Blot and Charbonnel represent two very particular cases, ideologically predisposed to move in their separate directions,[85] they demonstrate the difficulty for the RPR of managing an ambiguous ideological legacy. In its European dimension, the problem was dramatized most absurdly by the RPR's official television campaign for the Maastricht referendum, when half the allotted time *within the same broadcasts* was given over to urging a 'yes' vote, and half spent appealing for a 'no'!

RETHINKING EUROPE: IDEOLOGICAL RENEWAL IN THE GAULLIST PARTY

In a party where the leader is traditionally the driving force in policy making, and within a presidentialist culture which accentuates the importance of personal leadership, Chirac's signal ambivalence over Europe called his political vision into question. Seen in the light of his acknowledged long-term goal, the capture of the French presidency, his oscillations over Europe have a further significance. For they suggest the extent to which the European debate may be subordinated in France to domestic political considerations. The whole of the RPR's European strategy since the party's creation in 1976 has been dictated by another agenda: that of winning back political (primarily presidential) power in France and recovering the Gaullist hegemony of 1958–74. This has engendered an opportunistic attitude to ideology which, as Jean Baudouin argues, has led to 'doctrinal revisionism' not only in the RPR's European policy, but across the range of its economic and social policy making too.[86]

In the post-1981 contest between French socialism and a liberalism taking its cues from Thatcher's Britain and Reagan's United States, the RPR, seeking to capitalize on opposition to the governing Socialists and to consolidate its alliance with the UDF, abandoned past concerns for national unity through state interventionism and extolled instead the merits of deregulation, privatization and market forces. In the elaboration of party policy, economic liberalism began to go hand in hand with a much more pro-European emphasis, stressing the free-market aspects of the Community. A comparison between the RPR's 1979 European programme and the party's 1985–86 manifesto, *Le renouveau. Pacte RPR pour la France*, reveals the extent of the shift away from a protectionist discourse stressing French particularism towards a vigorous commitment to a free-market Europe, calling for 'the consolidation of a real single market', 'free movement of capital', 'the convergence of economic policy', 'the strengthening of the European monetary system', and 'the harmonization of legislation' controlling access to national markets.[87] Through a combination of ideological renewal and tactical expediency, the RPR had, by the mid-1980s, come to articulate a liberal, pro-European philosophy which was starkly at odds with its former nationalist and protectionist impulses. With the party's conversion to market economics and social conservatism, the appeal of Europe as an economic space came to outweigh the political threat posed to national sovereignty. When Séguin and Pasqua mounted their challenge to the leadership over Maastricht, they were taking issue not only with the RPR's direction on Europe but with the whole 'neo-liberal mutation' of the Gaullist Party,[88] the loss of its distinctive blend of *dirigiste* and free-market policies and its transformation into a classic conservative party with a classically conservative agenda.

In this regard, it is important to note the extent of the evolution which the Gaullist Party has undergone since the late 1970s, not just in terms of its ideology and policies but in terms, too, of its personnel. The RPR today is a party with a leadership team of younger, technocratic Gaullists, such as Alain Juppé and Jacques Toubon, who served their political apprenticeship not under the General but under Pompidou and Chirac, and whose allegiance to the tenets of historic Gaullism is tempered by an enthusiasm for free-market economics which leaves scant room for the interventionist and redistributive policies which were formerly at the base of the party's cross-class appeal. The onset of economic crisis in the 1970s, coupled with the failure of the Socialist experiment in France after 1981, prompted a major policy revision by the RPR and pushed the party to the right of the UDF in its economic liberalism and social conservatism. At the same time, a substantial renewal of membership changed the profile of the party, largely severing its roots with the UDR. A survey of the membership conducted in 1986 showed that over two-thirds of those interviewed had joined the party since 1981; only 10 per cent of the sample had been members before the party's relaunch in 1976.[89]

Such a fundamental recomposition of the party's leadership and membership, within the changed historical and political circumstances of the past two decades, has accelerated the weakening of traditional ties. The alliance with the UDF poses problems for detailed analysis of the RPR's evolving ideology and electorate; what emerges clearly, however, is that fidelity to the Gaullist legacy within today's RPR is fitful and selective. Of the Gaullists in the early 1960s, Philip Williams observed that 'the core of the party was still formed by men who had answered the call as Resisters or Free Frenchmen'.[90] Some thirty years later, the Gaullist Party had become a very different machine, managed by a new generation of cadres and balancing the classic themes of national unity, independence and *grandeur* against a market-orientated conception of Europe and an admiration for the United States as a model of economic liberalism.[91] Opinion polls in the mid-1980s showed strikingly high levels of support among RPR sympathizers for the 'construction of Europe', including a European defence system incorporating the French nuclear capacity, and for the broad lines of American economic and foreign policy.[92] Since then, the RPR has completed its official conversion to a vision of Europe far removed from that of its UNR or UDR predecessors, despite the emergence of a 'fundamentalist' Gaullist tendency in response to the party's evolution and the perceived dangers of the Maastricht Treaty. While the RPR continues to parade the symbols and references of its Gaullist heritage, the questions over its political identity and direction have been posed most acutely by the debate over Europe. The programme to which Chirac and his party subscribed for the European elections of June 1994, devoid of the merest reference to de Gaulle and his European project, confirmed that the RPR's agenda for Europe today remains 'Gaullist' in only the most tenuous sense.

NOTES

1 *Le Monde*, 7 September 1960. (All translations from French are the author's.)
2 See E. Jouve, *Le général de Gaulle et la construction de l'Europe (1940–1966)* (Paris, Librairie générale de droit et de jurisprudence, 1967), 2 vols.
3 *Le Monde*, 7 September 1960.
4 See de Gaulle's press conference of 15 May 1962 (*Le Monde*, 17 May 1962). Dante, Goethe and Chateaubriand, he protested, were Europeans *by virtue* of their respective national origins 'They would not have made much of a contribution to Europe if they had been stateless and if they had thought and written in some "esperanto" or "volapuk". . . . '
5 P. Cerny, *The Politics of Grandeur: Ideological Aspects of De Gaulle's Foreign Policy* (Cambridge, Cambridge University Press, 1980), p. 205.
6 P. Reynaud, *La politique étrangère du gaullisme* (Paris, Julliard, 1964), p. 217.
7 Cerny, *The Politics of Grandeur*, p. 48.
8 Ibid., p. 47; *Le Monde*, 17 May 1962.
9 Press conference of 12 November 1953 (*Le Monde*, 13 November 1953).
10 See the press conference of 15 May 1962 (*Le Monde*, 17 May 1962).
11 See de Gaulle's New Year address of 31 December 1964 (*Le Monde*, 2 January 1965). As Stanley Hoffmann noted, American dominance was the spectre hanging over and informing all of de Gaulle's European policy making ('The European process at Atlantic crosspurposes', *Journal of Common Market Studies*, vol. 3, no. 3, 1964–65, pp. 85–101).
12 Press conference of 12 November 1953 (*Le Monde*, 13 November 1953).
13 M. Couve de Murville, *Une politique étrangère 1958–1969* (Paris, Plon, 1971), pp. 366–76. See also de Gaulle's press conference of 15 May 1962 (*Le Monde*, 17 May 1962).
14 See J. Touchard, *Le gaullisme 1940–1969* (Paris, Seuil, 1978), pp. 115–17.
15 For an analysis of de Gaulle's European policy in the areas discussed, see S.J. Bodenheimer, *Political Union: A Microcosm of European Politics 1960–1966* (Leyden, Sijthoff, 1967), chapters 1–5.
16 The party went through a number of phases during the presidencies of de Gaulle and Pompidou: as the Union pour la nouvelle République (UNR), 1958–67, the Union des démocrates pour la Vᵉ République (UDVᵉ), 1967–68, and the Union des démocrates pour la république (UDR), 1968–76.
17 As Jean Charlot noted, discipline in the UNR was such that every deputy was constrained to sign a solemn pledge in support of de Gaulle and the parliamentary party (*L'Union pour la nouvelle République. Etude du pouvoir au sein d'un parti politique* (Paris, Armand Colin, 1967), pp. 143–5).
18 See J. Charlot/IFOP, *Les Français et de Gaulle* (Paris, Plon, 1971), pp. 81–3.

19　See J. Charlot, *Le phénomène gaulliste* (Paris, Fayard, 1970), pp. 60–1; D. Bahu-Leyser, *De Gaulle, les Français et l'Europe* (Paris, Presses Universitaires de France, 1981), pp. 201–3.

20　Comité d'action pour la Ve République, *Manifeste. Pour le progrès, l'indépendance et la paix avec le général de Gaulle*, cited in J. Charlot, *Le gaullisme* (Paris, Armand Colin, 1970), p. 127.

21　On the debate in France over direct elections to the European Parliament, see M. Leigh, 'Giscard and the European Community', *The World Today*, February 1977, pp. 73–80; J. Crandall Hollick, 'Direct elections to the European Parliament: the French debate', *The World Today*, December 1977, pp. 472–80.

22　See J. Crandall Hollick, 'The European election of 1979 in France: a masked ball for 1981', *Parliamentary Affairs*, vol. 32, no. 4, 1979, pp. 459–69.

23　*Le Monde*, 8 December 1978.

24　Ibid., 12 December 1978.

25　Ibid., 16, 21–22 December 1978.

26　'The Gang of Four': Marie-France Garaud, Pierre Juillet, Charles Pasqua and Yves Guéna. See ibid., 24–25 December 1978.

27　Ibid., 25 January 1979.

28　Ibid., 20 February 1979.

29　Ibid., 24, 26, 28 April 1979.

30　For a résumé of the DIFE's programme, see *Le Monde. Dossiers et documents* (June 1979), *Les premières élections européennes*, pp. 52–3.

31　Ministry of the Interior figures, published in *Le Monde*, 12 June 1979.

32　A poll in March 1979 showed 77 per cent of RPR sympathizers to be 'favourable' to the construction of Europe, as opposed to only 9 per cent against: SOFRES, *Opinion publique 1985* (Paris, Gallimard, 1985), p. 232.

33　The DIFE list, protested the former Gaullist minister Jean Charbonnel, represented not Gaullism but a form of neo-Poujadism (*Le Monde*, 2 May 1979).

34　A. Cole and P. Campbell, *French Electoral Systems and Elections since 1789* (Aldershot, Gower, 1989, 3rd edn) pp. 120–1.

35　*Le Monde*, 14 June 1983.

36　O. Duhamel and J.-L. Parodi, 'Les sondages et la campagne européenne de 1984 en France', *Pouvoirs*, no. 30, 1984, pp. 149, 150 n. 3.

37　*Le Monde*, 6 March 1984.

38　Cited by F. Saint-Ouen, 'Les partis politiques français et l'Europe. Système politique et fonctionnement du discours', *Revue française de science politique*, vol. 36, no. 2, 1986, p. 217.

39　See J.G. Shields, 'The politics of disaffection: France in the 1980s', in J. Gaffney and E. Kolinsky (eds), *Political Culture in France and Germany: A Contemporary Perspective* (London, Routledge, 1991), pp. 75–9.

40　Ministry of the Interior figures, published in *Le Monde*, 19 June 1984.

41　SOFRES, *Opinion publique 1985*, p. 178; *Le Monde*, 6 June 1984. An exit poll by the same agency on the evening of 17 June suggested that some 18 per cent of those who had voted for Chirac in the first round of the 1981 presidential election had switched their vote to the FN. See M. Charlot, 'L'émergence du Front national', *Revue française de science politique*, vol. 36, no. 1, 1986, pp. 39–40.

42　SOFRES, *Opinion publique 1985*, pp. 231–6. A poll conducted in May 1984 showed 85 per cent of the French to be in favour of the construction of Europe; among RPR sympathizers, the figure was as high as 86 per cent (ibid., p. 232).

43　The joint RPR–UDF platform for the legislative elections of 1986 seemed to confirm the Gaullists' new-found commitment to Europe, calling for European monetary union, institutional reforms to strengthen the Community, and a European defence strategy incorporating France's nuclear capability (RPR–UDF, *Plate-forme pour gouverner ensemble*, 1986, pp. 15–17).

44　See D. S. Bell, 'A hunger for power: Jacques Chirac', in J. Gaffney (ed.), *The French Presidential Elections of 1988: Ideology and Leadership in Contemporary France* (Aldershot, Gower, 1989), pp. 101–20.

45 For a brief discussion of the *rénovateurs* episode, see J.G. Shields, 'Disputing the General's mantle: France's Gaullists in disarray', *Contemporary Review*, vol. 256, no. 1493, 1990, pp. 281–6.

46 On the 1989 European election campaign in France, see P. Hainsworth, 'France', in J. Lodge (ed.), *The 1989 Election of the European Parliament* (London, Macmillan, 1990), pp. 126–44.

47 *Le Monde*, 8 April 1989.

48 This was precisely the line which the leader of the FN sought to take, making his own the 'Gaullist formula', as he put it. See J.-M. Le Pen, *L'espoir* (Paris, Albatros, 1989), pp. 98, 99.

49 A SOFRES survey suggested that some 10 per cent of those who had supported Chirac in the first round of the 1988 presidential election voted for the FN list in June 1989: SOFRES, *L'état de l'opinion 1990* (Paris, Seuil, 1990), p. 181. In the same elections, the Socialists and Left Radicals won 23.6 per cent (twenty-two seats), the Communist Party 7.7 per cent (seven seats), and the Greens 10.6 per cent (nine seats) (Ministry of the Interior figures, published in *Le Monde*, 20 June 1989).

50 Hainsworth, 'France', p. 132; F. Saint-Ouen, 'Le RPR est-il devenu européen?', *Revue politique et parlementaire*, vol. 90, no. 933, 1988, pp. 51–4.

51 See *Le Monde*, 6 and 7 December 1990. All of these themes were to find expression in the RPR's official manifesto, *La France en mouvement*, adopted by the October 1991 party congress (pp. 66–74).

52 Following the victory of the right in the 1986 legislative elections, Chirac was appointed prime minister at the head of a RPR–UDF government. When Mitterrand won the presidency for a second term in 1988, he dissolved the National Assembly and, in the wake of a stronger performance by the left, appointed Michel Rocard as prime minister over a new Socialist government.

53 H. Portelli, 'Le référendum sur l'Union européenne', *Regards sur l'actualité*, no. 184, 1992, pp. 6–7.

54 B. Criddle, 'The French referendum on the Maastricht Treaty, September 1992', *Parliamentary Affairs*, vol. 46, no. 2, 1993, p. 229.

55 Portelli, 'Le référendum sur l'Union européenne', p. 8.

56 On the 'democratic centralism' of the RPR and the emergence of factions, see A. Knapp, '*Un parti comme les autres*: Jacques Chirac and the Rally for the Republic', in A. Cole (ed.), *French Political Parties in Transition* (Aldershot, Dartmouth, 1990), pp. 164–71.

57 P. Séguin, *Discours pour la France* (Paris, Grasset, 1992), p. 17.

58 Ibid., pp. 9–81. For a detailed exposition of Séguin's anti-Maastricht stance, see also M.-F. Garaud and P. Séguin, *De l'Europe en général et de la France en particulier* (Paris, Le Pré aux Clercs, 1992).

59 C. Pasqua, *Que demande le peuple* . . . (Paris, Albin Michel, 1992), pp. 23–40, 70–74, 213–15.

60 *Le Monde*, 23 June 1992.

61 Ibid., 7 July 1992.

62 See Portelli, 'Le référendum sur l'Union européenne', p. 11; SOFRES, *L'état de l'opinion 1993* (Paris, Seuil, 1993), p. 86; *Le Monde*, 22 September 1992.

63 SOFRES, *L'état de l'opinion 1993*, p. 86.

64 Criddle, 'The French referendum', p. 238.

65 SOFRES, *L'état de l'opinion 1993*, pp. 98, 100.

66 See *Le Monde*, 23, 24, 25 September 1992.

67 The 1993 manifesto pledged allegiance to the Maastricht Treaty, promising the pursuit of European unification through greater monetary and political co-operation with Germany. It reiterated the call for a common security and defence policy within the framework of the Atlantic Alliance, and for enlargement of the European Union to the countries of Central and Eastern Europe (RPR–UDF, *Le Projet de l'Union pour la France*, 1993, pp. 20–1).

68 See P. Jarreau, 'Les européennes, dernière ligne droite avant la présidentielle de 95', *Revue politique et parlementaire*, vol. 96. no. 970, 1994, p. 18.

69 *Projet européen RPR/UDF* (Elections européennes 1994).

108 *James Shields*

70 *Le Monde*, 9 April 1994.

71 *Libératlon*, 8 April 1994.

72 Against 14.5 per cent (fifteen seats) for the Socialist list, 12 per cent (thirteen seats) for Bernard Tapie's 'Energie Radicale' and 6.9 per cent (seven seats) for the Communist list (results as published in *Le Monde*, 15 June 1994).

73 *Le Monde*, 14 June 1994.

74 See the CSA exit poll published in *Libération*, 14 June 1994. Without the presence of a de Villiers list in 1989, an estimated 16 per cent of RPR sympathizers had transferred their vote to the FN; in 1994, the figure dropped to some 4 per cent. See SOFRES, *L'état de l'opinion 1990*, p. 181; *Libération*, 14 June 1994.

75 BVA exit poll, published in *Le Monde*, 14 June 1994.

76 *Projet européen RPR/UDF* (Elections européennes 1994), p. 3.

77 The RPR's decision (criticized by UDF leaders) to go back on its electoral undertaking was prompted by resistance within the party to joining the Christian Democratic, pro-federalist European People's Party. With the UDF's Yves Galland joining the Liberal, Democratic and Reformist group, the twenty-eight MEPs from the RPR and UDF were spread, once again, across three different parliamentary groups. See *Le Monde*, 8, 9, 12, 14 July 1994.

78 The coexistence of different tendencies within the party has not fostered a culture of doctrinal debate, despite the granting of the right to form officially recognized *courants*. The RPR remains, in the tradition of previous Gaullist parties, a movement 'designed for winning power rather than debating policy' (Knapp, *'Un parti comme les autres'*, p. 174).

79 P.A. Gourevitch, 'Gaullism abandoned, or the costs of success', in W.G. Andrews and S. Hoffmann (eds), *The Fifth Republic at Twenty* (Albany, State University of New York Press, 1981), p. 114.

80 *Le Monde*, 15 January 1983.

81 See M. Meimeth, 'France gets closer to NATO', *The World Today*, May 1994, pp. 84–6.

82 J. Baudouin, '"Gaullisme" et "chiraquisme": réflexions autour d'un adultère', *Pouvoirs*, no. 28, 1984, pp. 59–60.

83 See on this point Saint-Ouen, 'Les partis politiques français et l'Europe', pp. 205–26. For the FN's express appeal to 'Gaullist' legitimacy, see Le Pen, *L'espoir*, pp. 98, 99.

84 See *Le Monde*, 2 June 1989 and 27 March 1990.

85 Blot had been director of the RPR secretary-general's office and president of the right-wing *Club de l'horloge* think-tank, while Charbonnel was a prominent left-wing Gaullist and former assistant secretary-general of the UDR.

86 J. Baudouin, 'Le "moment néo-libéral" du RPR. Essai d'interprétation', *Revue française de science politique*, vol. 40, no. 6, 1990, pp. 830–44.

87 See *Le Monde. Dossiers et documents* (June 1979), *Les premières élections européennes*, pp. 52–3; RPR, *Le renouveau. Pacte RPR pour la France* [1985–86], p. 105.

88 F. Haegel, 'Mémoire, héritage, filiation. Dire le gaullisme et se dire gaulliste au RPR', *Revue française de science politique*, vol. 40, no. 6, 1990, pp. 864–79. See also on this question H. Portelli, 'La résistible ascension du libéral-conservatisme', *Revue politique et parlementaire*, vol. 90, no. 935, 1988, pp. 23–8.

89 Knapp, *'Un parti comme les autres'*, p. 164. See also Baudouin, 'Le "moment néo-libéral" du RPR', pp. 834–5.

90 P.M. Williams, *Crisis and Compromise: Politics in the Fourth Republic* (London, Longman, 1964), p. 132.

91 On the influence of the American 'model' on party leaders such as Juppé and Toubon, see P. Fysh, 'Gaullism today', *Parliamentary Affairs*, vol. 46, no. 3, 1993, pp. 401–2.

92 SOFRES, *Opinion publique 1985*, pp. 231–6, 253–62.

SELECT BIBLIOGRAPHY

80
Appleton, A., 'Maastricht and the French party system: domestic implications of the treaty referendum', *French Politics and Society*, vol. 10, no. 4, 1992, pp. 1–18.

Bahu-Leyser, D., *De Gaulle, les Français et l'Europe*, Paris, Presses Universitaires de France, 1981.

Baudouin, J., '"Gaullisme" et "chiraquisme". Réflexions autour d'un adultère', *Pouvoirs*, no. 28, 1984, pp. 53–66.

Baudouin, J., 'Le "moment néo-libéral" du RPR. Essai d'interprétation', *Revue française de science politique*, vol. 40, no. 6, 1990, pp. 830–43.

Bodenheimer, S.J., *Political Union: A Microcosm of European Politics 1960–1966*, Leyden, Sijthoff, 1967.

Cerny, P., *The Politics of Grandeur: Ideological Aspects of De Gaulle's Foreign Policy*, Cambridge, Cambridge University Press, 1980.

Charlot, J., *Le phénomène gaulliste*, Paris, Fayard, 1970.

Charlot, J., 'Tactique et stratégie du RPR dans l'opposition', *Pouvoirs*, no. 28, 1984, pp. 35–46.

Crandall Hollick, J., 'Direct elections to the European Parliament: the French debate', *The World Today*, December 1977, pp. 472–80.

Crandall Hollick, J., 'The European election of 1979 in France: a masked ball for 1981', *Parliamentary Affairs*, vol. 32, no. 4, 1979, pp. 459–69.

Criddle, B., 'The French referendum on the Maastricht Treaty, September 1992', *Parliamentary Affairs*, vol. 46, no. 2, 1993, pp. 228–38.

Formesyn, R., 'Europeanisation and the pursuit of national interests', in V. Wright (ed.), *Continuity and Change in France*, London, Allen and Unwin, 1984, pp. 219–43.

Fysh, P., 'Gaullism today', *Parliamentary Affairs*, vol. 46, no. 3, 1993, pp. 399–414.

Garaud, M.-F. and Séguin, P., *De l'Europe en général et de la France en particulier*, Paris, Le Pré aux Clercs, 1992.

Guyomarch, A. and Machin, H., 'A history of hesitations on the road to Maastricht', *French Politics and Society*, vol. 10, no. 4, 1992, pp. 60–80.

Haegel, F., 'Mémoire, héritage, filiation. Dire le gaullisme et se dire gaulliste au RPR', *Revue française de science politique*, vol. 40, no. 6, 1990, pp. 864–79.

Hainsworth, P., 'France', in J. Lodge (ed.), *The 1989 Election of the European Parliament*, London, Macmillan, 1990, pp. 126–44.

Jouve, E., *Le général de Gaulle et la construction de l'Europe (1940–1966)*, Paris, Librairie générale de droit et de jurisprudence, 1967, 2 vols.

Knapp, A., '*Un parti comme les autres*: Jacques Chirac and the Rally for the Republic', in A. Cole (ed.), *French Political Parties in Transition*, Aldershot, Dartmouth, 1990, pp. 140–84.

Pasqua, C., *Que demande le peuple . . .* , Paris, Albin Michel, 1992.

Portelli, H., 'Le référendum sur l'Union européenne', *Regards sur l'actualité*, no. 184, 1992, pp. 3–12.

Reif, K., 'France', in K. Reif (ed.), *Ten European Elections: Campaigns and Results of the 1979/81 First Direct Elections to the European Parliament*, Aldershot, Gower, 1985, pp. 85–104.

Saint-Ouen, F., 'Les partis politiques français et l'Europe. Système politique et fonctionnement du discours', *Revue française de science politique*, vol. 36, no. 2, 1986, pp. 205–26.

Saint-Ouen, F., 'Le RPR est-il devenu européen?', *Revue politique et parlementaire*, vol. 90, no. 933, 1988, pp. 51–4.

Séguin, P., *Discours pour la France*, Paris, Grasset, 1992.

Stevens, A., 'France', in J. Lodge (ed.), *Direct Elections to the European Parliament 1984*, London, Macmillan, 1986, pp. 92–116.

PARTY DOCUMENTATION

RPR, *L'Europe, une volonté*, 1984

RPR, *Le renouveau. Pacte RPR pour la France*, s.d. [1985–86]

RPR–UDF, *Plate-forme pour gouverner ensemble*, 1986

RPR–UDF, *Pour une Europe unie* (plate-forme RPR–UDF pour l'Europe), 1989

RPR, *La France en mouvement* (projet pour la France du Rassemblement pour la République, adopté par le Congrès du 27 octobre 1991)

RPR–UDF, *Le projet de l'Union pour la France* (Elections législatives mars 1993)

RPR–UDF, *Projet européen RPR/UDF* (Elections européennes 1994)

6 The British Labour Party

Stephen George and Deborah Haythorne

The policy of the British Labour Party on the European Community (EC) has swung between outright opposition and wholehearted approval. This chapter will first chart the often tortuous course of the party's attitude on the European issue, and then try to find explanations for the sometimes rapid changes of policy.

LABOUR'S CHANGING ATTITUDE TO EUROPEAN INTEGRATION

Labour was in office immediately after the Second World War, when the first steps were taken towards closer European co-operation. However, the Labour government led by Clement Attlee opposed Britain playing any role in the creation of a federal Europe, either through the evolution in a federal direction of the Council of Europe or through participation in the European Coal and Steel Community.[1] When a Conservative government applied for membership in 1961, the then leader of the Labour Party, Hugh Gaitskell, spoke against membership as the betrayal of a thousand years of history.

Labour won the 1964 general election with a narrow majority under its new leader, Harold Wilson, who appeared to share the view that membership of the EC was undesirable. By the 1966 election, however, the Labour Party manifesto mandated the party to join the European Economic Community (EEC) 'provided essential British and Commonwealth interests are safeguarded'.[2] The application that was subsequently made by Wilson's government was vetoed by the French president, de Gaulle.

In the 1970 election, the Labour Party was committed to joining the EC in principle, but lost the election to the 'European' Edward Heath, who became the Conservative prime minister and subsequently applied for admission to the EC in 1971. Wilson, as Leader of the Opposition, criticized the terms of entry negotiated by Heath in 1972, and Labour committed itself to renegotiate them and to place the new terms before the British people for their judgement. By April 1972, the decision had been reached to do this in a referendum, and the October 1974 manifesto promised to give the British people the final say on membership of the EC.

Following victory in the 1974 election, these commitments were honoured. The terms were renegotiated and put to the British people in 1975 in a referendum which resulted in a large majority for entry from the country as a whole, although many members of the Labour Party had joined the campaign for a negative vote.[3]

Despite the referendum result, the Labour governments of Wilson and, after 1976, James Callaghan continued to be less than enthusiastic members of the EC.[4]

After the party lost office in 1979, and the anti-EC Michael Foot replaced Callaghan as leader in 1980, the party's attitude towards Europe became increasingly hostile. In November 1980 the Labour Party conference passed a resolution advocating withdrawal from the EC without a referendum, and a commitment to withdraw from the EC was included in the manifesto for the 1983 general election.

But after another humiliating defeat in that election, Labour was forced to re-examine a whole range of policies, including withdrawal from the EC. The election of Neil Kinnock as party leader to replace Michael Foot in 1983 initiated a new phase in Labour's attitude on this controversial issue.

In 1984 Labour Party policy towards Europe was unclear. The rhetorical calls for withdrawal became fainter, but outright demands for a policy of integration within the EC were not yet being heard in the mainstream of Labour politics. An article by Neil Kinnock in *New Socialist* at this time best sums up the wariness many on the left felt towards this issue:

> Britain's future, like our past and present, lies with Europe. But for us as socialists, it will still only lie within the EEC if the Common Market can be transformed to measure up to our wider vision of Europe's own future.[5]

Stephen Tindale believes there were two phases to Labour's European conversion.[6] The period 1983–87 marked the first phase, which reflected the feeling, outlined above, that while it was no longer electorally feasible to advocate withdrawal, there was not much enthusiasm for the EC either. The end of this first phase followed the third successive defeat at the polls when Labour's policy on Europe was blamed as part of the reason for defeat.

The 1984 European election manifesto reflected the ambiguity. It acknowledged that Britain had to remain in the EC, but insisted that the powers transferred to the European Parliament in the European Communities Act (1972) be repatriated. Such an unrealistic condition was incompatible with membership of the EC.

The 1987 Labour Party manifesto contained only three sentences regarding the issue of the EC:

> Labour's aim is to work constructively with our EEC partners to promote economic expansion and combat unemployment. However we will stand up for British interests within the European Community and will seek to put an end to the abuses and scandals of the Common Agricultural Policy. We shall, like other member countries, reject EEC interference with our policy for national recovery and renewal.[7]

This amazingly short statement fell short of either condemnation of membership or wholehearted approval.

Indeed, it was not until what Tindale describes as the second phase, from 1987, that a marked change occurred in Labour's European policy; but when it came it was a very significant change. The annual conference in October 1987 established a series of policy reviews. Every policy of the movement was examined, and each review contained a European dimension.[8] The overall thrust of these policy reviews legitimated the conversion of Labour to Europe.[9]

As a result, in the 1989 elections to the European Parliament, Labour was able to present itself as the European party and gained forty-five seats (40.2 per cent of the vote), a clear victory against the Conservatives' thirty-two seats (34.8 per cent).[10] At the Labour Party conference later in that year, John Smith, the shadow chancellor, persuaded the party to commit itself to entering the Exchange Rate Mechanism (ERM) of the European Monetary System.

The party also swung around to enthusiastic support for the idea of a social dimension to the EC. At the 1988 TUC conference held in Bournemouth, Jacques Delors, the President of the European Commission, received a standing ovation from the trades union audience for stating that the Single Market should benefit each and every citizen in the Community.[11] This, Delors believed, had to be achieved by the improvement of living and working conditions of workers within Europe.

When the Maastricht Treaty was debated in the House of Commons, early in 1992, the Labour Party opposed it only on the grounds that the Conservative government had insisted on the Social Chapter being taken out of the draft treaty and placed in a separate protocol, of which Britain was not a signatory. Labour officially supported the Treaty, including the Social Chapter. With the emergence of serious divisions in the Conservative Party on the issue of the EC, Labour was seen at this time as being more European than the Conservatives.

The conversion appeared complete. Yet after Labour's fourth election defeat in 1992, doubts were again raised about its conversion to Europe. Nevertheless, after the disappointment of defeat in the general election and the resignation of Kinnock, who was fully associated with Labour's conversion, the issue was reopened. One of the contenders in the campaign for the party leadership in June 1992, Bryan Gould, argued that Labour's support of the ERM made it difficult to take advantage of the failures of the government's economic policies. However, the election was won by the pro-European John Smith; and the indications were that the membership of the party was also by this time converted to support for the EC.[12]

EXPLANATIONS OF LABOUR'S POSITIONS ON THE EC

To explain the development of Labour's position on the EC it is first necessary to understand the traditions and culture of the party, because it was against this background that the debate was conducted. These traditions were very different from those of continental socialist parties. It is also necessary to understand how the issue of membership of the EC became tied up with factional power struggles within the party.

Until Britain joined the EC, the Labour Party, despite its membership of the Socialist International, had very little contact with continental socialist parties, and Labour's thinking owed little to continental socialist thought. The Labour Party was strongly influenced by the British tradition of non-conformist Christianity. It was rooted in the British working class, who formed the basis of its electorate, and specifically in the trades union movement. Indeed, unlike most other European socialist parties, the Labour Party was a product of the trades union movement.

This particular national history made it very difficult for Labour to adjust to the EC. The British working class were fully imbued with the spirit of imperialism, and the attitudes that were inculcated by imperialism: a sense of national superiority, and an assumption of a privileged position and a duty to spread enlightenment to others. These attitudes expressed themselves within the Labour movement in four ways: first in a strong sense of nationalism; second in the form of an attachment to the British and their kith and kin in the Commonwealth; third in a sense that Britain could show the way to others less fortunate; and fourth in attachment to a wider internationalism than was implied by the ideal of a united Europe.[13] It is therefore not surprising that the British Labour Party's initial attitude towards the EC was less than enthusiastic.

The attitudes of nationalism and attachment to Empire and Commonwealth that were prevalent within the Labour Party were typified by the speech made by the leader Hugh Gaitskell at the party conference of 1962. In rejecting British membership of the EC as a betrayal of 'a thousand years of history', Gaitskell constantly referred to the fear, widely felt within the Labour movement, of ties with the Commonwealth being loosened.

It is enlightening to examine the language used by Gaitskell. He spoke of Britain as the 'mother country' of the Commonwealth and stated that the link between Britain and other Commonwealth countries had to be 'protected' and 'safeguarded'. He expressed the fear that Britain would become a 'province of Europe'.[14] The speech, nationalistic and paternalistic in tone, found echoes throughout the Labour Party.

This speech was made in the context of a divided party which since its defeat in the 1959 general election had been tearing itself apart over a proposal from the leadership to abandon the commitment to the nationalization of key industries, and over the issue of unilateral nuclear disarmament. Not for the last time, rejection of membership of the EC became a useful unifying issue around which the Party could unite across its left–right divisions.

However, Gaitskell's attitude was also based on a pragmatic assessment of the national interest. Britain, a trading nation, relied on the markets of the Commonwealth not only to export, but also to import food. What was seen as a protectionist EC was not, it was felt, in the best interests of working-class people in Britain. Consequently, criticism was levelled at the Conservatives' unsuccessful attempt to join the EC in 1961. Protecting the national interest required steering Britain away from a European alliance and concentrating on the traditional trading relationship with the Commonwealth partners.

Protecting the Commonwealth was one of the fundamental conditions on which the Labour government entered into the unsuccessful membership negotiations of 1966. It was also one of the central objections of Labour in opposition to the terms of entry negotiated by the Conservative government of Edward Heath in 1972.

Even as late as 1975, during the renegotiation of the terms of entry, Harold Wilson made protection for agricultural exports to Britain from Australia and New Zealand one of the key issues at the summit meeting in Dublin to finalize the new terms. His statement that he had more relatives in New Zealand than he had in Huddersfield (his home town) struck exactly the right note with the British working classes: protecting the interests of 'our own people'. Large-scale emigration in the 1950s and 1960s from Britain to the white Commonwealth, mainly from working-class families, had reinforced this sense of kinship.

However, while Wilson talked of protecting the Commonwealth, he oversaw its decline. Britain's reciprocal markets shrank and the Commonwealth's importance declined to become merely symbolic. In its acceptance of membership at this stage, Labour's leadership can again be seen as acting in what was perceived to be the national interest. After the Suez debacle of 1956, Britain was forced to accept its declining position in the world and the grave problems that faced the British economy. Both Labour and the Conservatives were confronted with the reality of Britain as a declining power.

Following Labour's victory in the 1966 general election, Harold Wilson was able to persuade a significant section of his party to support entry into the EC on the grounds of economics: new markets, he promised, would be available to Britain upon membership. Labour Party members were sold the idea of Europe as a pragmatic necessity, but the conversion was by no means wholehearted.

As well as the commitment to the Commonwealth, there was also a commitment among the leadership of the Labour Party to protecting the Atlantic alliance with the United States in order to remain in the centre of the international stage. Loyalty to the Atlantic alliance was believed by the leadership to be incompatible with British membership of the EC.

The relationship between Britain and the United States remained special to Labour as much as to the Conservatives. Harold Wilson (prime minister 1964–70 and 1974–76) and James Callaghan (prime minister 1976–79) were both instinctive Atlanticists, and the Labour Party, until possibly as late as the 1980s, firmly believed that Britain had a leading role to play within the world, albeit as a junior partner to the United States. Such an attitude, which was prevalent within the British labour movement, seemed to be incompatible with the view that Britain should play a full and integral role within the EC. But soon after coming to office in 1964, Wilson, like Harold Macmillan before him, was persuaded that membership would not damage the alliance, and that the United States actually wanted Britain to become a member.

Nevertheless, divisions within the party continued during the 1966–70 Labour government. Because of his stance against membership of the EC, Peter Shore, a strong anti-European in the tradition of Gaitskell, was demoted by Prime Minister Wilson from his position as secretary of state for economic affairs to minister without portfolio. The majority, however, were persuaded by the advocacy of membership by Wilson and by the deputy leader of the party, George Brown. David Owen, a pro-European who was eventually to leave the party over the issue of EC membership, revealed that:

> All Wilson's political skills as Prime Minister and some of George Brown's oratorical skills had been deployed to persuade the majority of the Labour Party to subscribe to the view that entry was necessary.[15]

At this stage the Labour leadership was convinced of the necessity for Britain to join the EC, but the party membership, including significant sections of the parliamentary party, were unhappy with the idea for reasons that were deeply rooted in Labour's culture.

Opposition within the Labour Party to membership of the EC focused on a number of issues: the loss of sovereignty; the possibility that membership would increase unemployment and lead to a fall in industrial production; the high price of food under the Common Agricultural Policy; the unfairness to Britain of the then current budgetary arrangements; and the claim by many on the left that the EC was not a vehicle for socialist change. The sentiments expressed by one leading anti-marketeer were widely shared in the party:

I loathe the Common Market. It's bureaucratic and centralised, there's no political discussion, officials control Ministers, and it just has a horrible flavour about it.[16]

Into this context emerged a factional struggle for domination of the party. After defeat in the 1970 election, a new left analysis emerged of what had gone wrong, concluding that the government had failed to commit itself to genuine socialist goals. This analysis was particularly associated with the former cabinet minister Tony Benn, who in opposition emerged as the leading figure on the left.

The project of the left was to take control of the party and ensure that policies were enacted that would move Britain towards some form of state-directed capitalism, described as socialism by its advocates. Such a programme was unacceptable to the social democrats who occupied many of the leadership positions in the party, and it would probably not have received backing from a majority of the parliamentary party, although it was supported by a number of constituency parties and by enough of the large trades unions to make its imposition feasible.

The attraction for the left of the issue of membership of the EC was that it offered them the possibility of building a majority coalition against the leadership, because there were serious doubts about the EC among members of the party who did not support the more radical economic policies of the left. Thus there was the potential for a coalition that the left could lead and utilize to strengthen its position within the party. It was also an issue that might be used to lever out of key positions leading social democrats such as Roy Jenkins, deputy leader between 1970 and 1972, because the necessity of membership of the EC was an issue on which many of the social democrats felt extremely strongly.

Wilson's commitment to renegotiate the terms of entry to the EC, made when in opposition in 1970–74, can be seen as a tactical device to hold the party together. The decision to hold a referendum was a high-risk tactic to silence the left on the EC issue, and at first it appeared to have worked. However, the refusal of either Wilson or Callaghan to embrace the ideal of European unity and to give a strong lead to the party in this direction allowed the old cultural distrust to continue, and allowed the left to return to the issue again after the 1979 election defeat.

The coincidence of British membership of the EC with the onset of further economic problems fed prejudices within the Labour Party against membership, and in 1980–81 the left succeeded in using the issue to isolate leading social democrats in a way that drove them to leave the party. In August 1980 David Owen, William Rodgers and Shirley Williams, three leading members of the social democratic wing of the Labour Party, published an open letter in which they were critical of the drift of the party to the left. They were dubbed 'the Gang of Three' by their critics and by the media.

In January 1981, following the election of the left-wing and anti-EC Michael Foot as leader of the Labour Party, these three joined with the former Labour cabinet minister, Roy Jenkins, who had just returned to British politics after four years as President of the European Commission, in setting up a Council for Social Democracy. In March 1981 they announced the formation of an independent Social Democratic Party. The importance of the EC in these developments was clearly documented by David Owen: 'Europe was the first issue that was really divisive, and it was Europe that brought the Gang of Three together.'[17] After the departure of the chief defenders of the EC, it became possible for the left to get a commitment to withdrawal from the EC written into the manifesto for the 1983 general election. By 1983 the victory of the opponents of membership seemed to be complete. Why, then, did Labour shift so dramatically on the issue of Europe in the 1980s?

The implicit assumption, widespread in the British Labour movement, that it had a superior system of socialism on which the rest of world should model itself, became woefully out of date. Labour lost office at the end of the 1970s, and then saw many of the achievements of which the movement was so proud being dismantled. Low unemployment, high welfare and social rights, the prerogative of the trades unions to advise and influence government, all came under attack from Margaret Thatcher's Conservative government after 1979. Yet Labour seemed incapable of wresting power from the Conservatives, while at the same time socialist parties were winning elections and taking office in other European countries.

A change occurred in the thinking of the intellectual left in response to events. Throughout most of the 1970s the left had advocated what was known as the Alternative Economic Strategy, which proposed reconstructing the British industrial base behind a protectionist barrier. In the early 1980s this approach was abandoned because it was decided that it was not possible to implement socialism in isolation. This reorientation of thinking was particularly a result of the experience of the French socialist governments in the early 1980s, which tried unilateral reflationary policies with disastrous results:

> The economy was reflated, the minimum wage doubled and public expenditure increased by 27 per cent. However, France was reflating at a time when the world economy was in recession, and the resulting trade deficit, combined with inflation and a weakening of the franc due to loss of international confidence, forced the government into a humiliating U-turn.[18]

In the course of the 1980s the traditional view of the world system in which the sovereign nation states were all-powerful was coming into conflict with reality. Because of changing world circumstances, governments had to pool their resources and share power on a supranational basis. Ken Livingstone, previously a left-wing opponent of the EC, clarified the feeling of many on the left:

> In a world moving towards more protectionist regional blocs there is little attraction in being on the outside of one of these groups. If Britain pursues a path outside Europe, it will inevitably end up in a totally subordinate role to Japan or more likely the USA. It is better that we should fight instead to reform the EEC with a proper programme of democratic and social reforms, as well as seeking its enlargement to include the whole of Europe and become a common trading bloc with the USSR.[19]

To add to the pro-Europeans' arguments, concern was increasingly expressed about the power of multinational corporations, which could not be dealt with at a national level. Similarly, the issue of the environment, a subject that rose high on the political agenda in the 1980s, clearly could not be dealt with within national borders. It was evident that to tackle both of these problems, supranational controls had to be agreed and adhered to. David Martin, a leading Labour Member of the European Parliament (MEP), argued this case in 1988 in a Fabian pamphlet, a traditional forum for the airing of ideas within the Labour movement.[20]

How far the Labour MEPs played a role in the conversion of Labour towards Europe is a matter of some debate. Stafford Thomas suggested in 1992 that MEPs had little influence on policy in British politics.[21] David Martin, by this time the leader of the British Labour group in the European Parliament, took issue with this argument, claiming that many of the ideas in his 1988 Fabian pamphlet later became official Labour Party policy. In addition, Martin asserted that the three 'Martin Reports', reports of the European Parliament's Institutional Committee for which he acted as *rapporteur*, influenced the Labour Party's policy on economic and monetary union, majority voting on environmental and social policy, a common foreign policy, fundamental rights and freedoms for a citizens' Europe, more say for the regions of the EC, the right of the European Parliament to initiate legislation, and the right of the European Parliament to appoint the president of the Commission. All of these points were subsequently incorporated into Labour Party policy.[22]

How Labour MEPs were themselves converted to the EC is in itself revealing. It is not surprising, given the anti-EC attitude prevalent in the Labour movement in the early 1980s, that MEPs should have reflected this antagonism towards Europe. However, experience changed attitudes. Labour MEPs working alongside their European comrades in the socialist group learned that their aims could be achieved on a European basis. Ann Clwyd, an MEP who subsequently became an MP, outlined her conversion in a House of Commons debate:

> Members of this place who were formerly Members of the European Parliament will remember working with parliamentarians of other nationalities from day to day. I can assure the House that that is a sobering experience. Initially I was opposed to the European Community, but I found after a period as a Member of the European Parliament that there were advantages in working with people of other nationalities from day to day. . . . It had a profound effect on me and it changed my attitudes towards the European Community.[23]

She emphasized the importance of the multinational membership of the socialist group: 'I had an advantage over members of some other groups. That is because the members of the Socialist group worked with parliamentarians from 10 countries.'[24]

Richard Caborn MP, another former MEP, similarly acknowledged the influence his socialist colleagues had on his own conversion:

> Working and socialising with European colleagues, on a day-to-day basis, and hearing their own views of how the European Community can play a part in the aims and aspirations of a socialist, did play a part in my conversion to the workability of a European Community.[25]

Labour Members of the British Parliament increasingly developed links with socialists throughout Europe. The publication *Opportunity Britain* cited 'our strong links with our sister parties in Europe' as an advantage for Labour, making it more able than the Conservatives 'to defend Britain's interests and build a stronger Community'.[26]

The Labour Party recognized that mutual goals could be achieved through the EC. George Robertson MP, in a debate in the House of Commons, stated:

> In discussions with Social Democratic and Socialist colleagues it became clear that their priority is that of the Labour party, which is to use the engine of European economic growth to get our people back to work.[27]

Co-operation and consultation with European colleagues, meant Labour could have a voice again on issues of importance to itself.

The British trades union movement, with declining power as a result of anti-trades union legislation passed by the Thatcher government, began to look to Europe for support in implementing its own agenda.[28] Like Labour MEPs, British trades unionists found that whereas their views were totally ignored in the British arena, they were actively sought in the consensual framework of the EC, and actually influenced policy. Tony Benn outlined the mutual need of the British trades unionists and European integrationists: 'The TUC never gets invited to tea at No. 10 these days, but it is invited to three-course lunches in Brussels because M. Delors needs the TUC.'[29]

Probably the most important influence on the trades unions' conversion to the EC was the issue of the social dimension. The Single European Act, signed in 1986, was criticized by some in the movement for being an instrument of capitalism. Momentum grew for a 'human side' to the Single European Market that the Act would create, and in 1989 the European Commission, in response to such pressures from across Europe, produced a draft Social Chapter of workers' rights. The Social Chapter was eventually signed by all the member states except Britain. Labour MP George Foulkes articulated the views of the majority of his party, and a majority of both socialists and Christian democrats in the rest of Europe on this issue:

> But Europe must be a real community as well as a market. It must be a community of co-operation and diversity. The two concepts of economic efficiency and social justice are complementary. . . . We want a community in which the market works to the advantage of the people, not one in which the people serve the convenience of the market.[30]

The Social Chapter strongly influenced some of the remaining anti-EC factions in the Labour Party into becoming pro-European. It championed the rights of workers, women and pensioners, and it was therefore almost impossible for anyone on the left to oppose it, especially when Mrs Thatcher spoke so vehemently against it. 'Socialism through the back door' was how Thatcher saw the Social Chapter, and some within the Labour movement hoped her prediction would prove to be correct.

Opposition towards the EC never totally disappeared within the parliamentary Labour Party. Tony Benn, Dennis Skinner, Peter Shore and Austin Mitchell were among the better known MPs not to be convinced of the merits of Britain's integration with the rest of Europe; but no one with any real influence in the party's leadership took up the mantle of Euro-opposition throughout the late 1980s and early 1990s.

Mrs Thatcher's increasingly strident attacks on the way that the EC was developing led in November 1990 to her replacement as leader of the Conservative Party by John Major; but not before she had effectively split her party on the issue. The continuing divisions became the greatest weakness of the government, offering Labour an opportunity to make political capital that could not be turned down.

CONCLUSION

The British Labour Party approached the EC from a very distinctive national political tradition in which imperialism and nationalism featured strongly. There were no positive associations with Europe as a concept, and the experience of the early years of British membership, when a world economic crisis affected living conditions in Britain rather badly, reinforced a negative view. There was also considerable resistance to the surrender of national sovereignty, based on the belief that the British democratic tradition offered Labour an opportunity to realize its socialist aspirations in Britain, whereas the EC would act as a constraint on the achievement of those objectives.

Given this cultural context, the issue of whether Britain should even be a member of the EC became an internal political battle ground within the party, utilized by the left wing as a means of attracting support in their efforts to oust the social democrats from leadership positions.

The eventual victory of the left following the 1979 general election, after years of divisive and damaging struggle, contributed directly to the inability of Labour to present itself as a credible alternative party of government to the Conservatives, and in turn led to a reappraisal of policy on the EC. Under Neil Kinnock there was a steady adaptation to accepting the EC not only as a necessity, but eventually as a positive factor that could help Labour to achieve its objectives.

This new approach was fed by the experience of MEPs and trades unionists, who as a result of working within the European Parliament changed their attitudes to it. In the case of the constituency membership, it was helped tremendously by the opposition of Margaret Thatcher to developments in the EC, and particularly to the Social Chapter, which embodied most of the ideals that Labour wished to realize.

By the time that Kinnock stood down in 1992, the party had started to see EC membership as an opportunity rather than as a constraint, and to discuss the issue in terms of the type of Europe that it wanted to see rather than in terms of whether Britain ought to be a member of any type of EC.

When Bryan Gould stood for the leadership in 1992 on a platform that was critical of the EC, he was soundly beaten by the pro-European John Smith. When Smith died suddenly in 1994, none of the candidates to succeed him stood on a platform that was hostile to Europe. Indeed, it would have been exceptionally difficult for them to have done so, given that the leadership election followed hard on the heels of elections to the European Parliament in which Labour gained 42.7 per cent of the vote and sixty-two seats to the Conservatives' 26.9 per cent and only eighteen seats.

In those elections Labour stood on a manifesto that ended with the words: 'a Europe guided by Labour's values of community, opportunity and justice will benefit Britain, her people and her children'.[31] This was a far cry from the days of opposition to British membership. After a long and difficult evolution, Labour had apparently come into line with the positions of other European socialist parties.

NOTES

1 Stephen George, *Britain and European Integration Since 1945* (Oxford, Blackwell, 1991), p. 3.
2 Labour Party Manifesto, 1964, in F.W.S. Craig, *British General Election Manifestos 1900–1974* (London, Macmillan, 1975), p. 310.
3 David Butler and Uwe Kitzinger, *The 1975 Referendum* (London, Macmillan, 1976).
4 Stephen George, *An Awkward Partner: Britain in the European Community* (Oxford, Oxford University Press, 1990), pp. 96–136.

5 Neil Kinnock, 'New Deal for Europe', *New Socialist*, March/April 1984, pp. 9–15.
6 Stephen Tindale 'Learning to love the Market: Labour and the European Community', *Political Quarterly*, vol. 63, no. 3, 1992.
7 Labour Party, *Modern Britain in a Modern World: Labour Party Manifesto 1987*.
8 Martin J. Smith, 'A return to revisionism? The Labour Party's policy review', in Martin J. Smith and Joanna Spear (eds), *The Changing Labour Party* (London, Routledge, 1992), pp. 13–28.
9 Ben Rosamond, 'Labour and the European Community: learning to be European?', *Politics*, vol. 10, no. 2, 1990, p. 42.
10 John Gaffney, 'Labour Party attitudes and policy towards Europe', *Current Politics and Economics of Europe*, vol. 1, nos. 3–4, 1991, pp. 213–39.
11 George, *An Awkward Partner*, p. 193.
12 Patrick Seyd and Paul Whiteley, *Labour's Grass Roots: The Politics of Party Membership* (Oxford, Clarendon Press, 1992), pp. 47–8.
13 Tom Nairn, *The Left Against Europe?* (Harmondsworth, Penguin, 1973), pp. 42–77.
14 Hugh Gaitskell, *Labour and the Common Market*, Text of speech to the Labour Party Conference, 3 October 1962 (London, Labour Party, 1962).
15 David Owen and Kenneth Harris, *Personally Speaking* (London, Weidenfeld and Nicolson, 1987), p. 98.
16 Tony Benn, *Conflicts of Interest: Diaries 1977–1980*, edited by Ruth Winstone (London, Hutchinson, 1990), p. 234.
17 Owen and Harris, *Personally Speaking*, p. 165.
18 Stephen Tindale, 'Learning to love the Market', p. 283.
19 Ken Livingstone, *Livingstone's Labour: A Programme for the Nineties* (London, Unwin Hyman, 1989), p. 237.
20 David Martin, *Bringing Common Sense to the Common Market: A Left Agenda for Europe*, Fabian Tract 525 (London, Fabian Society, 1988).
21 Stafford T. Thomas, 'Assessing MEP influence on British EC policy', *Government and Opposition*, vol. 27, no. 1, 1992, pp. 3–18.
22 David Martin, 'Comment on "Assessing MEP influence on British EC policy" by Stafford T. Thomas', *Government and Opposition*, vol. 27, no. 1, 1992, pp. 23–6.
23 *Hansard* (Commons), 23 April 1986, col. 358.
24 Ibid.
25 Interview with authors, 2 May 1992.
26 Labour Party, *Opportunity Britain* (London, Labour Party, 1991), p. 52.
27 *Hansard* (Commons) 23 April 1986, col. 328.
28 Of course the position was more complicated than this; the trades union movement is not monolithic, and some unions adapted faster and further than others. For a detailed discussion see Ben Rosamond, 'National labour organizations and European integration: British trade unions and 1992', *Political Studies*, vol. 41, no. 3, 1993, pp. 420–34.
29 *Hansard* (Commons) 18 May 1989, col. 546.
30 *Hansard* (Commons) 23 February 1989, col. 1239.
31 Labour Party, *Make Europe work for you: Labour's Election Manifesto for the European Elections, June 1994* (London, 1994).

SELECT BIBLIOGRAPHY

Benn, T., *Conflicts of Interests: Diaries 1977–1980*, ed. Ruth Winstone, London, Hutchinson, 1990.
Bilski, R., 'The Common Market and the growing strength of Labour's left wing', *Government and Opposition*, vol. 12, no. 3, 1997, pp. 306–71.
Butler, D. and Kitzinger, U., *The 1975 Referendum*, London, Macmillan, 1976.
Byrd, P., 'The Labour Party and the European Community, 1970–1975', *Journal of Common Market Studies*, vol. 13, 1975, pp. 469–83.
Craig, F.W.S., *British General Election Manifestos 1900–1974*, London, Macmillan, 1975.
Gaffney, J., 'Labour Party attitudes and policy towards Europe', *Current Politics and Economics of Europe*, vol. 1, nos. 3/4. 1991, pp. 213–39.

George, S., *An Awkward Partner: Britain in the European Community*, Oxford, Oxford University Press, 1990.

George, S., *Britain and European Integration since 1945*, Oxford, Blackwell, 1991.

Grahl, J. and Teague, P., 'The British Labour Party and the European Community', *Political Quarterly*, vol. 59, no. 1, pp. 72–85.

Kinnock, N., 'New deal for Europe', *New Socialist*, March/April 1984, pp. 9–15.

Livingstone, K., *Livingstone's Labour: A Programme for the Nineties*, London, Unwin Hyman, 1989.

Martin, D., *Bringing Common Sense to the Common Market*, Fabian Tract 525, London, Fabian Society, 1988.

Martin, D., 'Comment on "Assessing MEP influence on British EC policy"', *Government and Opposition*, vol. 27, no. 1, 1992, pp. 23–6.

Nairn, T., *The Left Against Europe?*, Harmondsworth, Penguin, 1973.

Newman, M., *Socialism and European Unity: The Dilemma of the Left in Britain and France*, London, Junction Books, 1983.

Owen D. and Harris, K., *Personally Speaking*, London, Weidenfeld and Nicolson, 1987.

Robins, L., *The Reluctant Party: Labour and the EEC, 1961–1975*, Ormskirk, G. W. and A. Hesketh, 1979.

Rosamond, B., 'Labour and the European Community: learning to be European?', *Politics*, vol. 10, no. 2, 1990, pp. 41–8.

Seyd, P. and Whiteley, P., *Labour's Grass Roots: The Politics of Party Membership*, Oxford, Clarendon Press, 1992.

Smith, M.J. and Spear, J. (eds), *The Changing Labour Party*, London, Routledge, 1992.

Thomas, S.T., 'Assessing MEP influence on British EC policy', *Government and Opposition*, vol. 27, no. 1, 1992, pp. 3–18.

Tindale, S., 'Learning to love the Market: Labour and the European Community', *Political Quarterly*, vol. 63, no. 3, 1992, pp. 276–300.

Wheaton, M., 'The Labour Party and Europe, 1950–71', in G. Ionescu (ed.), *The New Politics of European Integration*, London, Macmillan, 1972.

7 The British Conservative Party

Peter Morris

INTRODUCTION: THE CONSERVATIVE PARTY AND BRITISH POLITICS

The Conservative and Unionist Party has dominated British electoral politics for over a hundred years and is one of the most durable political organizations in twentieth-century Europe. Conservatives have formed the largest single group in all but six of the twenty Parliaments elected since the end of the First World War and by 1994 Conservative prime ministers had resided in 10 Downing Street for sixty-three years this century. In 1992 the party won a fourth consecutive term in office, a victory that has no precedent in modern times and meant that by the end of the new Parliament the Conservatives would have been in office continuously for eighteen years, the longest period of one-party government since the 1832 Reform Act. In part, this success reflects the nature of the British electoral system. At no time since 1945 has the Conservative Party won a majority of the total votes cast in Great Britain and its electoral base is increasingly concentrated in the more prosperous regions of England.[1] Yet its electoral performance is by any standards, national or international, impressive. In 1992 the Conservatives won the highest number of votes ever obtained by a party in a British general election.

Although the resilience of British Conservatism is the result of many factors, one key element in its enduring success is the moderation of its doctrinal ambitions. Ever since the Duke of Wellington claimed in 1846, during the debate on the repeal of the Corn Laws, that the continuity of the Queen's government took precedence over any particular policy, most British Conservatives have been less concerned with realizing grand strategies than with occupying power so as to preserve their influence within the existing social and institutional order. They possess what Jim Bulpitt calls a 'governing code' rather than an ideological creed and are much more concerned, in J.H. Grainger's words, with what is to be done now than with theory.[2] Two contemporary Conservative intellectuals, and Members of Parliament, have made the same point. Robert Jackson asserts that 'to all ideas and values, including from time to time its own ... [Conservatism] opposes a realism which directs attention to facts, interests and the pressure of events' and David Willetts says that Tory principles emerge from political practice.[3] From outside the party, the political scientist Andrew Gamble observes that 'rationalist Conservatism in the grand Continental manner has never flourished in the ranks of the English Tories, who have generally preferred scepticism and philistine common sense'.[4] British Conservatism differs from the traditions of its continental counterparts in a number of ways. It has been less suspicious of parliamentary liberalism, less attracted to the politics of heroic leadership and, although committed to the defence of the established church, less interested in using the state to impose religious uniformity on society.

The consequences of a concern with the realities of power, and with the politics of presence (what Bulpitt calls 'being there') are clear. Conservatives have been prepared, as between 1915 and 1922, to serve in coalition governments under non-Conservative leaders and, when faced in 1974 with removal from office, to share power with another party. The will to govern led the party after the Second World War to accept the parameters of the new social and economic agenda laid down by the Labour government and, in 1990, to ditch Margaret Thatcher, its most dynamic leader this century, once her survival in office appeared to threaten its electoral prospects.

Doctrinal flexibility does not, however, mean that there is no corpus of values and attitudes to which all Conservatives appeal. The very fact that rival groups compete over the proper definition of what constitutes Conservative policy shows that ideas and traditions are important to the party's self-image. In the mid-nineteenth century, and again in the early 1900s, the party split over the issue of free trade versus protectionism and in the early 1930s there were internal tensions over the contours of foreign and defence policy. More recently, the celebrated disputes of the 1980s between 'wets' and 'dries' or, to use another cliché, between 'one nation' Tories and 'Thatcherite' liberals reflected rival traditions within the party about the proper management of industrial society that date back to the early nineteenth century, with each side claiming to articulate 'true' Conservative principles. We will see in this chapter that the recent intra-party conflicts over Britain's relations with the European Union derive from competing interpretations of what Conservative principles and priorities require.

Among the shared principles of Conservatism can be identified the following propositions:

1 Capitalism is the only efficient form of economic organization and private property is the only guarantee of a free society.
2 The United Kingdom is defined by its political unity, which transcends its multinationalism and sociological diversity and provides the basis for a state patriotism based on the Union of the four countries of England, Scotland, Wales and Northern Ireland. The Conservative Party regards itself as the defender of this patriotism of the Union – hence the inclusion of 'Unionist' in its title.
3 The constitutional order consolidated in the nineteenth century, namely, sovereignty of crown in Parliament and party-based government legitimized by free competitive elections, is the proper way to organize the United Kingdom's political affairs.
4 A strong state is essential to protect the national community from potential threats to its cohesion from inside and outside. The former requires a strong police force, the latter strong military defences and – since the late 1940s – an independent nuclear deterrent and membership of the Atlantic alliance.
5 The British state should not attempt to impose a centrally determined social order on the individually defined goals of its citizens. Government has a role to play in guaranteeing social cohesion and minimum welfare but should not try to interfere with the inevitability of human inequality.

To these principles can be added the governing code identified by Bulpitt and an internal political culture that emphasizes the leadership's right to determine the party's policy choices and to expect the loyalty of party members. The Conservative Party has rarely known the structured factionalism that exists in many left-wing parties and its internal policy conflicts have usually been over single issues. The party's claim to provide more competent government than its opponents, be they the Liberal Party in the late 1880s and 1920s or the Labour Party in the 1980s, has always been buttressed by congratulatory references to its unity. When the party chairman Sir Norman Fowler told the 1992 party conference that unity was the secret of Conservatism's success, he was giving voice to a potent myth.

THE 'EUROPEAN QUESTION' AND CONSERVATIVE POLITICS

The timing of Fowler's reference to party unity is significant. It was a response to an outbreak of internal conflict over a major policy area that has no parallel in the party's post-1945 history and derived from the Conservative government's attempt to win parliamentary approval for the treaty establishing a European Union negotiated by Prime Minister John Major at Maastricht in December 1991. By summer 1993, Major's political authority was under severe challenge from a section of the Conservative parliamentary party and the issue of Europe appeared to threaten not only his own survival in office but the future of the party itself. Only by making ratification of the Maastricht Treaty a matter of the government's continuation in office – and therefore appealing to the basic Conservative goal of 'being there' – was the Major government able to stay in office. Eight months later, in March 1994, the leadership once again came under severe pressure from inside the party over the question of qualified majority voting in the Council of Ministers of an enlarged European Union. The European question was not, moreover, a new one. The departure from office of senior party figures like Michael Heseltine and Leon Brittan (1986), Nigel Lawson (1989), Nicholas Ridley, Geoffrey Howe and Margaret Thatcher (1990) all stemmed from intra-party disagreements about the proper nature of British involvement in the institutions of the European Community. Nor is hostility to the official party line restricted, as is sometimes suggested, to an older generation of hitherto marginal Conservative politicians. The so-called Maastricht rebels or Eurosceptics of 1992 numbered, alongside three former party chairmen, MPs and activists whose political careers dated from the 1980s.

To say that the European question has presented the Conservative Party with serious problems is thus to state the obvious. The statement, however, raises more questions than it answers. In the first place it ignores the fact that, as we shall see, Conservative leaders were the driving force behind all the decisions whereby the United Kingdom linked itself to the European institutional structures and policies created by the 1957 Treaty of Rome, the 1985 Single European Act and the Maastricht Treaty. Second, it ignores the ease with which earlier Conservative leaders were able to overcome internal opposition to their policy of support for British membership of the European Community, to present Conservatism, with some justification, as the 'party of Europe' and to contrast the party's overall unity on European questions with the bitter conflict they provoked in the Labour Party. Third, it raises the linked questions of why the loyalty imperative which is, as we have seen, so important in the party's governing code weakened under the pressure of European issues.

This chapter aims to consider these three issues by studying British Conservatism's European record in the light of its principles and practices outlined earlier. The chapter looks first at the Conservative record on Europe in the period 1945–86 and then at the years that followed the implementation of the Single European Act. Our analysis focuses primarily on the party elite (leadership and MPs), for it is here that the key debates have occurred. This is not to deny the existence of grass-roots divisions over European issues, the anti-Europeanism that periodically erupts on the floor of Conservative conferences and the plethora of party pressure groups based around rival views of Europe. But it is suggested that such tensions are a response to elite divisions rather than their cause and that they originate within the party elite.

CONSERVATIVES AND EUROPEAN COMMUNITY MEMBERSHIP

Like their Labour opponents, most Conservatives refused to support the post-1945 efforts of many politicians and publicists in Western Europe to establish common European institutions. It is true that, while in opposition from 1945 to 1951, the party leader Churchill made a series of speeches urging European Union and even admitted, in his 1950 book 'Europe Unite' that a pooling of national sovereignty might be necessary.[5] Prominent party figures like Macmillan, Thorneycroft, Sandys, Maxwell-Fyfe and Boothby also gave support to movements for European unity. But once back in office in 1951, the Conservatives rejected the idea that Britain should participate in the moves to integrationism represented by the European Coal and Steel Community (1951), the European Defence Community (1954) and the European Economic Community (1957) The party's two most respected authorities, Churchill and Eden, are both identified with declarations that asserted a refusal to link Britain to any form of European integration. Churchill proclaimed that Britain's future depended on its role at the intersection of three international circles of influence – Commonwealth, United States, Europe – and that it must not privilege the latter at the expense of the other two. Eden in 1952 famously declared (to a United States audience) that joining a European federation was 'something we know, in our bones, that we cannot do'.[6]

This assessment of the national interest depended on a continuing belief in Britain's world role, on a confidence in the talents of British diplomacy and on a pride in the virtues of the Westminster model of parliamentary democracy. Not all Conservatives were happy with the new role of privileged, but subordinate, counsellor to the United States that Churchill and Eden seemed to relish after 1945. Very few, however, doubted that Britain was still a world, as well as a European, power and that the British Commonwealth and empire constituted a priceless political and economic asset that could not be sacrificed in the cause of binding ties with Western European states which looked fragile, were prone to support statist economic policies – and in some cases had dubious institutional and historical legitimacy. Confidence in the solidity and superiority of British institutions made the European vision of transcending existing political structures unacceptable.

Thus we see no evidence of any enthusiasm for the kind of supranationalism advocated by the Christian democratic parties which influenced continental conservative parties, and little interest in the creation of a Common Market. The possibility of British membership of the Common Market was not raised by Conservatives in the House of Commons until two backbenchers (Rippon and Boothby) spoke of the dangers of isolation a year after the 1955 Messina Conference opened the way to the signature of the Treaty of Rome. Shortly afterwards, the party's leading think tank, the Bow Group, gave broad (although not total) backing to membership, and a number of younger Conservative MPs tried to muster support within the House of Commons.[7] But the party grass roots remained unimpressed and so too did the leadership. The views of two future champions of Britain's European vocation are in this respect significant. Harold Macmillan told the House of Commons in 1956 that the importance of Commonwealth trade made British membership of the EEC impossible and Edward Heath said at the 1960 party conference that 'we are here with our Commonwealth, with our agriculture, with our well known Parliamentary system and our known attitude to supranational institutions'.[8] The EEC did not feature in the party's 1959 election campaign, except as a negative alternative to the European Free Trade Association which the Macmillan government had established in 1958.

Two years separate the 1959 election, in which EEC membership was not a Conservative theme, from the decision of the Macmillan government in 1961 to seek entry to the Community. This first application was vetoed by President de Gaulle of France in 1963, the year before the Conservatives lost power to the Labour government of Harold Wilson. When Mr Heath became Conservative prime minister in 1970, he placed Community membership at the centre of his programme for government and succeeded in negotiating terms for entry which 86 per cent of Conservative MPs accepted. By the time of the 1975 referendum on continuing British membership of the EEC, the Conservative Party was, as we shall see, identified as the European party in British politics and had become so without losing the support of the great majority of its electors, activists and parliamentarians. At the time of the original 1961 decision to investigate terms of entry, no government minister resigned. Only one Conservative MP voted against the decision and only twenty-nine abstained; the 1962 party conference easily passed a motion backing government policy on Europe. Macmillan's biographer, Alistair Horne, described party opposition to the idea of entry as 'remarkably feeble'.[9] There was more opposition to Heath's pro-Europeanism in 1971–72. Thirty-three Conservative MPs, plus the six Ulster Unionist MPs allied to the party, voted against the decisive 1971 House of Commons motion in support of entry and party managers had real difficulty in overcoming backbench opposition to the ratification of the Treaty of Accession. In a 1972 EEC related vote of confidence, fifteen backbench Conservative MPs voted against the government, the first time since 1945 that any Tory MPs had refused to support their government on a confidence issue.[10] Yet, as in 1961–62, the leadership was able to convince the bulk of the party of the rightness of Britain's entry into the Community. Only one junior government minister resigned over the issue and the 1971 party conference backed the policy by 3,474 votes to 324.[11]

This change in attitude towards EEC membership marked a clear break with some traditional assumptions about Britain's political and economic interests; and the fact that it occurred with such apparent ease should not obscure the misgivings that the new course aroused. In 1961–62, sections of Macmillan's Cabinet were sceptical about the new policy and there was outright opposition from within the parliamentary party, the constituencies and sections of the Conservative press, notably that controlled by Lord Beaverbrook. The Anti Common Market League, founded in August–September 1961, was originally a purely Conservative body whose members had to prove that they were paid up party members. President de Gaulle's 1963 veto on the British application was received with relief by grass-roots sentiment and by many Conservative MPs. Writing of the mid-1960s, Gamble observes that 'there is no doubt that an anti-Market leadership . . . would have received an overwhelming endorsement from Conservative conferences because they could have . . . played on all the attitudes and sentiments most dear to the rank and file supporters'.[12] In the early 1970s, the party's most effective orator, Enoch Powell, launched an all-out attack on the idea of British membership of the Community in the name of the Conservative principle of national independence existing through parliamentary sovereignty.

Conservative opposition to the principle of British entry could thus appeal to basic elements in the party's political code. In the early 1960s, it focused on the threat EEC membership allegedly posed to a key party interest, namely agriculture and to the party's claim to be the guarantor of low inflation; on the need to protect imperial and Commonwealth ties; and on a triumphalist reading of British nationalism that saw European countries as both unstable and hostile. One leading anti-Europeanist declared that 'those of us in Britain who oppose the Common Market don't want to subject ourselves to a lot of frogs and huns' and others still saw the six members of the European Community as 'a collection of losers'. The Conservative historian, Sir Arthur Bryant, summed up the threat apparently posed to the common civilization of the (white) Commonwealth by EEC membership when he wrote that it would 'discriminate against our own kind and children [and against] those nation members of the Commonwealth whose peoples derive from the same stock as ourselves and are every whit as much as we are the heirs of Alfred, Shakespeare, Hampden and Livingstone'.[13] By the early 1970s some of these themes – notably the sacredness of Commonwealth ties and the easy confidence in Britain's economic and political future – had lost their force. Enoch Powell, the party's most passionate opponent of entry, was notably contemptuous of the value of the Commonwealth as Bryant defined it and his efforts to link rejection of the Community with an ethnically defined British nationalism were decreasingly acceptable to mainstream Conservative opinion. Other anti-EEC arguments, however, retained their force. The emphasis on the threat to prices remained and was complemented by growing stress on the need to defend national sovereignty.

It could, therefore, be argued that membership of the European Community was not a 'natural' Conservative issue. Yet we have seen that Macmillan and Heath had little difficulty in selling the policy to the party and to the Conservative electorate. To explain their success we need to describe the strategies they employed to get their way and the similarities and differences in their policy ambitions.

Macmillan in 1961 was acutely aware of the negative historical legacies for the Conservative Party of earlier intra-party disagreements over strategic choices regarding Britain's role in the world political economy, namely the Corn Laws and tariff reform.[14] He responded by underplaying the political significance of Community membership and by emphasizing that his vision of the future had no place for the federalist ambitions of some continental conservatives. The ideologically neutral term Common Market was preferred to the more politically charged phrase European Economic Community. Macmillan dealt with intra-party opposition in a very emollient way and made no attempt to coerce the dissidents (it may be that he would have been firmer if the application had come close to success). Heath, too, minimized the federal implications by refusing to participate in the Community's 1973 attempt to establish monetary union and, on the surface, followed the Macmillan tactic of tolerating dissent by allowing a free vote in the October 1971 House of Commons vote to approve entry.[15] In fact, however, Heath was much tougher than his predecessor in using the party machinery, both central and local, to put pressure on potential opponents. He was only dissuaded from insisting on a 'yes' vote in the crucial 1971 vote by party managers' advice that to do so would make victory less, rather than more, certain by putting pressure on pro-EEC Labour MPs to vote against entry, and in 1972 told rebel Conservative MPs that if the government were defeated on the second reading of the European Communities Bill he would immediately seek a dissolution and a general election. Both Macmillan and Heath relied on the 'loyalty to the leader' principle and both sought to make Community membership a distinctively Conservative issue. In this they were helped by the adversarial conventions of British party politics which led the Labour opposition in both 1962 and 1971 to reject Tory terms for membership. At the time of the Macmillan application, the deputy prime minister, R.A. Butler, contrasted the Labour leader's anti-EEC appeal to 'a thousand years of history' with the forward looking nature of Conservatism, and in the difficult House of Commons votes on ratification in 1972, a number of potential Conservative rebels voted with the government out of anger at Labour's wrecking tactics.[16]

Why did EEC membership become a central policy goal of the Conservative leadership? Macmillan was responding to an intellectual appreciation of the difficulties Britain faced in a post-imperial world dominated by the two superpowers. The failure of Britain's attempt to play an independent global role in the 1956 Suez Crisis had alarmed him. He had initially shared the foreign office view that the European Economic Community would not work and it was his government, as we have seen, that set up the European Free Trade Association as an alternative, and a rival, trade organization. In 1960, however, the collapse of the Four Power summit held in Paris convinced him of Britain's inability to exercise an independent influence on superpower behaviour. Thus his overriding concern was political – to maintain a strategic role for Britain in changed international circumstances. Admittedly, the domestic political agenda was causing problems for the Conservatives in the early 1960s; inflationary pressures, relatively poor growth figures and a burgeoning culture of scandal threatened the party's claim to provide good government. Yet the real objective of membership was to find a way of restoring Britain's position within the three circles which the party's most authoritative leader, Churchill, had defined as being the source of its influence. The fact that the United States supported Britain's entry into the Community and that Commonwealth countries were kept closely in touch emphasized the continuities. EEC membership was not seen as involving a rethink of Britain's governing institutions; it was regarded as a means of strengthening trade and, above all, as a means of preserving diplomatic influence over a Washington that was strongly in favour of British engagement with the Community.

The position of Heath was in some ways more complex. For all his public caution as chief EEC negotiator between 1961 and 1963, he was a convinced European, willing to conceive of the Community as a new kind of political association rather than as a simple free trade area. As a newly elected backbencher in 1950, his first

House of Commons speech advocated British participation in the European Coal and Steel Community and the Godkin lecture he delivered at Harvard in 1968 placed Europe at the heart of his leadership vision. On becoming prime minister he made EEC membership the core of his policy programme, a goal to be achieved at almost any politically acceptable price.[17] Less interested, like his arch-adversary Powell, than any of his post-war predecessors in the myth of the special relationship with the United States, he was also (again like Powell) notably unimpressed with Commonwealth claims to influence British policy choices. In another break with traditional Conservative beliefs and allies, he took no account of the hostility of the Ulster Unionists to a European Community which they regarded, in a throwback to earlier definitions of British patriotism, as a Catholic conspiracy against Protestant liberties. Yet Heath did not, at this stage, challenge existing Conservative positions concerning the importance of the Atlantic alliance, the desirability of a global British security role (for example in the Gulf region) or even the continuing relevance of the Commonwealth. Nor did his Europeanism require the abandonment of the vocabulary of British patriotism in favour of a supranational ideal; the EEC was to be a mechanism whereby Britain could be 'Great' again rather than, as in the case of West Germany, a means of transcending a discredited patriotic ideal. In his House of Commons speech after the breakthrough in negotiations on membership, Heath underlined the importance of the 1966 Luxembourg Compromise enshrining governments' right of veto in Community decisions as the guarantor of essential national sovereignty against the ambitions of European federalists.[18]

THE PARTY OF EUROPE

By the time Mrs Thatcher replaced Edward Heath as party leader in February 1975, the attitude of the Conservatives towards the EEC can be summarized as follows. The party was now clearly identified in domestic politics as the 'party of Europe'. Joining the Community in 1973 was almost the only incontrovertible policy success in an otherwise traumatic term of office which did great damage to the party's reputation for competent government and culminated in the two election defeats of 1974. Conservatives could not abandon their pro-EEC stance without repudiating the record of a leader who, for all his unpopularity with many members of the parliamentary party, remained an influential figure of national, and international, standing and had strong support in the constituency associations. EEC membership did not feature prominently in the calculations of the backbench MPs who voted against Heath in the 1975 leadership contest. Only eight Conservative MPs voted against the revised terms for membership negotiated by the Labour Government in 1975 and the Conservative Party provided the bulk of the resources for the 'yes' campaign in the 1975 referendum on whether Britain should stay in the Community. An overwhelming 85 per cent of Conservative voters in the referendum supported continuing membership, with the five most Conservative counties recording a 75 per cent vote in favour.[19] In the first direct elections to the European Parliament in 1979, the Conservatives won sixty of the seventy-eight seats in mainland Britain on a pro-membership programme; the 51 per cent of the vote they gained was the highest share won by any party in a national election since 1931.[20] Although the Conservative MEPs remained outside the principal right-wing grouping in the European Parliament, the Christian democrat dominated European People's Party, they co-operated closely with it. In 1986 one of their number, Lord Plumb, was elected president of the Parliament.

Party managers had felt some unease about Conservatism's identification with a European cause which British public opinion did not, in the main, welcome, and anti-EEC sentiment within the parliamentary party did not wholly disappear. But the decision of Enoch Powell, the most influential Conservative opponent of entry, to leave the party and advocate a Labour vote in the 1974 general election did great damage to the anti-EEC cause in the party. By his actions, Powell broke the loyalty imperative which is so basic to Conservatism's governing code, and made anti-Europeanism seem suspect. The party's European profile was also helped by the increasing disarray of its principal opponent, the Labour Party, on the issue. The disagreements within the Labour Party between pro- and anti-Europeans, which culminated in the 1981 split and the creation of the Social Democratic Party, allowed the Conservatives to emphasise their unity and to brand anti-Europeanism as political extremism.

There were also clear limits to the European agenda of the Conservative Party. Once deposed from the leadership in 1975, Heath identified himself with the aspirations for a United Europe and was prepared to challenge the constitutional shibboleth of absolute parliamentary sovereignty. But apart from isolated MPs like Anthony Meyer (Clwyd North West) and Hugh Dykes (Harrow East) the revolutionary concept of a national interest separate from parliamentary sovereignty had no backers. EEC membership was welcomed because it spoke to the Conservative commitments to free trade (an argument that weighed heavily with future Eurosceptics like Norman Tebbit and Nicholas Ridley) and to the defence of regional security against the threat of Soviet communism. The explicitly federalist, and corporatist, themes of European Christian democracy had no appeal to mainstream party thinking. This helps to explain why Conservative MEPs were not, and are not, full members of the Christian democratic group in the European Parliament.[21]

The metaphor of revolution has been used so often by commentators, and by Mrs Thatcher herself, to describe her impact on the policy agenda of Britain, and the Conservative Party, that it is important to stress that in the case of Europe, continuities dominate. As party leader and, after 1979, prime minister she had majority party sentiment behind her in her coolness to Mr Heath's ardent Europeanism and in her conviction that Britain's membership of the European Community was essential on economic and political grounds. Her commitment was to the free market principles of the Treaty of Rome and to the value of the Community as a bulwark against the influence of communist parties in other member states.[22] Thus she welcomed the strengthening of European political co-operation within the Community and initiated the 1981 agreement on compulsory consultation between its member states during international crises. Despite her ardent support for President Reagan's anti-Sovietism, she also sided with her Community partners in their rejection of United States attempts to bar the construction of a gas pipe from Siberia to Western Europe.

It is, of course, true that during the early years of her premiership she launched an aggressive campaign against the size of Britain's contribution to the Community budget and linked this to the sensitive issue of the Common Agricultural Policy. Yet for all the fire and storm of her confrontation with other Community states, she never withheld British payments to the Community budget or practised de Gaulle's policy of the empty chair. At the 1984 Fontainebleau summit, the issue of Britain's budgetary contribution was resolved. Thereafter Mrs Thatcher co-operated fully with the ambitions of the European Commission to establish a proper internal market; the draughtsman of the 1985 Single European Act, Lord Cockfield, was a former member of her Cabinet. She used the full resources of party discipline to ensure that the Act, which contained a provision for majority voting in the Council of Ministers, was ratified by the Conservative majority in the House of Commons.

The strong intra-party opposition in the early 1980s to elements of the Thatcher programme did not, with the isolated exception of Mr Heath, focus on European issues. Though ministers like Carrington and Gilmour might complain about the aggressive style of Mrs Thatcher's European diplomacy, this merely reflected their belief that a more emollient approach would achieve results on which there was broad party agreement. The memoirs of Sir Ian Gilmour, Mrs Thatcher's arch-opponent among the party's traditional governing elite, are particularly significant in that they quote without disagreement a foreign office diplomat's view that the 1984 Fontainebleau Agreement was due to her 'courage and persistence'.[23] In her own memoirs, Mrs Thatcher speaks with pride of her role in the signing of the Single European Act and defends its inclusion of majority voting in the Council of Ministers.[24]

EUROPE: A CRISIS FOR THE CONSERVATIVE PARTY

With hindsight, the Single European Act can be seen as the high point of the Conservative Party's European strategy. It entrenched the free market and dereg-ulatory goals that were the central aim of the Thatcherite agenda; it came about as a result of intergovernmental co-operation; and it recognized the managerial role of the Commission in implementing and policing the policy. 'Europe' was thus a Conservative issue and one on which there was a broad intra-party consensus. The ease with which Conservative MPs could digest European questions was shown by their lack of interest in the detail of policy. Writing of the late 1980s, Nigel Ashford could observe that 'the (Conservative) parliamentary party does not give European issues a high priority, as evidenced by the low attendance at parliamentary debates'.[25]

After 1986, however, the question of Britain's relations with the institutions of the European Community became increasingly difficult for the leadership to handle and led, by the early 1990s, to deep internal divisions. It even began to look for a period as if 'Europe' might be as damaging to the Conservatives in the 1990s as it had been to Labour in the early 1980s. At Westminster, pro- and anti-European factions waged open war. Their conflicts spilled over into the parliamentary party's committee structure and backbench opponents of the official policy line like Bill Cash and Teresa Gorman acquired national prominence. Relations between Conservative MEPs and party managers deteriorated in the last years of Mrs Thatcher's premiership, particularly during the 1989 European elections, and came under renewed stress in 1992–93. The 1992 party conference, held at the start of the parliamentary debates on ratification of the Maastricht Treaty, and just after Britain's forced departure from the Exchange Rate Mechanism (ERM), was one of the most divisive in the party's history. Cabinet divisions over European policy in the late 1980s and after 1992 were obvious and public. Above all, the European issue became enmeshed in a debate over the party leadership. Europe played a large role in Mrs Thatcher's removal from office in 1990 and, after 1992, was responsible for a sharp decline in the political authority of her successor, John Major. After Britain's exit from the ERM, sections of the Conservative press made Europe the basis for a campaign against Mr Major's continuance as party leader that has no real parallel since the anti-Baldwin press agitation of 1930.

Many explanations of the apparent breakdown of the Conservatives' near consensus on Europe concentrate on the role of the Maastricht Treaty and it is easy to see why. In June 1992 eighty-four Conservative MPs mounted an open challenge to the central plank in the government's European policy by demanding a delay in the ratification of the treaty. A year later there occurred what one academic analysis calls the most serious parliamentary defeat suffered by a Conservative government this century when Mr Major was forced to resort to the ultimate – and humiliating – weapon of a parliamentary vote of confidence to save the treaty.[26] Only by making Maastricht an issue of the survival of a Conservative government was the prime minister able to save what had earlier been portrayed as the central achievement of his premiership.

There are, however, problems in limiting an explanation of the Conservatives' European difficulties to the Maastricht Treaty. Intra-party disagreements over Europe dominated the last years of Mrs Thatcher's premiership, and we have seen that at the time the treaty was signed, it was hailed as a triumph of Conservative statesmanship. Not only was Maastricht welcomed by the vast majority of Conservative candidates in the 1992 general election, only twenty-two Conservative MPs voted against the second reading of the ratifying bill in June of the same year. The rebellion was no greater in size than equivalent ones during the Heath govern-ment. It is, moreover, difficult to claim that Major's European policy broke with that of his predecessors. Dennis Kavanagh's observation on Mrs Thatcher's European record up to 1988 that 'the pattern has been one of resistance to proposals but, in the end, accepting compromise' could equally apply to Mr Major's Maastricht policy.[27] While accepting the creation at Maastricht of a European Union with enlarged powers, Mr Major obtained British opt outs over the issues of the Social Chapter and the timetable for monetary union and insisted on the removal from the text of any reference to the Union's federal vocation. He did so to preserve key elements in the Conservative code – the confederal nature of European institutions, the right of Parliament to determine the future of the currency, and hostility to any strengthening of the legitimacy of trades unionism.

Thus the real question about Maastricht is why the negotiated opt outs failed to swell a rising tide of internal conflict within the Conservative Party which some commentators likened to an incipient civil war. One part of the answer lies in the entangling of the European issue with broader questions of party leadership and policy. In recent decades, Conservative parliamentarians and activists have been more willing than in the past to challenge official leadership policies with which they do not agree. Mrs Thatcher's tendency to define policy choices in terms of first principles encouraged the sharpening of debate. To this assertiveness can be added the inevitable rivalries and resentments which exist in governing parties and which, in the Conservative Party, were exacerbated by Mrs Thatcher's style and the manner of her removal from office. Thus Europe became a weapon in the hands of those opposed, for whatever reason, to the leadership of Mrs Thatcher and Mr Major. In both cases, other problems (the poll tax, high interest rates, the prolonged recession, higher overall tax rates) were important in damaging prime ministerial authority. The narrowness of the government's majority (twenty-one seats) after the 1992 election also made problems of party management more difficult.

Yet the European problem cannot be reduced to issues of party management and leadership competence. Basic disagreements over the future functions and structure of the European Community came in time to separate Mrs Thatcher from her most senior ministers and spilled over into the government of her successor. Nor can the issue be seen as a simple repetition of the old left–right division that surfaced in the early 1980s as the conflict between 'wets' and 'dries', since by 1990 there was virtually no opposition from within the party (and not much outside) to the economic agenda of Thatcherism. While it is true that those who placed themselves on the left of the party were in favour of the European Union created at Maastricht, the 'dry' camp that had gained control of economic policy in the early 1980s were divided. Indeed, the disagreements over Europe between Mrs Thatcher and some of her erstwhile allies (Howe, Lawson, Cockfield, Brittan, Major) in the 1980s' redefinition of Conservative economic policy are among the most remarkable elements in the crisis.

The origin of the difficulties created for the Conservative Party by Europe lies in the new policy agenda developed by the Community after 1986. The conflict between Mrs Thatcher and her most senior colleagues (Howe, Lawson) over the desirability of British membership of the ERM was the first evidence of this. More fundamentally, the two intergovernmental conferences organized in the late 1980s to consider economic and monetary union and political union put the future competences and structure of the Community centre stage. Instead of being, as Mrs Thatcher had hoped, the final stage in the construction of a European Economic Community, 1992 became instead the launching pad for a new type of Union in which policy areas that had hitherto been the preserve of domestic high politics risked being annexed by the supranational institutions of Brussels. The new agenda, for which Maastricht became a shorthand term, plainly did not derive from mainstream Conservative thinking. David Howell, a senior Conservative backbencher and chairman of the House of Commons Foreign Affairs Committee was thus right to say in 1993 that 'the Conservative Party has never been the party of Maastricht . . . [and] from the very start . . . tried to resist the processes leading up to Maastricht'.[28] Neither Christian democratic aspirations for a federal constitution for Europe nor the free market cosmopolitanism of some liberals who regard the nation state as 'the ultimate supply side constraint' had any significant support within the party.[29] Few Conservatives, moreover, could welcome the emphasis in the Maastricht Treaty on the political identity and rights of Europe's regions, an emphasis that challenged the claim of unitary states, such as the United Kingdom, to govern multinational communities.

However unwelcome, the new European agenda was something with which British Conservatives would have to deal. A comparison of the responses of Mrs Thatcher and Mr Major can help to highlight how the party's governing code and principles could give rise to European policies that differed in some, but not all, respects. In her 1988 celebrated Bruges speech Mrs Thatcher sought to rally the party against any attempt to turn the European Community into anything more than a deregulated free trade area governed by a confederation of freely co-operating sovereign states. Her hostility to the deepening (*approfondissement*) of Community competences and institutions was absolute and was justified by core political principle. In condemning the 'socialist' policies of the Commission president and the 'anti-national' ambitions of the federalists, she emphasized a reading of British Conservatism as the party of British nationalism and economic deregulation. Her opposition to plans for a single European currency, in particular, united the claims of market liberalism and national independence. Explaining in her memoirs why she refused to nominate her former ally Lord Cockfield to a second term as a European Commissioner, she wrote that 'he tended to disregard the larger questions of politics – constitutional sovereignty, national sentiment and the promptings of liberty'.[30] Her support in 1992 for a referendum on the ratification of the Maastricht Treaty underlined her belief that what was being proposed did indeed mark a revolutionary break with British constitutional principle and thus represented the 'major strategic choice of the future role Britain should play in the world political economy' identified by Baker, Gamble and Ludlam.[31] Although Mrs Thatcher rejected the anti-Atlanticism which was part of General de Gaulle's European vision, there are obvious similarities between her belief that the nation state is the fundamental political reality and the Gaullist commitment to a *Europe des patries* (a term she quotes approvingly in her memoirs). The use in her memoirs of the chapter title 'Tower of Babel' for her account of the European Community harks back to de Gaulle's contemptuous reference, in a 1962 press conference, to the linguistic 'volapük' sought by the federalists. Thus the sanctity of the nation state was central to Mrs Thatcher's opposition to Maastricht. Free market and anti-corporatist arguments played a part; but the core concern was the threat to sovereignty and nationhood posed by the strengthening of Community institutions.[32]

Mrs Thatcher's definition of the European question in these terms helps explain the emergence of the so-called Eurosceptic constituency in the party which went beyond the traditional, but isolated, group of anti-marketeers. One of its members, Michael Spicer, identified four groups among the Eurosceptics – the traditional anti-marketeers, the English patriots, the free marketeers and the constitutionalists.[33] These groups identified with powerful traditions and values in the Conservative Party. Yet Mrs Thatcher's preferred successor as prime minister, the great majority of Conservative MPs and the 1992 and 1993 party conferences did not back the arguments that she and her supporters put forward. It may well be, as Baker, Gamble and Ludlam assert, that 'there can be little doubt that the majority of the Conservative Party would cheerfully [have] abandon[ed] the Maastricht Treaty if it were given the opportunity'.[34] The fact remains that it was given the opportunity and did not do so. To understand why this should be so, it is necessary to consider the arguments employed by Mr Major and his supporters and to highlight the themes in Conservatism to which they in turn were able to appeal.

Many Conservatives felt uneasy with the tone, and the implications, of the populist nationalism articulated by Mrs Thatcher and her supporters. Her demands for a referendum, for example, fitted in poorly with the Conservative claim to be the defenders of parliamentary sovereignty and the attacks on the authority of Mr Major angered those for whom loyalty to the leader is part of the Conservative code. The willingness of some Thatcherites to flirt with the language of xenophobia, while it might please some conference activists, was unappealing to moderate party opinion and alarming to Conservative business supporters who feared the consequences – falling export markets and inward investment – of a new isolationism.

Mr Major's decision to make party unity rather than ideology the basis of his European strategy left him open to attack from both the pro- and anti-European groups within the parliamentary party. Yet it spoke to the deep-rooted party concern with unity and with office holding; presence and pragmatism are powerful Conservative symbols. Two of Mr Major's declarations illustrate the point: his statement shortly after becoming prime minister that he wanted Britain to be 'at the heart of Europe' and his refusal, in the run up to the 1994 European elections, to rule out the possibility of future British participation in a single European currency. The first, with its echo of Churchill's 1950 observation on the European Coal and Steel Community that 'les absents ont toujours tort' (those who are absent are always wrong), signalled the need to 'be there'. The second is important not, as is often suggested, in its avoidance of a European commitment but in its refusal, at a time when Mr Major was under pressure from Eurosceptics to reject the very idea of a single currency, to see the question as one of basic political principle. Where Mrs Thatcher and her supporters used the heightened vocabulary of national independence in discussing a single currency, Mr Major sought to dedramatize the issue so that it became one of the calculation of technical advantage.

What made Mr Major's European strategy acceptable to majority party opinion was that it did not represent a break with past Conservative practice. It is true that, under pressure from the Eurosceptics, his pronouncements became more nationalistic in tone in 1993–94 than they had been earlier; but this was a change in tone rather than substance. At no time did Mr Major make concessions to the socialist or federalist agenda of the Europeans or even to the *esprit communautaire* of senior party figures like Heath and Howe and their supporters among Conservative MEPs. Thus his advertised support for the principle of subsidiarity enshrined in the Maastricht Treaty derived from the view that it was a Conservative measure to protect the rights of states and not, as European Christian democrats argued, the organizing principle of a future federal Europe. Increasingly, Mr Major sought to define a distinct Conservative agenda for Europe which could be opposed to the party's opponents at home and abroad. Based on deregulation and the assertion of the primacy of states' rights, this agenda sought to portray the integrationist ambitions of the Europeans as unrealistic and archaic and to weaken the political legitimacy of the European Commission. By vetoing the appointment of Jean Luc Dehaene as Commission president in 1994, Mr Major aimed to show the strength of Conservatism's hostility to federalism and to the pretensions of the Commission to provide political leadership. In a significant historical analogy that showed the depth of party suspicion of Jacques Delors, one Conservative MP said that the Commission president should no longer be a Napoleon-like figure.

CONCLUSION

An initial reading of the results of the 1994 European elections could suggest that Europe was destroying the Conservative Party. It polled 1.1 million votes fewer than it had done in the 1989 contest and the 28 per cent share of the vote it gained was its lowest ever in a national contest. In Scotland the Conservatives won only 14 per cent of the vote. Only two of the eighteen Conservative MEPs elected had a majority of over 5 per cent and a 2 per cent further swing would have reduced party representation at the Strasbourg Parliament to a derisory five seats.

The role of Europe in the European elections should not, however, be exaggerated. As with the 1992 Maastricht referendum in France, the 1994 elections were chiefly important in allowing a popular judgement to be passed on the incumbent government's overall performance. Although the impression of party disunity created by Europe unquestionably contributed to the bad result, poll evidence did not indicate that Mr Major's European policy was a principal element in voters' calculations. Nor did it suggest that the party was about to break up. No national or constituency organizations abandoned their party affiliation and there was no mass defection of Conservative voters to the overtly anti-European Union United Kingdom Independence Party. After the initial shock of the results, many Conservatives – but also many commentators – concluded that the party's performance was less awful than might have been expected.[35]

We may conclude, therefore, that despite the analogies made by historically minded commentators between the party's difficulties over Europe and the Conservative splits of 1846 and 1903, the leadership was still able in 1994 to contain the European question within manageable bounds. It did so partly by appealing to the loyalty code and partly by constructing a Conservative agenda for Europe which enabled the party to assert its preferred identity as guardian of the constitutional order. The Conservative principle of state patriotism could still operate in tandem with the belief in 'presence' which had led the party to take the European road in the 1960s and 1970s. Conservatives could still argue that the Europe they supported did not represent a break with party traditions which had been consolidated in the nineteenth century and maintained throughout the twentieth. Yet the Conservative elite continued to disagree over whether the approach to the European Union should be one of containment or rollback, terms which in their Cold War provenance are not inapt to describe the intra-party tensions. Given that one of the characteristics of Europe is that it is an evolving political association whose final shape is still indeterminate, the question of whether the Conservative Party can handle the European future, while remaining true to its national past, remains a live one.

NOTES

I am very grateful to John Gaffney for all his help in the preparation of this chapter. My thanks go also to Martin Ball, Neil Carmichael, Dennis Kavanagh and Lucy Morris.

1 D. Butler and D.A. Kavanagh, *The British General Election of 1992* (London, Macmillan, 1992), p. 286.
2 J. Bulpitt, 'Conservative leadership and the Euro-ratchet', *Political Quarterly*, vol. 63, no. 3, 1992, p. 265.
3 R. Jackson, *Tradition and Reality: Conservative Philosophy and European Integration* (London, The European Democratic Group, n.d.) *passim*; D. Willetts, *Modern Conservatism* (Harmondsworth, Penguin Books, 1992), p. 4.; see also J. H. Grainger, *Character and Style in English Politics* (Cambridge, Cambridge University Press, 1969), pp. 214–23.
4 A. Gamble, *The Conservative Nation* (London, Routledge and Kegan Paul, 1974), p. 2.
5 W.S. Churchill, *Europe Unite* (London, Cassell, 1948).
6 S. Greenwood, *Britain and European Cooperation since 1945* (Oxford, Blackwell, 1992), pp. 42–3.
7 Gamble, *The Conservative Nation*, pp. 190, 278 note 93.
8 R.J. Lieber, *British Politics and European Unity: Parties, Elites and Pressure Groups* (Berkeley, CA, California University Press, 1970), pp. 139, 143.

9 A. Horne, *Harold Macmillan*, vol. 2, *1957–86* (London, Macmillan, 1989), p. 261.
10 J. Campbell, *Edward Heath* (London, Pimlico, 1994), p. 439.
11 U. Kitzinger, *Diplomacy and Persuasion: How Britain Joined the Common Market* (London, Thames and Hudson, 1973), pp. 232–3.
12 Gamble, *The Conservative Nation*, p. 197.
13 Lieber, *British Politics*, p. 191. Many local Conservative Party officials had spent their working careers in the colonies as administrators or businessmen.
14 For an excellent study of the consequences for party unity of earlier 'strategic choices' made by Conservative leaders see D. Baker, A. Gamble and S. Ludlam, '1846 . . . 1906 . . . 1996: could European Union lead the Conservative Party into the wilderness again?', paper presented to the 1993 Conference of the Political Studies Association.
15 Greenwood, *Britain and European Cooperation*, p. 98.
16 Campbell, *Edward Heath*, p. 439
17 Ibid., p. 336.
18 Ibid., p. 360.
19 D. Butler and U. Kitzinger, *The British Referendum of 1975* (London, Macmillan, 1976), p. 271.
20 D. Butler and D. Marquand, *European Elections and British Politics* (London, Macmillan, 1981), p. 137.
21 N. Ridley, *My Style of Government* (London, Fontana, 1992); N. Tebbit, *Upwardly Mobile* (London, Weidenfeld and Nicolson, 1988).
22 I. Gilmour, *Dancing with Dogma* (London, Simon and Schuster, 1992), p. 233.
23 Ibid., p. 262.
24 M. Thatcher, *The Downing Street Years* (London, HarperCollins, 1993), p. 557.
25 N. Ashford, 'The political parties', in S. George (ed.), *Britain and the European Community: The Politics of Semi-Detachment* (Oxford, The Clarendon Press, 1992), p. 134.
26 D. Baker, A. Gamble and S. Ludlam, 'The parliamentary siege of Maastricht', *Parliamentary Affairs*, vol. 47, no. 1, 1994, p. 57.
27 D. Kavanagh, *Thatcherism and British Politics* (London, Macmillan, 1990), p. 268.
28 D. Howell, 'But we are good Europeans . . .', *The Independent*, 19 April 1993.
29 Willetts, *Modern Conservatism*, p. 171.
30 Thatcher, *The Downing Street Years*, p. 547.
31 Baker et al., '1846 . . . 1906 . . . 1996', p. 10.
32 P. Lynch, *Thatcherism and the Politics of Nationhood: An Overview*, Leicester University Discussion Papers in Politics no. P93/5. 1993, pp. 19–24.
33 T. Helm, 'A highly organised rebel band', *The Sunday Telegraph*, 1 November 1992.
34 Baker et al., '1846 . . . 1906 . . . 1996', p. 25.
35 D. Butler, 'Labour's triumph may still not lead to government', *Financial Times*, 22 June 1994.

SELECT BIBLIOGRAPHY

Baker, D., Gamble, A. and Ludlam, S., 'The parliamentary siege of Maastricht', *Parliamentary Affairs*, vol. 47, no. 1, January 1994.
Baker, D., Gamble, A. and Ludlam, S., '1846 . . . 1906 . . . 1996: Conservative splits and European integration', *Political Quarterly*, vol. 63, no. 4, 1993.
Bulpitt, J., 'Conservative leaders and the Euro-ratchet: five doses of scepticism', *Political Quarterly*, vol. 63, no. 3, 1992.
Campbell, J., *Edward Heath*, London, Pimlico, 1993.
Gamble, A., *The Conservative Nation*, London, Routledge and Kegan Paul, 1974.
Gilmour, I., *Dancing with Dogma*, London, Simon and Schuster, 1992.
George, S. (ed.), *Britain and the European Community: The Politics of Semi-Detachment*, Oxford, Clarendon, 1992.
Greenwood, S., *Britain and European Cooperation since 1945*, Oxford, Blackwell, 1992.
Horne, A., *Harold Macmillan*, London, Macmillan, 1988, 1989, 2 vols.
Kavanagh, D., *Thatcherism and British Politics*, Oxford, Oxford University Press, 1990, 2nd edn.

Kitzinger, U., *Diplomacy and Persuasion: How Britain joined the Common Market*, London, Thames and Hudson, 1973.

Lawson, N., *The View from Number 11*, London, Bantam Press, 1991.

Lieber, R., *British Politics and European Unity: Parties, Elites and Pressure Groups*, Berkeley, CA, California University Press, 1970.

Lynch, P., *Thatcherism and the Politics of Nationhood: An Overview*, Leicester, University of Leicester Discussion Papers in Politics no. P93/5, 1993.

Ridley, N., *My Style of Government: The Thatcher Years*, London, Fontana, 1992.

Thatcher, M., *The Downing Street Years*, London, HarperCollins, 1993.

Willetts, D., *Modern Conservatism*, Harmondsworth, Penguin Books, 1992.

8 The Italian Christian Democrats

Martin Bull

INTRODUCTION: EUROPE AND THE DC'S SIGNIFICANCE AS A REGIME PARTY

Between the 1950s and the early 1990s the Italian Christian Democratic Party (DC) proved to be one of the most successful parties in Western Europe, if viewed from the perspectives of electoral support and holding office. The party consistently obtained over a third of the vote and on three occasions over 40 per cent. It was the major party of every governing coalition and provided the prime minister for every government except two until the party's transformation into the Italian Popular Party (PPI, the name of the DC's pre-war predecessor) in January 1994. The principal reason for this persistence in office was the peculiarity of the Italian party system, and specifically the perceived need to exclude from power the largest communist party in the West, the Italian Communist Party (PCI), which consistently obtained over a quarter of the vote and as much as a third. In this situation the DC, as the largest party, governed in coalition with three or four other parties.[1] The DC's penetration and politicization of the state as a result of this permanence in office has been well-documented: the party was a regime party *par excellence*.[2]

This point underlines the significance to Italy of the DC's approach to European integration compared with other Italian parties. The lack of alternation in government gave the party a monopoly over key ministries and consequently over policy making. The European issue was no exception. Indeed, because it was long deemed to be an element of foreign affairs (governments only later viewed it as much a part of domestic as of foreign policy) it was an issue where DC hegemony was most complete because the 'blocked' nature of the party system had an international dimension to it: the ideological Cold War between East and West. Curiously, however, when we analyse the DC's foreign policy in general and its views on the European Union (EU) in particular, we find an effective absence of the first and a bland and unsophisticated – although unequivocally supportive – approach to the second. The reason for this lies in the party's lack of organizational instruments in foreign policy (until the 1980s) and its apathy with regard to foreign affairs in general, beyond a basic acceptance of the two tangible symbols of the post-war order, NATO and the EU. Variations in foreign policy depended less upon the DC or the government than upon the preferences and (often unco-ordinated) activities of various individuals: the prime minister, the minister for foreign affairs, the minister for overseas trade and, at times, those (such as Enrico Mattei) in charge of large state enterprises. Where the party did express preferences, they were determined more by internal needs than by external considerations: the maintenance of internal consensus and of the party's monopoly of power. Despite certain changes in the 1980s, the basic characteristic of the DC's post-war choice – a low-profile and underdeveloped foreign policy – remained substantially unchanged. The party's approach to – and its performance in – Europe, should be understood in this context.[3]

This chapter is divided into five sections. The first section analyses the DC's official position on Europe, the developments in this position and internal divisions over the issue. The second section attempts to flesh out the DC's position by looking at the sources of its Europeanism. The third, fourth and fifth sections evaluate the DC's performance in Europe: in its role in the European People's Party (EPP) and the European Parliament (EP); in its role in Brussels as the main party of Italian government; and in its action as the main party of government in Italy. It is argued that the DC's Europeanism was always flawed and that this flawed Europeanism represented a fundamental dilemma for the party. The conclusion assesses the prospects for this dilemma being resolved by the DC's successor, the PPI, in the context of the changes which the Italian political system underwent in the early 1990s.

THE DC'S APPROACH TO EUROPEAN INTEGRATION

The official position

In the post-war period, the DC's approach to the European issue reflected, to a large extent, its apathy regarding foreign policy. Excepting the period under De Gasperi (whose Europeanism will be touched on below), the party showed little real interest in Europe. Party literature on the issue until the 1980s was virtually non-existent and the party showed no interest in developing new ideas in the area of Community policy.[4] Yet, this did not mean that the DC was negative about Europe. On the contrary, of all Italian parties the DC was one of the most consistently pro-European. An analysis of the party's official position in the post-war period reveals constant support for the deepening of the integration process at the economic and political levels during all the key decisions in the integration process: the creation of the European Economic Community (EEC) in the 1950s, direct elections to the EP in the 1970s and the moves toward economic and political union in the late 1980s and early 1990s.[5] The issue was never the cause of a major division inside the DC (although, as will be argued below, differences in emphasis can be noted) and, in the 1980s, the DC placed itself in the vanguard of those supporting moves towards European union, as an analysis of the party's position before it transformed itself into the PPI confirms.

In economic terms, the DC was a strong supporter of the Single European Act (SEA) and the Maastricht Treaty, calling for the full opening of markets, greater integration of banking systems and the creation of an economic and monetary union with a single currency by 1999. It was also opposed to any notions of a 'two-speed' Europe. Regarding social and regional policy, the party believed in greater action in the social sphere to combat unemployment and was therefore fully supportive of the extensive social programme embodied in Maastricht's effective creation of a European Social Community by eleven of the member states. It was also a strong believer in the idea of 'regional harmonization', and was concerned that the creation of a Single Market could exacerbate the existing North–South divide in Europe. It therefore fully supported Article 130 of the SEA committing member states to reducing the disparities between regions through the use of structural funds, and the new Cohesion Fund established by the Maastricht Treaty to help the poorer countries.

At the external level, the party supported the extension of EU competence into the area of foreign and security policy with implementing moves taken by majority vote. Finally, at the political-institutional level, the DC long stressed the significance of political union embodied in the treaties setting up the EU. Its view was that the slow progress made on the issue of political integration (compared with economic integration) was the result of inadequate institutional mechanisms, and that there was a real danger of a 'democratic deficit' arising from the transfer of powers from the nation states to the Community level without a concomitant increase in democratic control at that level. The party believed that the European Commission should have effective power to initiate and implement European policy and that the Council should have decision-making powers free of the veto, meaning an extension of majority voting beyond the limited range of issues provided in the SEA. Moreover, it believed that the EP should be the institution which retained overall democratic control, meaning an extension of its powers. The party therefore supported the powers granted to the EP by Maastricht to amend and veto certain Council acts, to scrutinize Community finances, to set up committees of inquiry to investigate alleged contraventions or maladministration, and to have the power of a vote of confidence over the Commission.

Overall, the DC was deeply critical of the intergovernmental method which characterized the construction of the EU. Even the SEA (which was regarded by many as a milestone in the development of the EU) was judged by the DC to be a limited achievement, if not a mediocre product of the intergovernmental method. The party believed that member states would be unable to work towards integration in a coherent and binding fashion in the absence of better institutional mechanisms and decision-making structures. The response of the DC to the revolutions in Eastern Europe reflected its long-standing position on Europe. At a conference held in 1990 on international themes, Franco Maria Malfatti, then head of the DC parliamentary leadership, argued that the new European order could not be conceived of as a new era which should dispense with the two most significant constructions of the post-war period, the Atlantic alliance and the European Community (EC):

> The EC, first and foremost, has not been made superfluous by the new order, but rather finds in it further confirmation of its value. This is why an acceleration of the integration process is needed, transforming the Community of the twelve with maximum speed into economic and monetary union . . . rather than leaving European union as a vague objective with no specification of how and when it will be achieved.[6]

Internal variations in the official position

As argued earlier, open debate on foreign policy in the DC rarely existed and interest in international affairs was minimal. Nevertheless, some differences – or at least nuances – in the DC's Europeanism were identifiable, and they accounted for changes in emphasis in the party's position at different times in the post-war period. The chief tension focused on the degree to which the party's Europeanism and Atlanticism were compatible. Recent research has modified the view that the DC was nothing more than 'America's party' and has suggested that the first post-war DC leader, Alcide de Gasperi, viewed Italy's adhesion to the Atlantic alliance as a surrogate for the preferred European alternative, the latter offering the means by which Italy might find a new power base in the post-war order. He also viewed the Atlantic Treaty as a form of shell within which the European 'embryo' could develop.[7]

De Gasperi was able to provide a coherence and force to the DC's foreign policy which was never matched thereafter, and the potential incompatibility between Atlanticism and Europeanism became the principal source of tensions over foreign policy inside the party. Once the Cold War had declined in significance in the 1960s, the question of European integration became an economic, as well as a political, issue and different factions emerged within the party: the Atlanticists (who placed loyalty to the United States above all else), the *autonomisti* (who favoured rapid moves towards European integration as a means of resolving Italy's economic problems), the Mediterraneanists (who favoured closer collaboration with the Mediterranean and Third World states) and the federalists (who favoured a supranational federal state for political reasons). The strength of the right and of Atlanticism in the early 1970s was seen when, under a centre-right government led by Andreotti and Malagodi, Italy abandoned the European 'monetary snake'.

The extent of division inside the party, however, should not be exaggerated. First, the tone of the debate was never anti-European but rather revealed scepticism by a few about the creation of a European federal state. The prospect of the DC as a party opposing the basic principles of the EU was never likely. Second, the debate was never aired prominently in public; its main public effect was to cause more incoherence and reticence in the party over foreign affairs, leaving policy to be made by the DC ministers in charge. Third, and most important, the combination of a shift in the debate from political to economic issues, the modernization of the Italian economy in the 1950s and its subsequent crisis in the 1970s, resulted in support for Europe inside the party coming increasingly from those members who believed in carrying through economic reform, supported by the more progressive industrial interests. This identification of Europe with a more stable and equitable economy was to prove important and lasting. It meant that – although the balancing act between Atlanticism and Europeanism always continued – the party's pro-European elements could become more vocal. The collapse of communism in Eastern Europe and the transformation of the PCI into a non-communist party of the left reduced further the importance of the Italo-American link and confirmed the party's basic pro-European stance. In short, despite apathy and lack of organization in foreign affairs and the presence of some minor divisions over the issue, the DC's programmatic position on Europe in the post-war period was unequivocally supportive. Explaining and identifying the exact nature of this Europeanism is best done through an analysis of its sources.

THE NATURE AND SOURCES OF THE DC'S EUROPEANISM

The origins of the DC's Europeanism lay in six interrelated factors, the prominence of each of which changed throughout the post-war period.

International status and power

The EU was viewed as an essential means of raising Italy's, and the DC's, international stature and power. The rationale behind de Gasperi's goal of a united Europe was to raise Italy's status in the international community, bringing it back into the fold of the established and influential nations of Western Europe. This quest for greater international status (which, in turn, would buttress the DC's own monopoly of power) was subsequently ever present. As Maurizio Cotta notes, countries which already enjoy a high status in the international community stand to gain less from supranationalism than countries with a lower status: 'For the latter, joining a larger group may mean stepping at least indirectly (through the supranational union) into the "big game" of international politics.'[8] Italy's ambiguous position (i.e viewed as more significant than the small powers of Northern and Southern Europe but, at the same time, not regarded as a power ranking alongside Germany, Britain and France) acted as an incentive for the DC to attempt to enter the big league by promoting further integration. This, to a large extent, explained the desire on the part of Italian governments to be hyperactive during the periods when they held the leadership of the EU (via the presidency). Indeed, Italian support for an acceleration of the integration process after the unification of Germany was primarily motivated by the fear that Germany would lose interest in the EU and disrupt the balance in Europe generally through its increased political and economic weight. Hence, the DC wanted to tie Germany into a politically and economically united Europe through which lesser countries such as Italy could continue to exert their influence.[9]

Internal stability

Italy's nascent democracy was perceived by the DC as unstable (due to the Cold War and the strength of the PCI) and facing the prospect of a long period of consolidation, with a risk of democratic breakdown. A united Europe was seen as a means of tying Italy into a framework which would make the prospect of an internal communist transformation less tenable, at the same time as constituting a form of defence against communism in the East. It should be stressed, however, that – as with the question of international status – this reasoning was inseparable from concern about the power and electoral strength of the party (its first priority). Rightly or wrongly, the DC perceived – or claimed to perceive – the fate of Italy as bound up with its own, and this acted as an incentive for it to place the maintenance of its own power over all other considerations. If a united Europe aided the party's electoral struggle against the communist menace then it had to be supported at all costs.

Christian democratic 'doctrine'

Supranationalism was compatible with the DC's Christian doctrine, something which generally expressed hostility to the nation state, particularly in the writings of the party's founder, Don Luigi Sturzo.[10] Indeed, many members of the DC became active in, or at least influenced by, the European Federalist Movement (founded in Milan in 1943), and the 1950s saw the party espousing clearly federalist ideals while being happy for its government to pursue a more pragmatic European line.[11] These federal ideals tended to become submerged in the 1960s and 1970s to more pragmatic needs, yet party members never hesitated to resort to what they regarded as the essential Europeanism of Christian democratic thought to justify their party's credentials in Brussels.

Economic factors

From the 1960s onwards economic factors began to have an increasing influence in the European debate. The effect on the DC was primarily through the influence of different economic interests, rather than a result of a simple calculation of the benefit for Italy and the DC of pursuing further integration. Despite the scepticism shown towards the idea of a united Europe by small industry and agriculture in the immediate post-war period, once Italy's 'economic miracle' was under way the economic importance of the newly founded EEC became apparent, particularly to large sectors of industry, which had a growing influence inside the party. Being primarily export-driven, the economic miracle was given a major boost by the EEC's creation of a free trade zone, and the percentage of Italian goods exported to member states rose from 23 per cent in 1955 to 29.8 per cent in 1960 and 40.2 per cent in 1965.[12] The visible gains for Italy were such that supporting further integration was natural for a party committed to free trade.

The inadequacies of Italian policy making

From the 1970s economic factors took on a political or policy-orientated dimension. The economic crisis of the 1970s exposed the inadequacies of the Italian political system and a policy-making process where institutional inefficiency, ideological conflict and the prevalence of distributive interests resulted in incoherent economic policies and a growing budget deficit, something which the brief recovery in the 1980s did nothing to reverse. The EU and the economic commitments involved in further integration (particularly for European Monetary Union (EMU) to occur) were seen as a means by which harsh and unpopular economic measures could be legitimized and carried through. This became significant in the 1980s when real economic reforms were required to keep pace with other members of the EU. Giovanni Goria, for example (the DC prime minister in 1987–88) stated openly that he welcomed the economic constraints of the EU as a means of overcoming powerful domestic interests hostile to economic reform.[13] The prospect, otherwise, for the DC was to bear primary responsibility for relegating Italy to Europe's 'slow lane'.[14] Indeed, this factor intertwined with the first factor (the loss of status and power) to pose a daunting spectre which was used prominently in political debate.

Italian public opinion

The reason why the spectre of relegation to Europe's 'slow lane' could be used so prominently was because of the popularity of the EU with the Italian people. As regular surveys of *Eurobarometer* and Doxa polls since the 1970s have demonstrated, Italy has consistently been one of the nations most favourable to the EU both in the form of general support for the idea of European unity and specific support for increasing the power of European institutions such as the EP.[15] In the period since the Italian left (and particularly the PCI) began to shift its position on the EU, the consensus has been a broad one: from the general public to the media, interest groups, political parties and parliamentarians. As David Hine has commented:

> If a major element of European integration is the creation of a domestic political climate supportive of integration . . . [Italy's] . . . record is almost unimpeachable. It is the one country in the European Community where governments feel a constant pressure from Parliamentary opinion to be more incisive and more committed to the integration process.[16]

The DC, both in its role as a party in parliament and as the major party of government, felt these pressures for support of the EU. Like other Italian parties, it was aware that an anti-European stance was a potential – if not certain – vote loser.[17]

To summarize, the sources of the DC's apparently unqualified public commitment for European integration seem clear. Yet, the nature of these sources begs an analysis of the party's actions in Europe. A party's Europeanism is not judged solely by its programmatic position but also by its actions at the European level. Did the DC's actions match its apparent commitment to the European ideal? To answer this question, the next three sections will analyse the DC in the EPP and the EP, the action of DC governments externally (in Brussels) to further the integration process and the action of DC governments internally (in Italy) to further the integration process.

THE DC IN THE EUROPEAN PARLIAMENT AND EUROPEAN PEOPLE'S PARTY

The DC was – and its successor, the PPI, is – a member of both of the organizations which are the institutionalized expressions of the Christian democratic movement in Europe: the European Union of Christian Democrats (EUCD), and the European People's Party: Federation of Christian Democratic Parties of the European Community (EPP). The EUCD encompasses Christian democratic parties from all European countries, and was founded in 1965. It has twenty-eight member parties as well as eleven with observer status. The EPP is a supranational party of the EU with a federal structure and with a grouping based in the EP. It developed out of the EUCD as a federation of EU Christian democratic parties in 1976. The grouping is the second largest in the EP and consists of all Christian democratic parties of the member states, plus Greece's Nea Dimokratia (which joined in 1983), Spain's Partido Popular (1991) and the British and Danish Conservative Parties (1992) (although the last two are not, as yet, members of the federation itself).[18]

Of the three EU federations, there is little doubt that the EPP has been the most strongly and consistently pro-European and active in the cause of furthering integration. Its basic programme states that 'the EPP calls for the gradual – but resolute – transformation of the European Community into a genuine political union on a federal model . . . ' and that 'A federal Europe is now more than ever a necessary and realistic political objective.'[19] To reinforce this view the party produced at its VIIth Congress in 1988 a five-year Action Programme by which this goal could be achieved.[20] The party has also attempted to deepen the theoretical links between Christian democracy and European integration.[21] Finally, of the three existing federations, the EPP is the most federally (or supranationally) organized, an institutionalized expression of its commitment to a federal Europe.[22]

The DC was one of the most consistently active components of the EPP and the EPP (or CD) Group in the EP. The DC was, until the 1994 elections, the largest component of the parliamentary group (with twenty-six members), excepting the British Conservatives (who are not yet members of the federation). The PPI (the DC's successor) is, by comparison, a much smaller party with only eight seats. The DC component was one of the strongest supporters of European integration in the EP, with the party's MEPs according priority to their role in the EU over national and local concerns.[23] The DC was also active in attempting to mould a distinctive identity for the EPP, something which was perceived to be fundamental to the pursuit of European union. The main conflict inside the EPP has always been over its ideology and programme and the DC was one of the principal protagonists in this conflict, consistently fighting for a supranational party founded on two principles, Christianity and the social market economy. This vision tended to be restrictive towards European conservative parties with aspirations to join the EPP, an opening parties such as the German Christian Democrats always favoured.

There were few tensions existing between the DC in the EP and the DC at the national level. Indeed, in all of the direct elections to the EP, the DC adhered to the election manifesto approved by successive EPP congresses (even though the subsequent campaigns, as in other countries, tended to be conducted according to national issues).[24] The party used those manifestos as 'umbrella' platforms within which to develop election manifestos for national elections. Moreover, it adopted the EPP's Action Programme (see above) as its own. Links between the national party and the EPP were provided by the presence of Italian members of the EPP in the organs of the DC (there were no formal links between the DC national parliamentary group and the EPP group in the EP). The head of the delegation of the DC in the EP had formal speaking and consultative rights in the DC's executive (which also engaged in close political co-operation with the European Affairs Section of the Italian delegation in the EPP group). A percentage of MEPs (in 1986, for example, five out of twenty seven) had the same rights in the party's National Council. At the party's National Congress, MEPs could be given guest status which was equivalent to that of national deputies and gave them speaking rights. EPP group members who were members of a provincial party association had consultative rights on the DC's provincial committee, and those who were members of a regional party association enjoyed similar rights on the party's regional committee and regional executive. Finally, all EPP group members had speaking rights at the regional congress for the election of delegates to the National Congress.[25] The PPI has inherited these structural characteristics, and there has been no move as yet by the new party to make any radical changes.

How effective these formal mechanisms were – and are for the new PPI – in representing the European level in the decision-making processes of the national party is open to question. Generally speaking, the national level was always predominant in European affairs, even in the selection of candidates for European elections and the development of electoral platforms, but this is not to say that there was never any input of significance from the European level (the role of the EPP in the development of election manifestos has already been noted). Paradoxically, however, the influence that Italian members of the EPP wielded in the past was dependent less on their prominence at the European level than on their position in the national party, and specifically on the faction to which they belonged.

THE DC AND EXTERNAL GOVERNMENT ACTION TO FURTHER EUROPEAN UNITY

Sergio Pistone argues that the European policies of successive Italian governments, nearly all of which were directed by DC ministers and received unequivocal support from the party itself, were shaped by four characteristics which displayed more federalist traits than the European policies of any other member government during the post-war period.[26] First, the preference for a 'global' form of integration incorporating political, military and economic aspects; second, the belief that economic integration should occur not only through the removal of obstacles to the operation of a free market but also through the progressive unification of national economic policies and the removal of regional distortions created by the operation of a free market; third, support for the principle of the direct election of the EP and a strengthening of its powers with an aim to achieving democratization of the institutions of the EU; fourth, a preference for the participation of all forces and institutions in questions of European integration (rather than depending on the whims of intergovernmentalism), with the aim of realizing a federal European constitution.

Yet, these four traits were rarely pursued proactively until the 1980s. On the contrary, the chief characteristic of DC-led governments was a failure to impose any sort of coherence in Italian European policy, which inhibited the development of an Italian presence at the European level to match that of France and Germany. This can be explained by the lack of proper foreign policy instruments in the DC; the incoherence in DC policy produced by the attempt to support two ideas (Atlanticism and Europeanism) which were not always compatible; the high levels of inefficiency of the state bureaucracy; and the difficulties the DC faced in exerting influence when, for a long time, the party was viewed by others as representing the 'sick man of Europe'.[27] The effects of this negligence were at times damaging to Italy's economy and thus to the longer-term needs of the integration process. Perhaps the most striking example of this deficiency was in the negotiations over the setting up of the Common Agricultural Policy (CAP) in the 1960s, which had a decisively negative impact on Italian agriculture.[28]

Even the marked change in the level of European activism of Italian governments in the 1980s (best illustrated in the DC's handling of Italy's hosting of the EU presidency in 1985 and 1990)[29] was not without criticism. The persistent forwarding of 'maximalist' positions was viewed by many as lacking in realism and too often insufficiently backed up with measures at the concrete level. This was most visibly the case with respect to governmental action inside Italy, an issue which will now be explored.

THE DC AND INTERNAL GOVERNMENT ACTION TO FURTHER EUROPEAN UNITY

David Hine has pointed out that, as the integration process deepens, it is no longer sufficient for parties, governments or countries to claim and extol their European credentials simply through initiatives and action in Brussels to further European unity:

> European integration has now reached a level that requires that domestic policy and domestic legislative programmes are adjusted to Community policies on a very broad front. Increasingly, European integration requires a measurable internal commitment from national governments and legislatures. Awareness of the demands of integration must also penetrate throughout each country's system of public administration.[30]

In other words, there is an internal, domestic dimension to pro-European action, which, if absent, can undermine the putative European credentials of a country's external, supranational initiatives. There are, broadly speaking, two aspects to this domestic dimension: the politico-legal and the politico-economic. The first refers to the need for countries to ensure that Community law is implemented in their territories through translating EU directives into national law and through compliance with the decisions of the European Court of Justice. The EU's drive towards the achievement of the 1992 internal market programme since the passing of the SEA highlighted the importance of this aspect. Yet Italy's record on both counts was extremely poor, indeed, one of the poorest across the member states.[31] The second aspect refers to the need for countries to adjust their economic and budgetary policies to the needs of the EU to enable convergence of the economies of the member states (a prerequisite to economic and political union). The importance of this was highlighted with the formal moves taken by the EU to achieve economic union, with the formulation in the Maastricht Treaty of tough convergence criteria for membership. At the time, Italy passed on only one of the five criteria; the most alarming criterion was the stipulation that budget deficits should be no more than 3 per cent of GDP for convergence to occur (Italy's being nearer to 10 per cent).[32] Despite the fact that the need for action was evident long before Maastricht, successive governments took no serious measures until after the elections of April 1992 (which marked the beginning of the end of DC dominance). As Antonio Giolitti has noted:

> even though the Community was and still seems to be an essential foreign policy option for Italy, its governments hesitate to draw the consequences in terms of economic policy . . . rather than make a serious effort to overcome the divergences and its inferiority, Italy has sought recognition of [Community solidarity towards the 'less affluent' countries] and compensation in the form of exonerations, exceptions, aid (or, if necessary, by defaulting and not living up to its commitments).[33]

It might be added that, as noted earlier, the DC came to rely on the EU imposing discipline where it could not, as the need for action became more urgent. Certainly, serious measures will be required throughout the 1990s to bring the most alarming indicators of divergence in line with the Community average if Italy is to take part in EMU.[34]

The DC's failure to adapt Italy's political, economic and legal structures to the demands of the integration process called into question its European credentials and created scepticism about the sincerity of its commitment among its allies. Could the proposals of one of the strongest proponents of EMU and political union be taken seriously when Italy's economic and political system represented a significant stumbling block to the achievement of these goals? A response to this question might be that it was erroneous to identify the lack of concrete action in these fields with only one political party: the DC. Raising this point reintroduces the importance of regime parties with which this chapter began.

The issue is more profound and complex than simply assigning responsibility for Italy's failures on the European front to the party which dominated Italian government and policy making until the early 1990s. As indicated at the beginning of this chapter, it was not the case that the European issue was simply determined by the DC. Regime parties, particularly those which are present from the birth of a regime, are significant in the way in which they shape the political and economic system, and it is this perspective which is most relevant to the argument here. The DC's hold on power in the face of a strong delegitimized communist opposition, thus preventing genuine alternation in government, gave the political and economic system its essential characteristics: unstable governments but a failure to renew the political and administrative class; the politicization of the state; the 'sharing out' (*lotizzazione*) of the top ministerial posts; the clientelistic use of state agencies located outside the parliamentary system of government; and the 'immobilism' of successive governments in key policy areas such as health, welfare, education, the South and reforms of the state. A bloated, inefficient and (often) corrupt state distributed economic resources according to political rather than economic criteria and the greater the level of distortions in the system the stronger vested interests became in its maintenance.[35]

To be sure, the DC was not the only party which enjoyed the fruits of this system, and nor can other factors (such as the inhibiting nature of the legalistic tradition of the administration)[36] be overlooked in evaluating Italy's chronic inability to bring its economic and political structures up to the EU average. Nevertheless, the 'centrality' of the DC was a key feature of the system's inability to meet the demands of European integration. It followed, therefore, that the DC's removal from power would be an important part of any solution to this problem. This points to a long-term dilemma which was at work in the DC's Europeanism. To become a truly pro-European party which acted in government in a way which matched its initiatives and the activity of its representatives in Brussels, the DC needed to reform itself and the system which it had fashioned; yet, the achievement of both of these was not possible without it relinquishing power. Neither the DC nor the political system could begin to undergo genuine reform without the party first extracting itself from the state and going into a period of opposition. This explains why the failure to achieve this reform had been primarily due to the resistance of large sectors of the party. From this perspective the DC's Europeanism was deeply flawed.

The DC's dilemma exposed a deep paradox at work in its Europeanism. It was argued earlier that the DC's Europeanism in the post-war period was an important element in the party's monopoly of power. It can now be seen that the type of Europeanism essential to its dominance was flawed and that the transition from flawed to genuine Europeanism involved a concomitant transition for the party from government to opposition. This paradox was seen most clearly in the European strategy pursued by the last DC-led government (April 1991 – June 1992 under Andreotti). Andreotti's policy aimed to achieve a deepening of the integration process which would give Italy (and thus the DC) more influence in (an increasingly federal) Europe, at the same time as anchoring the country to Northern Europe, specifically through the influence of the Franco-German axis in the EU. Andreotti viewed, therefore, any faltering in the integration process as a threat (hence the government's disillusionment with the Danish referendum's rejection of the Maastricht Treaty in 1992). Yet, this strategy was also predicated on the assumption that anchoring Italy securely within a federated Europe would result in a painless compliance of the country itself with the requirements of closer integration. The strategy also assumed that Italy was essential to the achievement of political and economic union. The debate in the late 1980s and early 1990s on the prospects of a two-speed Europe, and the currency crisis of autumn 1992 (which resulted in the exit of the lira from the EMS), shattered these assumptions and showed that Italy was unlikely to achieve the political and economic modernization necessary to reaching the EU average without the removal from power of the regime party itself.[37] The DC was hoist on its own European petard.

CONCLUSION: FROM FLAWED TO GENUINE EUROPEANISM?

If, as this chapter has argued, the DC's flawed Europeanism was a product of its nature and development as a regime party, then a shift from flawed to genuine Europeanism is now possible. The early 1990s witnessed unprecedented changes in Italian politics as a result of the end of the Cold War, the transformation of the PCI into a non-communist party of the left and the exposure of a systematic network of corruption practised by Italian political parties, and particularly by the DC.[38] These changes caused the decimation of the DC. Most of its leading members' political careers were destroyed by the commencement of judicial investigations into their affairs, and party membership and votes plummeted. The DC's reformers were hindered in their attempts to change the party by the resistance of elements of the old guard. This conflict eventually came to a head in January 1994 when the party split: the majority changed the DC into the PPI (the name of the DC's pre-war predecessor), while a more right-wing minority broke away to form the Centre Christian Democrats (who were to become a component part of a right-wing alliance, including neo-fascists, in the national elections). Other members had already left to follow either the ex-christian democrat Mario Segni and his referendum movement (which was subsequently to form an electoral pact with the PPI), or the Social Christians (a left-wing group which had split from the party and entered a left-wing alliance for the elections); and some subsequently departed for Berlusconi's new centre-right *Forza Italia*! movement or the renamed neo-fascist National Alliance. As the official successor to the DC, the PPI's vote collapsed at the 1994 elections, the party obtaining only 11.1 per cent of the vote, compared with the DC's 29.7 per cent in 1992 (itself a drop from 34.3 per cent in 1987). In the subsequent European elections in June (in a campaign dominated by national issues) the PPI's vote plummeted to 10 per cent from the DC's 32.9 per cent in 1989. The consequence of the Italian elections was the formation of a right-wing government and the exclusion of the ex-DC (the PPI) from office for the first time in the post-war period.

The PPI, in short, must now develop its Europeanism as a party of opposition rather than as a permanent party of government. While this will probably not result in much change from its predecessor's official enthusiasm and support for European union (the PPI is still an active member of the EPP), the party is nevertheless freed from responsibility for successive governments' lack of concrete action in various areas to further the cause of a united Europe. Moreover, a subsequent return to office without its regime party status could complete the PPI's shift from flawed to genuine Europeanism by testing the new party's commitment in government. In the meantime, the main forces which gained from the DC's demise and went on to constitute the government (*Forza Italia!*, the Northern League and the National Alliance) were not as pro-European in their views as the old DC or the new PPI. Indeed, the new prime minister, Silvio Berlusconi, although not patently anti-European, was a pro-marketeer more along Thatcherite lines and no lover of intervention and standardization from Brussels. His movement, *Forza Italia!* set up its own group in the European Parliament.

The demise of the DC had two effects on the shape of EU politics. First, it sapped some of the strength of the EPP and introduced into the EP a new contingent of MEPs who were less enthusiastic about a federal Europe. Second, it increased the likelihood that, for the first time in the post-war period, Italy would be less pro-federalist – and less obliging towards its fellow member states – in its stance on European issues, even if, paradoxically, the new government achieved domestic changes which made convergence of the Italian economy with other EU countries more likely. For the PPI this would be quite a novelty: the party would find itself, for the first time, *opposing* the Italian government's European policy, rather than slavishly following it as the DC did for such a long period of time.

NOTES

The research for this chapter was completed during a Visiting Fellowship in the Department of Political and Social Sciences at the European University Institute, Florence. The author thanks Peter Kennealy, Emir Lawless, Simon Hix and the EUI's library for their bibliographic assistance and the University of Salford for financial assistance.

1 See Paolo Farneti, *The Italian Party System* (London, Frances Pinter, 1985).
2 It was not, of course, only this, but this aspect is the most important from the perspective of this chapter. For a good introduction in English to Italian Christian democracy see Robert Leonardi and Douglas A. Wertman, *Italian Christian Democracy: The Politics of Dominance* (London, Macmillan, 1989).
3 On Italian foreign policy in general see Carlo M. Santoro, *La politica estera di una media potenza. L'Italia dall'unità agli anni ottanta* (Bologna, Mulino, 1991).
4 As noted by Geoffrey Pridham in his review of party and other literature in 1980, 'Concepts of Italy's approach to the European Community', *Journal of Common Market Studies*, vol. 19, no. 1, September 1980, p. 81.
5 See the list of texts at the end of this chapter for some of the more useful documentary sources.
6 Franco Maria Malfatti, 'Un convegno della Dc sui temi internazionali. Nato e Cee vivono oltre la perestojka', *Il Sole 24 Ore*, 16 March 1990. See also Giulio Andreotti, 'Il ruolo dell'Italia nell'integrazione europea', *L'Italia e l'Europa*, 28–29, 1991 (Andreotti was, until the early 1990s, a key figure in shaping the DC's post-war foreign policy).
7 Severino Galante, 'In search of lost power: the international policies of the Italian

Christian Democrat and Communist Parties of the 1950s', in Ennio di Nolfo (ed.), *Power in Europe? II Great Britain, France, Germany and Italy and the Origins of the EEC, 1952–1957* (Berlin, De Gruyter, 1992), p. 410. For an example of the more conventional view see J. LaPalombara, 'Politica estera italiana. Immobolismo al tramonto', *Relazione Internazionali*, September 1989, p. 98.

8 Maurizio Cotta, 'European integration and the Italian political system', in Francesco Francioni (ed.), *Italy and EC Membership Evaluated* (London, Frances Pinter, 1992), p. 208.

9 See Philip Daniels, 'Italy and the Maastricht Treaty', in Stephen Hellman and Gianfranco Pasquino (eds), *Italian Politics: A Review*, Vol. 8 (Bologna, Mulino, 1993), p. 201.

10 For a summary of social christian political thought on Europe see Andrea Chiti-Batelli, 'Guido allo studio dell'unificazione europea. Bibliografia ragionata', *L'Italia e l'Europa*, vol. 8, nos 20–21, December 1981, part I ('Cristiano-Sociali').

11 For an analysis of the influence of the federalist movement in Italy see Sergio Pistone, 'L'Italia e l'integrazione europea', *L'Italia e l'Europa*, 28–29, 1991.

12 Paul Ginsborg, *A History of Contemporary Italy: Society and Politics 1943–1988* (London, Penguin, 1990), p. 214.

13 Philip Daniels, David Hine and M. Neri Gualdesi, *Italy, the European Community and the 1990 presidency: Policy Trends and Policy Performance*, Centre for Mediterranean Studies Occasional Paper no. 3, University of Bristol, June 1991, p. 16.

14 Cotta, 'European integration and the Italian political system', pp. 211–12.

15 For a useful summary see Douglas A. Wertman, 'Italian attitudes on foreign policy issues: are there generational differences?', in Stephen F. Szabo (ed.), *The Successor Generation: International Perspectives of Postwar Europeans* (London, Butterworths, 1983), esp. section 5.6 ('Attitudes toward European integration and patriotism').

16 David Hine, 'Italy and Europe: the Italian presidency and the domestic management of the European Community', in Robert Leonardi and Fausto Anderlini (eds), *Italian Politics: A Review*, vol. 6 (London, Frances Pinter, 1992), p. 53.

17 On the emergence of a consensus among the parties on Europe see Richard Walker, *Dal confronto al consenso. I partiti politici italiani e l'integrazione europea* (Rome, Istituto Affari Internazionali, 1976).

18 For a general analysis of the federations and EP groupings see Simon Hix's chapter in this volume; and Francis Jacobs, Richard Cobbett and Michael Shackleton, *The European Parliament* (Harlow, Longman, 1992, 2nd edn), chapter 5. For a succinct summary of the EUCD and EPP see Report of the Secretary General of the EPP / EUCD EPP-Political Bureau / Council EUCD, Joint Meeting Brussels, 14 January 1993 (EPP Documentation, mimeo). For other useful sources of information see the bibliography of this chapter.

19 Basic Programme of the European People's Party adopted by the IXth EPP Congress Athens, 11–13 November 1992, Version of 5 February 1993, EPP Documentation DOC-EN\DV\222\222009, mimeo, p. 7.

20 European People's Party, *On the People's side: Action Programme 1989–1994*, VIIIth EPP Congress, Luxembourg 1988, Documentation 8, European People's Party (Brussels, EPP group of the European Parliament, 1989).

21 See, for example, Clay Clemens, *Christian Democracy: The Different Dimensions of a Modern Movement*, Occasional Papers no. 1 (Brussels, Parliamentary Group of the European People's Party, 1989); and European People's Party, *Efforts to define a Christian Democratic 'Doctrine'*, Occasional Papers no. 2 (Brussels, Parliamentary Group of the European People's Party, 1989).

22 See Statuto del Partito Popolare Europea approvata dal VIII Congresso PPE, 14–16 novembre 1990, Dublino (marzo 1993), EPP Documentation, mimeo.

23 See, for example, the survey by Luciano Bardi, *Il Parlamento della Comunità europea. Legittimità e riforma* (Bologna, Il Mulino, 1989), which found the DC to be the fourth most pro-European out of the twelve major parties in Germany, France, Italy and Britain (p. 98). The DC's position is paralleled by high figures for the Italian parties as a whole (see p. 92).

24 On the 1984 and 1989 election campaigns see Geoffrey Pridham, 'Italy', in Juliet Lodge

(ed.), *Direct Elections to the European Parliament 1984* (London, Macmillan, 1986); and Philip Daniels, 'Italy', in Juliet Lodge (ed.), *The European Parliamentary Elections of 1989* (London, Macmillan, 1989).

25 See *Handbook of the European People's Party (CD-Group) of the European Parliament* (Luxembourg, 1986), pp. 329, 347–8.

26 Pistone, 'L'Italia e l'integrazione europea', pp. 179–82.

27 See, for example, Bino Olivi, 'L'Italia nella Cee degli anni '70. Problemi e prospettivi', in Natalino Ronzitti (ed.), Istituto Affari Internazionali, *La politica estera italiana. Autonomia, interdependenza, integrazione e sicurezza* (Varese, Edizioni di Comunità (Istituto Affari Internazionali), 1977), p. 205.

28 See Gisele Podbielski, 'The Common Agricultural Policy and the Mezzogiorno', *Journal of Common Market Studies*, vol. 19, no. 4, June 1981, p. 348; R. Galli and S. Torcasio, *La partecipazione italiana alla politica agraria comunitaria* (Bologna, Mulino, 1976), esp. pp. 21–45; and Massimo Roccas, 'Italy', in Dudley Seers and Constantine Vaitsos (eds), *Integration and Unequal Development: The Experience of the EEC* (London, Macmillan, 1980), especially pp. 109–11.

29 See Daniels et al., *Italy, the European Community and the 1990 Presidency*.

30 Hine, 'Italy and Europe', p. 52–3.

31 Hine's analysis found that Italy had (in late 1990) the lowest figures for implementation of the internal market programme, and the highest number of infringement proceedings against it for failing to comply with Community law (ibid., pp. 54–5).

32 By 1991 Italy had more outstanding debt than any country in the world except Japan and the United States. It was the biggest borrower in the EU and its ratio of outstanding debt to GDP was roughly double the average of the other eleven countries. It was also the only country where the debt was growing faster than the economy itself.

33 Antonio Giolitti, 'Italy and the Community after thirty years of experience', *International Spectator*, vol. 19, no. 2, April/June 1984, p. 76.

34 On the implications of the Maastricht Treaty for Italy and the inadequacies of existing government responses see Daniels, 'Italy and the Maastricht Treaty', esp. pp. 202–6.

35 See, for example, F. Cazzola (ed.) *Anatomia del potere DC. Enti pubblici e 'centralità' democristiana* (Bari, De Donato, 1979), and R. Orfei, *L'occupazione del potere. I democristiani 1945–1975* (Milan, Longanesi, 1976).

36 For the attempts so far to streamline the administration in so far as dealing with EU matters is concerned see Hine, 'Italy and Europe'.

37 On the suspension of the lira from the EMS see Daniels, 'Italy and the Maastricht Treaty', pp. 208–13.

38 Space does not permit a detailed treatment of these changes. For an overview see Martin J. Bull and James L. Newell, 'Italian politics and the 1992 elections: from "Stable Instability" to instability and change', *Parliamentary Affairs*, vol. 46, no. 2, 1993.

SELECT BIBLIOGRAPHY

Clemens, Clay, *Christian Democracy: The Different Dimensions of a Modern Movement*, Occasional Papers no. 1, Brussels, Parliamentary Group of the European People's Party, 1989.

Colarizi, Simona, 'The Italian political parties and foreign policy in the 1950s', in Ennio di Nolfo (ed.), *Power in Europe? II Great Britain, France, Germany and Italy and the Origins of the EEC, 1952–1957*, Berlin, De Gruyter, 1992.

Cotta, Maurizio, 'European integration and the Italian political system', in Francesco Francioni (ed.), *Italy and EC Membership Evaluated*, London, Frances Pinter, 1992.

Damilano, Andrea (ed.), *Atti e documenti della Democrazia Cristiana 1943–1967*, Rome, Edizioni Cinque Lune, 1968, 2 vols.

Daniels, Philip, Hine, David and Gualdesi, M. Neri, *Italy, the European Community and the 1990 presidency: Policy Trends and Policy Performance*, Centre for Mediterranean Studies Occasional Paper no. 3, University of Bristol, June 1991.

Daniels, Philip, 'Italy and the Maastricht Treaty', in Stephen Hellman and Gianfranco Pasquino (eds), *Italian Politics: A Review*, vol. 8, Bologna, Mulino, 1993.

European Parliament Directorate General For Research, *Research and Documentation Papers: Political Parties in the EC and European Unification*, Political Series no. 14, 10 1988, Luxembourg, European Parliament, 1988.

European People's Party, *Europe: The Challenge. The Principles, Achievements and Objectives of the EPP Group from 1979 to 1984*, Luxembourg, EPP Group (CD Group) of the European Parliament, 1983.

European People's Party, *Efforts to define a Christian Democratic 'Doctrine'*, Occasional Paper no. 2, Brussels, Parliamentary Group of the European People's Party, 1989.

European People's Party, *On the People's side: Action Programme 1989–1994*, VIIIth EPP Congress, Luxembourg 1988, Documentation 8, European People's Party, Brussels, EPP Group of the European Parliament, 1989.

Ferraris, Luigi Vittorio, 'Italian-European foreign policy', in F. Francioni (ed.), *Italy and EC Membership Evaluated*, London, Frances Pinter, 1992.

Galante, Severino, 'In search of lost power: the international policies of the Italian Christian Democrat and Communist Parties in the Fifties', in Ennio di Nolfo (ed.), *Power in Europe? II Great Britain, France, Germany and Italy and the Origins of the EEC, 1952–1957*, Berlin, De Gruyter, 1992.

Giolitti, Antonio, 'Italy and the Community after thirty years of experience', *International Spectator*, vol. 19, no. 2, April/June 1984.

Handbook of the European People's party (CD-Group) of the European Parliament, Luxembourg, The Group of the European People's Party (CD Group) of the European Parliament, 1986.

Hine, David, 'Italy and Europe: the Italian presidency and the domestic management of the European Community', in Robert Leonardi and Fausto Anderlini (eds), *Italian Politics: A Review*, Vol. 6, London, Frances Pinter, 1992.

Leonardi, Robert and Wertman, Douglas A., *Italian Christian Democracy: The Politics of Dominance*, London, Macmillan, 1989.

Malgeri, F. (ed.), *Storia della Democrazia Cristiana*, Rome, Cinque Lune, 1978–1989, 5 vols.

Pistone, Sergio, *L'Italia e l'unità europea. Dalle premesse storiche all'elezione del Parlamento europeo*, Turin, Loescher, 1982.

Pistone, Sergio, 'Italian pressure groups and political parties in the discussion on European Union', in Walter Lipgens and Wilfried Loth (eds), *Documents on the History of European Integration. Vol 3: The Struggle for European Union by Political Parties and Pressure Groups in Western European Countries 1945–1950*, Berlin, Walter de Gruyter, 1988.

Sbragia, Alberta, 'Italia/CEE. Un partner sottovalutato', *Relazioni Internazionali*, June 1992.

Walker, Richard, *Dal confronto al consenso. I partiti politici italiani e l'integrazione europea*, Rome, Istituto Affari Internazionali, 1976.

9 The Spanish Socialists

Richard Gillespie

Once described as 'the least typically Spanish and the most European of Spanish parties',[1] the Spanish Socialist Workers' Party (PSOE) can claim this distinction to have been applicable throughout its history. Created in 1879, and by far the oldest of Spain's parties, the PSOE has always been influenced by other European socialist forces. Early on, there was much imitation of the French socialist organization led by Jules Guesde, while after the demise of the Franco regime in 1975–76 the strongest external influence was the German Social Democratic Party (SPD). Within the PSOE both liberals and fundamentalists have looked to other parts of Europe for ideological inspiration.

More generally, there has been a tendency in modern Spanish political history for progressive, modernizing groups to identify with Europe, while conservative sectors have been more insular, or have sought to base foreign policy on the country's traditional links with former American colonies and the Arab world.[2] This dichotomy has been undermined in recent years by the democratization of the Spanish right and the consolidation of Spain's European involvement; but for most of the present century attitudes to Europe were largely an extension of domestic political differences.

The Spanish Socialists have a reputation for being among the leading advocates of European union. The purpose of this chapter is to analyse the development of the PSOE's attitudes to Europe in order to demonstrate that the common view should be qualified. There were deep ambiguities in the party's position before 1976 when the existence of the authoritarian Franco regime and a relatively strong rival Communist Party helped keep the PSOE on the far left of the European socialist movement.[3] These ambiguities appeared to have been resolved during the Spanish transition to democracy in the late 1970s, when Felipe González as leader overcame opposition from the militant grass roots of the party and imposed more moderate policies designed to appeal to a majority of the Spanish electorate. From being the main opposition party in 1977–82, the PSOE went on to win a huge electoral victory in 1982, on a decidedly pro-European programme. However, the experience of Spanish membership of the European Community from 1986 brought further shifts in PSOE attitudes towards Europe. In particular, it encouraged a more tenacious commitment to the defence of national interests, especially after the establishment of the European Union in 1993, with Spain by this time feeling threatened by plans to enlarge the Union.

EARLY AMBIGUITIES IN THE PSOE POSITION

Although the Socialist Party presents itself as always having been committed to the European ideal, its early reactions to the development of the EEC were in fact highly ambiguous. Until the death of General Franco in November 1975, the PSOE's central objectives were to survive his dictatorship – both in exile and as a modest clandestine force in parts of Spain – and to help to replace Francoism with a progressive democratic regime. The existence of democratic government throughout the EEC was an important cultivator of Community support within the PSOE, but insufficiently compelling for the party initially to support Spanish entry without reservation.

There were two reasons for this, the first historical, the second ideological. The party had felt betrayed on several occasions by the Western democracies: their policy of 'non-intervention' had helped the Axis-backed Francoist side win the civil war of 1936–39; moreover, the democracies had failed to act decisively against Franco at the end of the Second World War, had eventually admitted Francoist Spain to the United Nations in 1955, and went on to subscribe to a preferential EEC trade agreement with the regime in 1970.

For historical reasons, then, the Spanish Socialists were unsure about whether a pro-EEC stance would act as a lever against the Franco regime: it might, they feared, facilitate Spanish entry without prior democratization, and thus even strengthen the dictatorship, given the economy's increasing dependence on foreign investment and the European market.

At the same time, the party's long experience of hardship and clandestine activity left it broadly supportive of radical anti-capitalist positions. Although its own historical European leanings, reinforced by the presence in France of many exiled Spanish socialists and the aid received from socialists and trades unionists of the EEC more generally, left the PSOE sympathetic to the idea of European unity, the party was ideologically averse to the capitalistic orientation of the early Common Market. The resolutions on international affairs approved at successive PSOE congresses in France, usually held every three years, reveal rather different policy emphases at different times. Congress resolutions in 1958 and 1961 made no reference to the EEC, while at the ensuing 1964 congress there was controversy because party secretary Rodolfo Llopis had attended a pro-European meeting in Munich in 1962 without first obtaining the authorization of the party's directing committee. It was not until 1967 that a degree of support was registered, perhaps in response to the gentle urging of fellow members of the Socialist International. The resolution issuing from that congress at last mentioned the Treaty of Rome and supported European unity as a means of 'counteracting' the power of the USA and Soviet Union, although it insisted upon democratization as a precondition for Spanish entry and called for the EEC to become 'the main driving force for peace and progress in the underdeveloped countries'.[4]

However, this was the most supportive position adopted by a PSOE congress prior to the late 1970s. In the interval, party policy on Europe was marked by the wave of radicalism that accompanied the PSOE's renewal and the rise of Felipe González, as Llopis and the old guard lost authority. The resolution at the 1970 congress simply condemned the recent trade agreement between Spain and the EEC; two years later, 'without analysing ... the internal character of the Common

Market', an equivalent resolution just called for Spain's non-admission so long as Francoism survived. The 1974 resolution maintained that European unity could not be based on 'political and economic institutions serving international capitalism', although it did commit the PSOE to participation in the democratization of European institutions, 'freeing them from the domination of capital and directing them to benefit the legitimate interests of the workers'. For much of the 1970s, the PSOE claimed, in González's words at the 1972 congress, to be fighting for 'a workers' Europe with a truly socialist character'.[5]

Only after the PSOE had been drawn into the collaborative consensus politics of the early post-Franco years did it become more pragmatic and drop its ideological objections to the EEC. It was no doubt influenced here by the strong political support received from the Socialist International in 1976–77, and subsequently saw membership of the Community as a defence against the military threats to democratic consolidation, manifest in the coup attempt of February 1981.[6] Another consideration was a strong socialist desire for Spain to overcome its economic and military dependence on the USA, which was thought possible only if a European foreign policy was developed.[7] Besides, by the early 1980s the PSOE had accumulated an electoral majority and in 1982 won a general election in the middle of a serious economic recession. The Spanish experience of two decades earlier had been that economic recovery and fast growth benefited from a large influx of foreign capital and greater European economic involvement. Not surprisingly, then, entry to the EC became a central priority for the González government, and certainly one of its most trumpeted triumphs when finally achieved on 1 January 1986.

SOCIALIST POLICY MAKING AND THE EC

Before discussing PSOE attitudes towards Europe in more detail, it is important to establish the status of Spain's European policy since 1982: following the move into government, was this policy still that of the party, or did the centre of policy making shift to the government and public officials? Certainly, while the party was in opposition, from 1977 at least until 1979, its members exerted considerable influence over policy formation. Yet even before the Socialists took office, electoral and other considerations led many socialists to agree to González leading the party on his own terms. Thereafter, teams of political advisers, joined after 1982 by government think tanks and civil servants, had greater influence than ordinary party members, whose role became much more passive. Internally, the PSOE became an authoritarian party in which policy was decided by the leadership, which itself was subordinate to the González government.[8] This should be borne in mind when comparisons are made between the programmes of different Spanish parties. PSOE policies are often party policies only to the extent of party bodies endorsing policies formulated within the administration, where political appointees coexist with professional administrators and experts.

Particularly after entry into the Community in 1986, the party as such played no role in the formation of Spanish EC policy. This reflected not only party subordination to its leaders in government, but also the highly specialized and technical nature of many EC matters. Rather than party representatives exercise close control over the elaboration of Spain's European policy, it was they who occasionally went to the civil servants for detailed information, for example when preparing policy documents.[9] This applied to Spanish foreign policy making in general, although government ministers did discuss major issues with party leaders at PSOE executive meetings. Any notion that the party should determine policy, having received electoral support for its programme (i.e. the so-called 'mandate' theory of democracy), was rejected on the grounds that the government had a duty to represent the interests of the whole country.[10]

The lack of party influence created no tension between party and government for there was a broad consensus surrounding European policy, both in society and in the party, at least until the Maastricht Treaty on European Union provoked controversy. In July 1989 an opinion poll found a majority of Spaniards favouring European integration; 49 per cent were federalist enough to want to see a European president and 50 per cent wanted to see European parties and common elections throughout the Community.[11] An indication of the strength of PSOE support for further integration is that even when the government announced a very tough Convergence Plan in 1992, whose target for cutting the budget deficit exceeded the difficult economic targets set at Maastricht the previous year for participation in a European monetary union, only two members of the party's large federal committee (elected at the party congress, supposedly to supervise the work of the party executive committee) registered reservations by abstaining.[12] PSOE support for government European policy was quite genuine here, in contrast to the much more reluctant endorsement that the party had given to its leadership's volte face over NATO membership in 1984.

Besides the non-party, governmental input into Spanish policy, a further difficulty in identifying the PSOE's European policy is that, until the aftermath of Maastricht, there was considerable consensus among the Spanish parties on this issue. Even the Communist Party, identified in the 1970s with Eurocommunism, has not been opposed to the EC as a concept, only to the specific forms taken by the EU in the early 1990s. There has been no fundamentally anti-EC party in the Spanish Parliament, where annual 'state of the nation' debates have often been characterized by bipartisanship between the PSOE and the centre-right opposition over Europe.

However, if we focus on the 1989 and 1994 elections to the European Parliament, some differences of emphasis were evident among the Spanish parties. In 1989 the PSOE presented itself as the most European of Spain's parties. During the lead up to polling day, the party organized a conference on Socialism and Europeanism, with European Commission President Jacques Delors, SPD leader Oskar Lafontaine, and Spanish EC Commissioner Manuel Marín as speakers; and in the election itself the PSOE was the only Spanish party to stand on a trans-European programme, that of the Confederation of Socialist Parties of the European Community.[13] This was drafted by a working group headed by the then Spanish president of the European Parliament, Enrique Barón.

To the left of the Socialists, there was greater emphasis from the communist-led United Left (IU) on the need to develop a 'social Europe' than there was in the Euro-socialist programme.[14] The United Left claimed to be the only force on the Spanish left to offer an alternative to the socio-economic policies of the EC; it criticized the government's management of the Spanish presidency of the EC in early 1989 for not pushing the development of a social Europe, for being deaf to the demands of the European Parliament, and for a performance deemed 'more declaratory than operative' in relation to developing an EC foreign policy.

'Rhetorical Europeanism', as well as weakness in the defence of Spanish national interests, was also a criticism voiced by Adolfo Suárez's Social and Democratic Centre (CDS).[15] Meanwhile the programme of the centre-right People's Party (PP) was surprisingly quite compatible with the Socialists'. It called for a closer European union, the development of a European foreign policy, a strengthening of the European Parliament, the development of a citizens' Europe – but with a social and regional dimension – and a big increase in the structural funds with the aim of achieving 'cohesion' between the prosperous and underdeveloped areas. Only by dwelling on respect for the family and solidarity against terrorism did the PP programme differ much from the Socialist document.[16] In order to differentiate itself in the eyes of the voters, the PSOE ended up creating a straw man to fight against. The socialist campaign was based on the fiction that voters were being given a clear choice between a citizens' Europe, represented by the PSOE, and a Thatcherite Europe, the implication being that the PP was fully identified with Thatcherism.[17]

Only after the signing of the Maastricht Treaty in 1991 did inter-party differences become more significant, largely because the treaty had immediate consequences for Spanish economic policy, the programme for convergence among the European economies requiring the Spanish government to introduce a succession of economic austerity measures over the next few years. Not only did the party leaders clash more regularly over EC-related matters, but there was also considerable differentiation along party lines within the electorate. An opinion poll published in September 1992 suggested that if a referendum had been held on the treaty that González had signed, only 34 per cent of Spaniards would have voted for it. When the responses were identified with voting intentions, it was found that 56 per cent of PSOE voters were prepared to vote 'yes' in such a referendum, compared with only 37 per cent of PP voters and 28 per cent of IU voters.[18] This poll indicated that Spanish voters, including a large minority of PSOE supporters, were more reluctant to back further European integration than in the 1980s, the main reason being the economic sacrifices that were being demanded in the name of economic convergence.[19]

By the time of the European election in 1994, the policy divergence between Spain's two main parties was still not fundamental, but their differences with the United Left were more evident. The Communist Party, which dominated IU, was very critical of the project for European union designed at Maastricht: a Europe for the bankers, it claimed. Meanwhile the PSOE and PP both tried to present themselves as the best defenders of Spanish interests in Europe. PP leader José María Aznar's statements on Europe were somewhat inconsistent: in his bid for centre votes, he echoed the PSOE rhetoric in support of a united and progressive Europe, while to placate a group of Eurosceptics in his party leadership he accused González of conceding too much in European negotiations. Fortunately for the People's Party, the election was not decided on European issues – the economic recession and a series of government-related corruption scandals dominated the campaign, enabling the PP to inflict the first national election defeat on the PSOE since 1979.

PSOE OBJECTIVES IN EUROPE

From the late 1970s, as the party became much more moderate on virtually all issues, the PSOE's European postures evolved from an emphasis upon socialist ambitions to the assertion of national objectives, and from an emphasis upon the political benefits of membership to a perception of the EC as a catalyst of modernization. If in the late 1970s the party ideal was a 'democratic, socialist and non-imperialist Europe', overcoming an existing domination by large monopolies,[20] by the 1980s the capitalist framework was accepted. While there was still talk of the European context being a more appropriate arena than the national one for the implementation of much of the party programme, and there was an emphasis upon the need for social 'cohesion' as well as further political and economic integration, the PSOE basically came to accept the realities of the Community and to work for Spain to become a leading member of it.

During the 1980s a considerable strain of Euro-idealism ran through the party, its support for European federalism expressing the sentiments of a generation that had grown up identifying the relative backwardness of Spain with national isolation. That generation's sentiments were very much those expressed by the philosopher José Ortega y Gasset earlier in the century when he wrote 'Spain is the problem, Europe is the solution.'[21] This simple faith in Europe helped the PSOE to weather the arduous process of negotiating entry, and to accept terms that were in certain respects harmful to national interests, such as those of the fishing industry. Yet even as the calculations about national interest became more dominant, there was no immediate questioning of the federal European ideal. It was thought that the national interests of a country of intermediate size and status, such as Spain, lay in a strong union, whereas a mere increase in intergovernmental co-operation was considered likely to benefit only the more powerful countries.[22] The PSOE thus lent its express support to the notion of a federal Europe, although González recognized at the 32nd party congress in 1990 that this was a long way off and that the most that could be achieved in the meantime was the development of 'shared sovereignty'.[23]

The party's federalism was reflected in repeated calls during the 1980s for the Confederation of Socialist Parties of the EC to be transformed into a federal European socialist party, a theme pushed especially by deputy party leader Alfonso Guerra and contained in the party's Programme 2000 Manifesto.[24] The idealism behind such calls was not always matched in political practice, however. In May 1990 González admitted that on EC policy issues, his government often found itself closer to the Italian Christian Democrats than to the British Labour Party.[25] The internationalism upon which a genuine European socialist party would be based comes up against different national interests and the North–South cleavage, which for instance leaves the Northern European social democrats far less committed than the PSOE to a strengthening of the EC Mediterranean policy. It is therefore doubtful whether the Party of European Socialists, launched in November 1992, will function coherently.

PSOE pronouncements on the type of European Union it favours have been fairly vague. The more left-wing statements contained in party congress resolutions have insisted that Europe must speak with a single voice if it is to influence world affairs, and that this must be 'a progressive voice, a left-wing voice' (1988 congress). Also contained in such resolutions have been calls for an enhanced role for the European Parliament. Such an emphasis is not surprising from political actors who not so long ago contributed to democratization in Spain, and who would also like to see the strength of social democratic parties in the EU translated into comparable representation in European institutions.[26]

Yet since taking Spain into the EC, the PSOE's commitment to the development of a 'social Europe' has been limited to support for the Social Chapter, and the dominant theme in socialist discourse since the late 1980s has been that of a citizens' Europe rather than that of a social Europe. Thus a party congress resolution in 1990 supported the idea of a European Union based on 'three great pillars': monetary union, common citizenship and a common foreign and security policy. The idea of economic and social cohesion between richer and poorer regions and member states was added as something of an afterthought.[27]

The impediment to a greater emphasis upon a social Europe, especially if the notion extends to a reduction in class divisions, is that the Spanish Socialists' own governmental record on social protection was not outstanding. Growth rather than redistribution was the clear priority during the PSOE's first decade in office. Despite real improvements during the 1980s, Spain remained, next to Portugal, at the bottom of the EU social spending league table,[28] and unemployment benefits were even reduced at a time of recession in 1993. From early on, the trades unions, including the socialist General Workers' Union (UGT), became major critics of the government's social policies and what they saw as its neo-liberal economic strategy.[29] For the PSOE to have persisted with the rhetoric about a social Europe would have invited charges of hypocrisy.

A more constant feature of PSOE European policy since the late 1980s has been a defence of national interests. This was not made explicit at first, which probably explains why the Partido Popular decided to attack the government on the grounds that it was so full of utopian European notions that it was neglecting the defence of domestic interests. In practice, though, the Socialists showed a growing commitment to the furtherance of national interests, a concern perhaps first recognized on paper in 1988 in a discussion document that was used in the course of a programmatic renewal exercise. There was a reference there to the need to try to ensure that common decisions adopted by the EC reflected Spanish interests, especially in relation to important areas of national interest such as Latin America and the Mediterranean.[30] Since Spain's most durable traditional links have been with areas outside Europe, particularly Latin America and the Arab world, it is not surprising that it has become a prominent advocate of greater EC/EU external activity to assist the development of these regions, where Spanish involvement has grown since the late 1980s.

Other European issues over which Spanish national interests have been visibly pursued include resistance to Community efforts to limit CO_2 emissions, which Madrid has argued should be more lenient in the case of the less developed European economies;[31] Spanish blocking of the EC decision on internal frontiers, seen as compromising Spain's claim to Gibraltar;[32] arguments concerning the distribution of the structural funds; and, based on the Maastricht Treaty, the introduction of the Cohesion Fund to finance infrastructural improvements and environmental projects in the poorer states. Despite Spanish efforts to obscure the fact by presenting the Spanish share of structural funds as a proportion of GDP, Spain received the lion's share of such funds in the late 1980s and early 1990s.[33] Meanwhile, in the battle over the Cohesion Funds, the Spanish government used arguments based on size of population and territory in order to obtain 60 per cent of the money, although in GDP terms Spain was more prosperous than the other states qualifying for the funds (Ireland, Greece and Portugal).[34]

NATIONALIST AMBITIONS

There was some tension between PSOE insistence that European integration had to be based on reducing the developmental imbalances between member states and between regions, and the González generation's undisguised ambition for Spain to become a member of the leading group of EU states. After Spain's accession to the EC, this ambition led Spain's representatives to try to work with the German and French governments, rather than form a united front with the poorer Southern European states. However, after the transformation of Central–Eastern Europe, Spain's leaders found their traditionally good relations with German counterparts tested by the German desire to commit Community funds to Europe's eastern periphery at the same time as Spain was pressing for more attention to be given to the problems of the non-European Mediterranean states.

Spain and Germany found themselves on different sides in relation to the Cohesion Fund controversy of 1991–92. Spain momentarily became the standard bearer of the poorer EC states, and found that, even after the fund was accepted in principle, there was still a hard battle to fight to overcome Northern resistance to implementation. In May 1992 González threatened that Spain would hold up EU enlargement plans if its financial petitions were not taken more seriously.[35] However, this was a dangerous game for the Spaniards to play, especially following the currency crisis which affected the peseta in September, and which once again led to calls around Europe for a 'twin-track' approach to monetary union. Fearing that Spain might be left in the 'slow lane' more than he feared the loss of the Cohesion Funds, González ended up telling Helmut Kohl at a bilateral summit that in fact the Cohesion Fund was not vital for Spain, although it probably was for Ireland, Portugal and Greece.[36] This showed that proximity to the European political heavyweights was valued more than occasional Community pay-outs to the poorer states, because in the long term what mattered was to place Spain among the 'core countries' like Germany and France.[37]

During 1992 Spain's Socialists were so committed to meeting the convergence targets set as criteria for the next stage of monetary and economic union that they adopted draconian budgetary plans in the full knowledge that they thereby risked losing the next general election (in fact, in June 1993 the Socialists won the election, but lost their absolute parliamentary majority). Even so, in the context of Spain's worst recession for many years, the budget deficit remained stubbornly high, prompting government ministers during 1993 to echo the sentiments of those favouring a longer period of convergence before further steps were taken towards European Monetary Union (EMU).

Meanwhile, the Spanish Socialists became less definitely federalist with regard to European political union. One fear they had was that a federal Europe might strengthen the separatist movements based in some of Spain's regions, through diluting the authority of Madrid. Just as worrying was the prospect of EU enlargement, which promised to strengthen the north European presence and reduce the relative weight of the Union's southern member states. While González's government wanted to see the whole of Europe eventually forming part of the Union, it feared that Spain might lose influence and veto power as a result of concomitant changes in the decision-making mechanisms, designed to ensure the governability of the larger EU.[38] In 1993–94 the negotiations on the entry of the EFTA states saw most members of the EU wanting to increase from twenty-three to twenty-seven the minimum number of votes required for a blocking minority in qualified majority votes. In 1994 González temporarily vetoed this move, fearing that decisions unsympathetic to Spain might be taken on matters affecting crucial national interests, such as the rules concerning Mediterranean products.

The fact that Spain stood together with an anti-federalist member like the UK on this issue showed how the defence of national interests now overshadowed the commitment to European federalism. The Spanish Socialists still supported federalism in principle, but their leaders were searching for alternative formulae to a strong European presidency. For example, in May 1992 González endorsed a proposal to create a five-member European directorate, seen by Spain as just large enough (in the context of the Twelve) to include a Spanish member.[39]

It is likely that the retreat from federalism (or at least from advocating a strongly centralized EU) will continue, not least because of the declining electoral position of the PSOE and the strength of public support for displays of national assertiveness. Unless Spanish influence is institutionalized in some future European political architecture, governments in Madrid are likely to resist further European centralization and opt instead for a political system reliant on a considerable degree of inter-governmental co-operation.

Another important development in Spanish political life in the early 1990s was the rise of the nationalist parties, with the Catalan Convergence and Unity (CiU) alliance holding the balance of power in parliament from 1993. Dependence on Catalan nationalist support for a majority in parliament had the potential to force Spanish governments, whether based on the PSOE or the PP, to become more responsive to regionalist and micro-nationalist demands. At Maastricht, González co-sponsored the creation of the EU's Committee of the Regions, but this body was criticized by the Catalans for being purely advisory and for including representatives of local government as well as of the regions.

THE INFLUENCE OF THE PSOE IN EUROPE

The PSOE very quickly acquired a high profile in the EC following Spain's accession in 1986. There were several reasons for this. First, the party learned quickly that Spain's 'intermediate' position in Europe could be cleverly exploited to get the best out of both worlds: the economy was large enough for Spanish postures to be taken seriously by Community leaders, but at the same time Spain was sufficiently underdeveloped to act occasionally as a 'poor' state, yet certainly as the leading 'poor' state, able to mobilize the support of other 'cohesion' states even when Spanish postures were partly self-serving. Second, the PSOE received dividends from its domestic electoral success. Before Euro-elections were held in 1987,[40] the PSOE's representation in the European Parliament (EP) was determined on the basis of its national standing, which gave it thirty-six of Spain's sixty seats in Strasbourg. The party thus acquired for a while the largest presence within the European socialist group, itself the largest grouping in the EP.[41] Subsequently, the Spanish Socialists performed well in the EP elections in 1987 and 1989, on both occasions attracting more votes than the PP, CDS and IU together. In June 1987 the Socialists won 39.1 per cent of the vote and obtained twenty-eight seats; in June 1989 they took 39.7 per cent of the vote and won twenty-seven seats.[42] Before dropping to 30.7 per cent of the vote and twenty-two seats in 1994, the PSOE was thus one of the leading parties within the Socialist group. Third, the high degree of national consensus surrounding Europe during the early years of membership gave González a high degree of credibility as Spain's representative in the EC, as a leader who did not need to pay attention to an anti-European lobby back home. And fourth, the PSOE's success can be attributed to the high calibre of some of the people it sent to Brussels and Strasbourg, among them commissioner Manuel Marín, who had earned European respect during the hard negotiations on Spain's entry, the former foreign minister Fernando Morán, and former transport minister Enrique Barón, who became president of the European Parliament in 1989.[43]

The influence that Spanish Socialists have exerted in the EC has often been non-partisan, and only occasionally has a specific party interest been in evidence. Spanish representatives and officials have certainly lobbied effectively over the question of structural funds, obtaining the lion's share for their country in the late 1980s and early 1990s. Spanish parties share a common appreciation of these funds, just as they uniformly deprecate the Common Agricultural Policy, which does not function to Spain's advantage. However, the PSOE has a vested interest in the structural funds, for within Spain it is the region of Andalucía, the party's main stronghold since the late 1970s, that has done best out of the structural funds.[44] In this poor southern region, European aid helps to bolster up PSOE electoral support, for it is generally local Socialist officials who determine the allocation of public contracts, and there are many people who feel that their livelihoods depend on the continuation of the PSOE in office.

Two areas of foreign policy that were stressed by the PSOE far more than their centre-right rivals during the 1980s were Central America and the Mediterranean. Towards the end of the decade, Spanish conservatives had misgivings about the González government's support for the Central American peace process, fearing that it would be perceived as a challenge to the regional hegemony of the USA, which was still a crucial economic partner for Spain. Fernando Morán claimed to see some improvements in EC policy on Central America after just a year of Spanish membership.[45] Yet the largely unfulfilled desire to commit the EC to a more comprehensive policy of support for democracy and development in Latin America was still present in PSOE party congress resolutions early in 1988.[46] When in the first half of 1989 Spain gained its first opportunity to occupy the EC presidency, after just three years experience of Community matters, an aid plan for Central America was brought in. However, observers have judged that, for Latin America as a whole, there was less progress during the Spanish presidency than there was in relation to aid for North Africa, the latter already being a much more established area of EC external interest.[47]

In relation to the Arab world, the Spanish presidency of 1989 was also used to work for a Middle East peace settlement under UN auspices, a policy to which the PSOE had earlier helped to commit the Socialist International.[48] The Peace Conference that was eventually held in Madrid in late 1991 was organized on a different basis, but the choice of venue was a reward for constant Spanish diplomatic efforts on this issue and the fact that in recent years the government had established relations with Israel while skilfully managing to maintain its traditional Arab links. Overall, the PSOE was pleased with the 1989 Spanish presidency of the EC for maintaining the momentum of progress on European integration and for committing the Community to greater external activity.[49] The only area of policy where González admitted to little achievement was in relation to the Social Chapter.[50]

Between 1989 and 1992, the main question over which the Socialist government sought to exert influence was that of committing the EC to a reduction in the disparities not only between European regions but also between member states. Early in 1991 the Spanish government found no support among European leaders for a proposal for the Community to set up an interstate compensation fund, such as exists in Spain at the interregional level, to channel wealth from the relatively prosperous to the relatively poor areas.[51] However, at Maastricht the Spanish managed to get the principle of 'cohesion' established, addressing the problem of interterritorial developmental unevenness as opposed to social inequalities. The twelve member states agreed to create a Cohesion Fund to finance environmental projects and to develop trans-European communications networks in countries whose per capita income was under 90 per cent of average income in the Community; to revise the operation and volume of the structural funds; and to devise a system of contributions to the EC budget based on the relative prosperity of each state.[52] The Spanish Socialists regarded this as something of a triumph, only to find during 1992 that the wealthier partners, especially Germany and the UK, were strongly opposed to a real increase in aid to the poorer members, and certainly were not prepared to entertain the volume of funding aspired to by the Spaniards.[53]

The PSOE campaigned for the Cohesion Fund and managed to rally a degree of support for the idea in the Confederation of Socialist Parties of the EC.[54] Spain's non-Socialist Commissioner, Abel Matutes, and other conservatives criticized the idea of the fund, or ignored it, while defending cohesion in principle.[55] PP leader José María Aznar possibly underestimated popular approval of the fund when he described González as acting more like a beggar than a statesman at European summits.[56] Surprisingly, the Socialist Commissioner Marín was also openly critical of his government over this issue, possibly because the cool response that the Cohesion Fund proposal received within the Commission made it harder for him to enlist Community support for Spanish proposals in other areas.[57] Clearly, some Spanish Socialists were wary of persisting with a proposal that, while promising increased aid for Spain over the next few years, had a number of disadvantages: the proposal threatened to undermine the good relations developed by Spain with the German authorities; it had little chance of success except in a watered down form; and even if approved in full would still have meant far less of a transfer in resources than would realistically be necessary if interregional and interstate inequalities were to be tackled seriously. Nonetheless, the fact that the European Union has a Cohesion Fund is mainly attributable to Spanish Socialist influence.

CONCLUSION

Spain's membership of the EU enabled the PSOE to strengthen its international presence and exert an influence in matters of particular interest to both party and country. Party members supported the Community's eventual interest in Latin America, its increased co-operation with the Maghreb states, and its initiative over the question of cohesion. However, Felipe González as prime minister insisted that he would always put perceived national interests ahead of party interests in the event of any clash.[58] The context of this statement was provided by the very unpopular economic measures announced by his government during 1992, designed to meet the Maastricht criteria for economic convergence. The bottom line was that, if the poorer members' appeals for solidarity failed, the Spanish administration would seek to ensure that Spain was able to join the more prosperous members in further, more exclusive, integration moves.

Despite some signs of a domestic economic upturn by mid-1994, it was by no means certain that Spain would be admitted to the 'fast lane' if a 'twin-track' approach to EMU were adopted by the European Union. Moreover, the social costs of González's attempt to make the Spanish economy more competitive were likely to reduce the PSOE vote still further. If the party lost a general election as a result of EU-related policies, more critical attitudes towards European integration would be likely to be openly expressed in the party. Equally, if Spain continued to fall behind on the convergence criteria, there was the prospect of increased public disenchantment with Europe, which the Socialists could hardly ignore.

What had made the European dimension a potentially more controversial aspect of Spanish politics was the impact of European integration on the Spanish economy. The Maastricht-inspired move towards EMU affected the lives of all Spaniards much more directly and immediately than previous EC decisions had, through public sector cost-cutting measures. Public opinion was also influenced by the way in which the ERM crisis of 1992 brought instability to the peseta. Spaniards ceased thinking of Europe simply in terms of abstract notions of 'progress' and related unwelcome economic developments in Spain to European imperatives.

Subsequently, the Socialists had to face the threat represented by further enlargements of the Union. Having in the past always advocated more majority decision making for the EC, with the enlargement to fifteen members there was the un-welcome prospect of a more northern-dominated EU neglecting its southern members and channelling the bulk of its aid to the east rather than the south. There was already some hint of this in January 1992 when part of a new Mediterranean aid package was blocked in the European Parliament, among others by supposed socialist allies of the PSOE such as the SPD and British Labour Party. While these latter parties claimed to be acting out of concern for the human rights situation in Morocco, PSOE officials saw their behaviour as an example of northern reluctance to commit increased funds to the Mediterranean area.

In their efforts to maintain Spain's ability to block decisions in a larger EU, Spanish representatives found a strong nationalistic response at home. González eventually compromised on this issue in 1994, but public opinion remained a constraint upon Spain's parties and seemed to be a factor in the PSOE's increased nationalism on European issues. With the PP trying hard to reflect national sentiments on Europe, and emerging as an alternative party of government in 1994, the Spanish Socialists were left with little opportunity to allow government policy to follow ideological lines. Their experience supports the contention that ideology is an influence when parties are in opposition, or have recently come into office: being in government led the PSOE, to some extent, to 'nationalize' its European policy, while never questioning its underlying support for some form of a united Europe.

NOTES

1 J.J. Linz, *El sistema de partidos en España* (Madrid, Narcea, 1979), p. 89. Linz was referring to the 1930s.

2 B. Pollack and G. Hunter, *The Paradox of Spanish Foreign Policy* (London, Frances Pinter, 1987), chapter 6.
3 R. Gillespie, *The Spanish Socialist Party* (Oxford, Clarendon, 1989), chapters 4, 5.
4 PSOE, *Congresos del PSOE en el exilio*, vol. 2 (Madrid, Fundación Pablo Iglesias/PSOE, 1981), p. 126.
5 Ibid., pp. 158, 185, 205, 223.
6 K. Featherstone, 'Socialist parties in Southern Europe and the enlarged Community', in T. Gallagher and A.M. Williams (eds), *Southern European Socialism* (Manchester, Manchester University Press, 1989), p. 250.
7 J.M. Benegas, 'El papel de Europa en el concierto de las naciones', in A. Guerra et al., *El nuevo compromiso europeo* (Madrid, Sistema, 1987), p. 209.
8 R. Gillespie and T. Gallagher, 'Democracy and authority in the Socialist parties of Southern Europe', in T. Gallagher and A.M. Williams (eds), *Southern European Socialism*, pp. 163–87.
9 Interview with Gonzalo Bescós, Secretariat for Relations with the EC, Spanish Foreign Ministry, 28 May 1992.
10 Interview with Elena Flores, International Relations Secretary, PSOE, 20 February 1992.
11 C. del Arenal and J.A. Sotillo, 'Relaciones exteriores de España 1989', *Anuario Internacional CIDOB 1989* (Barcelona, CIDOB, 1990), p. 19.
12 *El País*, international edn (henceforth EPi), 22 June 1992.
13 Unión de los Partidos Socialistas de la Comunidad Europea, *Por una Europa unida, próspera y solidaria* (Brussels, 1989).
14 Izquierda Unida, *Elecciones Parlamento Europeo, Junio 1989, Programa*.
15 Centro Democrático y Social, *Paso al centro. Programa electoral para el Parlamento europeo, Elecciones '89*.
16 Partido Popular, *Europa unida democrática solidaria popular, Elecciones al Parlamento europeo, Junio 1989*.
17 R. Gillespie, 'Spain and Portugal', in J. Lodge (ed.), *The 1989 Election of the European Parliament* (Basingstoke, Macmillan, 1990).
18 *Cambio 16*, 14 September 1992.
19 It should be noted that poll results relating to Spanish attitudes on Europe show marked fluctuations and that September 1992 was a time of economic gloom in Spain. A *Financial Times* poll published on 1 June 1994 placed the Spaniards only second to the Italians in favouring 'a more integrated Europe as envisaged under Maastricht'. However, an examination of the European Commission's *Eurobarometer* for the period 1990–93 shows a significant decline in Spanish support for 'a European government responsible to the European Parliament'.
20 Pollack and Hunter, *The Paradox of Spanish Foreign Policy*, p. 138.
21 J. Ortega y Gasset, *Obras completas*, vol. 1 (Madrid, Revista de Occidente), p. 521.
22 M. Marín, 'La Comunidad Europea en 1992', *Anuario El País 1992*, Madrid, El País, 1992, p. 60.
23 *El Socialista* (henceforth ES), 15 November 1990.
24 A. Guerra, 'Hacia una acción política concertada en el espacio europeo', in Guerra et al., 1987, *El nuevo compromiso*, p. 271; ES, 30 June to 1 August 1990; EPi, 28 September 1987.
25 EPi, 28 May 1990.
26 ES, 1 December 1990.
27 PSOE, *32 Congreso. Resoluciones* (Madrid, PSOE, 1990), p. 9.
28 J.M. Maravall, 'Politics and policy: economic reforms in Southern Europe', in L.C. Bresser Pereira, J.M. Maravall and A. Przeworski (eds), *Economic Reforms in New Democracies: A Social Democratic Approach* (Cambridge, Cambridge University Press, 1993), p. 112; EPi, 26 August 1991, 17 August 1992.
29 R. Gillespie, 'The break-up of the socialist family: party–union relations in Spain, 1982–89', *West European Politics*, vol. 13, no. 1, 1990; D. Share, *Dilemmas of Social Democracy: The Spanish Socialist Workers Party in the 1980s* (New York, Greenwood, 1989), chapters 5, 6; *El Independiente*, 9 December 1988, 27 January 1989, 2 June 1989.

30 PSOE, *Programa 2000. Aspectos y problemas de la vida* (Madrid, Siglo XXI/Editorial Pablo Iglesias, 1988), p. 84.
31 EPi, 11 June 1990.
32 EPi, 1 July 1991.
33 EPi, 28 May 1990, 25 March 1991.
34 EPi, 27 July 1992.
35 EPi, 18 May 1992.
36 EPi, 21 September 1992.
37 Andrés Ortega, 'Spain in the post-Cold War world', in R. Gillespie, F. Rodrigo and J. Story (eds), *Democratic Spain: Reshaping External Relations in a Changing World* (London, Routledge, 1995). Despite recent bilateral tension, the German and Spanish governments agreed in June 1994 that they and the French would take advantage of their consecutive presidencies of the EU (July 1994 to December 1995) to ensure that the projected 1996 European Union conference on institutional reform would result in real progress towards European integration.
38 EPi, 27 December 1992.
39 EPi, 11 May 1992.
40 In 1986 Spain and Portugal decided to base their initial representation in the European Parliament on the distribution of seats in their national parliaments, but with EC-wide European elections not due before 1989 they went on to hold their own first European elections, in conjunction with domestic elections, in 1987.
41 ES, 28 February 1987.
42 ES, 15 June 1987, 15 January 1988, 15 June 1989; *Anuario El País 1990* (Madrid, El País, 1990), p. 138.
43 On the Spanish MEPs, see Jose M. Magone, *The Iberian Members of the European Parliament and European Integration*, Centre for Mediterranean Studies, University of Bristol, Occasional Paper no. 7, 1993, pp. 20–2.
44 ES, 15 March 1989.
45 ES, 31 May 1987.
46 ES, 31 January 1988.
47 J. Story and J. Grugel, *Spanish External Policies and the EC Presidency*, Centre for Mediterranean Studies, University of Bristol, Occasional Paper no. 2, 1991, pp. 37, 44.
48 ES, 15 May 1988.
49 ES, 15 May 1989, 30 June 1989, 30 September 1990.
50 ES, 30 November 1989.
51 EPi, 20 May 1991.
52 C. Alonso Zaldívar, 'El año en que acabó un mundo. La política exterior de España en 1991', *Anuario Internacional CIDOB 1991* (Barcelona, CIDOB, 1992); Alonso Zaldívar and M. Castells (eds), *Spain Beyond Myths* (Madrid, Alianza, 1992), p. 213; EPi, 16 December 1991.
53 EPi, 23 March 1992.
54 ES, 31 December 1991.
55 EPi, 8 July 1991.
56 EPi, 21 September 1992.
57 EPi, 8 July 1991, but for the government line from the same man cf. Marín, 'La Comunidad Europea', p. 60.
58 ES, 31 May 1992.

SELECT BIBLIOGRAPHY

Almarcha Barbado, M.A. (ed.), *Spain and EC Membership Evaluated*, London, Frances Pinter, 1993.
Alonso Zaldívar, C. and Ortega, A., *España, fin de siglo*, Madrid, Alianza, 1992 (also published in English by the same publisher under the title *Spain Beyond Myths*).
Featherstone, K., 'Socialist parties in southern Europe and the enlarged Community', in T. Gallagher and A.M. Williams (eds), *Southern European Socialism*, Manchester, Manchester University Press, 1989.

Gillespie, R., *The Spanish Socialist Party*, Oxford, Clarendon, 1989.

Gillespie, R., 'Spain and Portugal', in J. Lodge (ed.), *The 1989 Election of the European Parliament*, Basingstoke, Macmillan, 1990.

Gillespie, R., Rodrigo, F. and Story, J. (eds), *Democratic Spain: Reshaping External Relations in a Changing World*, London, Routledge, 1995.

Granell, F., 'Aims and outcome of the first Spanish presidency of the Council of the European Community', Centre for Mediterranean Studies, University of Bristol, unpublished MS, 1989.

Guerra, A. et al., *El nuevo compromiso europeo*, Madrid, Sistema, 1987.

Magone, J., *The Iberian members of the European Parliament and European integration*, Centre for Mediterranean Studies, University of Bristol, Occasional Paper no. 7, 1993.

Marín, M., 'La Comunidad Europea en 1992', *Anuario El País 1992*, Madrid, El País, 1992.

Morán, F., *Una política exterior para España. Una alternative socialista*, Barcelona, Planeta, 1982.

Morán, F., *España en su sitio*, Barcelona, Plaza & Janés, 1990.

Ortega, A., *La razón de Europa*, Madrid, El País/Aguilar, 1994.

Pollack, B. and Hunter, G., *The Paradox of Spanish Foreign Policy*, London, Frances Pinter, 1987.

PSOE, *Congresos del PSOE en el exilio*, 2 vols Madrid, Fundación Pablo Iglesias/PSOE, 1981.

Share, D., *Dilemmas of Social Democracy: The Spanish Socialist Workers Party in the 1980s*, New York, Greenwood, 1989.

Story, J. and Grugel, J., *Spanish External Policies and the EC Presidency*, Centre for Mediterranean Studies, University of Bristol, Occasional Paper no. 2, 1991.

10 The Greek Socialists

Susannah Verney

PASOK: THE DIFFICULT PARTNER

In October 1993, the dismayed reaction of much of the West European media to
the election of the new PASOK government revealed a widespread perception
of the Greek Socialists as difficult European Union partners. This controversial
reputation was largely acquired during the party's first term in office. During the
period 1981–85, the PASOK government had consistently refused to commit itself
concerning the future of Greece's relations with the then Community. At the same
time, it had continually insisted on special treatment for Greece, while displaying
a striking lack of Community consciousness. The latter was manifested not only in
an apparent insensitivity to EC rules, but also in the frequent vetoes which undermined European Political Co-operation (EPC) and hindered moves towards deeper
integration.

Particularly memorable was the Jumbo incident of 1983, when the PASOK
government had blocked a strong statement in EPC condemning the Soviet Union
for the shooting down of a civilian jet which had violated its airspace. In the words
of West German foreign minister, Hans-Dietrich Genscher, this incident had created
a 'confidence gap'.[1] In the UK, PASOK's stance during the Falklands War, when it
initially supported sanctions in EPC but later abstained during a vote against
Argentina in the UN, had also not been forgotten.

During its second term, from 1985–89, the party underwent a conversion. But
PASOK's increasingly enthusiastic pro-Europeanism did little to improve the country's
image. By this time, it was apparent that the development gap separating Greece
from its partners was widening instead of narrowing. While this was widely blamed
on PASOK's inflationary economic policies, in fact this was only part of the story.
Although the first oil price crisis of 1973 had made it clear that radical economic
restructuring was necessary, this had never taken place, either under PASOK or
under previous governments. As a result, an economy whose annual growth rates
had been approximately double the OECD average during the 1960s fell behind the
rest of Western Europe from 1980 onwards. Greece thus became established as a
problem Community member, which was encountering great difficulties in keeping
up with the pace of economic integration.

In the early 1990s, the re-emergence of that long-term apple of Balkan discord, the
Macedonian question, greatly aggravated the country's unpopularity within the EU.
As official opposition, PASOK adopted an inflexible stance on the recognition of the
Former Yugoslav Republic of Macedonia (FYROM) and played a leading role in

blocking a settlement with the new northern neighbour. After the party returned to power in 1993, its Macedonian policy brought the new Greek government into direct and open conflict with the recently rebaptized European Union. This created a climate in which part of the West European press even began to demand Greece's expulsion from the EU.[2] Thus, for many observers, the Macedonian issue consolidated the picture of PASOK as an intransigent and 'anti-European' party.

In fact, during PASOK's brief twenty-year history, its attitude towards the Community has continually shifted, covering the whole range from an adamant anti-integrationist stance to an apparently ardent pro-federalism. This evolution of its EC policy mirrored the different phases in the party's own development, as it moved from the self-proclaimed national liberation movement of 1974 to the full member of the West European socialist left of 1994. Hence, understanding the party's current attitudes towards the European Union and how this may change in the future requires some background. This chapter will explain the reasons behind PASOK's initial adoption of an anti-EC stance, and how and why the changes in its EC policy have taken place. This will be followed by a thematic treatment of the party's stance towards European Union, and a discussion of current and future developments. First, however, it would seem wise to describe the mechanisms of party decision making in relation to the EU.

POLICY-MAKING PROCESSES

Greece, with its clientelistic traditions, has a long history of leadership-dominated political parties without an organized popular base. The only real exception was the communist left, with its tight democratic centralist structures. Thus, during the 1970s, observers were invariably impressed by PASOK's rapid construction of a mass party machine, which was an innovation in the Greek context. By mid-1980, the party already claimed to have 75,000 members, organized into 1,500 local and sectoral organizations and 700 organizational cells.[3]

However, while PASOK always laid considerable verbal emphasis on decentralization and popular participation, in practice, its members did not play an active role in policy making. The party congress was called only three times in twenty years, and did not lay down policy guidelines. Its main task was to elect the central committee, which in turn chose the executive bureau. But the party's higher echelons were always tightly controlled by Andreas Papandreou, who did not hesitate, for example, to dissolve three central committees in the party's first ten months of existence. Perhaps it was not surprising that subsequently, the central committee became a rather passive institution which offered no serious challenge to the policy of the leadership. In turn, the executive bureau was always considerably less important than the group of current favourites clustered around Papandreou.

Papandreou himself never functioned as a member of an elected party organ, but as president of the movement, over and above the organization.[4] At all three congresses, he was reconfirmed as president by acclamation. Naturally, there were no other contenders. Dissidents rapidly found, in the immortal PASOK phraseology, that they had 'put themselves outside the party organization'. Meanwhile, any cadre who seemed to be developing an independent power base ran the risk of speedy demotion.[5]

As a result, and despite its very different structures, PASOK, like the 'personality parties' traditional in Greece, was from the beginning completely dominated by its founder and leader. Papandreou's hegemony was especially apparent in the ideological sphere. Although for some years the party had a theoretical section, Papandreou, the ex-Berkeley professor, was always the party's leading theoretician. Thus, major ideological statements and changes in the party's stands were traditionally announced by Papandreou himself. Perhaps his most frequent mode of operation was to bypass all organizational channels and communicate directly with the press. For example, the long-awaited public admission that Greece was in the European Community to stay was not made by any of the higher party organs, but finally occurred at a Papandreou press conference in Brussels in the spring of 1985.[6] Because of its importance, the EC is an issue area where the degree of personal control by Papandreou himself was always particularly pronounced. While the leader might consult his personal advisers, including MEPs such as Christos Papoutsis, neither the central committee nor the executive bureau seemed to play any role in shaping the party line on the EC.

A similar situation applied to PASOK's government policy. In the PASOK cabinets of the 1980s, there was no sense of collective responsibility for EC relations. According to the former national economy minister, throughout PASOK's crucial first term in office, the cabinet 'never' discussed general government strategy towards the Community, while issues related to the EC were raised 'only once or twice'.[7] The Committee of Community Affairs, which had previously met on a weekly basis to co-ordinate EC policy, ceased to function.[8] The result was a complete lack of institutional structures for intergovernmental consultation and decision making on EC matters. In practice, the day-to-day management of Greek–EC relations was left in the hands of the deputy foreign minister with responsibility for EC affairs, and to a handful of technocrats in the foreign ministry's EC service. Meanwhile, the overall political direction of Greek–EC relations remained more or less the exclusive preserve of Papandreou himself.

The perpetuation of this pattern following the party's return to power in 1993 was strikingly underlined in the case of the trade embargo against the Former Yugoslav Republic of Macedonia. This controversial decision, which was to bring Greece into such open disfavour with its EU partners, was apparently taken by Papandreou personally against the advice of the foreign ministry. It was then announced to the members of the government and assembled journalists at the beginning of a cabinet meeting, without any pretence at prior discussion, let alone agreement, among the ministers – and, naturally, no consultation with the party.

INTERNAL DISSENT

This does not mean there have been no internal disagreements on the EC. For example, in 1980, the abandoning of the old Third Worldist positions in favour of the new, more pro-European policy provoked a crisis in the Thessaloniki party organization. One year earlier, leading party cadre Kostas Simitis had been expelled from the executive bureau after he authorized the circulation of a poster bearing a slogan regarded as too openly pro-EC. In the early 1980s, a breakaway group headed by former central committee member, Nikos Kargopoulos, left the party to form a groupuscule, ASKE, which continued to contest elections on an anti-EC platform into the 1990s.

EC relations were also the cause of interministerial demarcation disputes. One example was the clash between national economy minister Arsenis and deputy foreign minister Varfis during PASOK's first term in power, concerning who had final jurisdiction over EC policy. In the first months after PASOK's re-election in October 1993, there was a well-publicized conflict within the foreign ministry, with rivalry between minister Papoulias and his deputy Pangalos over who had greater authority in EC affairs.[9] In the end the policy espoused by Andreas Papandreou always prevailed.

Although PASOK's EC policy was always made at the top and handed down from on high to the party base, this does not mean that the latter was completely ignored. Among the reasons why PASOK for so long avoided formally admitting that Greece would not be withdrawing from the Community was the fact that so many of its own supporters still clung to the old anti-EC line. Moreover, as a populist party, PASOK was always sensitive to changes in the political climate. The party did not simply lead public opinion, but also reflected it. In fact, one of Papandreou's greatest skills was his ability to capture and channel the mood of the moment. Because PASOK so often acted as a mirror of Greek society, the changes in its EC policy were closely related to the metamorphosis which Greece itself has undergone over the past twenty years.

FACTORS SHAPING THE ANTI-EC STANCE

PASOK's initial hostility to the EC was an expression of the more general anti-imperialist climate of the immediate post-dictatorship period. More specifically, it can be seen as part of an intense reaction against Greece's 150-year history of foreign intervention sparked by the events of the previous decade. Given his centrality to any discussion of PASOK, a description of Papandreou's own move to an anti-EC stance can illuminate his party's subsequent policy. This was not simply a personal change of course. The experiences which turned Papandreou against the EC between 1964 and 1974 also shaped the outlook of a whole generation.

After more than two decades in the USA, Andreas Papandreou returned to settle in Greece in 1961, the same year in which the Greek government signed its Association with the EC. Greece at this time was a rapidly developing country on the borderline between the two Cold War blocs. Like the rest of the non-communist political world, Papandreou supported the Association as a way to modernize the economy and reinforce the political orientation towards the West.

Greece in the early 1960s was entering a period of political ferment, encouraging widespread hopes for a democratization of the repressive parliamentarism which had prevailed since the 1940s Civil War. After he entered politics, Andreas Papandreou himself was hailed by some foreign observers as the potential 'Greek John Kennedy' who could help to introduce a new era. But this former campus liberal was soon radicalized by the downfall of his father's Centre Union government in July 1965. As a government minister, Papandreou had personally clashed with the Americans over Cyprus, and he believed that the USA, the dominant foreign power in Greece, had engineered the Centre's removal.[10] It was at this point that he began to regard foreign influence as a threat to Greek democracy and launched the rallying cry of 'Greece for the Greeks', which was to become one of PASOK's main slogans a decade later. It was also in this context that he started to question the policy of export-led development on which the Association with the EC was based, and to suggest the re-examination of the agreement.[11]

His conviction that external dependence was the root of Greece's problems was reinforced by the military coup of 1967, which Papandreou, like many Greeks, believed to be US inspired. Internationally, the Greek dictatorship of 1967–74 coincided with the student protest movement against the Vietnam War, and with Allende's overthrow in Chile. In this sense, the anti-imperialist platform adopted by Papandreou and his anti-Junta Panhellenic Liberation Movement, PAK, was very much a product of its era. In the early 1970s, Papandreou became attracted to dependence theory. This led him to adopt an analysis of Greece as a peripheral country in the world capitalist system, which could only maintain relations with metropolitan centres like the US and Western Europe on an unequal and exploitative basis. On these grounds, by early 1973 Papandreou was openly challenging the continuation of the Greek Association.[12] During the dictatorship, PAK's radical analysis elicited a limited response in Greece. But with the Junta's fall, it came much closer to the popular mood.

As a small, weak state occupying a strategic position, modern Greece has historically been the object rather than the subject of Great Power politics. Of course, Greece had never been a colony. Its post-war domination by the United States, for example, took the form of a patron–client relationship. But following the fall of the military dictatorship in the summer of 1974, the atmosphere in Greece was reminiscent of a country undergoing decolonization. In a society traumatized by the two Turkish invasions of Cyprus in July and August 1974, there was deep anger with the USA and NATO for failing to react more dynamically to the tragedy, coupled with rage at US support for the repressive military regime. Moreover, considerable fear was generated by the threat of war with Turkey and the latter's subsequent opening of a whole series of bilateral issues which essentially challenged the status quo in the Aegean. The resulting sense of national humiliation and of betrayal by the country's allies found its outlet in an anti-imperialist upsurge. It was in this climate that Papandreou dissolved PAK, and founded PASOK.

PASOK had no real Greek socialist tradition on which to build. Before 1974, the Greek left had been dominated by the Communist Party. Even today, the Greek word *Aristera* meaning 'left', is most often used to denote the communist area of the Greek political spectrum. PASOK, however, rejected both communism and social democracy, the two main strands of the twentieth-century European left, and was, therefore, outside the internationalist tradition associated with each of them. The party was particularly vehement in its opposition to social democracy, which Papandreou denounced as the 'noble face' or 'genteel mask' of capitalism.[13]

Thus, despite its socialist title, PASOK's founding *Third of September Declaration* included only a few, vague references to socialism. Instead, it emphasized external dependence as the cause of all Greece's ills, proclaiming national independence to be the top priority.[14] The party ideology, based on dependence theory, was a direct legacy of the Panhellenic Liberation Movement, complete with the latter's opposition to the EC. So when, soon after the Junta's fall, the new civilian government announced its intention of upgrading Greek–EC relations by seeking full membership, PASOK came out unhesitatingly against accession. The party argued that EC membership would complete Greece's historic subjugation to imperialism. As a result, Greece would be left at the mercy of foreign decision-making centres, which would distort or abolish democracy to allow multinational monopolies to plunder the economy. Moreover, PASOK claimed that as an EC member, the country would become even more vulnerable to imperialist pressures for a sell out of national interests in Cyprus and the Aegean. Hence, in the party's view, EC membership threatened Greece's economic development, democracy, national sovereignty and territorial integrity.

PASOK's anti-EC campaign did not rely solely on the foreign intervention syndrome. Its dire warnings that the EC would reduce the Greeks to a nation of hoteliers and waiters evoked considerable response in a transitional economy, where both the primary and secondary sectors were dominated by small-scale producers. Unlike many fraternal parties elsewhere, PASOK did not emerge from the trades union movement, and was not based on the organized working class. The latter had never been a major force in Greece, where a high proportion of the workforce was traditionally self-employed, and where rapid social mobility and multiple job holding blurred class identification. In Papandreou's own words, PASOK was 'a Movement which expresses the interests not of just one social class, but of all the working people ... the worker, the farmer, the wage-earner, the artisan, the small businessman, the graduate, and the young'.[15] A nationalist crusade against a foreign demon like the European Community offered an ideal way of cementing this broad coalition of disparate interests. In a society which had experienced a very fast post-war urbanization and rapid but highly uneven economic growth, all these groups were linked by a strong sense of economic insecurity and a widespread fear of foreign competition.

To sum up, Greek socialism, born in 1974, was shaped by recent Greek history and by the particular conditions of that time. These were likely to make it intro verted and hostile to West European integration. But this was to change as both PASOK and Greece began to move beyond the trauma of 1974.

'ONLY IN IT FOR THE MONEY'?

It is often suggested that PASOK revised its view of the EC because of Greece's high financial inflows from the Community budget. As early as 1983, for example, this view was expressed by *The Financial Times* when it headlined an article, 'Athens and the EC – only in it for the money'.[16] By 1985, net receipts from the EC, while far from the sums subsequently achieved, were already equivalent to 1.5 per cent of GDP. However, particularly in the early years, the economic record of Greek membership was mixed, owing to the serious deterioration in the balance of trade.[17] Moreover, the benefits of EC membership were not solely pecuniary.

In the 1970s for the forces which opposed EC membership the Community had appeared to be just another manifestation of the external intervention so familiar in Greece's past. But it soon became apparent that the country's relationship to Europe had changed radically. In 1981 the smooth transfer to a socialist government indicated that Greece was no longer a praetorian state with foreign powers meddling in its domestic politics. In the same year, accession to the EC gave Greece the chance to become a decision maker rather than decision taker in broader European affairs. That Community participation gave this small state the chance to play a part on a major stage seems to have been quickly appreciated by Papandreou after his first experience of EC summitry at London in 1981. In particular, the

PASOK government soon discovered that European Political Co-operation offered a privileged platform for its 'proud and independent foreign policy'.[18]

Besides the effects of EC membership itself, another influence was PASOK's changing relationship to other socialist parties and the resulting impact on its self-image. In the early years, PASOK sought close links with fraternal forces from other states which it regarded as peripheral.[19] Thus, during the 1970s, it participated actively in a series of conferences of Mediterranean Socialist and Progressive Parties, mainly composed of parties from the Mediterranean's North African shore. At this time, relations with the West European socialist parties were cool, apparently the result of Papandreou's own break with the Socialist International (SI) during the dictatorship. But in the late 1970s, with Greek accession imminent, the EC socialist parties began to woo PASOK as a potential member of their European Parliament group.

The subsequent realization that the second Enlargement opened the prospect of a new South European bloc within the EC led the five socialist parties approaching power in Greece, Spain, Portugal, France and Italy, to discover a new ideological affinity. In 1980–81, their leaders held a series of meetings, which PASOK used to attempt a subtle modification of its image, from Third Worldist movement to South European socialist party. Meanwhile, in December 1979, PASOK had already agreed to join the European Parliament's socialist group once Greece entered the EC. But initially, it retained the correct ideological distance by remaining outside the Confederation of Socialist Parties of the EC and the Socialist International. However, by the end of the 1980s, PASOK had applied for membership of both organizations and was proudly promoting itself as a fully fledged member of the West European socialist family.

This partly reflected the broader changes in Europe, which had turned the Socialist International into a magnet for a wide range of progressive parties.[20] But socialist solidarity in PASOK's hour of need also played a role. A few months before the election of June 1989 which PASOK, mired in scandals, was clearly about to lose, prominent members of the EP socialist group, including its leader Rudi Arndt, and former EP president Piet Dankert, spoke at PASOK rallies all over Greece.[21] Again, before the follow-up election in November, Papandreou flew to Paris for a well-publicized meeting with President Mitterrand, at which the two men apparently discussed their 'common ideals for Europe'.[22] Projecting the image of the international statesman, Papandreou, now out of power and already committed for trial by a special court, used his West European socialist links to repair his tarnished reputation. During this period, PASOK, which had lost votes to the Synaspismos coalition to its left in the June 1989 election, also made much of its potential leading role in the reshaping of the whole European left-wing movement.

Besides these special circumstances, over the course of the 1980s participation in the EP group seems to have had a socializing effect, helping to bring PASOK's self-image and EC policy closer to those of its West European counterparts. An indication of this change came when PASOK, albeit with some hesitation, endorsed the socialist group's manifesto for the 1989 European election campaign.

The evolution of PASOK's EC policy also appears to have been closely correlated with the party's own changing relationship to power. The period of obdurate anti-Community opposition was relatively short lived and coincided with the party's own youthful 'national liberation' phase. In breaking the pro-Western consensus which had united all the non-communist parties in Greece since the civil war, PASOK was iconoclastic. Thus, in the immediate post-dictatorship period, PASOK's rejection of the EC signalled a clear break with the pre-1967 past, and helped to establish the newborn party as a radical new force on the Greek political scene. But then the 1977 elections, which saw PASOK double its vote to emerge as official opposition, began its metamorphosis from a radical protest movement to a potential governing party. The growing ambiguity in PASOK's EC policy as it came closer to power was part of a more general toning down of its radical image, which also left greater margins for manoeuvre to a future PASOK government. This process of readjustment was described by Papandreou in an interview some months before the 1981 elections, in which he explained that:

> PASOK started out as a new movement which needed an identity and this was provided by our vision of our country's future, our founding Declaration. But a party which is approaching power or which takes power has to face medium-term aims. These medium-term aims are not defined only by the ultimate goal, but also by the strength of the prevailing winds encountered on the road.[23]

In line with this policy of adapting to existing conditions, during its first term, from 1981–85, PASOK reluctantly accepted Greece's EC entry, which had taken place ten months before the election. But with the self-confidence generated by the second election victory in 1985, which consolidated the party's hold on power, came the major U-turn towards a pro-European position.

Finally, the interparty environment was also a factor. After the dictatorship, accession was the major plank in the programme of the governing Nea Dimokratia (ND). In 1974–77, PASOK's relentless hostility to this project was part of the dynamic opposition which helped it to overshadow the pro-Community centre and establish itself as the second major pole in the emerging two-party system. Then, between 1977 and 1981, PASOK operated a careful balancing act, on the one hand attempting to attract the pro-EC former centrists whose votes would bring electoral victory, while on the other, trying not to alienate its radical constituency. The latter was particularly important, given the presence of the anti-EC Greek Communist Party (KKE) to PASOK's left. The Greek CP was one of the most orthodox, pro-Moscow parties in Western Europe. It was also Greece's third political force, usually gaining an approximately 10 per cent share of the vote in general elections. After 1981, the KKE's uncompromising opposition to the EC and criticism of PASOK's acceptance of membership acted as a brake, which helped to delay PASOK's move towards a more openly pro-EC policy. Of course, when the latter finally occurred in 1985, the KKE was still hostile to the EC. But the CP's modification of its own anti-EC line with the publication of its *Theses* on the 1992 programme in March 1987, facilitated PASOK's increasingly pro-European shift in the late 1980s.

Thus, a wide range of influences, and not simply the financial aspects of European Community membership, contributed to the amendment of PASOK's EC policy. Moreover, the party's attitude towards the EC did not change overnight, but, as we have shown, evolved over time.

THE CHANGE OF HEART

In its early years, PASOK did not simply fight accession and call for the renunciation of the Association.[24] It also declined to participate in Greek–EC affairs as a matter of principle. For example, in January 1977, the party withdrew from the Greece–EC Joint Parliamentary Commission which administered the Association, claiming that it was of historic importance to separate its responsibilities from those of the government.[25] But after 1977, the strategy of non-participation in EC affairs was generally abandoned, with one notable exception when the party walked out of Parliament before Greece's accession treaty was ratified in June 1979.

While PASOK continued to oppose accession, its central target gradually shifted from the Community itself to the way in which the Nea Dimokratia government was handling EC policy. In particular, it tried to transform the accession question into an issue of democratic government, by frequently reiterating the demand for a referendum. Meanwhile, the party blurred its intentions with regard to the EC by proposing a series of alternatives to full membership, beginning with the 'Norwegian' trade treaty first mentioned in 1976, followed by the 'Yugoslav' model proposed in early 1978, and succeeded by the especially vague 'special relationship' at the end of the same year.

Once in power, PASOK quietly forgot the referendum, a party election pledge in both 1977 and 1981.[26] Meanwhile, the 'special relationship' quickly metamorphosed into the even more imprecise 'special regulations'. With the Greek Government Memorandum, submitted in 1982, PASOK in essence asked its European Community partners to provide some kind of justification for the party's U-turn on EC withdrawal. The Commission's main answer came the following year with the promise of special Integrated Mediterranean Programmes, over 50 per cent of which would be allocated to Greece. But it took another two years and Papandreou's threat to veto Iberian entry before the Council finally approved funding for the IMPs in March 1985, allowing PASOK to openly admit that Greece was now in the EC to stay.

However, it was the 1.76 billion ECU Community loan a few months later which really turned the tide in Greece–EC relations. Although the loan was accompanied by an economic austerity policy, paradoxically it seems to have increased the EC's popularity in Greece. It appears that public opinion was convinced by Papandreou's declarations that without EC support, Greece would have been forced to resort to the IMF on even more onerous terms. Certainly, the EC's *Eurobarometer* surveys noted a rapid rise in the number of respondents who felt Greece had benefited from membership, from 42 per cent in November 1985 to 50 per cent in the spring of 1986 and 60 per cent by the following autumn.

For the next few years, PASOK continued to claim that EC membership had been a mistake, for which the previous Nea Dimokratia government was responsible. The party argued that, having come to power when Greece was already in the EC, its options were limited because the costs of EC withdrawal were higher than remaining inside. While this formula suggested no more than a grudging acceptance of a *fait accompli*, in reality PASOK's policy had changed deeply, as was to become apparent when the European Community agenda moved on to the discussion of European Union.

PASOK AND EUROPEAN UNION

Political union

During the 1970s, PASOK had been an advocate of 'Europessimism'. Maintaining that Western Europe was in deep crisis, the party regarded political union as a 'propaganda trick'[27] rather than a practical possibility. But it also opposed such a prospect as threatening the sovereignty of the nation state. During the early years of Greek EC membership, PASOK's attitude towards institutional reform was clearly coloured by the dependence syndrome. Declaring that EC decision-making procedures were already designed to favour the strong, the party was against further moves away from intergovernmentalism, on the grounds that this would aggravate the weaker members' domination by the 'directorate' of big Northern countries. Thus, PASOK initially opposed limiting the national veto in the Council of Ministers and extending the powers of the European Parliament. As a result, the party's MEPs voted against the Spinelli Report in 1983,[28] while two years later, the PASOK government lodged some fifteen official objections to the conclusions of the Dooge Report. But with its subsequent signature of the Single European Act, PASOK modified its earlier positions by accepting qualified majority voting (QMV) in Council for all issues connected with the Single Market, along with the new co-operation procedure which enhanced the EP's role.

In company with the UK and Denmark, the PASOK government had originally voted against the convening of the intergovernmental conference (IGC) to revise the Treaty of Rome. But like the other two Eurosceptics, it eventually took part. PASOK's participation was partly motivated by the perennial Greek fear of a two-speed Community, in which the other member states would proceed to a deeper level of integration without the dissidents. But in addition, the IGC, which coincided with the negotiation of the European Community loan to Greece, also provided the first opportunity for the manifestation of the party's new pro-EC stance. So, contrary to expectation, during the negotiations PASOK emerged in favour of the increased use of QMV and of extending the responsibilities of the Commission and European Parliament.[29] PASOK was not a direct participant in the next IGC, convened in 1990, because by this time it was back in opposition. However, within the European Parliament, the EP's socialist group and domestic fora, the party declared that the second renegotiation of the treaty was an opportunity to reduce the EC's democratic deficit, and pressed for the upgrading of the role of the European Parliament. It was especially concerned that the EC's move into Economic and Monetary Union (EMU) and a Common Foreign and Security Policy (CFSP) should be given a distinct supranational dimension. A particularly frequent demand was for the EP to gain substantial powers in relation to EMU. Just how much the party's view had developed in a decade was indicated by the fact that it now declared itself in favour of 'a political union of Europe with a federal character'.[30]

Common Foreign and Security Policy

In this area, the change in party policy was even more dramatic. Security was always a particularly sensitive issue for Greece, the only EC member to feel itself facing a clear and present external danger. But for PASOK in the 1970s, the EC was part of the problem: 'the other side of NATO',[31] and a junior partner in the Western imperialist machine held responsible for the dictatorship, the Cyprus tragedy, and the Greek–Turkish conflict. During its early years in government, PASOK seemed to see European Political Co-operation (EPC) as an attempt by the ex-imperialist powers to limit Greece's right to determine its own foreign policy. As a result, during the party's first term in office, Greece gained the reputation of a habitual dissident in EPC. As an East Mediterranean and Balkan state permanently pre-occupied with Cyprus and Turkey, Greece necessarily had different foreign policy priorities from the other EU members. But in the early stages, it sometimes seemed as if the PASOK government preferred to assert Greece's new independence by dramatically highlighting these differences instead of contributing to the search for consensus. However, during the party's second term in office, as part of its more general change of attitude towards the EC, PASOK generally avoided spectacular disagreements and pursued a much more conformist line in EPC.

Initially, PASOK had been suspicious of any attempts to move beyond EPC towards a common foreign policy. For example, Greece was one of the countries which appended its reservations to the Genscher–Colombo proposals in June 1983. Many of PASOK's disagreements in the Dooge Committee also concerned foreign policy issues. The party was also adamant, in the words of one of its MEPs, that 'national defence . . . lies outside the scope of the Community's competence'.[32] But already in 1984, moves to reactivate Western European Union (WEU) served as a warning that this was an area where the other EC states were prepared to advance without non-WEU members, Greece, Ireland and Denmark. Papandreou's stance at the European Council in Milan in June 1985 indicated a reassessment, with his agreement that EPC could extend its scope to cover security issues so long as Greece's special interests were taken into account. This was also the position which the party maintained during the negotiation of the Single European Act. How far the Greek prime minister's thinking on this issue had changed was indicated in 1987, when the PASOK government applied for WEU membership. However, this application was rejected on the grounds that Greece did not accept first use of nuclear weapons. Nor was Greece accepted subsequently, when PASOK amended Greece's nuclear weapons policy.

Then the collapse of the Cold War order brought a dramatic change in the Greek security situation. With the Balkans rapidly reverting to a political earthquake zone, European Community membership initially appeared to be one of the few strong cards Greece had to play. Under the new conditions, it seemed that the development of a real EC foreign and security policy might provide a solution to Greece's new problems. Thus, by the time of the second IGC in 1990, PASOK had become a firm supporter of the CFSP. In fact, PASOK's position, like that of the Nea Dimokratia government, had become fully 'Europeanist', in the sense that it preferred the CFSP to develop as an EU policy embedded in the latter's institutions.[33] Both parties were disappointed with the final compromise which allocated implementation to the WEU. PASOK, completely reversing its earlier attitude, also criticized the Maastricht Treaty for not establishing a common defence policy.[34]

Moreover, both PASOK and Nea Dimokratia had hoped that the CFSP would be based on the principle of solidarity between the member states and the inviolability of Community borders.[35] The Maastricht Treaty of course did not include any such declaration. However, it initially appeared that the problem would be solved through Greece finally being admitted to the WEU, whose charter includes a commitment to mutual defence (Article V). But with Turkey also invited to join as an associate,[36] in June 1992, the WEU Council of Ministers issued the Petersberg Declaration, stating that Article V would not apply in a dispute between two member states.[37] Hence, the CFSP offered no new guarantees for Greek security in the highly unstable post-1989 conditions. Instead, WEU's explicit declaration that its allies would not defend Greece in case of attack by the state regarded as its major external threat could even be seen as weakening Greek security.[38] These developments, adding to the uncertainties generated by the reopening of border questions in the Balkans, aggravated Greek fears about the future. This was to have repercussions on future Greek attitudes towards the EU, which will be discussed in the conclusions.

Economic and Monetary Union

Meanwhile, as in the other spheres, the party's changing attitude towards economic integration indicated an enormous shift in perspective. In the 1970s, PASOK had denounced EC membership as threatening a complete loss of economic sovereignty, with Greece's future development determined by external capitalist decision-making centres. Then, during its first years in power, the PASOK government appeared to resist full Greek involvement in the Common Market. A series of attempts to negotiate exceptions and postponements in the application of Community rules[39] apparently aimed at retaining national control for as long as possible. At this point, the party was less than enthusiastic about the prospect of deepening the integration process by moving beyond the customs union to the single market. Yet a decade later, in the early 1990s, PASOK accepted the much more ambitious project of Economic and Monetary Union envisaged in the Maastricht Treaty – even though this entailed transferring considerable economic policy responsibilities to a central bank over which national governments would have no control.

While this suggested quite a policy reversal, there was a notable element of continuity in PASOK's insistence that economic integration should not focus only on free trade and market liberalization. PASOK maintained that neither the Single Market nor EMU could be regarded as an end in themselves, and explicitly linked its acquiescence to both with the promotion of social and economic cohesion.

With regard to the former, the PASOK government made a significant attempt to promote the EC's social dimension when it adopted the 'social space' as a main theme of Greece's second presidency of the Council of Ministers in 1988. This brought few immediate results, partly due to Papandreou's heart surgery and resulting incapacitation. Given the way in which PASOK functioned, both as party and as government, the effective absence of the leader undermined the presidency's capacity to undertake major political initiatives. However, the Greek presidency's promotion of the issue helped to raise the profile of the social dimension and contributed to the climate in which the Social Chapter was drawn up the following year. PASOK criticized the latter for not going far enough and at the time of the Maastricht IGC, called for the introduction of QMV on social issues as the only way to develop an EC social policy.[40] Subsequently, the party supported the 1993 White Paper on Growth, Competitiveness and Unemployment. It was particularly in favour of the development of structural measures, such as trans-European networks. However, its objections to the reduction of working hours and wages highlighted the concerns of a socialist party from a less developed member state. As a result, the conclusions of the December 1993 Brussels summit included the new Greek government's declaration that it would not regard itself bound to implement the proposals on labour market flexibility.

Meanwhile, after 1981, the party's initial demands that Greece receive special treatment as compensation for participating in the Common Market had gradually mutated into a more general demand for redistribution in favour of the Community's South. While economic cohesion became a PASOK flagship, this in fact reflected a long-term Greek concern that economic integration threatened to marginalize the weaker economies.[41] During the 1985 IGC, the PASOK government submitted a memorandum with draft articles on cohesion to be considered for inclusion in the revised treaty.[42] This helped to influence the wording of Article 130A of the Single European Act which committed the Community to 'reducing disparities between the various regions and the backwardness of the least favoured regions'. Subsequently, PASOK pressed for this treaty commitment to find concrete expression with the doubling of the structural funds achieved with the first Delors package. At the time of the second IGC in 1990–91, PASOK adopted the view that the EMU could not be limited to the nominal convergence of macroeconomic indicators, but should also aim at real convergence of development levels. In pursuit of this aim, the party used every possible occasion, particularly in the European Parliament, to advocate a significant increase in the Community budget[43] and the development of new structural policies to help the less developed countries join the EMU.

It was always clear that the conditions laid down at Maastricht made Greek participation in stage 3 of EMU highly unlikely for the foreseeable future. But interestingly enough, during the national parliamentary debate before the ratification of the European Union Treaty, PASOK, as official opposition, did not focus on attacking the treaty provisions as such. Instead, the party directed its fire against ND's economic policy, claiming that under a different government with other economic priorities, it would be possible for Greece to meet the Maastricht criteria. PASOK's acceptance of the Maastricht settlement reflected a recognition that the dramatic changes in Europe since 1989 had left Greece with few options. As Papandreou put it during the debate, 'it is only possible to give a positive answer to the European challenge, and to participate actively in what is being created in Europe. There is really no alternative, except the marginalisation of our country.'[44]

CONCLUSION

Thus, following a decade of readjustment in PASOK's EC policy, the realities of the post-Cold War order seemed to consolidate the party in its pro-Community stance. With the East European states and the other European non-members all eager to enter the Community club, questioning Greek membership no longer appeared desirable. Instead, amid the debates about a new European architecture, the new concern became how to safeguard the country's privileged insider status. This view now seemed to be the subject of consensus among Greece's main political forces, including the Communist Party. In December 1988, the KKE joined former Eurocommunists and a range of minor parties and personalities from the broad left to found the Synaspismos coalition, which adopted an openly pro-EC line. As a result, in the 1989 European Parliament election, no party of significant size stood on an anti-EC platform. In contrast, in the first Greek Euro-election eight years earlier, the anti-EC KKE and PASOK had picked up 53 per cent of the vote. By the time of the 1990–91 IGC, Greece had become one of the most pro-federal states in the Community, with ND and PASOK now sharing a striking similarity of views concerning the Community's evolution and the need for an active Greek presence within it.

Ironically, however, the end of the Cold War, which initially seemed to confirm Greece's EC orientation, also created the conditions in which it could be shaken. The realization began to grow that in a restructuring Europe, Greece was likely to be relegated to the second or third speed. This was unlikely to enhance the popularity of an EU already associated with the economic austerity programme introduced after Maastricht. But what really began to shape a new mood was the changing situation in the Balkans. This brought Greek foreign policy aims into direct conflict with those of the country's EU partners, causing disappointment with a Union felt to have shown insufficient solidarity with Greek vital interests. When the EU failed to meet Greek expectations that it would act as a new protecting power, first the ND government and then its post-1993 PASOK successor made a distinct overture to the USA.[45] In PASOK's case, this was somewhat ironic, given the anti-Americanism which had been the party's original trademark. But while great things were apparently expected from a Clinton–Papandreou rapprochement, US Balkan policy also proved disappointing from a Greek viewpoint.

Meanwhile, the Yugoslav crisis and the EU role in it had reactivated memories of an era when outside powers determined the fate of the Balkan peoples. In Greece, the German insistence on the immediate recognition of Croatia and Slovenia in December 1991 was widely held responsible for the dissolution of the Yugoslav federation. Of course, German reunification had already resurrected a number of historical demons and fuelled fears of a Europe once again dominated by the big countries. While such concerns were also expressed elsewhere, they possibly had a greater resonance in Greece, given the strength of the dependence syndrome in the country's political culture. In December 1993, the PASOK deputy foreign minister, Theodoros Pangalos, provoked a diplomatic incident when he publicly described Germany as 'a bestial giant with the brain of a dwarf'. These echoes of the radical PASOK of the 1970s, with its denunciations of the big Western powers, had considerable domestic appeal, and Pangalos' remarks contributed to a rapid rise in his personal popularity.

As always, PASOK's shifting stance both mirrored and influenced trends in public opinion. Amid the new Balkan insecurities, Greek society was becoming more introverted, focused on the country's multiplying disputes with its neighbours rather than on the broader European picture. The reopening of the Macedonian question, with all its emotional overtones, created an ideal climate for a resurgence of nationalist populism, less similar to that which had nourished PASOK's rise two decades earlier in the backlash following the Cyprus invasion. During PASOK's period out of power between 1990 and 1993, the Macedonian issue proved an ideal oppositional tool against Nea Dimokratia. But now PASOK was competing for nationalist laurels with the newly formed Politiki Anoixi, essentially a single-issue party focused on Macedonia.

The contest for most obdurate defender of national interests inevitably affected relations with the EU. When the PASOK government's trade embargo against FYROM resulted in the country's referral to the European Court, this aggravated popular feelings that Greece was being hard done by. The next *Eurobarometer* poll recorded a 9 per cent fall in the Greek respondents who regarded EU membership as a good thing, a 10 per cent drop in those who felt the country had benefited from membership, and a significant 22 per cent less satisfied with the functioning of EU democracy.[46] It was in this climate that Pangalos declared to the third party congress in April 1994 that 'if the nation is going to be endangered, then it would be better for us to go forward alone'.[47] This was particularly striking coming from the main government cadre responsible for EC\EU relations in 1984–89 and from October 1993 to June 1994, and someone always so well known for his pro-EU stance. The response from the party base was indicated in the following day's central committee election, when Pangalos came second, emerging as one of Papandreou's leading heirs apparent.

But such playing to the gallery over the EU should not be confused with a serious change of direction. It should rather be seen as the nationalist garnish on what remains a fundamentally Europeanist policy. PASOK continues to be firmly anchored in the EP's socialist group and adopts group positions on most of the major issues concerning the EU's future. Naturally, its views are tempered by the special concerns of a party from a small state. As Pangalos put it in his own inimitable way, 'Greece is not prepared to become the errand boy of one or other of the big countries.'[48] It was already clear that in the 1996 IGC, if PASOK were still in power, it would oppose institutional changes which reduced the relative weight of the smaller states. But the Greek government was not alone in this. After all, the rise of a more critical stance towards integration had become a more general phenomenon in post-Maastricht Europe.

Despite the effects of the Macedonian issue, Greek public opinion still remains quite strongly in favour of the EU. Even after Greece was taken to the European Court, 64 per cent of Greek *Eurobarometer* respondents still thought EU membership was a good thing, 69 per cent felt that the country had benefited from membership, and 70 per cent supported a rapid advance towards European integration.[49] While standing up to the EU may be popular, apparently an explicit move away from it would not.

This is reflected in the attitudes of the main political forces. Of the five main parties, only the KKE has readopted an openly anti-EU stance, albeit one which emphasizes the iniquities of the Maastricht Treaty rather than Greek EU membership itself. But the KKE has been relegated to the position of fourth party, and its anti-EU platform attracted only 6.3 per cent of the vote in the 1994 European Parliament election. In contrast, the other four main parties, PASOK, ND, Politiki Anoixi and the Synaspismos, all supported a federal Europe. During the European election campaign, the main argument concerned which party was likely to take the toughest line in defending national interests within the EU. All of the four were emphatic that this was where Greece belonged.

Broader changes in Europe and their effects on Greece will clearly influence PASOK's future EU policy. For example, Greece's definitive demotion from the European core to a second-class status would probably encourage greater introversion and stimulate isolationist sentiment. This could also result from an intensification of the Balkan crisis. Another important influence will be the evolution of the party itself. Given PASOK's leader-dominated structures, much could depend on the personality and attitudes of the new leader. As PASOK finally moved towards the post-Papandreou era, it remained to be seen what effect the succession struggle would have on party unity and identity. But speculation about the likely pre-dominance of 'populist' or 'modernizing' wings and their potential impact on EU policy tended to overlook the fact that Greece's options were limited. There was no alternative orientation capable of replacing the multi-faceted relationship with the EU. To quote PASOK' s new *3 September Declaration*, issued in 1993 to replace the party's original ideological manifesto, 'our European road is given'.

NOTES

1 Quoted in *The International Herald Tribune*, 24 September 1983.
2 See *The Economist*, 5 March 1994 and *The Spectator*, 9 April 1994.
3 Beate Kohler, *Political Forces in Greece, Spain and Portugal* (London, Butterworth, 1982), p. 130.
4 Michalis Spourdalakis, *The Rise of the Greek Socialist Party* (London, Routledge, 1988), p. 89, p. 126.
5 A Greek journalist described this as the 'elevator syndrome', because any individual or group seen to be rising to the 'top floor' of the party edifice was likely to be sent plunging down to the bottom. See Stelios Kouloglou, *Sta Ikhni tou Tritou Dromou: PASOK, 1974–1986* (Athens, Odysseas, 1986), p. 25.
6 *The Financial Times*, 3 April 1985.
7 Gerassimos Arsenis, *Politiki Katathesi* (Athens, Odysseas, 1987), p. 168.
8 P.K. Ioakeimides, 'I elliniki dioikisi kai i diamorphosi tis evropaikis politikis', in Loukas Tsoukalis, *I Ellada stin Evropaiki Koinotita: I Proklisi tis Prosarmoyis* (Athens, Papazissis\EKEM, 1993), p. 216.
9 This clash was resolved when Pangalos was moved to the Ministry of Transport in the June 1994 cabinet reshuffle.
10 For Papandreou's own view of this period, see his memoir: Andreas Papandreou, *Democracy at Gunpoint: The Greek Case* (London, Andre Deutsch, 1971).
11 See Ilias Nachman, *L'évolution de la pensée économique de A. Papandreou*, Ph.D. thesis for the University of Paris X, and Michael Pateras, *From Association to Accession: Changing Attitudes of Greek Political Parties towards Relations with the European Community, 1957–1975*, PhD thesis for the London School of Economics, 1984.
12 See e.g. Andreas Papandreou, *Apo to PAK sto PASOK* (Athens, Ladia, 1976), pp. 21–4, and PAK bulletin *Exodos*, February 1973.
13 Andreas Papandreou, *I Ellada stous Ellines* (Athens, Karanassis, 1976), p. 593, and Andreas Papandreou, *Apo to PAK*, p. 231.
14 For an English translation, see Richard Clogg, *Parties and Elections in Greece* (London, C. Hurst, 1987), pp. 217–22.
15 Andreas Papandreou, *Apo to PAK*, p. 276.
16 6 May 1983.
17 In the first year after Greek accession, the deficit on trade with the Community increased by 86.5 per cent. Particularly striking was the effect on the agricultural trade balance, which went into the red for the first time. One estimate suggests that during the first five years of membership, the increase in Greek losses from trade with the EC was 'more or less equal to the financial transfers from the EC, and may actually have been greater': Heinz-Jurgen Axt, 'The costs and benefits of Greek EC membership', *Intereconomics*, vol. 22, Sept–Oct 1987, pp. 249–57. The same author has calculated that by 1988, Greece's trade deficit with other EC members was equivalent to 8.3 per cent of the country's GDP. Heinz-Jurgen Axt, 'Southern Europe and the EC: divergence and cohesion', *The South-East European Yearbook 1991* (Athens, ELIAMEP, 1992), p. 61. In contrast, one year later, Greek net receipts from the Community budget amounted to 4.9 per cent of GDP: see OECD, *Annual Report on Greece 1989/90* (Paris, OECD), p. 68.

18 1984 European election slogan.
19 A glance at a 1977 party publication about PASOK's international activities provides a good visual impression of where the party felt its ideological affinities lay. The booklet is illustrated with photographs of Papandreou with Bulgarian president, Todor Zhivkov; his Romanian counterpart, Nikolae Ceaucescu; PLO leader, Yasser Arafat; Vasso Lyssarides, leader of the Cypriot EDEK; the presidium of the Yugoslav League of Communists; the leadership of the Iraqi Ba'ath party; and finally, one West European leader, the Secretary of the French Socialist Party, François Mitterrand, on the very last page. See *To PASOK sto Diethni Khoro* (Athens, PASOK, 1977).
20 Papandreou himself claimed that in the past, the SI 'did not have the correct policy and direction. But this has changed. It changed a long time ago. We are talking about a new International, an International which also plays a role in national liberation movements . . . an International which in a little while will include among its members communist parties which have changed their titles.' Andreas Papandreou to the PASOK central committee, quoted in *Eleftherotypia*, 29 November 1989.
21 Moreover, at a socialist group meeting in Athens, Rudi Arndt made a highly supportive speech, praising the way in which 'the present Greek Prime Minister has struggled for his country and his people. Papandreou is a motivating force in the EC and thinks in a European way.' In contrast, Arndt claimed that the main opposition party, Nea Dimokratia, 'does not have a European programme'. See *Eleftherotypia*, 4 and 7 March 1989.
22 Papandreou quoted in *Kathimerini*, 17 October 1989.
23 *To Vima*, 26 April 1981. Equally revealing was the new prime minister's comment at a November 1981 press briefing following his first EC summit, when he declared that 'PASOK won elections, it didn't carry out a revolution', quoted in *Eleftherotypia*, 2 January 1987.
24 PASOK was later to claim it had never demanded the abrogation of the Association; but see e.g. Papandreou, *I Ellada stous Ellines*, p. 447.
25 See the speech by Papandreou, published in *To Vima*, 11 January 1977, and his statement recorded in the official debates of the *Greek Parliament*, 14 January 1977, pp. 2327–9.
26 In any case, it had always been well known that calling a referendum was the exclusive prerogative of the president of the Republic, and that President Karamanlis, who had made it his life's work to take Greece into the EC, was adamantly opposed to a popular vote on this issue.
27 PASOK, *Ellada-EOK: O Antilogos* (Athens, Pasok, 1976).
28 As well as other reports which suggested extending the EP's powers, e.g. the Abens Report in July 1981.
29 See P.K. Ioakeimides, *O Metaskimatismos tis EOK: Apo tin 'Entoli' stin Eniaia Evropaiki Praxi* (Athens, Papazissis, 1988), p. 326. As a member of the Greek Foreign Ministry's EC section, Ioakeimides was an active participant in the development of Greece's positions during the IGC.
30 PASOK Member Takis Roumeliotis in the debates of the *European Parliament*, 12 December 1990, p. 172 (Greek version). This reiterated Papandreou's position in a speech to socialist group leaders in Madrid two days earlier. See also the declaration by former deputy foreign minister Theodoros Pangalos during the national parliament debate to ratify the Maastricht Treaty, that 'the time was ripe for a major qualitative leap, for political unification. The European Union is the federal state of the future', *Greek Parliament*, 29 July 1992, p. 83.
31 Or, as another party slogan put it, 'EOK kai NATO to idio syndikato' ('the EC and NATO [are] the same gang').
32 Spyros Plaskovitis, *European Parliament*, 26 October 1983.
33 PASOK MEP, Takis Roumeliotis, proposed in the European Parliament that the Commission and the Council of Ministers should determine policy guidelines together and both have the right of initiative on foreign policy and security issues. Debates of the *European Parliament*, 12 December 1990, p. 171 (Greek version).
34 Gerassimos Arsenis, *Greek Parliament*, 27 July 1992, p. 10.
35 See Papandreou's speech to the meeting of socialist group leaders in Madrid, 10 December 1990.

36 At the time of writing, Turkey, as an associate, was participating fully in the work of the WEU but without the right of veto. Greek membership, in contrast, had still not been ratified.
37 Reprinted (in English) in *I Ellada kai O Kosmos 1993* (Athens, Hellenic Foundation for Defence and Foreign Policy (ELIAMEP)), pp. 233–5. The same issue also includes the 'Protocol of Accession of the Hellenic Republic to West European Union', pp. 241–2.
38 A message which does not appear to have been lost on the Turkish general staff, judging by January 1994 leaks in the Turkish press that they had proposed reopening the question of Greek sovereignty over the Aegean islands.
39 Two examples are the regulatory tax, which effectively allowed a five-year delay in the implementation of the Common Market for a wide range of industrial products, and the introduction of value-added tax, put off from January 1984 to 1986 and finally to 1987.
40 See Papandreou's speech to the 17th Congress of the Confederation of Socialist Parties of the EC, Berlin, 8 February 1990.
41 A view which had been expressed, for example, by the right-wing government of the 1950s in its White Book on *Greece, the European Economic Community and a Free Trade Area* (Athens, Ministries of Co-ordination and Foreign Affairs, 1959).
42 Ioakeimides, 'O Metaskimatismos', p. 300
43 In the October 1990 plenary session, Papoutsis called for the structural funds to be doubled again. In December 1992, he declared that Delors II would be inadequate to allow the weaker countries to participate in EMU.
44 *Greek Parliament*, 28 July 1992, p. 39.
45 See *To Vima*, 12 December 1993.
46 See *Eurobarometer*, 41, July 1994.
47 Quoted in *Avghi*, 17 April 1994.
48 Interview in *Eleftherotypia*, 9 December 1993.
49 *Eurobarometer*, 41, July 1994.

SELECT BIBLIOGRAPHY

Christodoulides, T., 'Greece and European Political Co-operation: The Intractable Partner' in N.A. Stavrou (ed.), *Greece Under Socialism: A NATO Ally Adrift*, New York, Aristide Caratzas, 1988, pp. 281–304.
European Commission, *Greece in the Community: Assessments and Proposals*, Brussels, COM(83) 134 final, 29 March 1983 (reply to the Greek Government Memorandum).
Featherstone, K., 'Greece', in Juliet Lodge (ed.), *Direct Elections to the European Parliament 1984*, Basingstoke and London, Macmillan, 1986, pp. 117–37.
Featherstone, K., 'Greece', in *Socialist Parties and European Integration: A Comparative History*, Manchester, Manchester University Press, 1988, pp. 170–90.
Featherstone, K. and Verney, S., 'Greece', in Juliet Lodge (ed.), *Euroelections 1989*, London, Macmillan, 1990, pp. 90–106.
Greek Government, 'Position of the Greek Government on Greece's Relations with the European Community' (Greek Government Memorandum), March 1982, reprinted in *The Greek Review*, 17 July 1982.
Ioakeimides, P.K., *O Metaskimatismos tis EOK: Apo tin 'Entoli' stin Eniaia Evropaiki Praxi*, Athens, Papazissis, 1988.
Ioakeimides, P.K., *Evropaiki Politiki Enosi: Theoria – Diapragmatevsi – Thesmoi kai Politikes: I Synthiki tou Maastricht kai i Ellada*, Athens, Themelio, 1993.
Kazakos, P., 'Socialist attitudes towards European integration in the eighties', in Theodore C. Kariotis (ed.), *The Greek Socialist Experiment: Papandreou 's Greece, 1981–9* New York, Pella Publishing Company, 1992, pp. 257–78.
Kazakos, P. and Ioakeimides, P.K. (eds), *Greece and European Community Membership Evaluated*, London, Frances Pinter, 1994.
PASOK, *Ellada-EOK: O Antilogos*, Athens, PASOK, 1978.
Psomiades, H.J. and Thomadakis, S.B. (eds), *Greece, The New Europe, and the Changing International Order*, New York, Pella, 1993.

Tsoukalis, L. (ed.), *I Ellada stin Evropaiki Koinotita: I Proklisi tis Prosarmoyis*, Athens, EKEM\Papazissis, 1993.

Verney, S., 'From the "Special Relationship" to Europeanism: PASOK and the European Community, 1981–89', in Richard Clogg (ed.), *Greece, 1981–89: The Populist Decade*, London, Macmillan, 1993, pp. 131–53.

Part II
Comparative perspectives

11 Irish political parties and the European Union

Michael Holmes

INTRODUCTION

The Republic of Ireland joined the European Union in 1973, at the same time as Britain and Denmark. But unlike both of those countries, Ireland has a reputation as an enthusiastic pro-European country, and there is a far-reaching consensus among Irish parties in favour of EU membership. All of them are in favour of European integration and the progressive development of the Union. Furthermore, there is an equally strong degree of consensus among them about the policies of the EU and about promoting national interests in the Union.

The attitudes of the Irish political parties towards the European Union have crystallized on a number of occasions. Three referenda have been held on the EU in Ireland, and these provide opportunities to assess the overall stance of Irish parties towards membership and integration, and towards specific policies of the EU. European Parliament elections present another angle for viewing party positions. The elections also focus on specific EU policies, and they bring in the issue of organizational adaptation by the parties to the EU. However, neither referenda nor elections give the full picture of Ireland's political involvement in the EU. It is also necessary to look at the development of the parties' relationships with the EU at the national political level.

THE IRISH PARTY SYSTEM

Any discussion of Irish political parties and the European Union must deal with the fact that the Irish party system eludes any neat categorization in terms of the usual models of party systems which are applied in Western Europe. Irish politics is dominated by two parties, Fianna Fáil and Fine Gael, both of which can be described as centre-right catch-all parties.[1] They are separated by a historical nationalist cleavage.

Fine Gael was formed in 1933 by the merger of two small parties with Cumann na nGaedheal, the party which had formed Ireland's first governments but which lost its parliamentary majority in 1932. Fine Gael has never been able to regain a majority, but has consolidated a position as the second largest party in Ireland. Support initially was drawn largely from conservative business interests and large farmers. However, in the 1960s, the party took in a number of new members who introduced a more radical strain to policies, particularly on social issues, and some even laid claim to a mild form of social democracy. The party continues to promote both a pluralist social agenda and conservative economic policies.[2]

Fianna Fáil has been the largest party at every general election since 1932 (see Table 11.1 for election results since 1973). Not surprisingly, it has also been the dominant party of government. However, it has failed to win an overall parliamentary majority at any election since 1977, and in 1989 it finally reversed a long-standing tenet by going into coalition government for the first time. Fianna Fáil was originally based on strongly nationalist policies which drew support from all sectors, but particularly among small farmers. However, from the 1960s on, policies became increasingly conservative, especially in the social sphere.[3]

The decline of Fianna Fáil's parliamentary majorities meant that smaller parties came to the fore as possible coalition partners. Of these, only the Labour Party has been present throughout Ireland's involvement with the EU. It was established by the trades union movement, but never enjoyed the electoral success of social democratic parties elsewhere in Western Europe. Its vote has always been below 20 per cent, and it has been limited to a minor role as the junior partner in coalition governments. The party relied on support from agricultural workers in rural market towns, and more recently from Dublin as well.

Only two other small parties have achieved prominence in the Dáil since EU membership.[4] Democratic Left emerged after a lengthy evolution and several name changes[5] as a party to the left of Labour, based in Dublin's working-class constituencies. The party first gained Dáil representation in 1981, and gradually consolidated and expanded its parliamentary strength through the decade, though it never exceeded 5 per cent of the vote. The other significant small party, the Progressive Democrats, split from Fianna Fáil in 1985, and built a position to the right in Irish politics, advocating a 'new right' economic agenda and liberal policies on social issues such as divorce. After an initial electoral surge, they fell back, but were the partners in Fianna Fáil's first ever coalition government, established in 1989.

The basic governmental equation from the 1960s to the 1980s was one of Fianna Fáil versus a Fine Gael–Labour coalition. The two big parties took over 70 per cent of the vote at every election from 1961 to 1989, and in most garnered over 80 per cent. Developments in the 1980s weakened Fianna Fáil's dominance. This offered alternative prospects to Fine Gael for coalition partners, but also introduced Fianna Fáil as rival suitor for those partners. But apart from whatever influence the Labour Party has managed to exert as a minority partner in coalition, Ireland has been entirely dominated by centre-right governments.

Table 11.1 Irish general election results, 1973–92

	FF	FG	LP	PD	DL	Other	Government	Taoiseach
1973	46.2	35.1	13.7	–	–	5.0	FG–LP	Cosgrave
1977	50.6	30.5	11.6	–	1.7	7.3	FF	Lynch, Haughey
1981	45.3	36.5	9.9	–	1.7	8.4	FG–LP	Fitzgerald
1982a	47.3	37.3	9.1	–	2.2	6.3	FF	Haughey
1982b	45.2	39.2	9.4	–	3.3	6.3	FG–LP	Fitzgerald
1987	44.1	27.1	6.4	11.8	3.7	6.9	FF	Haughey
1989	44.1	29.3	9.5	5.5	5.0	6.6	FF–PD	Haughey, Reynolds
1992	39.1	24.5	19.3	4.7	2.8	9.7	FF–LP	Reynolds

Source: J. Coakley and M. Gallagher (eds), *Politics in the Republic of Ireland* (Dublin and Limerick, PSAI Press, 1993), pp. 265, 272.

This is perhaps not surprising given the prevalent political culture in Ireland. Coakley suggests that nationalist and Catholic elements in Irish culture encourage a conservative outlook.[6] Political culture in Ireland also demonstrates an intensely local, clientelist conception of politics and politicians.[7] One consequence is that foreign policy is not an electorally important subject, with the vast majority of voters being more concerned with domestic issues. Since the EU is primarily seen as an external relations matter, interest in it is limited among the electorate and many politicians.

At the time when Europe was taking its first steps towards integration, Ireland's interest in the world was largely confined to seeking support against partition. The country joined the Council of Europe in 1949, but 'our parliamentary delegates to the Council of Europe seemed to devote their time to making speeches about partition: speeches which were designed to be read at home, but unfortunately had to be listened to abroad'.[8] For a while, the Council was Ireland's only involvement in integration in Europe.

At the start of the 1960s, Ireland began to reorient its economy, a development which created greater interest in Europe's economic integration. From a policy based on protectionism and self-sufficiency, Ireland moved towards an open, export-oriented trading policy. Ireland's position on membership was contingent upon that of the United Kingdom. The British decision in 1961 to seek membership of the EEC led to an application from Ireland as well. Throughout the 1960s, the progress of Ireland's application ebbed and flowed with Britain's, until accession in 1973.

The enthusiasm for accession was based very strongly on the perceived economic benefits that would accrue from membership, particularly in the agricultural sector and through regional redistribution programmes. Ireland had refrained from joining the European Free Trade Association because it had no agricultural component, although it had signed a free trade agreement with the United Kingdom in 1965. The political dimension of the EEC was given less attention, but emerged through EP elections and, initially, referenda.

REFERENDA ON INTEGRATION

The three referenda indicate that support for involvement in the EU is consistently high in Ireland (see Table 11.2). In fact, although the vote in favour has declined, support has grown among the political parties. In 1972, Labour led the opposition campaign; by 1992, only Democratic Left called for a 'no' vote.

Fianna Fáil had initiated moves towards the EEC in 1961, and was strongly supported by Fine Gael, so it was no surprise that both campaigned strongly for a 'yes' vote in the 1972 referendum. The case they put forward for membership

Table 11.2 Results of European referendums in Ireland, 1972–92

	For (%)	*Against (%)*	*Turnout (%)*
1972 (membership)	83.1	16.9	70.9
1987 (SEA)	69.9	30.1	43.9
1992 (Maastricht)	69.1	30.9	57.3

Source: J. Coakley and M. Gallagher (eds), *Politics in the Republic of Ireland* (Dublin and Limerick, PSAI Press, 1993), p. 269.

focused on the expected material advantages. They argued that Ireland stood to benefit strongly from the CAP, and from redistributive regional and social policies, while Irish industry would receive a valuable competitive stimulus.[9] They also contended that neutrality was not really at issue given the state and scope of the EC at that time,[10] and in general couched their support in terms of there being no viable alternative available for Ireland.

The only other party in the Dáil at the time was the Labour Party, which opposed membership in the referendum. This reflected both a strong isolationist tendency within the party and left-wing suspicions that the Community was no more than a capitalist 'rich man's club'. Labour argued that the political consequences of membership would threaten Irish neutrality, unemployment would increase because Irish industries were not strong enough to compete openly, and that the benefits likely to accrue from other programmes would not be sufficient to make up for these detrimental consequences. However, opposition was by no means undisputed in the party, and 'there were many leading members of the Labour Party whose hearts were not in the campaign'.[11]

It is probably the case that 'the opponents of membership offered a more accurate assessment of its consequences for Ireland than did those in favour of it'.[12] However, the vote in favour of joining was so conclusive that there was little point in continuing to oppose the Community and trying to reverse the decision. Labour immediately abandoned its opposition.[13] The concentration in the years after accession for all parties was on adapting to the EU. It was not until the mid-1980s that the prospect of a qualitative advance in integration emerged again.

The SEA of 1986 at first seemed likely to pass with only limited reaction in Ireland, but a court case found the Act to be unconstitutional, thus necessitating a referendum on the issue.[14] For a time there was a chance that the consensus on Irish membership might dissipate. The SEA had been negotiated under a Fine Gael–Labour government, and when it was initially discussed in the Dáil, Fianna Fáil leader, Charles Haughey, expressed reservations about some aspects of the Act dealing with a common foreign and security policy and with changes to decision-making procedures. By the time the referendum got under way, there had been a change of government, with Fianna Fáil replacing the coalition, but they did not pursue their objections any further, and indeed campaigned in favour of the SEA. They were joined in this by Fine Gael and also by the newly formed Progressive Democrats.

Labour found themselves in something of a bind. They had been part of the government that had negotiated the SEA,[15] and a number of leading party members favoured supporting the SEA in the referendum. However, the majority of party members were opposed to the SEA. The compromise that was reached saw Labour avoid adopting any official line and allowing members to choose as individuals to campaign for either side. This meant that the only major party to formally oppose the SEA was the Workers' Party. The opposition campaign drew in a very broad coalition of groups, who based their lobbies on diverse issues, including sovereignty, preservation of traditional Catholic values, and neutrality. The supporters of the Act presented the issue, somewhat disingenuously, as being about Ireland's continued membership of the EC, having 'wisely decided not to embark on the stony path of trying to engender popular enthusiasm for the Act's precise contents, which few either understood or cared about'.[16]

Despite the slight loss of support in the electorate, the SEA referendum showed an expanding party consensus in favour of integration. Fianna Fáil's criticisms were not sustained once the party reached government; Labour's policy showed signs of change; and even the Workers' Party couched its opposition in pro-integration language. Five years after the SEA referendum, the referendum on the Maastricht Treaty on European Union showed even greater moves towards this consensus. Four of the five parties campaigned in favour of Maastricht, and their party leaders issued a joint call for a 'yes' vote. For three of those, Fianna Fáil, Fine Gael and the Progressive Democrats, this was consistent with their support for European integration all along. The fourth was Labour, the culmination of an odyssey from opposition in the 1972 referendum, through the non-committal stance in 1987, to support for integration in 1992. The only major party to oppose the Treaty was Democratic Left, and even they 'argued from what they claimed was a fundamentally pro-European position that the Maastricht Treaty was inadequate and flawed'.[17]

The Maastricht debate also showed general agreement over most EU policies. All parties professed support for increased regional funds, for the principles of the Social Chapter, and for CAP reforms, while expressing their commitment to maintain Irish agricultural interests. On the issue of Economic and Monetary Union there was general consent, which became even more apparent in the aftermath of the referendum during the exchange rate mechanism crisis of September 1992, when all the parties affirmed their commitment to Ireland adhering to the Union's economic 'fast track'.

Even on the issue of neutrality, what was notable was not the divergence but the convergence of opinion. All parties declared their support for participation in European Political Co-operation. None interpreted neutrality as an obstacle to full participation in the Union. Instead, the collapse of communism in Eastern Europe and the subsequent instability in that region encouraged them to commit themselves fully to contributing to the debate about a common security policy, leading to the 1996 Intergovernmental Conferences.

Referendums have become an important mechanism for dealing with European affairs in Ireland, even though the government had not planned to hold a referendum on the SEA. The referendum on accession in 1972 was required because of clauses on sovereignty in the Irish constitution,[18] but it was phrased in such a way that future developments of the EU were not automatically covered. What began as a necessity became an advantage, because the need for subsequent referendums gave Irish membership a greater democratic basis.

THE EUROPEAN PARLIAMENT

The features evident in the referenda – growing consensus among the parties on the principle of integration and on most EU policies – appear again when the record of Irish parties in the European Parliament (Table 11.3) is examined. Once Ireland had joined, the parties immediately faced the challenge of finding suitable partners in the European Parliament. This task was easiest for the Labour Party, which already had ties with the socialist group. For the other two, it was slightly more problematic, partly because 'the two major parties in Ireland are ideologically aligned on a "national" issue which has no equivalent in other EC countries'.[19] Fine Gael joined the Christian Democratic group, while Fianna Fáil, who would probably have been

Table 11.3 Results of EP elections in Ireland, 1979–94

	1979		1984		1989		1994	
	Share of vote	Seats	Share of vote	Seats	Share of vote	Seats	Share of vote	Seats
FF	34.7	5	39.2	8	31.5	6	35.0	7
FG	33.1	4	32.2	6	21.6	4	24.3	4
LP	14.5	4	8.4	0	9.5	1	11.0	1
PD	n.a.		n.a		11.9	1	6.5	0
DL	3.3	0	4.3	0	7.5	1	3.5	0
Other[a]	14.4	2	15.9	1	17.9	2	19.7	3
Turnout (%)	63.6		47.6[b]		68.3[c]		44.2	

Notes: [a] Includes Green Party and Sinn Féin. In 1994, the Green Party won two seats. Otherwise, all seats won by 'Others' have been won by independent candidates.
[b] EP election held together with local election.
[c] EP election held together with general election.
Sources: European Parliament Office, 1984; *Irish Political Studies* data sections; *Irish Times* 14 June 1994.

equally at home there, sided with the French Gaullists in the European Progressive Democrat group.

In the first direct elections in 1979, the Labour Party's manifesto signalled clearly the change in policy to acceptance of membership, so all three major parties campaigned on pro-Community platforms. The consensus extended further, because the issues they pursued were widely similar – support for the CAP and for increased redistributive funds and reaffirmations of Ireland's neutrality. Only two major differences emerged. First, Fianna Fáil diverged from Fine Gael and Labour by opposing increased powers for the EP.[20] Second, all the parties brought up European party affiliations as an issue, arguing for both the merits of their own group and the failings of those of their opponents. Interestingly, this argument was conducted in terms of which grouping was best for the pursuit of Irish interests. Fianna Fáil argued that by being in a small grouping they had a greater say, and could thus ensure that Irish interests were given a high profile in the group. The other two parties argued that being attached to large groupings gave them far greater access to real influence, which would mean that Irish interests would be supported by more MEPs if accepted by the grouping.[21] Labour in particular emphasized the size and strength of their socialist group.

The election in Ireland was fought primarily on domestic issues, and the result was interpreted as a vote against the Fianna Fáil government. This primacy of national politics was evident also in the behaviour of the Irish MEPs through the five-year life of the EP. Despite the fact that the EP was intent upon applying its new-found democratic authority to increase its power and influence, and that the party groupings were trying to develop better cohesion, the Irish MEPs maintained a strongly national-oriented stance. This was most in evidence on agricultural issues, where the Labour Party in particular had difficulties adhering to socialist group policy. It was also evident in the practice of holding a dual mandate of a seat in both the Dáil and the EP: twelve of the fifteen MEPs originally elected in 1979 were TDs at the time too.

The dual mandate became an issue in the second direct EP elections in 1984, with all of the parties eventually moving away from the practice. Otherwise, not much changed in terms of party attitudes towards the EC. Fianna Fáil and Fine Gael still expressed enthusiastic support, Labour more critical support, and the same issues of the CAP, regional and social funding and neutrality came to the fore, but generally it was a 'very brief and lack-lustre European campaign'.[22] Labour lost all four of its seats, paying the penalty for having continually substituted its MEPs according to domestic political exigencies.[23] Labour's losses reflected a public perception of the EP as a 'gravy train' for greedy politicians.

By the 1989 direct elections, the Workers' Party was identifying itself as a committed pro-European party, though critical of aspects of the EU.[24] The 1989 direct elections showed that once again Irish concerns rather than questions of Europe's future were to the fore. The key issues were neutrality, the CAP reforms and resource transfers to Ireland. Despite the movement towards an intergovernmental conference on economic and monetary union, neither the Fianna Fáil nor the Fine Gael manifestos mentioned the topic, indicating the low priority that discussion of future developments in the EU held in Ireland.[25] But once again, an overriding feature was the precedence of domestic political issues in the campaign, despite the fact that a general election was being held concurrently, which might have served to free the EP campaign to discuss European issues.[26]

The results of the 1989 elections threw up the question of party affiliations once more, with two new parties gaining representation. The Progressive Democrats had already established links with the European liberal democrats group, and although an independent Irish MEP was already attached to the group, the PD member joined as well. The Workers' Party had more difficulty. They first joined the hardline communist Left Unity group, then switched to the reformist Group for a Unitary European Left, before ending the five-year stint unaffiliated. In the course of these changes, they had also approached the socialist group and the Greens at various times.

In the 1994 election, the Workers' Party, or Democratic Left as it had become, faced an additional problem. The party's well-known and charismatic leader, Proinsias De Rossa, had won the seat in 1989, but had given it up later on to a less well-known party member, Des Geraghty. Despite being recognized as a very good MEP, Geraghty was unable to gain a political profile in Ireland, and was replaced as the party's candidate in 1994 by a better-known figure from domestic politics.

Indeed, most of the parties sought high-profile candidates, and some went as far as inviting prominent personalities from outside the party to join and stand in the EP election. When this was combined with Ireland's electoral system, a form of proportional representation by single transferable vote which allows voters to express preferences for individuals and parties, it turned the 1994 election into a 'personality-driven campaign for Europe largely devoid of issues'.[27] But the parachutists landed badly – indeed, in a poll marked by the lowest turnout in a European election in Ireland, the eye-catching performance came from the little-known Green Party, which won two seats.

The new Green MEPs had no problem affiliating in the Parliament, with a ready-made Green group already there. But clearly, it is a problem for Irish MEPs and the EP to gain attention in Ireland. Media and public attention tend to concentrate on domestic matters, and, when they do turn to European matters, they focus on the Council of Ministers and the Commission. Second, the MEPs have struggled to gain attention within their own parties. This is more of a problem in the two larger parties, where effective structures to include them have not evolved. In the smaller parties, no such evolution has occurred either, but because of their size it is easier for an MEP to get noticed – there are fewer backbenchers and local councillors vying for attention.

Involvement in the EP has had a more significant influence in organizational terms, especially because of membership of the party groupings in Strasbourg. This is partly due to the efforts of the groupings themselves. They have gradually increased their role and authority, and have encouraged constituent parties to work together. This is most readily apparent in attempts to assemble common manifestos for the EP elections. But at the same time, Irish parties have perceived for themselves advantages of being associated with such groupings, as is evident from the manner in which they increasingly identify themselves in terms of their European party families.

However, MEPs of all parties face two overriding difficulties in gaining attention in Ireland, which apply also to their parties when it comes to European affairs. First, the EP elections in Ireland demonstrate that they remain secondary to national elections and domestic political concerns. Second, the conduct of Ireland's relations with the EU remains overwhelmingly in the hands of government rather than parliament, and the opportunity for anyone outside government to influence affairs, be they MEP or TD, is highly constrained. These two factors together highlight the importance of the national political arena for European affairs.

THE NATIONAL POLITICAL DIMENSION

In practical terms the EP has little power over the Union. This means that the primary focus for the parties is on the government's conduct of the country's membership. The scope for involvement in Union affairs by ordinary TDs is very limited. After accession, EU issues rapidly became the preserve of government ministers and senior civil servants.[28]

The structure of the Union itself encourages governments to act unilaterally. This is partly the result of the complex technical nature of much EU business, and is also a response to the demands of EU negotiation, where governments need a free hand to create compromise package deals. But the combination of an intergovernmental Council of Ministers and a small, elitist Commission has encouraged some states, including Ireland, to place strong emphasis on their government in dealings with the EU. This is exacerbated by a tendency to think of the EU as a foreign policy issue, which has always been seen as the exclusive preserve of government and as an area where secrecy is necessary to preserve national interests.

There are very few parliamentary mechanisms in Ireland to enhance scrutiny of government policy on the EU. Parliamentary debates on EU issues have become increasingly perfunctory, amounting to little more than statements from each party leader after European Council meetings. Question time has declined as a means of imposing control on the government, because there is insufficient time to deal adequately with all questions.[29] An effective committee system might have helped, but until 1993 there was no committee on foreign affairs, only a Joint Committee on Secondary Legislation of the EC. This tended to get bogged down in technical details of legislation, and had no time to discuss wider issues of integration. The debate on the annual report of the Joint Committee was shorn of much relevance by the fact that it normally took place long after the events in question. This heightens the importance of party differences over the decision-making structure of the Union. Fianna Fáil is the most reluctant to cede increased powers to the EP, and instead argues for the use of a *de facto* veto. All the other parties support an expansion in the EP's powers and curbs on national vetos. Fianna Fáil argues that one voice in the Council, with a possible veto, is better for a small country than fifteen seats in the EP. However, opposition to this comes not just from other parties but also from Fianna Fáil's own MEPs, who find their marginalization from party decision making a source of frustration.

MEPs form part of a small elite of those active on EU issues that has built up among members of all parties.[30] However, the ability of parties to influence EU affairs depends very strongly on being in government. This gives them access to appointments, and one function of the parties is as a source from which to recruit personnel, including EU Commissioners. But the latter post shows again how national political considerations can dominate. In 1982, Fine Gael's Richard Burke was appointed as Commissioner by the minority Fianna Fáil government, partly because they hoped to bolster their position by winning the subsequent by-election for Burke's Dáil seat.

National politics still dominate in Ireland, for parties and for the electorate. It remains very difficult to excite any public interest in EU issues. EP elections are fought largely on domestic political issues, and other elections hardly ever raise European issues. Even the 1989 general election, which was held on the same day as the EP election, failed to generate much interest in the Union, with opinion polls not even raising it as an issue. In the 1992 general election, held five months after the Maastricht referendum, one poll did ask respondents to rank 'management of our EC/European interests' alongside other election issues, but the category came sixth out of seven suggested topics.[31]

CONCLUSION

The discussion of the development of party attitudes towards the EU highlights a number of features of Irish political parties in the Union. The first point is the high degree of consensus in favour of Irish membership of the Union among the parties. For the three right-wing parties, Fianna Fáil, Fine Gael and the Progressive Democrats, this has been a constant feature. In the case of the two left-wing parties, Labour and Democratic Left, both have gradually shifted their position, from initial opposition to critical acceptance of the EU. All of the parties would describe themselves as pro-European and in favour of further integration. This is somewhat surprising, because although public sentiment in Ireland is strongly in favour of the EU, nonetheless, there was a vote of about 30 per cent against the SEA and Maastricht referenda, which none of the main parties has attempted to tap consistently.

The second feature of Irish parties' attitudes is that the high degree of consensus continues at the level of individual EU policies. There is a common pattern to the referenda and EP elections in Ireland. On most concrete policy issues, all the parties have found themselves in general agreement, for example on regional and social policy, the CAP and economic and monetary union. There are policy differences on these questions, but only on the details, not on the substantive issues involved. The only issues over which there are consistent and considerable divergences of opinion are on decision-making structures in the EU and on neutrality, although in the latter case there is even a growing consensus in favour of a common security policy, to add to the existing support for foreign policy co-operation.

This poses the question of why this wide-ranging consensus exists. The parties still perceive the Union in Irish terms rather than in party political terms. Once the basic consensus that Ireland should be a member of the EC was reached, after the 1972 referendum, all the parties focused on how best to use that membership for the country's benefit. Debate between them has leaned more towards arguing which party will do the best job in securing advantages from Brussels for Ireland. Since so many Community programmes do provide benefits for Ireland – the CAP and the redistributive funds to the fore – it is not surprising that the parties find themselves in general agreement about the value of these areas as well.

Even in the EP, which deliberately replaces national representation with party groupings, Irish MEPs regularly pursue a distinctly Irish line on certain issues. Although one Irish MEP argues that 'political group loyalties have the most consistent significance in affecting the outcome of votes in Parliament', he accepts that MEPs 'must be sensitive to national preoccupations'.[32] Particular Irish concerns can be found on agriculture and security questions.

The sharpest disagreements in attitude between the Irish parties occur on the question of decision making in the Union. The relationship of Irish parties to the EU is strongly affected by the dominance of the Irish government in dealing with EU matters that affect Ireland. This leaves very little room for influence by MEPs and TDs of any party, and also for party leaderships when in opposition. In the case of Fianna Fáil, who have been the dominant party of government throughout the years since membership in 1973, this has reinforced a predilection towards centralism in domestic political structures, and it is they who have been most strongly opposed to any concessions to the EP or to majority voting. Fianna Fáil have sought to portray this stance as the one best suited to protecting Ireland's interests in the Union.

In all Irish parties, it is clear that policy on the EU has emerged from a relatively small group within the party leaderships. Ordinary party members, including most backbench TDs, are not involved. This is perhaps no great surprise, given the lack of interest in foreign policy and EU affairs evident among most Dáil members. But even where the will to contribute to such issues exists, there can be problems gaining the attention of the policy-making elite. For instance, MEPs have found difficulties in getting themselves included in their parties' decision-making procedures, although as suggested earlier this applies more in the case of Fianna Fáil and Fine Gael than to the smaller parties.

Some external channels of influence on party decision making have emerged. This to some degree waters down the exclusiveness of the process, but in general policy making on Europe remains the preserve of a few in each party. The two major external influences are both pro-European ones. The Irish Council for the European Movement, which was active in all the referendums and in promoting participation in EP elections, is the main pro-integration pressure group in Ireland. It has successfully co-opted support and members from all the major parties. The European party groupings have also become important influences for the parties, particularly in drawing up EP election manifestos.

The party groupings are also significant in terms of policy articulation for parties. They have attempted to have their views incorporated into the stances of their grouping, and have used the EP as a major platform for the expression of policies on European issues. This reflects partly the weaknesses of the Oireachtas as a platform for the articulation of party policy, as outlined earlier. The Oireachtas is also more concerned with domestic political matters, and parties do not devote much energy to articulating their EU policies in domestic political contexts.

This can be seen in a number of cases. General elections are fought with little or no reference to Community or European issues on the part of either parties or electorate.[33] Similarly, the referenda that have been held on EU matters have been reduced towards simplified arguments of being pro- or anti-EU, rather than looking at details of EU policy. Thus, the standard of policy articulation does not encourage very sophisticated discussion of the Union.

Finally, we return to one particularly important feature for Irish parties *vis-à-vis* the EU. The government is clearly the dominant actor in relations with the Union, which curtails and constrains what parties can try to do. Articulation of party policy is primarily conducted at or through government, and the possibilities of influencing implementation of policy lie there too. This means that, to a considerable extent, the most important role of Irish political parties is simply to act as a recruitment source for governmental personnel, who then contribute directly to Ireland's dealings with the European Union.

Membership of the EU has changed Irish parties. They have been drawn out of their previous isolation and have found a place among the mainstream parties of Europe. They remain first and foremost domestic political actors, however. The EU has not supplanted local and national concerns in Irish politics, either for the parties or the electorate, and much of the response of the parties to the Union is dictated by national considerations. However, the parties have learned from their contact with other European parties. They are now more accustomed to identifying themselves in terms of their European party families.

The political parties in Ireland might also learn from another aspect of their involvement in the Union. The experience of being in the EP has introduced Irish politicians to a number of new mechanisms and procedures practised there, such as a far more extensive committee system than exists in Ireland. This might encourage the introduction of more effective means of parliamentary scrutiny in Ireland, which would resolve one outstanding problem.

This chapter has argued that Irish parties have shown a remarkable and growing consensus in support of the EU and European integration; but that major differences remain over the role of government, which to date has dominated EU affairs. Although Ireland has a better record of referring EU developments to public consideration and approval in referenda than most of its Union partners, the growing demand for greater democratic accountability in the EU is still echoed there. Participation in referenda has sanctioned the notion that there should be open consultation about European Union matters, yet referenda themselves provide only an infrequent tool to cater for such demands. For all of the political parties in Ireland, the development of greater parliamentary and public involvement in EU matters will remain an important issue.

NOTES

1　M. Laver and M. Marsh, 'Parties and voters', in J. Coakley and M. Gallagher, *Politics in the Republic of Ireland* (Dublin and Limerick, Folens and PSAI Press, 1993), pp. 120–1.

2　P. Mair, 'The party system and party competition', in J. Coakley and M. Gallagher (eds), *Politics in the Republic of Ireland* (Dublin and Limerick, Folens and PSAI Press, 1993), p. 97.

3　Mair, 'The party system', pp. 93–4.

4　The Dáil is the lower house of the Irish Parliament: the Seanad is the upper house. The collective name for the two houses is the Oireachtas. Members of the Dáil are known as TDs (*Teachta Dála* Dáil deputies). Prominence is here taken to mean having held more than one Dáil seat at two successive elections.

5　Democratic Left came into being in 1992, after a split in the Workers' Party. That party had previously been known as Sinn Féin the Workers' Party (1977–82), Official Sinn Féin (1970–77) and Sinn Féin (before 1970). In this chapter, all those parties will be referred to as the Workers' Party for simplicity's sake. In tables, the heading 'DL' will be used to refer to the earlier parties as well.

6　J. Coakley, 'Society and political culture', in Coakley and Gallagher, *Politics in the Republic of Ireland*, p. 45.

7　M. Gallagher and L. Komito, 'Dáil deputies and their constituency work', in Coakley and Gallagher, *Politics in the Republic of Ireland*, p. 151.

8　C.C. O'Brien, *To Katanga and Back* (London, Hutchinson, 1962), p. 14.

9　P. Sharp, *Irish Foreign Policy and the European Community* (Aldershot, Dartmouth, 1990), p. 101.

10　P. Keatinge, *A Singular Stance: Irish Neutrality in the 1980s* (Dublin, Institute of Public Administration, 1984), p. 101.

11　D. Keogh, *Ireland and Europe 1919–1989: A Diplomatic and Political History* (Cork and Dublin, Hibernian University Press, 1990), p. 246.

12　P. Sharp, *Irish Foreign Policy and the European Community*, p. 101.

13　T. Brown, 'Internationalism and international politics: the external links of the Labour Party', *Irish Studies in International Affairs*, vol. 1, no. 2, 1980, p. 92.

14　See J. Temple Lang, 'The Irish court case which delayed the Single European Act: *Crotty* v. *An Taoiseach and others*', *Common Market Law Review*, vol. 24, 1987, pp. 709–18.

15　Although the negotiations had been carried out almost entirely by Fine Gael ministers.

16　M. Gallagher, 'The Single European Act referendum', *Irish Political Studies*, vol. 3, 1988, p. 79.

17　M. Holmes, 'The Maastricht referendum', *Irish Political Studies*, vol. 8, 1993, p. 107.

18　B. McMahon, 'EEC membership and the Irish legal system', in P.J. Drudy and D. McAleese (eds), *Ireland and the European Community* (Cambridge, Cambridge University Press, 1984), pp. 58–61.

19　E. Moxon-Browne, 'Irish political parties and European integration', *Administration*, vol. 25, no. 4, 1977, p. 529.

20　N. Collins, 'Ireland', in K. Reif (ed.), *Ten European Elections* (Aldershot, Gower, 1985), p. 112.

21　J. Cooney, *The Race for Europe* (Dublin, Dublin University Press, 1979), pp. 30–2.

22　P. Keatinge, 'Ireland's foreign relations in 1984', *Irish Studies in International Affairs*, vol. 2, no. 1, 1985, p. 170.

23　Labour made seven replacements to its four original MEPs, so that those four seats mustered a total of eleven incumbents.

24　R. Dunphy, 'The Workers' Party and Europe: trajectory of an idea', *Irish Political Studies*, vol. 7, 1992, p. 28.

25　P. Keatinge and M. Marsh, 'The European Parliament election', in M. Gallagher and R. Sinnott (eds), *How Ireland Voted 1989* (Galway, Centre for the study of Irish elections, 1990), p. 133.

26　M. Holmes, 'The 1989 European Parliament election in the Republic of Ireland', *Irish Political Studies*, vol. 5, 1990, p. 87.

27　*Irish Times*, 9 June 1994, p. 1.

28 See B. Burns and T. Salmon, 'Policy-making coordination in Ireland on European Community issues', *Journal of Common Market Studies*, vol. 15, no. 4, 1977.
29 M. Holmes, N. Rees and B. Whelan, *The Poor Relation: Irish Foreign Policy towards the Third World* (Dublin, Gill and MacMillan/Trócaire, 1993), p. 51.
30 Moxon-Browne, 'Irish political parties and European integration', p. 523.
31 *Irish Political Studies* data sections, vol. 5, 1990, pp. 152–3, vol. 8, 1993, p. 201.
32 Chris O'Malley, *Over in Europe: The Issues facing Ireland in the European Community* (Dublin, the author, 1988), pp. 86, 87.
33 Holmes, 'The 1989 European election', p. 87.

SELECT BIBLIOGRAPHY

Brown, Tony, 'Internationalism and international politics: the external links of the Labour Party', *Irish Studies in International Affairs*, vol. 1, no. 2., 1980.

Chubb, Basil, *The Government and Politics of Ireland*, Oxford, Oxford University Press, 1993, 3rd edn.

Coakley, John and Gallagher, Michael (eds), *Politics in the Republic of Ireland*, Dublin/Limerick, Folens, PSAI Press, 1993, 2nd edn.

Coombes, David (ed.), *Ireland and the European Community: Ten Years of Membership*, Dublin, Gill and MacMillan, 1985.

Drudy, P.J. and McAleese, Dermot (eds), *Ireland and the European Community*, Cambridge, Cambridge University Press, 1984.

Dunphy, Richard, 'The Workers' Party and Europe: trajectory of an idea', *Irish Political Studies*, vol. 7, 1992.

Gallagher, Michael, *The Irish Labour Party in Transition: 1957–82*, Manchester, Manchester University Press, 1982.

Gallagher, Michael, *Political Parties in the Republic of Ireland*, Manchester, Manchester University Press, 1985.

Gallagher, Michael, 'The Single European Act referendum', *Irish Political Studies*, vol. 3, 1988.

Gallagher, Michael and Sinnott, Richard (eds), *How Ireland Voted 1989*, Galway, Centre for the study of Irish elections/PSAI Press, 1990.

Hainsworth, Paul (ed.), *Breaking and Preserving the Mould: The Direct Elections to the European Parliament (1989), the Irish Republic and Northern Ireland*, Belfast/Jordanstown, Policy Research Institute, 1992.

Hederman, Miriam, *The Road to Europe: Irish Attitudes 1948–1961*, Dublin, Institute of Public Administration, 1983.

Holmes, Michael, 'The 1989 European election in the Republic of Ireland', *Irish Political Studies*, vol. 5, 1990.

Holmes, Michael, 'The Maastricht referendum of June 1992', *Irish Political Studies*, vol. 8, 1993.

Keatinge, Patrick, *A Singular Stance: Irish Neutrality in the 1980s*, Dublin, Institute of Public Administration, 1984.

Keatinge, Patrick (ed.), *Ireland and EC Membership Evaluated*, London, Frances Pinter, 1991.

Keogh, Dermot (ed.), *Ireland and the Challenge of European Integration*, Cork and Dublin, Hibernian University Press, 1989.

Keogh, Dermot, *Ireland and Europe 1919–1989: A Diplomatic and Political History*, Cork and Dublin, Hibernian University Press, 1990.

Maher, D.J., *The Tortuous Path: The Course of Ireland's Entry into the EEC, 1948–73*, Dublin, Institute of Public Administration, 1986.

Mair, Peter, *The Changing Irish Party System: Organisation, Ideology and Electoral Competition*, London, Frances Pinter, 1987.

Manning, Maurice, *Irish Political Parties: An Introduction*, Dublin, Gill and MacMillan, 1972.

Marsh, Michael, *Irish Public Opinion on Neutrality and European Union*, Occasional paper no. 1, Dublin, Institute of European Affairs, 1992.

Moxon-Browne, Edward, 'Irish political parties and European integration', *Administration*, vol. 25, no. 4, 1977.

National Economic and Social Council, *Ireland in the European Community: Performance, Prospects and Strategy*, Report no. 88, Dublin, NESC, 1989.

Sharp, Paul, *Irish Foreign Policy and the European Community*, Aldershot, Dartmouth, 1990.

12 Scandinavian political parties and the European Union

Lars Svåsand and Ulf Lindström

INTRODUCTION

The Danish electorate rejected the Maastricht Treaty in 1992 and approved of the 'opt out' Edinburgh Agreement in 1993. Both the rejection and the approval were obvious reminders to the politicians of Finland, Norway and Sweden that they were heading for difficulties in convincing their electorates to vote in favour of EU membership in the referenda that were to be held between October and November 1994. Indeed, the margins of victory were narrow. In Finland and Sweden a majority of 57 and 52 per cent respectively, followed the recommendations of the powers that be to vote for EU membership, while the Norwegian electorate once again rejected membership, by 52.2 per cent.[1]

This chapter addresses the Nordic dilemma of combining representative and plebiscitary democracy in a democratic multiparty system. Why was it that the constituents of the parties did not easily abide by the stance of the party leadership on the European issue? What is so controversial about membership of the EU to make loyal party members and voters refuse to bow to pressure from their leaders?

FRAMEWORK AND THEORETICAL APPROACH

Denmark, Finland, Norway, and Sweden are small advanced capitalist countries with populations ranging between 4 and 9 million people; corporatist welfare states; and parliamentary democracies. The four countries have been eager participants in the international community. They are members of most intergovernmental organizations; their vital interest organizations take an active part among the networks of non-governmental organizations. Moreover, all four countries have party systems built upon the mass membership format that goes back a century in history. In short, if any countries were well prepared to confront the European issue in a way that complies with both the normative requirements and the empirically founded expectations of a sound democracy it should have been the Nordic states.[2]

This was far from being the case, however. Although referred to a referendum, the issue of EU membership threatened to rip party constituencies apart, to produce splits down the middle of parties, and encourage factions to defect to rival parties or to create new ones. The invoking of party loyalty was tantamount to throwing a boomerang. Delinkage, that is, issuing either everyone or selected parts of the constituency a temporary release from party bonds before the referendum, was an option that bought time, but not consensus.

Comparing the Scandinavian countries is often taken as an example of a 'most similar systems design'.[3] Yet, with regard to the EU, a comparison of the four countries reminds us more of a 'most different systems approach'.[4] They differ sharply from one another in their approach to EU membership, with external circumstances as much as domestic forces shaping the political parties' opinion on the EU.

Denmark, Finland, Sweden and Norway each has a different history in its EU relationship; each varies also in terms of both geopolitical position and economic integration with the global market; and the four countries have each evolved different patterns of party alliances.

One distinction is between Denmark and Norway on the one hand, and Sweden and Finland on the other. Danish and Norwegian EC membership first became possible with Britain's application in 1961. However, the issue 'disappeared' from the public agenda as long as British entry was blocked by de Gaulle's opposition. Again, when Britain's negotiations were reopened in 1969, Norway and Denmark followed suit. Put to a referendum, the issue led to a heated debate in both countries in 1972. In Denmark a relatively comfortable majority, 63 per cent, decided in favour of membership, while 53 per cent of the Norwegian electorate rejected membership – and effectively blocked debate over the issue for two decades.

For Sweden and Finland EC membership was not a viable option with the Cold War division of Europe. It was the international context of the late 1980s, the adoption of the Single European Act in 1986 and, ultimately, the East European Revolutions of 1989, that pulled the rug out from under the feet of Finnish and Swedish politicians and their previous positions on European integration. Until 1989, EU membership had been a non-issue, on account of the two countries' policies of non-alignment and neutrality, which, in the case of Finland, had the status of a formal agreement with the USSR (the FCMA Treaty of 1948). In Sweden and Finland, the debate on EC membership could be conducted without 'looking in the rear view mirror' – it had no history. Such retrospectiveness, however, was at the core of the problem in Norway; adults, reminding their offspring, still recalled their individual experience of the 1972 'civil war' at the ballot box. The division of the Norwegian electorate (and the parties) as the EU issue was again placed on the political agenda, seemed like a rerun of an old movie, with many of the same actors and the same arguments. Thus, with the experience of two decades outside of the EU, the arguments for and against membership were cast in a historic dimension.

The Scandinavian countries, and *ipso facto* the political parties, therefore have four separate paths to EU membership:

1   Denmark's and Norway's early application;
2   Denmark's acceptance and Norway's rejection of membership;
3   Sweden's and Finland's EC application, in 1991 and 1992 respectively, and Norway's reapplication in 1992;
4   The results of the 1994 referenda add a fourth phase: Finland's and Sweden's adaptation to the EU framework and Norway's search for a role outside the EU.

However, in spite of these different approaches there are also similarities with regard to the relationship between official party positions on the issue and the opinion among party voters; in a word, the elites have always been far more friendly to the EU than their electorates. This holds in all four countries and in all pro-EU parties.

Because of variations in the paths towards EU membership, the issues in the EU debate were also somewhat different. In Denmark the debate after 1973 centred on the depth and scope of integration, and less on Danish EU membership as such, while in the other Scandinavian countries the issue has focused upon the question of membership itself.

We will deal first with the cases of Finland, Norway and Sweden. These will then be contrasted with the Danish case.

THE EU MEMBERSHIP ISSUE IN THE SCANDINAVIAN CONTEXT

The issue of membership was fought against a backdrop that varied between the three countries.[5] Each had an economy more or less dependent on the European market; each country viewed its security interests differently; and each had unique experiences of putting a decision of this magnitude to be decided by the people.

Finland profited from its pampered position in the Soviet market, which absorbed about 20 per cent of total Finnish exports. But as the Soviet economy plummeted, orders for Finnish goods dried up and Finland slid into its worst depression since the 1930s: unemployment soared to nearly a fifth of the workforce in 1993. After a short period of initial relief from the latent threat of Soviet interference in Finnish internal affairs, a new spectre began to loom on the Eastern horizon: Russia in a state of permanent turmoil and the potential revival of Russian expansionism, as symbolized by the electoral success of Shirinovsky's party in the Russian parliamentary elections in December 1993. Finnish attempts to seek new security alliances found expression in Finland's decision to upgrade its air force with F-18 fighters and its acquired status as NATO observer and associate WEU member. By Nordic standards at least, Finnish foreign policy is run in an authoritarian fashion, especially when it comes to considering changes in the accepted truths. This habit had its own political liturgy before 1989. None of the major parties in Finland dared question the foreign policy prerogative of the presidency.[6] Political parties refused to discuss matters of foreign relations in the public agora. But none of the parties missed the opportunity offered by President Koivisto when, in his address opening the Parliament's 1992 session, he turned the EU issue over to the MPs for them to decide. His only cue was his comment that he would not have any objections should Parliament reach a decision to file for membership.

Within a remarkably short time, the parties developed a consensus to apply for membership. Official party positions prior to the changes brought on by the end of the Cold War had been equally unanimous: EU membership was not a possibility. Parties did not express strong opinions against membership; the issue simply did not exist. To the extent that there were differences, the Finnish Conservatives came out in favour earlier than the others. What set Finland apart from the rest of the countries was the speed with which it moved from the 'no issue' position to eagerness for joining. In contrast to the Norwegian situation, as we shall see, the Finnish centre party (Agrarians) joined the other parties in applying for membership. In the Finnish case, only the left party and the small Christian People's Party opposed EU membership. This contrasts with the situation in other countries, particularly with the Norwegian parties. Moreover, the Finnish EU debate first of all centred on the economic effects of membership on the agricultural sector and on regional development. The ambition behind economic, political and military integration as formulated in the Maastricht Treaty hardly figured as an issue.

The Swedish Social Democratic cabinet found itself in great difficulties during the autumn of 1990. The economy was getting out of control and capital was fleeing the country. The country's many transnational companies, realizing the substance of the Single European Act of 1986, were making new investments and entering into mergers with international finance institutions outside Sweden to an extent unparalleled in Swedish history.

Swedish neutrality had lost its rationale after the East European Revolutions of 1989. Although traceable to 1812, Sweden's policy of non-alignment had as its most important backdrop the bipolar division of post-war Europe. As a result of the breakdown of the old international order, the pro-EU forces which had been dormant in the Conservative, Liberal and Social Democratic parties were able to come out into the open.[7] The issue was seized upon by the Social Democratic government in 1990 as a new issue to remind the electorate of the party's long-standing tradition of responsible national leadership. As in Norway, a faction within the Social Democrats was opposed to Swedish EU membership but could not prevent the government from going ahead with its application. In Sweden, as well as in Finland, the centre party (the old Agrarian party), after hesitating, came on board the pro-EU coalition, thus reinforcing a strong foreign policy tradition in Sweden: domestic consensus has always been the best preserver of Swedish national interests. As in Finland, Swedish EU-friendly parties saw little reason to adopt a 'Danish solution' to their membership. Indeed, an immediate response to the Maastricht Treaty was support from the four major Swedish parties.

In the Norwegian case, the reopening of the EU membership question also had its rationale in the post-Cold War thaw, and was particularly spurred by the eager-ness with which Finland and Sweden dropped their old reservations against EU membership. To Norwegian decision makers, the prospect of being the one of two countries on the West European mainland outside the EU, looked increasingly discomforting. The potential political isolation was a stronger motivating factor than the economy or questions of national security. Given its increasing reliance on its oil economy Norway's affluence was not immediately at stake as the country considered its relationship to Europe; in 1990, oil and gas accounted for almost half of the nation's export revenues. Petroleum, its sources immobile and its output saleable at a decent price for the foreseeable future, was a sedative to Norway's public debate about the fundamental consequences of a global economy. Second, Norwegians still felt more comfortable with NATO than the European connection. This is explained by the limited scope of the NATO alliance and, more importantly, the hypothetical (though fatal) nature of the context in which the alliance would be brought into its full meaning.

The EU issue turned out to be particularly painful. The Conservatives had long secretly advocated EU membership, but it was not until 1989 that it was considered timely to again raise the issue in the party programme.[8] Labour had also been a pro-EC party in 1972, but was sharply divided. As a truce in the party, the issue was placed on the sideline for the next two decades. The party programme only accepted matter of factly that Norway's relationship to the EC should be regulated by a trade agreement. As co-operation between the EC partners widened to include foreign policy issues, the Norwegian parties followed suit. It is true that even as late as

1989, the Labour Party declined to offer membership as a desirable policy; however, an important rephrasing of the party programme indicated the shift: rather than specifying the trade agreement as the basis for co-operation, it now said, 'Norway should select the type of cooperation which is in its best interest.' Following the applications endorsed by the two Nordic sister parties, the Labour Party initiated a comprehensive debate in the party, resulting in a resolution at the 1992 convention to 'ask the government to apply for membership'. By now the 1972 coalitions were rapidly re-emerging: Conservatives and Labour in favour, with the Centre Party, Christian People's Party and the Left Socialist Party rallied against. The neo-liberal Progress Party also came out in favour, albeit more ambiguously than the other pro-EU parties.

These official positions, however, had little to do with the actual distribution of public opinion, a problem which was repeated across the three applicant nations as well as in Denmark. In Norway, where the electorate was never really demobilized after turning down membership in 1972, 'the legacy of 1972', the glorious victory of the people over the powers that be, legitimized disloyalty to one's party.[9]

The popular conflict over the European issue in Scandinavia in part reflects the paradoxically divisive nature of European integration itself. The EU is a project of and for *individual* Europeans already in possession of economic, cultural and/or political resources *or* European *states* within the reach thereof. Among the Nordic states, Finland was the one to which the national advantages of membership seemed to take precedence over those of individual citizens. To Finland as a neutral state – its border with Russia representing the geographically longest, but also the widest economic gap in standard of living on the Eurasian landmass – the full range of political resources accompanying membership in the EU appeared attractive. A basic problem in all three applicant countries was, as we shall see, that the consensus among party leaders on the attractiveness of EU membership was not shared by large parts of their electorates. In party terms, the EU issue was as much a question of elites versus grass roots *within* parties as it was a struggle *between* parties. The struggle between pro- and anti-EU forces was a struggle between coalitions where each side of the issue was made up of strange bedfellows. In other words, the EU issue was different from most other issues.

Whatever it is that made Norwegians hostile to the EU, it is *not* because they are a young nation, live in the periphery and are xenophobic. For one thing, the nation is old and heavily exposed to the rest of Europe, and its population is well travelled and knowledgeable about Europe. Finland, however, is a young nation, peripherally situated, and Finnish experience of Europe is too much dominated by Sweden as a bridgehead to the south. Yet, Finns – like other nationals on the fringe of Europe such as the Irish, Iberians and Greeks – are the most keen supporters of membership.

While across the region membership looked more attractive to some individuals than to others (see Table 12.4 in the appendix), the concern of the nation state interfered with this pattern to distort overall opinion. A crucial aspect of opinion formation on the EU has been the very large part of the population that did not have an opinion at all on the issue. The struggle for or against EU membership therefore was a struggle for the undecided. Analysis of Norwegian public opinion showed that roughly three-quarters of 'yes' and 'no' voters in 1972, were of the same opinion seventeen years later.[10] Of crucial importance for the outcome of the battle was which way those holding no opinion would lean in the end, and in the Norwegian case, whether the preferences of new voters since 1972 would differ substantially from those of voters leaving the electorate.[11]

Because such large segments of the electorates in the three applicant countries were undecided – even after the membership negotiations had been completed – parties and organizations became enormously important as opinion leaders and mobilizers. Yet the parties themselves faced internal as well as external competition for the votes. Overemphasizing the official party line might therefore jeopardize the long-term consideration of keeping the party together beyond the EU issue itself.

Spurious or not, there was a cognitive dimension to the European issue in the sense that citizens who did not take a firm opinion had few years of formal education beyond obligatory school. But other structural correlates with 'no opinion' did not lend themselves to this interpretation. These correlates formed a common pattern across the three countries: women were less decided than men; the youngest and the oldest voters were less decided than the middle aged; workers were less decided than either farmers or the urban petty bourgeoisie.

The difference between the classes may, of course, be rationalized as a reflection of individuals' economic interests and positions in the market. However, the difference also related to the standpoints of voters' 'natural' representatives in the party system.

Thus, formal education, gender, age, class and party contributed towards determining opinions on the issue. After the three countries had completed the membership negotiations and their governments recommended their voters to say 'yes', in Norway and Sweden the battle continued as the anti-EU movements gained strength during the spring and summer of 1994.

Ever since EU membership came on to the agenda of Nordic politics, the citizens of Finland have been more sympathetic to joining than those of Norway and Sweden. As Finns went to the polls in October 1994, Finland's agenda was still marked by the country's regaining full sovereignty as a nation state in the aftermath of 1989. Finland, in ways reminiscent of the situation that confronted Germany and Italy, Greece, Portugal and Spain after they had liberated themselves from their various yokes, was asking itself what to do with this opportunity. By contrast, in Sweden, the end of the Cold War era removed the *supporting* rather than restraining structures of its identity as a nation state.

With the decision to submit the EU membership issue to a popular referendum, the parties in a way placed themselves on the sideline. The referendum as an institution vastly increased the number of opinion leaders as well as participants, and created opportunities for *ad hoc* organizations and temporary alliances. Only in Denmark does the constitution require a referendum on EU matters involving the Danish constitution. In the three other Scandinavian countries referenda were arranged because of the saliency of the issue and the internal division within the political parties, which we shall analyse below.

DANISH DYNAMITE

While the debate in Norway, Finland and Sweden was focused on whether or not to be members of the EU, the Danish debate focused on the degree of integration.

After the 1972 decision to join the EU the Socialist People's Party was the only significant party to favour a break with the EU,[12] although Denmark has seldom been among the countries eager to push integration to higher levels. Public opinion had come to view EU membership positively (63 per cent in 1990).[13] Within this consensus, Branner classifies the Danish parties in three groups regarding the EU: a federalist group, comprising the Liberals (Agrarians), Conservatives and Centre Democrats, a pro-integrationist group based on inter-state co-operation, which includes the Social Democrats, Radicals and Christian People's Party, and in part the Progress Party, and finally the anti-integrationists consisting of the three parties on the left; the Socialist People's Party, Left Socialists and the Communist Party. The Danish government negotiating the Maastricht Treaty had some of the most EU-eager politicians in Denmark, Uffe-Ellemann Jensen (Liberal) as foreign minister and Poul Schluter (Conservative) as prime minister. However, they misjudged their ability to convince a sceptical electorate. The government had enjoyed a foreign policy victory in the 1986 referendum on the Single European Act (56 per cent 'yes') and may have been overconfident in its ability to 'deliver' the Danish voter. However, a combination of dissatisfied lower level elites within the Social Democrats, the Radical Liberals and virtually all of the Socialist and Progress parties joined forces with an extra-parliamentary movement to narrowly defeat the treaty; 47,000 votes out of a 4 million electorate.

According to Karen Sieune[14] the extensive political implications of the Maastricht Treaty were unacceptable to a majority of the Danes, even though the economics of the EU was beneficial for Denmark. The surprising defeat of the government was followed by a 'national compromise', initiated by the opposition parties, the Socialist People's Party, the Radicals and the Social Democrats. The governmental parties were more or less forced to accept. In essence, it called for a Maastricht 'light' version, in which Denmark was exempt from the common defence and security policy, the single currency, union citizenship and closer co-operation in police and judicial affairs. This pragmatic Europeanism was now embraced also by the Socialist People's Party leadership, which was seen by parts of the grass roots as an unacceptable turn around. Only the Progress Party on the far right and the minor parties on the far left refused to endorse the 'national compromise'. In essence, the Danes, whose concern about national security in its military connotation has been marked by fatalism (and Germanophobia) that goes back more than a century, voted 'no' to the bureaucratic half-measures behind the political visions of tomorrow's Europe. Of all the implicit political aims that are to be deciphered in the Maastricht Treaty, those suggesting something that may result in European federalism and citizenship were the least appreciated among the Danes. A coalition of nondescript Social Democratic patriots and left-wing radicals in Denmark turned against the transfer of sovereignty over matters in which, to the patriots, it seemed much wiser to maintain national authority and, to the radicals, to have no particularly authoritative institutions. In what amounted to a mob definition of the subsidiarity principle, a large number of voters seemingly conveyed an overload of confidence in the national political institutions.

The 'national compromise' was subsequently approved by the voters in May 1993. What made 57 per cent of the Danish electorate vote in favour of the Edinburgh Agreement?[15] First, it was a new and less federalist proposition that was put to the vote. Second, a 'no' majority would have put Denmark's membership of the EC in jeopardy. Third, in any event, it was feared that a 'no' majority would be harmful to the Danish economy and thus cause more lay offs.

When the Danish electorate returned to the polls to decide on ('light') EU membership, the issue was fought within a different setting. The electorate went to the polls under a Social Democratic prime minister and with a Socialist People's Party leadership committed to the Edinburgh Agreement. The Edinburgh Agreement was implicitly cast as an all-or-nothing proposition: accept a diluted EU or leave the increasingly appreciated Union. This implicit threat to national growth and jobs touched the social democratic constituency at grass-roots level, without further need of elaboration, initiated a complex process of re-evaluation of the issues at stake. To the otherwise loyal Social Democrats who voted 'no' in 1992, there was now a perfect excuse for setting things right: the fact that their own party had returned to cabinet position.

PARTY GRASS ROOT MEMBERS GO ASTRAY

The key to the final ruling on the European issue in Finland, Sweden and Norway was the Social Democratic constituency. In 1992 the majority of Danish Social Democratic grass root members turned against the Maastricht Treaty (see Table 12.1).

The Swedish Social Democrats barely managed to scrape together a majority of their own followers to vote for membership. Both the Finnish and Norwegian Social Democratic Parties, however, were able to mobilize substantial majorities of their regular voters in favour of membership (Table 12.2).

Table 12.1 Denmark's vote on the Edinburgh Agreement (1993), Finland's, Sweden's and Norway's vote on EU membership (1994), in total and by gender (%)

	Denmark			Finland			Norway			Sweden		
	Women	*All*	*Men*	*Women*	*All*	*Men*	*Women*	*All*	*Men*	*Women*	*All*	*Men*
Yes	52	57	63	34	57	46	43	48	52	47	52	57
No	48	43	37	42	43	39	57	52	48	52	47	42
Blank											1	
Don't know				24		15						

Note: The total vote is based on the final results. Data on gender for Denmark, Norway and Sweden are from exit polls; and for Finland from a pre-referendum opinion survey.

Sources: Denmark: H.J. Nielsen, *EF på valg* (Copenhagen, Columbus, 1993), p. 59. Finland: *Finnish EU Opinion, Autumn, 1994* (Centre for Finnish Business and Policy Studies (EVA), Helsinki, 1994). Norway: *Dagbladet, 29 November 1994*. Sweden: SVT/Valu94EU, Report no. 23, 1994 (exit poll Swedish Television).

The constituencies of the centre (agrarian) parties in Sweden and Finland were also less EU enthusiastic than the party elites. By contrast, the Norwegian sister party had the rare pleasure of having almost all its voters respond to the view of the leadership. The Christian Democratic Party of Sweden also saw its constituency split on the EU issue. The Norwegian Christian People's Party, by far the most significant of the Christian parties in Scandinavia,[16] enjoyed a fair response among its voters.

Table 12.2 Party support and vote against Maastricht Treaty (1992) and Edinburgh Agreement (1993) in Danish referendums; party support and vote against membership of the EU in Finland, Norway, and Sweden (1994) (%)

Denmark (voting 'no' on Maastricht)

Soc.P.P.	SD	Centre parties	Agr.Lib.	Cons.	Progr.
89	67	37	11	21	67

Denmark (voting 'no' on Edinburgh)

Soc.P.P.	SD	Centre parties	Agr.Lib.	Cons.	Progr.
85	50	31	11	14	55

Finland, estimate based on opinion poll August, 1994 (voting 'no')

Left	SD	Green	Agr.	Cons.
80	35	37	65	15

Norway, exit poll of those voting 'no'

Soc.Left	SD	Lib.(Green)	Agr.	Chr.	Cons.	Progr.
80	35	53	94	86	18	40

Sweden, exit poll ('no' votes; blank votes omitted)

Left	SD	Green	Lib.	Agr.	Chr.	Cons.	New Dem.
90	49	84	18	54	59	13	62

Sources: As for Table 12.1

Denmark: Soc.P. P. = Socialistisk Folkeparti (Socialist People's Party); SD = Socialdemokratiet (Social Democrats); Agr. Lib. = Venstre (Liberals); Cons. = Konservative Folkeparti (Conservatives); Progr.= Fremskridtspartiet (Progress Party). *Finland*: Left = Vasemmistpoliitto (left-wing Alliance); SD = Suomen Sosialdemokraattinen (Social Democrats); Green = Vihrevat (Greens); Agr. = Kekustapuolue (Centre Party); Cons. = Kansallinen Kokoomus (Conservatives). *Norway*: Soc. Left = Sosialistisk Venstreparti (Socialist Left party); SD = Det Norske Arbeiderparti (Labour); Lib. = Venstre (Liberals); Agr. = Senterpartiet (Centre Party); Chr. = Kristelig Folkeparti (Christian People's Party); Con. = Høyre (Conservatives); Progr. = Fremskrittspartiet (Progress Party). *Sweden*: Left = Vänsterpartier (Leftist Party); SD = Socialdemokratiska Arbetarepartiet (Social Democrats); Green = Miljøpartiet de grøna (Greens); Lib. = Folkpartiet (Liberals); Agr. = Centerpartiet (Centre Party); Cons. = Moderata Samlingspartiet (Conservatives); New. Dem. = Ny Demokrati (New Democracy).

The radical left-wing parties had a massive following among their constituencies. Between 80 and 90 per cent of the grass roots went against membership. This unity between the elite and the masses was also the case among the Conservative Parties. Among the neo-liberals, however, the picture was more fragmented.

The lack of a clear left–right dimension on the EU issue is demonstrated by the parties on the far right of the political spectrum. In Denmark the Progress Party officially rejected membership of the EU. In Sweden and Norway these parties were officially in favour of EU membership, but their sympathizers split. The Progress Parties contain two, possibly three streams of supporters. The liberal faction saw EU membership as completely natural, given its ideological orientation. However, to the populist faction, EU's freedom of movement of people involved the prospect of Scandinavia being overrun by immigrants. The third faction of the Progress Parties, the libertarians, would not subscribe to this as a cause of rejecting membership.

Rather, to this faction it was precisely the addition of yet another layer of government that was the problem. To them the EU just seems like another way of increasing bureaucracy and regulation, i.e. a new 'social democracy'.

If, and with good reason, some saw the EU as a new chance for the European social democratic parties to regain control of ever freer economic market mechanisms, why were the social democratic grass roots of Scandinavia so reluctant to join this new project of government? Why did the referendum split the social democratic constituencies along traditional lines: the 'no' vote among the working class against the 'yes' vote among the salaried employees; women against men, public against private employees, the grass roots of the northern peripheries against those of the capital areas?

For one thing, the days of party loyalty are gone. Party loyalty is a term associated with the 1950s and 1960s, when the working-class vote of the social democratic parties still accounted for 65–75 per cent of the party's total vote (see Table 12.3). The party of the 1990s is a catch-all party, in which the non-manual public employees have a prominent position.

This means that the world according to most social democratic grass roots is a world of politics instead of a world of market opportunities and risks to be faced and conquered. The long-nurtured perception of the EU among Nordic social democrats is that of a market, one in which goods are traded and politics always came second. This was confirmed as Finland, Norway and Sweden debated the issue of membership. Indeed, the terms of membership concluded in the negotiations focused exclusively on material issues. When these terms were brought into the campaigns they were translated into numbers: how many, how much, how long? How many new food additives would have to be readmitted? How many subsidies were to be collected by the peasants? For how long would the state liquor stores retain their monopolies? Not surprisingly, the few instances in which the EU would bring improvements to ordinary Scandinavians were brushed aside as irrelevant, and the number of drawbacks that were to accompany membership attracted all kinds of special interests into the campaign.

This pinpoints the second factor pivotal to the question of Social Democratic grass roots disloyalty: the end of the corporatist era. Until recently, the social democratic parties in Scandinavia had only one big interest organization to worry about. Indeed, the trades union central (TUC) was a source of joy rather than one of sorrow. Today, the arena of interest organization is overcrowded and multifaceted. There was not one single special interest that could not find a good reason to call upon their supporters to vote 'no' to EU membership. Worse still, the TUC in Sweden did not

Table 12.3 Working-class proportion of the social democratic vote (%)

	Denmark		Finland		Norway		Sweden	
Year	1966	1990	1966	1991	1965	1989	1966	1991
Working class	67	46	74	52	64	45	73	52

Sources: Denmark: J. Goul Andersen, in P. Gundelach and K. Siune (eds), *From Voters to Participants* (Aarhus, Politica, 1992), p. 104; Finland: T. Martikainen and R. Yrjönen, *Voting, Parties and Social Change in Finland* (Helsinki, Statistics Finland, Research Papers, 187, 1991), p. 60; Norway: H. Valen, B. Aardal and G. Vogt, *Endring og kontinuitet; Stortingsvalget 1989* (Oslo, SSB, 1990), pp. 99ff.; Sweden: M. Gilljam and S. Holmberg, *Väljarna inför 90-talet* (Stockholm, Norstedts Juridik, 1993), p. 198.

want to risk internal conflict to help the party to mobilize its rank and file. In Norway, the TUC in fact passed a resolution against membership of the EU at its national congress shortly before referendum day. Typically, it was the trades unions organizing public employees that won the vote. Only the Finnish TUC delivered support according to the old traditions in Nordic labour politics.

History was indeed part of the referenda. No one knew that better than the Norwegian Labour Party, for the reasons already mentioned above. Suffice it to add that the Labour Party faced an electorate that, even though twenty-two years older, had not changed much since 1972. The reason for this was uniquely Norwegian. A substantial portion of the petroleum revenues has been invested in the periphery. Unlike in many other countries, the population of Norway's remote areas have not been pushed to move away and settle in large urban areas. Local communities have retained their social fabric, and conserved political opinion as well. Using local government as units of analysis, an impressive correlation of 0.88 is found between the votes of the 1972 and 1994 referenda.

Yet, as a healthy balance to historical determinism, it is appropriate to remember the role of the social democratic parties themselves. The Finnish and Norwegian parties did considerably better among their own ranks than did the parties in Denmark and Sweden. In other words, hard and long work by the party leadership to make the rank and file cast a 'yes' vote did make a difference. For instance, in some of the legendary small industrial towns in which the labour movement has formed generations of voters, a majority was won for membership. By contrast, the Swedish Social Democratic Party opted for abdication. It never committed the party to an all-out campaign in favour of joining the EU, the kind of campaign the party was perfectly capable of organizing in a regular parliamentary election. This explains why there was only one single industrial town north of the Stockholm International Airport that (just) delivered a majority for membership. Instead, the grass roots of the Swedish labour movement were left to take their cues from individual leaders from the party and the trades unions. A few days before the referendum, the issue became one of personal trust, the party leader and party secretary appealing to the regular voters. In addition, three leaders of the most important public employees' unions (of whom two were women) came out to announce that they had decided to cast a 'yes' vote. This helped to narrow the gap between the vote of private and public employees in Sweden.

CONCLUSION

Surveying the Scandinavian countries for a pattern in the parties' view of the EU, there are only a few observations that hold across all the countries. The Conservatives everywhere were the most supportive of EU membership. Moreover, Conservative party elites were in tune with their mass following. In all four countries the Conservatives have been among the earliest advocates of EU membership and also among the most integrationist parties. There are, nevertheless, important variations in the timing of their EU standpoint which are linked to their individual national contexts. In Finland and Sweden the active advocacy of EU membership was contained by the Cold War. In Norway the breakdown of centre–right government co-operation in 1986–87[17] and the need to lift the profile of the Conservatives reopened the membership issue.

The socialist left parties, another group showing exceptional unity between the elite and the grass roots, all opposed EU integration, although the Danish party became part of the national compromise.

The pivotal social democratic parties in all countries except Finland were characterized by an ambivalent attitude towards the EU. In the Danish and Swedish parties this reluctance also trickled down to the masses. The Finnish and Norwegian parties proved that a more clear-cut stance on the issue, and a more vigorous campaign in favour of a 'yes' vote did make a difference.

Here, however, the similarities end. The political centre (liberal, agrarian, Christian, ethnic) in the four countries contains several parties that are unique to each country. But even where the same types of party appear, their standpoint on the EU varies. The most extreme example of difference in EU orientation is the case of agrarian oriented parties, of which the Danish party is the most federally inclined; the Norwegian adopts the completely opposite point of view, with the Finnish and Swedish parties being internally divided.

Knowing the ideological position of a party is normally a reliable cue to predicting its policies; but when parties confront Europe and the EU, ideology is a poor guide to prediction. There is no clear left–right dimension. Nor does the EU issue follow other cleavages, such as peasants versus workers versus public employees, in a consistent way across the Scandinavian countries. Rather, the internal geographic variation in each country is as relevant as the socio-economic position of the individual voters.

The variations in official party positions may be explained by differences in macropolitical factors, such as geo-political position, economic vulnerability among constituencies, and particular historical experiences. This chapter has pinpointed the most important of these variations as well as suggested the reasons behind them.

The long-term consequences of this battle remain to be seen. Finland and Sweden's elections to the European Parliament will doubtless follow the pattern of the Danish elections to the European Parliament: half-measures across the board. Since there will always be a more important ensuing national parliamentary election, the parties will not nominate their best and brightest candidates for the seats; and the parties will not waste too much energy in getting out the vote. In the European Parliament elections there will be once again an opportunity for those who voted 'no' to membership in the first place to express themselves. Parties and Europe do not mix easily.

APPENDIX

Table 12.4 Characteristics of supporters and opponents of EU membership in Finland, Norway and Sweden

	For	*Against*
Finland		
Greater Helsinki	74	17
Northern	44	43
Workers	50	36
Functionaries	65	26
Peasants	16	73
Compulsory education	51	36

Academic education	77	18
Age 18–24	66	28
Men	59	32
Women	49	36
Norway		
Oslofjord Area	62	38
Northern Provinces	29	71
Occupational sector:		
Industry	52	48
Farming	11	89
Health and education	46	54
Public administration	51	49
Banking/private business	63	37
Men	52	48
Women	43	57
Sweden*		
Stockholm	43	39
Periphery	20	57
Workers	19	51
White collar	39	38
Self-employed	55	32
Private employment	34	42
Public employment	23	48
Men	38	40
Women	22	47

Sources: Finland; Keskuskauppakamari, op. cit.; Norway; *MMI/Dagbladet* 29 November 1994; Sweden: *Göteborgs-Posten*.

* Survey, 'don't know' answers omitted from table.

NOTES

1 The referenda were held on 16 October in Finland, 13 November in Sweden and 28 November in Norway. The authors acknowledge the assistance of NSD/Opinion AS in supplying data used in this chapter. NSD, however, bears no responsibility for the selection and interpretation of these data.

2 For a general introduction to Nordic politics, see, for example, Alastair Thomas, *Nordic Politics and Government* (London, Routledge, forthcoming), or Eric S. Einhorn and John Logue, *Modern Welfare States: Politics and Policies in Social Democratic Scandinavia* (London, Praeger, 1989).

3 Adam Przeworski and Henry Teune, *The Logic of Comparative Social Inquiry* (New York, Wiley, 1970).

4 Ibid.

5 See e.g. Telja Tiilikainen and Ib Damgaard Petersen (eds), *The Nordic Countries and the EC* (Copenhagen, Copenhagen Political Studies Press, 1992) and also Clive Church, 'EFTA and the Nordic countries' responses to the EC in the early 1990's', *Journal of Common Market Studies*. vol. 28, no. 24, 1990, pp. 401–30.

6 See e.g. Dag Anckar, 'Finlands presidentmakt', in U. Lindström and L. Karvonen (eds), *Finland. En politisk loggbok* (Stockholm, Almqvist and Wiksell, 1987).

7 The Conservative Party and the Liberal Party had also a more positive view of Swedish EU membership in 1961, see Gullan Gidlund, *Partiernas Europa* (Stockholm, Natur och Kultur, 1992).

8 An internal party report which in 1976 had recommended a pro-EC stand caused a public commotion and had to be hurriedly shelved.

9 As demonstrated in September 1992 by the formation of the SME: Social democrats

against EC, a movement of Labour Party members bent on fighting their own party leadership (and government) on the EC issue.

10 See Gudrun Birkelund, *Norge og EF*, Thesis, Department of Comparative Politics, University of Bergen, 1989, p. 138.

11 Fifty per cent of the non-voters from 1972 were still undecided in 1989, with the rest almost evenly split between yes and no. Among the new voters about one third opposed membership, 28 per cent were in favour and 38 per cent undecided (ibid.).

12 In addition, a non-partisan list – Folkebevegelsen mod EU (People's Movement against the EU) – favouring Danish withdrawal from the EU has participated in the EP elections. It won four out of the total sixteen Danish seats in each of the 1979, 1984, 1989 EP elections, second only to the Social Democratic Party. In the 1994 elections it won only two seats, but the June Movement, the coalition that defeated the government in the Maastricht referendum in 1992, also won two seats, thus maintaining the strength of Danish EC scepticism in the European Parliament.

13 See Hans Branner, 'Danish European policy since 1945: the question of sovereignty', in M. Kelstrup (ed.), *European Integration and Denmark's Participation* (Copenhagen, Political Studies Press, 1992), p. 317.

14 'The Danes said no to the Maastricht Treaty: the Danish EC referendum of June 1992', *Scandinavian Political Studies*, vol. 16, no. 1, 1993, pp. 93–103.

15 See Palle Svensson, 'The Danish yes to Maastricht and Edinburgh: the EC referendum of May 1993', *Scandinavian Political Studies*, vol. 17, no. 1, 1994 pp. 69–83.

16 See Lauri Karvonen, 'In from the cold? Christian parties in Scandinavia', *Scandinavian Political Studies*, vol. 16, no. 1, 1993, pp. 25–48.

17 The Conservatives had co-operated with the Christian People's Party and the Centre Party in a government which was defeated in a parliamentary vote in 1986. The three parties made an unsuccessful attempt to unseat the Labour government in 1987, causing considerable turmoil within the Conservative party; see e.g. Kaare Strom, 'The Presthus debacle: intraparty politics and bargaining failure in Norway', *American Political Science Review*, vol. 88, no. 1, 1994 pp. 112–27.

SELECT BIBLIOGRAPHY

Branner, Hans, 'Danish European policy since 1945: the question of sovereignty', in Kelstrup, M. (ed.), *European Integration and Denmark's Participation*, Copenhagen, Copenhagen Political Studies Press, 1992, pp. 297–327.

Church, Clive, 'EFTA and the Nordic countries' responses to the EC in the early 1990s', *Journal of Common Market Studies*, vol. 28, no. 24, 1990, pp. 401–30.

Einhorn, Eric S. and Logue, John, *Modern Welfare States: Politics and Policies in Social Democratic Scandinavia*, London, Praeger, 1989.

Gidlund, Gullan, *Partiernas Europa*, Stockholm, Natur och Kultur, 1992.

Kelstrup, M. (ed.), *European Integration and Denmark's Participation*, Copenhagen, Copenhagen Political Studies Press, 1992.

Lindström, U., *Euro-Consent, Euro-Contract or Euro-Coercion? Scandinavian Social Democracy, the European Impasse, and the Abolition of Things Political*, Oslo, Scandinavian University Press, 1993.

Nelsen, Brent F. (ed.), *Norway and the European Community*, London, Praeger, 1993.

Nielsen, Hans Jørgen, 'The Danish voters and the referendum in June 1992 on the Treaty of Maastricht', in Kelstrup, M. (ed.), *European Integration and Denmark's Participation*, Copenhagen, Copenhagen Political Studies Press, 1992, pp. 365–80.

Sieune, Karen, 'The Danes said no to the Maastricht Treaty: the Danish EC referendum of June 1992', *Scandinavian Political Studies*, vol. 16, no. 1, pp. 93–103.

Svensson, Palle, 'The Danish yes to Maastricht and Edinburgh: the EC referendum of May 1993', *Scandinavian Political Studies*, vol. 17, no. 1, pp. 69–82.

Tiilikainen, Telja and Petersen, Ib Damgaard (eds), *The Nordic Countries and the EC*, Copenhagen, Copenhagen Political Studies Press, 1993.

Thomas, Alastair, *Nordic Politics and Government*, London, Routledge, forthcoming.

Government White Papers:
Finland: Statsrådets meddelande till Riksdagen om Finlands förhållande till integration-sutvecklingen i Västeuropa.
Norway: Norge, EF og europeisk samarbeid (Stortingsmelding no. 61, 1986–87).
Sweden: Sverige och den västeuropeiska integrationen (Regeringens proposition 1987/88:66).

13 Western communist parties and the European Union

David Bell

Communist parties were once part of a truly transnational political party. If a strict domestic yardstick is taken to measure whether or not an institution is a 'political party' then the communist movement has been the only real transnational political party. Communist parties moved with almost balletic precision in a co-ordinated manner orchestrated by Moscow for most of the history of the European institutions and this transnational political dimension was essential background in both Western communism and the integration of Europe.

The communist 'Third' International held its first meeting in Moscow in March 1919. Komintern was composed of parties, groups and individuals who supported Lenin's coup of October 1917. If many of these local sections were decentralized and ill-disciplined, by the mid-1920s true communist parties had been put in place and the discipline of the communist movement had been consolidated by the process of 'Leninization' (sometimes called 'bolshevization'), that is the centralization of world communism.[1] This is an important point. Communist parties are Leninist, totalitarian parties run by professional party bureaucracies. Although certain policies and programmes (like anti-Europeanism) had electoral pay offs the reasons for communist campaigns are not found in national electoral constraints. The parties were handed policy decisions from the centre leadership – the Communist Party of the Soviet Union (CPSU) – which were then applied with greater or lesser success in the countries of Western Europe. Their strategy might be successful or might be an electoral disaster (or worse) but it was applied for Moscow's own reasons.

Communism was a movement which looked to a political centre, Moscow, and which devoted itself to the interests of the Revolution as defined by the Kremlin. The Soviet Union was the workers' fatherland, the country of the successful Revolution, and its interests took precedence. There was some chaos in the world movement in the 1920s, largely the result of the indeterminate power struggle in the Soviet system. By 1928, however, this leadership conflict had been decisively resolved in Stalin's favour. National communist parties executed orders, which were sometimes suicidal, with exemplary discipline and, although there were local tactics, there are no examples of local autonomy in Western Europe after Stalin had become firmly established in power.

THE EUROPEAN ISSUE

For communists up until the Second World War, the European issue was a distraction or, perhaps worse, a reformist trap which fostered the 'unreal' social democratic expectation that peace could be obtained by ameliorative measures rather than through total revolution (hence communist opposition to the 1930 plan for European Union which Aristide Briand presented to the League of Nations). The essential task for communists was the protection of the heartland of the Revolution and the interests of the Soviet Union. In the communist vision all roads led to Moscow, and a European road could only be a useless diversion or else a dead end. Communists defined and rigorously interpreted the world as split between the capitalist or imperialist forces on the one side and the Socialist or Soviet forces on the other. There was no room in this simplistic divide for either an intermediary or for partial allegiances. Although this Manichean view did not exclude the use of tactical political ruse, the concealing of intentions (the better to deceive the 'bourgeois' enemy), or the use of diversionary tactics (of which there were many examples), the objective remained the same – the setting up of Soviet-type systems outside of the Soviet Union when the time was right.

THE COLD WAR

Communism in Western Europe emerged from the Second World War in a strong position. The exploits of the Red Army, the partnership of the Soviet Union with the Allies, their superior organization (which had flourished in clandestinity where other parties had not), the Resistance (often communist dominated) and the discredit of the right, all combined to place the Western parties in a favourable position for the electoral competitions at the Liberation.[2] To this must be added a Western misperception of communist parties not as revolutionaries but as determined reformers, social democrats who meant it. At that time communist parties had large memberships and polled respectably in Western Europe: 12.7 per cent in Belgium, 12.5 per cent in Denmark, 10.5 per cent in Luxembourg, 10.6 per cent in the Netherlands, 11.9 per cent in Norway, 10.3 per cent in Sweden and even 5 per cent in Switzerland and in Germany. In France, the French Communist Party (PCF) took 28 per cent of the vote in 1946 and claimed a membership of 800,000 – the communists' best ever poll in a free election until briefly bettered by the Italian Communist Party (PCI) with 34.4 per cent in June 1976. In Italy the PCI polled 18.9 per cent in 1946, in Finland the party took 20 per cent, and although in Southern Europe dictatorship and civil war prevented free votes it can be assumed that the communists were the best organized forces of the left.

The picture changed dramatically at the onset of the Cold War. Communist votes collapsed across the board (and most parties were reduced to a handful of activists). This did not mean that they were without influence, because communist positions in the unions remained crucial in a number of Western countries, but it did mean that communism as a parliamentary phenomenon was more or less eliminated except in France, Italy and Finland. These 'big parties' were later joined by the Greek, Portuguese and Spanish Communist Parties at the end of the 1970s when the Southern dictatorships fell. Apart from these only the Swedish Party by virtue of its hinge position, and the eccentric Icelandic and Luxembourg Parties were of note, but even these slowly weakened throughout the 1960s and 1970s.[3]

In this process of communist upsurge, of Cold War and communist decline, Europe plays a principal part. A substantial boost to European integration was precisely the fear of communism and communist take over of Western Europe. Although not the only factor, the Cold War did powerfully assist the integration process by providing both a common external enemy and, in the form of the USA, a sponsor of European integration. By the same token the communist parties, which had been initially indifferent to early Western moves to unity, became violently hostile to Europe after the founding of Komintern in September 1947. Europe was then identified, by all communist parties, as capitalist, Atlanticist, reformist and a rampart against the Revolution.[4] All this is well known, but a further qualification has to be made, and it is what gives communist attitudes to Europe contemporary relevance, Western Parties campaigned about Europe by appealing to defensive nationalism. The communist parties mobilized their supporters, often successfully, on the themes of the nation and of the protection of social and traditional institutions. Communist rhetoric tapped popular national feelings and played on xenophobic fears. National feeling and the fear of 'foreign' interference were easy targets in a Europe which had only recently suffered two catastrophic wars and where only the British Isles had escaped occupation.

Communist positions were defined in 1947 starting with the reaction to the Marshall Plan in November 1947 (quasi-insurrectional strikes) and then the denunciation of NATO as an aggressive military preparation for war against the USSR.[5] The Schuman Plan was greeted in the same way. This, announced the French and Italian communists, was the economic part of the NATO military machine which would reinforce American domination of Europe through its cat's paw, the German Federal Republic. The place of European institutions in the military reinforcement of Europe with an ultimately anti-Soviet war-like intent was continually emphasized by the communist parties.

Other arguments used to oppose the Schuman Plan stressed the benefits to Germany of the new institutions, and the detrimental consequences this development would have for the French and the Italian economies. The outcome of integration was depicted in lurid terms.[6] The effect that European competition would have on the French and Italian economies, it was contended, would be devastating, and for the French party this was a constant theme, although the Italian party ceased to stress this aspect in the 1970s. The French party portrayed the new Europe in terms of forced labour, deindustrialization and collapsing living standards. It was also stressed that France and Italy would be reduced to the status of second-class powers and that the sovereignty of states would be undermined. The alleged threat to national sovereignty proved to be a rich lode which was profitably mined on subsequent occasions by many European communist parties.[7]

The theme of the bellicose nature of the emerging Europe was naturally to the fore in the PCF's opposition to the European Defence Community.[8] Here, however, the threat to national sovereignty brought the PCF into an alliance with the Gaullists, a temporary coalition which defeated the treaty in the French Assembly. This was the harbinger of an 'objective' alliance between the USSR and the Gaullists which was to cause problems later for the PCF both because Moscow preferred the French right to the Atlanticist left and because of a convergence which made the communists the protectors of certain aspects of the General's legacy.

The Messina conference, which mooted the founding of the Common Market and Euratom produced a vigorous response from Moscow. The ECSC communist parties took the same view. They stated that:

These treaties [establishing the EEC and Euratom] lead to the formation of a military and political bloc under the leadership of the Bonn Republic of Germany and an accentuated division of the real Europe. The United States, which is at the origin of European 'integration' and which has in a more or less overt manner been directing the negotiations, is well placed to use these treaties for its own ends. Euratom delivers uranium and French scientists to the Bonn Republic of Germany and opens up to it the ability to make [nuclear] arms of mass destruction.[9]

1956 AND ALL THAT

The initial impetus to the parting of the ways in Western communism had come in 1956 and came to be interpreted as the French and Italian Communist Party 'routes'. The Khrushchev line of peaceful coexistence in Europe and of the 'parliamentary road to power' in the West implied that the communists' move out of isolation and form alliances.[10] In forming alliances the parties would inevitably have to bargain and could be sucked into the 'bourgeois' system. Yet in the beginning coalition bargains were thought to be compatible with Soviet interests. Khrushchev had ceased to demand the overthrow of the institutions of Europe and encouraged influence from the inside, as it were. However, one road (the French) meant the maintenance of the traditional Communist Party and a continuing commitment to the 'communist idea' (the Soviet system), the other (the Italian) meant the watering down and possible abandonment of Lenin's central tenets. The Italian communist strategy was to evidence a creeping reformism and could have led eventually to a form of social democracy with all the trappings of consensus-seeking gradualism. The events of 1989 and then the collapse of the communist regime in the Soviet Union accentuated this division although, of course, communist parties were in crisis well before the 1980s.

AFTER MESSINA

In 1959 the six communist parties of the EEC met in Rome and demanded the rejection of the Treaty. The 'parliamentary road' to power was not immediately applied to the European institutions. In 1957 the CPSU's '17 Theses' had seconded the Soviet view that integration was principally anti-Soviet and the tone was correspondingly hostile.[11] The innovative line on European institutions was introduced by the '32 Theses' of 1962 which recognized the 'economic reality' of the Common Market, in other words, that it was an organization with which the Soviet Union could and would deal. It was still an 'imperialist' institution but there were aspects of it which could be used for 'progressive' purposes to the extent to which institutions could be 'democratized' (that is, if there was communist influence). Nevertheless, the '32 Theses' redescribed European institutions as a way of keeping former colonies under control and of providing unskilled labour, and although the '32 Theses' were still marked by a hostility to a 'consolidating politico-military bloc', the parties hoped that duties and quotas would be changed to favour the USSR and to see trade extended to Eastern Europe. The Common Market, said the '32 Theses', has become a political and economic reality, namely a state and monopoly union of the financial oligarchies of Western Europe.

Communists could not view European institutions as anything other than the emanation of bourgeois society, but tactical considerations could always change how they were to be treated. This is the Leninist thin line between 'left-wing infantilism', which is the refusal to use the opportunities offered by bourgeois society and 'parliamentary cretinism' which is the embracing of those institutions. In Western Europe to get along you have to go along, so the danger of 'parliamentary cretinism' was ever present; but the lack of revolutionary possibilities in Western Europe (as a result of the consolidation of the Old Continent and the nuclear balance) was recognized in Khrushchev's change of line. The revolutionary hostility to the institutions of the West was replaced by a determination to enter them to use them for communist purposes. The long and, as it turned out, unsuccessful march through Western institutions began.

This position was reconfirmed by Brezhnev in 1972.[12] Communists remained hostile to the unification of capitalist Europe, but hoped for Community deals with the Eastern bloc and for party participation in the institutions. The Italian party, like the French, espoused this line, denouncing the capitalist aspects of European unification. In 1969 Giorgio Amendola led a group of seven Italian communist MEPs in Strasbourg and in 1973 they were joined by four French communists. The CGIL and CGT unions also asked to participate in the Economic and Social Council of the EEC.

The PCI and the PCF began to move apart as the Italian party groped its way towards increasingly supranational positions and moved from the critical to the constructive.[13] The French party's hostility was expressed in opposition to British membership (during the 1972 French referendum on enlargement), and in the crucial joint manifesto with the Socialist Party the PCF's objection to supranationalism was registered. Both the PCF and the PCI positions on Europe were broadly pro-Soviet, aiming to 'decouple' (in NATO jargon) the Community from the USA. The Italian position, however, involved a reinforcing of European co-operation against Atlanticist temptations and creating a neutral non-aligned Western movement. There was no real disagreement with the CPSU here even if there was discord on the details. It was, however, Jean Kanapa, the principal French communist and international theoretician of the 1970s, who elaborated on the further turn after the 1972 referendum in France on the first enlargement. Kanapa stated that

> today there exist possibilities to raise the class struggle of the Western European workers to a higher level to create a European Community free of the dominion of trust capital, respectful of the free determination of each people . . . A Europe which will not be a branch of the Atlantic bloc, but which will be really independent and capable of establishing relations as much with the United States of America as with the Socialist countries, relations founded on the strict equality of rights and in the interests of the peoples.[14]

Part of this declaration could be mistaken for a Gaullist Europe of nation states, and the party did emerge as a defender of the Gaullist status quo in French foreign policy in the late 1970s.

Hence in the mid-1970s the hostility to the Community among communist parties was still more or less uniform. The Communist Party of the Netherlands asserted that the Community was 'German neo-imperialism' and, moreover, that only reformists believed in the possibility of a united socialist Europe. The Danish and British parties opposed their country's entry into the Community and the Norwegian Communist Party briefly revived in 1972 as a result of its determined opposition to Norway joining Europe (it then disappeared again). The Swedish Communist Party was similarly opposed to any agreements with the Community, as was the Finnish party, and the Icelandic communists interpreted the Cod War over fishing rights as, partially at least, an anti-Community struggle. The Swiss Communist Party for its part objected to any form of association with the Nine of the EEC and opposed the free-trade pact with EFTA. The possibility of a Community-friendly policy emerging from the Western parties rested with the Spanish and Italian communists.[15]

The parting of the ways between the PCI and PCF when it materialized in the late 1970s involved a difference of perception.[16] The French party defined its problem as keeping external influences such as Europe and the USA (hostile to communists) out of the French political system. That meant, principally, overcoming American and to some extent Western European objections to communist demands (such as communist ministers in the French government). For the Italian communists, Italy already was influenced by its partners; the principal task was thus to persuade some of Italy's partners that communist participation in government was acceptable. The Italian party set out on a charm offensive, notably in the European Parliament, while the French party adopted an aggressive stance intended to defend the autonomy of the national political arena.

The 1980s were characterized by the French Communist Party's relentless pressing of the main lines of attack on the Community and by the Italian party's slow change of position.[17] Principal among these lines of attack were again the threats to national sovereignty from Europe. The French communist daily *L'Humanité* reported on 'two dangerous EEC projects': foreign teachers will come to France and trains will be driven by European railway workers.[18] The French party also opposed the Haagerup Report,which called for the co-ordination of defence policy (which would have been Atlanticist), with the arguments that these matters were the prerogative of individual states and that co-ordinated defence would recreate a Cold War atmosphere. In 1982 the Galizzi Report (by an Italian communist MEP) recommending a European strategy founded on 'the simultaneous affirmation of a policy of both defence and *détente*' was repudiated on the same grounds. The PCF argued that it was 'not a time for suspicion but for confidence, mutual confidence, which should open the way to disarmament. To brandish the threat of a European defence at the very time of agreement between America and the USSR would recreate suspicion and distrust.'[19]

The French party, however, used the European Parliament to promote Soviet campaigns. The Soviet invasion of Afghanistan was condemned by the European Parliament (including the PCI but excluding the PCF); the PCF's view, expressed by Gustave Ansart, was that this condemnation was news 'manipulation'. It was able to challenge the deployment of NATO Cruise and Pershing missiles even while this was supported by the Socialist government in Paris of which it formed a part. While the Polish communist government harassed and then suppressed Solidarity, the PCF launched a campaign on Human Rights in the Community (Northern Ireland in main part). The EP's resolution calling for the Polish communists to respect the Helsinki agreements on freedom and its subsequent condemning of the Polish 'state of emergency' again found the PCF isolated from the PCI.[20]

At a time in the late 1970s when the Spanish party supported the application of the new democracy to join the Community, the differences of view with the French became a major schism during the 1980s. The outcome in 1989 was the splitting of the communist group in the European Parliament into two, the Spanish and Italians on the one side and the French, Portuguese and Greek parties on the other. In 1989 the French, Portuguese and Greek Communists formed the Left Unity group and the Italians and Spanish communists formed the European Unitarian Left in the EP. The French-led group took a defensive line against the 'German dominated Europe of the monopolies' but the Spanish and Italian parties supported closer union. It was Altiero Spinelli, an MEP on the PCI's list, who tabled a project for European union – a proposal which was anathema to the French.

THE SOVIET BLOC COLLAPSE

If the collapse caught the parties in various conditions of decline, it also eliminated the Soviet model and created a new power balance in Europe. The Italian Communist Party, long thought to have been in the ante-chamber of social democracy, disbanded and re-emerged as the Party of the Democratic Left (PDS). A new player entered the Italian party system; the exclusion of the Italian Communist Party from the post-war Italian political system turned out to have been a slight advantage, the reasons for its exclusion (its position as the advance guard of the Soviet regime) having disappeared. All the same, it was not clear that the PDS had sloughed off its communist past sufficiently to satisfy the Italian voters, as the setback in the European elections of 1994 seemed to show.

The French Communist Party, and other Bolshevik parties which survived the end of communism with their bureaucracies and resources intact, faced a different problem: how to redefine the 'communist ideal' behind a plausible façade of continuity given that the fall of the USSR meant the end of communism, of the transnational communist movement and of the revolutionary ideal. The parties that followed the French route of readaptation within the Bolshevik framework were mostly those in Southern Europe: Portugal, Spain, Greece and Cyprus, but also Belgium.[21] The parties were aided by two factors. The first was that, as mentioned, their popular support came not because they were tied to the CPSU but despite those ties and despite their commitment to the Soviet model. The second was that these 'Southern' parties were assisted by the relative weakness of the socialist parties, and were able to continue presenting themselves as the radical left of the political spectrum. These 'Southern European' parties, although faced with the necessity to reorient themselves, felt no need for a complete overhaul.

In this process of communist redefinition after 1991, Europe operates as the political equivalent of the Red Headed League. Communist anti-Europeanism was always presented principally as a hypernationalism with populist symbols which echoed the fears of their supporters (who are to be found predominantly in the peasant farming and 'smokestack' sectors of European business) about increasing foreign competition. The 1992 Single Market, followed by the process of ratification by European states of the Maastricht Treaty, provided a potential opportunity to realign behind a populist and activist mobilizing barrage of nationalist and anti-European rhetoric. In an increasingly consensual European political spectrum the parties were again able to assert their differences radically and to offer an alternative – if vague – vision. This time the redefinition of the communist ideal was not just an abandonment of the Soviet model (the commitment to the Eastern bloc model had long been downplayed) but the parties' essential redefinition of themselves as reformist and not as revolutionary.

Communists, in the past, prided themselves on their revolutionary refusal to support the system. Communism, informed by Marxism, was the wave of the future; the wave was unstoppable and would sweep away old institutions. For communists, the key point was that under capitalism, a 'historically doomed' system, attempts to shore up the defences, to reform through palliatives, were bound to be ineffectual and, worse, would be irresponsibly putting off the day of the Revolution. The long-term perspective was of revolution, and this left no room for short-term reformist expedients. It is important to be clear about this position. Communist parties were not responsible for the welfare states or the mass of social legislation in Western Europe after the Second World War: the PCF, for example, opposed what it called the 'fascist social security laws' on the grounds that they were a mission to rescue capitalism. The communists saw themselves as the revolutionary vectors of a new society and not as social democrats; they were the Atlantic Ocean rolling in; the reformists, socialists, were like Mrs Partington trying to push it out with mops and buckets. The hesitant move towards new reformist positions has varied from party to party but if the old Adam of protectionism and central planning still lurks within, what was on offer from the remaining communist parties was a defensive form of Keynesianism in one country which emphasized the conquests of the welfare state and the threat to nations from the intruding 'capitalist Europe'.

It should be added, in parenthesis, that although the main surviving Communist Parties are in 'Latin' Europe, the Swedish and Finnish ex-communists have been subject to the same nationalist temptations over the enlargement of the European Union to include the Scandinavian countries. Both the former Swedish communists and the former Finnish Communist Party have exploited popular fears about what joining the European Union will mean and have almost succeeded in using this issue to distance themselves from their communist past and to create a space for themselves in the post-Cold War political systems.

The Portuguese case is rather different. The Portuguese Communist Party (PCP) has always emphasized Portugal's peripheral position as a poor economy in a distant part of Europe. The PCP had by the 1980s more or less accepted the European Community as an 'economic reality' but began to backtrack, during the debate in the late 1980s on 1992 and The Single Market, to argue that these new developments meant the end of Portuguese independence in foreign policy. The PCP argument was that the European Community would be transformed by the new market and that the Single Market's intensification of competition coincided with the end of the period of European transition for Portugal. The Maastricht Treaty, so the Portuguese party asserted, made no allowances for Portugal's difficulties. The Greek Communist Party, which underwent a hardening of line before the fall of the Soviet Union, took up a broadly similar position. The Greek Communist Party presented itself as the national champion against predatory Europe and as the defence against the internationalism (as it were) of the socialist PASOK. The Greek, Portuguese and French parties once formed, with East Germany, Cuba, North Korea and Vietnam a sort of Third-and-a-Half International which briefly flourished in the interval between the fall of the Berlin Wall and the fall of the East German regime. The remnants of the East German Communist Party joined the communist parties of Portugal, Greece, Spain, Belgium and France as well as Italian hardliners in the call for a referendum on Maastricht.[22] Even if the referendum were lost, as it was in France, the opportunities for draping themselves in the national flag would be valuable. The Spanish and Belgian cases are more intricate, because whereas the Portuguese and French parties have always been associated with stark anti-European stances, the Spanish and Belgian parties were more 'Italianate' and pro-integration in their response to the European challenge. However, the collapse of the Soviet Union turned them away from the potential pro-European path and towards the temptations of populist nationalism as a way of maintaining their separate identity on the left of the party system.

COMMUNIST OPPOSITION TO INTEGRATION: THE MAASTRICHT TRICK

The Maastricht Treaty, and the subsequent battle for its ratification across Europe, proved to be a rallying point for the remnants of the international communist movement. These groups, although but a shadow of their former selves, remained in the early 1990s important if marginal aspects of the Western European political scene. If the Italian ex-Communist Party is discounted (it subsequently joined the Second, social democratic, International), that left the communist parties of France, Portugal, Spain, Greece, Germany, Belgium and Italy (Refounders), and the left-wing, self-declared Marxist parties of Berlin, Germany and Ireland.

There are three aspects to the attacks of the extreme left on the Maastricht Treaty; they are a reprise of the essentially defensive, conservative case combined with both nationalism and reformism. The nationalist rhetoric of the extreme left has been sufficiently commented on elsewhere, but the 'reformist' case is novel on the communist left.

The Maastricht Treaty enabled the remaining communist parties to complete their shift to a reformist perspective. By the mid-1990s, communists were claiming to have been the builders of the welfare state society and its principal defenders. In politics the best way to make major changes of strategy is behind a covering attack – in this case the Maastricht Treaty enabled a continuation of this purpose. Thus the Maastricht Treaty was attacked because it undermined the purely national forms of defence available to the ordinary worker. This, of course, was said for France where the depredations of the free market which would be installed as a result of the application of the Maastricht Treaty were denounced in terms familiar from the debate on the Schuman Plan, but it also fits other communist parties. This is at odds with the former revolutionary perspective which did not differentiate between types of capitalism and which saw the purely local conquests of the reformists as being ways to divide – and hence rule – the potentially united proletariat.

Once again the reformist/revolutionary paradox arises. For communists, the advance of capitalism was, with remorseless logic, to lay the ground for the future revolution: the more widespread capitalism became, the closer the socialist revolution was. Yet here were the communist parties claiming that the workers have their own countries and that European unity will destroy the democratic control exercised by 'bourgeois' parliaments even though the Maastricht order would be a 'higher stage' of capitalism (see, for example, the KKE 'Our positions on the Maastricht Treaty'). The turnaround was almost complete with the Portuguese party which, like the Greek, saw itself as part of Southern 'colonized' Europe, and a victim to predatory US and German multinationals. The Portuguese party did say that it was neither against Europe (as it once was) nor against the increasing co-operation between sovereign states but was, it stressed, against European union on a federal basis.

All these parties emphasized the 'democratic deficit' in Europe which could be taken as an old-fashioned Leninist complaint about the lack of influence of the working class (communist parties). If taken at face value, however, the reinforcement of the EP is clearly at odds with state sovereignty: any reinforcement of supra-national institutions can only be to the detriment of state powers. By the same token, the European-wide realignment of social security and health benefits (condemned, for example, by the Belgian party) also means a severe restriction of state power and a redistribution of resources on a massive scale. State power is also at odds with the Belgian party's call for a new social, regional, citizens' Europe which would require a much more radical integration than the derided Maastricht Treaty. The Belgian party clearly has a more populist concept of Europe – that is a Europe of participation – and has linked the increased activity of the extreme right in Europe and the deflationary measures applied across Europe in the 1990s (the *Vlaamse blok* polled 20 per cent in Anvers and took twelve Assembly seats in the 1991 general elections). If the more 'liberal' of the communist parties, of which the Belgian is an example, emphasized the democratic deficit, other older themes such as anti-Americanism and opposition to a common foreign and military policy formed a part of the more conservative communist party opposition to Maastricht (such as that of PCP).

The PCE, PCP, PCB and PCI (renovators) were united in a call for a referendum on the Maastricht Treaty. In the Spanish case this represented a realignment behind the PCP and PCF with which they had spectacularly differed during the 1970s in their Eurocommunist phase (Europe being a main bone of contention). It also allowed the PCE to turn away from its previous pro-Europeanism, to call for a referendum on national defence, and to capitalize on the rising (if still small) doubts about Europeanism in Spain. The case of the Spanish party, which might have been expected to realign with the PDS Italian ex-communists, is explained by the domestic stance of the Spanish socialists (PSOE) which is committed to a Europeanization of Spain, and by the apparatus of the PCE, which looked into the abyss (dissolution) – and then recoiled.

The PCF's reaction to the Maastricht Treaty was a continuation of its traditional outlook: the forty-six strong parliamentary group voted against the ratification (with one abstention). The leadership declared that Maastricht (bearing the 'German imprint') meant agricultural quotas, unemployment, social reaction, a fall in living standards, the selling off of steel, textiles and shipbuilding, and a France in which millions of further jobs would be lost. The agreement at Maastricht was depicted as a brutally free market, and it was asserted that the complete deregulation of labour was foreseen by the EC. During the French referendum on the treaty it called for 'an uncompromising no'. In the PCF, the debate about the referendum and the Maastricht Treaty further intensified the split between the dissidents and the leadership of the French party; this was accentuated in the European elections of June 1994. The party leadership called for a referendum on the treaty and a radical 'no' to Europe. The party's line was consistent: Europe meant unemployment, reaction, rule by multinationals and bankers, a fall in standards of living and so on (old themes). The Maastricht Treaty meant a further intensification of competition and even such nineteenth-century relics as the legalization of child labour. For good measure, PCF leader Georges Marchais said, as we have mentioned, that the treaty had the 'German imprint' on it.

The PCF's dissidents were led on this issue by, among others, the party economist Philippe Herzog (one time leader of the party's European list) and while they opposed the Maastricht Treaty their position was flexible. The first clash came over the rejection, by Georges Marchais, of the right of Europeans to vote in local elections which, the dissidents noted, had been party policy until the Maastricht Treaty. The Herzog–Fiterman PCF dissidents wanted a renegotiation of the treaty and argued that any referendum should propose that possibility as well as an outright 'yes/no'. However, the main thrust of their argument was that the campaign should not be purely negative and should present some other prospect, in this case the idea of a left-wing Europe. This dissident faction asked for a democratic control of institutions and for a leftward shift of integration, a common money for businesses (not a common currency) and a European-wide reflation. This *non mais* approach linked up with a few in the French Socialist Party left (a small group around J.-P. Chevènement, former Socialist defence minister).[23] French communism was, in fact, split before the Maastricht Treaty became an issue and along the same lines, but the dissidents were isolated and the campaign only underlined their isolation. (Herzog's journal suffered a startling decline in subscriptions.) All the same, the dissidence in the PCF was more widespread, more vocal, and at a higher level than at any time since the mid-1920s; and never before had the party's rampant and negative anti-European nationalism been challenged from within. The Maastricht Treaty debate proved to be yet another indicator of the weakened condition of French communism and the declining audience for communist nationalist themes.

ALTERNATIVE EUROPE?

The communists declared themselves against 'false Europe', against 'little Europe' and against Europe of the multinationals. They also had a very distinctive vision of an alternative 'greater Europe', that is of a wider but Sovietized Europe. This was a well defined and coherent view, but one which became rapidly less attractive and more distant as the Cold War progressed, and it was eventually muted rather than vaunted and covered by references to a vague 'workers' Europe' or to a 'non-imperialist' West. The commitment to socialism remained the same, but the Soviet cast had been verbally softened over the years. Even the hardline communists ceased to promote the alternative and in their propaganda they preferred to point up the negative features of existing institutions. The collapse of the communist system after 1989 left the communists without this clear blueprint; but to what extent did it matter? Long before 1991 communist rhetoric had ceased to emphasize the priority in communist ideology given to the Leninist model, so that the need for a public change of presentation was not immediate. However, the underlying commitment to a socialist world, including Europe, had to be redirected. To what extent was this achieved?

All communist parties still claim to speak on behalf of an 'alternative Europe'

– with greater or lesser conviction – but this is given no firm contours nor is it explained how the parties could reach this 'alternative' destination. The French party, the principal force in the European Democratic Left coalition group in the EP, repeatedly emphasized this theme – alternative Europe – combining it with a fierce nationalism. These two themes were also deployed by the coalition group's other members.[24]

The answer seems to be that although a redefinition of the communist ideal was an imperative after the fall of the Soviet Union and Gorbachev's departure, there was only one position open to the communists – a defensive form of left-wing social democracy. That is the nationalistic 'Keynsianism in one country' which was once the property of the social democratic left. The propaganda of the remaining hardline communist parties displays a commitment to the welfare state and to social reform but also argues that existing European institutions make these impossible. The Maastricht Treaty, they say, imposes deflationary and monetarist policies on a Europe already in the throes of an unemployment crisis created by the right and social democrats.[25] The alternative Europe is portrayed as a positive vision (though not by the Portuguese party), and the promise of a people's Europe has been extended. The people's Europe still has to be defined but includes the assumption that the peoples of Europe – liberated from oppressive institutions – would be spontaneously predisposed to the sorts of policies advanced by the communists (this is not an orthodox communist assumption). Communist rhetoric does, however, now display a range of stances to the European Union. Some are overtly hostile while others, like the Spanish, present their positions as being an opposition to the current turn of events and not a root and branch condemnation of the institutions as a whole.

CONCLUSION

The transnational communist movement is not dead, but attempts to revive it have not, so far, been successful. The guiding star has been extinguished, and the end of the USSR has left the communist parties disoriented. Those still extant have reacted in a similar way. The French, Greek, Portuguese and Spanish parties reaffirmed their commitment to communist values. Other parties, like the Italian, disbanded or changed orientation. It is one of the minor ironies of the story that the PCI espoused Europeanism as a way of entering the Italian political system, while its PDS successor still found itself in opposition, only this time to a Eurosceptical right.

Of course, the notion of communist values unconnected with the Soviet Union and its system is a paradoxical, if not contradictory one. In this the communists, like other political parties, have been able to fall back on one old war-horse: a nationalist opposition to the European Union and its supranational characteristics. This retrenchment was less difficult than might have been expected because of the old but continuing anti-European fight by the parties, and the continuity of their essentially nationalist rhetoric. For communist parties, anti-Europeanism distinguishes them from the socialist parties and gives them a theme of genuine popular concern which enables them to make mischief among socialist voters; they also stand out in a Europe which is increasingly averse – at elite level – to shows of nationalism. Not the least of the ironies is the fact that the anti-European reflex puts them alongside the extreme right, which exploits the same nationalism (in some cases rather better). The short-term exploitation of nationalism has enabled the communists to claim that patriotism is their Ariadne's thread enabling them to trace a continuity with their past despite the eradication of their social model and an uncertain future. The parties can lay claim to the best in national life as they see it and pose as the defenders of the *essential* nation against encroaching Europeanism.

Hence anti-Europeanism, and its corollary, a fierce nationalism, give purpose and continuity at a time when both are in short supply. Nobody is in a position to say that the power of the nationalist emotion has been exhausted in Western Europe, and it could well be that the seizure of these themes will enable the communists to survive into the next millenium. If their future as communist parties is bleak, their future as populist nationalists might be rosier. It is ironic that this strategy is not open to the ex-Italian Communist Party (but is to its right-wing opponents), which by the mid-1990s was experiencing severe difficulties differentiating itself within the Italian system. Communists outside the European Union in Scandinavia also scented possibilities in anti-Europeanism and moved to anti-European positions reminiscent of the debates in the 1970s before the first enlargement.

In sum, if the collapse of the Soviet Union deprived the Western European communists of one of their reasons for unifying, it also gave freedom to local communist parties. They used their freedom to redefine themselves as left-wing nationalists. In the course of the 1990s, the disintegration of Europe's only true transnational political party gave rise to its opposite, a series of fiercely anti-European and dispersed, negative nationalisms.

NOTES

1 See J. Gotovitch, Pascal Delwit and J.-M. De Waele, *L'Europe des communistes* (Brussels, Editions Complex, 1993).
2 R.N. Tannahil, *The Communist Parties of Western Europe* (Westport, CT, Greenwood, 1975).
3 N. McInnes, *The Communist Parties of Western Europe* (Oxford, Oxford University Press 1975).
4 T. Nairn, *The Left Against Europe* (Harmondsworth, Penguin, 1974).
5 McInnes, *The Communist Parties*, chapter 4, pp. 183ff.
6 Like labour camps, deportation, and war. *L'Humanité*, 23 June 1950.
7 See F.D. Willis, *France, Germany and the New Europe* (Stanford, Stanford University Press, 1967), pp. 56, 67, 262.
8 Ibid., p. 141.
9 *L'Humanité*, 26 March 1957. The negotiations resulting in the Rome Treaties provoked a Soviet diplomatic protest (16 April 1957) against the signature.
10 See F. Fejtö, *The French Communist Party and the Crisis of International Communism* (Cambridge MA, MIT, 1967), chapter 4.
11 See McInnes, *The Communist Parties*, and E.F. Callot, 'The French Communist Party and Europe', *European Journal of Political Research*, vol. 16, 1988, pp. 301–16.
12 *L'Humanité*, 21 March 1972.
13 French Communist Party, *Changer de Cap*, p. 224.
14 J. Kanapa report to the Central Committee of the PCF in *L'Humanité*, 29 May 1973.
15 N. McInnes, *World Today*, February 1974, pp. 80–8.
16 See R.E.M. Irving, 'The European policy of the French and Italian Communists', *International Affairs*, vol. 53, no. 3, 1977, pp. 405–21.
17 Texts in English translation can be found in *The Communist Parties of Italy, France and Spain* edited by P. Lange and M. Vannicelli, (London, Unwin, 1981).

18 *L'Humanité*, 22 May 1987.
19 European Parliamentary debate of July 1993. The PCI approved the expansion of Community co-operation in foreign affairs and defence. See also *L'Humanité*, 22 May 1986 and 7 April 1989.
20 *L'Humanité*, 7 April 1985.
21 J. Gotovitch et al., *L'Europe des communistes*.
22 The documents used in the following passage are:
    La Belgique et le Traité de Maastricht (Dossier, Brussels, 1993); PCF *Faits et arguments*, no. 8 (Paris) January 1992; *Cahiers du Communisme*, May 1992 (no. 5) (Special issue on Maastricht); H. Steer (DKP) Declaration 'Referendum for or against Maastricht', Essen, June 1992; *Mundo Obrero* 11–12 August 1992 (no. 153); *Avante 12–13*, 12–13 September 1992; PCP *Sim Maastricht Nao*; Ireland September 1992 (Workers Party); *Berliner linke*, Special issue 1992; *Pressedienst*, Central Committee declaration on Maastricht treaty; P.C. Catalunya '*Maastricht Non*'; *Rizospastis* (KKE) September 1992.
23 J.-P. Chevènement, *Libération*, 11 September 1992.
24 See *L'Humanité*, 7 April 1989.
25 Sergio Garavini (Refounder) *L'Humanité*, 31 July 1992.

SELECT BIBLIOGRAPHY

Amodia, J., 'Izquierda Unida: second test, second failure', *Journal of Communist Studies* vol. 3, no. 4, 1987, pp. 170–3.
Arter, D., 'The Swedish Leftist Party', *Parliamentary Affairs*, vol. 44, no. 1, 1991, pp. 69–78.
Azcarate, M., *L'Europe de l'Atlantique à l'Oural*, Paris, Maspéro, 1979.
Blackmer, D.L. and Kriegel, A., *The International Role of the Communist Parties of Italy and France*, Cambridge, MA, CIA, 1975.
Blackmer, D.L. and Tarrow, S. (eds), *Communism in Italy and France*, Princeton, NJ, Princeton University Press, 1975.
Botella, J., 'Spanish Communism in Crisis', in M. Waller and M. Fennema (eds), *Communist Parties in Western Europe*, Oxford, Blackwell, 1988.
Bull, M.J., 'A new era for the non-rulers too', *Politics*, vol. 2, no. 1, 1991.
Callaghan, J., 'The long drift of the CPGB', *Journal of Communist Studies*, vol. 1, nos 3/4, 1985, pp. 171–4.
Callaghan, J., 'Further splits in the Marxist Left in Britain', *Journal of Communist Studies*, vol. 4, no. 1, 1988, pp. 101–4.
Callot, E.F., 'The French Communist Party and Europe', *European Journal of Political Research*, vol. 16, 1988, pp. 301–36.
Carrillo, S., '*Eurocommunism' and the State*, London, Lawrence and Wishart, 1978.
Claudin, F., *The Communist Movement from Comintern to Cominform*, Harmondsworth, Penguin, 1975.
Cline, R.S. et al. (eds), *Western Europe in Soviet Global Strategy*, Boulder, CO, Westview Press, 1987.
Copling, F. and Streiff, G., *Un marché des dupes*, Paris, Messidor, 1987.
Fennema, M., 'The end of Dutch Communism?', in M. Waller and M. Fennema (eds), *Communist Parties in Western Europe*, Oxford, Blackwell, 1988.
Gillespie, R., 'Izquierda Unida: the first test', *Journal of Communist Studies*, vol. 2, no. 4, 1986, pp. 441–4.
Gundle, S., 'On the brink of decline? The PCI and the Italian elections of June 1987', *Journal of Communist Studies*, vol. 3, no. 4, 1987, pp. 159–66.
Hassner, P., 'L'Euro-gauche entre les euro-missiles et la Pologne', *Politique étrangère*, March 1982.
Irving, R.E.M., 'The European policy of the French and Italian Communists', *International Affairs*, vol. 53, no. 3, 1977, pp. 405-21.
Logue, J., *Socialism and Abundance*, Minneapolis, University of Minnesota Press, 1982.
Machin, H. (ed.), *National Communism in Western Europe*, London, Methuen, 1983.
Marcou, L., *Les pieds d'argile*, Paris, Ramsay, 1986.
McInnes, N., *The Communist Parties of Western Europe*, Oxford, Oxford University Press, 1975.

Pasquino, B., 'Mid-stream and under stress: the Italian Communist Party', in M. Waller and M. Fennema (eds), *Communist Parties in Western Europe*, Oxford, Blackwell, 1988.

Patricio, M.T., 'Orthodoxy and dissent in the Portuguese Communist Party', *Journal of Communist Studies*, vol. 6, no. 3, September 1990, pp. 204–8.

Serafty, S., *The Foreign Policies of the French Left*, Boulder, CO, Westview, 1979.

Timmermann, H., *The Decline of the World Communist Movement*, Boulder, CO, Westview Press, 1987.

Urban, J.B., 'The PCI's 17th Congress', in P. Corbetta et al. (eds), *Italian Politics: A Review*, vol. 2, London, Frances Pinter, 1988.

Vega, P. and Erroteta, P., *Los Herejes del PCE*, Barcelona, Planeta, 1985.

Voerman, G., 'Le retour du communisme au sein du parlement Neerlandais', in *Communisme*, vol. 24, 1990, pp. 109–13.

Wettig, G.W., *Changes in Soviet Policy Towards the West*, London, Frances Pinter, 1991.

Whetten, L.L. (ed.), *The Present State of Communist Internationalism*, Lexington, MA, D.C. Heath, 1983.

14 Extreme right-wing parties and the European Union
France, Germany and Italy

Catherine Fieschi, James Shields and Roger Woods

DEFINITIONS

Classification of political parties on the far right is never straightforward. For the purposes of this analysis, we shall examine the German Republikaner, the French Front National (FN), the Movimento Sociale Italiano (MSI) and the Lega Nord in Italy as illustrative of the extreme right's relationship to Europe and the European Union. Stöss locates the German Republikaner on the 'extreme right' because they have a view of society which is anti-liberal, anti-socialist, and based on *völkisch*, ethnocentric nationalism. They also reject the universal human rights of freedom, equality and justice, and favour a hierarchically ordered, national community (*Volks-gemeinschaft*), and an authoritarian state with expansionist ambitions.[1] Uwe Backes shows up the shortcomings of clear categorizations, however, when he observes that the programme of the Republikaner contains many points also contained in the German Christian Democrats' programme. The Republikaner present themselves as a party 'with one foot in the majority democratic culture and one foot in the extreme right-wing subculture'. They appeal, therefore, not only to right-wing extremists but also to the democratic majority.[2] Many of the same comments can be made of the French Front National, in terms of both its extremist ideology and the ambivalence of its policies and appeal. As an heir to Mussolini's Fascism, it is easy to classify the Movimento Sociale Italiano (MSI) as a party of the extreme right. The case of the Lega Nord is more difficult to make. It has been portrayed as a tax-revolt movement which reflects the attitude of Italy's rich northern regions[3] and as a racist exclusionary party of the (northern) extreme right created to curtail the civil rights of immigrants from the south of Italy and from abroad.[4] Much of the Lega's language is overtly racist. The Lega advocates a separation between the North, the Centre and the South of Italy on the grounds that the North carries the weight of the parasitic South and a Centre mired in bureaucratic inertia. For the purposes of analysis here, we shall use the term 'extreme right' to apply to these various parties, while acknowledging that it does not entirely do justice to the situation of parties which have proclaimed a minimal commitment to the democratic order in which they operate, but which also draw much of their support from an anti-democratic political subculture.

EXTREME RIGHT-WING PARTIES IN THE EUROPEAN PARLIAMENT

Extreme right-wing parties started to gain ground in parts of the European Community in the mid-1980s. The Italian Movimento Sociale Italiano sent four representatives to the European Parliament in 1979,[5] and in 1984 Jean-Marie Le Pen's FN entered the European Parliament with ten seats. The German Republikaner gained 7.1 per cent of the vote and six seats in the 1989 election to the European Parliament.[6] In the June 1994 European elections, the Italian National Alliance (which embraced the MSI and other smaller right-wing parties) obtained 12.5 per cent of the vote and eleven seats; the FN obtained a total of 10.5 per cent of the votes and eleven seats; the Lega Nord stood separately and obtained six seats; the Belgian Vlaams Blok kept its one seat. Because the Republikaner obtained just 3.9 per cent of the vote in Germany, they failed to clear the 5 per cent hurdle and therefore lost their seats in the European Parliament.

In the aftermath of the 1984 elections to the European Parliament, a parliamentary group was formed from the members of the FN, the Italian MSI and the Greek EPEN (National Political Union).[7] The June 1989 elections brought more potential alliance partners into the European Parliament, even though the Greek EPEN MEP lost his seat. The FN still had ten MEPs, the MSI four, the Milan based Lega Lombarda two, the Republikaner six, and the Vlaams Blok one. Negotiations led to the creation of the Technical Group of the European Right, which included the Front National, the Republikaner and the Vlaams Blok. In the discussions between the parties, the leader of the Republikaner, Franz Schönhuber, brought the South Tyrol issue into play, declaring that it was impossible to form an alliance with people fighting his Tyrolean compatriots in Bozen (Bolzano) and Meran (Merano). As a result, the MSI did not join this new group in the European Parliament. Instead, it issued a statement rejecting discrimination against Italian workers living in Germany and attacking Schönhuber for suggesting that the party had links with the Mafia.[8]

The problems over establishing the parliamentary group were an early indicator of the limits to cross-national co-operation between parties whose assertive nationalism was to the fore in their ideological platforms. Historical enmities were clearly a major hurdle to any shared patriotism towards Europe. Like parties in other EP groups, the Republikaner stressed that the creation of the parliamentary group did not stop each partner having its own programme.[9] The fragility of the idea that there might be a shared ideology was revealed when Schönhuber accused some of his fellow Republikaner MEPs and the FN leader, Jean-Marie Le Pen, of racism. Schönhuber also attacked a Republikaner MEP for his vision of a Greater Germany which would include Austria, some Eastern territories and South Tyrol.[10] Schönhuber left the parliamentary group, taking three Republikaner with him, and explaining that he objected to the racist and chauvinist activities of the remaining two.[11] These two left the party but stayed in the Group.[12]

The extreme right not only encounters difficulties when it tries to cross national frontiers; it also experiences divisions within its own borders. In the 1970s, rivalry between the FN and the Parti des forces nouvelles (PFN) split the personnel and the meagre support of the French extreme right. In Germany, too, the Republikaner and the extremist Deutsche Volksunion (DVU) were openly hostile towards each other. At election time, this invariably converted into both parties standing and therefore a split vote.[13] In the case of the Lega and the MSI, their radically differing stances on institutional and constitutional reform in Italy, as well as their regionally and socio-economically contrasting bases of support, have resulted in constant enmity between them.

GERMANY AND EUROPE: A DILEMMA

The extreme right's attitude towards Europe attempts to reproduce the traditional platform of nationalism, ethnocentrism, protection of territory, struggle between nations, and centralized leadership in the European context. Thus, slogans such as 'Germany for the Germans' are complemented by the call for 'Europe for the Europeans'. Traditional nationalism coexists with the idea of the 'nation of Europe'. Schönhuber has called for a European patriotism and a Europe independent of the non-European world. One of the many theoretical journals of the right, *Nation und Europa*, argues that 'Europe was, is and will remain a continent of independent, distinctive peoples, cultures and identities, each with its own particular value system, traditions and way of life.'[14] Yet more profound than these differences between European peoples are supposedly shared 'European values', a 'European civilization' and a 'Western culture' which provide Europe's ideological foundation. Europe has to block immigration from Africa and Asia in order to avoid becoming a collection of multicultural societies. The proclaimed goal is an alliance of nations which retain their specific identity.[15] Thus Schönhuber can argue that one has to distinguish between foreigners from EU countries and 'other foreigners'. The French, Spanish, Italians, Greeks, he asserts, all have the same European culture behind them. The Turks do not share this culture, and, for Schönhuber, Europe ends at the Bosporus.[16]

The extreme right's commitment to a shared European civilization exists alongside an adamant rejection of any loss of national sovereignty to a centralized European bureaucracy. Reconciliation of the national and the European interest is expressed in the formula 'Europe of the Fatherlands' in contrast to that of a 'United States of Europe'.[17] It is always clear, however, that perceived national interest takes precedence over any European strand in the extreme right's thinking: until 1990, the Republikaner saw German reunification and the further integration of the Federal Republic into a European Union as mutually exclusive.[18]

Electoral successes of the extreme right in Germany attract attention because they stir memories of the Nazi past. Yet it appears that the more the German extreme right takes Nazism or fascism as a model, the less likely it is to succeed in elections.[19] Here it is possible to draw a theoretical distinction in ideological terms between the old and the new right.[20] While older parties such as the National-demokratische Partei Deutschlands (NPD) are clearly still intent on arguing that Germany was not solely responsible for the Second World War and that historical accounts of the Holocaust are exaggerated,[21] parties of the new right such as the Republikaner attempt to distance themselves from fascism and claim to embrace the idea of Europe. They look not to the National Socialists for their model but rather to intellectual movements of the right which had an ambiguous relationship with National Socialism, such as the Conservative Revolution during the time of the Weimar Republic.[22]

The choice of the Conservative Revolution is significant in two ways. First, it undermines the idea of a clean break with National Socialism. For example, the right-wing journal *Nation und Europa* takes Edgar Jung as a Conservative Revolutionary mentor and portrays him as an opponent of the Nazis.[23] Although Jung was indeed murdered by the Nazis in 1934, he also claimed with pride just two years before his death that 'we [Conservative Revolutionaries] prepared the day when the German people voted for the National Socialist candidates'.[24] Such ideological ambiguity prompts some political scientists to count the Republikaner among the old right.[25] Second, the choice of the Conservative Revolution as a model is significant because it embodies an ideological dilemma in the Weimar Republic when class-based socialism was the threat and traditional conservatism was abandoned as unable to meet it. This 'conservative dilemma' initially prompted the Conservative Revolutionaries to attempt to work out a political programme which would unite the forces of new nationalism and a redefined socialism. When they failed in this they went over to regarding all political programmes with contempt and advocating pure political activism instead.[26]

In the theoretical writings which inform the new right in Germany today, we see a parallel process at work. On the one hand, fascism is not an option but is ever present just beneath the surface; on the other, a right-wing vision of Europe is a theoretical construct which is undermined by nationalism. The resultant lack of ideological clarity is lamented, and the call goes out for a political stance which transcends mere rejection of the political opposition. It is admitted that the right has no idea of how to set about this task.[27] And it is this failure to provide an alternative political vision of Europe which is at the root of the extreme right's failure to collaborate in the European Parliament. Time and again the two key issues over which collaboration founders are the fascist past and the European future. Thus, Harald Neubauer was expelled from the Republikaner at the end of 1990 for descending, as the party's own newspaper put it, into crude 'right-wing extremism'. The leadership of the Republikaner censured him for publishing work by the controversial historian, David Irving, which amounted to a 'glorification of National Socialism'. Neubauer was attacked by his own former party as a 'Neonazi'.[28]

FRANCE AND EUROPE: THE IMPERATIVE AND THE PROBLEM

At the theoretical level, the French extreme right exhibits tensions similar to those shown by the German extreme right. 'There is no longer any obstacle to the creation of a Europe united in the face of the external threats which confront us. Such union is never a natural impulse. When people form a society, they do so because they do not have the means to act alone.' These words, written at the height of the European election campaign of 1984,[29] express both the imperative and the problem of Europe for Jean-Marie Le Pen: the imperative of a Europe united to face down the 'external threats' ranged against it; the problem of reconciling the 'natural' – nationalist – impulse with a reasoned political calculation transcending narrow state boundaries. 'People only unite', Le Pen went on, 'when they have a reason to do so, an objective. We must start by recognising that we are first and foremost Europeans, and that we should be intensely proud of this. For ours is the most extraordinary civilization in the world, with all its inestimably rich legacy.'[30]

These remarks articulate a notion of Europe as more than the sum of so many diverse nation states. The pre-eminence of a European civilization under threat, and the grounding of French national consciousness in a wider community of shared culture and identity, are the two interrelated notions upon which Le Pen claims to base his vision of Europe:

> In order for Europe to be a reality, there must be a genuine European sentiment; that is why we have expressed the wish to go beyond patriotism, beyond our

respective feelings of national patriotism, to achieve a European patriotism. Which is to say that there will be no Europe unless it is destined to become a Nation. This nation can only be brought about through the need to defend itself against the external threats confronting it – and God knows, the threats to Europe are real enough.[31]

This call for a 'European patriotism' as the binding agent of a European 'nation' implies an achievable fusion between French and European identity and interests. The fact that all of the foregoing extracts appear in a work bearing the defiant title *Les Français d'abord* (The French First), however, points up the essentially problematic nature of the relationship in question. 'I find no difficulty whatever', insists Le Pen, 'in reconciling the idea of a strong nation state with that of a strong Europe.'[32] Yet an analysis of the discourse and policies of the FN as they have evolved over the past decade throws light upon the difficulty encountered by a stridently nationalist party seeking to accommodate itself to Europe. The synthesis between 'French' and 'European' for Le Pen and his party holds up so long as it is a question of confronting a common enemy: 'What strikes at Europe strikes at France, and what strikes at France strikes at Europe.'[33] Yet the shared European heritage of which Le Pen makes such play, the commitment to the defence of 'Western civilization', cannot and must not intrude upon a national integrity which remains paramount.

The publications on Europe issued by the FN in the 1980s conjure up different avatars of the same 'external threat'.[34] Yet Le Pen's opposition to the construction of the European Community with which he claims such affinity, his denunciation of Maastricht as a 'national suicide', and of the European Union which it foreshadows as a 'supranational edifice built upon the shattered ruins of the nation',[35] illustrate the contradictions and ambiguities of his stance on Europe. In passing from ideology to practical politics, from the rarefied conception of Europe as 'a common fund of civilization'[36] to the concrete realities of the EU as a political and economic entity, the FN's vision undergoes a radical transformation. The party's appeals to Europeanism turn out, under scrutiny, to be little more than a rhetorical strategy deployed in the service of a discriminatory ideology, an amplified 'nationalism' projected on to the European stage.

The challenge for Le Pen and the Front National is to preserve the rich internal diversity within Europe, while resisting diversity from without. To create a 'European Europe', the FN urged in its manifesto for the 1993 French parliamentary elections, 'we should start from the inviolable principle that our Europe of nation-states can only include those European states with a common civilization whose roots are essentially Hellenistic and Christian'.[37] This 'inviolable principle' of neo-Hellenistic culture and Christian religion should serve not only as a strict criterion for the admission of states to the EU (and for the exclusion of others, such as Turkey notably): it consigns to an irredeemably alien status what the former president of SOS-Racisme, Harlem Désir, called the 'thirteenth state' of the Community, the immigrant population. Within this exclusionist perspective, the loss of 'national identity' and the onset of 'European decadence' become two elements of the same discourse. Witness the close correlation which Le Pen perceived in 1984 between the dangers confronting France and those confronting Europe as a whole:

My European programme is a faithful extrapolation from the national programme of the Front National, since the same dangers which threaten France threaten Europe. Communism and revolutionary Marxism, two sides of the same coin, threaten to bring about the collapse of our most deeply held values, the breakdown of our social, national, family and moral discipline. One of the gravest threats of all arises from the fundamental imbalance between demographic levels in Europe and demographic levels in the Third World.[38]

If the collapse of the Soviet Union and the progressive abandonment of socialism in France deprived the FN of two of its privileged themes, the threat of foreign invasion merely expanded to fill the space vacated by the retreating spectre of Marx. In November 1991, the deputy leader of the FN, Bruno Mégret, published a policy paper entitled 'A contribution to solving the immigration problem: 50 concrete measures'. In this, he called for the restriction of nationality to those born of French parents, a review of all naturalizations granted since 1974, a policy of 'national preference' in employment and welfare provision, a quota system for immigrant children in French schools, and a rigorous medical examination for all foreigners entering France, including a mandatory AIDS test. While the document held immigrants up as the gravest threat to 'French identity' and the 'national community', its sweeping prescriptions were prefaced with a carefully defined exception: 'We should add here that, since we consider France an intrinsic part of Europe, the measures proposed in this document clearly do not apply to EC nationals or, more broadly, to those of our European community who share our destiny, culture, religion and civilization.'[39]

This conception of France as part of a greater European community finds expression across a range of policy areas, as defined in the FN's official programmes of 1985–86 and 1993. In these, the party calls for 'a coherent political project' for Europe,[40] comprising a common European defence and nuclear strategy, a common foreign policy, common immigration controls, a common anti-terrorist policy, a common (as opposed to single) currency, and the establishment of an external European border under supranational control and of a clearly defined 'European citizenship' (the concept, we may note in anticipation of later remarks, which lies at the very heart of the Maastricht design).[41] Economic recovery, we further read, must be buttressed by measures to protect Europe against competition from the USA and Japan, while a policy of 'European preference' should be set in place to complement that of 'national preference'.[42]

As for France's role in the construction of this Europe, it is clearly set out by Le Pen and developed in the FN's electoral programmes. France must be the 'driving force of Europe', its 'leader' and its inspiration. 'Without having any wish to dominate, France's position makes her in every sense the federator of Europe. What is certain is that there will be no Europe without France. There will be no Europe if France is weakened or corrupted. France is too much of a model for too many countries, starting with her neighbours.'[43] While such a discourse on France's place within Europe has become the common currency of parties across the French political spectrum,[44] it is especially significant coming from the nationalist right. As in the earlier conception of de Gaulle, France thus becomes the central protagonist of Europe, while Europe provides the stage on which *le génie français* may be liberally deployed. As we read in the FN's 1985–86 manifesto, 'The rebirth of France, with her culture, her language, her traditions and her essential spirit of liberty, will lead Europe to open a new chapter in her history and in the dissemination of her culture throughout the world.'[45]

ITALY: A CASE OF REGIONAL EUROPEANISM

The case of the extreme right in Italy is interesting both from a comparative perspective and in terms of its attitude toward Europe and the European Union. The context of the extreme right's position on Europe is the overwhelming cross-party support in Italy for the Common Market, the European Community and later the European Union. This accurately reflects national popular support for Europe, which is consistently higher than in other European countries.[46] These factors contributed to the positive European stance taken by both extreme right parties, the Lega and the MSI. Italy was one of the earliest supporters of the European Community and of the idea of a unified Europe. Although enthusiasm went well beyond Italy's own capacities, Europe was seen by the parties as a means of justifying the imposition of domestic standards and unpopular austerity measures, and, just as in the case of Spain, as a guarantor of democratic government.

Italy's extreme right is represented by two parties: the MSI headed by Gianfranco Fini after 1987, and the Lega Nord, an electoral umbrella organization for the various northern regional leagues, such as the Lega Lombarda and the Lega del Veneto, led by the controversial Umberto Bossi. Whereas the MSI is a seasoned political actor, the Lega's politics date from the late 1980s. The two political groups are different from one another in a variety of ways. The MSI is nationalistic and corporatist, and is electorally based in the South of Italy, as well as in Rome and its immediate surroundings. The Lega is too politically opportunistic to be ideologically coherent, hence its relatively chaotic ideological references. Liberal in its stance towards the economy, it emerged around a programme of institutional and territorial reform which would turn Italy into a federal state comprising three regions (roughly North, Centre and South). Political and economic ties between the regions would be kept to a minimum through supranational government via the European Parliament. The Lega Nord has sought to tackle national politics on a regional platform destined to sever ties between what it sees as the rich and industrially developed northern areas of Italy, and the dependent southern regions and costly and corrupt Roman administration. There are therefore two extreme rights in Italy whose ideological and political stances diverge significantly, even though both support the idea of Europe – if not Maastricht – in various ways and for various reasons.

The MSI portrays itself as the direct ideological heir to Mussolini's *Fasci*, and little revision of the fascist doctrine has taken place. The reasons for this are largely historical. Despite the defeat of the fascist forces by the Allies, Italy experienced a fascist revival as early as 1946 when the MSI was once again represented in Parliament. Two factors account for this: first, the Allied presence and the influence of American foreign policy initiatives in Italy were guided by the fear of communist expansion in Western Europe. The second factor, a consequence of the first, was that the attitude encouraged by the Allies allowed fascist war criminals to go unharmed in Italy after the war. As Franco Ferraresi and others have pointed out, the absence of a formal condemnation of fascist war criminals in Italy contributed to the ease with which the MSI re-entered the realm of formal, parliamentary politics. The sabotage of anti-fascist legislation, and the distortion of the legal framework when applied to fascist leaders such as Borghese and Almirante (who went virtually unquestioned despite public knowledge of their actions during the war) added to the impression that 'the fascists' could get away with anything. Such immunity contributed to the legitimation of some of their war-time attitudes and policies.[47] Authors such as Norberto Bobbio and Francesco Sidoti[48] have imputed the persistence of authoritarian attitudes in Italian culture to the failure to formally denounce and discredit the fascist regime after the war.

Support for the MSI has varied over the years. After a strong showing in the late 1940s and mid-1950s, party support waned during the 1960s as factionalism and discord ravaged its rank and file. The radical youth wing of the party became more and more opposed to what it saw as the party's co-option by bourgeois politics. This opposition expressed itself through the creation of various groups such as Ordine Nuovo and Avanguardia Nazionale. The early 1970s saw a renewal of public support, particularly in the 1972 election. The reprise, however, was short lived, and by 1976 support was again on the wane. The situation worsened until the unforeseen increase in support in the elections of autumn 1993. This trend was confirmed in the national elections of March 1994, when the MSI became a crucial coalition partner for Berlusconi's *Forza Italia!* with 13 per cent of the popular vote.

In the context of Italian politics, and given that a negative stance on Europe was untenable, Europe posed two main problems. The first was the same as that faced by Le Pen and the FN. On the one hand, Le Pen was unable to reconcile the FN's platform with a Europe in which national sovereignty is curtailed by supranational government. On the other, he promoted a vision of Europe as an instrument to arrest the flow of Third World immigrants into France. The MSI and Fini found themselves in the same situation: the benefits of an exclusionary Europe were imperilled by the relinquishing of national sovereignty. The MSI differed from the Front National in its stance on liberal economics. As a true perpetrator of fascist policy, the MSI always expressed mixed feelings towards the EU's liberal economic stance. Because no revision of the basic fascist doctrine has occurred within the MSI, Giovanni Gentile, Ugo Spirito and Alfredo Rocco remain the ideological mentors of the party. Moreover, because of its overwhelmingly southern-based support, the MSI had to use the defence of sectoral interests as a crucial electoral appeal. These factors contributed to the development within the party of a diverse set of ideological inclinations, enough to lead some MSI leaders and supporters to adopt views very similar to those of a left-wing party. Italian commentators have remarked that the 'left wing' of the MSI – sometimes encompassing as much as 45 per cent of members on certain issues – is to the left of the PSDI and the PSI.[49] It is important to emphasize, however, that their stance, which leads them to be more lenient toward some forms of trades unionism, for example, stems from adherence to corporatist precepts of state management.

The Lega Nord presents a different political profile and an interesting case for comparison with the MSI. The main area of contention between the two is the European question itself. Both parties view Europe as a venue for domestic institutional reform, but in different ways. Unlike the MSI, the Lega is not only a regionally based movement, but a regional*ist* movement. Consequently, it has no recourse to a discourse of national unity, nor to the defence of the nation against external enemies. What it shares with the MSI is fear of the enemies that are to be found within the nation. For the Lega these are, first, the corrupt Italian state – more particularly the Rome-based national administration – and, second, the southern regions which are portrayed as both corrupt (because of the presence of the Mafia) and inefficient – due to a combination of factors of which corruption is but one.[50]

Since its creation, the party's share of the vote has risen from less than 1 per cent to 20 per cent of the Lombard electorate. In the national elections of March 1994, the Lega became Italy's third largest party after Berlusconi's *Forza Italia!* and the MSI. Difficulties in the formation of a national governing coalition under Berlusconi, however, proceeded from a reluctance by the two extreme right-wing parties to govern together, given their differing stances on both Europe and domestic constitutional reform.

The MSI has championed both electoral and constitutional reform. It has supported Europe partly because it appreciates the efficiency stemming from European pressures. It severely criticized the Maastricht Treaty, however, for the loss of sovereignty it implied. Bossi, on the other hand, denounced Maastricht for the insufficient powers granted to the European Parliament, and condemned the stance adopted by the MSI on the grounds that it 'smacks of a certain type of Right which is antithetical to democracy'.[51] According to Dwayne Woods, the Lega's success 'does not depend on organizational ability to mobilize a distinct ethnic and linguistic group, but on its ability to constitute a regional identity'.[52] Hence the Lega's stance on Europe has been conditioned by its allegiance to northern Italy and its electoral commitment to bring about a fundamental modification of the status of the northern regions through a form of federalism.

RELATIONSHIP TO EU INSTITUTIONS AND PROCESSES

How do these tensions in the thinking of the extreme right work themselves out in practical politics? The German dilemma of being cut off from the fascist past and unable to generate a durable vision of a European future shapes the attitude of the Republikaner towards the European Union. The German extreme right in the European Parliament deals with this by attacking the ideological enemy in its own terms. It has been suggested that the extreme right can be characterized by its anti-parliamentarianism, anti-pluralism and anti-partyism, that it encourages distrust for the parliamentary system and criticizes excessive freedom, the weakness of the state, and unnatural egalitarianism.[53] Yet one of the distinctive features of the Republikaner is its deployment of the opposition's own ideology. Thus, if the European Union presents itself as a democratic structure, the Republikaner attack it as undemocratic. The party newspaper, *Der Republikaner*, stresses that the EU commissioners are not subject to parliamentary control and that the 'will of the people' counts for little in the minds of the 'Eurocrats'. The European Commission is criticized for operating a kind of state socialism against which the European Parliament can do little. The constitution of the European Parliament itself is criticized for giving excessive weight to the smaller countries and leaving Germany underrepresented.[54] Schönhuber explained his opposition to Turkey joining the European Union by declaring that it was not a democratic state.[55]

This tendency to appeal to the values of democracy reflects, in fact, the new right's difficulty in generating an ideology; in both national and European terms, negative xenophobia remains its only real organizing principle. The Republikaner oppose European union on the grounds that it will lead to the importation of crime and an influx of immigrants. Germany should not be seen as an 'immigration country' for others but as the Germans' own country. After a year of unemployment, foreigners should be obliged to return home, and Germans should be given preference when it comes to allocating jobs.[56] Schönhuber has declared that EU policies are leading to increasing 'foreignization' (*Überfremdung*) and endangering Germany's sense of national identity.[57] His antagonism towards foreigners has even led him to declare that if large-scale immigration from Africa and Asia were allowed to continue, the result would be xenophobia.[58] The Republikaner play upon German fears of uncontrolled immigration into Germany by refugees and asylum seekers. As the number of asylum seekers rose dramatically through the early 1990s, *Der Republikaner* made much of the 'misuse of the right to asylum' and linked it with the image of a European Union about to throw open its borders.[59] Thus the Technical Group of the European Right brought a draft resolution before the European Parliament in September 1992 expressing concern over acts of violence committed against foreigners, but also by foreigners, criticizing 'one-sided reporting in the media of these events' in Germany, and declaring that 'only a complete ban on immigration into EC states and the return of most economic refugees and non-EC citizens to their country of origin could put an end to xenophobia and prevent the colonization of Europe by Africa and Asia'. The draft resolution also called for political refugees to be taken in by states where they could expect to find a culture and religion closer to their own.[60] A recommendation contained in a 1992 European Parliament subcommittee's report on racism and xenophobia that immigrants in Europe should be allowed to obtain citizenship after five years was condemned for 'destroying European identity'. The proposal to extend voting rights to those resident in Europe for five years was attacked for destroying the Europeans' right to self-determination. Measures designed to encourage integration of ethnic minority children in European schools were dismissed as lowering standards in order to accommodate non-Europeans.[61]

Other issues taken up by the extreme right in the European Parliament were welfare, falling birth rates, and communism.[62] Like part of the Italian extreme right, Schönhuber also indulged in the vague anti-capitalism characteristic of extreme right-wing thought in the past: 'who benefits from the EC? Primarily the Euro-multinationals, big business, but not small-scale craftsmen, farmers or workers'.[63] The creation of the Single Market at the start of 1993 was attacked for opening the door to a flood of foodstuffs produced in countries where lax regulations allowed chemically polluted foods to be sold. Such moves were denounced for slavishly bowing to the requirements of 'big business' at the expense of the consumers and small-scale family businesses.[64]

The conflict between nationalism and a European vision is as much in evidence in the thinking of the FN as in that of the Republikaner. For a party espousing pro-Europeanism in principle, the FN has done all in its power to thwart the major initiatives (Single European Act, Schengen Agreements, Maastricht Treaty) which seek to give political expression to this vision of a united Europe. The reasons for this lie partly in the difficulty for the FN of translating ideology into policy at the European level, and partly in the nature of the party's domestic political agenda. The difficulty over policy is simply put: how does an ultra-nationalist party such as the FN reconcile its platform with a convincing Europeanism? How, for example, can the principle of 'national preference' leave room for any meaningful policy of 'European preference'? Set against the FN's repeated calls for the allocation of economic resources, jobs and welfare benefits on the basis of French nationality, the notion of 'European preference' appears little more than an empty formula.[65]

In the FN's 1985–86 programme *Pour la France*, we read: 'European union will remain a Utopian dream until such time as the Community has at its disposal sufficient resources, a common currency, a defence capability and the political will to deploy it, a common police force and a European judiciary equipped with the means to defeat terrorism.'[66] Yet how might such 'European union' be achieved without reinforcing the very structures (legislative, administrative, judicial) for which Le Pen reserves his most savage criticism?

Since the first direct elections to the European Parliament in 1979, when the FN mounted its ill-starred campaign under the slogan 'Building Europe without undoing France',[67] the problem has been one of keeping its Europeanism in line with nationalist dictates. The unwieldy title of the failed alliance for these elections between the FN and the Parti des forces nouvelles – 'The French Union for a Euro-Right of Nation States' – indicated the scant place accorded to Europe in the preoccupations of the 'national right'.[68] This points to the second reason for the FN's ambivalence over Europe: it is in the nature of the party's oppositional role that it should exploit the European issue for its own domestic political advantage. Whatever the ideological significance of Europe for the FN, its political agenda is primarily a domestic one.

In the European elections of June 1984, which saw the emergence of the FN as a national political force and of Le Pen as a focus of media attention, the party concentrated on internal issues to the near exclusion of Europe. Exploiting the deep unpopularity of President Mitterrand and the Socialists after three years in office, the FN ran a campaign focused on resistance to socialism, on law and order, immigration, unemployment, the defence of private education and a return to 'traditional values'. Setting itself up as the most radical pole of opposition to the government, the FN sought to turn these elections into an indictment both of the governing Socialists and of the mainstream opposition parties. The strategy paid dividends. With 10.95 per cent of the ballot, some 2.2 million votes, the FN list captured ten seats in the European Parliament with its National Opposition Front for a *Europe des patries*. The success of the FN in 1984 showed how readily Europe could be sacrificed to domestic political expediency. The title of Le Pen's book, *Les Français d'abord*, published in May 1984 and used as an election slogan, implied a European dimension to the FN's campaign, but with clearly negative connotations.

The 1989 Euro-elections saw the FN devote much more attention to European issues than formerly, although the title of the party's list, *Europe et Patrie*, again signalled the nature and limits of its Europeanism. By the late 1980s, with the Single European Act nearing implementation and the Gaullist leader, Jacques Chirac, evincing a more accommodating attitude to European integration, the field was open for the FN to pose once again as the most resolute champion of a Europe of nation states. Confident of his national political standing in the wake of his 1988 presidential result (14.4 per cent in the first round), Le Pen used the 1989 Euro-elections to publish a book of reflections on Europe's place in the world and France's place within Europe. He argued that the construction of Europe was essential, but that the principle of subsidiarity should prevail. Invoking the 'Gaullist formula',[69] as he put it, he developed his vision of a 'confederal' Europe, insisting that supranational control should extend only to those areas (chief among them defence) where government authority was best pooled. In no circumstances, he insisted, was national sovereignty to be the price of closer European integration.

Here was a Le Pen anxious to dispel the extremist label and adopt the posture of a statesman of global political vision. So Europeanist did he appear, indeed, that he incurred criticism from other components of the French extreme right. In a series of articles published in the Maurrassian royalist weekly, *Aspects de la France*, Pierre Pujo took Le Pen to task for failing to choose clearly between a nationalist and a pro-European stance. Le Pen's appeals to a 'common European identity', charged Pujo, were at odds with the preservation of an authentic 'national identity', while his calls for a common European defence and security policy could not be achieved without the sacrifice of national sovereignty.[70] Pujo's criticism, however partisan in its motivation, found its target. For it discerned in Le Pen and the FN two quite distinct discourses on Europe, neither of which amounted to a clearly defined position. At the same time as Le Pen was presenting himself as the statesman with a European vision, he was posing as the intransigent defender of 'national identity' before the crowds gathered in Paris on 1 May to honour Joan of Arc, that symbol of the French national populist right. The European elections, intoned Le Pen, were 'first and foremost a battle for France'; the FN, he insisted, would not allow the French to be sold out to a 'cosmopolitan and multi-racial Europe'.[71]

Where the French extreme right displays ambivalence, the Italian counterpart displays indifference. The contribution of the MSI and the Lega to EU institutions and processes has been almost insignificant. In the case of the MSI, the tenuous relationship with the rest of the European extreme right has contributed to an isolated position within the EP. Whereas until the mid-1970s the MSI had powerful international allies, Salazar's fall in Portugal in 1974, the end of rule by the military junta in Greece, and General Franco's death in 1975, contributed to the party's international isolation. This was compounded by the MSI's decision not to join the Technical Group of the European Right in the EP over the South Tyrol issue. Finally, the MSI's refusal to distance itself from classic fascist precepts and ideology resulted in the other parties consciously seeking to distance themselves from it in order to maintain the distinction between 'old right' and 'new right', and in order to avoid a discourse too explicitly reminiscent of the Second World War.

On issues such as immigration and immigrant rights, which both the German and the French extreme right have repeatedly addressed in the European forum, the MSI and the Lega have remained more subdued. The MSI has indeed a xenophobic streak and anti-immigrant tendencies, but its racism is underplayed and is often less strident than that of the Lega. Two factors account for this attitude. First, Italy has not been a land of immigration but of emigration – especially in the regions from which the MSI draws its support. As a result, immigrant workers are a relatively recent phenomenon in comparison with France and Germany, and the backlash against them has not reached full force.[72] Second, since the October 1993 elections, the MSI has sought to demarcate itself from the discourse of the Lega, which although similarly subdued in the European context can be quite vehemently racist in the national. It is also worth pointing out that in Italy there is no anti-semitic tradition of the type found in both France and Germany.

Southerners (or, as they are pejoratively referred to in northern Italy, *i terroni* – those who scrape the earth) are the Lega's target. The discourse surrounding the *terrone* is the same as that surrounding the Republikaner's and FN's immigrant figure: the *terrone* is lazy, profiteering, parasitic, and often unfit for the privileges conferred by citizenship. What differs, however, is that whereas the FN and the

Republikaner are responding to a national phenomenon which they seek to influence via supranational initiatives and cross-national assaults, essentially through the EP, the Lega works at a subnational level, thus largely without reference to the EP. Few policy statements relating to European institutions have been made by either party. Even Bossi's federalism has never been defined with any precision and tends to represent a defiant rallying cry for Italy's northern provinces rather than a specific programme of action or a coherent body of policy proposals. Although each of the three countries examined in this chapter presents an extreme right whose actions are often guided by domestic concerns, the case of Italy is more extreme in its domestic narrowness. The Republikaner and the FN attempt to use the arena of the EP and their MEPs to influence European policy, or at the very least to influence domestic politics from a supranational platform; they can do this largely because of a relative consensus on what constitutes the nation, both historically and institutionally. The Lega and the MSI have far less grip upon European issues, given that Italy's very nationhood remains contested.

The European elections of June 1994 confirmed the trends in Italian politics. Of the three allied parties which formed the Italian government (Sylvio Berlusconi's *Forza Italia!*, the Lega Nord and the MSI) *Forza Italia!* emerged with 31 per cent of the popular vote.[73] The MSI saw a slight erosion of its support from 14 per cent in the March 1994 legislative elections to 12–13 per cent. The Lega was in retreat, falling from 8.4 per cent of the vote in the March 1994 legislative elections to just under 7 per cent.[74] Italians were not put off by the international unease at the MSI's success in the legislative elections, and for Fini, the party's leader since 1987, the European election results were a clear vote of confidence. The Lega, Berlusconi's most reluctant ally, lost part of its electoral support to *Forza Italia!*[75] In the light of the 1994 European elections, the Lega seemed increasingly like a protest movement unable to sustain support in the face of more established parties of the right – including the extreme right – despite its strong support for federalism and a powerful European Parliament.

FROM A EUROPE UNDER THREAT TO THE THREAT OF EUROPE: THE MAASTRICHT REFERENDUM

Alongside the mythical, visionary Europe which informs much of the discourse of the extreme right, there is a constant denunciation of the *real* Europe, in its institutions, its policies and its personnel. The charges were clearly set out in the FN's 1985–86 manifesto:

> The European Parliament too often offers the spectacle of an assembly sensitive to Marxist reasoning and responsive to Third World ideology. The Commission in Brussels is an organization labouring under the weight of bureaucratic socialism. No: there is more to Europe than this – more to Europe than shopkeepers, trade unions, theoreticians and technocrats! It is a community whose destiny stretches back a thousand years and whose construction, as the final great project of the twentieth century, can hold out to our young a future worthy of their legitimate ambitions.[76]

The decision by President Mitterrand of France to put the ratification of the Maastricht Treaty to referendum in September 1992, thus forcing the FN to forsake its abstractions and articulate a view on closer integration of the real Europe, exposed the bankruptcy of the FN's avowed Europeanism. Denouncing the Maastricht Treaty as a 'conspiracy against the peoples and nations of Europe', Le Pen and his party mounted a vigorous campaign under the slogan 'No to Maastricht – yes to a *Europe des patries!*'[77] Gone were the emollient tones of 1989 and the vision of a common European endeavour; gone, too, the calls for a 'European patriotism' transcending national sentiment; in their place, a hard-right discourse reminiscent of the imprecations which had attended French withdrawal from Indo-China and Algeria in the 1950s and 1960s, with Le Pen's party denouncing 'this French capitulation, this national abdication, this selling-out of France'. The time had come to rescue France (more echoes, this time of Poujadism) 'from the hands of foreigners, from the faceless representatives of global capitalism, from state-less bankers and Brussels technocrats'.[78] Here was the French extreme right at its most doggedly entrenched behind the old redoubt of nationalism, drawing upon a long tradition of virulent opposition and mobilizing all of the symbols at its disposal (Vercingetorix, Clovis, Saint Louis, Joan of Arc, Roland at Ronceveaux, the defenders of Verdun, 'the betrayed soldiers of Indochina and Algeria').[79] The consequences of a 'yes' vote, warned Le Pen, would be 'worse than losing a war', the triumph of an 'international conspiracy' mounted by 'hidden forces and vested interests against our nations', the end of 'France eternal'.[80] Le Pen's anti-Maastricht speech in La Trinité-sur-Mer, with its apocalyptic vision of a post-Maastricht Europe, was a model of the paranoia which besets the French extreme right: 'plots', 'treason', 'traitors', 'felony', 'hidden forces', 'international conspiracy'.[81] More specifically, the ratification debate became for the FN a platform on which to parade the evils threatening France: 'In concrete terms, it means more immigration, more insecurity, more unemployment, and more taxes . . . less democracy and less freedom, the death knell of France's History!'[82]

Behind the extravagant language and imagery (Maastricht as a *coup d'état*, as an AIDS epidemic, as 'the end of France'),[83] behind Le Pen's denunciations of 'euristocrates', 'fédérastes' and 'Maastricheurs', lay a systematic assault on the project of European integration. Backed by the FN's propaganda machine and by the editorials of François Brigneau in the party's semi-official organ, *National-Hebdo*, the French contingent within the Technical Group of the European Right published in September 1992 a special twenty-three-page issue of the Group's bulletin, *Europe et Patries*, in which it lambasted the Community and its institutions – 'l'Europe de Bruxelles', a Europe of bureaucrats and bankers.[84] Were Maastricht to be ratified, argued this booklet, France's European partners would conspire to bring about her ruin. Britain, Portugal and the Netherlands would serve as conduits for immigrants from ex-colonial territories wishing to exploit their future voting rights in France; Spain and the Netherlands would be routes for drug-trafficking; the power of the German mark would hold the French economy to ransom; while Ireland, Greece, Spain and Portugal would soak up subsidies from revenue raised by taxing the French.[85] Such were the consequences of Maastricht, argued Le Pen in a special issue of the bi-monthly *Lettre de Jean-Marie Le Pen*, that it could be compared to the 'infamous Treaty of Troyes', which had ceded the French throne to Henry V of England in 1420 – a wrong which it had been Joan of Arc's historic mission to right.[86]

Both the Italian MSI and the Lega pronounced themselves similarly against

Maastricht, although their negative stances were informed by radically diverging attitudes; for the MSI, Maastricht represented a loss of sovereignty too severe for a nationalist party, however pro-European it might be. For the Lega on the other hand, Maastricht did not go far enough in ceding powers to the European Parliament and fell short of providing a vehicle for domestic reform.

The Technical Group of the European Right demanded a referendum for Germany on Maastricht, claiming that most Germans rejected their own government's policy on Europe.[87] The extreme right in Germany could report with pleasure how near the French came to rejecting Maastricht in their referendum. Despite the concerted attack on the European Community, lack of agreement on Europe demonstrated the limits of co-operation on the extreme right.[88]

The extreme right in France and Germany found their credibility stretched to breaking point on the issue of Europe, for each had sought to sustain two quite divergent postures: a pro-Europeanism grounded in concepts of ethnic and cultural kinship, and an anti-Europeanism drawing its rationale from the perceived threat of integration on the Maastricht model, as well as deep antipathy to any form of political federalism. If the novel aspect of the extreme right in post-war France is, as Malcolm Anderson has argued, its Europeanism,[89] then Maastricht demonstrated clearly the practical limits of what remains a Europeanism of principle alone.

NOTES

1 Richard Stöss, *Die 'Republikaner'* (Cologne, Bund-Verlag, 1990 2nd rev. edn), p. 81; Bettina Westle and Oskar Niedermayer, 'Contemporary right-wing extremism in West Germany: "The Republicans" and their electorate', *European Journal of Political Research*, vol. 22, no. 1, 1992, pp. 83–100.
2 Uwe Backes, 'Extremismus und Populismus von rechts: Ein Vergleich auf europäischer Ebene', *Aus Politik und Zeitgeschichte*, B 46–47/90, 9 November 1990, pp. 3–14.
3 See R. Mannheimer's *La Lega Lombarda* (Milan, Feltrinelli, 1991).
4 See L. Balbo and L. Manconi, *I razzismi possibili*, (Milan, Feltrinelli, 1990) and V. Moioli, *I nuovi razzismi. Miserie e fortune della Lega Lombarda* (Rome, Edizioni Associate, 1990).
5 Almirante, leader of the MSI/AN before Fini, had also founded Eurodestra in 1978 with some French and Spanish support. See M. Caciagli 'The Movimento Sociale Italiano: Destra Nazionale and Neo-fascism in Italy" in K. Von Beyme (ed.), *Right-wing Extremism in Western Europe* (London, Cass, 1988).
6 The EC's *Eurobarometer* studies indicate that support for the Republikaner comes disproportionately from working-class voters, people with a low level of formal education, men, and those aged between forty-five and sixty-four. See Oskar Niedermeyer, 'Sozialstruktur, politische Orientierung und die Unterstützung extrem rechter Parteien in Westeuropa', *Zeitschrift für Parlamentsfragen*, vol. 4, 1990, pp. 564–82.
7 See Backes, 'Extremismus und Populismus von rechts', pp. 3–14.
8 Reuter Textline, 19 July 1989.
9 See Backes, 'Extremismus und Populismus von rechts', p. 5. Benno Hafeneger, 'Die Vernetzung der extremen Rechten in Westeuropa', in Martina Kirfel, Walter Oswalt (eds), *Die Rückkehr der Führer* (Vienna, Zurich, Europaverlag, 1991, 2nd edn), pp. 185–94.
10 Franz Schönhuber, 'Die europäische Rechte was ist das?', *Der Republikaner*, no. 1, January 1991, p. 3.
11 'Interview mit dem Bundesvorsitzenden Franz Schönhuber', *Der Republikaner*, no. 12, December 1990, p. 3.
12 There is much to suggest that the antagonisms within the Group and the feuds among the Republikaner themselves had as much to do with clashes of personalities as with

ıdeological differences. See, for example, Johanna Grund, 'Frischer Wind in Straßburg', *Der Republikaner*, no. 8, July 1990, p. 5.

13 See Theo Tannert, 'Eurorechte im Blickpunkt, Deutschland', *Nation und Europa. Deutsche Monatshefte*, vol. 42, no. 4, April 1992, pp. 44–5.

14 Quoted by Hafeneger, 'Die Vernetzung der extremen Rechten in Westeuropa', p. 193.

15 Ibid., pp. 193–4.

16 'Un entretien avec Franz Schönhuber', *Der Republikaner*, no. 2, 9 February 1992, p. 4.

17 *Die Republikaner, Parteiprogramm* 1990, ed. Bundesgeschäftsstelle der Republikaner, Erich Schmidt Verlag, 1990, p. 10.

18 See Norbert Lepszy, 'Die Republikaner: Ideologie, Programm, Organisation', *Aus Politik und Zeitgeschichte*, B41–42/89, 6 October 1989, pp. 3–20.

19 See Piero Ignazi and Colette Ysmal, 'Extreme right-wing parties in Europe: Introduction', *European Journal of Political Research*, vol. 22, no. 1, 1992, pp. 1–2; Backes, 'Extremismus und Populismus von rechts', pp. 3–14. The Republikaner have often used the Deutsche Volksunion to emphasize their own distance from National Socialism, accusing the DVU leader, for example, of being a dealer in Nazi relics. Stöss contrasts the DVU's relatively poor showing in the 1989 European elections with the success of the Republikaner and points to the DVU's neo-fascist image among the German electorate. Both parties together obtained 8.7 per cent of the total vote, with 7.1 per cent going to the Republikaner and 1.6 per cent going to the DVU-Liste D. (Richard Stöss, *Die 'Republikaner'*, p. 45).

20 This distinction is offered, for example, by Piero Ignazi, 'The silent counter-revolution: hypotheses on the emergence of extreme right-wing parties in Europe', *European Journal of Political Research*, vol. 22, no. 1, 1992, pp. 3–34.

21 The contrast between old and new right becomes apparent in the German context if one compares the traditional *Deutsche National-Zeitung* with the more recently founded *Der Republikaner*. The *National-Zeitung* regularly carries articles with titles such as 'Those really responsible for the Second World War' (see, for example, no. 48, 20 November 1992, p. 3).

22 On the Conservative Revolution see Roger Woods, 'The Radical Right: The "Conservative Revolutionaries" in Germany', in Roger Eatwell and Noel O'Sullivan, *The Nature of the Right* (London, Frances Pinter, 1989), pp. 124–45.

23 Gerwin Steinberger, 'Edgar Jung und der organische Staat', *Nation und Europa*, no. 9, September 1992, p. 49.

24 Quoted by Woods, 'The Radical Right', p. 140.

25 Richard Stöss thus puts the Republikaner in the company of the NPD and the DVU. See Westle and Niedermayer, 'Contemporary right-wing extremism', p. 89.

26 On the conservative dilemma see Martin Greiffenhagen, *Das Dilemma des Konservatismus* (Munich, Piper, 1971).

27 Steinberger, 'Edgar Jung und der organische Staat', p. 50.

28 Ralph Lorenz, 'Aus Neubauers Blatt trieft braune Jauche', *Der Republikaner*, no. 12, December 1990, p. 7.

29 Jean-Marie Le Pen, *Les Français d'abord* (Paris, Carrère-Lafon, 1984), p. 155.

30 Ibid., p. 158.

31 Ibid., p. 163.

32 Ibid., p. 164.

33 Ibid., p. 164.

34 See for example, Jean-Marc Brissaud, *L'Europe face à Gorbatchev. Une stratégie impériale contre l'impérialisme* (Paris, Groupe des Droites européennes (GDE), 1989); Jean-Marie Le Chevallier, *Immigration en Europe. Attention, danger* (Paris, GDE, 1989).

35 *Le Monde*, 25 August 1992.

36 See Le Pen's 1988 presidential manifesto, *Passeport pour la victoire*, p. 58.

37 *300 mesures pour la renaissance de la France. Front National: programme de gouvernement* (Paris, Editions Nationales, 1993), p. 365. Cf. Jean-Marie Le Pen, *Europe. Discours et interventions 1984–1989*, ed. Jean-Marc Brissaud, (Paris, GDE, 1989), p. 149.

38 *Les Français d'abord*, p. 163.

39 Front National: colloque 'Immigration: les solutions', Marseille, 16 November 1991,

intervention de Bruno Mégret: 'Contribution au règlement du problème de l'immigration: 50 mesures concrètes', p. 1.

40 Front National, *300 mesures pour la renaissance de la France*, p. 363.

41 See Jean-Marie Le Pen, *L'Espoir* (Paris, Albatros, 1989), pp. 86, 96, 97, 100.

42 Front National, *300 mesures pour la renaissance de la France*, pp. 364, 371–2.

43 *Les Français d'abord*, p. 159–60; *Pour la France: Programme du Front National* (Paris, Albatros, 1985), p. 187.

44 Compare, for example, the PS's designation of France as 'the driving force at the heart of the European Community', or Giscard d'Estaing's claim that France's 'vocation' was to 'lead' in Europe. See on this question François Saint-Ouen, 'Les partis politiques français et l'Europe. Système politique et fonctionnement du discours', *Revue française de science politique*, vol. 36, no. 2, 1986, pp. 205–26.

45 *Pour la France. Programme du Front National*, p. 192.

46 In a series of surveys between autumn 1987 and spring 1989, Italian support for a 'European government by 1992' remained within the 68–77 per cent range, as against 49–56 per cent for the EC as a whole (*Eurobarometer*, 31, Annex 22). Taking the most general indicator – overall support for the integration process – and using the *Eurobarometer* scale (from 4 'very much in favour' to 1 'very much against') the Italian average for 1973 to 1986 was 3.32, bettered only by Luxembourg's 3.37. (*Eurobarometer*, 25 June 1986, pp. 52–3). All figures drawn from David Hine, *Governing Italy: The Politics of Bargained Pluralism* (Oxford, Oxford University Press, 1993), p. 341.

47 Franco Ferraresi, 'The radical right in postwar Italy', *Politics and Society*, vol. 16, 1988, pp. 71–117.

48 See the chapter by Francesco Sidoti 'The extreme right in Italy: ideological orphans and counter-mobilization' in P. Hainsworth (ed.), *The Extreme Right in Europe and the USA*. (London, Frances Pinter, 1992). Also see Norberto Bobbio, 'Chronaca', *L'Opinione*, July 1989, p. 24.

49 Sidoti, 'The extreme right in Italy'.

50 For a comparison between the Front National and the Lega see Paolo Flores d'Arcais and Marc Lazar, 'Derives italiennes: entretien' in *Esprit*, July 1992, pp. 30–41. Also for a discussion of inefficiency and fiscal parasitism, see R. Mannheimer, 'Chi vota Lega e perche', in R. Mannheimer (ed.), *La Lega Lombarda* (Milan, Feltrinelli, 1991).

51 Marco Moussanet, 'Un Bossi durissimo promette: "Mai con la destra forcaiola"', in *Il Sole-24 Ore*, 29 March 1994, p. 2.

52 Dwayne Woods, 'The crisis of the Italian party-state', *Telos*, vol. 25, no. 3, 1992, pp. 111–26.

53 Piero Ignazi, 'The silent counter-revolution', p. 12.

54 Klaus Zeitler, 'Das Märchen von einem zukünftigen Europa der Regionen und einem demokratisch gewählten Europaparlament!', *Der Republikaner*, no. 11, November 1992, p. 6.

55 Franz Schönhuber, 'Europa JA – Diese EG – NEIN', *Der Republikaner*, no. 10, 8, October 1991, p. 4.

56 *Die Republikaner, Parteiprogramm 1990*, pp. 53–5.

57 See Stöss, *Die 'Republikaner'*, pp. 65–74.

58 'Un entretien avec Franz Schönhuber', p. 4.

59 *Die Republikaner, Parteiprogramm 1990*, p.19.

60 'Das Europäische Parlament', *Nation und Europa*, vol. 42, no. 10, October 1992, p. 47.

61 Klausdieter Ludwig, '"Antirassismus" ganz offiziell. Eine Studie des Europaparlaments', *Nation und Europa*, vol. 42, no. 4, 1992, pp. 37–8.

62 Hafeneger, 'Die Vernetzung der extremen Rechten in Westeuropa', p. 187.

63 Ibid., p. 192.

64 'Der Widerstand der Ökologen gegen die EG', *Der Republikaner*, no. 10, October 1992, p. 3.

65 On the FN's calls for 'une véritable priorité d'emploi pour les nationaux', and 'la réservation des allocations familiales et de l'aide sociale aux ressortissants français', see *Pour la France. Programme du Front National*, pp. 116–17, 159–62.

66 Ibid., p. 191.

67 *Le Monde*, 6 April 1979. The veteran campaigner of the nationalist right, Jean-Louis Tixier-Vignancour, eventually headed a PFN Eurodroite list which won 1.3 per cent of the vote, demonstrating the continued marginality of the French extreme right in the late 1970s.

68 *Le Monde*, 12 May 1979.

69 *L'Espoir*, pp. 98, 99.

70 See Pierre Pujo, 'Jean-Marie Le Pen entre la France et l'Europe', *Aspects de la France*, 20 April 1989; 'Le Front national devra choisir', ibid., 11 May 1989; 'L'Europe de Jean-Marie Le Pen', ibid., 15 June 1989.

71 See *Le Monde*, 3 May 1989.

72 Conversely, of course, it could be argued that precisely because of the absence of a tradition of immigration, Italy's population might be less tolerant towards foreigners.

73 *Le Monde*, 14 June 1994 'Silvio Berlusconi en plein état de grâce', p. 53.

74 Ibid. and *Il Sole-24 Ore*, 29 March 1994, front page.

75 This is not surprising, given that the European elections are typically less 'clientelistic' than national elections. For the Lega, whose support is based exclusively in the North and dependent on local dissatisfaction, this translates into a loss of votes.

76 *Pour la France: Programme du Front National*, pp. 188–9.

77 *Le Monde*, 17–18 May 1992.

78 Ibid. Interestingly, by contrast, Poujade's UDCA came out in favour of a 'yes' vote. See *Le Monde*, 20–21 September 1992.

79 See the reports on Le Pen's Reims speech in *Le Monde*, 8 September 1992, and *Libération*, 7 September 1992.

80 *Le Monde*, 25 August 1992; *Libération*, 24 August 1992.

81 *Le Monde*, 25 August 1992. See in similar vein Jacques Ploncard d'Assac, 'Maastricht, un complot maçonnique contre les nations', *Minute-la France*, 19–25 August 1992.

82 See Le Pen's Nice speech of 4 July, reported in *Le Monde* of 7 July 1992. See also Le Pen's speech of 22 August in La Trinité-sur-Mer, where he denounced the treaty as 'plus d'immigration, plus d'insécurite, plus de drogue, plus de sida', an open door through which 'la Mafia pourra s'installer calmement et officiellement chez nous' (*Le Monde*, 25 August 1992).

83 See *Le Monde* of 29 August 1992 and 15 September 1992. See also the interview with Le Pen in *Le Quotidien de Paris*, 5 September 1992.

84 'Maastricht – Avant d'aller voter. Les questions que vous vous posez. Les réponses que vous recherchez', *Europe et Patries*, no. 46, September 1992.

85 Ibid., pp. 8–9, 12–13, 15, 18-19. Among the more hysterical fears expressed was that, should a future Labour government grant British nationality to members of the Commonwealth, 827 million Indians, 116 million Bangladeshis and 123 million Pakistanis would have the right to vote in France and throughout the Community (ibid., p. 8).

86 *La Lettre de Jean-Marie Le Pen*, no. 160, July 1992, p. 2.

87 'Dem Volk das Wort', *Nation und Europa*, vol. 43, no. 1, January 1993, p. 60.

88 'Eurorechte im Blickpunkt', *Nation und Europa*, vol. 42, no. 10, October 1992, p.48.

89 Malcolm Anderson, *Conservative Politics in France* (London, Allen and Unwin, 1974), p. 298.

SELECT BIBLIOGRAPHY

Caciagli, Mario, 'The Movimento sociale italiano: destra nazionale and neo-fascism in Italy' in K. Von Beyme (ed.), *Right-wing Extremism in Western Europe*, London, Cass, 1988.

Cheles, L., Ferguson R. and Vaughan, M. (eds), *Neo-Fascism in Europe*, London, Longman, 1991.

Diamanti, Ilvo, *La Lega. Geografia, storia e sociologia di un nuovo soggetto politico*, Roma, Donzelli Editore, 1993.

Eatwell, Roger and O'Sullivan, Noel, *The Nature of the Right*, London, Frances Pinter, 1989.

'Extreme Right in Europe', special issue of *Parliamentary Affairs*, vol. 45, no. 3, 1992.

Ferraresi, Franco, 'The radical right in post-war Italy', *Politics and Society*, vol. 16, 1988, pp. 71–115.

Front National, *Pour la France*, Paris, Albatros, 1985.

Front National, *300 mesures pour la renaissance de la France*, Paris, Editions Nationales, 1993.

Furlong, Paul, 'The extreme right in Italy: old orders and dangerous novelties', *Parliamentary Affairs*, vol. 45, no. 3, July 1992, pp. 345–56.

Galli, Giorgio, *La Destra in Italia*, Milan, Gammalibri, 1983.

Greiffenhagen, Martin, *Das Dilemma des Konservatismus*, Munich, Piper, 1971.

Greiffenhagen, Martin and Greiffenhagen, Sylvia, *Ein schwieriges Vaterland. Zur politischen Kultur im vereinigten Deutschland*, Munich, List Verlag, 1993.

Greß, Franz, Jaschke, Hans-Gerd and Schönekäs, Klaus, *Neue Rechte und Rechtsextremismus in Europa, Bundesrepublik, Frankreich und Großbritannien*, Opladen, Westdeutscher Verlag, 1990.

Griffin, Roger, *The Nature of Fascism*, London, Routledge, 1993.

Hainsworth, Paul, *The Extreme Right in Europe and America*, London, Frances Pinter, 1992.

Ignazi, P. and Ysmal, C. (eds), *Extreme Right-wing Parties in Europe*, special issue of *European Journal of Political Research*, vol. 22, no. 1, 1992.

Kirfel, Martina and Oswalt, Walter (eds), *Die Rückkehr der Führer*, Vienna, Zurich, Europaverlag, 1991, 2nd edn.

Le Pen, J.-M., *Les Français d'abord*, Paris, Carrère-Lafon, 1984.

Le Pen, J.-M., *L'Espoir*, Paris, Albatros, 1989.

Le Pen, J.-M., *Europe. Discours et interventions 1984–1989*, Paris, Groupe des Droites européennes, 1989.

Maier, Charles, *The Unmasterable Past*, Cambridge MA, Harvard University Press, 1988.

Mannheimer, Roberto, 'I metalmeccanici della Lega Lombarda', *Istituto Italiano di Sociologica*, Milan, 1990.

Mannheimer, Roberto (ed.), *La Lega Lombarda*, Milan, Feltrinelli, 1991.

Moioli, V., *I nuovi razzismi*, Rome, Edizioni associate, 1990.

Niedermayer, Oskar and Von Beyme, Klaus (eds), *Politische Kultur in Ost- und Westdeutschland*, Berlin, Akademie Verlag, 1994.

Padgett, Stephen (ed.), *Parties and Party Systems in the New Germany*, Aldershot, Dartmouth, 1993.

Poche, Bernard, 'La Ligue Nord face à l'état italien. Entre la décomposition territoriale et la recomposition institutionelle', *Revue politique et parlementaire*, 968, Nov–Dec 1993.

Revelli, M., *La cultura della destra radicale*, Milan, Angeli, 1985.

Ricolfi, Luca, 'Politica senza fede. L'estremismo dei piccoli leghisti', *Il Mulino*, vol. 1, 1993.

Stöss, Richard, *Die 'Republikaner'*, Cologne, Bund-Verlag, 1990, 2nd rev. edn.

Tassani, Giovanni, *Vista da sinistra. Ricognizioni sulla 'nuova destra'*, Florence, Arnaud, 1986.

Von Beyme, Klaus (ed.), *Right-wing Extremism in Western Europe*, London, Cass, 1988.

Weidenfeld, Werner (ed.), *Deutschland. Eine Nation – doppelte Geschichte*, Cologne, Wissenschaft und Politik, 1993.

15 Green parties and the European Union

Wolfgang Rüdig

INTRODUCTION

During the 1980s, a new brand of a political party, usually called 'Green' or ecological parties, emerged throughout Western Europe. These new parties were chiefly motivated by the environmental and anti-nuclear concerns which had given rise to substantial protest movements in the 1970s, and they also benefited from the emergence of the peace movements in the early 1980s.[1] Despite repeated predictions about their imminent demise, Green parties had established themselves as relatively stable new political actors in many European party systems by the early 1990s. Green representatives had been sitting in the European Parliament since 1984. After the very successful 1989 European elections, the Greens were also able to form their own Green group in the European Parliament whose importance in European politics was reconfirmed in the 1994 elections.

The interrelationship between Green parties and Europe is extremely complex and varied, involving many processes at national and European level.[2] Through their role in local, regional and national political systems, Green parties are involved in domestic aspects of European policy making. With their representation in the European Parliament, Green parties have also been playing their part in the political process at European level. While there are instances where Green parties have influenced the formulation and implementation of European legislation, arguably more important has been the impact of European integration on Green parties. Most pertinent in this context has been the introduction of direct elections to the European Parliament, starting in 1979. Green parties were able to take advantage of European elections to raise their own profile and use these elections as a springboard for their establishment within national political systems. The results of the four direct elections to the European Parliament (see Table 15.1) demonstrate quite well that Green parties have succeeded in establishing themselves as permanent fixtures of the political system in many European countries. Green parties are also represented in the national parliaments of the three countries who joined the European Union (EU)[3] in 1995, Austria, Finland and Sweden. This EU enlargement will thus strengthen the Green group in the European Parliament even further.

While Green parties have thus undoubtedly benefited from certain aspects of the European integration process, the attitudes of Green parties to the EU have often been critical. Over the years, Green parties have developed a range of positions, ranging from embracing the EU as an agent of environmental reform to demands for secession from the EU. Common to all Green parties, however, is an alternative vision of a 'Green' Europe based on the concept of a Europe of the Regions. This Green European vision is very often overlooked in accounts of discourses of European integration. But, as will be shown, to some extent Green parties themselves have to take some blame for this because they have historically given little attention to developing their European policies.

Table 15.1 Green European election results, 1979–94[a]

	1979 %	1984 % (seats)	1989 % (seats)	1994 % (seats)
Belgium	3.4	8.2 (2)	13.9 (3)	11.5 (2)
France	4.4	6.7 (0)	10.6 (9)	5.0 (0)
Germany	3.2	8.5 (7)	9.1 (8)	10.9 (12)
Greece	–	–	2.6 (0)	0.8 (0)
Ireland	–	1.9 (0)	3.7 (0)	7.9 (2)
Italy	–	–	6.2 (5)	3.2 (3)
Luxembourg	1.0	6.2 (0)	11.3 (0)	10.9 (1)
Netherlands	–	6.9 (2)	7.0 (2)	6.3 (1)
Portugal	–	–	* (1)	* (0)
Spain	–	–	2.5 (0)	0.8 (0)
UK	0.1	0.5 (0)	14.5 (0)	3.1 (0)

Notes: [a] Figures represent the combined results of all Green groups and parties fielding candidates in each country. I am very grateful to T.T. Mackie for his help in compiling these figures.
* Participated in coalition with the Communist Party.
There are no results for Denmark. The Danish Greens were formed in 1983 but fielded no candidates in European elections.

Source: Own calculations based on official election results.

In this chapter, I will chart the development of the relationship between Green parties and the EU, concentrating mainly on two countries whose public discourse over Europe provides a vivid contrast: Britain and Germany. The British Greens have consistently been more sceptical about European integration than their German counterparts. To a major extent, Green party attitudes thus appear to reflect the national context of the political discourse. But we will also have to examine the role of the success of the German Greens in establishing themselves in the German polity which contrasts starkly with the British Greens' failure to make a lasting impact on British politics. Following these two national case studies, I will look at other Green parties in the EU and their current policies, particularly in the context of the debate about the Maastricht Treaty, and also examine the extent to which the European positions of Green parties reflect the views of their electorates.

THE BRITISH GREENS AND EUROPE

Ever since its formation, the British Green Party has struggled with the issue of Europe, and its policies have seen a few changes.[4] While there appears to be broad agreement about the criticism of the EU's ecological and democratic deficits, the key question remains to what extent the party advocates Britain leaving the EU or changing existing EU institutions from within.

The party's[5] first ever national election manifesto, entitled *Manifesto for Survival* published in June 1974, called for the secession of Britain from the EU: 'The EEC will hamper the adoption of survival policies unless a majority of member states also adopt the principle on which PEOPLE is founded and it is therefore necessary to secede from it.'[6] One year later, the party published a more comprehensive fundamental programme, the *Manifesto for a Sustainable Society*, which accepted Britain's EU membership and set out a programme for the greening of the Union: 'The Ecology Party accepts the democratic decision of the British people to remain within the EEC and will actively work towards achieving a self-sufficient Europe based upon the principles of the Ecology Party.'[7] While the manifesto warned of 'EEC technocratic elitism', the chances of reforming its nature were seen in quite a positive light: 'it is envisaged that ultimately it will be possible for Britain to be part of a European Political Community within which conservationist principles are paramount'.

The differences between the 1974 and 1975 documents are associated with the main ideological schisms within the party at that time. For the 'survivalists' who were expecting the almost imminent collapse of industrial society, the need to build environmentally sustainable local communities was paramount. The development of the EU was at best irrelevant, at worst highly damaging for those advocating a strict decentralization of all political decision making. For others in the party opposed to 'survivalist' thinking, opposition to the EU was less of a foregone conclusion, and after Britain's referendum on EU membership in June 1975, a secessionist position was difficult to sustain. As the party turned increasingly away from the survivalist position in the late 1970s with an attempt to boost its political respectability, a reformist position towards European matters came to prevail.

The party's 1979 General Election manifesto embodied such a position, summing up neatly what Greens thought good and bad about the EU:

> The Ecology Party acknowledges that the UK has an important role to play within Europe, and that it will continue to do so in the future. The nature of that involvement must, however, be reviewed, for in its present state the Common Market demonstrates the worst failings of an over-centralised growth-orientated bureaucracy. The Common Agricultural Policy is quite simply a disaster.
>
> As such, the EEC is merely a reflection of its member states. But there is no fundamental reason why the EEC should be slower to adopt ecological principles tha[n] any national government. Indeed, current directives on pollution control require some governments to do more than they would if left to their own devices.[8]

The manifesto went on to call for the promotion of the development of the EEC 'as a federation of self-reliant regions' and the preparation of 'coherent European policies on energy, raw materials, the environment, and especially agriculture and food, working together to establish a stable and self-sufficient European Union'.[9] The party's 1979 European Election manifesto reiterated and expanded on many of these points, and called for greater powers for the European Parliament to control the Council and the Commission.[10] At that time, the Greens clearly saw the EU as an at least potentially pro-environmental force, and explicitly acknowledged the benefits of EU environmental legislation.

By the early 1980s, this had changed, and a more hostile attitude to the EU came to dominate. This was partly due to the influence of a new generation of party members who had joined after 1979. Many of those had broadly 'left anarchist' political views, and the balance of party opinion shifted again towards a more fundamentalist position on Europe. The 1983 General Election manifesto stated bluntly that 'most people in the green movement are strongly opposed to the Common Market – there never was a less ecological document than the Treaty of Rome!'[11] The manifesto explicitly demanded Britain's withdrawal from the EU: 'We should withdraw from the EEC. We would seek instead to establish a European Federation, non-aligned in defence matters, opposed to reliance on economic growth, with its emphasis on the regions of Europe, and not its nation states, and committed to sustainability and justice, both in Europe and the Third World.'[12] By that time, the original pro-EU passage in its fundamental programme dating from 1975 had been deleted. The replacement stated clearly that 'the Ecology Party is opposed to Britain's continued membership of the European Economic Community'.[13] That policy was by no means uncontroversial within the party. Some members argued strongly that Britain leaving the EU was not only unrealistic but would have undesirable ecological consequences. But attempts to change the policy failed, and opposition to EU membership was reiterated again in the 1987 General Election manifesto: 'The Green Party believes that Britain must leave the Common Market . . . .'[14]

It was only towards the end of the 1980s that the force of anti-EU feeling mellowed. In the spring 1989 edition of the fundamental programme, the demand for taking Britain out of the EU was qualified with the sentence '. . . unless reconstituted as a neutral, non-aligned Confederation of European Regions, which would be base[d] on sound ecological principles'.[15] Entering the 1989 European Election campaign, the party leadership made an explicit decision not to emphasize the EU membership issue as this was thought to be 'too negative' and would also have injected a dissonant note for relations with EU sister parties.[16]

The 1989 European Election manifesto avoided any explicit reference to leaving the EU. Instead, it provided a detailed and balanced assessment of the pros and cons of the EU from a green point of view. The manifesto stated that Green MEPs would support the proper enforcement of EU environmental policies and demand greater rights for the European Parliament. It expressed strong criticism of the Single Market: 'With an end to monetary barriers, wealth will migrate even more quickly to those areas which are already wealthy, while the "peripheral areas" will continue to be fed grudgingly with money for inappropriate projects like wall-to-wall holiday apartments and nuclear waste dumps.'[17] But rather than demand the complete severing of links with the EU, the manifesto on the same page promised to stress those aspects of the Single European Act that made a commitment to protecting Europe's environment and to work so that 'Europe can look forward to a truly democratic, truly green future.' The rest of the document reiterated the Greens' long-standing reservations about the Common Agricultural Policy and also expressed concern about the EU becoming a vehicle for a nuclear-armed European army, but it also stated: 'The Green Party recognises that without EEC regulations Britain's environmental record would be even worse than it is.'

In the 1989 European elections, the Green Party achieved the best national election result by far of its history. There had been some voices before the elections that had argued for the party to boycott the elections in the light of the party's policy to leave the EU. But, as in 1984, a pragmatic approach of using the European elections as an opportunity to present Green policies to the electorate prevailed. However, party policy with its ambivalence over EU membership was still in force, although it was 'well concealed'[18] in the 1989 European election campaign. The electoral success strengthened the forces in the party that worked towards what they regarded as a more pragmatic and realistic position. The 1989 autumn conference adopted a range of new additions to the *Manifesto for a Sustainable Society* which expressed a desire to change the EU from within. The key passage read:

> The Green Party proposes the creation of a European Confederation of Regions. The Confederation would have a European Parliament; the extent of its powers would be governed by its constituent regions. The Green Party opposes the structure of the European Community as presently constituted but favours continued membership seeking reform from within.[19]

The programme also set out specific proposals for institutional reform, such as the abolition of the Council of Ministers and a strengthening of the role of the European Parliament. The expansion of the EU to include the newly democratic countries of Eastern Europe was stated as a 'primary foreign policy objective', and support for 'the principle of a Social Chapter and community-wide social policies' was expressed.

Despite its record vote of 14.5 per cent nationwide, the British majority voting system denied the Green Party any representation in the European Parliament. In recognition of the achievement of the British Greens, the Green Group in the European Parliament was willing to give the party an institutionalized role and 'allowed for one or two Group members to share their voting rights within Group meetings with the [British] Green Party Representative'.[20] The party committed resources to this in creating a paid position for this purpose and sent one of its most experienced politicians, Jean Lambert, to play this role. Despite high hopes that this would raise the party's profile as it demonstrated its international acceptance and active participation in European affairs, the effect was short lived. The British Greens' involvement did not attract any substantial publicity or other benefits for its standing back in the UK. While the Green Group developed numerous activities, it suffered from the relative inattention of the national media to European Parliament matters unless they directly concerned atopical domestic political issues.[21]

The Green boom of 1989 and 1990 had been based on the increased salience of a variety of environmental issues. By the early 1990s, the political agenda in Britain changed substantially with the onset of the economic recession, and the Green Party's standing suffered as a result. One of the issues which dominated much of the debate in the early 1990s was Europe, with the negotiation and ratification of the Maastricht Treaty creating major difficulties for the government. In that context, one might have expected that the Greens could have benefited from the groundswell of anti-EU feeling, particularly as none of the established parties campaigned openly on an anti-Maastricht ticket. However, this was not to be the case.

The British Green Party opposed the Maastricht Treaty on the grounds that it centralized decision making, failed to provide adequate democratic accountability, paved the way for Western Europe to become an armed superpower, aimed to further economic growth which the party regarded as unsustainable and promoted policies which were likely to have a damaging effect on the environment.[22]

The 1992 General Election manifesto expressed clear opposition to the aims of the Maastricht Treaty:

substantial powers of self-determination should be devolved away from both the central British government and the European Commission, back to the hands of local people. Those who urge economic and political union in pursuit of the European Community's present aims do the world no service.[23]

However, by that time the Greens had become a marginal force in British politics, commanding no more than 1–2 per cent of the vote. Completely ignored by the media, their views on Europe did not gain them any publicity and brought no electoral benefits in 1992.

The Green Party went on to call for a referendum on the Maastricht Treaty in October 1992 and opposed its ratification.[24] A policy document, *Green Europe?*, was published in September 1993, setting out the party's objections to Maastricht in more detailed form.[25] But as the party kept being ignored by the media and with its following in the country remaining very small, it did not have any real influence on the Maastricht debate and the ratification process.

Arguably, the party did quite well in trying to adapt its European policies to the political realities of the day, fudging its commitment to leaving the EU in 1989 and emphasizing its critical stances towards the EU at the time of the Maastricht debate. With the presence of two passages in its fundamental programme with a somewhat different emphasis, activists could quote their favourite policy as desired. Despite its new European policy of accepting the EU as a framework for reform as adopted in 1989, the party's programme still contained the passage 'the Green Party is opposed to Britain's continuing membership of the European Economic Community, unless reconstituted on sound ecological principles'.[26] The 1992 General Election manifesto of the Green Party did not provide clarification, although it clearly veered towards the reformist approach. It stated: 'The European Community will need a radical reform of many of its policies, procedures and institutions.'[27] 'Ultimately, it is hoped the European Community will be replaced by a confederation of European regions, based on ecological and cultural boundaries.'[28]

But, clearly, the question remained whether the desired EU reforms were seen as a condition of continued EU membership or not. It was only with the 1994 European elections approaching that a clarification was finally considered necessary. The autumn conference of 1993 decided to combine the two previous statements on membership in the following new passage:

> As presently constituted, the European Community is fundamentally flawed, in its objectives, its structure, its relations with the rest of the world, and its impact on the biosphere. The Green Party favours continued membership of the EC while seeking reform from within, but opposes Britain's membership continuing in the long-term if the EC is not reconstituted on sound ecological principles.[29]

While this new version may have kept both camps of the debate happy, the problems of coming to a position on the EU reflected a genuine difference of opinion on European issues in the membership of the party.

A survey of Green Party members[30] asked about their attitude to Europe in November 1992. Table 15.2 compares their answers with those of the general population, with results from a survey taken shortly after the General Election of April 1992.[31] Overall, Greens are slightly more anti-European than the general public, but quite a sizeable part of their membership, almost 20 per cent, would like to go all the

Table 15.2 View of European integration in Britain

Question: What do you think Britain's long-term policy should be with regard to the European Community?

	Green Party members (1992)	General public (election study 1992)
Britain should leave the European Community	16.5	10.9
Britain should stay in the European Community but reduce its powers	41.3	31.8
Britain should leave things as they are	8.4	16.6
Britain should stay in the European Community and increase its powers	15.8	30.1
Britain should work for a single European government	18.0	10.5
	N = 1328	N = 2855

Sources: Green Party Membership Survey, 1992; British Elections Study, 1992.

way to a United Europe. Only a minority of Green Party members favour the extreme option of leaving the EU, but together with those seeking a reduction of powers, those wanting to reduce Britain's involvement are in a majority. We found that activists generally hold stronger anti-EU views than ordinary members. How to respond to EU developments is thus likely to be a question which will be of continued importance for the internal debate of the Greens.

THE GERMAN GREENS AND EUROPE

In Germany, Europe was never a serious political issue before the early 1990s. For *Die Grünen*, the EU was part of the established polity which was fiercely criticized, but it was rarely singled out for particular attention. The Greens were always highly critical of any form of renewed nationalism, and to most Greens, as for most other Germans, the EU provided a suitable international safety net within which the country could develop. The question of German membership of the EU thus never arose as a political issue in Germany. For the Greens, the main themes of its international policies were NATO and the stationing of nuclear weapons in Germany, Third World issues, and more recently, German unification. Beyond that, Green activists were almost exclusively oriented towards domestic policy issues, and the EU did not figure prominently in the Greens' political activity. Nevertheless, the history of the Greens is interlinked with European developments from the very start.

In Germany, the environmental conflicts of the 1970s had involved a wide variety of groups with different political orientations. Their coming together in a new party was by no means an easy or automatic process, particularly after a series of rival environmental parties had been formed at local and regional level. The first direct elections to the European Parliament in 1979 provided a focus for a temporary coalition of groups to come together for the first time at national level to fight a national-level election, facilitated by the less rigorous conditions which had to be met for lists to be admitted onto the ballot.

A number of Green parties and lists as well as other individuals and organizations not previously associated with party politics had come together in the summer of 1979 to form the 'Other Political Organization – the Greens' to contest the 1979 European elections. They did not include the anarchists and far left groups that were to join the Greens later. Nevertheless, the European election programme entitled *The Greens: Alternative for Europe* formulated many of the key policies which were to determine German Green thinking for many years. The first paragraph defined the key principles of Green politics: ecology, social responsibility, grass-roots democracy and non-violence. As for Europe itself, the programme proposed a 'Europe of the regions'.[32] The colour green was chosen for the party to stand for 'life, future and hope'.[33]

The Greens' first programme contained the key demands of the anti-nuclear movement for a non-nuclear, decentralized energy policy, and emphasized the complete reorganization of the economy according to ecological principles. While environmental demands dominated, the programme also devoted space to social and employment policy with an emphasis on the 'humanization of labour' and the reduction of working hours, human rights, the rights of minorities, the emancipation of women, children and youth, education and research, and information and media policy. The Greens rejected any notion of the EU being used for the creation of a European military bloc.

The programme contained remarkably few criticisms of the EU. The motivation of forming the EU as a bulwark against war in Europe was recalled, and the fight for the EU to remain a civil-economic alliance rather than military alliance was emphasized. Otherwise, the Greens saw the European Parliament as a force to push forward an ecological transformation process, and many measures clearly assumed major advances of the European unification process along ecological lines. The Greens demanded that the European Commission be accountable to the European Parliament which was to be elevated to supersede the Commission in importance. The programme foresaw a range of European initiatives, particularly in the areas of renewable energy sources, energy conservation, transport policy and health policy. A common taxation system was to be introduced throughout the EU, with only some minor variation in the size of tax rates according to regional conditions. The introduction of a new taxation regime was envisaged, providing incentives for the reduced use of energy and raw materials.

This generally benevolent view of European integration reflected to a major extent the generally favourable view prevalent in Germany at the time, but also the specific perception of many of those critical of German political institutions that a Europeanization of policy was to be welcomed. Petra Kelly, who played a crucial role in the early years of Green party politics, worked as an EU civil servant and had campaigned on various political issues within an EU context, including as a member of the Young European Federalists.[34]

The new Green organization scored 3.2 per cent in the elections, a good result for a new national group on its first attempt. The foundation of a new party, Die Grünen, in January 1980, followed on from this success.

The introduction of direct elections to the European Parliament thus had a profound effect on Green developments in Germany, providing an ideal political environment for the emergence of the new party. The substance of European policy, however, clearly played a very marginal role. The concept of the Europe of the Regions was not really elaborated, and the political context of the coming years provided no incentives for the German Greens to devote much attention to such a task.

With the integration of a variety of far left groups, the Green agenda had shifted markedly to the left since the 1979 European campaign. The first major programme of the political party Die Grünen, the Federal Programme of 1980, devoted just four out of forty-six pages to international issues. The theme of Europe only featured in terms of the debate about military security: the Greens demanded a demilitarized, neutral Europe free of nuclear weapons. The EU was not mentioned once in the entire programme.[35]

The European Election manifesto for the 1984 elections provided a more comprehensive statement of Green policies on Europe. The general tone of this document was different from that of the 1979 manifesto. The EU was now attacked quite vigorously. European institutions were accused of being remote, costly, bureaucratic and democratically unaccountable. The main focus of attack was, however, reserved for the EU's supposed attempt to create a European superpower which was roundly rejected. Even the plans for a further increase of the powers of the European Parliament were condemned as being not motivated by an attempt to democratize the EU but as part of the plan to develop the EU into a European superpower. The Greens explicitly presented themselves as 'part of a comprehensive movement which questions the European Community in its present form'.[36] This undesirable reality of the EU was contrasted with a 'Europe of the regions', involving a decentralization of decision-making processes to give primary powers to the 'historically grown regions'. Such a Europe could not be imposed from above, but had to grow from the grass roots, with local and regional movements seeking to replace 'capitalist competition' with a 'domination-free way of living and producing'.[37]

The 1984 programme demonstrates how the Green agenda had shifted to the left, with a fundamentalist critique of political institutions being combined with an essentially utopian political strategy, relying on the continued power of the 'new social movements' to challenge political systems. The fundamentalist position was increasingly challenged by the 'realists' as the 1980s progressed, but European issues were by no means central to that debate. Green party activists were largely uninterested in statements on European policy, and they were hardly discussed at party congresses. In the rest of the 1980s, the EU does not figure prominently in the Greens' programmatic development. But as the dominance of fundamentalist-utopian positions waned and 'realist' positions gained ground, policy positions on Europe tended to reflect a more pragmatic attitude.[38]

One key step in this process was the Reconstruction of Industrial Society programme passed in 1986. Here, the EU was mentioned more regularly, reflecting its importance for a range of policy issues. The programme mentioned the EU in the context of a damaging technological and economic race between the EU, Japan and the USA,[39] and it criticized the Common Agricultural Policy.[40] While it advocated a reorientation of the CAP along ecological lines, the programme did not demand any specific changes in EU policy making. Instead, it 'left open' the question of whether an ecological agricultural policy would be 'politically implementable' within the CAP.[41] Furthermore, the Greens complained about the lack of implementation of the EU drinking water directive[42] and declared their opposition to EU policies on the irradiation of food.[43] In terms of the formulation and implementation of ecological policies, the Greens demanded that the German government take the initiative at European level to push through strict regulations.[44] The EU was thus clearly accepted as part of the polity; membership was not an issue, and while some firm criticisms were made, the shape of EU institutions was not seen as a major political issue.

With Europe remaining a non-issue for most party activists and the national party showing little inclination to devote much attention to it, German Green MEPs were largely left to their own devices which allowed them to pursue their own political hobbyhorses. As Bomberg shows, the German MEPs in the Green Group developed radically different styles of dealing with the EU, ranging from an 'obstructionist' rejection of all EU institutions to 'reformists' and 'colluders' who saw some value in working within the EU framework to work for either reform from within or concrete policy results, such as the strengthening of EU environmental legislation.[45] However, German Green MEPs generally did not have a very high standing in the party and at home their activities were largely ignored.

Europe became a more important issue, however, with the revolutionary changes in Eastern Europe, German unification, and the debate about the Maastricht Treaty. From the very start, the position of the German Greens on the future shape of the EU was dominated by their social concerns for East Germany, and for other East European states. The image of (West) German industry colonizing Eastern Europe and taking advantage of low wages and lower environmental standards dominated Green perceptions of these issues.

A fairly comprehensive policy document dealing with the EU in the context of foreign economic policy was published by the German Green parliamentary group in the Bundestag in the 1990 election year. The *Concept for a Green Foreign Economic Policy* along the principles of 'ecology' and 'social justice' reiterated the usual Green criticisms of the EU but developed the lines of a policy of opening up the EU to Eastern Europe as the main policy tool. The document demanded the inclusion of all Eastern European states including the states of the former Soviet Union in an enlarged EU reconstituted along a federalist and decentralist concept of a 'whole' Europe.[46] The Greens' General Election manifesto again reiterated Green opposition to a militarization of the EU and the creation of a European superpower seeking economic and military dominance.[47]

The 1990 elections in a unified Germany were dominated by the electorate's embrace of unification, and the Green position was not rewarded. But it was only Maastricht, or, more precisely, the emergence of strong resistance to Maastricht in other European countries, which brought Europe onto the Green agenda in a more central way in the 1990s. The Maastricht Treaty forced the Greens for the first time to develop a more coherent European perspective. The main policy statement of the Greens was a motion adopted by the *Land* Council[48] of the party on 11 October 1992. The document is instructive in that it demonstrates very clearly the major differences between the German and British approaches. In the first part of the statement, the German Greens sought to demonstrate their pro-European credentials. In a key passage, the particular national context of German European policy was alluded to:

> Especially in view of increasing nationalistic and racist opinions and attacks in Germany and elsewhere, the Greens emphasize the importance and necessity of a European integration.[49]

Having established the necessity to proceed with European integration, the statement then reiterated the main criticisms (centralist, undemocratic, unecological, militaristic/repressive), but concentrated most strongly on the need to look towards Eastern Europe and the Third World. The main task of any European Union was not to close itself off from outside influences but to open up to assist the ecological and social reconstruction of Europe as a whole. The Greens were particularly critical of Sweden and Austria being singled out as first negotiation partners for the expansion of the Union.

Unlike the British Greens, the German statement also put particular emphasis on the social dimensions of the Treaty. While the British Greens had welcomed John Major's opt-out clause on the Social Chapter because it went beyond the competence the EU should have,[50] the German Greens strongly attacked the British opt out as an unwelcome attempt to exclude social concerns from the European project. They also criticized the provisions for employers and trades union associations to negotiate about social standards without the involvement of the European Parliament. Social policy was devolved to market forces at the time when the trade unions had been severely weakened.

Despite these strong reservations about Maastricht, there was little enthusiasm for an anti-Maastricht campaign. In June 1992, a 'left-alternative' alliance called 'Maastricht – not this way!' was formed which included the Greens, the Party of Democratic Socialism (the successor party of the East German Communist Party, the SED) and environmental and civil rights movements. The alliance demanded a referendum on Maastricht, but the response from the grass roots was muted. The main environmental groups soon found more important campaigns to devote their attention to, and the campaign just managed to convene one expert symposium. With all the major parties solidly behind Maastricht, there was never any realistic chance of preventing ratification with parliamentary means.

Then, suddenly, a new opportunity presented itself. After the Treaty had been ratified by both houses of parliament, four German Green MEPs went to the German Federal Constitutional Court to challenge the constitutional legality of the Maastricht Treaty with the argument that its provisions violated the 'eternal' German constitutional principles of 'federalism' and 'democracy'.[51] Rather than ruling that all complaints were 'inadmissible', as some had expected, the Federal Constitutional Court took up the points raised by the Greens and gave them prominence of place in a two-day hearing which, according to all German press reports, provided a moral victory for the Green case against Maastricht.[52] In the end, the court ruled in October 1993 that the Maastricht Treaty was compatible with the German Basic Law, but strongly affirmed that the further development of the European Union had to go hand in hand with a strengthening of democratic institutions, and stressed in particular the continued role of the Federal Parliament in such a process. Constitutional changes and other legislation enacted as part of the ratification process had already created new institutions to ensure the full participation of both houses of parliament and enhance the role of the *Länder* in the further development of the EU.

After their poor performance in 1990, the Greens had to come to terms with the political realities of the 1990s which included a unified Germany and the creation of the European Union. With internal reforms introduced in 1991 and most fundamentalists having left the party, and after merging with the political representative of the East German civil rights movements, Alliance '90, in 1993, the German Greens of the mid-1990s were a considerably more pragmatic force than in the 1980s. The 1994 European elections offered the opportunity, in the election programme of the new party Alliance '90/the Greens, to come to a new definition of European policy. The party did so in an extremely detailed and weighty programme.[53]

There are substantial continuities in the Green position: the critique of existing EU institutions and practices as insufficiently democratic and ecological was maintained. But compared with the utopian approach of the early 1980s, the 1994 programme set out quite detailed policy positions in a pragmatic way relating to the current framework of EU policy making. The concept of a Europe of the Regions was seen to have made a contribution to the debate leading to greater powers being given to the representation of regional and local interests in the Maastricht Treaty. The Greens demanded that even more powers should be given to the Regions, with the creation of a regional chamber playing a full part in the legislative process. But the programme acknowledged the differences between countries in the definition of what such 'regions' consisted of. In explicit recognition of criticisms made of the Greens' previous Europe of the Regions policy, the programme acknowledged the problem of how such regional bodies should be constituted in each case and left the solution open to be dealt with by future policy processes. This is indicative of the 'realistic' tone of the document which effectively refused to be drawn into a discussion of precisely what the 'ideal' Green EU would look like.

The Greens rejected the notion of the EU developing into a new superstate, a United States of Europe, and instead firmly embraced the principle of subsidiarity. Designs for a democratic, ecological Europe thus had to focus essentially on the role of the nation state and subnational government, and not on grandiose constitutional plans for the European level. The Greens here latched on to the judgement of the Federal Constitutional Court and the success of the German *Länder* in being recognized as important partners in the EU decision-making process both at European and at national level. The concept of subsidiarity was thus chiefly interpreted as part of a democratization and decentralization process, and not as an argument to weaken social and environmental standards agreed at EU level. Where the Greens wanted to see more forceful development was in the further enlargement of the EU. The Greens demanded that the EU draw up a specific timetable regarding the membership of East European countries after the EFTA countries joined.

The Greens made an explicit commitment to European integration which should embrace the whole of Europe. Despite the variety of criticisms of the EU, the Greens appeared to be reasonably well pleased with the way the EU decision-making process had taken shape in Germany.

The 1994 European Election programme could thus be interpreted as further evidence of the turning away from the moral fundamentalism which characterized the Green treatment of international issues in the 1980s towards more 'pragmatic' policy positions. However, such a change was clearly easier to undertake with regard to European issues which did not arouse the passions of party activists. The continued commitment to aims such as the abolition of NATO and the German Federal Army in the 1994 General Election manifesto[54] demonstrates that the new 'realist' leadership still had to contend with the political demands that fed the rise of the Greens in the early 1980s. The manifesto had its own section on foreign policy, but Europe again did not figure prominently. Perhaps significantly, the main

European passages can be found in a section entitled 'Against nationalism – in favour of Europe', containing a strong 'yes' to European integration, with most emphasis being placed on a 'democratization' of European institutions.[55] While the usual criticisms of the EU were reiterated, Alliance '90/the Greens announced their participation in the up-coming 'constitutional debate' about Europe to press home their demands for a democratic and ecological reform of the Union.

GREEN POLITICS AND EUROPEAN INTEGRATION: A COMPARATIVE ANALYSIS

The respective German and British Green party positions reflect the different histories and ideological roots of the parties and the national contexts of the European debates. The German Greens have a higher commitment to the welfare state and are generally more inclined to accept European integration as a basic premise for further policy development. While the particular national background made a radical anti-EU position more unlikely, Green European policy changed in line with the institutionalization of the party as an accepted part of the established polity. The different influence of left–right divisions is also striking: the German Greens are closer to traditional, state-oriented left thinking, as evidenced by their support for the Social Chapter and the position of trades unions. For the British Greens, it is the more left-anarchist wing of the party which has mobilized most strongly against European integration, while the more pragmatic 'right' is more pro-European but at the same time much less inclined to accept the imposition of what they would see as 'corporatist' principles in social policy.[56]

To what extent are the differences between the policy positions of the British and German Greens reflected in the views of their political supporters? Support for further European integration[57] is generally much stronger in Germany than in Britain. If we compare Green supporters with the general population (Table 15.3), we can find virtually no difference between the two groups in Germany. In Britain, on the other hand, Green supporters are even more sceptical of 'European government' than the rest of the population.

The opinion survey results presented in Table 15.3 allow us to draw some broader comparisons across the EU. Clearly, Denmark stands out in its opposition to the idea of 'European government', and Green supporters are even more strongly opposed to Europe. UK Green supporters are second after the Danes in terms of their anti-EU opinions. In the rest of the EU, the position of Green supporters appears to be generally in line with national sentiments. But, importantly, nowhere do Green parties clearly appear as rallying forces of a distinctive anti-EU position.

This result is generally matched by the policy positions adopted by Green parties. The key European policy issue of the 1990s was the Maastricht Treaty, and all Green parties across Europe opposed the Treaty in line with the general criticisms of Maastricht as expressed by the German and British Greens. The degree to which these parties could affect the outcome of national debates on the ratification of Maastricht varied enormously, however. In those countries where Green parties were represented in parliament, they generally voted against Maastricht in the full knowledge that the ratification of the Treaty would not be affected by this action. Therefore, generally more pro-European Green parties in the Benelux countries, Italy, and also Germany could live with this as a symbolic protest against the

Table 15.3 Support for European government, Spring 1992

Question: Are you for or against the formation of a European Union with a European government responsible to the European parliament?

		For (%)	Don't know (%)	Against (%)
Belgium	All	64.1	28.6	7.3
	Greens[a]	61.1	31.1	7.8
Denmark	All	25.8	9.8	64.4
	Greens	5.6	14.6	79.8
France	All	58.8	20.3	20.8
	Greens	62.8	24.4	12.8
Germany	All	57.3	23.3	19.4
	Greens	61.5	26.0	12.5
Greece	All	62.7	18.0	19.3
	Greens	63.4	3.4	33.2
Ireland	All	53.4	30.0	16.6
	Greens	62.7	11.3	26.0
Italy	All	76.2	15.0	8.9
	Greens	87.9	0.0	12.1
Luxembourg	All	57.2	20.0	22.8
	Greens	52.9	21.0	26.1
Netherlands	All	61.3	15.1	23.7
	Greens	63.9	7.8	28.3
Spain	All	64.7	24.5	10.8
	Greens	63.6	25.2	11.2
UK	All	36.0	28.4	35.6
	Greens	44.2	10.5	45.3

Notes: N = 12,774 (All EU countries)

[a] Supporters of Green parties were identified with the standard question: 'If there were a general election tomorrow, which party would you support?'

There are no figures for Portugal because the survey did not list the Green Party as one of the electoral choices.

Sources: Eurobarometer, vol. 37, March–April 1992; Reif 1993. I am grateful to the ESRC Data Archive for making this dataset available.

undemocratic aspects of the EU.[58] But in those countries where the ratification decision was left to a referendum, the choice of Green parties could have been rather more important.

The Danish Greens were clearly anti-Maastricht, but were only a marginal force in Danish politics, and the party has never managed to gain the 2 per cent of the national vote necessary to enter the national parliament. In Ireland, the Greens were also a rather marginal force at the time of the referendum: their national share of the vote was just 1.4 per cent in the November 1992 general elections. Irish Green supporters in spring 1992 were clearly rather positively inclined towards further European integration, with supporters outstripping opponents by 2 to 1. The Irish Green Party opposed Maastricht, but the anti-Maastricht campaign was dominated by forces seeking to protect Ireland's conservative stance on abortion and contraception. The referendum on 15 June 1992 brought a clear 69 per cent to 31 per cent majority in favour of ratification.

Perhaps the most interesting Green debate about Maastricht took place in France. Unlike in most other countries, the Greens' voice could have made some difference in the Maastricht debate. Following its success in the 1989 European elections, the French Greens managed to hold their poll standing up above 10 per cent. Faced with a referendum on Maastricht, the Greens were called to provide a recommendation to their supporters on how to vote. The usual arguments were listed for a rejection of the Treaty, but others within the Greens thought that the damage caused by toppling Maastricht would outweigh its costs. After an acrimonious discussion, the national decision-making body of Les Verts failed to come to a clear decision. The party split on the usual left–right lines, with Waechter for, Cochet against the Treaty. As a compromise, the Greens left it to the individual conscience of their supporters to make up their mind about Maastricht. Les Verts' rival for the ecological vote, Génération Ecologie led by Brice Lalonde, recommended voting in favour of the Treaty.[59] Opinion polls showed clearly that Lalonde's supporters were 2:1 in favour of the Treaty while Les Verts supporters were virtually evenly divided between supporters and opponents (53 per cent in favour, 47 per cent against) (*Paris Match*, 3 September 1992). France voted narrowly in favour of the ratification of Maastricht, 51 per cent to 49 per cent, on 20 September 1992.[60]

CONCLUSION

The Green campaign against the Maastricht Treaty had quite a limited effect on the ratification process. In no country did the Greens play a pivotal role in anti-Maastricht actions. It was usually other groups, such as sections within the British Conservatives or the French neo-Gaullists, that were at the forefront of opposition and gained most attention. Anti-EU sentiments were strong in countries such as the UK and Denmark,[61] but in both countries Green parties have remained relatively marginal and had no significant impact on the debate. The Maastricht debate could have provided a difficult problem for the established Green parties in Germany and the Benelux countries. But as all other major parties supported ratification, Green parties were spared any difficult choices which could have upset their attempts to present themselves as responsible and moderate political forces pursuing pragmatic policies.

In the future, Green parties may not find it so easy to draw up a common position on Europe.[62] There is a clear difference between the consistently Eurosceptical parties in the Scandinavian countries and in Britain and the established Green parties in Germany and the Benelux countries with their federalist position and greater willingness to work 'within' the EU. But, with time, the secessionist option is likely to be increasingly discredited, and it can be expected that eventually all European Green parties will concentrate more closely on the practical options available for the reform of existing institutions.

NOTES

1 There is a substantial comparative literature on the development of Green parties. Broad international overviews are given by S. Parkin, *Green Parties: An International Guide* (London, Heretic Books, 1989); F. Müller-Rommel (ed.), *New Politics in Western Europe: The Rise and Success of Green Parties and Alternative Lists* (Boulder, CO., Westview Press, 1989); and most recently, D. Richardson and C. Rootes (eds), *The Green Challenge: The Development of Green Parties in Europe* (London, Routledge, 1995).

2 For a book-length study of this topic, see E. Bomberg, *Green Parties and Politics in the European Community* (London, Routledge, 1995).

3 To avoid confusion, I use the term European Union also for all pre-Maastricht EU predecessors (EEC, EC, etc.) throughout this chapter, except, of course, in verbatim quotations pre-dating Maastricht.

4 However, the problems of the Green party to create a consensus position on Europe were arguably rather minor compared with the difficulties experienced by Labour and the Conservatives.

5 The party was formed as 'People' in 1973. It changed its name to Ecology Party in 1975 and to Green Party in 1986. In 1989, the Scottish Green Party became a fully independent, separate party. All post-1989 references thus exclude the Scottish Greens.

6 *A Manifesto for Survival* (Coventry, People, 1974), p. 25.

7 *Manifesto for a Sustainable Society* (Leeds, The Ecology Party, 1975), not paginated.

8 *The Real Alternative, Ecology Party 1979 Election Manifesto* (Birmingham, Ecology Party, 1979), p. 14.

9 Ibid.

10 *It's Your Europe, Your Future, Ecology Party Manifesto, European Elections 1979* (no place of publication, no date).

11 *Politics for Life, 1983 Election Manifesto* (London, Ecology Party, 1983), p. 20.

12 Ibid., p. 27.

13 *Manifesto for a Sustainable Society* (London, Ecology Party, n.d. (1983/4 version)), paragraph F200.

14 *The Green Party General Election Manifesto* (London, The Green Party, 1987), p. 21; cf. also pp. 24–5.

15 *Manifesto for a Sustainable Society* (London, The Green Party, 1989), p. 91.

16 Interview with Jean Lambert, Chair, Green Party Executive, 30 November 1993.

17 *Don't let your World turn Grey: The Green Party European Election Manifesto* (London, The Green Party, 1989), not paginated.

18 S. Dawe, 'Greens and the European Community', *Green Line*, no. 80, July/August 1990, p. 10.

19 *Manifesto for a Sustainable Society* (London, The Green Party, 1991), p. 30.

20 S. Lambert, 'The impact of the Green Group in the European Parliament', paper presented at ECPR, Colchester, March 1991, p. 3.

21 Within the Green Party, the reasons for this 'failure' to capitalize on the European election success are mainly discussed in terms of attributing blame to 'internal' factors, such as the lack of interest shown in Europe by party activists or the actions of the party's representative in Europe. However, as with most other aspects of the recent development of the party, the hostile external conditions appear to play a far more important role in explaining the party's failure: see W. Rüdig, L.G. Bennie and M.N. Franklin, *Green Blues: The Rise and Decline of the British Greens*, Strathclyde Papers in Government and Politics, no. 95 (Glasgow, Department of Government, University of Strathclyde, 1993).

22 'The Maastricht Treaty', Policy statement of the Green Party Regional Council, October 1992, reprinted in *Manifesto of Policy Statements 1990–3*, compiled by J. Morrissey (London, Green Party, 1993), pp. 9–11.

23 *New Directions: The Path to a Green Britain Now, General Election Policy Manifesto 1992* (London, The Green Party, 1992), p. 16.

24 'The Maastricht Treaty'.

25 *Green Europe? A Green View of European Integration* (London, The Green Party, 1993).

26 Ibid., p. 26.

27 *New Directions: The Path to a Green Britain Now, General Election Campaign Manifesto 1992* (London, The Green Party, 1992), p. 10.

28 Ibid., p. 17.

29 *Final Agenda, Green Party AGM*, Hastings I, 1993, p. 49; and *List of Conference Decisions*, complied by D. Johnson (London, Green Party, 1993). The party's European Election manifesto provided a summary of Green criticism of the EU and proposals for a reform of EU institutions but did not mention the issue of continued membership.

Instead, the emphasis now appears to be firmly on specific proposals involving reviews of individual pieces of EU legislation; The Green Party, *European Election Manifesto 1994: the Green Vision of Europe* (London, The Green Party, 1994).

30 For details of the surveys, see Rüdig et al., *Green Blues*, and *Green Party Members: A Profile* (Glasgow, Delta Publications, 1991).

31 Data: British Election Study. I am grateful to John Curtice for providing me with the results for this question.

32 *Die Grünen. Alternative für Europa* (Bonn, Bundesbüro der Grünen, not dated, [1979]), p. 1. I am grateful to the archive of the Greens for making a copy of this document accessible to me. All translations of German texts are mine.

33 Ibid., p. 2.

34 S. Parkin, *The Life and Death of Petra Kelly* (London, Pandora, 1994), p. 71.

35 *Bundesprogramm 1980* (Bonn, Die Grünen, 1980), pp. 18–21.

36 *Global denken – vor Ort handeln! Erklärung der GRÜNEN zur Europawahl am 17. Juni 1984* (Bonn, Bundesvorstand der Grünen, 1984), p. 10.

37 Ibid., p. 39.

38 E.G. Frankland and D. Schoonmaker, *Between Protest and Power: The Green Party in Germany* (Boulder, CO, Westview Press, 1992), chapter 6.

39 *Umbau der Industriegesellschaft. Schritte zur Überwindung von Erwerbslosigkeit. Armut und Umweltzerstörung* (Bonn, Die Grünen, 1986), p. 6.

40 Ibid., p. 25.

41 Ibid., p. 27.

42 Ibid., p. 19.

43 Ibid., p. 29.

44 Ibid., p. 108.

45 Bomberg, *Green Parties and Politics*.

46 *Auf dem Weg zu einer ökologisch-solidarischen Weltwirtschaft. Konzept für eine grüne Außenwirtschaftspolitik* (Bonn, Die Grünen im Bundestag, 1990), p. 35.

47 Die Grünen, *Das Programm zur 1. gesamtdeutschen Wahl 1990* (Bonn, Die Grünen, 1990).

48 This body consists of representatives of the leadership of Green *Land* parties and was created as part of the organizational reforms of 1991 which led to the exodus of most members of the fundamentalist wing of the party; see T. Poguntke, *Alternative Politics: The German Greens* (Edinburgh, Edinburgh University Press, 1993), p. 168.

49 'Die Grünen zu den Maastricher Beschlüssen: So nicht!, beschlossen auf dem Länderrat am 11.10.1992 in Kassel', reprinted in Breyer, H., Graefe zu Baringdorf, F.-W., Roth, C. and W. Telkämper, *Europa Ja – Maastricht Nein. Dokumentation der Verfassungsbeschwerde gegen die Maastricher Verträge* (Bonn, Europagruppe Die Grünen, 1993), p. 46.

50 This position is, however, controversial within the Greens. Others approve of the Social Chapter. (Interview with Jean Lambert, 30 November 1993).

51 Apart from the Green MEPs, others challenged Maastricht in the Court, mainly from the far right of the political spectrum. British accounts of this episode generally gave far more prominence to these nationalistic elements and often did not mention the Greens at all.

52 See the press documentation in Breyer et al., *Europe Ja – Maastricht Nein*.

53 *Lieber Europa erweitern als Demokratie beschränken, Programm zur Europawahl 1994* (Bornheim, Bündnis '90/Die Grünen, 1994).

54 *Nur mit uns. Programm zur Bundestagswahl 1994* (Bornheim, Bündnis '90/Die Grünen, 1994).

55 Ibid., pp. 56–7.

56 See L.G. Bennie, M.N. Franklin and W. Rüdig, 'Green dimensions: the ideology of the British Greens', in W. Rüdig (ed.), *Green Politics Three* (Edinburgh, Edinburgh University Press, 1995), pp. 217–39. for an analysis of the ideological dimensions of British Green politics.

57 There are numerous measurements of 'support for European integration'. The one I chose for the analysis in Table 15.3 seemed most likely to capture the basic attitudes on the future of the EU.

58 In Belgium, for example, there was a debate amongst Greens about whether they should vote in favour of Maastricht to express fundamental support for the concept of European integration. The fact that their vote had no practical impact on the ratification decision clearly made it easier for all Green MPs to vote against; interview with Pierre Jonckheer, ECOLO, Member of the Sénat, 3 November 1993.

59 'Traité de Maastricht, Résolution du Conseil national interrégional des Verts: 30 août 1992', in: *Recueil (non-exhaustif) de textes des Verts sur Maastricht* (Gentilly, Les Verts, Secrétariat national, 1992), pp. 4–5; interview with Niki Kortvelyessy, Green Party International Secretary, September 1992.

60 A. Duff, 'Ratification', in A. Duff, J. Pinder and R. Pryce (eds), *Maastricht and Beyond: Building the European Union* (London, Routledge, 1994), pp. 53–68.

61 Attitudes in the UK and Denmark have consistently been less supportive of European integration than in other members states throughout the 1970s and 1980s; see R.C. Eichenberg and R.J. Dalton, 'Europeans and the European Community: the dynamics of public support for European integration', *International Organization*, vol. 47, 1994, pp. 507–34.

62 For a detailed analysis of the programmatic developments of the European co-ordination bodies of Green parties, see Bomberg, *Green Parties*.

SELECT BIBLIOGRAPHY

Anderson, J.G., 'Denmark: environmental conflict and the "greening" of the Labour movement', *Scandinavian Political Studies*, vol. 13, 1990, pp. 185–210.

Ashford, N., 'The political parties', in George, S. (ed.), *Britain and the European Community: The Politics of Semi-Detachment*, Oxford, Clarendon Press, 1992, pp. 119–48.

Bennie, L.G., Franklin, M.N. and Rüdig, W., 'Green dimensions: the ideology of the British Greens', in W. Rüdig (ed.), *Green Politics Three*, Edinburgh, Edinburgh University Press, 1994, pp. 217–39.

Bomberg, E., 'The German Greens and the European Community: dilemmas of a movement-party', *Environmental Politics*, vol. 1, no. 4, 1992, pp. 160–85.

Bomberg, E., *Green Parties and Politics in the European Community* (London, Routledge, 1995).

Dawe, S., 'For a green EEC', *Green Line*, no. 20, March 1984, pp. 14–15.

Dawe, S., 'Greens and the European Community', *Green Line*, no. 80, July/August 1990, pp. 10–11.

Duff, A., 'Ratification', in Duff, A., Pinder, J. and Pryce, R. (eds), *Maastricht and Beyond: Building the European Union* (London, Routledge, 1994) pp. 53–68.

Eichenberg, R.C. and Dalton, R.J., 'Europeans and the European Community: the dynamics of public support for European integration', *International Organization*, vol. 47, 1994, pp. 507–34.

Frankland, E.G. and Schoonmaker, D., *Between Protest and Power: The Green Party in Germany*, Boulder, CO, Westview Press, 1992.

Hubert, H.P./Bundesarbeitsgemeinschaft Frieden und Internationalismus der Grünen (eds), *Grüne Aussenpolitik: Aspekte einer Debatte*, Göttingen, Verlag Die Werkstatt, 1993.

Hugenroth, R. (ed.), *Kein leichter Weg nach Eurotopia. Maastricht – so nicht*, Bonn, Pahl-Rugenstein Nachfolger, 1993.

Lambert, J., 'The impact of the Green Group in the European Parliament', paper presented at the ECPR Meetings, Colchester, March, 1991.

Marsh, M., 'Ireland', *European Journal of Political Research*, vol. 24, 1991, pp. 455–66.

Müller-Rommel, F. (ed.), *New Politics in Western Europe: The Rise and Success of Green Parties and Alternative Lists*, Boulder, CO, Westview Press, 1989.

Parkin, S., *Green Parties: An International Guide*, London, Heretic Books, 1989.

Parkin, S., *The Life and Death of Petra Kelly*, London, Pandora, 1994.

Poguntke, T., *Alternative Politics: The German Greens*, Edinburgh, Edinburgh University Press, 1993.

Reif, K., *European Unity, Environmental Concern, Alcohol and Drug Use, March–April 1992* [computer file], Colchester, ESRC Data Archive, 1993.

Richardson, D. and Rootes, C. (eds), *The Green Challenge: The Development of Green Parties in Europe*, London, Routledge, 1995.

Rüdig, W., Bennie, L.G. and Franklin, M.N., *Green Party Members: A Profile*, Glasgow, Delta Publications, 1991.

Rüdig, W. and Franklin, M.N., 'Green prospects: the future of green parties in Britain, France and Germany', in W. Rüdig (ed.), *Green Politics Two*, Edinburgh, Edinburgh University Press, 1992, pp. 37–58.

Rüdig, W., Franklin, M.N. and Bennie L.G., *Green Blues: The Rise and Decline of the British Greens*, Strathclyde Papers in Government and Politics, no. 95, Glasgow, Department of Government, University of Strathclyde, 1993.

Rüdig, W. and Lowe, P., 'The "withered" greening of British politics: a study of the Ecology Party', *Political Studies*, vol. 34, 1986, pp. 262–84.

Part III
The European Union

16 How European are European elections?

Julie Smith

European elections provide an arena for national and European political parties to co-operate. The aim of this chapter is to consider how far they interact, how far this takes us towards truly transnational elections and what the implications are for electoral politics at the European level. Taking the 1994 election to the European Parliament (EP) as a case study, we look particularly at what it shows about: the evolution of European political integration; and the difference between political cultures in the European Union (EU) and nation states.

The nature and scope of formal party links in terms of transnational manifestos and other forms of joint activity are outlined briefly. However, the main focus is on activity in the twelve member states, looking especially at Britain, France, Germany and Spain. The reason for this approach is that in 1994, as on previous occasions, European elections were dominated by domestic issues and national political parties. Nevertheless, it is our contention that by 1994 the situation was changing: domestic and European politics were becoming ever more intertwined and the role of European political parties was growing.

HISTORY

> What is lacking under the present system is an election about European issues. Such a campaign would force those entitled to vote to look at and examine the questions and the various options on which the European Parliament would have to decide in the months and years ahead. It would give the candidates who emerged victorious from such a campaign a truly European mandate from their electors; and it would encourage the emergence of truly European political parties.[1]

So wrote former President of the Commission, Walter Hallstein, in 1972, prior to the introduction of direct elections to the European Parliament. The underlying implication of his words is obvious: direct elections would foster just the sort of campaign on European issues which Professor Hallstein sought. Yet when electors cast their votes in June 1994, this scenario still seemed to lie in the future.[2] People across the European Union had the opportunity to vote as 'citizens of the Union' for the first time in the 1994 European Parliament election.[3] Direct elections had been held on three previous occasions – 1979, 1984 and 1989 – and the experience of those elections did not offer much cause for celebration among advocates of transnational democracy. While the prospect of direct elections had been greeted with enthusiasm by Members of the European Parliament (MEPs), this emotion was not shared by voters or national politicians.

Turnout in 1979 (with an EC average of 65.9 per cent) was lower than MEPs and the Commission had hoped for; in 1984 and 1989 it fell still further. Moreover, although transnational party federations had been created in the mid-1970s, the elections right across the European Community (EC)[4] were characterized by a focus on national issues; national parties tended to fight on national manifestos, paying only lipservice to the manifestos produced by the European party federations; and national politicians tended to dominate the campaigns. Small, new and protest parties such as the German Greens performed well at the expense of large parties, whether of government or opposition.[5] This led Karlheinz Reif to describe them as 'second-order elections', more like local elections than national general elections. Since there was less at stake than in general elections, citizens were both less inclined to vote and, when they did vote, more prone to cast protest votes.[6]

Although the idea of direct elections to a European assembly was enshrined in a treaty as early as the 1951 Treaty of Paris establishing the European Coal and Steel Community (ECSC), moves towards such elections were painfully slow. Even when elections were finally introduced, in 1979, the rules were determined nationally.[7] Despite the treaty provision for the EP to draw up proposals for a uniform electoral system, by 1994 there was still little uniformity in the electoral rules in force.[8] Eleven of the twelve member states used some form of proportional representation (PR), but there were considerable differences in the electoral rules in force. Denmark, France, Germany, Greece, Luxembourg, the Netherlands, Portugal and Spain all used single national constituencies;[9] Belgium, Ireland and Italy had regional constituencies. Ireland used the single transferable vote (STV) system, while the other ten countries used list forms of PR. In some cases voters had a choice of candidates, in others they were presented with a rigid party list, allowing no choice of candidates. Legal thresholds for representation – for example a 5 per cent threshold in France and Germany – were in force in some states. Great Britain continued to use the single member plurality ('first-past-the-post') system, although the three seats in Northern Ireland were allocated by a form of proportional representation.

The absence of a common electoral system, coupled with the fact that, given differing national traditions, elections did not take place on the same day, was seen by some commentators as a way of explaining the difficulties experienced in organizing common election campaigns.[10] Problems undoubtedly do arise from the lack of a common electoral system. The British system had a particularly large effect, with small changes in votes in Britain causing large shifts in the balance of party groups in the EP.[11] However, other factors are more significant in giving the elections a national focus:

1　The fact that European elections did not directly lead to a change in government nor to major changes of direction in policy making, and the perception of the EP as a powerless institution made it difficult to mobilize voters by campaigning on 'European' themes.
2　The nature of European identity, at best very weak, ensured that it was hard to interest voters in elections on European issues. Indeed, we argue that this is indicative of how different the European Union still is from traditional states.

3 The lack of transnational media, in turn a result of the absence of a common European language, meant that cross-border activity would be unlikely to gain coverage.[12]

These factors largely explain the nature of the early European elections: the EP had few powers in 1979 and, despite the impartial information campaigns under-taken by the Commission in the run up to the elections, there was little awareness of the elections.[13] European elections did not have any major impact on how the European Community was governed and it was not therefore surprising that other issues should predominate. By the 1989 elections, the powers of the European Parliament had been considerably strengthened by the Single European Act (SEA) and it might have been expected that this would lead to increased interest in European elections.

How had the situation changed by 1994? How much transnational activity was there? Were the campaigns more integrated and more directed towards the European Union? Were the results significant in domestic or European terms?

THE 1994 ELECTIONS

Background

Several positive factors gave politicians reason to hope that greater interest would be evoked by the 1994 elections than had previously been the case. Three points are of particular importance in this respect. First, the powers of the European Parliament had been substantially increased under the provisions of the Maastricht Treaty. For the first time, the incoming Parliament would have a vote of confir-mation of the Commission and could veto legislation in certain policy areas (true of the 1989–94 Parliament from 1 November 1993).[14] Following changes in their Rules of Procedure, Members of the outgoing Parliament expressed their intention of holding Congressional style hearings for the nominees for the College of Commissioners, and of voting on the presidential candidate separately. Although only granted the right of consultation over the choice of president, parliamentarians felt that a candidate rejected by the EP was unlikely to persist in his or her quest for the presidency. MEPs initially expressed the hope that the composition of the Commission and the choice of president could be linked to the EP election. Thus, a Parliament with a socialist majority would have pressed for a candidate of the left, such as the Spanish prime minister, Felipe González, as Commission President, whereas a majority for the EPP might have resulted in the selection of a Christian democrat, the most frequently postulated at the time being the outgoing Dutch prime minister, Ruud Lubbers. Such a campaign could have given voters a sense that there was a clear-cut choice at the polls and, perhaps, a sense that the elections mattered. It soon became clear, however, that this would not happen in the 1994 elections and by the time the election campaigns began the issue was scarcely mentioned.[15] The co-decision procedure introduced by the Maastricht Treaty gave the Parliament a more important role in the legislative process of the Union than had previously been the case. While still unable to introduce legislation, by 1994 the Parliament could veto legislation in several policy areas, giving it significant leverage over the Commission and the Council of Ministers. Thus, voters had the opportunity to elect an institution which was gradually being taken far more seriously by the other European institutions, to which it had traditionally been very subordinate. European elections still did not lead to European government formation – indeed the concept of 'government' at the European level remains blurred – or to a direct impact on policy formation. However, the growing influence of the EP meant that the elections would affect European decision making. Again, this influence on the policy process offered the potential for a shift towards more coherent transnational party campaigning.

Second, with a new intergovernmental conference (IGC) to revise the Maastricht Treaty and discuss institutional reform of the Union scheduled for 1996, there was scope for discussion of the future direction of the European Union. Complications surrounding ratification of the Maastricht Treaty (which was rejected in the first Danish referendum on 2 June 1992) partly resulted from a sense of elites running ahead of their peoples. The 1994 elections could have been an ideal opportunity for the future of the Union to be discussed and for proposals to be put to voters before any new decisions were taken in 1996. Indeed, this would have been the only opportunity for voters in some member states to be consulted at all.

Finally, the depth of the recession led many to argue that the solution to the problem of unemployment was only to be found at the European level. In his white paper published in December 1993, Commission President Delors proposed a set of policies to help reduce unemployment across the EU.[16] The political parties all suggested that it was an issue to be tackled at the European level.

Apart from the greater interest in the elections that these issues might have been expected to bring about, there was reason to think that more emphasis might be placed on European issues. Environmental policies had already come to be considered as European issues. Now, unemployment and immigration could be considered in the same category. The problems of immigration varied between member states (for example, the French are concerned about an influx from North Africa, the Germans about immigrants from East/Central Europe), but could nevertheless be viewed as problems best tackled on an EU-wide basis.

There were thus several reasons for thinking both that the 1994 election might raise more interest than previous EP elections, and that more 'European' issues might be raised. Such a scenario would have fulfilled the hopes of former president of the European Parliament, Emilio Colombo, when he declared in 1977 that:

> The election of the European Parliament by direct universal suffrage provides an opportunity of bringing debate on Europe into the public forum and of enlisting the active support of the man in the street for the construction of Europe.[17]

However, unlike the 1989 election which took place in a period of relative Euro-euphoria in the wake of the Single European Act, the election of 1994 took place against a background of disillusionment with politics and politicians, a long-term recession, high unemployment and increasing hostility towards the European Union. These factors had an impact not only in countries traditionally sceptical about European integration, notably Britain and Denmark, but also in France, Germany and Italy.

Two somewhat contradictory forces were therefore in evidence in 1994. The European Parliament was more important than in the past and there was an expanding number of policy areas that could be seen as 'European', providing a positive dimension to European elections. Against this must be set the declining support for further European integration, seen across the Union. The impact of these factors on the elections in terms of national versus transnational activity and interest in the elections is the question to which we now turn.

THE TRANSNATIONAL PARTY DIMENSION

As Simon Hix's chapter in this volume points out, the main political families responded to the prospects of direct elections by strengthening their formal links.[18] Initially, this took the form of party federations – the Socialists formed the Confederation of Socialist Parties (CSP) in 1974, the Christian democrats the European People's Party (EPP) in 1976, the year also when the various liberal parties established the Federation of European Liberals, Democrats and Reformers (ELDR). Green Parties followed suit in 1993, with the formation of the European Federation of Green Parties. By 1994, the three larger federations had all officially become political parties. There were several reasons for the change. One in particular was the reference to political parties in the Maastricht Treaty.[19] This first mention of political parties in the context of a European treaty led some people to predict that this might prefigure funding of European political parties. As shown below, however, the question of funding political parties is a thorny issue. As of 1994, the formal shift from federation to party had not had a major impact on the activities of the Party of European Socialists (PES), the EPP or the ELDR party at least in electoral terms.[20]

Manifestos

Transnational parties bring together parties from the member states and the party groups which sit in the European Parliament, acting as a conduit between them. Their most significant role in the European elections is to co-ordinate transnational party manifestos.[21] National parties have accepted the manifestos of the transnational parties they belonged to with varying degrees of enthusiasm. Since the European Parliament does not set the legislative agenda of the Union, the manifestos have tended to be more symbolic than statements of intent. Differing political traditions in member states and the consequent need for compromise, plus the use of several languages in negotiating the manifestos mean that the documents which emerge offer little more than platitudes.[22]

Over the years, the socialists evolved from a fairly loose confederation of parties to become the most coherent transnational party, partly because of a shift in the direction of the Community from one which focused on free-market issues, to one with a social dimension. In contrast to the first three elections, when the British and Danish Labour Parties opted out of large sections of the CSP manifesto, the 1994 document contained only one footnote, to the effect that the manifesto should be read in the light of the Edinburgh Conclusions.[23] The ELDR party objected to a similar point being inserted into its manifesto, since members felt that it would imply tacit support for more opt outs in the future. This led the left-wing Danish Liberals, Det Radikale Venstre, to vote against the entire manifesto.

The various liberal parties had the greatest difficulty in negotiating their common manifesto. Member parties of the ELDR reflect widely diverging political cultures: the German Free Democrats and Dutch Liberals (VVD) are more traditional economic liberals than the Liberal Democrats or the smaller Dutch party D'66, which is also a member of ELDR. British Liberals have non-conformist origins, marking them out from many of their continental colleagues who come from anti-clerical backgrounds. In addition, the desire to exclude the Walloon Liberals from the party added a further complication to the negotiations for the 1994 manifesto.

Originally the most cohesive of the parties in ideological terms, the EPP's homogeneity gradually eroded with the entry of Greek, Spanish and French MEPs whose approaches to European integration were frequently at odds with those of the traditional Christian democrat members.[24] Nevertheless the party produced a manifesto strong on federalist rhetoric in 1994. Because its candidates fought on a joint list with the Union pour la démocratie française (UDF), even the Gaullist Rassemblement pour la république (RPR), traditionally in favour of a Europe of nation states, adopted the EPP manifesto.

The European Federation of Green Parties was the only other group to put forward a transnational manifesto.

The EPP, PES and ELDR manifestos differed from each other in detail rather than major substance; the Green manifesto was significantly different in terms of its vision of Europe. The manifestos all mentioned the main policy issues at stake – unemployment; environmental policy; institutional reform, especially in terms of a reduction of the so-called 'democratic deficit' in European decision making; economic and monetary union; a common foreign and security policy; asylum and immigration policy; and enlargement of the Union.[25] 'European' issues were thus raised at least in the context of the transnational manifestos.

Funds

The party groups in the European Parliament receive funds for secretarial and information purposes. Originally the groups tended to distribute the information money to their constituent national parties, which then used them to fund the European election campaigns. However, the European Court of Justice (ECJ) upheld a case brought by the French Greens that this discriminated against parties not already represented in the EP.[26] Subsequently, money was distributed to the groups as a whole for information activities; such funding stops at the end of February prior to the European elections.[27]

Campaign activities

Attempts to extend the role of the European parties have been fraught with difficulties. The PES did arrange several meetings, focused on specific issues, such as women's rights, in the run up to the elections. By contrast, the ELDR considered the idea of a transnational rally but could not decide on a venue or what sort of activity should be undertaken. The parties offered member parties facilities for inviting speakers from other countries to election rallies, but logistics, especially in terms of timing and language, meant such activities remained limited. One small example demonstrates the complexities of EU-wide co-operation. When trying to compile an electoral map of Europe, an official from one of the main party groups encountered a whole set of complications: the Greeks objected to the use of the name 'Macedonia' for the former Yugoslav republic; the Irish to the listing of member parties and so on.[28] Such matters, while apparently minor, are symptomatic of the problems facing elections above the national level.

The ELDR produced a common poster for the first time since 1979. The PES adopted a logo (three red roses), to be used by all the member parties, and a slogan: 'A Europe for the People'. Like the EPP, the PES had common leaflets to be distributed in the member states. These differed only slightly in order to accommodate regional politico-linguistic differences. In addition, there were support materials, such as videos, which could be used as appropriate for the different member states, for example in the form of party political broadcasts in Britain. Although the role of the transnational parties had increased by 1994, they still played a very subordinate part compared with national parties. It is to the role of national parties in the European campaigns that we now turn.

THE NATIONAL DIMENSION

There are, of course, direct links between the national and European parties in the elections. National parties which are members of the transnational parties are expected to accept their European manifestos, or at least not to contradict them. In practice, as implied earlier, the manifestos have tended to count for little. It was hard to distinguish between the parties on the basis of rather bland manifestos, which in any case serve to inform the activists, not the voters. Just how much emphasis was placed on European issues and manifestos varied from state to state and from party to party. Where elections took place at the same time as national elections, national matters invariably overshadowed European issues and elections. In 1994, only Luxembourg had national and European elections coinciding. The creation of European citizenship was a major election issue in Luxembourg, because it heightened awareness among Luxembourgers about the numbers of non-nationals living and working there. It is hard to categorize such an issue as European or domestic; rather it is an example of just how far domestic and European politics had become enmeshed.

Occurring in the wake of general elections in the Netherlands and Italy, the European elections took second place to continuing debates over the formation of governments. In Italy they were a test for the new *Forza Italia!* movement of media magnate Silvio Berlusconi. The campaign suggested a shift away from the traditionally pro-integration stance of post-war Italian politicians, with the new foreign minister openly anti-Maastricht. There was an added twist in the European elections: the old regional list system of proportional representation, abandoned for national elections, was used. There was thus a possibility that the alliances forged for the general election held under a first-past-the-post system might break down. With the composition of the government still not clear following the general election of 3 May, the Dutch elections were even more low key than usual, a point reflected in a turnout figure of 35.6 per cent for the European election.

National electoral cycles had a significant impact in other member states as well. In Britain, the election was the only nationwide test of the Conservative government between general elections and John Major's future as prime minister was seen to be at stake. The two main opposition parties were both keen to play down the

European aspect of the campaign in favour of using the elections as a mid-term referendum on the Major government. Facing record low levels of support in the opinion polls, the Conservatives hoped to minimize their losses by concentrating on European issues. By attacking the opposition parties who, they claimed, wanted to give up Britain's veto, the Tories hoped to woo back those voters hostile to further European integration. However, the deep divisions which campaign managers hoped had been overcome in the aftermath of the Maastricht ratification debate re-emerged. To an extent, the election did offer some sort of European debate, but it fell far short of giving voters a clear pro-system, anti-European or anti-Maastricht choice; indeed splits within the Conservative Party proved to be deeper than those between the parties. The British electoral system ensured that such intra-party differences could not be translated into choices for the voters.

Labour and the Liberal Democrats adopted the PES and ELDR transnational manifestos respectively, but supplemented them with national ones. The Labour Party demonstrated its recently found commitment to the EU by making use of PES material. The party's campaign was overshadowed by the death of its leader, John Smith, and by the race for his successor. Although no campaigning for the leadership was supposed to start until after the European elections, the issue was simmering throughout June. In the hope of maximizing its support, the most pro-European of the British parties, the Liberal Democrats, played down its European credentials, with a manifesto emphasizing national issues.

National considerations initially looked set to overshadow the elections in France as well. The parties of the moderate right, the UDF and RPR formed a joint list, and pledged to fight on an EPP platform for the 1994 elections. This represented a large shift for the RPR, the Gaullist party, traditionally opposed to a federal Europe. Such a shift was a price the RPR was willing to pay to secure UDF support for its presidential candidate in 1995. As a result of this arrangement, a rather bizarre situation arose with the list of candidates being composed alternately of pro- and anti-Maastricht candidates.

Domestic politics also played a part when a group of intellectuals threatened to put up a list, Europe begins at Sarajevo, which called for the arming of Bosnian Muslims. While the substantive issue related to European defence, the response of Socialist leader, Michel Rocard, reflected his anxiety over whether he would be the left's candidate for the 1995 presidential election. Two new lists emerged, however, which did not arise directly from domestic politics. Anti-Maastricht campaigner, Philippe de Villiers, formed a Eurosceptic list, L'autre Europe, with Sir James Goldsmith. Businessman Bernard Tapie created a left-wing, pro-European list, Energie radicale, based on the old Mouvement des radicaux de gauche. The presence of these very different lists distinguished the elections from both national elections and the European election in other countries, where traditional national parties continued to dominate.

The two largest Spanish parties, the Popular Party (PP) and the Socialists, showed that the use of transnational manifestos, which would seem to imply strong European credentials, may mean little in practice. For the Popular Party (which comprises conservatives, liberals and Christian democrats), divided over European issues, there was little to gain from fighting a campaign on European issues, since that would only reveal its divisions. The elections offered the PP a chance to defeat the Socialists in a national poll for the first time. Corruption scandals, in which certain prominent Socialists were implicated, came to light during the election and dominated the campaign. The focus of the elections, therefore, was much more on national than European politics.

Germany had nineteen elections scheduled in 1994, with the European elections falling in the middle of the election period. This raised the prospect both of voter fatigue and of elections which were viewed as an indicator for the October election to the Bundestag. The elections also took place in the context of declining support for Europe among voters. Nevertheless, the Christian Democrats (CDU), the Social Democrats (SPD) and the Free Democrats (FDP) fought strongly pro-European campaigns. They were opposed by a burgeoning number of anti-European or, more accurately, anti-Maastricht parties, especially in Bavaria, the home of the far right Republikaner Party, and of Manfred Brunner's newly formed League of Free Citizens. The CDU's sister party, the Christian Social Union (CSU), only presents lists in Bavaria and so needed to obtain around 40 per cent of the Bavarian vote to ensure it reached the 5 per cent national threshold. Following German unification in 1990, this task had become harder. In an apparent attempt to woo some of the anti-European vote and retain his party's representation in Strasbourg, Edmund Stoiber, minister president of Bavaria and CSU leader, made some speeches rejecting a federal approach to Europe. This approach put him somewhat at odds with coalition partners, especially the extremely pro-European Chancellor Kohl.

CAMPAIGN ISSUES

We can see that in 1994 national actors still dominated European campaigns, despite a slight shift towards more transnational activity. Yet this situation did not necessarily entail a situation of domestic issue predominance. Whether an issue becomes salient in an election depends very much on the media, which focus on some issues more than others. In 1994 this meant that an issue such as institutional reform of the European Union was not the main topic for debate in any of the member states. The main exception to this was Britain where, although the campaigns were primarily related to domestic politics, the Conservatives did succeed in putting the issue of the 'veto'[29] on the agenda.

On the rare occasions, such as in the Netherlands in 1979, when questions relating to European integration were raised, the outcome has been one of resounding voter apathy. The exceptions to the pattern have been few and far between: in their first European elections in 1981, the Greek parties differed significantly in their attitudes towards the European Union. Since the elections coincided with national elections, the European poll was largely overshadowed.

Denmark is the only country where voters have traditionally had an opportunity to vote on European integration in the EP elections. Voters hostile to the EC could vote for the People's Movement Against the EC, in elections which have been fought like reruns of the 1972 referendum. After the referendums on Maastricht, the People's Movement shifted to a position of 'thus far and no further'. This led to the emergence of newer anti-Maastricht parties, in particular the June Movement. For the first time, in 1994 voters hostile to the Union or to further integration had two lists to choose from.

In the main, issues concerning the future direction of the Union were still not a part of the electoral process, although issues with a European dimension were. One of the unusual features about the German election was the attention paid to bananas. Germany has traditionally been a large banana importer and there was dissatisfaction with the agreement reached in the General Agreement on Tariffs and Trade. The EU was seen as the guilty party in this matter, hence the problem could be seen as a European affair.

An even more clear-cut case of European issues emerging is in the poorest states of the Union – Greece, Spain, Ireland and Portugal – where government and opposition parties could fight on the question of which party would win the most money from the European structural funds for their country, and who would make best use of the funds.[30] This sort of debate shows the interaction between domestic and European politics as more policy areas are tackled, at least partially, at the European level. We may expect this sort of mingling to increase with further integration, giving a more European aspect to the elections.

WHY THE LACK OF A TRANSNATIONAL APPROACH?

There are several reasons why the elections did not result in transnational campaigns or focus on European issues in any systematic way:

1 The most obvious reason is that the rewards of European elections were perceived to be slim. European elections have no direct impact on government formation[31] and the impact on the policy agenda of the Union is limited. The Maastricht provisions may alter this in due course: the role of the Parliament within the Union is increasingly important and the balance of the parties matters much more than in the past. But while the reality is changing, perceptions had not caught up by 1994.
2 National politicians still dominated the political process and this fed through to European elections. Since most national politicians tend to view the EP with a mixture of ignorance and anxiety, there was a reluctance to stress the importance of European affairs. Part of this stemmed from a widespread, although not necessarily accurate, belief that an increase in the powers of the European Parliament necessarily involves a reduction of the role of national parliaments. However, if issues being dealt with at the European level cannot be scrutinized by national legislatures, granting the EP a larger role in these areas would not reduce the powers of national MPs further. Thus, a misplaced fear contributed to an unwillingness to inform voters about the importance of the elections.
3 Different approaches to European integration often came within rather than between parties. Parties were therefore reluctant to discuss European issues in order not to jeopardize their domestic positions. This was particularly true of the parties of the right in France, of the two larger British parties, and, in 1989, even in the Netherlands, where parties faced with a general election in the autumn were reluctant to focus on European issues for fear of antagonizing potential government partners.
4 The lack of common media made it hard to ensure coverage of any pan-European debate or activity, possibly reducing any incentives parties might have had to engage in such activities. Regional media, on the other hand, tend to be interested in reporting events which are not national and would cover European matters, thus to a certain extent overcoming the media problem. The absence of

a common language complicated matters further, making common media more tricky to organize and reducing the scope for bringing speakers to other countries.

5 After forty years of European integration, there was still only a relatively weak sense of European identity as compared with national identities in the member states. In 1990, 88 per cent of respondents to *Eurobarometer* questions said that they felt attached to their country, as against 48 per cent who admitted to feelings of attachment to the European Community.[32] It would not be surprising, therefore, if it were hard to interest voters in European affairs, particularly European elections which are not seen by many voters as directly affecting their lives.

DOES THE LACK OF A GENUINELY TRANSNATIONAL DIMENSION MATTER?

Should we be concerned that there is still only a relatively limited transnational aspect to European elections? The answer partly depends on what one is looking for in transnational elections, particularly elections which do not lead to executive formation. Here comparison with the United States is helpful. The USA, often portrayed as having a two-party system, has nothing of the sort. Parties can better be viewed as mechanisms coming together for the limited purpose of electing a president. Congressional elections are very different, with candidates, although nominally standing as Republicans or Democrats, largely campaigning on who can get the best deal for the constituency. Even in European countries, domestic elections reflect a range of interests, with the issues tackled not exclusively local or national. Viewed in this light, the European elections were not so unusual. Yet, the limited nature of transnational activity does matter in the European context. Several very large questions about the future of Europe had still to be addressed in 1994. Such matters, including the possible drafting of a European constitution, had been tackled in neither national nor European elections, contributing to the malaise affecting Western Europe and beyond. In a speech to the European Parliament in 1988, Commission President Jacques Delors stated: 'We are but a year from the European elections and we must give the people their say. They will find our problems very remote.'[33] Six years on there was still a need to give voters their say. The problems of the Union were still remote for most people. European elections could be the ideal arena for such matters to be raised, giving voters in all member states, not just those such as France and Denmark which make use of the referendum device, a say in decisions which will have a major effect on their lives. Of course it is difficult to interest voters in institutional issues; the number of votes necessary for Parliament to block a Commission proposal is not of obvious concern to the man or woman on the street. However, major changes like the Maastricht Treaty, seen – rightly or wrongly – as curtailing national sovereignty, undoubtedly do interest voters.

The European Union in 1994 differed from traditional nation states in several ways which made it desirable that certain issues; be raised in European elections:

1 The very nature of the Union was still disputed: many British and Danish voters in particular supported entry to the EC for the economic advantages which were

likely to accrue. This is not surprising when we consider that the referendums in these two countries focused primarily on these economic matters,[34] but it did mean a certain amount of confusion and hostility about the political dimension of the European Union.

2 Huge changes were taking place within the Union on which voters were not being consulted. The Maastricht Treaty was a prime example of this, but with a new IGC pending in 1996 when the institution questions which were ducked in Maastricht looked likely to be addressed, European elections offered an ideal opportunity for voters to express their views on the future direction of the Union. Yet such debate did not occur.[35]

CONCLUSION

The 1994 European elections brought together the voters in twelve very different countries, with very different electoral traditions. Fifteen years after the first European elections, there was still a considerable emphasis on domestic issues, with national parties playing a more important role than European parties. However, there was already a perceptible shift in European elections in 1994, as parties, and to an extent voters, began to realize that many problems, most notably the environment and unemployment, had at least a partial solution at the European level. Policy issues were increasingly being discussed at the European level, in a way which would have been unthinkable in 1979.

The impact of European politics on domestic politics was still of prime importance, enabling the implications of EP elections to be assessed in largely national terms. Yet here, too, there was change. Initially, the composition of the EP mattered little; by 1994 it did. The Maastricht Treaty altered the powers of the Parliament significantly: the right to veto legislation in certain areas and the vote of confirmation of the Commission both gave MEPs a certain degree of leverage in the Union. MEPs in the outgoing Parliament were increasingly willing to make maximum use of their powers. A similar attitude on the part of the new Members would have meant that a clear majority of left or right could have helped determine the composition of the Commission.

A clear majority for one party or homogeneous group of parties could have facilitated a legislative bias towards a more free market or a more socially orientated approach to European policy making. The potential implications are important in terms of the future direction of the Union. Future elections may give scope for voting for a slate for the Commission – that at least is what many of those responsible for drafting the Maastricht Articles concerning the EP and also the new Rules of Procedure hope. In that case the party balance will matter greatly and the Conservative Party's slogan, 'Europe right or left?' rather than the more traditional theme of 'Europe right or wrong?' would be appropriate. In 1994, it was somewhat premature.

European elections had begun to matter, and to matter for 'European' reasons, by 1994. Yet, we must conclude that Professor Hallstein's words were not entirely out of place after fifteen years of direct elections to the European Parliament. By 1994, there still had not been 'an election campaign about European issues', but the situation was changing.[36]

NOTES

1 Walter Hallstein, *Europe in the Making* (London, George Allen and Unwin, 1972), p. 74.
2 The elections took place between the 9 and the 12 June to allow for differing national traditions regarding work- or rest-day voting. Voters in the United Kingdom, Ireland, Denmark and the Netherlands went to the polls on Thursday 9 and voters elsewhere on the 12. All votes were counted after the polls closed on the 12 to ensure the results in the states voting on 9 did not affect the outcome in the other states.
3 European citizenship was established under Article 8 of the Maastricht Treaty on European Union (TEU), which came into force on 1 November 1993. The Treaty provides for citizens of one EU country resident in another member state to vote and stand in European and municipal elections in their country of residence. The change was not without its problems. Luxembourg and the area around Brussels in Belgium have large numbers of resident non-nationals and the idea of the extension of the right to vote raised anxiety among nationals. In Luxembourg the difficulty was partly overcome by introducing minimum residency requirements.
4 European Community is used for events prior to 1 November 1993. Thereafter the term European Union is used, except when the European Community pillar of the Union is being referred to, usually in the context of legislative activity. The other two pillars created under the provisions of the Maastricht Treaty – the Common Foreign and Security, and Justice and Home Affairs pillars – work on an intergovernmental basis, with only a consultative role for the European Parliament.
5 For a full assessment of the campaigns in the 1979, 1984, 1989 and 1994 elections see Valentine Herman and Juliet Lodge, *Direct Elections to the European Parliament: A Community Perspective* (London, Macmillan, 1982); Juliet Lodge, *Direct Elections to the European Parliament 1984* (London, Macmillan, 1986); Juliet Lodge, *The 1989 Election of the European Parliament* (London, Macmillan, 1990); Juliet Lodge, *The 1994 Election of the EU Parliament* (London, Frances Pinter, 1995).
6 See for example Karlheinz Reif (ed.), *Ten European Elections: 1979/81 and 1984, Campaigns and Results* (Aldershot, Gower, 1985); Karlheinz Reif, 'National electoral cycles and European elections 1979 and 1984', *Electoral Studies*, vol. 3, no. 3, 1984, pp. 244–55.
7 The idea of direct elections to a European Parliament was first raised at the 1948 Hague Conference. Article 21(3) of the Treaty of Paris establishing the European Coal and Steel Community (1951) calls for the Assembly (as the EP was then known) to draw up proposals for direct elections with a uniform procedure. The Treaties of Rome establishing the European Economic Community and Euratom (1957) had similar provisions.
8 The European Parliament had on more than one occasion drawn up proposals for a uniform electoral system. The most recent attempt to introduce a common system, the De Gucht Report, was passed by the EP in March 1993. However, the proposals must then be agreed by the Council of Ministers; this had not happened by the time of the 1994 elections.
9 Germany had a single national constituency for European elections. Parties may put forward lists on a regional, rather than a national basis. The Christian Democratic Union put up lists in all the *Länder* except Bavaria, where its sister party, the Christian Social Union, put up a list.
10 See for example, Juliet Lodge and Valentine Herman, 'Direct elections to the European Parliament: a supranational perspective', *European Journal of Political Science Research*, vol. 8, 1980, pp. 45–62.
11 Between 1979 and 1994, the British Labour Party increased its representation in the European Parliament from seventeen to sixty-two (albeit in a slightly enlarged parliament in 1994), giving the Labour Party, as the largest single party from 1989, a disproportionately large amount of influence.
12 *The Financial Times* does have a European readership, being published in Germany as well as London; other trans-European media do exist, e.g. *Euro-News* and *Euro-Sport*, but reach a limited audience.
13 See *Eurobarometer* 10 and 11. Indeed, as Reif and Schmitt pointed out, Sørensen (*Campaign Analysis Report on the Danish Direct Election to the European Parliament,*

June 7th, 1979, University of Aarhus, Institute of Political Science) 'attributed part of Denmark's low participation rate to what he called "information overkill" due to the intensive but very boring TV and radio campaign'. They then suggested that, 'This explanation could also be applicable in The Netherlands, where more than average information was provided by the media, government and EC-agencies.' See Karlheinz Reif and Hermann Schmitt, 'Nine second-order elections: a conceptual framework for analysis of European election results', *European Journal of Political Research*, vol. 8, 1980, pp. 3–44.

14 Articles 158 and 189b of the Treaty on European Union respectively.

15 Indeed, when the heads of state and government met at the European Summit in Corfu three weeks after the elections to choose the new Commission president, the arguments for or against certain candidates were put in national terms; the results of the EP elections had no discernible impact on the discussion.

16 Commission White Paper on *Growth, Competitiveness, Employment*.

17 Emilio Colombo, President of the European Parliament, Directorate-General for Research and Documentation, *Elections to the European Parliament by Direct Universal Suffrage* (Luxembourg, European Parliament, 1977), cited in Herman and Lodge, *Direct Elections*.

18 The main political strands in European politics are brought together in the more broad-based Socialist International, the Liberal International and the Christian Democrat International. The transnational parties are more tightly organized than the Internationals, due to their more specific role in European elections. They also include parties from non-EU European states. For example socialist and social democrat parties from the then four EFTA applicant countries – Austria, Finland, Norway and Sweden – were full members of the Party of European Socialists which voted on the 1994 manifesto.

19 Article 138a of the TEU states: 'Political parties at European level are important as a factor for integration within the Union. They contribute to forming a European awareness and to expressing the political will of the citizens of the Union.'

20 Away from the electoral arena, there was a growing role for the transnational parties at pre-summit meetings, where ministers try to co-ordinate with ministers of the same political persuasion from other states.

21 In 1979, the socialists produced a less formal 'Appeal to the Electorate'. Subsequently, they published manifestos, like the EPP and ELDR.

22 This is even more inevitable when one considers that most national parties are themselves made up of various sections of opinion.

23 This is the document which clarifies the Danish position *vis-à-vis* the Maastricht provisions.

24 The British and Danish Conservative MEPs are not members of the EPP: they sit as 'allied members' of the EPP group and are therefore not technically involved in the manifesto process. This arrangement enables the parties' MEPs to take a full part in the activities of the EPP group – provided they 'subscribe to the basic policies of the Group of the European People's Party and if they accept the Rules of Procedure' (Article 5b of the Rules of Procedure of the Group of the European People's Party (Christian Democratic Group) in the European Parliament) – while not having to make a commitment to the whole EPP programme.

25 The 'democratic deficit' was defined by the EP as 'the combination of two phenomena: a) the transfer of powers from the member states to the European Community; and b) the exercise of these powers at the Community level by institutions other than the European Parliament, even though, before the transfer, the national parliaments held power to pass laws in the areas concerned.' *European Parliament Report drawn up on behalf of the Committee on Institutional Affairs on the Democratic Deficit in the European Community:* PE 111.236/fin. 1 February 1988, pp. 10–11.

26 *Les Verts vs EP* (1986) ECR 1339 Case 294/83, which relates to reimbursement of election campaign expenses, judging them to fall within the remit of the member states. For a fuller comment, see Martin Westlake, *A Modern Guide to the European Parliament* (London, Frances Pinter, 1994).

27 See F. Jacobs, R. Corbett and Michael Shackleton, *The European Parliament* (London,

Longman, 1992, 2nd edn) for the legal position. In fact much election material is produced in advance of the cut-off date, using EP information money (personal information).

28 Interview with the author in April 1994.

29 This issue refers to the possibility of groups of ministers vetoing issues in the Council of Ministers. It was raised as an issue by the Conservatives following the debate about the 'blocking minority' in the Council which arose during the negotiations for enlargement. Both issues seemed to rally the Conservatives, whether pro- or anti-European, and were therefore seen by John Major to be advantageous.

30 Structural funds may be in the form of the European Regional Development Fund, the European Social Fund and the Guidance Section of the European Agricultural Guidance and Guarantee Fund. Following the Single European Act and the introduction of 'Economic and Social Cohesion', spending on structural funds was increased to a quarter of the Community budget. Greece, Spain, Portugal and Ireland are the main beneficiaries of the funds.

31 In 1979 Helen Wallace wrote that the executive of the EC was not clearly defined, noting that there were no direct links between the EP and the executive. By 1994, the situation was, if anything, more confused. See Helen Wallace, 'The European Parliament: the challenge of political responsibility', *Government and Opposition*, vol. 14, no. 4, 1979, pp. 433–43.

32 For a fuller analysis of this issue see Karlheinz Reif, 'Cultural convergence and cultural diversity as factors in European integration' in Soledad García (ed.), *European Identity and the Search for Legitimacy* (London, Royal Institute of International Affairs, 1993).

33 Address by M. Jacques Delors, President of the European Commission to the European Parliament, 6 July 1988, cited in *Documents on Political Union* (Dublin, European Parliament, 1992), p. 11.

34 This issue was to come back to haunt British politicians who had campaigned on the economic benefits of membership of the EEC in the 1975 referendum, even though they, but not the voters, knew the longer term political goals of European integration.

35 UK government minister, David Heathcoat-Amery, did suggest that the European Commission's sole right of legislative proposal should be removed, echoing ideas put forward by the European Policy Forum (Frank Vibert, *The Future Role of the European Commission* (London, EPF, 1994). This was not followed up, as would have been feasible, by, for example, the Liberal Democrats supporting proposals by the European Movement in favour of streamlining the Commission (*Reform of the European Union: Proposals of the European Movement for British Policy Towards the Intergovernmental Conference of 1996* (London, The European Movement, 1994), hence engendering debate.

36 See note 1 above.

SELECT BIBLIOGRAPHY

Documents on Political Union, Dublin, European Parliament, 1992.

Elections to the European Parliament by Direct Universal Suffrage, Luxembourg, European Parliament Directorate-General for Research and Documentation, 1977.

European Parliament Report drawn up on behalf of the Committee on Institutional Affairs on the Democratic Deficit in the European Community: PE 111.236/fin. 1 February 1988.

Hallstein, Walter, *Europe in the Making*, London, George Allen and Unwin, 1972.

Herman, Valentine and Lodge, Juliet, *Direct Elections to the European Parliament: A Community Perspective*, London, Macmillan, 1982.

Jacobs, Francis, Corbett, Richard and Shackleton, Michael, *The European Parliament*, London, Longman, 1992, 2nd edn.

Lodge, Juliet (ed.), *Direct Elections to the European Parliament 1984*, London, Macmillan, 1986.

Lodge, Juliet (ed.), *The 1989 Election of the European Parliament*, London, Macmillan, 1990.

Lodge, Juliet (ed.), *The 1994 Elections of the European Parliament*, London, Frances Pinter, 1995.

Lodge, Juliet and Herman, Valentine, 'Direct elections to the European Parliament: a supra-national perspective', *European Journal of Political Science Research*, vol. 8, 1980, pp. 45–62.

Reform of the European Union: Proposals of the European Movement for British Policy Towards the Intergovernmental Conference of 1996, London, The European Movement, 1994.

Reif, Karlheinz, 'National electoral cycles and European elections 1979 and 1984', *Electoral Studies*, vol. 3, no. 3, 1984, pp. 244–55.

Reif, Karlheinz, (ed.), *Ten European Elections: 1979/81 and 1984 Campaigns and Results*, Aldershot, Gower, 1985.

Reif, Karlheinz, 'Cultural convergence and cultural diversity as factors in European integration', in Soledad García (ed.), *European Identity and the Search for Legitimacy*, London, Royal Institute of International Affairs, 1993.

Reif, Karlheinz and Schmitt, Hermann, 'Nine second-order elections: a conceptual framework for analysis of European election results', *European Journal of Political Research*, vol. 8. 1980, pp. 3–44.

Vibert, Frank, *The Future Role of the European Commission*, London, European Policy Forum, 1994.

Wallace, Helen, 'The European Parliament: the challenge of political responsibility', in *Government and Opposition*, 1979, pp. 433–43.

17 Political parties in the European Parliament

Robert Ladrech

INTRODUCTION

Since the introduction of direct elections to the European Parliament (EP) in 1979, the potential for a European-level party system has focused upon the presence and activities of the EP party groups.[1] To the extent that a European party system may contain characteristics resembling national systems, a minimum set of properties should include a range of political parties operating and competing in an organized pattern.[2] Further, elections should contain the promise of gaining primary influence within the decision-making apparatus of the governance structure. Indeed, the institutional enhancement of the EP itself is viewed as the primary prerequisite for an emergent party system, and the adoption of characteristics similar to those of national parliaments in relation to governmental power.[3] Since the late 1970s, with the establishment of transnational party federations, and, more recently, changes within the federations as they have sought the more explicit appearance of party organizations,[4] analysis of transnational party co-operation has broadened beyond the institutional confines of the EP. Nevertheless, as the most explicit site for European-level party political dynamics, the evolution of EP party groups in the 1990s has come to be seen as of prime importance for partisan articulation and influence at the European level.

As the scope of the EP widened during the 1980s — for example, its institutional enhancement *vis-à-vis* the Council of Ministers,[5] the role of the party groups altered. Politicization (discussed below), however, did not occur in the sense of establishing a European party system; it did, however, begin to structure a left–right dimension more clearly at the European level, and, of itself, lead to more explicitly partisan dynamics in other areas of EC decision making. In this chapter, we shall consider the role of the party groups; factors inhibiting their direct transformation into party organizations; and events signalling the more politicized nature of European-level politics, and thus the altered significance of the groups. Finally, consideration will be given to developments which may give a more prominent role to the EP party groups in European politics.

ROLE OF THE PARTY GROUPS

Party groups in the European Parliament were formally recognized by the Common Assembly of the European Coal and Steel Community. The first three groups to be founded, in June 1953, were those representing the traditional European political families, the socialists, Christian democrats and liberals. Over the next twenty years, others formed, the minimum number required to form a group changing up and down. With the first direct elections in 1979, the number of members more than doubled from 198 to 410, and over the course of the next two elections, in 1984 and 1989, other groups formed, most notably the Greens. As of the 1989 elections, the EP consisted of 518 MEPs and nine groups.

The groups' direct importance derives from their responsibility for the work of the EP. Indeed, the groups play:

> the decisive role in changing the Parliament's leaders . . . The Groups also set the parliamentary agenda, choose the rapporteurs and decide on the allocation of speaking time. They have their own large and growing staff, receive considerable funds from the Parliament and often have an important say in the choice of the Parliament's own top officials. The power of the Groups is also shown by the powerlessness of those non-attached members who are not in Political Groups, who are highly unlikely, for example, ever to hold a powerful post within the Parliament . . .[6]

The role of the party groups extends beyond their statutory responsibilities within the EP, though in a more indirect manner. As political entities operating within a European-level environment, they reap the benefits accruing to the EP in its drive for institutional enhancement relative to other EU as well as national bodies. According to Lodge, the development of the EP's powers and the role of the party groups 'are mutually dependent: the politicization of the Commission's role and of the EP's growing legislative role has significant implications for inter-institutional relations as well as for the EP's relationship with national parliaments.'[7] As national parliaments begin to engage in EU policy making, their relations with the EP are at times channelled into the political dynamics expressed at the European level, i.e. political rather than national affiliations. For example, at the Assizes held in Rome in November 1990 which brought national and European MPs together to discuss problems of parliamentary democracy in the EC, the parliamentarians sat according to political family, rather than in national delegations. Direct elections to the EP compelled national parties to consider their European platform (in some cases this being the first time serious consideration was given to positions on EC integration). However remote the EP and its party groups remained from national politics, since the launch of the Single Market initiative in the mid-1980s, the increased prominence of the EP, and the EU in general, has focused national attention in this direction.[8] The party groups, especially the socialists and Christian democrats, play a role in imparting a partisan motif to this interaction.

From its inception, the EP party groups/national parties relationship was relegated to a low priority by national party leaderships. This is explained by the attitude on the part of party elites toward the European Union in general, and toward the EP specifically. As long as European Union affairs were considered of marginal importance in domestic policy making, attention to the EP and its relevant actors remained relatively modest. The attitudes of national party leaderships toward the EU, and thus the EP, acted as a constraint on the formation of more defined EP party group identities.

Other chapters in this volume examine national party attitudes towards the EU, and on such topics as European federalism these attitudes spanned the spectrum from highly supportive (in terms of further EP institutional power) to highly critical of existing relations. Nevertheless, national attitudes were generally a small portion of party strategies, concerned as they were with domestic elections and politics. Despite the Single European Act generating renewed interest and raising the profile of the EU, attitudes toward the EP were still encapsulated within the broader context of EU integration. Consequently, those parties (and national political perspectives) desiring a more limited role for Brussels generally supported an inter-governmentalist approach to EU decision making, thus marginalizing the EP. Those supporting a more federalist vision for the EU also promoted designs for enhancing the EP. The 1984 Spinelli Draft Treaty on European Union was an example of successful manoeuvering by EP committees and federalist organizations such as the Crocodile Club.[9] Attention by the national parties towards the development of party group identity was therefore connected to views on the appropriate role for the EU itself. Change in the profile of the EP party groups was thus dependent not only on intra-institutional amendments, but also on the connection and influence of the national parties, for in the final analysis it was generally they who controlled the nomination and candidate selection process for EP elections. Change in national party elite views on issues of European integration – a response to its politicization – should then affect the priority given to their respective party groups in the EP, especially at the time of EP election campaigns.

The party groups play a critical role in the administration and daily work of the European Parliament. They represent the political forces found in European politics at the national level, whether this is social democratic, Green, regionalist, Christian democratic, liberal, or neo-fascist. The fact that MEPs of various ideological hues arrange themselves in transnational rather than national delegations is significant for the symbolic enhancement of European-level political dynamics in the public realm. Despite the transnational complexion of the party groups and the socialization of MEPs into this work environment, national considerations remain part of intra-group dynamics.[10] Finally, as the EP itself became more and more a critical part of the EU decision-making process, especially after the Maastricht Treaty on Political Union,[11] the visibility of the groups as well as intergroup relations took on added importance. This added importance was still mediated by the variability of national political perspectives on EU development as well as specific party-ideological positions.

LIMITATIONS ON EURO-PARTY FORMATION BY THE GROUPS

As we pointed out above, the EP party groups were considered potential vehicles for the emergence of a European-level party system. The advent of direct elections to the EP increased this potential, for a popular sanction now legitimated the activities of MEPs. The hopes of federalists and others who sought to strengthen the representative dimension of policy making in Brussels were disappointed, though, when EP elections failed to provide a linkage between public opinion and EU decision making. In other words, political organizations and dynamics approxi-mating a party system did not emerge.[12] Part of the explanation was that party groups never developed campaign organizations and strategies, owing both to the primacy of the national party and the existence of transnational party federations, ostensibly created for this exact purpose.

Euro-parliamentary groups versus Euro-party organization

Hix, and Pridham and Pridham[13] have made clear that when the topic of transnational parties in the EU is addressed, in reality a triangular relationship is in operation. The actors in this relationship are the EP party groups, the transnational party federations (primarily the socialists and Christian democrats), and the relevant national parties. The relationship between the EP groups and the party federations rests upon a division of responsibilities. The domain of responsibility for election campaign co-ordination lies with the party federations, while the EP groups focus on EU legislative matters. This of course does not mean that a great deal of interaction by the two groups does not occur, and indeed the party federations remained financially dependent on their respective EP groups.[14] The EP party groups themselves did not have the intention of organizationally combining their parliamentary activities with a campaign/electioneering machine. In this sense, the actions taken by the EP socialist and the EPP groups to breath new life into their transnational party federations – allowing a degree of organizational enhancement and more financial independence – suggests a differentiation reminiscent of national parties with regard to the parliamentary group and the party organization proper.

By relinquishing primary responsibility for EP election campaign co-ordination to the party federations, the EP groups emphasized the parliamentary-specific nature of their role.[15] This organizational division of labour did, on the other hand, stress the importance the groups placed on the elections, for it recognized the need for a more advanced and defined political profile at EP elections and therefore the efficiency that a campaign organization, strictly speaking, can bring.

If the party groups intend to be the 'parliamentary wing' of more developed transnational European parties, have they succeeded? Two considerations should be addressed. First, has a political-ideological identity emerged? Second, in the context of EU legislation and policy making, do the party groups, through the EP, exert any influence? These two considerations will lead the following discussion of the limitations on the party groups in their quest to define their role more straightforwardly.

Constraints on party groups

As parliamentary wings of a political party, we should have expected the groups to conduct themselves according to a set of propositions and perhaps even to an electoral manifesto. Put another way, the party groups in the EP should have been active in trying to implement or influence the EU policy-making process according to a programme. Various factors prevented the groups from developing this type of parliamentary identity. Briefly, they were:

1 The absence of a parliamentary division between government and opposition (due to lack of EU government drawn from EP).
2 The more heterogeneous nature of the EP, with cross-group and intra-group national pressures; the wide ideological spectrum within groups; and political-cultural differences, i.e. consensual versus confrontational.
3 Co-operation between socialist group and Christian democratic group (EPP) on voting in EP co-operation procedure, e.g. budgetary issues.

These factors complicated the development of the party groups into more identifiable party entities. Further, they 'have tended to undercut the importance of left–right divisions in the European Parliament'.[16] This is an important point, for, in the light of the heterogeneity of the groups and the absence of a government/ opposition polarity, the left–right division could serve as the means by which public opinion comprehends not only the role of party groups within the EP but EU policy issues in general. The diffuse political complexion of the EP contributes, then, to its lack of resonance among the EU public. This, in turn, has affected the public's grasp of European integration issues in general, and the nature of the integration process by political elites. According to Weiler, 'despite the growing centrality of Community activity to important decisions of social choice, there has been . . . a near absence of overt debate on the left–right spectrum'.[17] Weiler has suggested that this:

> neutralization of ideology has conditioned . . . the belief that an agenda could be set for the Community, and the Community could be led toward an ever closer union among its peoples without having to face the normal political cleavages present in the member states. Thus, the Community political culture that developed in the 1960s and 1970s saw an habituation of the political class in Europe to the idea of European integration as ideologically neutral regarding, or ideologically transcendent over, normal debates on the Left–Right spectrum.[18]

The parliamentary wing of a party seeks to have its programme translated into legislation, and thus the need to differentiate its policy views from competitors is a necessary exercise. The constraints noted above make this process of differentiation difficult. The development of a structured left–right bipolar EP environment would have, at the very least, provided a general coalescence of issues around two competing political perspectives. In this fashion, although details of EP work may have been lost on the average EU citizen, the choice offered by a broad distinction between two competing groups (or coalitions) traditionally expressed in left–right terms, could have allowed for some semblance of a parliamentary identity, at least on the part of the major party groups.

When we turn to how effective the party groups were in terms of EU policy making (and thus what heightened profile accrued), the picture is complex. Following from the third factor listed above – voting co-operation between the socialist and Christian democratic groups, especially on budgetary matters – a situation exists which, paradoxically, has blunted the organizational evolution of groups into 'party organizations' but fulfils EP procedural requirements. On certain essential issues, the EP is obliged to garner a qualified majority vote – 284 – to pass legislation, e.g. on budgetary matters. Since neither of the two largest groups alone or in a broad left or right coalition was in a position to accomplish this, the socialists and Christian democrats agreed to co-operate in this area with the greater goal of advancing the EP's stature and power. Inability to pass such legislation would have undermined the EP's position in inter-institutional dynamics.

Having to build and maintain a co-operative relationship between two groups that would otherwise form the main opposing blocs in the EP prohibited the process of differentiation and identity formation. According to one observer, this 'dual strategy brought us more responsibilities and more difficulties'.[19] The necessity of supporting the overall influence of the EP, namely, the institutional logic of EU governance, and the goal of enhancing EP power and increasing the profile of the party groups, introduced a prioritization which rendered partisan goals secondary.

The ambiguity, and sometimes open hostility, on the part of the other party groups toward the European Union or further integration (with the partial exception of the liberals), allowed more ideological tendencies to dominate, which contributed to the problems of coalition building for the pro-European socialists and Christian democrats.

In keeping with the underlying assumption that further development towards Euro-parties and a party system is dependent upon the future of EU integration, and in particular the role of the EP, the emergence of a left–right dimension on issues under the growing purview of EU policy would seem to have been a prerequisite for more defined party-specific activities. Although it would be incorrect to state that a rudimentary left–right division did not exist within the EP, it was not until the ratification process of the Maastricht Treaties that the nature and indeed future of EU integration became a highly politicized issue. This state of affairs began to change with the ratification campaigns for the Maastricht Treaties, especially in Denmark, France, Britain and Germany. Politicization of EU institutional power and development affected the ideological nature and relationship among the EP party groups, which led the socialists and Christian democrats to reformulate their pro-EU positions on more explicitly partisan bases. The following section examines events and underlying changes which account for the resumption of the politicized nature of EU integration and the consequences for the party groups.

EU POLITICIZATION AND EP PARTY GROUPS

In their analysis of growing transnational party co-operation, Pridham and Pridham concluded that it was 'the closer interlinkage between the three dimensions of transnational activity – the Euro-parliamentary, the transnational party-organizational and the national party frameworks – which promoted this process within the wider context of politicization in the EC as a whole'.[20] Specifically addressing the EP party groups, they added that:

> politicisation has had two competitive characteristics: on the one hand, the emergence of an active political role and clearer profile of the groups; on the other, the increasing articulation of national interests and approaches and party-political pressures which more overtly challenged their unity and cohesion. The basis of this dual development has been the growing interlinkage between national and European politics arising from the greater political relevance of the Community as a whole.

By the end of the 1970s, with the establishment of the transnational party federations and the prospect of direct elections, the EP as well as the main party groups had indeed developed a higher profile.[21] In the light of the Maastricht Treaties, what changed, if anything? A new wave of politicization occurred, the result of the elite bargain being in the Single European Act[22] together with wider environmental factors. This means that the emergence of a more defined left–right dimension within the EP is a by-product of European integration – especially the experiences of the Maastricht ratification process – and of global changes in the late 1980s and early 1990s, changes which include the demise of the communist states in Eastern Europe.[23] Thus, rather than changes derived from amendments to the operation of the EP itself, which Pridham and Pridham and others analysed at the end of the

1970s, these changes originated from a wider and more complex environment. The Maastricht ratification process was a turning point during these years in that the EU itself now entered national politics, and not solely as a foreign policy issue. We now turn to an explanation of how Maastricht laid the foundation for future EU partisan dynamics, in particular the effect upon the party groups as they reacted to this politicization.

Maastricht and political mobilization

We noted above that the increasing attention of national interests, including party political pressure, was a factor constraining the EP party groups from more rapid transformation into transnational parties (together with the party federations). The difference between the 1990s and the late 1970s concerns the significance of the EU in national politics, the 'greater political relevance of the Community as a whole'.[24] Unlike the previous period, however, the tension that came to the fore during the Maastricht negotiations and the subsequent ratification process concerning the future of the EU ended an extended period in which public opinion remained dormant or outside the integration process. In a sense, the legitimacy of further EU development was tested, and the opportunity provided by the Danish (2 June 1992) and French (20 September 1992) referendums and the British and German parliamentary debates during 1992 and 1993, in particular, did much to politicize, through anti-Maastricht mobilization, the meaning and role of the EU and its relations with its member states.[25] The relative inattention by national party elites to issues of EU integration and its growing policy domain had returned to haunt them.

The anti-Maastricht arguments ranged from the inadequacy of democratic decision making in the EC to nationalist polemics in favour of defending national sovereignty. Occurring at a time of deepening economic recession, a 'blame it on Brussels' attitude was also promoted by opponents. There were also criticisms, especially of the Treaty on Political Union, based on the inadequacy of transforming the Union into a more democratic, transparent and responsible entity, and impediments to the move towards some type of federal system. As an institutional actor, the EP criticizes the treaties, especially on political union, most forcefully in the Martin IV Report.[26]

The essentially intergovernmentalist nature of the treaties, then, hid deeper issues at hand, and the surprise by most political elites at the vociferous response of the public, which had been assumed to be pro-EC up to this point, demonstrated the volatile nature of the EC issue in national politics.[27] Wallace framed this affair as a debate about:

> the shift from policy to polity and the broaching of the metaphysical or basic political values. In other words it is not merely a matter of adjusting institutional rules and procedures or legal powers to act, important as these are. On the contrary, a political union . . . would need a constitution . . . founded on some set of shared values and to express commitment to some form of collective identity.[28]

How did this situation work to the benefit of the party groups, or contribute to defining a left–right dimension in the EP? We suggest three reasons:

1 EP/party group mobilization during the 1991 IGCs;

2   national parties' unpreparedness during 1992–93 for defence of the EU;
3   post-1989 loosening of Cold War pattern coalition dynamics.

EP/party group mobilization during intergovernmental conferences

The European Parliament, though not a formal participant in the 1991 IGCs leading to the Maastricht Treaties, nevertheless sought to influence the direction and content of these negotiations.[29] Primarily interested in the Treaty on Political Union, since this document would define any changes in its relationship toward the other EU institutions, the EP mobilized its supporters in various quarters, including individuals within the European Commission. The EP also drew upon support in several national political systems, especially the Belgian, Dutch, Italian and German, and a promise was made by the Belgian and Italian Parliaments not to ratify the treaties unless the EP had approved of them.[30]

In addition to enlisting the support of national parliaments, EP mobilization also indirectly emphasized the party groups, as they were in a position to generate information on, if not interest in, the EP's case with their respective national parties and government negotiating positions.[31] The importance of political parties was recognized in this respect by the EP Committee on Institutional Affairs. One of its reports specifically mentioned the formation of alliances 'with the federations of political parties at European level, since they are in the best position to provide a link between national democracy and European democracy'.[32] The potential for an upgraded EP also meant that those national party delegations not part of one of the major party groups now explicitly sought membership. The British Conservatives, who had been seated in the EP as the European Democratic Group (EDG), although interacting closely with the EPP for a number of years,[33] joined the EPP in 1992. This occurred after their group diminished in size following the 1989 elections and suffered defections to the EPP, as was the case with the Spanish Partito Popular immediately after the elections.[34]

Finally, through the support of the leaders of the three largest party groups – socialist, EPP and liberal – the president of the EP during 1991, Spanish Socialist Enrique Baron Crespo, was able to have inserted in the Treaty on Political Union Article 138a: 'Political parties at European level are important as a factor for integration within the Union. They contribute to forming a European awareness and to expressing the political will of the citizens of the Union.' The inclusion of this article had the potential for formally asserting the rights of transnational party federations in political activities beyond simply EP elections. The three party groups responsible for assisting in this effort co-operated in determining matters of funding and other consequences that could potentially flow from Article 138a, for instance the legal status of the party federations.[35]

National party confusion regarding the EU

Uppermost in our consideration of the socialist and EPP party groups is the changed nature of European integration by 1993. We have already mentioned the entry of public opinion into the integration process beginning in 1991, ranging from concern with preserving national identity to fears of economic dislocation. Issues outside the more narrow focus on monetary and other technical matters shifted the debate on ratification from elite confines to the public forum, from the media to protest demonstrations. The debate, however, did not emerge around a clear partisan theme. Political elites, as Weiler suggested, were generally united in favour of the treaties. Opponents, on the other hand, emerged from across the political spectrum, and declared or undeclared alliances were established, e.g. among British Conservative and Labour Eurosceptics and French Communist and National Front individuals.

The apparent inability of party elites to mobilize public opinion in favour of Maastricht ratification reflected two factors. First, their relative inattention over the years to details of EU integration, seen primarily as 'technical matters', was translated into an absence of developed arguments comprehensible to a cross-section of the population. Second, as Wallace suggested, the implications of the Maastricht Treaties went beyond simple institutional tinkering and instead, unintentionally, engaged much deeper and more profound aspects of the national–supranational relationship. Again, most national parties were completely unprepared to address the sensitivities expressed by many people. Into this intellectual vacuum, one which was made even more apparent and immediate by the inclusion of socio-economic issues related to the recession of the first half of the 1990s, entered the party groups, primarily the socialist and EPP. The 1994 EP elections presented an opportunity for these groups to assert themselves as authoritative actors on a matter of urgency to their national counterparts.

The EPP, especially its major component – Christian democrat parties – had a long-standing commitment to European unification,[36] therefore substantial programmatic and organizational change was not considered to be an acute need.[37] Beginning in 1989, the socialist group and the Confederation of Socialist Parties of the EC (CSPEC) undertook several initiatives. These included sponsoring the organizational enhancement of the CSPEC, renamed the Party of European Socialists in November 1992, with the EP group renamed the Group of the Party of European Socialists; active involvement by national delegations of the socialist group in national party conferences on the EU, the first time for some (e.g. the British Labour Party in 1992); participation by the chair of the socialist group in the party leaders conference convened before each semi-annual European Council summit; and formulation of policy papers developed from contributions by many national quarters presented as potential alternative programmes at the European level.[38] These activities represented the efforts and initiative of socialist actors at the European level to bring a sense of both intellectual coherence as well as organizational definition to the national–supranational connection.

It is important to bear in mind that, apart from the actual substance contained in the treaties, the ratification process, whether by national referendums or national parliamentary approval, transformed the EU into a domestic political issue beyond its previously distant reference. Consequently, national party leaderships were required to spend more time considering the relevance of EP positions (and their national delegation's position on party group policies) on issues which now resonated in domestic politics.[39] The parties also found that Maastricht ratification had entered into intra-party division.

In the UK the Conservative Party was racked by internal conflict throughout 1992 and 1993 over Maastricht ratification and the general direction of European integration. The threat to the authority of prime minister John Major was such that a vote of confidence was employed to secure final passage of the Maastricht Bill, 23 July 1993.

In France two of the major parties – the Socialists and the Gaullists (RPR) – suffered defections over support for Maastricht. In the Socialist case, a splinter group formed an independent party led by former government minister J.-P. Chevènement. A breakaway group from the RPR–UDF alliance formed an anti-Maastricht party to contest the 1994 EP elections.

To reverse the referendum failure to ratify Maastricht, Danish pro-EU parties undertook a campaign to convince voters that new compensations were sufficient. The Conservative-led government coalition was defeated on 13 January 1993. A second referendum was held on 18 May 1993. A new anti-Maastricht left-wing party formed, and, together with the original anti-Treaty party, secured 25 per cent of the vote at the June 1994 EP elections.

Public opinion polls in Germany detected worry over the 'loss' of the deutschmark in a future monetary union. The major parties sought to clarify this position and link it with future parliamentary approval. A new 'anti-Maastricht' party formed in Bavaria.

These examples demonstrate how divisive and significant Europe as an issue became within parties which had hitherto confined the European Community to a technical issue appropriate only for expert consideration and public ritual. The unpreparedness of the national parties in the realm of EU activities and long-range perspectives allowed the main EP party groups, and in particular national MEP delegations, to strengthen their presence in the national party organization.

Loosening of Cold War pattern coalition dynamics

Changes in domestic political landscapes after 1989 as a result of the end of the East–West conflict engendered realignments in the EP party groups; one of the consequences was a more pronounced left–right division. The national party system alignments structured by a Cold War logic, in particular Italy with its exclusion of the former Communist Party, the Partito Democratico della Sinistra (PDS), began to alter as those aspects of party identity related to these relationships lost their defining *raison d'être* with the collapse of the Soviet Union. New opportunities (as well as dangers) arose from possible coalition strategies heretofore unavailable. For instance, in the case of socialists, according to Ware:

> some of the previous constraints on . . . electoral strategies have been eroded within the last few years. Socialist parties in Europe are more free to develop new strategies than they have been in the preceding 50 years. For in some ways the cold war served to make party competition even more fixed than it had been in the interwar years. Take away the cold war dimension and there are greater alternatives for attempting to expand the electoral base – and, equally, corresponding greater threats to that base from other parties.[40]

An example of this new freedom to redirect party strategies and build new alliances occurred within the EP socialist group. The Italian PDS formally joined the socialist group in October 1992, leaving the group it had dominated, the group of the United European Left. This switch was part of a larger shift for the PDS as it was also welcomed into the Socialist International. Together, then, with the affiliation of the

British Conservatives to the EPP and the PDS to the socialist group, the number of groups dropped from ten to nine; more importantly, consolidation of the bipolar nature of the EP 'party system' was intensified. The post-Cold War environment, in a paradoxical manner, freed national strategies and alliances while consolidating others in the EP.

Apart from the numerical growth of the two largest groups, a growing left–right dimension also gained further impetus from the content of group legislative actions during the 1989–94 EP session. The close relationship between the German CDU and the British Conservative EP delegations which began in the mid-to-late 1980s allowed for the pursuit of more straightforwardly conservative economic policies, rather than the more socially oriented Christian democratic approach – hence the hostility of the Belgian, Dutch and Italian Christian democrats to British Conservative admission to the EPP. The EPP's more explicitly anti-socialist orientation narrowed the type of voting coalitions within the EP between the EPP and the socialist group, for with an increase in group discipline came less of the traditional Christian democratic party tendency to seek compromises and build coalitions (a hallmark of their national strategies), and a more ideological stance.

Likewise, the admission of the Italian PDS into the socialist group reinforced the effort by the group leadership to stress a left identity. The motivation to do so was fed by the perception of intellectual disarray and policy drift by national parties on issues which had been framed by a social democratic orientation. By the late 1980s such an identity in various national settings had become problematic.[41] Issues of a socio-economic nature that appeared in the EP – proposals arising from the European Commission or the Economic and Social Committee – such as an EU minimum wage, and spending on an EU recovery programme, pitted the two groups in a higher profile left–right contrast than before. Increasingly, issues were fashioned in such a way as to emphasize the contrast between the two groups. One consequence of this was to strengthen the public's impression of the EP's concerns and involvement. In some cases, national parties were able to adopt positions and arguments that had been politically impossible for coalition reasons. For instance, from September 1993, the socialist group '[chose] a key political theme for each part-session designed to mobilise the Left and able to be exploited by our parties'. The group also stated:

> Thanks to our control of important reports in the committees concerned and control of the part-session agenda, we shall select topics which will give us an opportunity to differentiate ourselves clearly from the other groups and present ourselves to voters as a quite distinct party of the Left on European issues.[42]

The partisan formulation of EU policy, as this quote attests, became a conscious part of group strategy, both within the EP and in the presentation of a consistent image to a public audience.

Ironically, the end of the Cold War introduced a degree of fluidity into national party system patterns, and yet at the same time contributed to consolidating the mainstream left and right at the European level. This meant that the necessity for the two groups to collaborate on those issues requiring an absolute majority – 284 votes – stood in even greater contrast than before.[43] Apart from this exception, the constraints loosened by the demise of the Cold War which led to a reconfiguration of forces and relationships within the EP also lent it a higher visibility because of

the urgency generated in domestic politics by the Maastricht debates. The polariz
ation within the European Parliament was therefore reflected in national settings
as the EU increasingly became part of the domain of domestic politics. In the early
1990s, H. Wallace was able to write, 'in retrospect we may come to see the 1970s
and 1980s as an unusually quiescent period in which tolerance for indirect
legitimacy still hung on the legacy of post-war reconstruction and the apparent
immobility in East/West relations'.[44]

CONCLUSION

After Maastricht, several developments offered potential for further EP activism,
and that of the party groups in particular. They were: (1) Article 138a acknowledging the role of European-level political parties; (2) the October 1993 German
Constitutional Court ruling emphasizing parliamentary involvement in EU matters;
and (3) the 1994 EP elections.

The most significant contribution of Article 138a was the institutionalisation of
relations between the party groups and the party federations. A secure base of funding derived from the Treaty allowed the party federations to consolidate and develop
their activities beyond campaign co-ordination at EP elections. The daily legislative
work of the party groups brought the supranational dimension into organizational
contact with the problems and prospects of similar issues in national settings.
Consequently, Article 138a provided a means for transmitting the work of the EP to
the public through the strengthened position and activities of the transnational party
federations.

The German Constitutional Court ruling of 12 October 1992 finalized German
ratification for the Maastricht Treaties. The ruling also served to bolster the hopes of
EP supporters, for the Court confronted the question of parliamentary democracy
in an evolving European Union. Asserting that '[i]f an association of democratic
states takes on sovereign tasks and exercises sovereign powers, it is principally
the peoples of the member states who must legitimate this through their national
parliament'.[45] Referring specifically to the EP, the Court stated:

> Increasingly as European nations grow together . . . democratic legitimation is
> conveyed by the European parliament elected by the citizens of the member
> states. . . . It is of decisive importance that the democratic basis of [European]
> Union should keep pace with integration, and that a vital democracy should be
> maintained as the integration of member states continues.[46]

The EP, and the party groups in particular, seized upon this ruling as a victory in their
effort to raise the profile of the EP. The immediate impact of the Court's ruling was
the completion of the ratification of the Maastricht Treaties. The emphasis of the
Court upon the role of parliaments, both national and European, in the decision-
making process did provide an impetus for the EP in its drive to develop ties to
national parliaments. In this regard, various EP committees have sought to establish
meetings with national counterparts on a systematic basis (while still protecting EP
prerogatives in EU policy making). An example of this 'outreach' was a 1993 meeting of the EP Committee on Legal Affairs organized with members of the
Parliaments of the member states 'with a view to preparation of the report . . . on the
application of Community law'.[47] Other joint meetings were also proposed. The party

groups contributed as well to this process of deepening ties with national parliamentary groups. For example, the EPP organized joint meetings with presidents of the Christian democrat and Conservative groups from national parliaments. A meeting in May 1993 revolved around issues relating to European integration and Union legislation, e.g. subsidiarity.[48] Ultimately, the issue of the proper scope of European and national parliamentary power may engage the European Court of Justice.

The 1994 EP elections followed two years of high public attention to European integration and related national political dynamics. Both the socialist group and EPP viewed these elections as opportunities for pushing even further for EP enhancement, especially as a run up to the scheduled 1996 intergovernmental conference on EU institutions.

The results of the elections did further define a left–right continuum, particularly on economic policy. This was reflected less in the programmatic positions of the two largest groups and instead in the results of the election. The socialists campaigned with a manifesto devoid of the national party opt outs of past elections, and included references to the European Employment Initiative of 9 December 1993.[49] The EPP produced a manifesto that essentially maintained a Christian democratic social-market approach to economic policies. The results of the elections, however, provided the real substance of a polarizing trend within the EP. This can be summarized as follows. The socialist group remained the single largest group in the EP, composed roughly of the same number of seats. Together with allies such as the French Energie Radicale,[50] communists such as the Spanish Izquierda Unida and Italian Rifondazione Comunista, and certain social liberal parties within the liberal group, for example the Dutch D'66, British Liberal Democrats, etc., a centre-left economic majority may emerge over time. This is in contrast to the effects of the elections on the right overall. The traditional Christian democratic parties were confronted with a much larger conservative orientation, ranging from the British Conservatives to the Italian *Forza Italia!*, with the German CDU sympathetic on certain issues. Thus the right appeared both to fragment and polarize, especially on economic matters and future institutional development of the Union, the role of the Parliament a particular area of division between federalist Christian democrats and Eurosceptics such as the French RPR and British Conservatives.

Finally, the Maastricht Treaty on Political Union gave the EP the ability to grant approval of a new incoming Commission, and for its term of office to be linked with that of the Parliament. The potential for this approval to evolve in the direction of a parliamentary vote of investiture, linked to parliamentary majorities supporting the work programme of the Commission, added to the significance of the 1994 elections for the development of competing political programmes and a growing left–right dimension.

The role of EP party groups has unfolded in two general phases. The first concerned the establishment of their authority within the framework of EP legislation and interinstitutional relations in the 1960s and 1970s. The second phase began after the first direct EP elections in 1979, and accelerated beginning in the late 1980s as the prominence of the EU increased by virtue of the Single Market initiative and the Maastricht Treaties ratification. This chapter has demonstrated that the party groups, although operating at the supranational level, are linked to their national counterparts in a complex fashion. This complexity is seen in their growing authority on specialized questions of EU governance within their respective national parties' policy making bodies. The continued expansion of the EU into previously domestic policy areas initiated a reappraisal of the EP (and therefore the party groups) by national elites. The blurring of left–right positions in national settings has, para-doxically, become more defined at the European level, no doubt as a result of the developing partisanship introduced by the activities of the party groups themselves. The party groups must, therefore, be viewed as actors in an evolving party system that operates in a multidimensional though interrelated manner. In this fashion, the national–supranational connection should become increasingly a point of departure in analyses of EU politics.

NOTES

1 See, *inter alia*, J. Fitzmaurice, *The Party Groups in the European Parliament* (London, Saxon House, UK, 1975), and G. Pridham and P. Pridham, *Transnational Party Cooperation and European Integration* (London, Allen and Unwin, 1979).
2 Additional properties could include an ideological dimension structuring electoral competition and policy formulation, the number of parties, etc.
3 The case that European parties, or the party groups in the EP, cannot develop full attributes as parties due to the lack of a European-level government is found in K. Reif and O. Niedermayer, 'The European Parliament and the political parties', *Journal of European Integration*, nos. 2–3, Winter 1986, pp. 157–72.
4 See the chapter by Hix in this volume, and R. Ladrech, 'Social democratic parties and EC integration: transnational party responses to Europe 1992', *European Journal of Political Research*, vol. 24, 1993, pp. 195–210.
5 See F. Jacobs, R. Corbett and M. Shackleton, *The European Parliament* (London, Longman, 1992, 2nd edn).
6 *The European Parliament*, p. 56.
7 Juliet Lodge, 'EC policymaking: institutional dynamics', in J. Lodge (ed.), *The European Community and the Challenge of the Future* (New York, St Martin's Press, 1993, 2nd edn), p. 25.
8 Moravcsik asserts that EC member states have in fact used the EC, perhaps increasingly since the mid-1980s, to carry out policies difficult to achieve at the national level. Though Moravcsik grounds this behaviour in an intergovernmentalist mode, the interaction with EC institutions and policy making requires attention to be paid to its actors, including the EP, and thus the major groups. See Andrew Moravcsik, 'Preferences and power in the European Community: a liberal intergovernmentalist approach', *Journal of Common Market Studies*, vol. 31, no. 4, 1993, pp. 473–524, especially pp. 514–17.
9 See J. Lodge, 'The European Parliament: from "assembly" to co-legislature: changing the institutional dynamics', in J. Lodge (ed.), *The European Community*, especially pp. 64–8.
10 See *Eurobarometer* surveys which point to the relatively high level of public identifi-cation with the EP rather than with the Commission, Court or Council, e.g. no. 39, June 1993.
11 The extent of the increase in the powers of the EP is noted in J. Lodge, 'The European Parliament and the authority–democracy Crises', *Annals, American Academy of Political and Social Science*, no. 531, January 1994, pp. 69–83, as well as *The European Parliament*, 2nd edn.
12 The evaluation of EP elections as essentially national referenda on incumbent govern-ments is found in K. Reif and H. Schmitt, 'Nine second-order national elections: a conceptual framework for the analysis of European election results', *European Journal of Political Research*, vol. 8, no. 1, 1980, pp. 3–44.
13 S. Hix, chapter in this volume, and Pridham and Pridham, *Transnational Party Cooperation and European Integration*.
14 This changed with Article 138a of the Maastricht Treaty on Political Union.
15 For the 1994 EP election, the socialist group turned over the moulding campaign of

propaganda for national-specific settings to the national parties, e.g. posters, etc. Comment made during interview by socialist group chair Jean-Pierre Cot, 8 January 1993, Brussels.

16 *The European Parliament*, p. 85.

17 Joseph H.H. Weiler, 'After Maastricht: Community legitimacy in post-1992 Europe', in James Adams (ed.), *Singular Europe: Economy and Polity of the European Community after 1992* (Ann Arbor, MI, University of Michigan Press, 1992), p. 33.

18 Weiler, 'After Maastricht', p. 32.

19 Jean-Pierre Cot, *Overview of the Achievements of the Group of the Party of European Socialists in the European Parliament Since the June 1989 Elections*, submitted to the Second Congress of the Party of European Socialists, Brussels, 5–6 November 1993, p. 1.

20 Pridham and Pridham, *Transnational Party Cooperation and European Integration*, p. 278.

21 Pridham and Pridham noted six features of party group development: (1) organizational dominance of the party groups in the EP; (2) formation of group-based majorities; (3) growing importance of cohesion; (4) more elaborate formulation of group policies; (5) the role of group leadership; and (6) new interest in their external relations (pp. 42–74).

22 See W. Sandholtz and J. Zysman, '1992: recasting the European bargain', *World Politics*, vol. 42, 1989, pp. 95–128.

23 Helen Wallace contends that potential EU enlargement should also be added, considering that the political conditions under which Austria and the Nordic countries negotiated during 1993 were different from the period in which Spain and Portugal entered. See Helen Wallace, 'Deepening and widening: problems of legitimacy for the EC', in S. Garcia, *European Identity and the Search for Legitimacy* (London, Frances Pinter, 1993), pp. 95–105.

24 Pridham and Pridham, *Transnational Party Cooperation*, p. 278.

25 The concept of subsidiarity was seized by opponents of Maastricht and used to defend national interests, primarily by the British Conservative government.

26 European Parliament Resolution of 7 April 1992. The 'major shortcomings' as seen by the Parliament are expressed succinctly in this report. See Richard Corbett, *The Treaty of Maastricht: From Conception to Ratification: A Comprehensive Reference Guide* (Harlow, Longman, 1993).

27 Pro- and anti-Maastricht opinions cut across partisan identifications.

28 Wallace, 'Deepening and widening', p. 101.

29 See R. Corbett, 'The Intergovernmental Conference on Political Union', *The Journal of Common Market Studies*, vol. 30, no. 3, September 1992.

30 The resolutions of both parliaments were adopted on 21 March 1990.

31 As an example of party group influence on negotiating positions leading to the 1991 IGCs, see the EPP document *For A Federal Constitution of the European Union*, adopted by the 8th Congress of the EPP 14–16 November 1990, *Agence Europe Documents*, no. 1665, 5 December 1990. The development of this document was no doubt a factor 'in preparing crucial European Council meetings, as in October 1990 when the EPP leaders agreed to press the case for a strict timetable for monetary union at the subsequent European Council in Rome [in December]. This was the so-called "ambush" of Margaret Thatcher who was left isolated at the Summit.' *The European Parliament*, pp. 86–7.

32 F. Herman, *The Strategy of the European Parliament for Achieving European Union*, Report on Behalf of the Committee on Institutional Affairs of the EP, Doc. A2–322/88, 1989.

33 See M. Burgess, 'The convergence of the British and European conservative traditions', in *Federalism and the European Union*, (London, Routledge, 1989), pp. 147–62.

34 Individual members of the Conservative national delegation joined as a result of negotiations with the EPP. Many EPP national delegations objected to their membership because of conservative antipathy toward the federalist orientation of Christian democratic parties. It was the influence of the German CDU delegation that acted as a mediator in this regard.

35 For instance, the inclusion of Article 138a in the section of the treaty concerned with the EP might be read as a restriction to solely EP-related activities, rather than to a broader mandate.

36 See R.F.M. Irving, 'The Christian Democrats and European integration', in *The Christian Democratic parties of Western Europe* (London, George Allen and Unwin, 1979), and Michael Burgess, 'The European tradition of federalism: Christian Democracy and federalism', in M. Burgess and A.-G. Gagnon (eds), *Comparative Federalism and Federation: Competing Traditions and Future Directions* (Toronto, University of Toronto Press, 1993), pp. 138–53.

37 The organizational linkages among the Christian democratic parties profited from the fact that they participated in most government coalitions throughout the 1980s, allowing their leaders many other occasions to confer beyond transnational party congresses.

38 See, *inter alia*, 'The European Employment Initiative', Declaration of the Party Leaders' Conference, Brussels, 9 December 1993.

39 The growing symbolic importance of EP votes on certain issues, and the effects of this within a national context, led British Labour Party leader John Smith to criticize Labour MEPs for 'their lack of assiduity and their absence in certain important votes'. The affair was triggered by rejection of a socialist draft resolution condemning plans to close pits in the UK. See *Agence-Europe*, no. 5892, 7 January 1993, p. 4.

40 A. Ware, 'Transcontinental socialism', book review, *Government and Opposition*, vol. 28, Winter 1993, p. 133.

41 For a sample of the literature in this area, see C. Lemke and G. Marks (eds), *The Crisis of Socialism in Europe* (Durham, NC, Duke University Press, 1992), and M. Telo (ed.), *De la nation à l'Europe. Paradoxes et dilemmes de la social-démocratie* (Brussels, Bruylant, 1993).

42 *Overview of the Achievements of the Group of the Party of European Socialists*, p. 13.

43 It also adds to the motivation of the EP to change the requirements in negotiations with the other institutions and in intergovernmental conferences.

44 Wallace, 'Deepening and widening', p. 100.

45 'German court's Maastricht ruling a win for all,' *The Financial Times*, 13 October 1993, p. 3.

46 *The Financial Times*, 13 October 1993.

47 *Agence-Europe*, no. 6128, 13–14 December 1993.

48 *Agence-Europe*, no. 5981, 15 May 1993.

49 A report commissioned by the Party of European Socialists. The working group was headed by Swedish Social Democrat A. Larsson, a former cabinet minister.

50 Led by French businessman Bernard Tapie, this list incorporated socialists left off their official list and left radicals represented in French domestic politics by the MRG (Mouvement des radicaux de gauche).

SELECT BIBLIOGRAPHY

Adams, J. (ed.), *Singular Europe: Economy and Polity of the European Community after 1992*, Ann Arbor, MI, University of Michigan Press, 1992.

Anderson, S. and Eliassen, K. (eds), *Making Policy in Europe: The Europification of National Policy-making*, London, Sage, 1993.

Bulmer, S. and Scott, A. (eds), *Economic and Political Integration in Europe: Internal Dynamics and Global Context*, Oxford, Blackwell, 1994.

Burgess, M., *Federalism and the European Union*, London, Routledge, 1989.

Burgess, M. and Gagnon, A.-G. (eds), *Comparative Federalism and Federation: Competing Traditions and Future Directions*, Toronto, University of Toronto Press, 1993.

Corbett, R., *The Treaty of Maastricht: From Conception to Ratification*, Harlow, Essex, Longman, 1993.

Dinan, D., *Ever Closer Union? An Introduction to the European Community*, Boulder, CO, Lynne Rienner, 1994.

Garcia, S., *European Identity and the Search for Legitimacy*, London, Frances Pinter, 1993.

Haahr, J., *Looking to Europe: The EC Policies of the British Labour Party and the Danish Social Democrats*, Aarhus, Denmark, Aarhus University Press, 1993.

Hanley, D., *Christian Democracy in Europe*, New York, Frances Pinter, 1994.

Irving, R.E.M., *The Christian Democratic Parties of Western Europe*, London, Allen and Unwin, 1979.

Jacobs, F., Corbett, R. and Shackleton, M., *The European Parliament*, Harlow, Essex, Longman, 1993, 2nd edn.

Lodge, J., (ed.), *The European Community and the Challenge of the Future*, New York, St Martin's Press, 1993.

Martin, D., *Europe: an Ever Closer Union*, Nottingham, Spokesman, 1992.

Pridham, G. and Pridham, P., *Transnational Party Co-operation and European Integration*, London, Allen and Unwin, 1979.

Sbragia, A., *Euro-politics: Institutions and Policymaking in the 'New' European Community*, Washington, DC, Brookings, 1992.

Telo, M. (ed.), *De la nation à l'Europe. Paradoxes et dilemmes de la social-démocratie*, Brussels, Bruylant, 1993.

Wilde, L., *Modern European Socialism*, Aldershot, Dartmouth, 1994.

18 The transnational party federations

Simon Hix

There are four party federations in the European Union: the Party of European Socialists (PES) (see Table 18.1), which until November 1992 was the Confederation of Socialist Parties of the European Community (CSP); the European People's Party: Federation of Christian Democratic Parties of the European Community (EPP) (see Table 18.2); the Federation of European Liberal, Democrat and Reform Parties (ELDR) (see Table 18.3); and the European Federation of Green Parties (EFG) (see Table 18.4). There are also a number of other transnational party groupings: the European Democratic Union (EDU) (see Table 18.2), a broad right-wing group of conservative, Christian democrat and right-liberal parties; the European Free Alliance (EFA) (see Table 18.5), a group of regionalist and nationalist parties; and various transnational links between nationalist and neo-fascist parties, and communist and former communist parties. However, only the CSP, the EPP, the ELDR and the EFG possess all the elements of a transnational party federation: a statute, a common programme, a secretariat, an executive body, a party assembly, a hierarchical leadership structure, the ability to make decisions binding on the member parties, and the aspiration to become a fully fledged European political party.[1]

Other party families, such as the regionalists, the conservatives, the radical right and the communists, may also establish transnational federations.[2] However, for these party groups there are ideological and organizational reasons which make the formation of a party federation problematic. On the ideological side, these other party families either oppose supranational party integration, as do the conservatives and radical right, or are fundamentally divided over the question of European integration, as are the communists. Moreover, on the organizational side, these other party families only exist as a major force in a few member states (the conservatives and the communists), or exist in a number of countries but only as small parties (the regionalists and the radical right). In fact, after the collapse of international communism perhaps the regionalists can claim to be the only truly transnational party families apart from the socialists, the liberals, the Christian democrats and the Greens. In addition to these internal constraints, a further barrier to these other party families (and to the institutionalization of the Green Federation) is the emergence of a stable 'core' of the EU party system.[3] The core of the system includes the organizations of the three main party federations (the PES, EPP and ELDR) and the major alignments between these federations. Hence, in the EU as in most party systems, the dominance of the core parties and alignments constitute a significant barrier against the entry of new parties. This was the case, for example, during the

Table 18.1 Member parties of the Party of European Socialists[a]

Country	Party (date of joining PES, if not a founder member)	Abbreviation
Full members		
Austria	Socialistische Partei Österreichs (1990)	SPÖ[a]
Belgium	Parti Socialiste	PS
	Socialistische Partij	SP
Denmark	Socialdemokratiet	S
Finland	Soumen Sosialidemokraattinen Poulue (1992)	SSDP[a]
France	Parti socialiste	PS
Germany	Socialdemokratische Partei Deutschlands	SPD
Greece	Panellinio Socialistiko Kinima (1989)	PASOK
Ireland	The Labour Party	LP
Italy	Partito Socialista Italiano	PSI
	Partito Socialista Democratico Italiano	PSDI
	Partito Democratico della Sinistra (1992)	PDS
Luxembourg	Parti Ouvrier Socialiste Luxembourgeois	POSL
Netherlands	Partij van de Arbeid	PvdA
Norway	Dct Norske Arbeiderpartei (1993)	DNA[a]
Portugal	Partido Socialista (1979)	PS
Spain	Partido Socialista Obrero Español (1979)	PSOE
Sweden	Sveriges Socialdemokratiska Arbetareparti (1992)	SAP[a]
UK	The Labour Party (1976)	LP
Northern Ireland	Social Democratic and Labour Party (1976)	SDLP
Associate members		
Switzerland	Sozialdemokratische Partei der Schweiz	SPS
Iceland	Althyduflokkurinn	Alt
Cyprus	Socialist Party of Cyprus	EDEK
Observer status		
Israel	Israel Labour Party	ILP
	United Workers' Party of Israel	MAPAM
Malta	Malta Labour Party	MLP
San Marino	Partito Socialista Sammarinese	PSS
Turkey	Sosyaldemokrat Halkçi Parti	SHP

Note: [a] The Austrian Socialistische Partei, the Finnish Sosialidemokraattinen Poulue, the Norwegian Arbeiderpartei and the Swedish Sveriges Socialdemokratiska Arbetareparti were the first non-EC parties to be full members of a European party federation. This set the precedent for the membership of the Federation of Green Parties.

Sources: Agence-Europe; F. Jacobs (ed.), *Western European Political Parties: A Comprehensive Guide* (Harlow, Longman, 1989); L. Bardi, 'Transnational party federations in the European Community', in R.S. Katz and P. Mair (eds), *Party Organizations: A Data Handbook on Party Organizations in Western Democracies 1960–1990* (London, Sage, 1992); Confederation of Socialist Parties, *Declaration: Party Leaders' Summit*, Lisbon, 15–16 June 1992; Party of European Socialists, *Statutes of the Party of European Socialists* (PES, 1993).

negotiation of the Maastricht Treaty in the intergovernmental conferences (IGCs), which were launched at the Rome summit on 15 December 1990 and were concluded at the Maastricht summit on 11 December 1991.

Acknowledging the first direct elections to the European Parliament (EP) as the impetus for the formation of the party federations, the initial research on trans-national party co-operation concentrated on the electoral role of the federations.[4]

Table 18.2 Member parties of the European People's Party

Country	Party (date of joining EPP, if not a founder member)	Abbreviation
Full members		
Austria	Österreichische Volkspartei (1995)	ÖVP*
Belgium	Parti Social Chrétien	PSC
	Christelijke Volkspartij	CVP
Denmark	Det Konservative Folkeparti (1995)	KP*
Finland	Kansallinen Kokoomus (1995)	KK[a]*
France	Centre des démocrates sociaux	CDS
Germany	Christlich Demokratische Union	CDU*
	Christlich Soziale Union	CSU*
Greece	Nea Dimokratia (1981)	ND*
Ireland	Fine Gael	FG
Italy	Democrazia Cristiana	DC
Luxembourg	Chrëstlech Sozial Vollekspartei	CSV**
Netherlands	Christen Demokratisch Appèl	CDA
Portugal	Partido do Centro Democrático Social (1986)	CDS*
Spain	Partido Democràtica Popular (1986)	PDP
	Partido Popular (1992)	PP*
	Uniò Democràtica de Catalunya (1986)	UDC
	Partido Nacionalista Vasco (1986)	PNV
Sweden	Kristdemokratisk Samhällspartiet (1995)	KDS
	Moderata Samlingspartiet (1995)	MS[a]*
Associate member		
Malta	Partit Nazzjionalista	PN**
Observer status		
Norway	Høyre	H*
Sit with EPP group in the European Parliament		
France	Union pour la Démocratie Française	UDF[b]
United Kingdom	Conservative Party	CP*
Northern Ireland	Ulster Unionist Party	UUP
Other members and observers of the EUCD		
Bulgaria	Union Agriare Nationale Bulgare	BANU†
	Parti Démocratique	DP†
	Centre Démocratique Uni	ODZ†
	Union Démocrate Chrétienne	UDC†
Croatia	Hrvatska Demokratska Zajednica	HDZ†
	Hrvatska Krscanska Demokratska Strana	HKDS†
Cyprus	Democraticos Synagermos	DS*
Czech Republic	Krestanska a demokraticka unie	KDU
	Krestansko Demokraticka Strana	KDS†
Denmark	Kristelige Folkeparti	KrF
Estonia	National Coalition Party (ISAMAA)	EKL
Finland	Soumen Kristillinen Liito	SKL†
Hungary	Magyar Demokrata Forum	MDF
	Kereszténydemokrata Néppart	KDNP
	Independent Smallholder's Party	ISP†
Lebanon	Union Chrétienne Démocrate Libanaise	UCDL†
Lithuania	Lietuvos Kriksconiu Demokratu Partija	LKDP
Norway	Kristelig Folkeparti	KF
Poland	Porozumienie Centrum	PC†
	Kongres Chrzescijanskiaj Demokracij	KCD†

Romania	Partidul National Taranesc, crestind i democrat	PNT-cd
	Romania Magyar Demokrata Szövetseq	RMDSZ†
San Marino	Partito Democratico Cristiano Sammarinese	PDCS
Slovakia	Krestanskodemokraticke Hnutie	KDH
	Magyar Keresztenydemokrata Mozgalom	MKDM†
Slovenia	Slovenski Krscanski Demokrati	SKD
Switzerland	Christlich-demokratische Volkspartei der Schweiz	CVP**

Notes:
 * Member party of the European Democratic Union (EDU)
 ** Party with observer status to the European Democratic Union (EDU)
 † Party with observer status to the European Union of Christian Democrats (EUCD)
 a The Finish Kansallinen Kokoomus and the Swedish Moderata Samlingspartiet have 'permanent' observer status; which means that (unlike other observer parties) they did not automatically become full members of the EPP when Finland and Sweden joined the EU.
 b Only some of the members of the Union pour la démocratie française alliance sit with the EPP. Significantly, however, these include Giscard d'Estaing, the leader of the UDF.

Sources Agence-Europe; F. Jacobs (ed.), *Western European Political Parties: A Comprehensive Guide* (Harlow, Longman, 1989); L. Bardi, 'Transnational party federations in the European Community', in R.S. Katz and P. Mair (eds), *Party Organizations: A Data Handbook on Party Organizations in Western Democracies 1960–1990* (London, Sage, 1992); European People's Party, *List of Members of EPP and EUCD* (EPP, 1993).

Indeed, in the late 1970s, it was even fashionable to predict a *Europe des partis* (in contrast to de Gaulle's proposal for a *Europe des patries*) as a result of European elections.[5] However, because of the limited role of the party federations in all the EP elections, and their inability to produce European-wide party political alignments, most authors reluctantly admit that real political parties at the European level are a distant prospect.[6] However, drawing such conclusions solely on the basis of the role of the party federations in the EP elections may be premature. It is true that the EP elections are unlikely to lead to European parties because they will not develop beyond 'second-order national contests'.[7] However, this is not unexpected given the EU's institutional arrangements – a collegiate executive (the Commission), whose membership cannot be changed by direct elections, and a directly elected chamber (the EP) with less legislative power than an indirectly elected chamber (the Council of Ministers).

Furthermore, even within this institutional framework, the party federations have evolved towards European parties. In all party systems, party activity is directed in a number of different arenas, such as the electoral arena, the legislative arena and the governmental arena. Depending on the nature of the political system, one or other of these arenas is the primary focus of party behaviour. For example, in Switzerland, which has a similar institutional structure and decision-making environment to the EU,[8] parties at the federal level play a limited role in the elections to the Nationalrat (National Council), but are active agents in both chambers of parliament and in policy development and issue bargaining.[9] Consequently, the new policy and issue-orientation roles of the EU party federations in the IGCs may be more important indicators of the emergence of nascent European parties than the limited function of the federations in the EP elections.

Table 18.3 Member parties of the Party of European Liberals, Democrats and Reformers

Country	Party *(date of joining ELDR, if not a founder member)*	Abbreviation
Full members		
Belgium	Parti des Réformateur Libéral	PRL
	Vlaamse Liberale Demokraten	VLD
Denmark	Venstre, Danmarks Liberale Parti	V
	Det Radikale Venstres (1991)	RV
Finland	Suomen Keskuta (1995)	SK
France	Parti républicain	PR
	Parti radical	RAD
Germany	Freie Demokratische Partei	FDP
Greece	Hellenic Liberal Party (1983)	HLP
Ireland	Progressive Democrats (1988)	PD
Italy	Partito Liberale Italiano	PLI
	Partito Repubblicano Italiano	PRI
Luxembourg	Demokratesch Partei	DP
Netherlands	Volkspartij voor Vrijheid en Democratie	VVD
Portugal	Partido Social-Democratico (1986)	PSD
Spain	Centro Democrático y Social	CDS
Sweden	Folkspartiet Libralerna (1995)	FP
UK	Social and Liberal Democrats	SLD
Northern Ireland	Alliance Party of Northern Ireland (1984)	APNI
Observer status		
Hungary	Fiatal Demodratak Szövetsége	FiDeSz

Sources: Agence-Europe; F. Jacobs (ed.), *Western European Political Parties: A Comprehensive Guide* (Harlow, Longman, 1989); L. Bardi, 'Transnational party federations in the European Community', in R.S. Katz and P. Mair (eds), *Party Organizations: A Data Handbook on Party Organizations in Western Democracies 1960–1990* (London, Sage, 1992); Federation of European Liberal, Democrat and Reform Parties, *Vade–Mecum* (ELDR, 1993).

THE EVOLUTION OF THE PARTY FEDERATIONS

The recent history of transnational party co-operation in the EC has three fairly distinct phases. First, there was a period of optimism, from the birth of the federations in the early 1970s to the first EP elections in 1979, when it was hoped that the new party federations would establish a role in the EC institutional framework. Second, there was a period of stagnation, from the aftermath of the first European elections to the third European elections in 1989, when it became clear that it would be difficult for the federations to develop beyond umbrella organizations for the drafting of perfunctory EP election programmes. Finally, however, there was a period of renaissance, from the start of the IGC negotiations in December 1990 to the end of the ratification process of the Maastricht Treaty in 1993, where there was a renewed interest in the work and potential of the federations, and which has led to their 'widening and deepening' (increased membership and organizational development). Above all, during the negotiation of the Maastricht Treaty the party federations emerged as a crucial forum for the co-ordination of national party policies towards the IGCs, and facilitated the development of divisions in the negotiations along party-ideological lines as opposed to the traditional conflicts over 'national interest'.

Table 18.4 Member parties of the European Federation of Green Parties

Country	Party	Abbreviation
Full members		
Austria	Die Grün-Alternativen	GA
Belgium	Ecolo	Eco
	Agalev	Aga
Bulgaria	Green Party of Bulgaria	GP
Denmark	De Grønne	G
Estonia	Estonian Greens	EG
Finland	Vihreä Liitto	VL
France	Les verts	V
Germany	Die Grünen	G
Georgia	Georgian Greens	GG
Ireland	Green Alliance (Comhaontas Glas)	GA
Italy	Federazione dei Liste Verdi	FLV
Luxembourg	Dei Grëng Alternativ	GA
	Glei	G
Malta	Alternattiva Demokratika	AD
Netherlands	De Groenen	G
	Groen Links	GL
Norway	Miljöpartiet de Gronne	MG
Portugal	Os Verdes	V
Spain	Los Verdes	V
Sweden	Miljöpartiet de Gröna	MG
Switzerland	Parti écologiste suisse	PES
United Kingdom	Green Party	GP

Sources: F. Jacobs (ed.), *Western European Political Parties: A Comprehensive Guide* (Harlow, Longman, 1989); European Federation of Green Parties, *Statuts de la fédération européenne des partis verts* (FEG, 1993).

Phase One: optimism – the birth of the federations

The catalyst for the formation of the party federations was the decision to hold direct elections to the EP, which was taken at the December 1974 Brussels summit. However, unlike the Federation of European Liberals and Democrats and the European People's Party, the Confederation of Socialist Parties was formed before the Brussels summit. Hence, although the elections were a major impetus for the formation of the federations, they were not the sole reason for their creation. Nevertheless, the main catalyst was the 1969 Hague summit, which made a commitment to directly elect the EP, and hence facilitated a 'new departure' in transnational party co-operation in the EC, from the party internationals to the party federations.[10]

In 1957 the Socialist International (SI) established a special interparty liaison bureau for co-operation between the EC member parties; and as early as 1968 the SI began to prepare for the formation of a European Socialist Party. Following the Hague summit, however, the Liaison Bureau became the Office of the Social Democratic Parties in the EC. In 1973 it was entrusted with drafting a report on the formation of a Confederation of Socialist Parties. After the report had been circulated to the EC member parties for comments and recommendations, a redrafted version was adopted by the SI Bureau on 5 April 1974 and the CSP was thus formally established.[11]

Table 18.5 Member parties of the European Free Alliance

Region (country)	Party	Abbreviation
Alsace (France)	Elzaessiche Union/Union pour l'Alsace	EU
Andalucia (Spain)	Partido Andalucista	PA
Basque (France)	Eusko Alkartasuna-Iparraide	EAI
Basque (Spain)	Eusko Alkartasuna	EA
Brittany (France)	Union Démocratique Bretonne	UDB
Catalonia (Spain)	Esquerra Republicana di Catalunya	ERC
Cornwall (UK)	Mebyon Kernow	MK
Corsica (France)	Unione di u Populu Corsu	UPC
Flanders (Belgium)	Volksunie	VU
Flanders (France)	Vlaams Federalistische Partij	VFP
Friesland (Netherlands)	Fryske Nasjonale Partij	FNP
Fruili (Italy)	Union Furlana	UF
German-Wallonia (Belgium)	Partei der deutschsprachigen Belgier	PDB
Ireland	Independent Fianna Fàil	IFF
Lombardy (Italy)	Lega Lombarda	LL
Occitania (France)	Partito Occitan	PO
Perpignan (France)	Unitat Catalana	UC
Piedmont (Italy)	Movimento Autonomista Occitano	MAO
Sardinia (Italy)	Partito Sardo d'Azione	PSA
Savoy (France)	Mouvement Région Savoie	MRS
Scotland (UK)	Scottish National Party	SNP
Slovene-Fruili (Italy)	Slovenska Skupnost	SS
South Tyrol (Italy)	Union für Süd-Tirol	UST
Val d'Aosta (Italy)	Union Valdôtaine	UV
Venice (Italy)	Union del Populo Veneto	UPV
Wales (UK)	Plaid Cymru	PC

Sources: F. Jacobs (ed.), *Western European Political Parties: A Comprehensive Guide* (Harlow, Longman, 1989); European Free Alliance, *Les membres de l'ALE* (EFA, 1993).

Also following the Hague summit, the European Union of Christian Democrats (EUCD) established a Standing Conference and a Political Committee of the Christian democratic parties in the EC. At the 19th EUCD Congress in Bonn, in 1973, seven working groups were set up on different issues in the EUCD, including one on closer party co-operation. Enough progress was made by September 1975 for a new working group to be set up by the political committee, which was explicitly charged with drafting a statute for a European Christian Democratic Party. The statute was ready by February 1976, but the formal establishment of the EPP was delayed until 29 April 1976 because of a prolonged dispute over its name.[12]

Also in the wake of the Hague summit, the 1972 Congress of the Liberal International (LI) adopted a resolution asking the party leaders to examine the possibility of a federation of liberal parties in the EC, but only as a regional organization of the LI. However, in May 1973, Liberal leaders proposed the creation of an EC-based federation of parties, with a separate identity from the LI. A working group was subsequently created to prepare a statute, which was adopted at the LI Congress in Florence in 1974. However, due to the requirement that the statute should be ratified by individual parties, and because of arguments over the national parties' representation, the Federation of European Liberals and Democrats (ELD) was not formally established until 26 March 1976.[13]

Although no more 'federations' were established, a number of other party families also developed transnational links prior to the first EP elections. In the build up to the EP elections, the PCI and the PCF held several summits, but refused to set up a formal EC party organization because of fundamental ideological differences between the parties and because they 'excluded the idea of a simple decision centre for the European or world communist movement'.[14] In 1978, a number of regionalist parties established the European Free Alliance, and signed a Charter for Europe – which was more a call for a Europe of the Regions than a common political programme. Prior to the first EP elections, there was only very limited co-operation between the Green parties, and there was no co-ordination among parties of the extreme right.[15] Consequently, the only other formal transnational party organiz-ation created was the European Democratic Union (EDU), which was established in Salzburg (outside the EC!) in April 1978. Apart from the immediacy of the direct elections, however, the decision to form a broad right-wing alliance arose from a number of imperatives: the enlargement of the EC in 1973 to include Britain and Denmark, neither of which had Christian democratic parties; the particular desire of the CDU and the British Conservatives to overcome Conservative Party isolation in the EC; the formation of the CSP, with members in every member state; and the threat of a left-wing majority in the first elections.[16] The EDU was unlike the party federations in two key ways. First, the EDU was never meant to be anything more than a loose grouping of all the elements of the centre-right, including non-EC parties. Second, and ironically considering the impetus for its formation, the EDU played no role in the EP elections.[17]

Even for the party federations, however, the question of their exact status was unclear. This was highlighted by the controversies over names. This was a salient issue because of the implications of the title on the structure and membership of the federations. Upon its inauguration, when the first President of the CSP, Wilhelm Dröscher, described the confederation as a 'family of parties' rather than a 'European Socialist Party', he was clearly addressing the ambivalence of several member parties towards the establishment of supranational political structures.[18] These sensitivities were also reflected in the various descriptions of the socialist organization; where the English (confederation) and Danish (*samenslutingen*) titles imply a looser arrangement than the French (*union*), the German (*Bund*), and the Dutch (*federatie*).

For the liberals, the main problem was the ideological heterogeneity of liberal forces in the EC. The word 'democratic' was added to the original title because a number of member parties did not call themselves 'liberal'. To resolve the compli-cated problem of membership, however, the ELD allowed a 'period of application', between the inauguration congress in March 1976 and the first formal congress in the Hague in November 1976, which allowed parties interested in joining the ELD to prepare their arguments and make the necessary arrangements in the national arena. However, after the French PR had decided to join the ELD – which was not a member of the LI, was ideologically close to French neo-Gaullism, and had links with the British Conservatives – the more left-liberal French MRG withdrew in protest.

For the Christian democrats, the controversy over the name delayed the inaugur-ation by several months. The final version – the European People's Party: Federation of Christian Democratic Parties of the European Community – clearly illustrated the divisions within the group. The German CDU (and CSU) wanted a title that would not alienate the Conservative parties, whereas the more programmatic Christian democratic parties from the Benelux countries and Italy insisted on the inclusion of 'Christian'. The fact that 'EPP' appeared first, therefore, implied a victory for the more conservative parties. However, the choice of 'party', rather than 'federation' or 'confederation', reflected the unanimous supranational aspirations of the member parties.

Despite these problems, there was considerable optimism about the future role of the federations. The fact that the EP elections had encouraged national parties to become integrated in transnational party structures appeared to suggest that there would be a considerable amount of campaign co-ordination during the elections. Then, the aspiration that the federations wanted to be more than simply election-fighting coalitions was clear from their statutes. Even the least federalist CSP 'rules of procedure' provided for majority decision making in the executive bureau, and committed the confederation to drafting a Common Manifesto. Moreover, Article 2 of the ELD statutes stipulated that the federation would, 'seek a common position on all important problems affecting the Community . . . and inform the public and involve it in the construction of a united Europe'.[19] In a similar manner, Article 3 of the EPP statutes proclaimed that the party would ensure, 'close and permanent collaboration between its member parties . . . in order to implement their common policy in the construction of a federal Europe'.[20]

Finally, EC watchers openly predicted that the new European party structures and the direct elections to the EP would launch a fundamentally new and demo-cratic phase of European integration. What Henk Vredeling had described in 1971 as a 'common market of political parties', which would automatically 'arise from the shift in the structure of power in the EC from the national to the European level', at last seemed a possibility.[21] As a result of EP elections and the new European-level party structures, it was argued that political conflict in the EC would emerge along party political lines; and even that political alignments at the European level would be based on the divisions and alliances between the transnational party feder-ations.[22] The hopes for a new and democratic 'Europe of the Parties' were summed up by Leo Tindemans, the former Belgian prime minister and the new chairman of the EPP, who proclaimed that, 'only European political parties can bridge the gap between the hopes of public opinion and the powerlessness of governments to turn these expectations into proposals for concrete policies'.[23]

Phase two: stagnation – the European election campaigns

These optimistic predictions, however, collapsed with the reality of the first three EP elections, in 1979, 1985 and 1989. In the drafting of election manifestos, all three federations were deeply divided. Furthermore, the role of the federations in the election campaigns was minimal. Finally, a 'party Europe' could not emerge without a clear role for the federations in the EC's institutional framework.

In drafting a common electoral programme, even the EPP, with the most supra-nationally oriented member parties, had problems resolving opposing ideological views. An election manifesto was unanimously adopted by the EPP political bureau in February 1976, but the final political programme was not completed until March 1978. The reason for the delay was a protracted disagreement between the Dutch CDA and the German CDU/CSU over the place of 'Christian' principles in the programme.[24] In addition, whereas the German parties insisted on the importance of building an 'anti-socialist' bloc in the elections, such a strategy for the Belgian, Dutch and Italian parties would have contradicted alignments in the national arena, where Christian–socialist alliances are not only common but form the basis of party-system stability. Moreover, the salience of these ideological and strategic differences meant that they re-emerged in the 1984 and 1989 campaigns.

The ELD election manifesto aspired to be the most federal, with all the sections in bold type binding on the member parties. However, because of the ideological diversity of the liberal parties, and the insistence of most member parties on retaining their autonomy, the binding sections were no more than universally acceptable vague statements on such matters as pluralism, human rights and democracy. Nevertheless, the ELD programme was adopted without much disagreement in November 1977. However, differences that had been suppressed at the adoption Congress continually resurfaced until the elections, which eventually led to the withdrawal of the Danish Radikale Venstre in May 1978. Moreover, whereas EPP and CSP cohesion partially increased in the build up to the second and third EP elections, divisions in the ELD widened, particularly over the questions of economic policy and nuclear disarmament.[25]

For the socialists, the difficulties of drafting a common electoral programme were so great that the 1977 Congress, which was due to adopt the election manifesto, was postponed to avoid drawing attention to the open divisions in the newly formed CSP.[26] Moreover, as a result of continued disagreement, the draft election manifesto was abandoned in favour of a short and extremely vague Political Declaration, which was adopted by the party leaders in June 1978, and an Appeal to the Electorate passed by the CSP Congress in January 1979. However, the CSP succeeded in adopting a common electoral programme for the 1984 and 1989 EP elections. Nevertheless, the national parties were allowed to opt out of particular commitments in the programme by registering their opposition in a footnote, and there was no binding commitment on the member parties to use the transnational manifestos in the elections.

On top of the lack of internal solidarity in drafting the election programmes, the transnational party dimension of the election campaigns was almost non-existent. The EP elections were fought in the nation states, by the national parties, with national candidates and on national issues. With limited financial resources and rudimentary organizational structures, the transnational party federations could be nothing more than clearing houses; providing information, campaign materials, and organising (poorly attended) conferences and candidate exchanges. Most voters and party activists in almost all member states were unaware of the work of the federations, despite the use of some of the federation symbols, especially by the member parties of the EPP.[27] In all three elections, the national parties jealously guarded their control of the electoral campaign and agenda. Moreover, most parties were not prepared to pass up the opportunity to present the European elections as nationwide referenda on the incumbent government. Consequently, a commonly used theoretical framework for analysing the EP elections is the concept of 'second-order national elections', which has four main characteristics: there is a lower turnout than in first-order elections, campaigns are fought on first-order issues, governing parties lose votes, and there are brighter prospects for small and new parties.[28]

Consequently, despite the optimism of 1979, by the third direct elections it was increasingly acknowledged that the EP elections would not facilitate a 'party Europe' based on the party federations. At the European level, the EP groups predominated over the national parties, and the national parties had no real incentive to involve themselves in EC politics beyond the EP elections. A fundamental problem was that it was impossible to envisage a role for the federations in everyday EC business without a fundamental reform of the EC's institutional structures.[29] As Pridham noted after the second elections, 'although parties, whether transnational or national, have an institutional point of focus in the EP, they do not have an institutional point of focus within the EC system as a whole'.[30]

Nevertheless, despite the limited prospects of party development as a result of the direct elections, there were some indications that the transnational party federations might develop further given the right institutional circumstances. In the 1989 elections, all three federations had agreed common election manifestos, and for the first time there were two supranational themes in all the national campaigns: the environment and the Single European Act.[31] Moreover, in the national parties there was increased awareness of the work of the federations, particularly among the upper- and middle-level party elites.[32] Finally, the party leaders' summits began to emerge as important federation arenas. This was perhaps the most significant development for two reasons. First, like the EC summit meetings, because of the leadership position of the actors, the party leaders' meetings could set the general political agenda of the federations and make policy decisions which would be accepted by the national parties. Second, by holding leaders' summits before every European Council meeting, the federations began to establish a role in EC executive decisions and in setting the general EC agenda. Hence, by recognizing the inability of the EP and the direct elections to mobilize party political alignments at the European level, the federations turned their attention to the more crucial EC institutional arenas. This strategy began to bear fruit in the intergovernmental conferences.

Phase three: renaissance – the negotiation and ratification of Maastricht

The negotiation and ratification of the Maastricht Treaty[33] in the IGCs facilitated the renewed interest in the party federations for two main reasons. Given the political nature of the IGC agenda (preparing the political and economic union of Europe) the actors in the conferences were eager to seek alliances along ideological lines, rather than on issues of purely national interest. Second, because the outcome of the conferences had to be ratified in all the member states' parliaments, the national political parties were eager to have an input into the IGCs. This was particularly true of the opposition parties, which had no formal say in the negotiations.

The IGCs met once every month at ministerial level and the general agenda was agreed at the four European Council meetings prior to and during the negotiations. As a result, the usual federation party leaders' summits before each European Council became arenas for the development of joint policies to be presented in the IGCs. The federations' executive meetings were also rearranged to coincide with the ministerial-level IGC business. Hence, by manipulating their institutional organization, the party federations emerged as fora for coalition building before every major meeting of the IGC.

Moreover, the party environment of the federation meetings was perhaps better suited to complex coalition building than the 'defence-of-national-interest' environment of the IGCs. An example of the potential of the party federation arenas was demonstrated at the Rome summit, on 27 October 1990, which set the agenda for the IGC on Economic and Monetary Union. An EPP party leaders' summit had been held on 25 October, where the Christian democrat leaders, which included six EC heads of government, agreed unanimously to support a fixed timetable for EMU in the EC summit. In the build up to the summit, the British government had been preparing to oppose any such move. However, the use of qualified majority at the Rome summit meant that the EPP agenda was accepted almost in its entirety, which left the British prime minister feeling that she had been 'ambushed'. Margaret Thatcher had been unprepared for this show of solidarity by the Christian democrats because her advisers had underestimated the importance of the EPP meeting. The effectiveness of the October 1990 EPP leaders' summit hence led the socialist and liberal federations to adopt similar strategies and arrange their meetings to coincide with the IGC timetable and agenda.[34]

A further significant force behind the institutionalization of the party federations during the IGCs was the opposition parties in the member states. Out of office in the national arena, the opposition parties were unable to participate formally in the IGCs. Hence, the federations provided an important back-door into the conferences. This was particularly important for large and traditionally influential parties which were in opposition, such as the British Labour Party and the German Social Democratic Party. Both parties submitted proposals to the CSP leaders' summits, which the French and Spanish prime ministers agreed to support in the IGCs if adopted by the federation.[35] Indeed, this procedure was used to varying degrees by almost all socialist, liberal and Christian democratic parties in opposition. A measure of the success of this strategy was the fact that all parties which were members of the party federations accepted the outcome of the IGCs and hence supported the ratification of the Maastricht Treaty, regardless of whether they were in government or opposition.

An additional implication of the new institutional role of the party federations was that they helped facilitate the emergence of political alignments along party political lines. For example, the differences between the EPP and the CSP on Economic and Monetary Union constituted a classic left–right conflict. The socialists argued for: 'convergence criteria' based not simply on economic indicators; a Cohesion Fund for 'real fiscal transfers'; the transformation of the Council of Ministers for Economics and Finance (EcoFin) into a permanent and fixed member organization; an independent EC Central Bank, but 'accountable' to EcoFin; the 'control' of medium-term economic policy and medium-term exchange-rate policy by EcoFin; and the possibility of binding minimum taxation rates, to avoid 'tax-cut competition'. In contrast, the Christian democrats supported convergence criteria based on strict economic targets; the possibility of a Cohesion Fund, but only within the existing structural fund framework; the continuation of EcoFin as a regular meeting of the Council of Ministers; a fully independent central bank, under a statute similar to the German *Bundesbankgesetz*; the co-ordination of medium-term economic policy and long-term exchange-rate policy in EcoFin; and no policy on taxation rates.[36]

In addition, the divisions and alignments between the three federations were reflected in the outcome of the IGCs. The general structure of competition between the federations was similar to the 'triangular' alliances of the German party system (see Figure 18.1).[37] Along one side of the triangle, the EPP and the CSP opposed the ELDR[38] on corporatist issues (for example the socialists and christian democrats supported a more *dirigiste* industrial policy than the liberals). Along the second side, the EPP and ELDR opposed the CSP on free market issues, for example on EMU convergence criteria based purely on economic indicators as opposed to also including social indicators. Finally, along the third side, the CSP and ELDR opposed the EPP on democracy–citizenship issues, such as on the right for EC citizens to vote in EP and local elections in any member state. As can be seen in the Maastricht Treaty, on each of these issues the majority coalition position was successful, because the treaty contained an interventionist section on industrial policy,[39] convergence criteria based purely on economic targets,[40] and the right to vote in EP and regional elections in any member state.[41]

Hence, transnational party co-operation received a new impetus as a result of the IGCs. Because of the operation of the party federations, for the first time the national party elites were involved in the development of EC policy. Furthermore, the federations provided an arena for the development of party political positions towards EC integration which facilitated the emergence of a new cleavage in the IGCs based on ideology rather than national interest. Finally, the renewed interest in the work of the federations as a result of the process of negotiating and ratifying the Maastricht Treaty led to their 'widening and deepening'. The British and Danish Conservative MEPs decided to join the EPP Group in the EP, and the national parties began the process of becoming members of the EPP Federation. With the British and Danish parties, the EPP would have member parties in all EC states, like the CSP and the ELDR. In addition, after the Italian PDS (the former PCI) joined the CSP, all major centre-left parties were members of the Socialist Confederation. Finally, as regards the deepening of the federations, in November 1992 the CSP became the Party of European Socialists and preparations were made at the end of 1992 for the formation of a European Liberal Party.[42] The statute of the PES provides for majority decision making in all areas of EC policy where qualified majority is used in the Council of Ministers, and in certain areas decisions can be made which are binding on the national socialist parties.[43] Finally, in June 1993, twenty-three European Green parties established the European Federation of Green Parties. In organizational terms the Green Federation is more like the

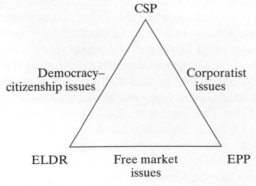

Figure 18.1 The triangular alliances in the intergovernmental conferences

early structures of the other federations than the new 'federal-type' statutes of the European socialist, Christian democrat and liberal parties.[44] Nevertheless, the establishment of a fourth federation may suggest that the core of the EC party system will now include alignments and conflicts on environmental issues.

THEORIZING ABOUT THE EUROPEAN PARTY FEDERATIONS

Despite this renaissance of transnational party co-operation, what exactly are the European party federations? The following theories range from a 'minimalist' view, which sees the federations as no more than transnational interest groups, to a 'maximalist' view, which regards them as European-level political parties. The opposing conceptions of the party federations also arise from differing theoretical positions in international relations (IR) and comparative politics. Within the pluralist paradigm of IR, the federations are either transnational organizations and/or reflections of intra-state conflicts. In comparative politics, on the other hand, there are two basic models of party development: the institutional model, which concentrates on the emergence of legislative and executive party functions; and the genetic model, which concentrates on the emergence of social and political cleavages.[45]

Against the realist paradigm of IR, the pluralist school challenges the concept of the state as a unitary actor in the international system. Hence, one area of interest is the development and operation of transnational non-state actors, such as the transnational party federations.[46] To avoid the concept of non-state actor, however, Rosenau proposes the use of 'sovereignty-free' actors, which he uses for multinational corporations and political parties, and 'sovereignty-bound' actors, which are the nation states.[47] In this framework, therefore, the transnational party federations would have a high degree of freedom but would not possess the legitimacy to make policy decisions. Moreover, most transnationalist literature suggests that, unlike corporations, there are unlikely to be strong transnational party organizations because of the desire of the national parties to preserve their autonomy.[48]

However, also within the pluralist paradigm, neo-functionalism argues that European (and party) integration arises from competition between national political elites.[49] In the neo-functionalist approach, 'political parties are far more crucial carriers of political integration or disintegration than even supranationally organised interest groups'.[50] Political parties are the only institutions capable of linking competition between elites at the national and European levels, and facilitating, 'the process whereby political actors in several distinct national settings are persuaded to shift their loyalties, expectations and activities towards a new centre'.[51] Hence, the transnational party federations emerge as a result of 'political spill-over',[52] whereby in order to obtain an advantage in the national party arena, parties become integrated into transnational groups. Integration in the party federations not only makes the European policy of a party more legitimate, but also eases the development of often difficult and complex policies.[53] Hence, in the neo-functionalist theory, the transnational federations will continue to develop as long as the national parties can gain in the national arena from integration into the party federations. For example, the renewed development of federations in the IGCs arose from the national parties' desire to establish a role in the new institutional framework. However, under this model the federations are no more than European arms of the national political parties and may thus be unlikely to emerge as full European parties.

Turning to models of party formation, one of the main theories argues that parties evolve as a result of institutional development.[54] As legislative and executive institutions develop, parties emerge to fulfil the necessary functions of democratic government. Under this argument, the party functions can broadly be categorized into three main groups: representation and aggregation, integration and education, and governing.[55] The primary institutional catalyst for the evolution of these party functions, however, is the introduction of competitive elections. Universal elections facilitate a change from caucus to mass parties, as more complex and broader party organizations are required to provide a link between society and the state.[56] Moreover, Duverger also makes a distinction between internally created parties, emerging from the parliamentary party groups, and externally created parties, emerging from non-parliamentary organizations such as trades unions.[57] Hence, where the party federations are concerned, they were established as a direct result of the decision to hold direct elections to the EP. Moreover, the federations were internally created, that is, out of the groups in the EP. The groups provided a framework for transnational co-operation, broadly determined the membership of party federations, and provided most of the necessary finances.

However, an alternative theory of party development, argues that parties evolve as a result of political conflict.[58] Under this model, parties emerge to occupy a space in a matrix of cross-cutting cleavages. The cleavages arise from dichotomous conflicts created by 'critical junctures' in the historical development of a system.[59] For example, the National Revolution produced church versus state and centre versus periphery conflicts, and the Industrial Revolution produced landed versus urban and middle-class versus working-class conflicts.[60] Hence, in the EU system, there are two fundamental lines of conflict produced by different critical junctures. First, as with the process of national integration,[61] supranational integration produces a centre versus periphery conflict; between national interest and European interest, and thus between pro- and anti-integration forces. Second, the politicization of the EU, as a result of increasing supranational decisions on questions of distribution,[62] facilitates socio-economic conflict at the European level, and the development of a classic left–right cleavage.[63] The governments of the EU member states in the Council of Ministers are the actors which articulate the centre–periphery conflict. However, because of the 'political' nature of the Maastricht Treaty negotiations, the party federations developed a new institutional role and new functions to articulate the left–right conflict. Nevertheless, under this elaboration of the genetic model, the party federations would not necessarily develop beyond vehicles for expressing the socio-economic conflict at the EU level.

An alternative ('maximalist') view claims that the party federations are fully-fledged political parties. The federations already possess all 'three faces of party organization':[64] the party as a membership organization (the corporate membership of the national parties, and the introduction of procedures for 'individual membership' in the 1992 federation statutes); the party as a governing organization (the policy development function during the IGCs); and the party as a bureaucratic organization (the increased number of staff in the federations' central offices).[65] However, without a direct link to the EU executive, the governing organization of the party federations may be severely circumscribed. Nevertheless, the governing function of parties in Switzerland, in a similar institutional environment, is also restricted to policy formulation and conflict regulation.[66] Moreover, all three party federations have developed more integrated hierarchical leadership structures, which under the new federation statutes allow certain supranational party decisions to be imposed on the member parties.[67] Furthermore, as regards the external element of party activity, party competition developed in the IGCs as a result of the triangular alliances between the three federations. Finally, for the first time in EU treaties or legislation, the Maastricht Treaty contains an explicit reference to 'European Parties'. In a similar fashion to the 'party article' of the German Basic Law, Article 138a of the Maastricht Treaty states that: 'Political Parties at European level are important as a factor for integration within the Union. They contribute to forming a European awareness and to expressing the political will of the citizens of the Union'.[68]

CONCLUSION

The party federations have evolved from organizations for transnational party co-operation, with a limited electoral role, to nascent European parties, with certain policy development and agenda setting functions. Furthermore, whereas initial transnational party co-operation was facilitated by the introduction of direct elections to the European Parliament (in line with the 'institutional model' of party formation), the development of more cohesive party structures and party competition between the federations was facilitated by the emergence of the left–right conflict in the negotiation of the Maastricht Treaty (in line with the genetic model of party formation). Rather than the party federations actually producing the conflicts in the IGCs, however, they acted as channels for the development of European and national party positions towards European integration, thus solidifying political conflict along party ideological lines (a socio-economic cleavage) in contrast to the traditional conflict between pro- and anti-integration positions (a centre–periphery cleavage). It is the case, therefore, that even if the federations are still only nascent European parties, increased politicization of conflict in the EU is likely to lead to further party integration.

However, there are two important sources of constraint which will restrict further development of the party federations. First, it will be difficult for the federations to establish a role in everyday EU business within the present institutional arrangements. With a fixed member executive, whose members are appointed primarily on the basis of their national (as opposed to party) affiliation, and who cannot be removed by direct elections, the governmental function of political parties at the European level will remain limited. Moreover, as long as the Council of Ministers is the main legislative arena, political conflict will fundamentally be along national interest lines (the centre–periphery cleavage), with left–right conflicts distinctly secondary.

Second, it is unlikely that the national party systems will be replaced as the first-order political arena. Because of the historical concentration of national parties and the media on the national arena, and the question of national identity, it will be difficult for European political parties to supplant the national parties. Moreover, even if some of the 'high politics' issues, such as foreign and defence policies, are handed to the European level, the national arena will still be concerned with fundamental party political questions of redistribution, such as health and education policies. Furthermore, with the 'pillarization' in the EU's consociational system along national lines, the member states' governments are already the functional equivalent of political parties. Whereas in societally fragmented systems, such as the Netherlands, political parties are responsible for the representation and accommodation of each pillar, in the EU these functions are fulfilled by the executives of the member states in the Council of Ministers.

However, like national political parties, the European party federations may have a certain degree of autonomy.[69] Like most institutions, the party federations have been able to establish their own internal dynamic.[70] For example, the institution of the party leaders' summits has developed independently of the original role in the initial federation statutes. Like the EU summit meetings, by involving the top national figures and deciding on the general direction of institutional development, the party leaders' summits have provided a motor for further party co-operation and a focus for national party (and media) attention. It is not surprising, therefore, that with the politicization of EU conflicts in the IGCs, the federation leaders' summits became the new arena for coalition building. Hence, despite writing in the 'optimistic' period surrounding the birth of the federations, the Pridhams were correct to suggest that, 'the very existence of . . . the European party federations, does itself provide a motor for further (party) integration'.[71]

Finally, a further institutional feature with a degree of independence, and which may thus reinforce the federations, is the emergence of an EU party system 'core'; based on the triangular system of alliances between the PES, the EPP and the ELDR. In addition to preserving the role of the federations in the EU system as coalition-building arenas, the stability of these alliances helps to reinforce the position of the three party federations *vis-à-vis* the other party families. For example, the outcome of the Maastricht Treaty did not significantly enhance EU policy in areas outside the core coalitions, such as in environment and regional policies. Furthermore, following the Treaty ratification, the Conservative Parties in Britain and Denmark, which were isolated in the negotiation of the Maastricht Treaty not only as the only fundamentally anti-integration governing parties, but also because they were outside the party system core, made significant moves towards becoming full members of the EPP. Finally, despite the existence of Green and regionalist groups in the EP, the development from *ad hoc* alliances for fighting EP election campaigns to fully fledged federations has been slow. Because there were no Green or regionalist parties in government in any of the member states during the IGCs, from December 1990 to December 1991, there was no motivation to develop transnational links in order to build coalitions for the negotiations. However, as with the limited independence of the party federations themselves, this nascent party system core is also ultimately dependent upon EU institutional arrangements and the Council of Ministers remaining the major arena of political conflict in the EU. In a different institutional configuration, and with more powers for the EP, the shape of the EU party system core might be very different, and include alignments on environmental and regional issues.

NOTES

1 Because of the *sui generis* nature of transnational party activity in the EU, it is problematic basing the difference between 'party co-operation' and 'party federation' on analogies drawn from the development of national parties. Nevertheless, certain comparisons can be made with systems where parties existed at the regional level before becoming

established at the national level, such as Switzerland. See, in particular, H. Gruner, *Die Parteien in der Schweiz* (Berne, Franke Verlag, 1969, rev. edn in 1977). Second, this list of elements is also derived from the five criteria proposed by Pridham and Pridham for measuring the development of transnational party co-operation in the unique environment of the EC: titular and cosmetic, a common title and label; programmatic, a common programme with some definition of ideological orientation and policies; electoral-organizational, a degree of central control of electoral organization and candidate selection; political-organizational, the creation of some form of integrated hierarchical structure; and a 'political power structure of leadership' at the European level. See G. Pridham and P. Pridham, *Transnational Party Cooperation and European Integration: The Process Towards the Direct Elections*, (London, Allen and Unwin, 1981) pp. 115–16.

2 For the historical and ideological definitions behind the concept of 'party family', see K. von Beyme, *Political Parties in Western Democracies* (London, Gower House, 1985), pp. 29–136.

3 In party system theory, the idea of 'core persistence' is developed by Gordon Smith. He distinguishes two main elements of a party system core: the major political parties (the largest and most influential parties for the functioning of the system); and the major (divisive and coalitional) alignments between these parties. See G. Smith 'Core persistence: system change and the "People's Party"', *West European Politics*, vol. 12, no. 4, 1989, pp. 161–2.

4 See, for example: P.-H. Claeys and N. Loeb-Mayer, 'Trans-European party groupings: the emergence of new and alignment of old parties in light of the direct elections to the European Parliament', *Government and Opposition*, vol. 4, no. 4, 1979, pp. 456–78; G. Pridham and P. Pridham, 'Transnational parties in the European Community II: the development of the European party federations', in S. Henig (ed.), *Political Parties in the European Community* (London, Croom Helm, 1979), and J. Lodge and V. Herman, *The Direct Elections to the European Parliament* (London, Macmillan, 1982).

5 H. Vredeling, 'The Common Market of political parties', *Government and Opposition*, vol. 6, no. 4, 1979, D. Marquand, 'Towards a Europe of the parties', *Political Quarterly*, vol. 49, no. 4, 1978, pp. 443.

6 See, for example, O. Niedermeyer, 'The transnational dimension of the election', *Electoral Studies*, vol. 3, no. 3, 1984; G. Pridham and P. Pridham, *Transnational Party Cooperation and European Integration: The Process Towards the Direct Elections* (London, Allen and Unwin, 1981); and J. Lodge (ed.), *Direct Elections to the European Parliament 1984* (London, Macmillan, 1986).

7 Cf. K. Reif and H. Schmitt 'Nine second-order national elections: a conceptual framework for the analysis of European election results', *European Journal of Political Research*, vol. 8, no. 1, 1980, pp. 6–15.

8 In terms of institutional arrangements, Switerland and the EU both have a collegiate executive, with fixed representation under the principle of 'proportionality' and with fixed tenure; and in both cases elections to the lower chamber of parliament cannot change the make up of the executive. In terms of the decision-making environment, Switzerland and the EU both display elements of 'co-operative federalism' and 'consociationalism'. For discussion of co-operative federalism in the EU, see F.W. Scharpf, 'The joint-decision trap: lessons from German federalism and European integration', *Public Administration*, vol. 66, no. 2, 1988, pp. 239–78, and A.M. Sbragia, 'Thinking about the European future: the uses of comparisons', in A.M. Sbragia (ed.), *Euro-Politics: Institutions and Policymaking in the 'New' European Community* (Washington, DC, The Brookings Institution, 1992); and for the application of consociationalism to the EU see P. Taylor, 'The European Community and the state: assumptions, theories and propositions', *Review of International Studies, 1991*, vol. 17, no. 2, 1991, pp. 109–25.

9 See H.H. Kerr, 'The Swiss party system: steadfast and changing', in H. Daalder (ed.), *Party Systems in Denmark, Austria, Switzerland, The Netherlands and Belgium* (London, Frances Pinter, 1987), pp. 180–4.

10 Cf. G. Pridham and P. Pridham, 'The new European party federations and direct elections', *The World Today*, vol. 35, no. 2, 1979, p. 63.

11 For more on the birth of the CSP see: Lodge and Herman, *Direct Elections*, pp. 131–52;

326 *Simon Hix*

Pridham and Pridham, 'Transnational Parties', p. 283–7; J. Fitzmaurice, *The European Parliament* (London, Saxon House, 1978), pp. 104–11; J. May, 'Cooperation between socialist parties', in W.E. Paterson and A.H. Thomas (eds), *Social Democratic Parties in Western Europe* (London, Croom Helm, 1977); K. Featherstone, 'Socialist parties and European integration: variations on a common theme', in W.E. Paterson and A.H. Thomas (eds), *The Future of Social Democracy: Problems and Perspectives of Social Democratic Parties in Western Europe* (Oxford, Clarendon Press, 1986), and K. Featherstone, *Socialist Parties and European Integration: A Comparative History* (Manchester University Press, 1989), pp. 339–49.

12 For more on the birth of EPP see: Lodge and Herman, *Direct Elections*, pp. 153–71; Pridham and Pridham, 'Transnational parties', pp. 279–83; Fitzmaurice, *The European Parliament*, pp. 112–15; R.E.M. Irving, *The Christian Democratic Parties of Western Europe* (London, Allen and Unwin, 1979), pp. 243–52; G. Pridham, 'Christian Democrats, Conservatives and transnational party cooperation in the European Community: centre-forward or centre-right?', in Z. Layton-Henry (ed.), *Conservative Politics in Western Europe* (London, Macmillan, 1982); and B. Kohler and B. Myrzik, 'Transnational party links' in R. Morgan and S. Silvestri (eds), *Moderates and Conservatives in Western Europe: Political Parties, the European Community and the Atlantic Alliance* (London, Heinemann, 1982).

13 For more on the birth of the ELD see Lodge and Herman, *Direct Elections*, pp. 189–209; Pridham and Pridham, 'Transnational parties', pp. 287–90; Fitzmaurice, *The European Parliament*, pp. 115–18; and R. Hrbek 'Transnational links: the ELD and the Liberal group in the European Parliament', in E.J. Kirchner (ed.), *Liberal Parties in Western Europe* (Cambridge, Cambridge University Press, 1988).

14 See Fitzmaurice, *The European Parliament*, p. 104.

15 See Claeys and Loeb-Mayer, 'Trans-European party groupings', pp. 474–7.

16 Cf. Fitzmaurice, *The European Parliament*, pp. 119–20; Lodge and Herman, *Direct Elections*, pp. 171–86; Pridham and Pridham, 'Transnational Parties', pp. 293–4; Pridham and Pridham, *Transnational Party Cooperation*, chapter 3; Kohler and Myrzik, 'Transnational party links', pp. 200–3; Pridham, 'Christian Democrats', pp. 331–42.

17 There were a number of reasons for this, the most prominent of which were pressures on the CDU from within the EPP, and the British Conservative Party's refusal to make any supranational electoral commitments.

18 Indeed, the British Labour Party refused to participate formally in the work of the CSP until 1976.

19 Federation of European Liberal and Democratic Parties (1976) *ELD Statutes*, ELD Publication.

20 European People's Party (1976) *EPP Statutes*, EPP Publication.

21 Vredeling, 'The Common Market of political parties', p. 448, 460.

22 Cf. Fitzmaurice, *The European Parliament*, pp. 90–130; Marquand 'Towards a Europe of the parties', pp. 438–45; D. Marquand, *Parliament for Europe* (London, Jonathan Cape, 1979), pp. 111–28; Pridham and Pridham 'Transnational parties', pp. 294–6; Pridham and Pridham 'European party federations', pp. 62–7; and Pridham and Pridham, *Towards Transnational Parties in the European Community* (London, Policy Studies Institute, 1979), pp. 11–17.

23 *CD-Europe Bulletin*, publication of the Christian Democratic Group of the EP, June 1976, p. 1.

24 Cf. Pridham, 'Christian Democrats', pp. 322–3.

25 The most divisive issue for the ELD in the second EP elections was NATO's 'twin-track' policy. Hrbek, 'Transnational links', p. 463.

26 Lodge and Herman, *Direct Elections*, p. 140.

27 See the European Elections Studies (EES): K. Menke and I. Gordon, 'Differential mobilisation and Europe: a comparative note on some aspects of the campaign', *European Journal of Political Research*, vol. 8, no. 1, 1980 pp. 63–89; M. Steed 'Failure or long-haul? European elections and European integration', *Electoral Studies*, vol. 3, no. 3, 1984, pp. 225–34; and O. Niedermeyer, 'The 1989 European elections: campaign and results', *European Journal of Political Research*, vol. 19, no. 1, 1989, pp. 3–15.

28 See Reif and Schmitt, 'Nine second-order national elections', pp. 9–12; and K. Reif 'National electoral cycles and European elections 1979 and 1984', *European Journal of Political Research*, vol. 3, no. 3, 1984, p. 247.

29 On this point see in particular V. Bogdanor, 'The future of the European Community: two models of democracy', *Government and Opposition*, vol. 21, no. 2, 1986, pp. 161–76; and V. Bogdanor, 'Direct elections, representative democracy and European integration', *Electoral Studies*, vol. 8, no. 3, 1989, pp. 1–12.

30 G. Pridham, 'European elections, political parties and trends of internalization in Community affairs', *Journal of Common Market Studies*, vol. 24, no. 4, 1986, p. 285.

31 Cf. J. Lodge, '1989: edging towards "genuine" Euro-elections?', in J. Lodge (ed.), *The 1989 Elections of the European Parliament* (London, Macmillan, 1989), pp. 213–17; and J. Curtice, 'The 1989 elections: protest or Green tide?', *Electoral Studies*, vol. 8, no. 3, 1989, pp. 217–30.

32 Contrast Niedermeyer, 'The 1989 European elections', pp. 6–8, with K. Reif, R. Cayrol and O. Niedermeyer, 'National political parties' middle level elites and European integration', *European Journal of Political Research*, vol. 8, no. 1, 1980, pp. 91–112.

33 This section is adapted from S. Hix, 'The emerging EC party system? The European party federations in the intergovernmental conferences', *Politics*, vol. 13, no. 2, 1993, pp. 38–46.

34 For an analysis of the developments surrounding the October 1990 EPP and Rome Summits see *Agence-Europe*, 22 October 1990, p. 4; 24 October 1990, p. 5; 25 October 1990, p. 5; 27 October, p. 3; and, *Agence-Europe: European Documents*, 29 October 1990, p. 1.

35 See *Agence-Europe*, 12 December 1990, p. 4; and 5 June 1991, p. 5.

36 These differences are based on my own observations as an EC political consultant during the IGCs. A similar picture is formed on the reading of the French, Spanish, German and French governments' submissions to the IGCs, and the declarations of the socialist and EPP leaders' summits.

37 The idea of a 'triangular' party system in Germany is proposed by Pappi. See F.-U. Pappi, 'The West German party system', *West European Politics*, vol. 7, no. 4, 1984, pp. 7–26.

38 In 1986, with the membership of the Spanish and Portuguese parties, the name of the Liberal federation was changed from the ELD to the Federation of European Liberal, Democrat and Reform Parties (ELDR).

39 In the Maastricht Treaty, Title XIII: Industry, Article 130 states that: to 'ensure that the conditions necessary for the competitiveness of the Community's industry exist', the Council can take action in the following areas: 'speeding up the adjustment of industry to structural changes; encouraging an environment favourable to initiative and to the development of undertakings throughout the Community . . . ; fostering better exploitation of the industrial potential of policies of innovation, research and technological development'; Council of the European Communities, *Treaty on European Union* (Luxembourg, Office for Official Publications, 1992), pp. 52–3.

40 Article 109j of the Maastricht Treaty lists the four convergence criteria for admission to the final stage of EMU. The criteria are based on targets for price stability, budgetary discipline, exchange-rate stability, and level of interest rate. See Council of the European Communities, ibid., pp. 40–2. The CSP argued for additional criteria based on the level of 'social and economic convergence', which would include levels of unemployment and regional economic disparities.

41 Article 8b(1) of the Treaty states that: 'Every citizen of the Union . . . shall have the right to vote and to stand as a candidate at municipal elections in the Member State in which he resides.' Article 8b(2) extends this right for elections to the European Parliament. See Council of the European Communities, ibid., pp. 15–16.

42 The decision to establish a European Liberal Party was taken at the ELDR leaders' summit on 7 December 1992; see *Agence-Europe*, 9 December 1992, p. 5.

43 *Agence-Europe*, 11 November 1992, p. 5. Also see Article 9.4 of the PES Statutes.

44 See European Federation of Green Parties (1993) *Statuts de la fédération européenne des partis verts*, FEG Publication.

45 Cf. J. LaPombara and M. Weiner, 'The origin and development of political parties', in J. LaPalombara and M. Weiner (eds), *Political Parties and Political Development* (Princeton, Princeton University Press, 1966), pp. 7–21.

46 Cf. M. Clarke, 'Transnationalism', in S. Smith (ed.), *International Relations: British and American Perspectives* (Oxford, Basil Blackwell, 1985).

47 J.N. Rosenau, *Turbulence in World Politics: A Theory of Change and Continuity* (New York, Harvester Wheatsheaf, 1990), p. 36.

48 P. Willets (ed.), *Pressure Groups in the Global System: The Transnational Relations of Issue-Oriented Non-Governmental Organisations* (London, Frances Pinter, 1982), p. 8.

49 The theory of neo-functionalism was first elaborated in E.B. Haas, *The Uniting of Europe: Political, Social and Economic Forces, 1950–57* (London, Stevens and Sons, 1958); and L.N. Lindberg, *The Political Dynamics of European Economic Integration* (Oxford, Oxford University Press, 1963).

50 Haas, *The Uniting of Europe*, p. 437.

51 Ibid., p. 16.

52 Lindberg defines 'spill-over' as, 'a situation in which a given action, related to a specific goal, creates a situation in which the original goal can be assured only by taking further actions, which in turn creates a further condition and a need for more action, and so forth'; Lindberg, *Political Dynamics*, p. 9.

53 In the original formulation of neo-functionalism, parties (like government agencies) tend to delegate difficult problems to the European level. See Lindberg, *Political Dynamics*, pp. 10–11.

54 This approach is associated with Maurice Duverger. See M. Duverger, *Political Parties: Their Organization and Activity in the Modern State* (New York, John Wiley, 1954).

55 Cf. S. Neumann, 'Towards a comparative study of political parties', in S. Neumann (ed.), *Modern Political Parties: Approaches to Comparative Politics* (Chicago, Chicago University Press, 1956); Duverger, *Political Parties*; L.D. Epstein, *Political Parties in Western Democracies* (New Brunswick, Rutgers University Press, 1967); and R.C. Macridis, Introduction, in R. C. Macridis (ed.), *Political Parties: Contemporary Trends and Ideas* (New York, Harper & Row, 1967).

56 Duverger, *Political Parties*, pp. xxxvi–xxxvii.

57 Ibid., pp. 1–37.

58 This approach is primarily associated with the seminal work of Lipset and Rokkan. See S.M. Lipset and S. Rokkan, 'Cleavage structures, party systems and voter alignments: an introduction', in S.M. Lipset and S. Rokkan (eds), *Party Systems and Voter Alignments: Cross-national Perspectives* (New York, Free Press, 1967).

59 Ibid., pp. 3–9.

60 Ibid., pp. 13–23.

61 S. Rokkan, 'Electoral mobilisation, party competition, and national integration', in J. LaPalombara and M. Weiner (eds), *Political Parties and Political Development* (Princeton, Princeton University Press, 1966).

62 Cf. H. Wallace, 'Direct elections and the political dynamics of the European Communities', *Journal of Common Market Studies*, vol. 17, no. 4, 1979, pp. 283–9.

63 The two dimensions of conflict in the EU coincide with the 'two fundamental cleavage lines', the 'centre–periphery' and the 'functional', that Lipset and Rokkan derive from Parsonian social theory. Lipset and Rokkan, 'Cleavage structures', p. 10.

64 See R.S. Katz and P. Mair, 'Introduction: the cross-national study of party organizations', in R.S. Katz and P. Mair (eds), *Party Organizations: A Data Handbook on Party Organizations in Western Democracies, 1960–90* (London, Sage, 1992).

65 During the IGCs all three party federations took on new staff. Moreover, from 1976 until the start of the conferences, the number of central office staff had already increased from three to fourteen for the socialists, three to ten for the Christian democrats, and three to six for the liberals. See L. Bardi, 'Transnational party federations in the European Community', in R.S. Katz and P. Mair (eds), *Party Organizations: A Data Handbook on Party Organizations in Western Democracies, 1960–1990*, (London, Sage, 1992), pp. 942–4.

66 F. Lehner and B. Benno-Homan, 'Consociational decision-making and party government

in Switzerland', in R.S. Katz (ed.), *Party Government: European and American Experience* (Berlin, Walter de Gruyter, 1987).
67 See the new statute of the Party of European Socialists: *Agence-Europe*, 11 November, p. 5.
68 Council of the European Communities, *Treaty on European Union*, p. 62. Article 2(1) of the German Basic Law states that: 'The political parties shall participate in the forming of the will of the people'; the Federal Republic of Germany, *The Basic Law of the Federal Republic of Germany* (Bonn, Press and Information Office of the Federal Government, 1986), p. 23.
69 Sartori has pointed out that traditionally political parties have been treated as 'dependent' variables; whereas in fact they are somewhat 'independent' of societal and institutional factors. See G. Sartori 'From the sociology of politics to political sociology', in S.M. Lipset (ed.), *Politics and the Social Sciences* (Oxford, Oxford University Press, 1969).
70 Cf. J.G. March and J.P. Olsen, 'The new institutionalism: organizational factors in political life', *American Political Science Review*, vol. 78, no. 2, 1984, pp. 734–49.
71 Pridham and Pridham, 'Transnational parties', p. 298.

SELECT BIBLIOGRAPHY

Agence-Europe, Brussels: Agence internationale d'information pour la presse.
Bardi, L., 'Transnational party federations in the European Community', in R.S. Katz and P. Mair (eds), *Party Organizations: A Data Handbook on Party Organizations in Western Democracies, 1960–1990*, London, Sage, 1992.
Beyme, K. von, *Political Parties in Western Democracies*, London, Gower House, 1985.
Bogdanor, V., 'The future of the European Community: two models of democracy', *Government and Opposition*, vol. 21, no. 2, 1986, pp. 161–76.
Bogdanor, V., 'Direct elections, representative democracy and European integration', *Electoral Studies*, vol. 8, no. 3, 1989, pp. 1–12.
CD-Europe Bulletin.
Clarke, M., 'Transnationalism', in S. Smith (ed.), *International Relations: British and American Perspectives*, Oxford, Basil Blackwell, 1985.
Confederation of Socialist Parties, *Declaration: Party Leaders' Summit*, Lisbon, 15/16 June 1992.
Council of the European Communities, *Treaty on European Union*, Luxembourg, Office for Official Publications, 1992.
Curtice, J., 'The 1989 elections: protest or Green tide?', *Electoral Studies*, vol. 8, no. 3, 1989, pp. 217–30.
Duverger, M., *Political Parties: Their Organization and Activity in the Modern State*, New York, John Wiley, 1954.
Epstein, L.D., *Political Parties in Western Democracies*, New Brunswick, Rutgers University Press, 1967.
European Federation of Green Parties, *Statuts de la fédération européenne des parties verts*, FEG Publication, 1993.
European Free Alliance, *Les membres de l'ALE*, EFA Publication, 1993.
European People's Party, *EPP Statutes*, EPP, 1976.
European People's Party, *List of Members of EPP and EUCD*, EPP, 1993.
Featherstone, K., 'Socialist parties and European integration: variations on a common theme', in W.E. Paterson and A.H. Thomas (eds), *The Future of Social Democracy: Problems and Perspectives of Social Democratic Parties in Western Europe*, Oxford, Clarendon Press, 1986.
Federal Republic of Germany, *The Basic Law of the Federal Republic of Germany*, Bonn, Press and Information Office of the Federal Government, 1986.
Federation of European Liberal and Democratic Parties, *ELD Statutes*, ELD, 1976.
Federation of European Liberal, Democrat and Reform Parties, *Vade-Mecum*, ELDR, 1993.
Fitzmaurice, J., *The European Parliament*, London, Saxon House, 1978.
Gruner, H., *Die Parteien in der Schweiz*, Berne, Franke Verlag, 1969, rev. edn in 1977.

Haas, E.B., *The Uniting of Europe: Political, Social and Economic Forces, 1950–57*, London, Stevens, 1958.

Hix, S., 'The emerging EC party system? The European party federations in the inter-governmental conferences', *Politics*, vol. 13, no. 2, 1993, pp. 38–46.

Hrbek, R., 'Transnational links: the ELD and the liberal group in the European Parliament', in E.J. Kirchner (ed.), *Liberal Parties in Western Europe*, Cambridge, Cambridge University Press, 1988.

Irving, R.E.M., *The Christian Democratic Parties of Western Europe*, London, Allen and Unwin, 1979.

Jacobs, F. (ed.), *Western European Political Parties: A Comprehensive Guide*, Harlow, Longman, 1989.

Katz, R.S. and Mair, P., 'Introduction: the cross-national study of party organizations', in R.S. Katz and P. Mair (eds), *Party Organizations: A Data Handbook on Party Organizations in Western Democracies, 1960–90*, London, Sage, 1992.

Kerr, H.H., 'The Swiss party system: steadfast and changing', in H. Daalder (ed.), *Party Systems in Denmark, Austria, Switzerland, The Netherlands and Belgium*, London, Frances Pinter, 1987.

Kohler, B. and Myrzik, B., 'Transnational party links', in R. Morgan and S. Silvestri (eds), *Moderates and Conservatives in Western Europe: Political Parties, the European Community and the Atlantic Alliance*, London, Heinemann, 1982.

LaPalombara, J. and Weiner, M., 'The origin and development of political parties', in J. LaPalombara and M. Weiner (eds), *Political Parties and Political Development*, Princeton, Princeton University Press, 1966.

Lehner, F. and Benno-Homan, B., 'Consociational decision-making and party government in Switzerland', in R.S. Katz (ed.), *Party Government: European and American Experience*, Berlin, Walter de Gruyter, 1987.

Lindberg, L.N., *The Political Dynamics of European Economic Integration*, Oxford, Oxford University Press, 1963.

Lipset, S.M. and Rokkan, S., 'Cleavage structures, party systems and voter alignments: an introduction', in S.M. Lipset and S. Rokkan (eds), *Party Systems and Voter Alignments: Cross-national Perspectives*, New York, Free Press, 1967.

Lodge, J. (ed.), *Direct Elections to the European Parliament 1984*, London, Macmillan, 1986.

Lodge, J., '1989: edging towards "genuine" Euro-elections?', in J. Lodge (ed.), *The 1989 Elections of the European Parliament*, London, Macmillan, 1989.

Lodge, J. and Herman, V., *The Direct Elections to the European Parliament*, London, Macmillan, 1982.

Macridis, R.C., 'Introduction', in R.C. Macridis (ed.), *Political Parties: Contemporary Trends and Ideas*, New York, Harper and Row, 1967.

March, J.G. and Olsen, J.P., 'The new institutionalism: organizational factors in political life', *American Political Science Review*, vol. 78, no. 2, 1984, pp. 734–49.

Marquand, D., 'Towards a Europe of the Parties', *Political Quarterly*, vol. 49, no. 4, 1978, pp. 425–45.

Marquand, D., *Parliament for Europe*, London, Jonathan Cape, 1979.

May, J., 'Cooperation between socialist parties', in W.E. Paterson and A.H. Thomas (eds), *Social Democratic Parties in Western Europe*, London, Croom Helm, 1977.

Menke, K. and Gordon, I., 'Differential mobilisation and Europe: a comparative note on some aspects of the campaign', *European Journal of Political Research*, vol. 8, no. 1, 1980, pp. 63–89.

Neumann, S. (ed.), *Modern Political Parties: Approaches to Comparative Politics*, Chicago, Chicago University Press, 1956.

Niedermeyer, O., 'The 1989 European elections: campaigns and results', *European Journal of Political Research*, vol. 19, no. 1, 1989, pp. 3–15.

Pappi, F-U., 'The West German party system', *West European Politics*, vol. 7, no. 4, 1984, pp. 7–26.

Party of European Socialists, *Statutes of the Party of European Socialists*, PES, 1993.

Pridham, G., 'Christian Democrats, Conservatives and transnational party cooperation in the European Community: centre-forward or centre-right?', in Z. Layton-Henry (ed.), *Conservative Politics in Western Europe*, London, Macmillan, 1982.

Pridham, G., 'European elections, political parties and trends of internalization in Community Affairs', *Journal of Common Market Studies*, vol. 24, no. 4, 1986, pp. 279–96.

Pridham, G. and Pridham, P., 'Transnational parties in the European Community II: the development of the European Party federations', in S. Henig (ed.), *Political Parties in the European Community*, London, Croom Helm, 1979.

Pridham, G. and Pridham, P., 'The New European party federations and direct elections', *The World Today*, vol. 35, no. 2, 1979, pp. 62–70.

Pridham, G. and Pridham, P., *Towards Transnational Parties in the European Community*, London, Policy Studies Institute, 1979.

Pridham, G. and Pridham, P., *Transnational Party Cooperation and European Integration: The Process towards the Direct Elections*, London, Allen and Unwin, 1981.

Reif, K., 'National electoral cycles and European elections 1979 and 1984', *European Journal of Political Research*, vol. 3, no. 3, 1984, pp. 244–55.

Reif, K. and Schmitt, H., 'Nine second-order national elections: a conceptual framework for the analysis of European election results', *European Journal of Political Research*, vol. 8, no. 1, 1980, pp. 3–44.

Reif, K. Cayrol, R. and Niedermeyer, O., 'National political parties' middle level elites and European integration', *European Journal of Political Research*, vol. 8, no. 1, 1980, pp. 91–112.

Rokkan, S., 'Electoral mobilisation, party competition, and national integration', in J. LaPalombara and M. Weiner (eds), *Political Parties and Political Development*, Princeton, Princeton University Press, 1966.

Rosenau, J.N., *Turbulence in World Politics: A Theory of Change and Continuity*, New York, Harvester Wheatsheaf, 1990.

Sartori, G., 'From the sociology of politics to political sociology', in S.M. Lipset (ed.), *Politics and the Social Sciences*, Oxford, Oxford University Press, 1969.

Sbragia, A.M., 'Thinking about the European future: the uses of comparisons', in A.M. Sbragia (ed.), *Euro-Politics: Institutions and Policymaking in the 'New' European Community*, Washington, DC, The Brookings Institution, 1992.

Scharpf, F.W., 'The joint-decision trap: lessons from German federalism and European integration', *Public Administration*, vol. 66, no. 2, 1988, pp. 239–78.

Smith, G., 'Core persistence: system change and the "People's Party"', *West European Politics*, vol. 12, no. 4, 1989, pp. 157–68.

Steed, M., 'Failure or long-haul? European elections and European integration', *Electoral Studies*, vol. 3, no. 3, 1984, pp. 225–34.

Taylor, P., 'The European Community and the state: assumptions, theories and propositions', *Review of International Studies*, vol. 17, no. 2, 1991, pp. 109–25.

Vredeling, H., 'The Common Market of political parties', *Government and Opposition*, vol. 6, no. 4, 1971, pp. 448–61.

Wallace, H., 'Direct elections and the political dynamics of the European Communities', *Journal of Common Market Studies*, vol. 17, no. 4, 1979, pp. 281–96.

Willets, P. (ed.), *Pressure Groups in the Global System: The Transnational Relations of Issue-Oriented Non-Governmental Organisations*, London, Frances Pinter, 1982.

Index